E46

# The New York Times
# Year in Review
# 1986

# The New York Times
# Year in Review
## 1986

NYT/FRED CONRAD

EDITED BY ADAM CLYMER

Times BOOKS

Copyright © 1987 by Adam Clymer

All rights reserved under International and Pan-American Copyright Conventions. Published in the United States by Times Books, a division of Random House, Inc., New York, and simultaneously in Canada by Random House of Canada Limited, Toronto.

All material in this book previously appeared in *The New York Times*. Copyright © 1986, 1987 by The New York Times Company. Reprinted by permission. All rights reserved.

**Library of Congress Cataloging-in-Publication Data**
The New York times year in review 1986
Includes index.
1. Almanacs, American.   I. Clymer, Adam.
II. New York times.
AY67.N5N49   1987     071′.471     86-14561
ISBN 0-812-91632-8

Manufactured in the United States of America

9 8 7 6 5 4 3 2

First Edition

DESIGNED BY BARBARA MARKS

FOR ANN

# Contents

Introduction  ix

1. International  1

2. National  83

3. Public Opinion  201

4. Business and Industry  235

5. Finance and Markets  265

6. Sports  313

7. Culture  373

8. Miscellany and Living  395

Index  437

# Introduction

*The New York Times* used to be known as the "newspaper of record." The phrase is rarely heard around the newsroom these days, perhaps because it sounds ponderous, dull, or old-fashioned. But it is still an apt and proud description. Some specialized journals may print more names and numbers concerning their field of interest, but *The Times* is the newspaper for the general reader to turn to for everything from election results to tabulations of public opinion to lists of stock-market winners and losers or the biggest trees in America.

When I started reading *The Times* more than forty years ago, there were more lists in it than there are today, and less explanation. We no longer report the names of all graduates of the service academies, or all ships coming in and out of New York harbor every day. But we print lots of lists and try to put them in a readable context. The collection in the book includes, for example, a list of Rhodes scholars that includes one remarkable service academy senior, Hoang Nhu Tran of the Air Force Academy, and an excerpted version of the article that noted that he is the first Rhodes Scholar born in Vietnam. And while it does not have lists of every day's ships, it has a finely illustrated list of the stately tall ships that sailed into New York Harbor on the Fourth of July, the ceremonial centennial birthday for the Statue of Liberty.

The way that list of tall ships appears in this book illustrates another change from *The Times* I first read to the one I now work for. Those lists appeared in agate type. A few of the ones in this book did, too, but far more care is now given to how they look in the paper, to the artwork and design that helps make the names and numbers meaningful. For example, it is one thing to report in words that President Reagan's approval rating had declined 21 percentage points in a month. It is more emphatic to do it in Anne Cronin's front-page graphic, whose pointed lines measured that steep decline. Throughout this book are many of the graphics that Andy Sabbatini and his colleagues in our Map Department executed to make the words more telling, and that Andy and his colleagues searched out from their files for this volume.

But this is not just an illustrated book of lists. Traditional almanacs certainly carry more names and numbers. At *The Times* and in this book these tables or lists are used with articles. They almost never stand by themselves, but accompany an article to emphasize key points, or to furnish more detail than a story could swallow, or to tell a piece of the overall story in staccato paragraphs that leave the analysis, the tone, the music of the event to the main story.

In this book nearly all of the lists—of names, of names and numbers, of events—follow edited versions of the stories they accompanied. The point was to give the heart of the matter, and *Times* writers are skillful enough so that their first few paragraphs almost always succeed in doing just that.

Another heavy emphasis in this book that could not have been found in *The Times* of many years ago is reporting on public opinion. Polling at *The Times* in its current form dates from 1975, when the first New York Times/CBS News Poll appeared. That one dealt with the nation's attitudes on aid to New York City. This book covers attitudes on politics, farmers, terrorism, immigration, drugs and even pro football. And the publics polled are not only Americans but also Mexicans, Japanese, British, French and German. The results of questions and answers often appear more fully here than they did in the paper. Tables can effectively compress and paraphrase a poll question in the context of a 1,500-word story that puts all the questions and answers together. But where those stories have been shrunk to 200 to 400 words, as they had to be here, the full text of the questions used usually seemed necessary, and Marjorie Connelly and Amy Solas of the News Surveys Department at *The Times* prepared those tabulations.

There are no lists here of things that did not appear in *The Times,* but occasionally a series of events that happened on different days—like the games in the World Series or the announcements of Nobel prizes—have been collected into one list that stitches numbers and even paragraphs from different days' papers into a single "list." Once or twice a list has been organized in a way that seemed clearer than the version put together under deadline pressure. And sometimes a list appears here in a more complete version than the one that ran in the daily paper. One example is the list of 1986 best-selling books, which listed as many books in each category as the Sunday *Book Review* lists every week. Mary Ann Rennick, who sends the weekly list to the *Book Review,* assembled the annual list, too.

Finally, in this new, reflective almanac, as in *The Times* these days, not everything carries the weight of the world with it. An accounting of the events that set records for garbage collection in New York City, or a collection of the worst statistical failures of the baseball season, not to mention those big trees or tall ships, conveys a lighter side of the world, and of *The Times* these days.

# The New York Times
# Year in Review
# 1986

# PART 1
# International

# Skirmishes on the Economic Frontier

**By CLYDE HABERMAN**

TOKYO—Japan seems resigned to the prospect of a continuing deterioration in its trade relations with the United States, possibly at a faster pace this year. Politicians and business leaders assume that the two countries will stop well short of an all-out trade war, but some wonder how long the tension can persist before it starts to undercut the foundation of an otherwise friendly relationship.

To them, the next few months seem riddled with hard-to-pass tests. By spring, the Government must make a decision on the emotional issue of whether to continue its quotas on automobiles exports to the United States. Car manufacturers and the Ministry of International Trade and Industry have begun the process, tentatively suggesting in the Japanese press that it may be time to lift so-called voluntary restraints. Such a move would add considerably to the pressures for protectionist legislation in Washington.

Congressional elections this year are expected to complicate matters. So are trade figures for 1985, which will be announced soon. They are all but certain to show an overall United States trade deficit of more than $140 billion. Japan's share should come to about $50 billion, or roughly one third. Even optimists such as Mike Mansfield, the United States Ambassador in Tokyo, worry about the emotional consequences of the statistics. Mr. Mansfield said recently that there has been "very good progress" on several trade fronts, notably negotiations to open Japan on behalf of American telecommunications companies that feel excluded.

But, he acknowledged, "When that $50 billion figure hits the front page, you're going to hear a lot of grumbling. There'll be a lot of finger-pointing at Japan."  JAN. 5

## What the U.S. sells Japan
The 10 leading United States exports to Japan (in millions of dollars)

|  | 1982 | 1983 | 1984 | 1985* |
|---|---|---|---|---|
| Corn and seed for planting | 1,290 | 1,764 | 1,999 | 686 |
| Soybeans | 970 | 1,209 | 1,172 | 465 |
| Coal | 1,635 | 1,133 | 986 | 491 |
| Logs | 846 | 699 | 642 | 333 |
| Cotton (short fiber thread) | 495 | 494 | 590 | 245 |
| Office machine parts | 443 | 467 | 582 | 364 |
| Wheat | 564 | 589 | 534 | 227 |
| Aircraft | 380 | 786 | 527 | 541 |
| Aircraft parts | 469 | 500 | 522 | 280 |
| Electronic tubes (other than TV tubes) | 235 | 332 | 499 | 222 |

*January through June   Source: Department of Commerce

JAN. 5

## Libyan economic ties
Tripoli's major trading partners in 1984 (in millions of U.S. dollars)

|  | Imports from Libya | Exports to Libya |
|---|---|---|
| Italy | 2,527 | 1,826 |
| West Germany | 1,996 | 885 |
| Spain | 969 | 293 |
| France | 753 | 233 |
| Turkey | 655 | 155 |
| Yugoslavia | 407 | 225 |
| Switzerland | 402 | 110 |
| Netherlands | 366 | 204 |
| Greece | 326 | 120 |
| Rumania | 311 | 140 |
| Industrialized nations | 7,737 | 5,086 |
|   United States | 9 | 220 |
|   European Economic Community | 6,428 | 3,817 |

|                     | Imports from Libya | Exports to Libya |
|---------------------|-------------------:|-----------------:|
| Developing nations  | 2,090              | 1,340            |
| East bloc           | 746                | 444              |
| Total Libyan trade  | 10,519             | 6,869            |

Source: International Monetary Fund

JAN. 12

# Big Banks Upgrade Argentina

By ERIC N. BERG

It was only one year ago that American bankers were girding themselves to write off billions of dollars in Argentine loans. But now, one major bank after another is reporting sharply higher profits, thanks in part to the interest earned from those same loans.

In year-end earnings reports released in the last week, four of the nation's largest banks—Chemical, Chase Manhattan, Morgan Guaranty, and Irving Trust—said that in the fourth quarter they placed more than $500 million in Argentine loans back on "accrual" status. That meant that the banks resumed reporting interest on the loans. In the next few days, moreover, other multinational banks are expected to announce that they, too, resumed booking profits on their Argentine loans.

On average, fourth-quarter earnings at big American banks will be about 10 percent higher on a pretax basis than they would have been otherwise because of the switch in accounting for Argentine loans, said James J. McDermott, director of research at the New York brokerage firm of Keefe, Bruyette & Woods Inc.

What made the change possible was two payments that Argentina made to its creditor banks: one for $800 million Sept. 30 and another for $340 million Nov. 26. Together, the payments enabled Argentina to declare itself paid up on virtually all the overdue interest on its public-sector debt. Not all of the Argentine public and private loans were on a nonaccrual basis. But the reclassification of those loans that were in arrears amounted to hundreds of millions of dollars for some big banks. The interest on those loans can now be fully booked into quarterly profits.

Some banking experts, however, say that the switch resulted from nothing more than bankers using their own money to repay themselves. Significantly, Argentina made the payments in a period when it received nearly $3 billion in new loans from commercial banks worldwide.

"Unless the banks had extended the $3 billion, there is no way Argentina, even with its reduced level of imports, could have serviced its debt in full," said Christine A. Bogdanowicz-Bindert, a former economist at the International Monetary Fund who is now a senior vice president at Shearson Lehman Brothers. "It's an accounting gimmick, absolutely."

JAN. 15

## U.S. Loans to Argentina

Estimated Argentine exposure of U.S. banks, in billions of dollars as of Dec. 31, 1984

| Manufacturers Hanover | $1.3 |
|-----------------------|-----:|
| Citicorp              | 1.1  |
| Chase Manhattan       | 0.8  |
| Morgan Guaranty       | 0.7  |
| Continental Illinois  | 0.4  |
| Chemical Bank         | 0.4  |
| Bank of Boston        | 0.2  |
| Irving Trust          | 0.2  |

Source: Keefe, Bruyette & Woods

JAN. 15

## U.S. Observers for Philippine Election

Senator Richard G. Lugar, Republican of Indiana and chairman of the Senate Foreign Relations Committee, and Representative John P. Murtha, Democrat of Pennsylvania, co-chairmen of the delegation.

Others are: Fred F. Fielding, counsel to the president; Adam J. Maida, the Roman Catholic Bishop of Green Bay, Wisconsin, and senators Thad Cochran, Republican of Mississippi, and John F. Kerry, Democrat of Massachusetts; and representatives Robert L. Livingston, Jr., Republican of Louisiana; Bernard J. Dwyer, Democrat of New Jersey; Samuel S. Stratton, Democrat of upstate New York, and Jerry Lewis, Republican of California.

Also, Allen Weinstein, president of the Center for Democracy; Adm. Robert Long, retired; Norma Paulus, former Oregon Secretary of State; Jack Brier, Kansas Secretary of State; Natalie Meyer, Colorado Secretary of State; Larry Niksch, director of Asian affairs at the Congressional Research Service; Mortimer B. Zuckerman, publisher of U.S. News & World Report; Ben J. Wattenberg, American Enterprise Institute; and Van Smith, former president of the United States Chamber of Commerce.

FEB. 2

## North Sea Oil Production

North Sea oil production has not slowed, despite the sharp drop in oil prices.
The leading companies producing oil in the British sector of the North Sea, ranked by their current output, in thousands of barrels per day.

| Company | 1985 | 1986* |
|---|---|---|
| British Petroleum | 495 | 430 |
| Royal Dutch Shell | 460 | 485 |
| Exxon | 455 | 480 |
| Britoil | 162 | 162 |
| Mobil | 140 | 168 |
| Texaco | 121 | 114 |
| Conoco | 116 | 136 |
| Phillips | 108 | 93 |
| Chevron | 104 | 112 |
| Occidental | 90 | 80 |
| Total average daily production in British sector, in millions of barrels daily | 2.56 | 2.50 |

*Estimate    Source: Wood Mackenzie & Co.

FEB. 3

## Senate Condemns Philippine Result as Rife with Fraud

By STEVEN V. ROBERTS

WASHINGTON, Feb. 19—The Senate voted overwhelmingly today to condemn corruption in the Philippine election, as sentiment mounted on Capitol Hill to restrict American aid to the Manila Government and to try to force President Ferdinand E. Marcos from power.

By a vote of 85 to 9, the Senate adopted a resolution declaring that the Philippine presidential elections on Feb. 7 were "marked by such widespread fraud that they cannot be considered a fair reflection of the will of the people of the Philippines."

No senator defended the Marcos Government, and the negative votes were cast by eight conservative Republicans and one Democrat.

The resolution has no force of law, but it reflects a rising sense of outrage over the Philippine situation that has washed over Capitol Hill this week since the lawmakers returned from the Washington's Birthday recess. On Saturday, the Philippine National Assembly, controlled by supporters of Mr. Marcos, declared him the winner of the election over Corazon C. Aquino.

FEB. 20

## Senate Vote

Following is the roll-call vote on a nonbinding U.S. Senate resolution that condemned the Philippine elections as "marked by such widespread fraud that they cannot be considered a fair reflection of the will of the people of the Philippines":

### FOR THE RESOLUTION—85

#### Democrats—42

Baucus, Mont.
Bentsen, Tex.
Biden, Del.
Bingaman, N.M.
Boren, Okla.
Bradley, N.J.
Bumpers, Ark.
Burdick, N.D.
Byrd, W. Va.
Chiles, Fla.
Cranston, Calif.
DeConcini, Ariz.
Dixon, Ill.
Dodd, Conn.
Eagleton, Mo.
Ford, Ky.
Gore, Tenn.
Harkin, Iowa
Hart, Colo.
Hollings, S.C.
Johnston, La.
Kennedy, Mass.
Kerry, Mass.
Lautenberg, N.J.
Leahy, Vt.
Levin, Mich.
Long, La.
Matsunaga, Hawaii
Metzenbaum, Ohio
Mitchell, Me.
Moynihan, N.Y.
Nunn, Ga.
Pell, R.I.
Proxmire, Wis.
Pryor, Ark.
Riegle, Mich.
Rockefeller, W. Va.
Sarbanes, Md.
Sasser, Tenn.
Simon, Ill.
Stennis, Miss.
Zorinsky, Neb.

#### Republicans—43

Abdnor, S.D.
Andrews, N.D.
Armstrong, Colo.
Boschwitz, Minn.
Chafee, R.I.
Cochran, Miss.
Cohen, Me.
D'Amato, N.Y.
Danforth, Mo.
Dole, Kan.
Domenici, N.M.
Evans, Wash.
Garn, Utah
Gorton, Wash.
Gramm, Tex.
Grassley, Iowa
Hatch, Utah
Hatfield, Ore.
Hawkins, Fla.
Heinz, Pa.
Humphrey, N.H.
Kassebaum, Kan.
Kasten, Wis.
Laxalt, Nev.
Lugar, Ind.
Mattingly, Ga.
McClure, Idaho
McConnell, Ky.
Murkowski, Alaska
Nickles, Okla.
Packwood, Ore.
Pressler, S.D.
Quayle, Ind.
Roth, Del.
Rudman, N.H.
Simpson, Wyo.
Specter, Pa.
Stafford, Vt.
Stevens, Alaska
Trible, Va.
Warner, Va.
Weicker, Conn.
Wilson, Calif.

### AGAINST THE RESOLUTION—9

#### Democrat—1

Melcher, Mont.

#### Republicans—8

Denton, Ala.
East, N.C.
Goldwater, Ariz.
Hecht, Nev.
Helms, N.C.
Symms, Idaho
Thurmond, S.C.
Wallop, Wyo.

### VOTING PRESENT

#### Democrat—1

Heflin, Ala.

### NOT VOTING—5

#### Democrats—3

Exon, Neb.
Glenn, Ohio
Inouye, Hawaii

#### Republicans—2

Durenberger, Minn.
Mathias, Md.

FEB. 20

# Gorbachev's Fast Start Puts New Team in Charge

**By SERGE SCHMEMANN**

**M**OSCOW, Feb. 23—In less than a year in power, Mikhail S. Gorbachev has achieved a shake-up of the top ranks of the Soviet leadership that has been more thorough than any of his predecessors managed in so short a time.

Many diplomats rank the mass replacement of officials from the Politburo down through the party apparatus, the ministries and the republic and regional organizations as probably the most impressive achievement of the new leadership so far.

The Communist Party Congress that begins here Tuesday is expected to consolidate the changes by naming a central committee with a sizable block of new members—as many as half, according to some projections. The committee's 300 or so members set the policies of the party between congresses and make up the primary pool from which top national leaders are drawn.

More than 30 percent of the 319 members named at the last party congress in 1981 have died, retired or lost the positions that entitled them to a seat on the Central Committee, and many more are likely to be removed to make room for Mr. Gorbachev's people.

The shake-up began almost as soon as Mr. Gorbachev was appointed General Secretary of the Communist Party on March 11, and it quickened in the weeks before the party congress. Among the most recent victims was Viktor V. Grishin, the former Moscow party chief, who was dropped from the Politburo last week. Mr. Grishin was the third full member removed under Mr. Gorbachev, joining the former Leningrad party chief, Grigory V. Romanov, and the former Prime Minister, Nikolai A. Tikhonov.

In their stead, Mr. Gorbachev has promoted his own men, including Yegor K. Ligachev, his second-in-command and chief ideologist; Nikolai I. Ryzhkov, the new Prime Minister; Foreign Minister Eduard A. Shevardnadze; Nikolai V. Talyzin, the new head of Gosplan, the economic planning agency; and Boris N. Yeltsin, head of the Moscow party organization.

What has impressed diplomats more than the changes at the top, where Mr. Gorbachev would be expected to bring in his own men, has been the shake-up of the vast machinery of state below. It is there, in the central party apparatus, in the many ministries, in far-flung republics, cities, oblasts and other subdivisions of the Soviet state that the ambitions of the leadership can be stymied or advanced, and it was there that Mr. Gorbachev and Mr. Ligachev staged their major offensive.

Mr. Gorbachev signaled his intentions in unadorned terms in a talk last May in Leningrad.

"We must, of course, give a chance, as it were, to all our cadres to understand the demands of the moment and this stage, and to adjust," he said. "But those who do not intend to adjust and who, moreover, are an obstacle to the solution of these new tasks, simply must get out of the way, get out of the way and not be a hindrance." FEB. 24

## The Soviet Hierarchy: Who's In and Who's Out

Following is a list of key members of the Soviet Communist Party apparatus and the Soviet Government, members who have been appointed since Mikhail S. Gorbachev took office in March 1985 and others who have left office since then.

A party congress opens Tuesday. Such meetings are called once every five years to approve party programs and policies. Congress delegates, chosen by party organizations around the country, also approve the choices of Central Committee members from among their own numbers.

■ Left office after Gorbachev came to power

☐ Came to office or was promoted after Gorbachev came to power

### THE PARTY

Holds all political power, centered in the Politburo and the Secretariat of the Central Committee. All important decisions—on foreign policy, the economy and social affairs—are made there and carried out by the Government.

**Politburo** Sets the overall policy for the Soviet Union. Consists of about a dozen full (voting) members and about eight or nine candidate (nonvoting) members, all of whom are among the leading political figures. Membership is not a full-time position in itself; all members hold regular duties elsewhere in the party or the Government.

#### Full Members

Mikhail S. Gorbachev, party leader

Geidar A. Aliyev, First Deputy Prime Minister

☐ Viktor M. Chebrikov, K.G.B. chief

■ Viktor V. Grishin, retired Moscow city chief

☐ Andrei A. Gromyko, President

Dinmukhamed A. Kunayev, Kazakhstan chief

☐ Yegor K. Ligachev, second-ranking party leader, in charge of ideology and party personnel

■ Grigory V. Romanov, retired national party secretary

☐ Nikolai I. Ryzhkov, Prime Minister

Vladimir V. Shcherbitsky, Ukrainian party chief

☐ Eduard A. Shevardnadze, Foreign Minister

Mikhail S. Solomentsev, party control commission chief

■ Nikolai A. Tikhonov, former Prime Minister

Vitaly I. Vorotnikov, Premier of Russian Republic

**Candidate Members**

Pyotr N. Demichev, Culture Minister
Vladimir I. Dolgikh, a national party secretary
Vasily V. Kuznetsov, the First Vice President
Boris N. Ponomarev, a national party secretary
☐ Sergei L. Sokolov, Defense Minister
☐ Nikolai V. Talyzin, a First Deputy Prime Minister
☐ Boris N. Yeltsin, Moscow city party chief

**Secretariat.** Actually in charge of day-to-day affairs of the Soviet Union. Headed by General Secretary, Mr. Gorbachev. He is assisted by a number of national secretaries and a large permanent staff.

Gorbachev, General Secretary
Doigikh, industry
Ivan V. Kapitonov, light industry
Ligachev
☐ Viktor P. Nikonov, agriculture, previously Russian Republic's Agriculture Minister
Ponomarev, relations with nonruling Communist parties
■ Romanov
■ Konstantin V. Rusakov, retired
☐ Lev N. Zaikov, military industries, previously Leningrad Province party chief
Mikhail V. Zimyanin, internal propaganda

**THE GOVERNMENT**

Carries out decisions made by the Communist Party. Directed by Council of Ministers. The nominal Parliament, the Supreme Soviet of the U.S.S.R., meets perfunctorily twice a year. Its Presidium represents state authority between sessions and performs the functions of the collective presidency. Listed below are the key ministers of the Government under Gorbachev.

Nikolai I. Ryzhkov, Prime Minister
■ Nikolai A. Tikhonov, former Prime Minister

**First Deputy Prime Ministers:**

Aliyev
Ivan V. Arkhipov
☐ Vsevolod S. Murakhovsky, heads agribusiness sector
☐ Talyzin, economic planning

**Deputy Prime Ministers:**

Aleksei K. Antonov, East European economic relations
■ Nikolai K. Baibakov, retired chairman, State Planning Committee
☐ Yuri P. Batalin
■ Ivan I. Bodyul, retired
■ Veniamin E. Dymshits, retired
Guri I. Marchuk, science and technology
■ Nikolai V. Martynov, retired head of materials allocation
☐ Yuri D. Maslyukov, military industry
■ Ziya N. Nuriyev, retired head of agriculture
Boris Y. Shcherbina, oil and gas industries
☐ Ivan S. Silayev, machinery industries
■ Leonid V. Smirnov, retired head of military industry
☐ Lev A. Voronin, materials allocation

FEB. 24

# Marcos Flees and Is Taken to Guam; U.S. Recognizes Aquino as President

**By SETH MYDANS**

MANILA, Wednesday, Feb. 26—Ferdinand E. Marcos fled the Philippines Tuesday, ending 20 years as President. Corazon C. Aquino succeeded him, saying "a new life" had begun for her country.

Mr. Marcos, facing pressure from all sides to step down, left the presidential palace shortly after 9 P.M. (8 A.M. Eastern Standard Time) and traveled by helicopter to Clark Air Base.

There, accompanied by his wife, Imelda, and Gen. Fabian C. Ver, a close associate and former chief of the Philippines military forces, he boarded an American Air Force plane for Guam, a United States territory in the Pacific.

[A Defense Department statement said 55 people were in Mr. Marcos's party aboard two aircraft, The Associated Press reported from Agana, Guam.]

Mr. Marcos arrived at Andersen Air Force Base in Guam this morning, where he was greeted by Acting Gov. Edward D. Reyes.

In Washington, officials said the 68-year-old leader, who reportedly suffers from a kidney ailment, would receive treatment at the Naval Medical Center on Guam. One official described his hospitalization as precautionary.

According to a Defense Department spokesman in Washington, Mr. Marcos was to leave Guam this evening (between 5 A.M. and 8 A.M. E.S.T.) for an unspecified air base near Honolulu.

The departure of Mr. Marcos from Manila ended a day in which he pleaded with Washington for help in clinging to office, then went through an inaugural ceremony that was held apparently after he had decided to leave.

Mrs. Aquino was also inaugurated in the morning to head what was dubbed a provisional government, and although Mr. Marcos made no public resignation when he departed, the United States immediately recognized her administration.

The news of Mr. Marcos's departure set off celebrations in the capital as hundreds of thousands of Filipinos surged into the streets, honking horns, setting off firecrackers and burning tires.

As crowds converged on the presidential palace, fighting broke out between supporters and opponents of Mr. Marcos. Stones and knives were used in the clashes, and a number of injuries were reported. Eventually, a noisy crowd surged into the palace, tearing down portraits of Mr. Marcos and his wife and helping themselves to souvenirs.

Earlier, three civilians were reported killed in Manila during a pitched battle between loyalist and rebel troops for control of a television transmitting tower.

In Washington, the Reagan Administration hailed Mrs. Aquino for "her commitment to nonviolence" while praising Mr. Marcos for a

## A Tally of Latin Debtors

| | External Debt* | | | Use of IMF credit** | | |
|---|---|---|---|---|---|---|
| | Total Debt | Owed To Banks | % Debt Owed U.S. Banks | Loans Outstanding | Potential Borrowings | Repayments Scheduled |
| Argentina | $ 49.0 | $ 26.6 | 30.4% | $ 2.31 | $ 3.45 | $ 1.33 |
| Bolivia | 4.2 | 0.7 | 23.2 | 0.05 | 0.37 | 0.05 |
| Brazil | 103.9 | 77.9 | 30.5 | 4.62 | 3.13 | 2.30 |
| Chile | 21.1 | 13.4 | 49.4 | 1.09 | 1.25 | 0.70 |
| Colombia | 13.1 | 6.9 | 38.5 | 0.0 | 1.73 | 0.0 |
| Ecuador | 7.7 | 5.0 | 43.7 | 0.36 | 0.40 | 0.22 |
| Mexico | 96.7 | 71.8 | 36.0 | 2.97 | 2.15 | 0.91 |
| Peru | 14.0 | 5.5 | 38.2 | 0.70 | 1.05 | 0.42 |
| Uruguay | 4.7 | 2.0 | 50.1 | 0.35 | 0.49 | 0.19 |
| Venezuela | 31.9 | 25.1 | 42.2 | 0.0 | 6.03 | 0.0 |
| Total | 346.3 | 235.0 | 35.3 | 12.45 | 20.04 | 6.11 |

*As of mid-1986, in billions of dollars except as noted
**As of Dec. 31, 1986, in billions of dollars

Source: Morgan Guaranty Trust Co.

FEB. 25

decision "characterized by the dignity and strength that have marked his many years of leadership."

The official said that even after Mr. Marcos arrived at Clark Air Base, he asked if he could remain in his home province in northern Luzon, but that the Aquino side refused.

Legal questions remained to be resolved about Mrs. Aquino's mandate following the Feb. 7 election in which Mr. Marcos was proclaimed the winner by the National Assembly, which he controlled, on the basis of a vote count marred by widespread fraud and violence by his supporters.

Thirty people were taken by helicopter from the palace to the United States Embassy and 80 others were evacuated down the Pasig River and then by car convoy to the embassy, according to Mrs. Aquino's new military chief, Gen. Fidel V. Ramos.

General Ramos did not say who was evacuated besides Mr. Marcos and his family, which includes his wife, Imelda, a son, Ferdinand Jr., two daughters, Imee Manotoc and Irene Araneta, and three grandchildren.

Mrs. Aquino, wearing a yellow dress, as she did throughout her campaign, appeared on television in the early hours of the morning to tell the nation, "The long agony is over. A new life starts for our country tomorrow."

For her 52-second address, which was repeated periodically, Mrs. Aquino removed her glasses, as she does for photographers when she wants to look her best.

"We are finally free, and we can be truly proud of the unprecedented way in which we achieved our freedom, with courage, with determination and most of all in peace," she said, smiling at the camera.

"A new life starts for our country tomorrow, a life filled with hope and I believe a life that will be blessed with peace and progress."

Her sentiments appeared to be reflected throughout Manila, where there was a tangible sense of elation and relief. "We are free now," cried a man who had worn a "Marcos for President" button throughout the campaign.

Late into the night, cars traveled the streets of Manila honking their horns, as people shouted to each other, "Happy New Year!" and "Happy Birthday!"

"This was their show," said a senior American Embassy official this morning. "They deserve all the credit. We find the whole thing an engulfing human experience."

He praised Mrs. Aquino's patience and serenity throughout the pressures of the election and its aftermath, and the courage of Defense Minister Juan Ponce Enrile and General Ramos in challenging the power of Mr. Marcos.

The official also praised the democratic drive of the Filipinos against the forces of Mr. Marcos and his military.

The groundswell of support that has carried Mrs. Aquino into office appears to have left no doubts here about her mandate, despite her inability to win a formal proclamation of victory from the Marcos-controlled National Assembly, the nation's parliament.

The desire of many Filipinos for change and their frustration with Mr. Marcos's long years in power were heightened over the past three weeks as he openly manipulated the forces at his command to deny Mrs. Aquino her victory.

The role of the popular will, rather than political dealings, in her victory was underscored over the past four days by the massing of hundreds of thousands of Filipinos in the streets to protect a group of breakaway military officers who challenged Mr. Marcos.

It was this final challenge by Mr. Enrile and General Ramos that helped force Mr. Marcos out of power.

The two men, who were named Tuesday morning to Mrs. Aquino's new Cabinet as her Defense Minister and military Chief of Staff, barricaded themselves in a military base. Although their forces were far inferior to those of Mr. Marcos and General Ver, the massed presence of the people around them made retaliation by the Government impossible.

Speaking on television this morning, General Ramos said that "pockets of resistance" remained but that "99.5 percent" supported the new Government.

Throughout the campaign, and as late as his final statements before leaving the country, Mr. Marcos made it plain that although he had called this special election 16 months before the end of his six-year term, he had no intention, whatever the outcome, of relinquishing office.

He continued to struggle with all the legal and military forces at his command for a technical victory, long after it had become clear that the national will was not with him.

In the face of his stubbornness, Mrs. Aquino's victory was seen as victory for the millions of people who protected their right to vote in the face of intimidation by Mr. Marcos's backers.

"Now he is one of the soon-to-be-forgotten exiles," said Homobono Adaza, an Assemblyman who supported Mrs. Aquino. "I never thought Marcos would go along the same classical way the others have gone, the Somozas and the Batistas."

He said legislators supporting Mrs. Aquino, who hold only one third of the National Assembly seats, would meet today to seek an agreement with the majority to gain parliamentary proclamation for the new President.

Mrs. Aquino has said that if the legislature stands in the way of reforms she intends to institute, she will use Mr. Marcos's special decree-making powers, which she has opposed, for one last time before abolishing them.

She and her supporters have also said a priority of her new Administration would be the drafting of a new constitution to replace the one Mr. Marcos fashioned under martial law.

At her inauguration Tuesday morning, Mrs. Aquino named Mr. Enrile and General Ramos to their new posts, and said her Vice President, Salvador H. Laurel, would also hold the position of Prime Minister.

She called for the resignations of high public officials and Supreme Court justices, but assured civil servants that they could keep their jobs if they had not violated the law.

On the question of the Communist insurgency, Mrs. Aquino has said she will declare a six-month cease-fire and an amnesty for insurgents who lay down their arms and renounce violence.

On the issue of Clark Air Base and the American naval base at Subic Bay, Mrs. Aquino has said she will allow the current agreement to run its course through 1991 and then seek to negotiate a full-fledged treaty rather than the current executive agreement.

In the early hours of Tuesday morning, Mr. Marcos made a number of telephone calls to both Filipinos and Americans, seeking some way to remain in office, if only as the shell of a President, giving all the real power to Mrs. Aquino.

"It's too late," Mr. Enrile said he told Mr. Marcos when he telephoned him.

"I said I thought that was impractical," said Senator Paul Laxalt, Republican of Nevada, who had visited Mr. Marcos as a special envoy of Mr. Reagan.

"Then he asked me the gut question, 'Senator, what should I do?' " Mr. Laxalt said. "I wasn't bound by diplomatic niceties. I said, 'Cut and cut cleanly. The time has come.'

"There was the longest pause. It seemed to last minutes. It lasted so long I asked if he was still there. He said, 'Yes,' and then he said, 'I am so very, very disappointed.' "

The conversation ended without Mr. Marcos's saying what he intended to do.

Before leaving Clark Air Base for Guam, Mr. Marcos told American officials he had made a last plea to Mrs. Aquino's supporters to be allowed to retire to his home province of Ilocos Norte, in northern Luzon, a senior State Department official said.

The President was quoted as having said he

was told the idea was not "practical."

In holding an inauguration, which came at noon Tuesday, Mr. Marcos left office in much the same way he had held it, with a tenacious insistence on the forms and legalisms of government, though holding a less firm grasp of the spirit of the law.

Though his mandate has slipped away, he stood firmly and confidently on a low platform in the reception hall of the palace. Hundreds of supporters—though no foreign representatives and few of his own officials—sat on the floor and on chairs and cheered as he looked directly into a television camera and raised his right hand to take the oath.

His wife stood smiling radiantly in a white dress just behind him, and at one point kissed him on the cheek. His son, dressed in green fatigues, stood behind her. At their side, his daughters, both in white, sat on velvet chairs, smiling at their supporters and sometimes quietly joining them in calling "Mabuhay," or "Hooray."

"No man can be more proud than I am at this moment," Mr. Marcos said, as if forcing himself to proceed with the forms of the leadership he now knew he had lost.

"Whatever be the challenges, whatever be the obstacles before us, I say to you as I say to everybody else that we will overcome," he said.

His supporters cheered, and one whispered, "Just like Lincoln."

But in a final indignity, as he stood with his right hand raised, his opponents, who had been waging a pitched battle for the television station, disconnected it at the very moment he was to take the oath of office, and television screens went blank.

The battle for the television transmitter, which began at 7 A.M., was one of the few real military engagements of the change in government.

Forces under the command of General Ramos surrounded the 1,000-foot television tower, with an armored car with machine guns and small cannons, and exchanged fire with government troopers positioned at the station.

The thousands of people gathered in the street, part of the masses who have made "people power" the catchword of this political event, threw themselves onto the ground screaming. Three were killed.

The confrontation calmed as a priest, the Rev. Nestor Rabon, came forward to negotiate, a symbol of the decisive role the church has played in the election and its aftermath.

Television reporters said it was not the battle itself that disconnected transmission at the moment of Mr. Marcos's inauguration, but technicians who managed to cut the microwave signal from the palace at the decisive moment.

Coverage of the inauguration was replaced by a John Wayne movie.  FEB. 26

## 30 Months in Manila: From a Death to a Presidency

**Aug. 21, 1983** Benigno S. Aquino, Jr., the opposition leader, returns to the Philippines from self-imposed exile in the United States and is shot dead as he leaves his plane at Manila International Airport. Rolando C. Galman, the man the Government says is the assassin, is immediately shot dead by guards on the tarmac.

**Aug. 31, 1983** A million Filipinos take part in the 10-hour funeral procession for Mr. Aquino, largest in the Philippines' history. Jaime Cardinal Sin, the Archbishop of Manila, presides at obsequies and calls for liberation "from tyranny and oppression."

**Oct. 22, 1983** A civilian board is named by President Ferdinand E. Marcos to investigate the Aquino slaying. Mr. Aquino's widow, Corazon, says she expects no justice while Mr. Marcos is President.

**Feb. 14, 1984** The anti-Marcos side scores gains in elections for National Assembly.

**Oct. 24, 1984** Majority on investigation board finds a military conspiracy in the slaying of Mr. Aquino and names Gen. Fabian C. Ver, the Chief of Staff, as having been involved. General Ver goes on leave of absence.

**Jan. 23, 1985** General Ver and 25 others, mostly military officers, are charged in Mr. Aquino's death. The case is assigned to three-judge court named by President Marcos.

**Oct. 16, 1985** President Reagan sends Senator Paul Laxalt, Republican of Nevada, to voice American concern over President Marcos's ability to govern in the face of continuing economic crisis.

**Nov. 3, 1985** Mr. Marcos announces that he will call an election before end of his six-year term in 1987. National Assembly later sets an election date: Feb. 7, 1986.

**Dec. 2, 1985** General Ver and all other defendants in Aquino slaying are acquitted. Court finds that shooting was the work of a lone gunman. The United States Government cautiously criticizes verdict. General Ver is reinstated as Chief of Staff.

**Dec. 3, 1985** Mrs. Aquino announces that she will run for President of the Philippines.

**Dec. 12, 1985** Mrs. Aquino opens her campaign and calls for justice for her husband and "all the victims" of Mr. Marcos.

**Feb. 6, 1986** The campaign ends amid signs of seriously eroded support for Mr. Marcos. Cardinal Sin says Mrs. Aquino will "make a good President."

**Feb. 7, 1986** Voters flock to polls amid charges of large-scale intimidation and fraud on the part of Marcos partisans. According to the Aquino camp, voter lists disappear, ballots are stolen and Marcos supporters cast multiple votes.

**Feb. 10, 1986** Independent observers report that the election was marked by fraud and violence on the Marcos side, including killings and beatings of known Marcos opponents.

**Feb. 11, 1986** President Reagan seems to endorse Mr. Marcos when he suggests at a news conference that fraud and violence could have taken place on "both sides" in Philippine election.

**Feb. 15, 1986** The National Assembly proclaims Mr. Marcos the winner of the election. President Reagan now blames Mr. Marcos for fraud and violence during the balloting.

**Feb. 16, 1986** Mrs. Aquino says she won election and calls for nationwide nonviolent campaign of strikes and boycotts to bring down the Marcos Government.

Philip C. Habib, President Reagan's special envoy, begins "fact-finding" mission and talks to both Mr. Marcos and Mrs. Aquino. He is reportedly in the Philippines to urge Mr. Marcos to step down.

**Feb. 19, 1986** Secretary of State George P. Shultz cites "fraud and violence on a systematic and widespread scale" in the election by Marcos supporters.

**Feb. 21, 1986** Mr. Marcos calls foreign critics "modern-day imperialists" and warns he will charge his opponents with sedition if they resort to civil disobedience.

**Feb. 22, 1986** Defense Minister Juan Ponce Enrile and Lieut. Gen. Fidel V. Ramos, Deputy Chief of Staff, occupy the Defense Ministry and resign from Marcos Government to protest what they call election fraud and years of Government misconduct.

**Feb. 24, 1986** Marcos troops tentatively attack garrison held by troops loyal to Mr. Enrile and General Ramos. Washington threatens to cut off all military aid to Philippines if violence persists.

**Feb. 25, 1986** Mr. Marcos and Mrs. Aquino stage rival inaugurations. The United States steps up pressure on Mr. Marcos to quit, offering a plane and asylum. Later in the day, he accepts the offer and is flown to Clark Air Base and then to Guam. Mrs. Aquino is hailed as legitimate President. Crowds surge into the streets all over the Philippines as 20 years of Marcos rule ends.

FEB. 26

## A Growing Deficit

Trade balances in January 1986
(in millions of dollars)

**... with selected countries and regions**

| | |
|---|---:|
| Canada | −1,712 |
| Japan | −5,465 |
| Mexico | −499 |
| Taiwan | −1,243 |
| South Korea | −530 |
| Western Europe | −3,049 |
|     European Economic Community | −2,504 |
|     West Germany | −1,308 |
|     Britain | −494 |
| OPEC countries | −1,832 |
| Developing countries | −6,034 |
| TOTAL | −16,500 |

## ... for selected products

| | |
|---|---:|
| Petroleum and petroleum products | −4,761 |
| Passenger cars | −3,142 |
| Clothing | −1,395 |
| Telecommunications equipment | −1,282 |
| Iron and steel mill products | −704 |
| Electrical machinery | −516 |
| Office machinery (including computers) | −98 |
| Agricultural products | +351 |

Source: Commerce Department

**MARCH 9**

# The Marcos Retinue

On March 10 the State Department released a list of the people who accompanied Ferdinand Marcos, the former president of the Philippines, into exile in Hawaii in February. While most of those on the list are domestic servants, guards and personal aides of the Marcos family, it also included Eduardo Cojuangco, a Manila business executive who has been accused of collaborating with Mr. Marcos to divert millions of dollars from the nation's coconut industry. Also, General Fabian C. Ver, the former chief of staff, was accompanied by at least seven members of his family.

This is the list released by the State Department:

ANTONIO, Fe
AQUINO, Agripina
ARANETA, Gerogrio
ARANETA, Irene
ARUZA, Arturo
ASUNCION, Rosa
AZURIN, Ramon
BATANT, Emilio
BAUTISTA, Maria
BAYLEN, Evelina
BENITEZ, Jose
BOLIBO, Ferdinand
BONDOC, Griselda
CALAPINI, Ricardo
CINCO, Romeo
COJUANGCO, Carlos
COJUANGCO, Carmen
COJUANGCO, Danielle
COJUANGCO, Eduardo
COJUANGCO, Marcos
COJUANGCO, Paola
COJUANGCO, Soledad
CORPUZ, Minerva
DELEAR, Ricardo (since returned to the Philippines)
ESPADERO, Mervyn
ESPINELI, Menandro
ESTABILLO, Alberto
FLORA, Manuel
FELIX, Alfredo
FULE-FORONDU, Laureauo
FULE-FORONDU, Octavio
FULE-FORONDU, Paloma
GALLEGO, Maria
GANUT, Alejo
GIMENEZ, Fe
HUPPANDA, Teresita
ISIDERIO, Neinita
LABAN, Agnes
LAGUARDIA, Pacita
LUGA, Jovercio
LUMAKANG, Olivia
MAGNO, Delmar
MANOTOC, Ferdinand
MANOTOC, Fernando
MANOTOC, Imee
MANOTOC, Tomas
MARANON, Ramona
MARCOS, Aimee
MARCOS, Ferdinand Jr.
MARCOS, Imelda
MARCOS, Restituto
OCAMPO, Prospedo (since returned to the Philippines)
OCHINANG, Dari
ORTALEZA, Buenaventura
PANARIGAN, Salvador
PASCUA, Eufemio
PINEDA, Narciso
QUIRAO, Eva
RAMOX, Cloven
RANADA, Herminia
RATLIFF, Rudy
RAZA, Nora
RESURRECCION, Faida
RESURRECCION, Male
RESURRECCION, Nephthys
RUIZ, Agnes
SADLARIN, Nestor
SANIDAD, Eustacia
TAGAL, Lucile
TAUQUERIDO, Bernadette
TUASON, Anna
TUASON, Fabian
TUASON, Helma
TUASON, Mark
TUASON, Reina
TUASON, Reynaldo
VALDOZ, Ana
VELASCO, Geronimo
VILLA, Gil
VILLA, Orlanac
VER, Aida
VER, Fabian C.
VER, Irwin P.
VER, Maria Agnes
VER, Maria Ramona
VER, Marita E.
VER, Rexor
VER, Wyrlo
VERIDIANO, Monino
ZAGALA, Juanita

**MARCH 11**

# Marcos Papers Show a Fortune Around World

By JOEL BRINKLEY

WASHINGTON, March 19—Documents found among the personal effects of Ferdinand E. Marcos show that he and his family maintained bank accounts and other investments around the world worth hundreds of millions of dollars.

One document, apparently found in Mr. Marcos's own suitcase when he arrived in Hawaii last month, lists balances totaling $88.7 million in five banks in the United States, Switzerland and the Cayman Islands, a British possession in the Caribbean. Handwritten notes indicate that $35 million more had been deposited but not yet credited to the accounts.

The suitcase also contained negotiable stock certificates from Philippine corporations, all countersigned and made out to a variety of names. Together they carry a par value of $1.9 million. This is the nominal value assigned to shares of stocks regardless of their trading value on stock exchanges.

MARCH 20

## Marcos List of Payments

WASHINGTON, March 19—Following is a list of payments and deposits found in ledgers and other documents among Ferdinand E. Marcos's belongings made available to *The New York Times*:

### "Commissions" Received from Westinghouse 1976–1982:

|      | Received in Switzerland | Received in Philippines | Total |
|------|------------------------|------------------------|-------|
| 1976 | $4,050,460.86 |  | $ 4,050,460.86 |
| 1977 | $1,000,000.00 |  | $ 1,000,000.00 |
| 1979 |  | $2,756,105.11 | $ 2,756,105.11 |
| 1980 |  | $2,077,581.68 | $ 2,077,581.68 |
| 1981 |  | $1,136,590.88 | $ 1,136,590.88 |
| 1982 |  | $ 186,685.01 | $ 186,685.01 |
| TOTAL: | $5,050,460.86 | $6,156,962.68 | $11,207,423.54 |

### Record of Bank Deposits:

| | |
|---|---|
| Swiss Bank Corp. | US$9,350,418.00 |
| Credit Swiss | US$37,655,000.00 |
| Paribas | US$32,403,000.00 |
| Grand Cayman | US$4,296,887.00 |
| TOTAL: | US$88,745,446.88 |

### Payments from Japanese Companies:

| | | |
|---|---|---|
| 1. | Kawatetsu Bussan Co., Ltd. | US$311,874.08 |
| 2. | Sumitomo Corporation | US$212,708.75 |
| 3. | Kanematsu-Gosho, Ltd. | US$404,747.00 |
| 4. | Ace Lines-Freight | US$51,611.90 |
| 5. | Toyo Corporation | US$53,421.17 |
| | TOTAL: | US$1,034,362.90 |

### Government Share from Casino Earnings as of July 31, 1981:

| | Pesos |
|---|---|
| 1976 | 142,997,449.05 |
| 1977 | 170,547,996.08 |
| 1978 | 167,334,058.37 |
| 1979 | 158,012,737.39 |
| 1980 | 128,870,381.35 |
| TOTAL: | 767,762,622.24 |

MARCH 20

## Denationalization for France

### By PAUL LEWIS

PARIS, March 11—Some of the best-known companies in French industry and banking will shortly be coming onto the auction block if, as the polls predict will happen, France's right-wing opposition alliance wins next Sunday's parliamentary election.

That alliance has pledged to sell back to private investors the major industrial groups and banks nationalized by President François

Mitterrand's Socialists in 1981, when they came to power committed to "a rupture with capitalism."

The conservative alliance also plans to sell off other banks and enterprises nationalized by earlier governments.

In fact, the denationalization pledge represents a historic new commitment by the French right to economic deregulation that reverses a centuries' old tradition of state involvement in industry and finance.

"Our aim is to change the course of French economic history," says Alain Juppé, the economic spokesman for the opposition alliance, which consists of Jacques Chirac's Rally for the Republic and the Union for French Democracy, led by former President Valéry Giscard d'Estaing.

In denationalizing, France would become the latest country to join the long list of industrial and developing nations now selling off state-owned enterprises in a bid to make their economies more efficient and create additional wealth and jobs. Britain's Conservative Government, for instance, has already sold more than $25 billion worth of nationalized companies and Japan, West Germany and Italy plan similar programs. Even the Reagan Administration is in the process of selling its stake in Conrail, a freight railroad.

In France, the plan is to sell more than $20 billion worth of nationalized assets during a new government's five-year life at a rate of about $4 billion a year. The money from the sales will go to finance cuts in taxes and reduce the budget deficit.

The Socialists strongly oppose denationalization, but would continue to run state-owned companies as if they were private in the unlikely event they win the election. Already they have told the heads of most nationalized industries to get their companies into the black or lose their jobs, and the managers have been given freedom to restructure the companies, dismiss workers and raise capital on the private market. MARCH 12

## French-owned companies in line for privatization

Estimated value of the main state-owned companies eligible for denationalization, in millions of dollars at current exchange rate

**Insurance**

| | |
|---|---|
| Union des Assurances de Paris | $2,514 |
| Group des Assurances Nationales | 1,900 |
| Assurances Générales de France | 1,214 |

**Banks**

| | |
|---|---|
| Banque Nationale de Paris | 2,714 |
| Société Générale | 1,857 |
| Crédit Lyonnais | 1,714 |
| Crédit Commercial de France | 357 |

**Investment banking groups**

| | |
|---|---|
| Suez | 2,143 |
| Paribas | 829 |

**Industrial companies**

| | |
|---|---|
| Rhône-Poulenc | 1,714 |
| Pechiney | 1,357 |
| Compagnie Générale d'Electricité | 1,357 |
| Thomson | 1,000 |
| Saint-Gobain | 786 |
| **Total** | **$21,456** |

Estimated value of state-owned stakes, eligible for denationalization, in companies listed on the French stock exchange*

| Company | State-Owned Percentage | Value |
|---|---|---|
| Elf Acquitaine | 66 | 1,957 |
| Avions Marcel Dassault | 46 | 814 |
| Roussel-Uclaf | | |
|   Regular shares: | 40 | 486 |
|   Special shares: | 64 | |
| Compagnie Française | | |
|   des Pétroles | 40 | 457 |
| Matra | 51 | 200 |
| **Total** | | **$3,914** |

*Valuations as of December 1985
Source: "Dénationaliser," Jean Loyrette

MARCH 12

## Chirac Becomes France's Premier and Forms Conservative Cabinet

By RICHARD BERNSTEIN

PARIS, March 20—Jacques Chirac, the leader of the neo-Gaullist party, formally assumed the post of Prime Minister today and formed a new, conservative Government.

On Tuesday, President François Mitterrand, the Socialist leader, invited Mr. Chirac to become Prime Minister after a right-of-center coalition narrowly won parliamentary elections held Sunday.

The new Government formed by Mr. Chirac signaled a major shift in the political life of France, back to the conservatives who had governed uninterruptedly for 23 years before elections in 1981 swept a Socialist administration into power.

Mr. Chirac's formal acceptance today was accompanied by his presentation to Mr. Mitterrand of a list of the new Cabinet members. It marked the formal beginning of what the French call "cohabitation," a power-sharing arrangement between a leftist President and a rightist Prime Minister that had never been tried in this country before.

The new Prime Minister said he would ask the Parliament for blanket authorization to put nationalized businesses back into private hands and to reinstitute a majority system of voting, replacing the proportional system instituted by the Socialists a year ago.

"The French people have made a choice," Mr. Chirac said. "They have elected a new majority to the National Assembly and in so doing they have approved new policies for our country."     MARCH 20

## The New French Cabinet

On March 20 this new French cabinet was announced, with the listing below indicating political party affiliation and other background:

**Prime Minister**—Jacques Chirac, Rally for the Republic, Mayor of Paris.

**Foreign Affairs**—Jean-Bernard Raimond, unaffiliated career diplomat, most recently Ambassador to the Soviet Union.

**Minister of Economics, Finance and Privatization**—Edouard Balladur, Rally for the Republic, close Chirac adviser.

**Defense**—André Giraud, Republican, architect of nuclear energy program.

**Interior**—Charles Pasqua, Rally for the Republic, party leader in the Senate.

**Justice**—Albin Chalandon, Rally for the French Republic, former chairman of the Government oil company Elf-Aquitaine.

**Culture and Communications**—François Léotard, Republican, a rising young member of the political right.

**Housing and Transportation**—Pierre Méhaignerie, Center for Social Democrats, former Agriculture Minister.

**Overseas Departments and Territories**—Bernard Pons, Rally for the Republic, party's second-ranking leader, 1979–84.

**Education**—René Monory, Senator from Vienne Department.

**Social Affairs and Employment**—Philippe Séguin, Rally for the Republic, Mayor of Epinal.

**Industry and Tourism**—Alain Madelin, Republican, National Assembly member from Ille-et-Vilaine Dept.

**Agriculture**—François Guillaume, unaffiliated, former Farm Union head.

**Cooperation**—Michel Aurillac, Rally for the Republic, former National Assembly member from Indre Dept.

**Relations with Parliament**—André Rossinot, Radical, Deputy Mayor of Nancy.

MARCH 21

## Marcos Linked to Four Manhattan Sites

By JANE PERLEZ

The Philippine Government made public a document yesterday that it said linked Ferdinand E. Marcos to ownership of four Manhattan buildings thought to be worth hundreds of millions of dollars.

The document submitted as part of a deposition in a Federal District Court in New York, was identified as a trust agreement signed by Joseph E. Bernstein, a New York realtor. It says that Mr. Bernstein was empowered to act on behalf of Mr. Marcos.

Mr. Bernstein and his brother, Ralph, also a realtor, were cited for contempt of Congress recently after refusing to discuss allegations that they acted on Mr. Marcos's behalf.

Mr. Marcos and his wife, Imelda, have denied that they own property in the United States.

In the court proceedings, lawyers for the Philippine Government said the trust agreement and other papers found in the presidential palace in Manila constituted a "smoking gun" that proved that the Marcoses owned the four Manhattan buildings.

As part of the deposition, the Philippine Government submitted handwritten notes and checks that it said documented purchases by Mrs. Marcos of more than $2 million in one month at New York jewelers, including Cartier, Van Cleef & Arpels, Fred Leighton and La Vieille Russie.

According to Jovito R. Salonga, a Philippine official who heads a commission investigating the Marcoses' wealth, the documents show that Mrs. Marcos spent $3.3 million during a trip to New York in May 1983.

MARCH 21

## Reagan Defeated in House on Aiding Nicaragua Rebels

By STEVEN V. ROBERTS

WASHINGTON, March 20—The House of Representatives today rejected President Reagan's request to send $100 million to the rebels fighting to overthrow the Nicaraguan Government. The vote was 222 to 210, with 16 Republicans joining 206 Democrats in rebuffing the President on what he described as a major test of his presidency.

Forty-six Democrats and 164 Republicans supported Mr. Reagan, who was calling wavering lawmakers right up until the vote and asking for their backing.

Democrats and Republicans alike said that the outcome reflected a deep-seated confusion and uneasiness in the country over the President's policy toward Central America. Mr. Reagan, congressional leaders agreed, failed to convince enough House members that he has seriously tried to negotiate a peaceful settlement in the region.

"The public," said Representative Thomas S. Foley of Washington, the Democratic whip, "is not ready to engage in the escalation of military violence in Central America until other avenues are fully explored."

However, leaders in both parties also agree that a majority of Congress supports military aid for the rebels in some form. In the weeks ahead, they said, the lawmakers are likely to approve compromise legislation containing such aid.

"It's not a one-shot thing, it's not over now," said Representative Dick Cheney of Wyoming, a senior member of the Republican leadership. "I think eventually we'll pass a package for Central America and it will include military aid."

Whatever aid package does emerge from Congress is likely to delay the release of military support while the Administration is urged to pursue negotiations more vigorously. Under most proposals now being advanced on Capitol Hill, the money would be spent only if Congress determined that the Sandinista Government in Nicaragua was not bargaining in good faith.

Even while they were rejecting the Administration's approach to Nicaragua, many lawmakers expressed their deepening frustrations today over a situation that seems increasingly intractable.

Representative Dave McCurdy, an Oklahoma Democrat who is helping to draft an alternative to Mr. Reagan's plan, expressed the mood of many members of Congress when he said: "There's no magic solution out there. It's a very complex, complicated problem."

The vote today was the latest chapter in a long-running story on Capitol Hill. Congress voted to cut off all aid to the Nicaraguan rebels in 1984, but agreed last year to send $27 million in nonmilitary help. In the meantime, private supporters of the guerrillas organized a fund-raising drive to finance the purchase of weapons and other supplies.

President Reagan renewed his appeal for military support this year and went on national television Sunday night to press his case with the people. But in most congressional offices the phone calls opposing Mr. Reagan outnumbered those that supported him.

Representative Cheney cited this lack of public response as a major reason for today's vote. "It's a difficult issue to explain to the public," he said. "It's not on the front burner of public consciousness."

Many Democrats also say that the harsh language emanating from the White House, which accused opponents of giving aid and comfort to the Communists, alienated some potential supporters of the President.

"I think their tactics definitely backfired in some areas," said Representative W. G. Hefner, Democrat of North Carolina. "People just said, enough's enough. I think guys screwed up their courage and said, 'I'm not going to be intimidated; I'm not going to be bullied.'"

## House Roll Call on Aid to the Contras

On March 20, the House voted 222 to 210 to reject President Reagan's request for $100 million in aid to the Nicaraguan rebels. Two hundred and six Democrats and 16 Republicans opposed the aid, while 46 Democrats and 164 Republicans voted for it. In the list below, a "yes" is a vote for the aid, a "no" is a vote against it, and "xxx" indicates the member did not vote.

### ALABAMA
**Democrats**—Bevill, yes; Erdreich, yes; Flippo, yes; Nichols, yes; Shelby, yes.
**Republicans**—Callahan, yes; Dickinson, yes.

### ALASKA
**Republican**—Young, yes.

### ARIZONA
**Democrat**—Udall, no.
**Republicans**—Kolbe, yes; McCain, yes; Rudd, yes; Stump, yes.

### ARKANSAS
**Democrats**—Alexander, no; Anthony, no; Robinson, yes.
**Republican**—Hammerschmidt, yes.

### CALIFORNIA
**Democrats**—Anderson, no; Bates, no; Beilenson, no; Berman, no; Bosco, no; Boer, no; Brown, no; Burton, no; Coelho, no; Dellums, no; Dixon, no; Dymally, no; Edwards, no; Fazio, no; Hawkins, no; Lantos, no; Lehman, no; Levine, no; Martinez, no; Matsui, no; Miller, no; Mineta, no; Panetta, no; Roybal, no; Stark, no; Torres, no; Waxman, no.
**Republicans**—Badham, yes; Chappie, yes; Dannemeyer, yes; Dornan, yes; Dreier, yes; Fiedler, yes;

Hunter, yes; Lagomarsino, yes; Lewis, yes; Lowery, yes; Lungren, yes; McCandless, yes; Moorehead, yes; Packard, yes; Pashayan, yes; Shumway, yes; Thomas, yes; Zschau, yes.

### COLORADO
**Democrats**—Schroeder, no; Wirth, no.
**Republicans**—Brown, yes; Kramer, yes; Schaefer, yes; Strang, yes.

### CONNECTICUT
**Democrats**—Geidenson, no; Kennelly, no; Morrison, no.
**Republicans**—Johnson, yes; McKinney, no; Rowland, no.

### DELAWARE
**Democrat**—Carper, no.

### FLORIDA
**Democrats**—Bennett, yes; Chappell, yes; Fascell, yes; Fuqua, yes; Gibbons, yes; Hutto, yes; Lehman, no; MacKay, no; Mica, yes; Nelson, yes; Pepper, yes; Smith, yes.
**Republicans**—Bilirakis, yes; Ireland, yes; Lewis, yes; Mack, yes; McCollum, yes; Shaw, yes; Young, yes.

### GEORGIA
**Democrats**—Barnard, yes; Darden, yes; Fowler, no; Hatcher, yes; Jenkins, yes; Ray, no; Rowland, yes; Thomas, yes.
**Republicans**—Gingrich, yes; Swindall, yes.

### HAWAII
**Democrats**—Akaka, no; Heftel, no.

### IDAHO
**Democrat**—Stallings, no.
**Republican**—Craig, yes.

### ILLINOIS
**Democrats**—Annunzio, no; Bruce, no; Collins, no; Durbin, no; Evans, no; Gray, no; Hayes, no; Lipinski, yes; Price, no; Rostenkowski, no; Russo, no; Savage, no; Yates, no.
**Republicans**—Crane, yes; Fawell, yes; Grotberg, xxx; Hyde, yes; Madigan, yes; Martin, yes; Michel, yes; O'Brien, yes; Porter, yes.

### INDIANA
**Democrats**—Hamilton, no; Jacobs, no; McCloskey, no; Sharp, no; Visclosky, no.
**Republicans**—Burton, yes; Coats, yes; Hiler, yes; Hillis, yes; Myers, yes.

### IOWA
**Democrats**—Bedell, no; Smith, no.
**Republicans**—Evans, xxx; Leach, no; Lightfoot, no; Tauke, no.

### KANSAS
**Democrats**—Glickman, no; Slattery, no.
**Republicans**—Meyers, yes; Roberts, yes; Whittaker, yes.

### KENTUCKY
**Democrats**—Hubbard, no; Mazzoli, no; Natcher, no; Perkins, no.
**Republicans**—Hopkins, no; Rogers, yes; Snyder, yes.

### LOUISIANA
**Democrats**—Boggs, no; Breaux, yes; Huckaby, yes; Long, no; Roemer, yes; Tauzin, yes.
**Republicans**—Livingston, yes; Moore, yes.

### MAINE
**Republicans**—McKernan, yes; Snowe, no.

### MARYLAND
**Democrats**—Barnes, no; Byron, yes; Dyson, yes; Hoyer, no; Mikulski, no; Mitchell, no.
**Republicans**—Bentley, yes; Holt, yes.

### MASSACHUSETTS
**Democrats**—Atkins, no; Boland, no; Donnelly, no; Early, no; Frank, no; Markey, no; Mavroules, no; Moakley, no; O'Neill, no; Studs, no.
**Republican**—Conte, no.

### MICHIGAN
**Democrats**—Bonior, no; Carr, no; Conyers, no; Crockett, no; Dingell, no; Ford, no; Hertel, no; Kildee, no; Levin, no; Traxler, no; Wolpe, no.
**Republicans**—Broomfield, yes; Davis, yes; Henry, yes; Pursell, yes; Schuette, yes; Siljander, yes; Vander Jagt, yes.

### MINNESOTA
**Democrats**—Oberstar, no; Penny, no; Sabo, no; Sikorski, no; Vento, no.
**Republicans**—Frenzel, no; Stangeland, yes; Weber, yes.

### MISSISSIPPI
**Democrats**—Dowdy, yes; Montgomery, yes; Whitten, no.
**Republicans**—Franklin, yes; Lott, yes.

### MISSOURI
**Democrats**—Clay, no; Gephardt, no; Skelton, yes; Volkmer, no; Wheat, no; Young, no.
**Republicans**—Coleman, yes; Emerson, yes; Taylor, yes.

### MONTANA
**Democrat**—Williams, no.
**Republican**—Marlenee, yes.

### NEBRASKA
**Republicans**—Bereuter, yes; Daub, yes; Smith, yes.

### NEVADA
**Democrat**—Reid, no.
**Republican**—Vucanovich, yes.

### NEW HAMPSHIRE
**Republicans**—Gregg, yes; Smith, yes.

### NEW JERSEY
**Democrats**—Dwyer, no; Florio, no; Guarini, no; Howard, no; Hughes, no; Rodino, no; Roe, no; Torricelli, no.
**Republicans**—Courter, yes; Gallo, yes; Rinaldo, yes; Roukema, yes; Saxton, yes; Smith, yes.

### NEW MEXICO
**Democrat**—Richardson, no.
**Republicans**—Lujan, yes; Skeen, yes.

### NEW YORK
**Democrats**—Ackerman, no; Addabbo, xxx; Biaggi, no; Downey, no; Garcia, no; LaFalce, no; Lundine, no; Manton, no; McHugh, no; Mrazek, no; Nowak, no; Owens, no; Rangel, no; Scheuer, no; Schumer, no; Solarz, no; Stratton, yes; Towns, no; Weiss, no.
**Republicans**—Boehlert, no; Carney, yes; DioGuardi, yes; Eckert, yes; Fish, yes; Gilman, yes; Green, no; Horton, no; Kemp, yes; Lent, yes; Martin, yes; McGrath, yes; Molinari, yes; Solomon, yes; Wortley, yes.

### NORTH CAROLINA
**Democrats**—Hefner, no; Jones, no; Neal, no; Rose, no; Valentine, no; Whitley, no.
**Republicans**—Broyhill, yes; Cobey, yes; Coble, yes; Hendon, yes; McMillan, yes.

### NORTH DAKOTA
**Democrat**—Dorgan, no.

### OHIO
**Democrats**—Applegate, no; Eckart, no; Feighan, no; Hall, no; Kaptur, no; Luken, no; Oakar, no; Pease, no; Seiberling, no; Stokes, no; Traficant, no.
**Republicans**—DeWine, yes; Gradison, yes; Kasich, yes; Kindness, yes; Latta, yes; McEwen, yes; Miller, yes; Oxley, yes; Regula, yes; Wylie, no.

### OKLAHOMA
**Democrats**—English, yes; Jones, yes; McCurdy, no; Synar, no; Watkins, no.
**Republican**—Edwards, yes.

### OREGON
**Democrats**—AuCoin, no; Weaver, no; Wyden, no.
**Republicans**—D. Smith, yes; R. Smith, yes.

### PENNSYLVANIA
**Democrats**—Borski, no; Coyne, no; Edgar, no; Foglietta, no; Gaydos, yes; Gray, no; Kanjorski, no; Kolter, no; Kostmayer, no; Murphy, no; Murtha, yes; Walgren, no; Yatron, no.
**Republicans**—Clinger, yes; Coughlin, yes; Gekas, yes; Goodling, yes; McDade, yes; Ridge, no; Ritter, yes; Schulze, yes; Shuster, yes; Walker, yes.

### RHODE ISLAND
**Democrat**—St Germain, no.
**Republican**—Schneider, no.

### SOUTH CAROLINA
**Democrats**—Derrick, no; Spratt, no; Tallon, yes.
**Republicans**—Campbell, yes; Hartnett, yes; Spence, yes.

### SOUTH DAKOTA
**Democrat**—Daschle, no.

### TENNESSEE
**Democrats**—Boner, no; Cooper, no; Ford, no; Gordon, no; Jones, no; Lloyd, no.
**Republicans**—Duncan, yes; Quillen, yes; Sundquist, yes.

### TEXAS
**Democrats**—Andrews, no; Brooks, no; Bryant, no; Bustamante, no; Chapman, no; Coleman, no; de la Garza, no; Frost, no; Gonzalez, no; R. Hall, yes; Leath, yes; Leland, no; Ortiz, yes; Pickle, no; Stenholm, yes; Wilson, yes; Wright, no.
**Republicans**—Archer, yes; Armey, yes; Bartlett, yes; Barton, yes; Boulter, yes; Combest, yes; DeLay, yes; Fields, yes; Loeffler, yes; Sweeney, yes.

### UTAH
**Republicans**—Hansen, yes; Monson, yes; Nielson, yes.

### VERMONT
**Republican**—Jeffords, no.

### VIRGINIA
**Democrats**—Boucher, no; Daniel, yes; Olin, no; Sisisky, yes.
**Republicans**—Bateman, yes; Bliley, yes; Parris, yes; Slaughter, yes; Whitehurst, yes; Wolf, yes.

### WASHINGTON
**Democrats**—Bonker, no; Dicks, no; Foley, no; Lowry, no; Swift, no.
**Republicans**—Chandler, yes; Miller, yes; Morrison, yes.

### WEST VIRGINIA
**Democrats**—Mollohan, no; Rahall, no; Staggers, no; Wise, no.

### WISCONSIN
**Democrats**—Aspin, no; Kastenmeier, no; Kleczka, no; Moody, no; Obey, no.
**Republicans**—Gunderson, yes; Petri, yes; Roth, yes; Sensenbrenner, yes.

### WYOMING
**Republican**—Cheney, yes.

MARCH 21

## Exploding the bomb
(Known nuclear tests, 1945–1985)

| | United States | Soviet Union | Britain | France | China | India |
|---|---|---|---|---|---|---|
| 1945 | 3 | 0 | 0 | 0 | 0 | 0 |
| 1946 | 2 | 0 | 0 | 0 | 0 | 0 |
| 1947 | 0 | 0 | 0 | 0 | 0 | 0 |
| 1948 | 3 | 0 | 0 | 0 | 0 | 0 |
| 1949 | 0 | 1 | 0 | 0 | 0 | 0 |
| 1950 | 0 | 0 | 0 | 0 | 0 | 0 |
| 1951 | 16 | 2 | 1 | 0 | 0 | 0 |
| 1952 | 10 | 0 | 0 | 0 | 0 | 0 |
| 1953 | 11 | 4 | 2 | 0 | 0 | 0 |
| 1954 | 6 | 7 | 0 | 0 | 0 | 0 |
| 1955 | 18 | 5 | 0 | 0 | 0 | 0 |
| 1956 | 18 | 9 | 6 | 0 | 0 | 0 |
| 1957 | 32 | 15 | 7 | 0 | 0 | 0 |
| 1958 | 77 | 29 | 5 | 0 | 0 | 0 |
| 1956–58* | | 18 | | | | |
| 1959 | 0 | 0 | 0 | 0 | 0 | 0 |
| 1960 | 0 | 0 | 0 | 3 | 0 | 0 |
| 1961 | 10 | 50 | 0 | 2 | 0 | 0 |
| 1962 | 96 | 44 | 2 | 1 | 0 | 0 |
| 1963 | 43 | 0 | 0 | 3 | 0 | 0 |
| 1964 | 29 | 6 | 1 | 3 | 1 | 0 |
| 1965 | 29 | 9 | 1 | 4 | 1 | 0 |
| 1966 | 40 | 15 | 0 | 6 | 3 | 0 |
| 1967 | 29 | 16 | 0 | 3 | 2 | 0 |
| 1968 | 39 | 13 | 0 | 5 | 1 | 0 |
| 1969 | 29 | 15 | 0 | 0 | 2 | 0 |
| 1970 | 33 | 13 | 0 | 8 | 1 | 0 |
| 1971 | 15 | 20 | 0 | 5 | 1 | 0 |
| 1972 | 15 | 22 | 0 | 3 | 2 | 0 |
| 1973 | 12 | 14 | 0 | 5 | 1 | 0 |
| 1974 | 12 | 20 | 1 | 7 | 1 | 1 |
| 1975 | 17 | 15 | 0 | 2 | 1 | 0 |
| 1976 | 15 | 17 | 1 | 4 | 4 | 0 |
| 1977 | 12 | 18 | 0 | 6 | 1 | 0 |
| 1963–77** | | 16 | | | | |
| 1978 | 16 | 27 | 2 | 8 | 3 | 0 |
| 1979 | 15 | 29 | 1 | 9 | 0 | 0 |
| 1980 | 14 | 21 | 3 | 13 | 1 | 0 |
| 1981 | 16 | 21 | 1 | 12 | 0 | 0 |
| 1982 | 18 | 31 | 1 | 6 | 0 | 0 |
| 1983 | 17 | 27 | 1 | 7 | 2 | 0 |
| 1984 | 17 | 27 | 2 | 8 | 2 | 0 |
| 1985 | 15 | 8 | 1 | 8 | 0 | 0 |
| Total | 799 | 604 | 39 | 141 | 30 | 1 |

*Stockholm International Peace Research Institute and the Swedish National Defense Research Institute report 18 additional Soviet tests conducted between 1956 and 1958.

**French Ministry of Defense reports 16 additional Soviet tests conducted between 1963 and 1977.

Since 1962 British underground nuclear tests have been conducted jointly with the United States in Nevada.

Source: Natural Resources Defense Council

MARCH 23

### Key Libyan military forces

Troop and equipment count before confrontation with U.S. forces.

**AIR FORCE**

| | |
|---|---|
| Forces | 8,500 |
| Fighter interceptors | |
|   MIG-23 | 143 |
|   MIG-21 | 55 |
|   MIG-25 | 55 |
|   Mirage F-1 | 32 |
| Attack fighters | |
|   Sukhoi 20/22 | 100 |
|   Mirage 5 | 58 |
| Bombers | |
|   TU-22 | 7 |
| Air defense | |
|   SAM-2 missiles | 72 |
|   SAM-3 missiles | 4 |
|   SAM-5 missiles | 18* |

*Estimate

**Sukhoi attack fighter**

**NAVY**

| | | | |
|---|---|---|---|
| Forces | 6,500 | Mine layers | 6 |
| Foxtrot class | | Fast attack ships | 46 |
| attack submarines | 6 | Amphibious ships | 25 |
| Frigate | 1 | | |
| Corvettes | 8 | | |

**Nanuchka class missile corvette**

**ARMY**

| | |
|---|---|
| Forces | 58,000 |
| Tank battalions | 20 |
| Mechanized infantry battalions | 30 |
| Artillery battalions | 10 |
| Special forces battalions | 10 |

Sources: International Institute for Strategic Studies, Jane's Fighting Ships and All the World's Aircraft

MARCH 26

# 6 Are Acquitted in Plot on Pope; Ruling Ambiguous

By JOHN TAGLIABUE

ROME, March 29—An Italian court today acquitted three Bulgarians and three Turks of conspiring to assassinate Pope John Paul II. The court ruled that the evidence against them was ambiguous.

The acquittal for lack of proof is a formula under Italian law implying that evidence exists to support both the guilt and innocence of a defendant and that the court is unable to decide. The verdict is therefore unlikely to end the debate over the case.

The court found another Turk guilty of storing and delivering the weapon used to shoot the Pope in 1981. Mehmet Ali Agca, one of the Turks acquitted on the conspiracy charges, who is serving a life sentence for the attack, was convicted of complicity in smuggling the weapon into Italy.

The verdict on the conspiracy charges followed a bitterly contested legal battle that lasted nearly four years and posed a serious irritant to East-West relations. The implication behind the charges against the Bulgarians was that the Soviet bloc had ordered the Pope's assassination by a right-wing Turkish gunman to wipe out resistance to Communist rule in Poland, the Pope's native land.

In a statement released to coincide with the verdict, the Soviet press agency, Tass, said, "The West's reactionary quarters failed to further their sordid aims of smearing the Bulgarians.

"The so-called Bulgarian connection charge crumbled to nothing."

The Bulgarian press agency issued a similar statement.

In a session lasting about six minutes, the

court found Mr. Agca, who shot and wounded the Pope in St. Peter's Square on May 13, 1981, guilty of the gun-smuggling charge.

The court sentenced Mr. Agca, 28 years old, to one year in prison and two months of solitary confinement on the charge, which he had admitted during the trial.

Mr. Agca was the Government's leading witness against the Bulgarians, but he damaged its case by his erratic courtroom behavior, including assertions that he was Jesus Christ.

The fourth Turkish defendant, Omer Bagci, 40, was convicted of storing the gun and illegally delivering it to Mr. Agca at a meeting in Milan in early 1981. He was sentenced to three years in prison.

But the court said the sentence could not be imposed because Mr. Bagci had been extradited from Switzerland only on the conspiracy charges, of which he was acquitted.

The jury of two judges and six lay jurors deliberated for six days before acquitting the defendants in the 10-month trial.

These were the defendants:

**MEHMET ALI AGCA**
28 years old . . . Was convicted in 1981 of shooting and wounding Pope John Paul II in St. Peter's Square and sentenced to life imprisonment . . . Was the key state's witness in current trial, but also was charged with conspiring with others to kill the Pope and illegally smuggling into Italy the gun he used . . . Admitted charges and was sentenced to one year in prison and two months in solitary confinement.

**SERGEI I. ANTONOV**
Former Rome station chief of Bulgarian airline . . . Arrested in Italy Nov. 25, 1982 . . . Accused of helping plan the assassination and driving Mr. Agca and a second Turkish accomplice to St. Peter's Square . . . Acquitted.

**TODOR S. AIVASOV**
Bulgarian diplomat and former cashier at the embassy in Rome . . . Left Italy in 1982, now in Sofia . . . Charged with helping procure guns and a sealed truck for the would-be assassins' getaway . . . Acquitted.

**ZHELYO K. VASILEC**
Former aide to the military attaché at the Bulgarian Embassy in Rome . . . Left Italy in 1982, now in Sofia . . . Charged with organizing meetings with conspirators in Rome and helping plot the Pope's death . . . Acquitted.

**OMER BAGCI**
A Turkish laborer arrested in Switzerland and extradited to Italy . . . Convicted of delivering to Mr. Agca the gun used to shoot the Pope . . . Sentenced to three years in jail, but sentence cannot be imposed.

**MUSA SERDAR CELIBI**
The former head of a right-wing "Gray Wolves" group of Turkish workers in West Germany . . . Accused of channeling money to Mr. Agca . . . Said he never knew Mr. Agca intended to kill the Pope . . . Acquitted.

**ORAI CELIK**
Right-wing Turkish activist and suspected drug smuggler sought in several countries . . . Accused by Mr. Agca of being a backup gunman in St. Peter's Square . . . Now at large . . . Acquitted.

MARCH 30

## Attack on the Pope: How Case Developed

The verdict yesterday in the case arising from the shooting of Pope John Paul II came nearly five years after the assassination attempt. These were some of the key developments in the case:

**May 13, 1981**—Mehmet Ali Agca shoots and seriously wounds Pope John Paul II in St. Peter's Square.

**July 22, 1981**—Mr. Agca is convicted of the attempted assassination of the Pope and is sentenced by Judge Severino Santiapichi to life imprisonment. The convicted assailant continues to insist he acted alone.

**Sept. 25, 1981**—Judge Santiapichi delivers a 50-page verdict in the first papal shooting trial asserting that the attack was the result of an armed conspiracy and declaring that the investigation will remain open.

**May 1982**—Mr. Agca begins giving details to the investigating magistrate, Ilario Martella, of the involvement of the Bulgarian secret service in a purported conspiracy to assassinate the Polish-born Pope, in what he says was an effort to crack resistance to Communism in Poland.

**June 2, 1982**—Omer Bagci, a Turkish migrant laborer in a Swiss glass factory, is arrested by the Swiss police and extradited to Italy to stand trial for complicity.

**Nov. 3, 1982**—Musa Serdar Celibi is arrested in Frankfurt and later extradited by West Germany to Italy to stand trial.

**Nov. 25, 1982**—Sergei I. Antonov is arrested in Rome.

**Dec. 17, 1982**—Todor Aivasov, Zhelyo M. Vasilev and Bekir Celenk appear at a specially arranged news conference in a downtown Sofia hotel to declare their innocence. Bulgaria refuses to extradite the three to Italy to stand trial and demands the release of Mr. Antonov, asserting he is the victim of a plot by Western intelligence services to smear Bulgaria.

**Oct. 26, 1984**—Judge Martella orders three Bulgarians and five Turks to stand trial for conspiring to assassinate the Pope.

**May 27, 1985**—Trial of the eight defendants begins in a special high-security courtroom converted from a sports gymnasium. Only four defendants are in Italy; the other four are tried in absentia.

**July 7, 1985**—Bulgaria sends Bekir Celenk back to Turkey, asserting that it has no evidence he has been involved in any wrongdoing.

**September 1985**—Mr. Celenk dies of heart failure in a military prison near Ankara.

**March 29, 1986**—Three Bulgarian and three Turkish defendants are acquitted of conspiracy charges. Mr. Bagci and Mr. Agca are convicted of smuggling the weapon used in the shooting into Italy.

MARCH 30

# Terror's Victims: 3 Generations of a Family . . .

**By SARA RIMER**

ANNAPOLIS, Md., April 4—In a well-kept house on Lafayette Avenue, with family photographs on the walls and daffodils blooming in the front yard, friends and relatives of three American victims of terrorism gathered today in shared sorrow.

Like others before them, they asked questions without seeming to expect answers.

"We're good people," said Virginia Shultz. "What did we do to deserve this?"

Mrs. Shultz's brother-in-law, Paul Alexiou, is the brother of Demetra Stylian, 52, who was killed on Wednesday along with her daughter, Maria Klug, 24, and her nine-month granddaughter, Demetra Klug, when a bomb exploded aboard Trans World Airlines Flight 840. The three were from Annapolis; the fourth victim, Alberto Ospina, was from Stratford, Conn.

Mrs. Shultz recalled someone else's question: "One of the men said this morning—don't those terrorists have wives and brothers and sisters?"

APRIL 5

# . . . and a Businessman Worried about Travel

**By DIRK JOHNSON**

STRATFORD, Conn., April 4—Alberto Ospina stood in a Federal courtroom six years ago, his right hand held high, and recited the oath of United States citizenship.

"He was so proud," said Carmela Cardiello, a neighbor of the emigrant from Colombia. "Being an American meant good things. It meant opportunity."

It has come to mean danger, as well, for those traveling abroad. Mr. Ospina, 39 years old, was one of four American passengers killed Wednesday when a bomb exploded aboard a Trans World Airlines Boeing 727 bound for Athens from Rome.

Mr. Ospina, an international sales representative for a manufacturer of medical supplies, had talked about the risks before making what would be his final business trip to the Mediterranean. When the bomb exploded he was just beginning the journey, which was to have taken him to Athens, Istanbul and Ankara.

In the last year, he had made about 15 trips

abroad, to South America as well as to Europe, for Frigitronics Inc., a medical supplies company based in Minneapolis that has offices in Shelton, Conn.

"He was quite worried about this last trip," said Gloria Cavallaro, the personnel manager at Frigitronics. "But he said, 'If your time has come, it's come.'"

APRIL 5

---

**The four victims, all American, of the explosion on TWA Flight 840 on April 2:**

Alberto Ospina, 39, Stratford, Conn.

Demetra Stylian, 52, Annapolis, Md.; her daughter, Maria Klug, 24, also of Annapolis; and her granddaughter and Mrs. Klug's daughter, Demetra Klug, 9 months, also of Annapolis.

APRIL 3

---

## 12 Months of Terror: The Mideast Connection

Links between groups and countries made by American experts on terrorism.

### 1985

**April 12, Madrid.** Bomb explodes at restaurant outside city frequented by U.S. servicemen, killing 18 Spaniards and wounding 82 people, including 14 Americans.
**Claim:** Islamic Holy War.
**Link:** Syria and Iran.

**April 13, Paris.** Bombs explode at branch of Israeli-owned Bank Leumi and National Immigration Office and at offices of rightist weekly newspaper *Minute* the next day.
**Claim:** Direct Action, a French guerrilla group, says attacks were carried out by "Sana Mheidleh commando," a reference to a Lebanese woman who carried out suicide bomb attack in Lebanon.
**Link:** Libya and Syria.

**June 14, Athens.** Two Lebanese Shiite gunmen hijack TWA jetliner on Athens-to-Rome flight with 104 Americans aboard and force it to fly to Beirut. United States Navy diver, Robert Dean Stethem, is killed. A Shiite Amal militia leader, Nabih Berri, negotiates on behalf of hijackers; hostages released after 17 days.
**Link:** Syria.

**June 19, Frankfurt.** Bomb explodes at Frankfurt's international airport, killing 3 and wounding 42.
**Claim:** Arab Revolutionary Organization, which some experts believe is the Palestinian Abu Nidal group.
**Link:** Libya and Syria.

**July 1, Madrid.** Terrorists bomb building housing offices of TWA and British Airways and attack offices of Jordanian national airline, Alia. One killed and 27 wounded.
**Claim:** Organization of the Oppressed.
**Link:** Unknown.

**Aug. 8, U.S. Rhein-Main Air Base,** near Frankfurt. Car bomb explodes, killing 2 Americans and wounding 20 Americans and Germans.
**Claim:** Direct Action and the Red Army Faction.
**Link:** Libya.

**Sept. 3, Athens.** Two grenades are thrown into lobby of Greek hotel, wounding 18 British tourists.
**Claim:** None, but telephone caller tells Greek newspaper that unless unidentified Palestinian is released, Black September guerrilla group "would fill Athens with bombs."
**Link:** Libya.

**Sept. 16, Rome.** Grenades are thrown into Café de Paris, wounding 38 people, including 9 Americans.
**Claim:** Revolutionary Org. of Socialist Moslems.
**Link:** Unknown.

**Sept. 25, Rome.** Bomb explodes in Rome ticket office of British Airways, killing 1 and wounding 14.
**Claim:** Palestinian teenager who says he is a member of Revolutionary Organization of Socialist Moslems is arrested and confesses to police.

**Oct. 7, Mediterranean.** Four hijackers seize *Achille Lauro* cruise ship. An American, Leon Klinghoffer, is killed a day later; hijackers surrender in Egypt Oct. 9.
**Claim:** Hijackers say they are members of Palestine Liberation Front, a faction of the P.L.O.
**Link:** Tunisia, Libya, Syria.

**Nov. 23, Athens.** Egyptair jetliner is hijacked on flight from Athens to Cairo and forced to land in Malta. Five passengers are shot, 2 fatally, including an American, Scarlett Marie Rogenkamp; Egyptians then storm plane; 58 people are killed.
**Claim:** Hijackers say they are members of a group called Egypt's Revolution, but Abu Nidal's Arab Revolutionary Command and the Organization of Egypt's Revolutionaries also issue statement taking responsibility.

**Nov. 24, Frankfurt.** Car bomb explodes at U.S. military shopping center, wounding 35, including 33 Americans.
**Claim:** None, but Abu Nidal group is suspected of involvement.

**Dec. 7, Paris.** Bombs explode at Galeries Lafayette and Printemps department stores, 39 people wounded.
**Claim:** Palestine Liberation Front.

**Dec. 27, Rome and Vienna.** Gunmen attack airports and 20 people are killed, including 4 terrorists and 5 Americans, and more than 110 others are wounded.
**Claim:** Surviving gunmen say they are members of the Fatah Revolutionary Council, a Palestinian group headed by Abu Nidal.

### 1986

**Feb. 3, Paris.** Bomb explodes on Champs-Elysées, wounding 8 people.
**Claim:** Committee of Solidarity with Arab and Middle Eastern Political Prisoners, which demands release of 2 Arabs and 1 Armenian jailed in France, including leader of Lebanese Armed Revolutionary Factions.

**Feb. 4, Paris.** Bomb explodes in crowded bookshop in Latin Quarter, wounding 4 people. That evening, bomb is discovered in Eiffel Tower, but police defuse it.
**Claim:** None issued.

**Feb. 5, Paris.** Bomb explodes in Forum des Halles shopping mall, wounding 9.
**Claim:** None.

**March 20, Paris.** Bomb explodes on Champs-Elysées, killing 2 and wounding 28. Second bomb found in a subway station is defused.
**Claim:** Committee of Solidarity with Arab and Middle Eastern Political Prisoners.

**April 5, West Berlin.** Bomb explodes in a discothèque popular with American troops, killing one American serviceman and a Turkish woman and wounding 204 people, including more than 50 Americans.
**Claim:** West German terrorist groups and previously unknown group calling itself Anti-American Arab Liberation Front. U.S. officials say there are clear indications of Libyan responsibility for attack.

APRIL 8

## Still Missing: The Hostages in Lebanon

### AMERICAN

**Terry A. Anderson,** chief Middle East correspondent for The Associated Press, kidnapped March 16, 1985.

**William Buckley,** a political officer at the United States Embassy in Beirut, abducted March 16, 1984.

**David P. Jacobsen,** director of the American University Hospital in Beirut, kidnapped May 28, 1985.

**The Rev. Lawrence M. Jenco,** head of the Beirut office of Catholic Relief Services, abducted Jan. 8, 1985.

**Thomas M. Sutherland,** dean of agriculture at the American University, kidnapped June 9, 1985.

### BRITISH

**Alec Collett,** New York-based freelance journalist on a writing assignment for the United Nations Relief and Works Agency, kidnapped March 25, 1985.

**John McCarthy,** cameraman for the London-based Worldwide Television News Agency, kidnapped April 17, 1986.

### IRISH

**Brian Keenan,** professor at the American University in Beirut, kidnapped April 11, 1986.

### FRENCH

**Marcel Fontaine,** vice consul of the French Embassy, kidnapped March 22, 1985.

**Marcel Carton,** protocol officer of the French Embassy, kidnapped March 22, 1985.

**Jean-Paul Kauffmann,** correspondent for the French weekly *L'Evénement du Jeudi*, kidnapped May 22, 1985.

**Michel Seurat,** researcher at the French Center for Studies and Research of the Contemporary Middle East, kidnapped May 22, 1985.

**Philippe Rochot,** correspondent for the French network Antenne 2, kidnapped March 8, 1986.

**Georges Hansen,** cameraman for the French network Antenne 2, kidnapped March 8, 1986.

**Aurel Cornea,** soundman for the French network Antenne 2, kidnapped March 8, 1986.

**Jean-Louis Normandin,** lighting engineer for French network Antenne 2, kidnapped March 8, 1986.

### ITALIAN

**Alberto Molimari,** businessman who dealt in insurance and import-export and lived in Beirut for 20 years, kidnapped Sept. 11, 1985.

### SOUTH KOREAN

**Do Chae Sung,** second secretary at the South Korean Embassy, kidnapped Jan. 31, 1986.

APRIL 18

## Air Raid on Libya: Minute by Minute*

**12:13 P.M.** Twenty-eight KC and KC135 refueling planes leave from Royal Air Force bases Fairford and Mildenhall.

**12:36 P.M.** Twenty-four F-111 bombers leave from R.A.F. base Lakenheath and five EF-111 Raven electronic jamming planes take off from R.A.F. base Heyford. Four silent refuelings take place on the way to the target area. Six of the F-111's were spare planes that returned to Britain, as planned, after the first refueling. One spare EF-111 also returns.

**5:45–6:15 P.M.** The aircraft carrier *America* launches six A-6E strike and six A-7 strike support aircraft.

**5:20–6:20 P.M.** The carrier *Coral Sea* launches eight A-6E strike and six F/A-18 strike support aircraft.

**6:54 P.M.** Three EF-111's commence electronic jamming while A-7's and F/A-18's begin missile attacks on SAM missile sites. The fourth EF-111 is held in reserve.

**7:00 P.M.** Simultaneous attacks begin at Benghazi and Tripoli. The Benina Airfield and military barracks near Benghazi are hit by bombs from twelve A-6E's and the Azzizyah barracks and the Sidi Bilal training camp near Tripoli are attacked by eight F-111's.

**7:06–7:11 P.M.** Five F-111's bomb the Tripoli military airport, the final target.

**7:13 P.M.** All Navy strike aircraft confirm "feet wet" (over the ocean, away from Libyan land). Unable to confirm all Air Force aircraft "feet wet."

**7:15 P.M.** Search and rescue forces are alerted to search for a possible missing aircraft.

**7:46 P.M.** All *Coral Sea* strike aircraft are back on deck.

**7:53 P.M.** All *America* strike and primary support aircraft are back on deck.

**8:14 P.M.** First return refueling confirms one F-111 is missing.

**10:16 P.M.** One F-111 returning to Britain is diverted to Rota, Spain, because of an overheated engine.

**11:24 P.M.** The diverted F-111 is reported safe at Rota.

*All times are Eastern Standard.

Source: Defense Department

APRIL 18

## Six Hostile Years

### 1981

**May**—The United States orders Libya to close its diplomatic mission in Washington, citing "support for international terrorism."

**August**—American Navy jets shoot down two Libyan warplanes off Libya after being fired on. Qaddafi urges Arab "active forces" to retaliate.

### 1982

**March**—Reagan Administration imposes embargo on Libyan oil, curtails exports of technology to Libya.

### 1983

**February**—Libya says U.S. is jamming its communications, warns that Gulf of Sidra will be bay of "blood and fire" if U.S. carrier enters.

**August**—Navy jet fighters from carrier *Eisenhower* intercept two Libyan MIG-23's off Libya's coast; MIGs turn away.

### 1984

**May**—Qaddafi denounces Reagan as the "worst terrorist in the world," following attack by anti-Government guerrillas on a barracks usually used by Qaddafi.

**July**—Fighter planes from carrier *Saratoga* fly over the Gulf of Sidra; no incidents reported.

### 1985

**December**—State Department says Soviet Union provided SA-5 long-range ground-to-air missiles to Libya that would pose a threat to aircraft in disputed Mediterranean areas.

**December**—United States accuses Libya of aiding terrorists who staged attacks at the Rome and Vienna airports two days after Christmas, says it will work with other governments to "exert pressure" on Libya to halt export of terrorism

### 1986

**January 9**—American banks freeze Libyan assets under Reagan order.

**March 24**—United States Navy planes attack two Libyan patrol boats near "line of death" in Gulf of Sidra waters claimed by Libya; Libyan shore batteries and radar also attacked.

**April 5**—United States blames Libya for blast that kills one American, injures 230 people in West Berlin discothèque.

**April 9**—Reagan calls Qaddafi "mad dog of the Middle East." Qaddafi replies Reagan is "old man."

**April 14**—U.S. planes bomb Libya, killing Qaddafi's adopted infant daughter, injuring two of his sons and at least a dozen other people. Senior White House official says, "We were showing him that we could get people close to him."

**April 18**—Reagan says, "We weren't out to kill anybody."

APRIL 20

## Unpaid bills

Assessments and contributions to the United Nations regular budget for selected countries (in millions of U.S. dollars)

| | Assessment as percent of U.N. budget | Contributions due Jan. 1, 1986 | Contributions outstanding on March 31, 1986 | | |
|---|---|---|---|---|---|
| | | | Prior years | Current year | Total |
| Brazil | 1.40 % | $ 9.806 | $ 15.978 | $ 9.806 | $ 25.784 |
| Britain | 4.86 | 34.041 | 0 | 25.531 | 25.531 |
| Cambodia | 0.01 | 0.70 | 0.177 | 0.70 | 0.247 |
| Canada | 3.06 | 21.433 | 0 | 0 | 0 |
| China | 0.79 | 5.533 | 1.859 | 5.333 | 7.392 |
| France | 6.37 | 44.618 | 0 | 4.357 | 4.357 |
| Iran | 0.63 | 4.413 | 3.500 | 4.413 | 7.913 |
| Israel | 0.22 | 1.541 | 2.998 | 1.541 | 4.539 |
| Italy | 3.79 | 26.546 | 0 | 26.546 | 26.546 |
| Japan | 10.84 | 75.927 | 0 | 56.548 | 56.548 |
| Libya | 0.26 | 1.821 | 2.430 | 1.821 | 4.251 |
| Mexico | 0.89 | 6.234 | 0.012 | 6.234 | 6.246 |
| Netherlands | 1.74 | 12.187 | 0 | 9.033 | 9.033 |
| Poland | 0.64 | 4.483 | 4.990 | 4.483 | 9.473 |
| Saudi Arabia | 0.97 | 6.794 | 0 | 6.794 | 6.794 |
| Spain | 2.03 | 14.219 | 0 | 14.219 | 14.219 |
| South Africa | 0.44 | 3.082 | 24.484 | 3.082 | 27.566 |
| Soviet Union* | 11.82 | 82.791 | 48.949 | 82.791 | 129.741 |
| Sweden | 1.25 | 8.755 | 0 | 0 | 0 |
| United States | 25.00 | 210.277 | 43.226 | 210.277 | 253.503 |
| West Germany | 8.26 | 57.856 | 0 | 28.576 | 28.576 |
| Total, all member countries | 100.00 | 735.609 | 176.359 | 566.019 | 742.878 |

*Includes the Soviet Union, Byelorussian Soviet Socialist Republic and Ukranian Soviet Socialist Republic

Source: United Nations

APRIL 27

## Changing South Africa

### 1983

**Nov. 2:** White referendum approves limited political role for mixed-blood and Indian groups; blacks still excluded.

### 1985

**Feb. 1:** Government says it will no longer forcibly relocate blacks living near white cities.

**March 29:** Opposition group meetings banned for three months in Johannesburg and Eastern Cape.

**May 25:** Government announces repeal of ban on multiracial political parties.

**June 13:** Ban on interracial sex and marriage revoked.

**July 21:** Emergency police powers imposed in Johannesburg, Eastern Cape.

**July 31:** Outdoor funerals banned in Johannesburg and Eastern Cape.

**Aug. 28:** Congress of South African Students banned.

**Sept. 11:** Discussions begin on restoring South African citizenship to eight million blacks in so-called homelands.

**Nov. 2:** Reporting on unrest restricted.

### 1986

**March 7:** State of emergency lifted; the last of 8,000 detainees released. Police may still detain people without filing charges.

**April 23:** Government announces it will abolish "pass" laws restricting movement of blacks; residential areas remain segregated.

APRIL 27

## Libya's primary trading partners
For year 1984

**Main origins of imports:**

| | |
|---|---|
| Italy | 32.1% |
| West Germany | 12.3% |
| Britain | 6.2% |
| Japan | 5.6% |
| France | 4.2% |
| Spain | 4.0% |
| Others* | 35.6% |

**Main destinations of exports:**

| | |
|---|---|
| Italy | 20.2% |
| West Germany | 18.1% |
| Netherlands | 7.3% |
| Spain | 7.2% |
| Turkey | 6.7% |
| Britain | 1.8% |
| Others* | 38.7% |

*U.S. portion of Libya's imports estimated to be 2.5 percent by Organization for Economic Cooperation and Development; U.S. shows virtually no imports from Libya after banning its crude petroleum in 1982 and refined petroleum in 1985.
Source: The Economist Intelligence Unit; O.E.C.D.

MAY 2

## Nuclear Disaster: Looking Backward; Nuclear Accident in the Ukraine: The Soviet Account

In the last week, Soviet officials and the Soviet press have issued a trickle of facts about what happened at the Chernobyl atomic power station in the Ukraine. The following is a reconstruction of the accident drawn mainly from these accounts.

Saturday, April 26: At 1:23 A.M., an explosion of undetermined source touches off a fire in the roofing of the engine room of the No. 4 reactor at the Chernobyl power station at Pripyat. The reactor is functioning at a low output of 200 megawatts.

Firefighters, working in extreme heat, battling flames as high as 100 feet, keep the blaze from spreading. But the reactor becomes exposed, a fire breaks out inside and radioactive material escapes. The reactor is shut down, but the graphite moderator core appears to continue burning. Two people die fighting the fire, and 204 are hospitalized with radiation sickness, 18 of them in serious condition.

How quickly the word spreads is unclear. Assistance is summoned from fire departments as far away as Kiev, 70 miles to the south. Police officers from neighboring towns converge on Pripyat, set up roadblocks and maintain order. *Pravda*, the Soviet party paper, later reports some isolated panic.

Preparations are made for a mass evacuation. Hundreds of buses start arriving in Pripyat.

A government commission is appointed under Boris Y. Shcherbina, a Deputy Prime Minister. Members arrive in Pripyat and find that local officials have not made a proper assessment of the dangers.

Sunday, April 27: At 1:50 P.M., 36 hours after the accident, the local radio announces the start of the evacuation of Pripyat, and party workers fan out through all the buildings of the city of 40,000. Marshaling points are avoided to prevent panic, and buses pick up people at their buildings.

The evacuation gets under way at 2 P.M., and by 4:20 P.M. the city is empty except for workers who remain to maintain basic services. They will leave two days later.

A total of 1,100 buses take part, and in Kiev residents note that some bus services are disrupted.

Monday, April 28: In the morning, Swedish monitoring stations report heightened radiation levels. The Swedes conclude that the radioactivity is coming on prevailing winds from the Soviet Union and demand information. The Russians deny any emission of radioactive material.

At 9 P.M., the Soviet press agency, Tass, and the evening television news programs issue a brief statement saying that there has been an accident at the Chernobyl plant and that a reactor was damaged. They say aid is being given to those affected. No mention is made of radioactive emissions.

Tuesday, April 29: An international outcry begins, and rumors begin to circulate about the accident. United Press International reports that 2,000 have been killed.

Reports from Sweden and West Germany say Soviet diplomats have approached private nuclear agencies for advice on fighting graphite fires.

At 9 P.M., the Soviet Government issues its second bulletin, disclosing "a certain leak of radioactive substances," the evacuation of Pripyat and three other settlements, the two deaths and the makeup of the government commission. It reports that the three other reactors have been shut down.

Western tourists in Kiev call their embassies in Moscow seeking information and make preparations to leave. They report life in Kiev is normal.

Wednesday, April 30: The daily government bulletin says there has been no fission chain reaction. It says that in addition to 2 dead, 197 were hospitalized and 49 of them were discharged. The bulletin says the water and air in Kiev are safe.

Envoys of Britain, the Netherlands, France and Austria are summoned to the Foreign Ministry in Moscow and briefed about the accident. They report no new information.

Thursday, May 1: The government bulletin says that 18 people are in critical condition and that radioactivity is decreasing in the area of the power station. Mikhail S. Gorbachev presides over May Day celebrations. The departure of Western students and tourists gathers pace. A large group of students arrive in Moscow, then board planes for London.

Friday, May 2: In Hamburg, West Germany, the Moscow party chief, Boris N. Yeltsin, says radioactivity levels at the plant are falling but are still too high for people to enter.

Saturday, May 3: Prime Minister Nikolai I. Ryzhkov, Yegor K. Ligachev, the second-ranking member of the Politburo, and Vladimir V. Shcherbitsky, the Ukrainian party chief, head a high-ranking team that inspects the region of Chernobyl.

A four-man United States Army team arrives to start monitoring conditions in Moscow.

Monday, May 5: The government announces that dikes are being built along the Pripyat River to prevent potential contamination.

Hans Blix, head of the International Atomic Energy Agency, arrives in Moscow for discussions of the accident.

Tuesday, May 6: *Pravda* and *Izvestia*, the government paper, publish extensive accounts of what happened at Chernobyl, and officials hold a press conference at which they reveal that the evacuation did not take place until 36 hours after the accident. They also suggest that local officials underestimated the scope of the accident in their initial reports. MAY 7

## The Menu at the Banquet

TOKYO, May 6—Following is the menu for the banquet given tonight at the Imperial Palace by Emperor Hirohito at the end of the economic summit conference:

Swallow's Nest Soup

Harvest Fish in White Wine
Leg of Lamb
Salad

Ice Cream Mount Fuji
Melon and Strawberries

The Wines

Bernkasteler Doktor 1982

Château Margaux 1979

Moët & Chandon

Dom Perignon 1976

Sake

MAY 7

# Foreign Aid Is Now an Even Tougher Sell

**By BERNARD GWERTZMAN**

WASHINGTON, May 18—Ever since the United States began giving military and economic assistance to other countries at the end of World War II, there have been those who vigorously opposed it. This year, as the budget-cutting atmosphere in Washington makes it harder to justify giving away billions in foreign aid while funds are being slashed from programs to aid Americans at home, there seem to be more doubters than ever.

The chairman of the House Appropriations subcommittee for foreign operations, David R. Obey, Democrat of Wisconsin, was blunt: "I can't pass a foreign-aid bill on the House floor no matter what shape it is in, so long as the members of the House see that we're increasing foreign aid and we're paying for that increase by gutting cancer research, gutting educational opportunity and things of that nature."

In the current climate, the cuts may go beyond foreign aid to the funds for diplomatic missions abroad. In the aftermath of the attacks on United States embassies and diplomats, Congress had virtually promised to provide a blank check for a comprehensive security plan. But when presented with a five-year, $4.4-billion proposal for enhanced protection and embassy furnishings—in addition to foreign-aid funds—Congress balked.

Except for aid to Israel, Egypt and a few other nations, the foreign-aid portion of the $22-billion State Department package is clearly in deep trouble. Old arguments about having too many embassies and about waste and fraud in foreign-aid programs abound on Capitol Hill. Congressional reluctance has angered Secretary of State George P. Shultz. He told reporters he was considering "dropping

### On the receiving end

Ten largest recipients of direct U.S. economic and military aid (in thousands of dollars, fiscal years)

| 1984 | | 1985 | | 1986* | |
|---|---|---|---|---|---|
| Israel | $2,610,000 | Israel | $3,350,000 | Israel | $3,621,000 |
| Egypt | 2,482,877 | Egypt | 2,479,883 | Egypt | 2,497,060 |
| Turkey | 857,777 | Turkey | 879,490 | Turkey | 738,841 |
| Pakistan | 578,133 | Pakistan | 638,013 | Pakistan | 628,460 |
| Greece | 501,406 | El Salvador | 561,076 | El Salvador | 435,695 |
| Spain | 414,988 | Greece | 501,366 | Greece | 431,894 |
| El Salvador | 408,931 | Spain | 414,926 | Spain | 396,581 |
| Sudan | 237,306 | Honduras | 282,571 | Philippines | 240,894 |
| South Korea | 231,786 | Philippines | 269,676 | Portugal | 188,912 |
| India | 202,786 | Sudan | 253,220 | Honduras | 187,794 |
| Total, all countries | 11,993,953 | | 13,733,961 | | 12,728,267 |

*Estimate

Source: Agency for International Development

MAY 18

everything" to lobby for foreign aid, embassy security and other State Department appropriations such as the Peace Corps and food for peace. The State Department, after all, is the smallest Cabinet-level agency. And, as Mr. Shultz noted at a press conference on Wednesday, "only 2 percent of the Federal budget goes to all activities directly in support of our foreign policy." "So the budget issue comes down to this question," he said: "Are we willing to devote 2 cents of every budget dollar to our foreign policy goals?"

The argument is reminiscent of other eras.

MAY 18

## Farmers' Slipping Share of the Market

By CLYDE H. FARNSWORTH

WASHINGTON—Hard times on the farm and political backlash from farmers in an election year have stirred new militancy in United States agricultural trade policy. Against a backdrop of mounting farm debt, price-depressing crop surpluses and shrinking land values, the Reagan Administration has moved closer to combat with some of its most valued foreign allies.

Washington is trying to increase farm exports in a world awash in food. India is one of 30 countries that were formerly importers of food and have now become exporters. For decades, American farmers advocated free trade and prospered in a relatively open world trading system. Farm exports nearly tripled in the 1970s. But since 1981, although still the leading export item, farm shipments have fallen 30 percent to $31.2 billion last year, contributing to the trade deficit and triggering rising demands for protection.

The Democrat-controlled House of Representatives has weighed in with its own program. The farm provisions of trade legislation, approved by the House by 295 to 115 votes last week, would increase costly export subsidies and curb imports of products ranging from

## Corn, wheat and soybean production
(in millions of metric tons)

| | U.S. | World | U.S. as a percentage of world | U.S. | World | U.S. as a percentage of world | U.S. | World | U.S. as a percentage of world |
|---|---|---|---|---|---|---|---|---|---|
| | Corn | | | Wheat | | | Soybeans | | |
| 1976 | 160 | 354 | 45% | 58 | 421 | 14% | 42 | 66 | 64% |
| 1977 | 165 | 363 | 45 | 56 | 384 | 15 | 35 | 59 | 59 |
| 1978 | 185 | 390 | 47 | 48 | 447 | 11 | 48 | 72 | 67 |
| 1979 | 201 | 421 | 48 | 58 | 424 | 14 | 51 | 77 | 66 |
| 1980 | 169 | 404 | 42 | 65 | 443 | 15 | 62 | 94 | 66 |
| 1981 | 206 | 436 | 47 | 76 | 448 | 17 | 49 | 81 | 60 |
| 1982 | 209 | 438 | 48 | 75 | 479 | 16 | 54 | 86 | 63 |
| 1983 | 106 | 346 | 31 | 66 | 491 | 13 | 60 | 94 | 64 |
| 1984 | 195 | 457 | 43 | 71 | 515 | 14 | 45 | 83 | 54 |
| 1985 | 225 | 480 | 47 | 66 | 503 | 13 | 51 | 91 | 56 |
| 1986* | 192 | 464 | 43 | 59 | 510 | 12 | 58 | 96 | 60 |

*Forecast

Source: Department of Agriculture

MAY 25

beef to honey and roses. Both approaches have substantial support among farmers. "Like any industry, agriculture is for free trade as affects exports, and protection as affects imports," said John A. Schnittker, a Washington-based agricultural consultant.   MAY 25

## Africans Unhappy on Replies at U.N. Aid Session

**By ELAINE SCIOLINO**

UNITED NATIONS, N.Y., May 28— Many African delegates expressed disappointment today at the failure of the industrialized donor countries to commit themselves to specific financial targets requested by African nations at the General Assembly special session on the African economic crisis.

"I am still waiting for a commitment, and I am not yet satisfied," said Foreign Minister William Eteki Mboumoua of the Cameroons. Another African official called positions outlined by the United States and Japan "totally reactionary."

In the first two days of speeches before the five-day session, officials from donor countries, including the United States, Japan, Britain, France and West Germany, praised Africa's willingness to develop free markets and encourage individual initiative.

But they have strongly suggested that the specific requests for huge amounts of new aid and debt relief cannot be met, at least not at this time.

"Let's be candid about the resource issue," Secretary of State George P. Shultz said in a toast prepared for a buffet luncheon today for 60 foreign and economic ministers. "We all agree that Africa needs resources; but those resources must be well used.

"In the United States, our own budgetary constraints dictate major cutbacks in domestic programs as well as in international commitments. If we expect to maintain current aid levels to Africa, the American people will insist that our assistance be well used."

MAY 29

## Africa's Economy in Crisis: The Facts and Figures

Figures are from 1984. South Africa and Morocco are not included; they are not members of the Organization of African Unity.

| Country | Per capita production level (dollars) | Debt (millions of dollars) | Net aid (millions of dollars) |
|---|---|---|---|
| **Indian Ocean countries** | | | |
| Comoros | 235 | 203.0 | 24.4 |
| Madagascar | 245 | 2,119.8 | 159.6 |
| Mauritius | 1,004 | 560.0 | 19.6 |
| Seychelles | 2,296 | 57.5 | 2.2 |
| **East Africa** | | | |
| Ethiopia | 114 | 1,550.2 | 397.2 |
| Burundi | 214 | 346.0 | 160.5 |
| Tanzania | 219 | 2,600.0 | 81.4 |
| Uganda | 237 | 1,031.0 | 146.0* |
| Kenya | 261 | 3,811.0 | 414.6 |
| Somalia | 275 | 1,429.0 | 303.0 |
| Rwanda | 293 | 281.0 | 149.4 |
| Djibouti | 313 | 179.0 | 40.1 |
| Sudan | 393 | 7,892.0 | 542.0 |
| **Southern Africa** | | | |
| Mozambique | 147 | 1,044.0 | 250.0 |
| Malawi | 177 | 885.0 | 163.0 |
| Lesotho | 214 | 140.0 | 103.0 |
| Zambia | 410 | 4,775.0 | 255.0 |
| Angola | 568 | 859.0 | 92.0 |
| Swaziland | 669 | 278.9 | 29.0 |
| Zimbabwe | 740 | 2,124.0 | 282.0 |
| Botswana | 1,210 | 356.1 | 101.0 |
| **Central Africa** | | | |
| Equatorial Guinea | 65 | 126.0 | 11.2 |
| Zaire | 93 | 5,001.0 | 238.0 |
| Central African Republic | 241 | 277.2 | 120.0 |
| São Tomé and Principe | 343 | 75.2 | 7.9 |
| Cameroon | 792 | 2,729.0 | 142.0 |
| Congo | 1,100 | 1,603.0 | 44.0 |
| Gabon | 2,618 | 975.0 | 73.0 |
| **Sub-Saharan Africa** | | | |
| Chad | 116 | 157.9 | 115.0 |
| Burkina Faso | 119 | 529.9 | 188.0 |
| Mali | 137 | 1,176.0 | 278.0 |
| Guinea-Bissau | 174 | 214.2 | 66.0 |
| Niger | 243 | 668.1 | 251.0 |
| Cape Verde | 256 | 118.0 | 39.9* |
| Gambia | 272 | 311.7 | 42.7 |
| Senegal | 364 | 2,026.0 | 32.7 |
| Mauritania | 425 | 1,700.0 | 156.0 |
| **West Africa** | | | |
| Guinea | 153 | 1,306.9 | 44.0 |
| Benin | 265 | 685.0 | 81.0 |
| Togo | 268 | 843.4 | 69.2 |
| Sierra Leone | 287 | 593.7 | 27.7 |
| Liberia | 390 | 1,027.0 | 139.0 |
| Ghana | 628 | 2,013.6 | 229.3 |
| Ivory Coast | 671 | 7,431.0 | 91.0 |
| Nigeria | 795 | 22,616.0 | 30.0 |
| **North Africa** | | | |
| Egypt | 1,021 | 22,482.5 | 1,394.6* |
| Tunisia | 1,136 | 4,032.0 | 222.3* |
| Algeria | 2,116 | 16,615.8 | 160.4* |
| Libya | 7,111 | 797.8 | — |

*Estimate

Source: Organization of African Unity

MAY 29

# At U.N., Africa Spells Out Its Shortcomings; A Continent's Weakening Grip on Survival

Partly because of widespread environmental destruction and uncontrolled population growth, Africans are growing less food per capita than they did 20 years ago. The decline has brought a heavy toll in malnutrition, illness and shortened lives.

The failures were spelled out last week at a special session of the United Nations General Assembly. President Abdou Diouf of Senegal, chairman of the Organization of African Unity, termed improving agriculture the "priority of priorities."

To pay for remedies, the organization called on Africans to invest $80 billion on their own. It urged outsiders to give $45.6 billion in new aid while forgiving $35 to $55 billion in debt over five years.

The richer countries praised the Africans for promising to foster free markets and individual initiative. But pledges of big money were scarce. "In the United States, our own budgetary constraints dictate major cutbacks in domestic programs as well as international commitments," said Secretary of State George P. Shultz. The Reagan Administration hopes to fend off congressional cuts and keep economic aid to Africa at $1 billion a year, well below the level proposed by the Africans.

JUNE 1

## Brief and painful lives
(1983)

|  | Birth rate per thousand | Life expectancy at birth, in years |
|---|---|---|
| U.S. | 16 | 75 |
| Mauritius | 25 | 67 |
| Congo | 43 | 63 |
| Botswana | 44 | 61 |
| Ghana | 49 | 59 |
| Kenya | 55 | 57 |
| Zimbabwe | 53 | 56 |
| Swaziland | 51 | 55 |
| Cameroon | 46 | 54 |
| Lesotho | 42 | 53 |
| Ivory Coast | 46 | 52 |
| Tanzania | 50 | 51 |
| Zaire | 46 | 51 |
| Zambia | 50 | 51 |
| Gabon | 35 | 50 |
| Liberia | 49 | 49 |
| Madagascar | 47 | 49 |
| Nigeria | 50 | 49 |
| Togo | 49 | 49 |
| Uganda | 50 | 49 |
| Benin | 49 | 48 |
| Central African Rep. | 41 | 48 |
| Sudan | 46 | 48 |
| Burundi | 47 | 47 |
| Ethiopia | 41 | 47 |
| Rwanda | 52 | 47 |
| Mauritania | 43 | 46 |
| Mozambique | 46 | 46 |
| Senegal | 46 | 46 |
| Niger | 52 | 45 |
| Mali | 48 | 45 |
| Somalia | 50 | 45 |
| Burkina Faso | 47 | 44 |
| Malawi | 54 | 44 |
| Angola | 49 | 43 |
| Chad | 42 | 43 |
| Guinea-Bissau | 47 | 38 |
| Sierra Leone | 49 | 38 |
| Guinea | 47 | 37 |
| Gambia | 49 | 36 |

Note: Subject countries vary from one study to another.
Source: The World Bank

JUNE 1

## Profile in poverty
(1980–82)

| | Daily calorie consumption per capita | Percent of requirement |
|---|---|---|
| **U.S.** | **3,630** | **138** |
| Mauritius | 2,811 | 124 |
| Ivory Coast | 2,658 | 115 |
| Congo | 2,466 | 111 |
| Madagascar | 2,522 | 111 |
| Swaziland | 2,526 | 109 |
| Botswana | 2,468 | 106 |
| Niger | 2,462 | 105 |
| Tanzania | 2,409 | 105 |
| Nigeria | 2,444 | 104 |
| Lesotho | 2,355 | 103 |
| Burkina Faso | 1,922 | 102 |
| Burundi | 2,244 | 102 |
| Senegal | 2,364 | 99 |
| Sudan | 2,332 | 99 |
| Liberia | 2,261 | 98 |
| Guinea-Bissau | 2,230 | 97 |
| Malawi | 2,220 | 96 |
| Zaire | 2,155 | 96 |
| Mauritania | 2,186 | 95 |
| Central African Rep. | 2,151 | 95 |
| Benin | 2,142 | 94 |
| Togo | 2,160 | 94 |
| Cameroon | 2,148 | 93 |
| Gambia | 2,223 | 93 |
| Rwanda | 2,115 | 91 |
| Zimbabwe | 2,164 | 91 |
| Angola* | 2,110 | 90 |
| Somalia | 2,077 | 90 |
| Zambia | 2,124 | 90 |
| Kenya | 2,036 | 88 |
| Guinea* | 1,934 | 84 |
| Sierra Leone | 1,936 | 84 |
| Mozambique | 1,864 | 80 |
| Uganda | 1,781 | 76 |
| Chad | 1,808* | 75 |
| Ethiopia* | 1,729 | 74 |
| Mali | 1,749 | 74 |
| Ghana | 1,657 | 72 |

*1980
Sources: Food and Agriculture Organization; World Health Organization

JUNE 1

## Going to sleep hungry
(1984 estimates)

| | Malnourished children 6 to 60 months (in thousands) | Percent of all children 6 to 60 months |
|---|---|---|
| **U.S.** | **n.a.** | **n.a.** |
| Mauritius | 1 | 2 |
| Cape Verde | 3 | 5 |
| Gabon | 6 | 10 |
| Ivory Coast | 230 | 15 |
| Cameroon | 240 | 16 |
| Swaziland | 20 | 17 |
| Botswana | 30 | 18 |
| Lesotho | 45 | 19 |
| Togo | 100 | 20 |
| Sudan | 710 | 22 |
| Kenya | 820 | 23 |
| Liberia | 90 | 23 |
| Nigeria | 3,520 | 23 |
| Rwanda | 210 | 23 |
| Guinea-Bissau | 20 | 24 |
| Namibia | 40 | 24 |
| Senegal | 240 | 24 |
| Zaire | 1,270 | 24 |
| Zimbabwe | 350 | 24 |
| Burundi | 190 | 25 |
| Congo | 70 | 25 |
| Madagascar | 400 | 25 |
| Tanzania | 870 | 25 |
| Benin | 180 | 26 |
| Niger | 280 | 26 |
| Zambia | 300 | 26 |
| Uganda | 690 | 27 |
| Sierra Leone | 180 | 28 |
| Somalia | 250 | 28 |
| Mozambique | 570 | 29 |
| Angola | 400 | 30 |
| Mauritania | 100 | 30 |
| Malawi | 380 | 31 |
| Gambia | 40 | 34 |
| Mali | 440 | 34 |
| Chad | 280 | 36 |
| Guinea | 330 | 36 |
| Ethiopia | 2,230 | 37 |
| Burkina Faso | 520 | 40 |

Source: Cornell University

JUNE 1

# Senate Upholds Arms for Saudis, Backing Reagan

By STEVEN V. ROBERTS

WASHINGTON, June 5—President Reagan won a narrow victory in the Senate today as his supporters mustered enough votes to allow the sale of advanced missiles to Saudi Arabia. The margin was a single vote. Last month both houses of Congress approved a resolution blocking a stripped-down version of the arms package, and President Reagan vetoed that resolution. The vote today to override that veto was 66 to 34, but because a two-thirds vote is required, the President's opponents fell one vote short.

Leaders in both parties agreed that critical to the outcome was President Reagan's argument that a defeat on such a highly visible foreign policy issue would undermine his international credibility and destroy his role as a mediator in the Middle East.

Senator Richard G. Lugar, the Indiana Republican who led the fight for the President, said after the vote: "Do you want to let this President, this Secretary of State, have a shot at the peace process or not? That was the question."

Opponents of the arms sale also claimed a significant victory. Originally Mr. Reagan wanted to sell the Saudis several billion dollars' worth of equipment, including tanks and helicopters, according to Senator Alan Cranston, the California Democrat who led the opposition to the sale.

In the face of heated opposition, the package was reduced to $354 million worth of missiles of types that were already in the Saudi arsenal. These included the hand-held Stinger antiaircraft weapons, Harpoon air-to-ship missiles and Sidewinder air-to-air missiles.

Last month, before the first Senate vote, Mr. Reagan retreated again and withdrew the Stingers from the deal.

"They didn't get what they wanted," Senator Cranston said. "They got 10 percent of what they wanted." JUNE 6

## Senate Roll Call on Arms for Saudi Arabia

On June 5 the Senate sustained President Reagan's veto of a resolution that would have prohibited the sale of missiles to Saudi Arabia. While the vote was 66 to 34 in favor of overriding Mr. Reagan's veto, a two-thirds majority, or 67 votes, was required to override. The vote:

### FOR THE ARMS SALE—34

**Democrats—5**

Bentsen, Tex.
Exon, Neb.
Long, La.
Stennis, Miss.
Zorinsky, Neb.

**Republicans—29**

Armstrong, Colo.
Chafee, R.I.
Cochran, Miss.
Denton, Ala.
Dole, Kan.
Domenici, N.M.
East, N.C.
Evans, Wash.
Garn, Utah
Goldwater, Ariz.
Gramm, Tex.
Hatch, Utah
Hecht, Nev.
Helms, N.C.
Humphrey, N.H.
Kassebaum, Kan.
Laxalt, Nev.
Lugar, Ind.
Mathias, Md.
McClure, Idaho
McConnell, Ky.
Quayle, Ind.
Roth, Del.
Simpson, Wyo.
Stafford, Vt.
Stevens, Alaska
Thurmond, S.C.
Wallop, Wyo.
Warner, Va.

### AGAINST THE ARMS SALE—66

**Democrats—42**

Baucus, Mont.
Biden, Del.
Bingaman, N.M.
Boren, Okla.
Bradley, N.J.
Bumpers, Ark.
Burdick, N.D.
Byrd, W. Va.
Chiles, Fla.
Cranston, Calif.
DeConcini, Ariz.
Dixon, Ill.
Dodd, Conn.
Eagleton, Mo.
Ford, Ky.
Glenn, Ohio
Gore, Tenn.
Harkin, Iowa
Hart, Colo.
Heflin, Ala.
Hollings, S.C.
Inouye, Hawaii
Johnston, La.
Kennedy, Mass.
Kerry, Mass.
Lautenberg, N.J.
Leahy, Vt.
Levin, Mich.
Matsunaga, Hawaii
Melcher, Mont.
Metzenbaum, Ohio
Mitchell, Me.
Moynihan, N.Y.
Nunn, Ga.
Pell, R.I.
Proxmire, Wis.
Pryor, Ark.
Riegle, Mich.
Rockefeller, W. Va.
Sarbanes, Md.
Sasser, Tenn.
Simon, Ill.

**Republicans—24**

| | | |
|---|---|---|
| Abdnor, S.D. | Grassley, Iowa | Packwood, Ore. |
| Andrews, N.D. | Hatfield, Ore. | Pressler, S.D. |
| Boschwitz, Minn. | Hawkins, Fla. | Rudman, N.H. |
| Cohen, Me. | Heinz, Pa. | Specter, Pa. |
| D'Amato, N.Y. | Kasten, Wis. | Symms, Idaho |
| Danforth, Mo. | Mattingly, Ga. | Trible, Va. |
| Durenberger, Minn. | Murkowski, Alaska | Weicker, Conn. |
| Gorton, Wash. | Nickles, Okla. | Wilson, Calif. |

JUNE 6

# Why Investors Are Sour on China

By JOHN F. BURNS

PEKING, June 8—To many people, the opening of China to foreign investors at the outset of the 1980s seemed like one of the most promising political and economic developments since World War II. But now, fresh on the heels of the American Motors Corporation's well-publicized problems with its Jeep-making venture here, there is a growing sense among Americans and Chinese alike that the lure of investing in China has dimmed.

In public, at least, the Chinese continue to stress their successes. According to Chinese Government statistics, 2,300 joint ventures between foreign companies and Chinese state enterprises had been approved by the end of 1985, drawing $6 billion in foreign equity investment to China. Of this, about $1.4 billion was American, including investments by such Fortune 500 corporations as McDonnell-Douglas, A.M.C., Pepsi-Cola, Coca-Cola, Atlantic Richfield and Occidental Petroleum.

But now—despite the Chinese decision to meet A.M.C.'s threat of a pullout with concessions that at least temporarily resolve the problems—there is widespread doubt among foreign investors whether their efforts to establish a foothold here are worthwhile. Many are increasingly doubtful that their dream of gaining access to the vast Chinese market will ever materialize. All but a handful of them remain plagued with the same foreign exchange problems, disputes over contract interpretation, inflexible bureaucracy and high costs that have shadowed A.M.C.

Currency remains the major sticking point. Only a few investors—mainly owners of luxury hotels built to accommodate foreign tourists and business executives, which have guaranteed hard-currency earnings—are untouched by the problem. The 1,000-room Holiday Inn–Lido Hotel in Peking enjoyed a profit rate of more than 50 percent on revenues last year of nearly $38 million. Robert Lo, the Singapore millionaire who is the majority owner, is said to be confident that he can pay off his investment in three and a half years, faster than hotels in Hong Kong. But most joint ventures have yet to show a profit in anything other than the inconvertible Chinese currency, the renminbi. To some executives the compromise with A.M.C., which involved a pledge to resume payments to that company in dollars, represented the first hope that the Chinese, after years of promising investors at least a "reasonable" hard-currency profit, might be preparing for more than the half-measures adopted hitherto. But to others the deal looked like an exceptional fix, made to avoid the ripple effect of a pullout by A.M.C. "A happy ending? Don't bet on it," said one American executive.

JUNE 8

## Largest Sino-American joint ventures

Projects ranked by estimated investment by United States company

| U.S. Company | U.S. Company's Investment ($ millions) | U.S. Company's Equity Stake in Project | Nature of Project |
|---|---|---|---|
| Occidental Petroleum | $175 | 25% | Develop the Antaibao open pit coal mine |
| Atlantic Richfield | 170 | 35% | Develop offshore gas field in South China Sea |
| John Portman Associates | 170 | n.a. | Manage a hotel and foreign trade complex |
| Mutual Petroleum | 100 | n.a. | Construct deep-water berths for container ships |
| Beatrice Companies | 60 | 60% | Develop food-processing and light industrial products |
| Eastman Kodak | 50 | n.a. | Build production line for color photographic materials |
| E-S Pacific Development | 35 | 49% | Construct and initially manage the Great Wall Hotel |
| Sheraton Corporation | 35 | n.a. | Manage Hua Ting hotel (under construction) |
| Empire Trading Company | 30 | n.a. | Build hotel and commercial complex |
| American Motors | 16 | 31% | Manufacture 4-wheel drive vehicles |

n.a. not available

Source: National Council for U.S.–China Trade

JUNE 8

## Trade with South Africa

### What the U.S. Exports

Top 1985 merchandise exports to South Africa; millions of dollars

| | |
|---|---|
| Military goods | $282.1 |
| Computers | 121.4 |
| Chemicals (unfinished) | 83.4 |
| Aircraft parts | 57.8 |
| Industrial machinery | 51.2 |

### What the U.S. Imports

Top 1985 merchandise imports from South Africa; millions of dollars

| | |
|---|---|
| Precious metals (not gold) | $572.3 |
| Diamonds | 274.2 |
| Ferro-alloys | 147.3 |
| Nuclear fuel materials | 138.7 |
| Numismatic coins | 99.8 |

JUNE 22

# House Votes, 221–209, to Aid Rebel Forces in Nicaragua; Major Victory for Reagan

**By LINDA GREENHOUSE**

WASHINGTON, June 25—The House of Representatives handed the Reagan

Administration a major victory today by voting to provide military aid to the Nicaraguan rebels.

The vote was 221 to 209. The Democrat-controlled House, which only three months ago rejected military aid, reversed itself in the face of personal lobbying by President Reagan.

Fifty-one Democrats voted for aid, and 11 Republicans against.

A White House official said President Reagan, over the last two days, had been instrumental in gathering eight to ten votes in favor of aid through personal telephone calls and other efforts.

Even as he was flying across the country today, he was telephoning House members and succeeded in changing the minds of some. One Democrat who was persuaded to change sides was Representative Mario Biaggi of the Bronx, who voted in March against aid.

Mr. Reagan, who was at a fund-raising dinner in Las Vegas en route to a vacation at his Santa Barbara ranch, said the vote was "only round one, but, oh boy, what a round."

"It does represent a giant bipartisan effort," he said. "We hope the coalition will hold together."

The vote came on an Administration plan to aid the rebels, known as contras. The plan, backed by a coalition of Republicans and conservative Democrats, provides $70 million in military aid and $30 million in nonmilitary aid in three installments, with the first weapons to reach the rebels starting Sept. 1.

Eleven House members, six Democrats and five Republicans, who voted against aid in March voted for it today. In addition to Mr. Biaggi, the Democrats were: Les Aspin of Wisconsin, Albert G. Bustamante of Texas, Carroll Hubbard, Jr., of Kentucky, Marilyn Lloyd of Tennessee and Richard B. Ray of Georgia.

The Republicans who changed their votes were: Larry J. Hopkins of Kentucky, Bill Frenzel of Minnesota, Olympia J. Snowe of Maine, Chalmers P. Wylie of Ohio and John G. Rowland of Connecticut.  JUNE 26

## House Roll Call on Aid to the Contras

On June 25 the House reversed itself and voted to approve $100 million in military and logistical aid for the Nicaraguan rebels. Fifty-one Democrats and 170 Republicans voted for the aid and 198 Democrats and 11 Republicans voted against it. In the listing below, a "yes" vote is in support of the aid, a "no" is against it, and "xxx" shows that a member did not vote.

### ALABAMA
**Democrats**—Bevill, yes; Erdreich, yes; Flippo, yes; Nichols, yes; Shelby, yes.
**Republicans**—Callahan, yes; Dickinson, yes.

### ALASKA
**Republican**—Young, yes.

### ARIZONA
**Democrat**—Udall, no.
**Republicans**—Kolbe, yes; McCain, yes; Rudd, yes; Stump, yes.

### ARKANSAS
**Democrats**—Alexander, no; Anthony, no; Robinson, yes.
**Republican**—Hammerschmidt, yes.

### CALIFORNIA
**Democrats**—Anderson, no; Bates, no; Beilenson, no; Berman, no; Bosco, no; Boxer, no; Brown, no; Burton, no; Coelho, no; Dellums, no; Dixon, no; Dymally, no; Edwards, no; Fazio, no; Hawkins, xxx; Lantos, no; Lehman, no; Levine, no; Martinez, no; Matsui, no; Miller, no; Mineta, no; Panetta, no; Roybal, no; Stark, no; Torres, no; Waxman, no.
**Republicans**—Badham, yes; Chappie, yes; Dannemeyer, yes; Dornan, yes; Dreier, yes; Fiedler, yes; Hunter, yes; Lagomarsino, yes; Lewis, yes; Lowery, yes; Lungren, yes; McCandless, yes; Moorhead, yes; Packard, yes; Pashayan, yes; Shumway, yes; Thomas, yes; Zschau, yes.

### COLORADO
**Democrats**—Schroeder, no; Wirth, no.
**Republicans**—Brown, yes; Kramer, yes; Schaefer, yes; Strang, yes.

### CONNECTICUT
**Democrats**—Geidenson, no; Kennelly, no; Morrison, no.
**Republicans**—Johnson, yes; McKinney, no; Rowland, yes.

### DELAWARE
**Democrat**—Carper, no.

### FLORIDA
**Democrats**—Bennett, yes; Chappell, yes; Fascell, yes; Fuqus, yes; Gibbons, yes; Hutto, yes; Lehman, no; MacKay, no; Mica, yes; Nelson, yes; Pepper, yes; Smith, yes.
**Republicans**—Bilirakis, yes; Ireland, yes; Lewis, yes; Mack, yes; McCollum, yes; Shaw, yes; Young, yes.

### GEORGIA
**Democrats**—Barnard, yes; Darden, yes; Fowler, no; Hatcher, yes; Jenkins, yes; Ray, yes; Rowland, yes; Thomas, yes.
**Republicans**—Gingrich, yes; Swindall, yes.

### HAWAII
**Democrats**—Akaka, no; Heftel, no.

### IDAHO
**Democrat**—Stallings, no.
**Republican**—Craig, yes.

### ILLINOIS
**Democrats**—Annunzio, no; Bruce, no; Collins, no; Durbin, no; Evans, no; Gray, no; Hayes, no; Lipinski, yes; Price, no; Rostenkowski, no; Russo, no; Savage, no; Yates, no.
**Republicans**—Crane, yes; Fawell, yes; Grotberg, xxx; Hyde, yes; Madigan, yes; Martin, yes; Michel, yes; O'Brien, yes; Porter, yes.

### INDIANA
**Democrats**—Hamilton, no; Jacobs, no; McCloskey, no; Sharp, no; Visclosky, no.
**Republicans**—Burton, yes; Coats, yes; Hiler, yes; Hillis, yes; Myers, yes.

### IOWA
**Democrats**—Bedell, no; Smith, no.
**Republicans**—Evans, yes; Leach, no; Lightfoot, no; Tauke, no.

### KANSAS
**Democrats**—Glickman, no; Slattery, no.
**Republicans**—Meyers, yes; Roberts, yes; Whittaker, yes.

### KENTUCKY
**Democrats**—Hubbard, yes; Mazzoli, no; Natcher, no; Perkins, no.
**Republicans**—Hopkins, yes; Rogers, yes; Snyder, yes.

### LOUISIANA
**Democrats**—Boggs, no; Breaux, yes; Huckaby, yes; Long, no; Roemer, yes; Tauzin, yes.
**Republicans**—Livingston, yes; Moore, yes.

### MAINE
**Republicans**—McKernan, yes; Snowe, yes.

### MARYLAND
**Democrats**—Barnes, no; Byron, yes; Dyson, yes; Hoyer, no; Mikulski, no; Mitchell, no.
**Republicans**—Bentley, yes; Holt, yes.

### MASSACHUSETTS
**Democrats**—Atkins, no; Boland, no; Donnelly, no; Early, no; Frank, no; Markey, no; Mavroules, no; Moakley, no; O'Neill, xxx (by tradition, the House Speaker seldom votes); Studds, no.
**Republican**—Conte, no.

### MICHIGAN
**Democrats**—Bonior, no; Carr, no; Conyers, no; Crockett, no; Dingell, no; Ford, no; Hertel, no; Kildee, no; Levin, no; Traxler, no; Wolpe, no.
**Republicans**—Broomfield, yes; Davis, yes; Henry, yes; Pursell, yes; Schuette, yes; Siljander, yes; Vander Jagt, yes.

### MINNESOTA
**Democrats**—Oberstar, no; Penny, no; Sabo, no; Sikorski, no; Vento, no.
**Republicans**—Frenzel, yes; Stangeland, yes; Weber, yes.

### MISSISSIPPI
**Democrats**—Dowdy, yes; Montgomery, yes; Whitten, no.
**Republicans**—Franklin, yes; Lott, yes.

### MISSOURI
**Democrats**—Clay, no; Gephardt, no; Skelton, yes; Volkmer, no; Wheat, no; Young, no.
**Republicans**—Coleman, yes; Emerson, yes; Taylor, yes.

### MONTANA
**Democrat**—Williams, no.
**Republican**—Marlenee, yes.

### NEBRASKA
**Republicans**—Bereuter, yes; Daub, yes; Smith, yes.

### NEVADA
**Democrat**—Reid, no.
**Republican**—Vucanovich, yes.

### NEW HAMPSHIRE
**Republicans**—Gregg, yes; Smith, yes.

### NEW JERSEY
**Democrats**—Dwyer, no; Florio, no; Guarini, no; Howard, no; Hughes, no; Rodino, no; Roe, no; Torricelli, no.
**Republicans**—Courter, yes; Gallo, yes; Rinaldo, yes; Roukema, yes; Saxton, yes; Smith, yes.

### NEW MEXICO
**Democrat**—Richardson, no.
**Republicans**—Lujan, yes; Skeen, yes.

### NEW YORK
**Democrats**—Ackerman, no; Blaggi, yes; Downey, no; Garcia, no; LaFalce, no; Lundine, no; Manton, no; McHugh, no; Mrazek, no; Nowak, no; Owens, no; Rangel, no; Scheuer, no; Schumer, no; Solarz, no; Stratton, yes; Towns, no; Weiss, no.
**Republicans**—Boehlert, no; Carney, yes; DioGuardi, yes; Eckert, yes; Fish, yes; Gilman, yes; Green, no; Horton, no; Kemp, yes; Lent, yes; Martin, yes; McGrath, yes; Molinari, yes; Solomon, yes; Wortley, yes.

### NORTH CAROLINA
**Democrats**—Hefner, no; Jones, no; Neal, no; Rose, no; Valentine, no; Whitley, no.
**Republicans**—Broyhill, yes; Cobey, yes; Coble, yes; Hendon, yes; McMillan, yes.

### NORTH DAKOTA
**Democrat**—Dorgan, no.

### OHIO
**Democrats**—Applegate, no; Eckart, no; Feighan, no; Hall, no; Kaptur, no; Luken, no; Oakar, no; Pease, no; Selberling, no; Stokes, no; Traficant, no.
**Republicans**—DeWine, yes; Gradison, yes; Kasich, yes; Kindness, yes; Latta, yes; McEwen, yes; Miller, yes; Oxley, yes; Regula, yes; Wylie, yes.

### OKLAHOMA
**Democrats**—English, yes; Jones, yes; McCurdy, no; Synar, no; Watkins, yes.
**Republican**—Edwards, yes.

### OREGON
**Democrats**—AuCoin, no; Weaver, no; Wyden, no.
**Republicans**—D. Smith, yes; R. Smith, yes.

### PENNSYLVANIA
**Democrats**—Borski, no; Coyne, no; Edgar, no; Foglietta, no; Gaydos, xxx; Gray, no; Kanjorski, no; Kolter, no; Kostmayer, no; Murphy, no; Murtha, yes; Walgren, no; Yatron, no.
**Republicans**—Clinger, yes; Coughlin, yes; Gekas, yes; Goodling, yes; McDade, yes; Ridge, no; Ritter, yes; Schulze, yes; Shuster, yes; Walker, yes.

### RHODE ISLAND
**Democrat**—St. Germain, no.
**Republican**—Schneider, no.

### SOUTH CAROLINA
**Democrats**—Derrick, no; Spratt, no; Tallon, yes.
**Republicans**—Campbell, yes; Hartnett, yes; Spence, yes.

### SOUTH DAKOTA
**Democrat**—Daschle, no.

### TENNESSEE
**Democrats**—Boner, no; Cooper, no; Ford, no; Gordon, no; Jones, no; Lloyd, yes.
**Republicans**—Duncan, yes; Quillen, yes; Sundquist, yes.

### TEXAS
**Democrats**—Andrews, no; Brooks, no; Bryant, no; Bustamante, yes; Chapman, no; Coleman, no; de la Garza, no; Frost, no; Gonzalez, no; R. Hall, yes; Leath, yes; Leland, no; Ortiz, yes; Pickle, no; Stenholm, yes; Wilson, yes; Wright, no.
**Republicans**—Archer, yes; Armey, yes; Bartlett, yes; Barton, yes; Boulter, yes; Combest, yes; DeLay, yes; Fields, yes; Loeffler, yes; Sweeney, yes.

### UTAH
**Republicans**—Hansen, yes; Monson, yes; Nielson, yes.

### VERMONT
**Republican**—Jeffords, no.

### VIRGINIA
**Democrats**—Boucher, no; Daniel, yes; Olin, no; Sisisky, yes.
**Republicans**—Bateman, yes; Bliley, yes; Parris, yes; Slaughter, yes; Whitehurst, yes; Wolf, yes.

### WASHINGTON
**Democrats**—Bonker, no; Dicks, no; Foley, no; Lowry, no; Swift, no.
**Republicans**—Chandler, yes; Miller, yes; Morrison, yes.

### WEST VIRGINIA
**Democrats**—Mollohan, no; Rahall, no; Staggers, no; Wise, no.

### WISCONSIN

**Democrats**—Aspin, yes; Kastenmeier, no; Kleczka, no; Moody, no; Obey, no.

**Republicans**—Gunderson, yes; Petri, yes; Roth, yes; Sensenbrenner, yes.

### WYOMING

**Republican**—Cheney, yes.

JUNE 26

# Southeast Asia's Economic Downturn

Despite the many problems facing the Philippines, Secretary of State George P. Shultz feels "bullish" about the country, and he said so last week in Manila. During discussions of economic strategies and efforts to end the Communist insurgency with President Corazon C. Aquino and her top aides, he also signed an agreement to deliver $200 million in aid.

The Secretary was less sanguine after talks with Prime Minister David Lange of New Zealand. Mr. Shultz was unable to alter Mr. Lange's policy of requiring visiting United States ships to declare if they are carrying nuclear weapons. As a result, he said, Washington will no longer feel bound to assist New Zealand under the 1951 Anzus treaty.

Mr. Shultz also visited Singapore, where President Lee Kuan Yew told him that protectionist trade legislation now under consideration in Congress could encourage Soviet inroads in the region. The Reagan Administration also opposes the measures.

Trade issues were dominant, too, as Mr. Shultz met with foreign ministers of the Association of Southeast Asian Nations, which in addition to Singapore and the Philippines includes Thailand, Malaysia, Brunei and Indonesia. All these nations are suffering an economic slowdown after years of strong growth, as these charts indicate. JUNE 29

## Gross domestic product (in billions of dollars)*
## Real Growth (in percent)

|  | 1980 | | 1981 | | 1982 | | 1983 | | 1984 | | 1985 | |
|---|---|---|---|---|---|---|---|---|---|---|---|---|
| Brunei | $4.9 | −7.9% | $4.4 | −19.8% | $4.3 | 4.0% | $3.9 | 0.5% | $3.9 | 0.3% | $4.0 | −4.4% |
| Indonesia | 72 | 9.9 | 86 | 7.9 | 90 | 2.2 | 81 | 4.2 | 84 | 6.5 | 79 | 1.0** |
| Malaysia | 24 | 7.9 | 25 | 6.9 | 27 | 5.6 | 30 | 6.3 | 34 | 7.6 | 31 | 2.7 |
| The Philippines | 35 | 4.4 | 38 | 3.3 | 39 | 1.9 | 34 | 1.2 | 32 | −5.2 | 33 | −4.0** |
| Singapore | 11 | 10.3 | 14 | 9.9 | 15 | 6.3 | 17 | 7.9 | 19 | 8.2 | 18 | −1.8 |
| Thailand | 33 | 5.8 | 36 | 6.3 | 37 | 4.1 | 40 | 5.8 | 42 | 6.2 | 39 | 4.0 |

*Adjusted for inflation
**Projection

Sources: International Monetary Fund; Bank of America

JUNE 29

# "Star Wars" Debate; Question Is Whether to Accept Limits on Research as Part of a Soviet Deal

By MICHAEL R. GORDON

**W**ASHINGTON, July 2—Recent Soviet initiatives at the Geneva arms talks have stirred a debate within the Reagan Administration over whether it is prepared to accept limits on its antimissile research program in return for cuts in strategic arms. Up to now, the United States has not confronted such a decision.

Previously the Soviet Union did not make an offer that is so attractive that the United States feels compelled to rethink its position on the space-based missile defense program.

The program is known officially as the Strategic Defense Initiative and popularly as "Star Wars."

When the Soviet Union first said last year that it would agree to deep reductions in strategic weapons, as the Americans had proposed, it asked for too much in return: a total ban on all antimissile research. Neither the Administration nor most of its critics were prepared to abandon research.

But with the recent Soviet proposals, the situation may be starting to change, officials say. To be sure, they note that the Soviet proposals are not acceptable in their entirety. The offer, which pertains to strategic or long-range weapons, is noteworthy because it removes stumbling blocks and hints at the possibility of further concessions.

"There are no breakthroughs," an official said of the Soviet proposals. "But they have the look and smell of opening moves in a real negotiation."

JULY 3

## Bargaining over arms: How Kremlin and White House proposals compare

The Soviet Union has recently made some significant shifts in its position at the Geneva arms talks. Administration officials say that the Soviet offers still cannot be accepted in their entirety, but that they may pave the way for progress in the talks. Some previous offers, such as the U.S. offer on medium-range forces and the Soviet offer on strategic forces and the Strategic Defense Initiative, remain on the negotiating table as an alternative approach. Here is how the latest Soviet offers compare with previous proposals and with past and present ones from the United States.

| | Soviet positions | | U.S. positions | |
|---|---|---|---|---|
| | **Latest** | **Previous** | **Latest** | **Previous** |
| **Strategic weapons** Total number of missile launchers and bombers | 1,600 for each side (but would also freeze U.S. medium-range forces in Europe and fighter-bombers on aircraft carriers close to the Soviet Union) | U.S.: 1,680 (would count U.S. medium-range forces in Europe and fighter-bombers on aircraft carriers close to the Soviet Union), Soviet: 1,250 | Breaks them down as indicated below | Breaks them down as indicated below |

|  | Soviet positions | | U.S. positions | |
|---|---|---|---|---|
|  | Latest | Previous | Latest | Previous |
| Intercontinental ballistic missiles (ICBMs) and submarine-launched ballistic missiles (SLBMs) | Included in totals for all missiles and bombers | Same | 1,250–1,450 for each side | 1,250 for each side |
| Long-range bombers | Included in totals for all missiles and bombers | Same | 350 for each side, including Soviet Backfires | 400 for each side, including Backfires |
| All missiles and bomber warheads | 8,000 for each side | 6,000 for each side | Broken down as indicated below | Same |
| ICBM and SLBM warheads | Included in total for all warheads and bombs | Same | 4,500 for each side | 5,000 for each side |
| Long-range air-launched and sea-launched cruise missiles (ALCMs and SLCMs) | Limits long-range ALCMs and SLCMs on submarines. Bans long-range cruise missiles on ships. | Bans all long-range ALCMs and SLCMs | 1,500 ALCMs for each side. Does not address SLCMs | Implicit limit of 8,000 ALCMs for each side. Does not address SLCMs |
| Limits on ICBM warheads | 4,800 for each side | 3,600 for each side | 3,000 for each side | 2,500 for each side |
| Missile throw weight | No proposal; reductions would follow from overall cuts | Same | Reduces Soviet throw weight by 50 percent, to about 3,000 tons for each side | About 2,000 tons for each side |
| New systems | Bans all new types of ICBMs, SLBMs and bombers with cutoff dates to be negotiated | Same | Bans all new "heavy" ICBMs (modernized Soviet SS-18) and mobile missiles (modernized Soviet SS-24, SS-25 and U.S. Midgetman) | Bans all new "heavy" ICBMs (such as Soviet SS-18) |
| Medium-range forces | Eliminates all U.S. and Soviet medium-range missiles in Europe, freezes Soviet SS-20 missiles in Asia. British and French must agree to limit their missiles to current levels. U.S. must agree not to transfer missiles to "third parties." Does not limit short-range missiles. | Equal number of warheads for U.S., British and French forces. No increase in Asian based SS-20s if "strategic situation" unchanged. Same on short-range missiles. U.S. allowed 100 to 120 ground-launched cruise missiles, but Pershing 2 missiles banned. | A 3-part plan calling for eventual elimination of all U.S. and Soviet medium-range missiles in three years. Short-range systems would be restricted. British and French systems excluded. | A limit of 140 on U.S. and Soviet medium-range missiles in Europe. Total number of warheads would be between 420 and 450 for each side. Proportional reductions of Soviet missiles in Asia. |

|  | Soviet positions | | U.S. positions | |
| --- | --- | --- | --- | --- |
|  | **Latest** | **Previous** | **Latest** | **Previous** |
| Strategic Defense Initiative | Each side to pledge not to withdraw from ABM treaty for period of 15 to 20 years. Some antimissile research can be conducted in laboratory. Proposes a strict interpretation of ABM treaty terms in order to block significant testing of ABM systems in space. Ban on antisatellite weapons. | A ban on all "Star Wars" research, including that in laboratory. | Rejects notion that progress on reducing arms should be contingent on limits on antimissile research. Seeks to discuss a cooperative transition to a world in which both sides have antimissile defenses. | Same |

Sources: Arms Control Association, Reagan Administration officials and Soviet and American government statements.

JULY 3

# Report Shows U.S. Was Outvoted In the U.N. through Most of 1985

by ELAINE SCIOLINO

UNITED NATIONS, N.Y., July 3—The United States Mission issued a report today that it said showed that most of the world voted against the United States most of the time during the 1985 United Nations General Assembly session.

The study of voting patterns, which was made by the United States Mission, says member countries on average vote on the same side as the United States only 22.5 percent of the time.

The overall voting pattern has fluctuated little since 1983, when the first such report was submitted to Congress. It reflects the tendency of countries to vote in regional blocs, especially among developing nations, the report said. Such solidarity against the United States is often cited as one of the reasons why Congress voted last year to withhold part of the annual financial contribution to the United Nations, even though such a step violates international treaty obligations.

**AFRICA**
Ivory Coast, 27.3
Malawi, 26.9
Liberia, 23.7
Zaire, 23.1
Mauritius, 22.1
Swaziland, 22.0
Equatorial Guinea, 21.2
Central African Rep. 20.9
Gabon, 19.7
Senegal, 19.3
Togo, 19.0
Sierra Leone, 18.3
Cameroon, 18.0
Chad, 18.0
Niger, 17.6
Botswana, 17.4
Rwanda, 17.4
Kenya, 16.7
Somalia, 16.3
Mauritania, 16.1
Lesotho, 16.0
Burundi, 15.9
Morocco, 15.9
The Sudan, 15.5
Egypt, 15.3
Gambia, 14.9
Zambia, 14.9
Nigeria, 14.7
Zimbabwe, 14.6
Djibouti, 14.3
Tunisia, 13.9
Ghana, 13.2
Uganda, 13.2
Burkina Faso, 13.1
Guinea Bissau, 12.2
Comoros, 12.1
Guinea, 12.1
Cape Verde, 11.9
The Seychelles, 11.9
Congo, 11.3
Tanzania, 11.3
Mali, 11.1
Madagascar, 10.6
Sao Tome and Principe, 10.3
Ethiopia, 9.3
Benin, 8.8
Libya, 6.9
Mozambique, 5.9
Algeria, 5.1
Angola, 3.5

**ASIA, MIDDLE EAST AND THE PACIFIC**
Japan, 66.3
Australia, 60.2
New Zealand, 55.3
Solomons, 48.1
Samoa, 27.4
Fiji, 26.0
Singapore, 23.6
Papua New Guinea, 23.1
Thailand, 22.4
Philippines, 22.3
Cambodia, 21.4
Nepal, 18.0
Burma, 17.1
Sri Lanka, 16.8
Malaysia, 16.3
Bangladesh, 16.1
Pakistan, 16.1
China, 15.9
Brunei, 15.3
Indonesia, 14.3
Jordan, 14.2
Bhutan, 13.9
Oman, 13.6
Saudi Arabia, 13.6
Vanuatu, 13.4
Lebanon, 13.1
Bahrain, 12.8
Qatar, 12.8
United Arab Emirates, 12.8
Maldives, 12.5
Kuwait, 12.2
Cyprus, 11.6
Iran, 11.3
Mongolia, 9.9
Yemen, 9.0
India, 8.9
Iraq, 8.7
Syria, 8.1
Vietnam, 6.5
Afghanistan, 6.2
Laos, 5.9
Southern Yemen, 5.7

**THE AMERICAS**
Grenada, 71.7
Canada, 69.8
St. Christopher and Nevis, 50.0
Belize, 37.8
Paraguay, 35.4
St. Vincent and Grenadines, 32.7
Chile, 31.4
El Salvador, 30.2
Honduras, 29.8
Costa Rica, 29.1
Colombia, 27.9
St. Lucia, 26.2
Guatemala, 25.2
Antigua and Barbuda, 25.0
Dominican Republic, 25.0
Ecuador, 24.6
Dominica, 24.2
Haiti, 23.8
Jamaica, 22.7
Barbados, 20.3
Panama, 19.7
Venezuela, 19.0
Bahamas, 18.6
Bolivia, 18.5
Uruguay, 18.1
Trinidad and Tobago, 17.9
Peru, 17.8
Argentina, 16.4
Suriname, 16.2
Brazil, 16.0
Mexico, 14.5
Guyana, 13.9
Nicaragua, 8.4
Cuba, 6.2

**WESTERN EUROPE**
Britain, 86.6
West Germany, 84.4
France, 82.7
Belgium, 82.3
Italy, 81.9
Luxembourg, 80.2
The Netherlands, 76.3
Portugal, 75.0
Iceland, 62.4
Norway, 61.2
Denmark, 58.3
Spain, 55.6
Ireland, 51.0
Sweden, 42.2
Austria, 40.0
Finland, 39.8
Turkey, 38.1
Greece, 33.3
Malta, 16.5

**NO AFFILIATION**
Israel, 91.5

**EASTERN EUROPE**
Poland, 14.8
Romania, 14.6
Hungary, 12.3
Ukraine, 12.3
Bulgaria, 12.2
Byelorussia, 12.2
Czechoslovakia, 12.2
East Germany, 12.2
Soviet Union, 12.2
Yugoslavia, 11.9
Albania, 6.7

JULY 4

## South African trade
Strategic imports (Averages, in percent, 1981–84)

| | Industrial diamond stones | Platinum group metals | Chromium | Vanadium | Manganese | Uranium | Gold |
|---|---|---|---|---|---|---|---|
| Share of U.S. imports originating in South Africa | 67 | 67 | 56 | 38 | 33 | 24 | n.a. |
| South Africa's share of world reserves | 7 | 81 | 84 | 47 | 71 | 14 | 55.1 |
| South Africa's share of world production | 14.8 | 43.2 | n.a. | 42.2 | 14.7 | 14.8 | 47.0 |

Sources: U.S. Department of Commerce; U.S. Bureau of Mines; Organization for Economic Cooperation and Development

JULY 20

# President Wins Test in Senate on Contra Aid

By STEVEN V. ROBERTS

WASHINGTON, Aug. 13—The Senate gave President Reagan a major foreign policy triumph tonight by approving his request for $100 million in aid to the Nicaraguan rebels.

The vote was 53 to 47, as 11 Democrats joined 42 Republicans in voting for aid.

Republican leaders fought successfully all day to thwart Democratic attempts to amend the aid package, which was attached to a bill appropriating money for military construction. The construction bill was then adopted, 59 to 41.

The aid deal approved tonight is identical to the one adopted by the House earlier this summer, and Republican leaders hope that a House-Senate conference on the measure will move swiftly.      AUG. 14

## Senate Roll Call on Aid to Contras

On August 13 the Senate votes, 53 to 47, to approve $100 million in aid to the Contra rebels in Nicaragua. This is the roll-call vote:

### FOR THE AID—53

**Democrats—11**

Bentsen, Tex.
Boren, Okla.
Bradley, N.J.
Chiles, Fla.
Dixon, Ill.
Heflin, Ala.
Hollings, S.C.
Johnston, La.
Long, La.
Nunn, Ga.
Stennis, Miss.

**Republicans—42**

Armstrong, Colo.
Boschwitz, Minn.
Broyhill, N.C.
Cochran, Miss.
Cohen, Me.
D'Amato, N.Y.
Danforth, Mo.
Denton, Ala.
Dole, Kan.
Domenici, N.M.
Evans, Wash.
Garn, Utah
Goldwater, Ariz.
Gramm, Tex.
Grassley, Iowa
Hatch, Utah
Hawkins, Fla.
Hecht, Nev.
Heinz, Pa.
Helms, N.C.
Humphrey, N.H.
Kassebaum, Kan.
Kasten, Wis.
Laxalt, Nev.
Lugar, Ind.
Mattingly, Ga.
McClure, Idaho
McConnell, Ky.
Murkowski, Alaska
Nickles, Okla.
Pressler, S.D.
Quayle, Ind.
Roth, Del.
Rudman, N.H.
Simpson, Wyo.
Stevens, Alaska
Symms, Idaho
Thurmond, S.C.
Trible, Va.
Wallop, Wyo.
Warner, Va.
Wilson, Calif.

### AGAINST THE AID—47

**Democrats—36**

Baucus, Mont.
Biden, Del.
Bingaman, N.M.
Bumpers, Ark.
Burdick, N.D.
Byrd, W.Va.
Cranston, Calif.
DeConcini, Ariz.
Dodd, Conn.
Eagleton, Mo.
Exon, Neb.
Ford, Ky.
Glenn, Ohio
Gore, Tenn.
Harkin, Iowa
Hart, Colo.
Inouye, Hawaii
Kennedy, Mass.
Kerry, Mass.
Lautenberg, N.J.
Leahy, Vt.
Levin, Mich.
Matsunaga, Hawaii
Melcher, Mont.
Metzenbaum, Ohio;
Mitchell, Me.
Moynihan, N.Y.
Pell, R.I.
Proxmire, Wis.
Pryor, Ark.
Riegle, Mich.
Rockefeller, W.Va.
Sarbanes, Md.
Sasser, Tenn.
Simon, Ill.
Zorinsky, Neb.

**Republicans—11**

Abdnor, S.D.
Andrews, N.D.
Chafee, R.I.
Durenberger, Minn.
Gorton, Wash.
Hatfield, Ore.
Mathias, Md.
Packwood, Ore.
Specter, Pa.
Stafford, Vt.
Weicker, Conn.

AUGUST 14

# Out of Africa? Well, Not Really

By KEITH H. HAMMONDS

JOHANNESBURG—Three months ago, Stanley Works pulled out of South Africa. The New Britain, Conn., manufacturer of hand tools sold its local subsidiary to three senior managers. Stanley kept a foot in the door, though. Its former subsidiary, Stanley Tools S.A., is now Tuf Tools—but it has an exclusive, long-term distribution contract that lets it assemble and sell American and European-made Stanley hammers, drills and tape measures, just as before.

"Basically, Stanley wanted to keep their product in the country, but they wanted to take their name off because of the political pressure," said Bob Frost, one of the executives who purchased the Stanley business here.

Except for the reduction in paperwork, Mr. Frost says, he hardly notices the absence of his American corporate parent. Management is the same, and the 24 employees at the warehouse and assembly operation outside Johannesburg are paid the same, except for two salesmen who were made commissioned agents.

Mr. Frost would not discuss the terms of the sale, except to say his group is paying for its purchase out of profits: Every month, part of the company's receipts go into a special account that will be transferred to the parent when the purchase price is reached—by Christmas, he hopes.

In the last two years, the movement to get American corporations to shed their South African operations has gained strength and credibility on university campuses and at shareholder meetings—becoming, in the process, a highly emotional issue that executives at leading companies must take seriously. Indeed, 55 American companies have closed or sold their South African operations since 1984, according to the Investor Responsibility Research Center, a not-for-profit study group in Washington.

But so far, the disinvestment campaign in the United States has had little practical effect on the way business is done in South Africa.

## This year's exodus

The U.S. companies that have divested South African subsidiaries so far in 1986

| U.S. Company | Subsidiary | Buyer | Nationality of Buyer |
|---|---|---|---|
| Applied Power | Applied Power | Jenda Holdings | Liechtenstein |
| Ashland Oil | Valvoline | Shell South Africa | Netherlands |
| Ashland Oil | MikroPul* | Hosakawa Micron | Japan |
| Bell & Howell | Micrographics | Ronnie Price Group | South Africa |
| Bell & Howell | TL Electronics | Ronnie Price Group | South Africa |
| CBS | Gramaphone | Gallo Africa | South Africa |
| Cooper Industries | Gardner-Denver | Local managers | South Africa |
| Eaton | Cutler-Hammer | North. Engineering | South Africa |
| Eaton | Eaton Truck | North. Engineering | South Africa |
| GTE | Valenite-Modco | Gillis-Mason | South Africa |
| General Electric | G.E. South Africa | Local managers | South Africa |
| MacMillan | P. F. Collier | Proash Pty. | South Africa |
| Manpower | Parker Pen S. Africa* | Parker Pen U.K. | Britain |
| Pennwalt | Pennwalt S. Africa | Local managers | South Africa |
| Phillips Petroleum | Phillips Carbon Black | Degussa | West Germany |
| Rohm & Haas | Rohm & Haas S. Africa | Local managers | South Africa |
| Scovill | Schrader Bellows* | Parker-Hannifin | United States |
| Scovill | Schrader Scovill* | Arvin Industries | United States |
| W. R. Stamler | Stamler S. Africa | Liquidated | |
| Stanley Works | Stanley Tools S. Africa | Local managers | South Africa |
| VF Corporation | Berkshire Int'l. | Local managers | South Africa |

*Disinvestment part of a worldwide divestiture that included South African operations.

Sources: Investor Responsibility Research Center; company executives

AUGUST 17

For in most cases the disinvestment has been along the lines of Stanley Tools.

In fact, of the 17 companies that have disinvested in 1986, 13 have retained substantial business connections through distribution, licensing or technology agreements. South African consumers can still buy CBS records, Lee jeans and Collier encyclopedias, even though the American companies behind those products no longer operate here. "With very few exceptions, the products and services of companies that have withdrawn are still available," said a United States Government official here.

Only one of the 17, W. R. Stamler, has actually shut down its local operation this year —and it had just eight employees. For most companies, management and employment have remained intact under new ownership. In fact, six of the subsidiaries were purchased by their own managers. "In the end, the fact that Ashland is no longer here has had very little effect beyond the cosmetic," observed Robin Martin, managing director of the Valvoline subsidiary sold by Ashland Oil last June. . . . The two largest companies to pull out of South Africa this year were General Electric and the VF Corporation—but neither has cut all ties.

G.E., for example, negotiated 42 distribution agreements covering the wide range of electrical, electronic and industrial products it ships to Genwest Industries, the subsidiary it sold to nine South African managers in April. G.E. products and components still make up 95 percent of the company's sales, said Genwest's managing director, Rob Hofman.

It seems to be a good arrangement for the parent company, which is getting the same prices for its products under the distribution agreements that it got when it owned Genwest —but no longer takes the losses Genwest has suffered for two years.

VF sold its subsidiary, Berkshire International—the South African manufacturer and distributor of Lee jeans—to Corder Tilney, the chairman of Berkshire, for 1.1 million rand, or about $220,000. But the payment of the purchase price, plus interest, has been deferred until 1988, and Lee products still account for three quarters of Berkshire's sales. AUG. 17

---

## Superpower Contacts: A Variety of Forums

*American and Soviet negotiators are holding talks on arms control, regional issues and other matters, including human rights. Besides those negotiations, there are several specially convened meetings to prepare for talks scheduled in Washington on Sept. 19 and 20 between Secretary of State George P. Shultz and Foreign Minister Eduard A. Shevardnadze. That meeting is to prepare for a possible summit conference between President Reagan and Mikhail S. Gorbachev, the Soviet leader. Here is a list of the talks in progress.*

### ARMS-PACT NEGOTIATIONS

**NUCLEAR AND SPACE ARMS TALKS**
**Goal:** Agreements on three separate issues—strategic long-range arms, space and defensive systems and medium-range arms. The American goal is to negotiate a treaty reducing strategic arms that does not block President Reagan's Strategic Defense Initiative, the space-oriented missile defense research program popularly known as "Star Wars." The Soviet Union seeks to reduce arms and also to restrict the "Star Wars" program. The two sides are working on a separate treaty to limit American and Soviet medium-range arms.
**Site:** Geneva
**History:** Talks on long-range and medium-range arms were carried out in first term of Reagan Administration, but were broken off by the Russians in late 1983 after the United States began deploying medium-range missiles in Europe. Talks resumed in March 1985; sixth round is scheduled to begin Sept. 18.
**Chief negotiators:** Max M. Kampelman (U.S.), Viktor P. Karpov (Soviet Union).

**CONFERENCE ON DISARMAMENT**
**Goal:** A total ban on chemical weapons
**Site:** Geneva
**History:** A United Nations forum that first met in 1979; last meeting, June 9–Aug. 29; another session is scheduled at end of year.
**Negotiators:** Donald S. Lowitz (U.S.), Viktor L. Israelyan (Soviet Union) and negotiators from 38 other countries.

## CONFERENCE ON CONFIDENCE- AND SECURITY-BUILDING MEASURES AND DISARMAMENT IN EUROPE

**Goal:** Reducing the risk of accidental war by working out arrangements so NATO and the Warsaw Pact notify each other of troop movements and military exercises
**Site:** Stockholm
**History:** First met in January 1984; current meeting Aug. 19–Sept. 19.
**Negotiators:** Robert L. Barry (U.S.), Oleg A. Grinevsky (Soviet Union) and delegates from 33 other countries in Europe and North America.

## MUTUAL AND BALANCED FORCE REDUCTION

**Goal:** Reducing the number of NATO and Warsaw Pact troops stationed in Central Europe
**Site:** Vienna
**History:** First met in 1973; will meet for 40th time Sept. 25–Dec. 4.
**Negotiators:** Robert D. Blackwill (U.S.), Valerian V. Mikhailov (Soviet Union) and representatives of 19 other countries, including 13 from NATO and 6 from the Warsaw Pact.

## PREPARATORY TALKS

**Goal:** Finding a basis for progress at Shultz-Shevardnadze meeting and at next round of Geneva arms talks beginning Sept. 18. They are part of the larger Geneva negotiations.
**Site:** Washington and Moscow
**History:** Experts met in Moscow Aug. 11–12; will meet again in Washington Sept. 5–6.
**Chief negotiators:** Paul H. Nitze (U.S.) and Viktor P. Karpov (Soviet Union) at Moscow meeting.

## CHEMICAL WEAPONS

**Goal:** Curbing the spread of chemical weapons
**Site:** Bern
**History:** Experts met March 5–6, scheduled to meet Sept. 4–5.
**Negotiators:** John H. Hawes (U.S.), Viktor L. Israelyan (Soviet Union).

## NUCLEAR TESTING

**Goal:** Agreement on technical issues concerning verification of measures on underground testing and nuclear weapons. The United States is seeking Soviet agreement on additional verification measures for two treaties of the 1970s that limit the size of nuclear explosions. The Soviet Union has argued for a total ban on testing.
**Site:** Geneva
**History:** Technical experts met July 25–Aug. 1. Another meeting scheduled Sept. 4.
**Negotiators:** Robert Barker (U.S.); Andronik M. Petrosyants (Soviet Union).

## NUCLEAR RISK REDUCTION CENTERS

**Goal:** Establishing centers in Washington and Moscow, separately manned by American and Soviet officials, to lessen the chances of accidental nuclear war. The centers would be used, for example, to exchange information about strategic exercises and missile tests.
**Site:** Geneva
**History:** Met May 5–6 and Aug. 24–25
**Negotiators:** Assistant Secretary of Defense Richard N. Perle and Col. Robert E. Linhard of the National Security Council (U.S.), Aleksei A. Obukhov (Soviet Union).

## STANDING CONSULTATIVE COMMISSION

**Goal:** Discussion of concerns about compliance with treaties and other technical arms control issues
**Site:** Geneva
**History:** Commission set up under 1972 ABM treaty; first met in 1973. A special meeting requested by Russians was held July 22–30. Next meeting scheduled to start about Oct. 1.
**Negotiators:** Gen. Richard H. Ellis (U.S.), Maj. Gen. Vladimir I. Medvedev (Soviet Union).

## NUCLEAR ENERGY

**Goal:** American-Soviet agreements on atomic energy issues
**Site:** Washington and Moscow
**History:** First meeting in 1974. Latest meeting Aug. 18–22; next meeting tentatively scheduled for fall 1987.
**Negotiators:** Dr. Alvin W. Trivelpiece (U.S.), Andronik M. Petrosyants (Soviet Union).

## U.S. AND SOVIET NAVIES

**Goal:** Minimizing risk of unintended confrontations at sea and notifying mariners of actions on high seas that represent a danger to navigation or aircraft in flight
**Site:** Washington and Moscow
**History:** Annual talks began in 1972. Last round held June 9–13.
**Negotiators:** Vice Adm. Henry C. Mustin (U.S.), Adm. Pyotr N. Navoitsev (Soviet Union).

## REGIONAL ISSUES

**Goal:** Discussion of differences over regional problems
**Site:** Washington and Moscow
**History:** Meeting held Aug. 26–28 in Washington. Talks previously held this year on southern Africa, the Middle East, Central America, the Caribbean, East Asia and the Pacific. Afghanistan will be subject of talks in Moscow Sept. 2–3.
**Negotiators:** Under Secretary of State for Political Affairs Michael H. Armacost (U.S.), Deputy Foreign Minister Anatoly L. Adamishin (Soviet Union) at Washington meeting; Arnold L. Raphel, Deputy Assistant Secretary of State for Near Eastern and South Asian Affairs

(U.S.), no confirmation on Soviet representative at Moscow.

**OTHER ISSUES**
**Goal:** Identifying differences on issues such as cultural and scientific exchanges, trade and human rights, including reunification of divided families.
**Site:** Washington and Moscow
**History:** Talks took place week of July 22 in Moscow and July 25–29 and Aug. 12–15 in Washington. A meeting in near future is expected. Talks on people-to-people exchanges took place July 29–Aug. 5 in Washington; another meeting is expected in September in Moscow.
**Chief Negotiators:** Thomas W. Simons, Jr., Deputy Assistant Secretary of State for European and Canadian Affairs (U.S.); Vitaly A. Mikolchak, Deputy Chief of the Foreign Ministry's Department of United States and Canada, and Aleksandr A. Bessmertnykh, Deputy Foreign Minister.

Sources: Arms Control and Disarmament Agency, Department of Defense and State Department

AUG. 31

Soviet officials said that at this time of year, the peak vacation period, the ship was probably filled to capacity.

The *Admiral Nakhimov*, a 61-year-old German-built passenger ship, had been used in recent years during the summer months on the regular coastal service between Odessa, its home port, and Batumi, near the Turkish border, a six-day round-trip, with stops in Sevastopol, Yalta, Novorossisk, Sochi and Sukhumi.

Many Soviet vacationers use Black Sea passenger ships during the summer for round-trip cruises. The *Admiral Nakhimov* had cabin berths for 870 passengers, but it is customary during this peak travel season to add several hundred deck-chair seats at the lowest fares.

The *Admiral Nakhimov* was reported to have collided near Novorossisk with the freighter *Pyotr Vasev*.

SEPT. 2

# Soviet Liner Sinks in Black Sea

**By PHILIP TAUBMAN**

MOSCOW, Sept. 1—A Soviet passenger ship collided with a freighter in the Black Sea last night and sank, with an unspecified loss of life, the Soviet Union announced today.

The gravity of the accident was underscored by the fact that the announcement was issued jointly by the government and the Central Committee of the ruling Communist Party, a device sometimes used to brace the country for a major accident.

A top government official has been appointed to head a commission of inquiry, and a shipping official described the accident as a "real tragedy."

The four-deck ship, the *Admiral Nakhimov*, could accommodate about 1,000 passengers.

## Recent Maritime Disasters

Reports of the sinking of a Soviet passenger ship in the Black Sea with up to 1,000 people aboard indicated substantial loss of life. Here are some notable maritime disasters of the last three decades.

**July 26, 1956**—The Italian liner *Andrea Doria* sinks, a day after colliding with the Swedish liner *Stockholm* off Cape Cod. Fifty-two people are killed, most of them on the Italian vessel.

**July 14, 1957**—The Soviet ship *Eshghabad* sinks in the Caspian Sea, and 270 people are killed.

**April 10, 1961**—The British liner *Dara* sinks in the Persian Gulf, with a reported loss of 212 lives, two days after a bomb explosion aboard.

**July 8, 1961**—The Portuguese ship *Save* runs aground and breaks up off Mozambique; 259 killed.

**April 10, 1963**—The American nuclear submarine *Thresher* sinks in the North Atlantic; 129 killed.

**Feb. 10, 1964**—The Australian destroyer *Voyager* sinks after colliding with the aircraft carrier *Melbourne* off New South Wales; 82 killed.

**April 10, 1964**—An Iranian motor launch burns and sinks in the Persian Gulf; 113 dead.

**Nov. 13, 1965**—The cruise ship *Yarmouth Castle*

burns and sinks en route from Miami to the Bahamas; 90 dead.

**Dec. 8, 1966**—A Greek ferry sinks in the Aegean; 241 killed.

**Jan. 25, 1968**—The Israeli submarine *Dakar* vanishes; 69 lost.

**Jan. 27, 1968**—The French submarine *Minerve* vanishes in the Mediterranean; 52 dead.

**May 21, 1968**—The American nuclear submarine *Scorpion* sinks southwest of the Azores; 99 dead.

**June 2, 1969**—The United States destroyer *Evans* is cut in half by the Australian carrier *Melbourne* in the South China Sea; 74 dead.

**March 4, 1970**—The French submarine *Eurydice* sinks off Toulon; 57 dead.

**Dec. 15, 1970**—A South Korean ferry sinks in the Korea Strait; more than 260 dead.

**Feb. 1, 1973**—A ferry sinks in the harbor of Rangoon, Burma; more than 200 dead.

**Dec. 24, 1973**—A ferry sinks off Guayaquil, Ecuador; 109 dead.

**May 1, 1974**—A motor launch capsizes off Bangladesh; 250 dead.

**Sept. 26, 1974**—A Soviet destroyer burns and sinks in the Black Sea; about 200 dead.

**Dec. 25, 1976**—The Egyptian liner *Patra* burns and sinks in the Red Sea; about 100 dead.

**Jan. 27, 1981**—The Indonesian passenger ship *Tamponas II* catches fire and sinks in the Java Sea; 580 dead.

**Aug. 10, 1983**—The United States reports that a Soviet nuclear-powered submarine sank in the North Pacific two months earlier with the loss of most or all of the 90-member crew.

SEPT. 2

# Push on Hiring Bias in Ulster

**By STEVE LOHR**

LONDON, Sept. 3—Encouraged by the success of the campaign to get American investors to pull out of South Africa, a coalition of Irish human rights advocates and politicians is mounting a drive to prod American companies doing business in Northern Ireland to combat discrimination against Roman Catholic workers. The Northern Ireland campaign would place American investors and companies, once again, at the forefront of a sensitive social issue.

The effort is based on the "MacBride Principlas," a nine-point set of guidelines for fair employment in the predominantly Protestant British province, also known as Ulster. Drafted by four Irish activists led by Sean MacBride, a Nobel Peace Prize winner, the guidelines are patterned after the Sullivan Principles, which were presented in 1977 as an alternative to divestment in South Africa for companies doing business there.

The year-old MacBride campaign is trying to convince American states and municipalities, whose pension funds are invested heavily in American companies that do business in Northern Ireland, to support the principles. In addition, the MacBride advocates are marshaling support for shareholder initiatives that criticize the employment practices of selected American companies in Northern Ireland and urge them to support the principles.

Each company signing the MacBride Principles would agree, for instance, to make "every reasonable lawful effort to increase the representation of underrepresented religious groups at all levels of its operations in Northern Ireland."

Although there are no official unemployment figures by religion, studies have concluded that the unemployment rate for Catholics in Northern Ireland is about twice that of Protestants. Twenty-four American companies—led by American Brands, Du Pont, General Motors and Ford—employ 11 percent of the manufacturing work force in Northern Ireland. The overall unemployment rate in the province is 22 percent, the highest in Western Europe.   SEPT. 4

## The MacBride Principles

Following is the text of the MacBride Principles:

In light of decreasing employment opportunities in Northern Ireland and on a global scale, and in order to guarantee equal access to regional employment, the undersigned propose the following equal opportunity affirmative action principles:

1. Increasing the representation of individuals from underrepresented religious groups in the work force, including managerial, supervisory, administrative, clerical and technical jobs.

2. Adequate security for the protection of minority employees both at the workplace and while traveling to and from work.

3. The banning of provocative religious or political emblems from the workplace.

4. All job openings should be publicly advertised and special recruitment efforts should be made to attract applicants from underrepresented religious groups.

5. Layoff, recall and termination procedures should not, in practice, favor particular religious groupings.

6. The abolition of job reservations, apprenticeship restrictions and differential employment criteria, which discriminate on the basis of religion or ethnic origin.

7. The development of training programs that will prepare substantial numbers of current minority employees for skilled jobs, including the expansion of existing programs and the creation of new programs to train, upgrade and improve the skills of minority employees.

8. The establishment of procedures to assess, identify and actively recruit minority employees with potential for further advancement.

9. The appointment of a senior management staff member to oversee the company's affirmative action efforts and the setting up of timetables to carry out affirmative action principles.

SEPT. 4

## Terror in Istanbul

By HENRY KAMM

ISTANBUL, Turkey, Sept. 6—Two Arab terrorists invaded a Sephardic synagogue during Sabbath services in the Jewish quarter here today and, after locking the doors with iron bars, attacked the congregation with submachine guns and hand grenades.

At least 21 worshipers, including 7 rabbis, were killed, and 4 others were wounded in the massacre, a blaze of gunfire and explosions that went on for three to five minutes and left the newly refurbished synagogue on fire. The bodies of both gunmen were found in the carnage.

Witnesses described scenes of horror as bullets from automatic weapons raked the benches, worshipers in prayer shawls screamed and fell and blasts shook the Neve Shalom Synagogue, the city's largest, in the Karakoy district near the Galata Tower. One report said the killers also poured gasoline on some victims and tried to burn the bodies.

"It's horrifying," Hasan Ali Ozer, Istanbul's deputy governor, said after visiting the scene. Interior Minister Yildirim Akbulut said the killers had barred the synagogue's main doors to keep people from escaping the bullets and grenades. Only 4 of the 29 worshipers escaped unhurt.

Turkish security officials said two Czechoslovak-made submachine guns, seven unexploded Soviet-made hand grenades and more than 100 spent cartridges were found inside the synagogue after firemen put out the flames in the single-story building.

Police officials described the gunmen as Arabs in their twenties and said they were on an apparent suicide mission. A teenaged survivor, Gabriel Shaun, said they spoke Arabic to one another. Some witnesses said the gunmen entered by posing as photographers or tourists who wanted to take pictures of the interior, but others said they wore masks and dark clothing and simply burst in and began firing.

Bodies and parts of bodies were strewn about the synagogue and many of the dead could not be immediately identified. The bodies were taken away in blood-spattered pine boxes. The four wounded, one seriously hurt, were taken to a hospital.

All the victims were men, most of them

elderly, the authorities said. Friends of the victims said that those killed included a visiting Israeli rabbi of Iranian origin, Raphael Nesim, and Rabbi Yuda Adoni, who was leading the morning prayers.  SEPT. 7

## Synagogue Victims

This is a list of the worshipers killed or wounded in the attack on Neve Shalom Synagogue in Istanbul. The list was provided by local Jewish leaders, and all are Turkish citizens except where indicated otherwise:

**Dead**
ALHALEL, Jozef
ANJEL, Salamon
ATALAY, Yuda Levi
BABAZADE, Mirva (Iranian)
BAROKAS, Izak
BARUH, Danyel Daryo
BEHAR, David, a cantor
CITTONE, Selim Salom
ERESKENAZI, Binyamin
ERGUN, Aser, a cantor
ERGUN, Ibrahim
GERSON, Izak
HARA, Elyezer
LEVI, Moiz
LEVI, Rensiyon
MATALON, Yakov
MUSAOGLU, Leon Levi
NESIM, Rafael (Iranian)
OZFINS, Robert Israel
SAUL, Moiz
SENKAL, Sefanya

**Wounded**
ERESKENAZI, Avram
GENC, Yasef Levi
SAMRANO, Jak
SITRAN, Moiz

SEPT. 9

## Hijacking in Karachi

By STEVEN R. WEISMAN

KARACHI, Pakistan, Sept. 6—The Pakistani authorities, revising the details of the capture of a hijacked Pan American jumbo jet on Friday, said tonight that all four gunmen who had seized the plane were alive and had been taken into custody by government security forces.

Contradicting an earlier report that two of the gunmen had been killed, law enforcement officials also said one of the four was seriously wounded. They said one of the four was from Syria, one from Bahrain and one was Palestinian.

But other sources indicated that all four were from Beirut, Lebanon, and that they had entered Pakistan last month on false Bahrain passports.

Airport security officials today put the number of dead at 16, including 14 passengers, one member of the Pan American cabin crew and one ground crew employee.

Officials said the number of critically wounded was less than 50, but others said more than 100 had been wounded or otherwise injured.  SEPT. 7

## Hijacking in Karachi
## 16 Hours of Terror: The Pakistani Account

At a news conference in Karachi yesterday, the Pakistani authorities gave an account of the hijacking Friday of Pan American World Airways Flight 73. Here are the key developments; all times are approximate.

**6 A.M. (9 P.M. Thursday, New York time.)**—The hijacking begins as four gunmen speed onto the tarmac at Karachi International Airport in a blue van. Firing into the air, they clamber aboard the Pan Am jumbo jet, taking it over. The two pilots and the flight engineer, hearing the shots, flee through an emergency hatch over the cockpit.

**8:30 A.M.**—The first communication with the hijackers is established as Viraf Daroga, director of Pan Am in Pakistan, goes out to the tarmac with a megaphone to open discussions, finding the hijackers "in a very high state of agitation," according to Air Vice Marshal Kurshid Anwar Mirza, chairman of the Pakistan Civil Aviation Authority. Shortly after this time the hijackers locate Rajesh Kumar, an American citizen, and shoot him in the back of the head, throwing him out of the plane, according to Vice Marshal Mirza. Soon afterward the hijackers ask for an Arabic speaker to communicate with them, and airport authorities recruit Nasim Khan, a ground manager for Saudi Arabian Airlines. The hijackers demand to be flown to Cyprus and vow to shoot passengers unless their demand is met. The hijackers are told that a crew is coming, and Vice Marshal Mirza says, "I believe that we were able to calm them down." The hijackers maintain contact with ground authorities every half hour or hour for the rest of the morning and afternoon. The hijackers set a deadline of 7 P.M. for their demands to be met.

7 P.M.—The hijackers are informed that the crew has not arrived and that they will have to wait further. The hijackers convey a new deadline of 11 P.M. to midnight for their demands to be met, according to Vice Marshal Mirza.

8 P.M.—The ground center loses radio contact with the hijackers and discerns that "their mood was apparently turning ugly."

9 P.M.—After the plane's lights begin to dim as the on-board generator runs out of fuel, the hijackers herd the passengers to the middle of the plane. By this time they have collected most of the passengers' passports. The passengers are apparently huddled in the middle third of the plane so most of them are around three escape hatches. Some are sitting and some are squatting.

10 P.M.—The hijackers open fire on the passengers and throw two hand grenades, apparently one in the front and one in the rear of the plane, according to some passengers and officials. The passengers manage to break open one safety door on the right side of the plane and scramble down an emergency chute.

10:15 P.M.—According to Vice Marshal Mirza, the commandos who had been gathered in the area outside the plane finally reach the plane after a 15-minute delay and capture or shoot the hijackers who remain on the plane. They also climb up one of the chutes and open a second safety door to allow passengers to escape, according to airport security officials.

SEPT. 7

## A Partial Casualty List

Following is the partial list of casualties in the hijacking of Pan American Flight 73 in Karachi, Pakistan, as released by the airline.

**Dead**
KHARAS, Pakistan (Pan Am ground crew member).
KUMAR, Rajesh, U.S.
MULLOR, T., India
NAGATHOLY, Mrs. E., India
SINGH, Mrs. Kalpana, India
SUNDRESAN, Miss Meera, India
MISRAN, N., India (Pan Am flight crew member)

**Wounded Americans**
DASGUPTA, Mrs. A.
SINGH, Sameer

**Uninjured Americans**
BHADREJA, G. M.
DASGUPTA, A. M. S.
DODGE, C. (flight crew)
GOLDSTEIN, M.
HUSSAIN, Mrs. Farat
HUSSAIN, A. (infant)
KHATRI, Dr. A. A.
KIANKA, W. (flight crew)
MAJID, Mr. A.
MALONEY, Mr. C.
MEHRA, Deepa
MELHART, Mr. Richard
RIDGWAY, J. (flight crew)

**Status Unknown**
AHMED, Mr. S.
ALLISON, D. A. V.
ANURADHA, J.
ANURADHA, N.
BHANDARI, J. M.
BHANDARI, S. R.
DASGUPTA, D. M. S.
DUMAS, C.
GAYATRI, D. A. V.
HARPER, Mr. T.
HUSSAIN, W.
HUSSAIN, Ms. N.
KHAN, Mr. Z. N.
MAHMOOD, Naseeruddin
PATEL, Mr. Srekantbhal
PATEL, Ms. Shetal
PIEPER, Mr. D.
PRIYA, Joyce
SUNDERESAN, Mr. E.
SUNDERESAN, Mrs. S.
SUNDERESAN, Miss Minu
SURESH, Raj

SEPT. 7

## The U.N.'s Complicated Brand of Office Politics

By ELAINE SCIOLINO

UNITED NATIONS, N.Y.—According to the Russians, Gennadi F. Zakharov is an international civil servant who was trying to learn all he could for his job in an obscure scientific office of the United Nations. According to the Federal Bureau of Investigation, he is a spy who bought classified information and should be tried and punished.

The Zakharov case dramatizes the flaws and pitfalls of an international civil service that employs nationals of countries with widely different ideologies, values and economic and political systems. Its members are supposed to work harmoniously, free from constraints or orders from home. That goal is rarely achieved in the United Nations Secretariat, which has 12,400 employees.

Most of the world organization's members agree that the personnel system is deeply flawed and that politics and expediency outweigh competence in hiring and promotions. A report to the General Assembly by 18 international experts calls on the Secretary General, Javier Perez de Cuellar, to "exercise greater leadership in personnel matters and insure that the selection of staff is done strictly in accordance with the charter." SEPT. 21

### Team Players
Number of full-time workers at U.N. Secretariat*

United States, 1,740
France, 959
Thailand, 624
Britain, 618
Philippines, 605
Ethiopia, 535
Chile, 458
Soviet Union, 411
Lebanon, 383
Kenya, 364
China, 288
Egypt, 252
Switzerland, 240
India, 233
Spain, 201
Italy, 197
Jordan, 184
Canada, 165
Jamaica, 164
West Germany, 162
Austria, 154
Syria, 152
Japan, 141
Argentina, 127
Colombia, 126
Mexico, 121
Trinidad and Tobago, 115

*Countries with 100 workers or more; does not include employees of independent U.N. organizations

Source: United Nations

SEPT. 21

## Russians Set Daniloff Free and He Flies to Frankfurt; Not a Trade, President Says

By BERNARD GWERTZMAN

The Soviet Union yesterday freed Nicholas S. Daniloff, the American journalist who had been confined to Moscow for the last month on spying charges.

Mr. Daniloff was allowed to leave without standing trial. He flew to Frankfurt, West Germany, for an overnight stay on his way to the United States.

His release seemed to remove an obstacle to setting a date for a meeting between President Reagan and Mikhail S. Gorbachev later this year.

Reagan Administration officials said that as part of the arrangement on Mr. Daniloff worked out in talks in New York, Gennadi F. Zakharov, a Soviet citizen accused of espionage, would be allowed to plead no contest in court and be sent back to the Soviet Union in exchange for a group of Soviet dissidents.

Mr. Daniloff's release occurred suddenly, without public announcement, and appeared to end a dispute that had threatened to paralyze and worsen Soviet-American relations.

SEPT. 30

## The Daniloff Affair: Four Tense Weeks

**Aug. 30**—Nicholas S. Daniloff, correspondent for *U.S. News & World Report*, is detained in Moscow after a Soviet acquaintance handed him a package containing two maps marked "top secret." The arrest follows by one week the arrest in New York of Gennadi F. Zakharov, a Soviet employee of the United Nations, on charges of espionage.

**Aug. 31**—American officials call the arrest a "frame-up" and rule out a direct Daniloff-Zakharov exchange.

**Sept. 5**—Secretary of State George P. Shultz says Mr. Daniloff is a Soviet hostage and demands his release.

**Sept. 6**—President Reagan assures Mikhail S. Gorbachev in a message that Mr. Daniloff is not a spy and that Soviet-American relations are too important to be affected by this matter.

**Sept. 7**—The Soviet Union formally charges Mr. Daniloff with being a spy and says he will be tried.

**Sept. 9**—A Federal grand jury in Brooklyn indicts Mr. Zakharov on espionage.

**Sept. 12**—Under a Soviet-American arrangement, Mr. Daniloff and Mr. Zakharov are freed from prison in the custody of their embassies.

**Sept. 15**—The United States orders 25 members of the Soviet Mission to the United Nations to leave by Oct. 1.

**Sept. 18**—Mr. Gorbachev, in a rebuff to President Reagan, calls Mr. Daniloff "a spy caught red-handed." Moscow says the expulsion of the 25 will "not go without consequences."

**Sept. 19**—President Reagan meets with the Soviet Foreign Minister, Eduard A. Shevardnadze, at the White House.

**Sept. 20**—Secretary of State Shultz and Foreign Minister Shevardnadze say progress has been made in laying the groundwork for a summit meeting, but they say the Daniloff case is an obstacle.

**Sept. 21**—A Soviet Foreign Ministry spokesman says that the Daniloff case is an unnecessary obstacle to talks on substantial issues and that a way may soon be found to free Mr. Daniloff.

**Sept. 22**—President Reagan, in a speech at the United Nations, voices new hope on American-Soviet arms control talks, but he says Mr. Daniloff's arrest "cast a pall" on American relations with the Soviet Union.

**Sept. 23**—Mr. Shevardnadze calls a summit meeting "a realistic possibility." The State Department says that the main obstacle—the release of Mr. Daniloff—has not yet been resolved.

**Sept. 24**—Contrary to expectations, and acting on a request from the United States Attorney for the Eastern District of New York, a Federal judge in Brooklyn sets no date for a trial of Mr. Zakharov.

**Sept. 28**—Mr. Shultz and Mr. Shevardnadze meet late into the night, holding the longest of four meetings on the case.

**Sept. 29**—Mr. Daniloff is allowed to leave the Soviet Union and flies to Frankfurt.

SEPT. 30

## House, 313 to 83, Affirms Sanctions on South Africa

**By STEVEN V. ROBERTS**

WASHINGTON, Sept. 29—The House of Representatives brushed aside a new proposal by President Reagan today and voted decisively to override his veto of a bill imposing stiff economic sanctions on the South African government.

The vote was 313 to 83, or 49 more votes than the two thirds of those voting needed to override the veto. The President picked up six votes from the initial vote in the House, but supporters of the bill added five votes, so Mr. Reagan's appeal today had virtually no effect.

"This bill will send a moral and diplomatic wake-up call to a President who doesn't understand the issue," Representative William H. Gray 3d, a Pennsylvania Democrat, said in the debate today. "Sometimes we need to feel good about who we are and what we stand for."

SEPT. 30

# House Vote on Overriding Veto of South African Sanctions

This is the roll call by which the House overrode President Reagan's veto of a bill imposing economic sanctions on South Africa.

### ALABAMA
**Democrats**—Bevill, yes; Erdreich, yes; Flippo, yes; Nichols, yes; Shelby, yes.
**Republicans**—Callahan, no; Dickinson, no.

### ALASKA
**Republican**—Young, yes.

### ARIZONA
**Democrat**—Udall, yes.
**Republicans**—Kolbe, yes; McCain, yes; Rudd, no; Stump, no.

### ARKANSAS
**Democrats**—Alexander, yes; Anthony, xxx; Robinson, yes.
**Republican**—Hammerschmidt, no.

### CALIFORNIA
**Democrats**—Anderson, yes; Bates, yes; Beilenson, yes; Berman, yes; Bosco, yes; Boxer, yes; Brown, yes; Burton, xxx; Coelho, yes; Dellums, yes; Dixon, yes; Dymally, yes; Edwards, yes; Fazio, yes; Hawkins, yes; Lantos, yes; Lehman, yes; Levine, yes; Martinez, yes; Matsul, yes; Miller, xxx; Mineta, yes; Panetta, xxx; Roybal, yes; Stark, yes; Torres, yes; Waxman, yes.
**Republicans**—Badham, xxx; Chappie, no; Dannemeyer, no; Dornan, no; Dreier, no; Fiedler, xxx; Hunter, no; Lagomarsino, yes; Lewis, no; Lowery, yes; Lungren, no; McCandless, no; Moorhead, no; Packard, no; Pashayan, yes; Shumway, no; Thomas, xxx; Zschau, xxx.

### COLORADO
**Democrats**—Schroeder, yes, Wirth, yes.
**Republicans**—Brown, yes; Kramer, xxx; Schaefer, no; Strang, no.

### CONNECTICUT
**Democrats**—Geidenson, yes; Kennelly, yes; Morrison, yes.
**Republicans**—Johnson, yes; McKinney, yes; Rowland, yes.

### DELAWARE
**Democrat**—Carper, yes.

### FLORIDA
**Democrats**—Bennett, yes; Chappell, yes; Fascell, yes; Fuqua, yes; Gibbons, yes; Hutto, no; Lehman, yes; MacKay, yes; Mica, yes; Nelson, yes; Pepper, yes; Smith, yes.
**Republicans**—Bilirakis, no; Ireland, yes; Lewis, yes; Mack, no; McCollum, no; Shaw, no; Young, no.

### GEORGIA
**Democrats**—Barnard, yes; Darden, yes; Fowler, xxx; Hatcher, xxx; Jenkins, yes; Ray, yes; Rowland, yes; Thomas, yes.
**Republicans**—Gingrich, yes; Swindall, no.

### HAWAII
**Democrats**—Abercrombie, yes; Akaka, yes.

### IDAHO
**Democrat**—Stallings, yes.
**Republican**—Craig, no.

### ILLINOIS
**Democrats**—Annunzio, yes; Bruce, yes; Collins, yes; Durbin, yes; Evans, yes; Gray, yes; Hayes, yes; Lipinski, yes; Price, yes; Rostenkowski, xxx; Russo, yes; Savage, yes; Yates, yes.
**Republicans**—Crane, no; Fawell, yes; Grotberg, xxx; Hyde, no; Madigan, yes; Martin, yes; Michel, no; Porter, no.

### INDIANA
**Democrats**—Hamilton, yes; Jacobs, yes; McCloskey, yes; Sharp, yes; Visclosky, yes.
**Republicans**—Burton, no; Coats, yes; Hiler, yes; Hillis, yes; Myers, no.

### IOWA
**Democrats**—Bedell, yes; Smith, yes.
**Republicans**—Evans, yes; Leach, yes; Lightfoot, yes; Tauke, yes.

### KANSAS
**Democrats**—Glickman, yes; Slattery, yes.
**Republicans**—Meyers, yes; Roberts, yes; Whittaker, no.

### KENTUCKY
**Democrats**—Hubbard, yes; Mazzoli, yes; Natcher, yes; Perkins, yes.
**Republicans**—Hopkins, yes; Rogers, no; Snyder, no.

### LOUISIANA
**Democrats**—Boggs, yes; Breaux, xxx; Huckaby, xxx; Long, yes; Roemer, yes; Tauzin, yes.
**Republicans**—Livingston, no; Moore, xxx.

### MAINE
**Republicans**—McKernan, yes; Snowe, yes.

### MARYLAND
**Democrats**—Barnes, yes; Byron, yes; Dyson, yes; Hoyer, yes; Mikulski, yes; Mitchell, yes.
**Republicans**—Bentley, yes; Holt, no.

### MASSACHUSETTS
**Democrats**—Atkins, yes; Boland, yes; Donnelly, yes; Early, yes; Frank, yes; Markey, yes; Mavroules, yes; Moakley, yes; O'Neill, yes; Studds, yes.
**Republican**—Conte, yes.

### MICHIGAN
**Democrats**—Bonior, yes; Carr, yes; Conyers, yes; Crockett, yes; Dingell, yes; Ford, yes; Hertel, yes; Kildee, yes; Levin, yes; Traxler, yes; Wolpe, yes.
**Republicans**—Broomfield, no; Davis, yes; Henry, yes; Pursell, yes; Schuette, yes; Siljander, xxx; Vander Jagt, xxx.

### MINNESOTA
**Democrats**—Oberstar, yes; Penny, yes; Sabo, yes; Sikorski, yes; Vento, yes.
**Republicans**—Frenzel, yes; Stangeland, xxx; Weber, yes.

### MISSISSIPPI
**Democrats**—Dowdy, yes; Montgomery, no; Whitten, yes.
**Republicans**—Franklin, yes; Lott, no.

### MISSOURI
**Democrats**—Clay, yes; Gephardt, yes; Skelton, xxx; Volkmer, yes; Wheat, yes; Young, yes.
**Republicans**—Coleman, xxx; Emerson, no; Taylor, no.

### MONTANA
**Democrat**—Williams, yes.
**Republican**—Marlenee, no.

### NEBRASKA
**Republicans**—Bereuter, yes; Daub, yes; Smith, yes.

### NEVADA
**Democrat**—Reid, yes.
**Republican**—Vucanovich, no.

### NEW HAMPSHIRE
**Republicans**—Gregg, xxx; Smith, no.

### NEW JERSEY
**Democrats**—Dwyer, yes; Florio, yes; Guarini, yes; Howard, yes; Hughes, yes; Rodino, yes; Roe, yes; Torricelli, yes.
**Republicans**—Courter, yes; Gallo, yes; Rinaldo, yes; Roukema, yes; Saxton, yes; Smith, yes.

### NEW MEXICO
**Democrat**—Richardson, yes.
**Republicans**—Lujan, yes; Skeen, no.

### NEW YORK
**Democrats**—Ackerman, yes; Biaggi, yes; Downey, yes; Garcia, yes; LaFalce, yes; Lundine, yes; Manton, yes; McHugh, yes; Mrazek, yes; Nowak, yes; Owens, yes; Rangel, yes; Scheuer, yes; Schumer, yes; Solarz, yes; Stratton, yes; Towns, yes; Waldon, yes; Weiss, yes.
**Republicans**—Boehlert, yes; Carney, yes; DioGuardi, yes; Eckert, no; Fish, yes; Gilman, yes; Green, yes; Horton, yes; Kemp, no; Lent, yes; Martin, xxx; McGrath, yes; Molinari, yes; Solomon, no; Wortley, yes.

### NORTH CAROLINA
**Democrats**—Hefner, yes; Jones, xxx; Neal, yes; Rose, xxx; Valentine, yes; Whitley, yes.
**Republicans**—Cobey, no; Coble, no; Hendon, no; McMillan, no.

### NORTH DAKOTA
**Democrat**—Dorgan, yes.

### OHIO
**Democrats**—Applegate, yes; Eckart, yes; Feighan, yes; Hall, yes; Kaptur, yes; Luken, yes; Oakar, yes; Pease, yes; Selberling, yes; Stokes, yes; Traficant, yes.
**Republicans**—DeWine, no; Gradison, yes; Kasich, yes; Kindness, xxx; Latta, no; McEwen, no; Miller, no; Oxley, xxx; Regula, yes; Wylie, yes.

### OKLAHOMA
**Democrats**—English, yes; Jones, yes; McCurdy, yes; Synar, yes; Watkins, yes.
**Republican**—Edwards, xxx.

### OREGON
**Democrats**—AuCoin, yes; Weaver, xxx; Wyden, yes.
**Republicans**—D. Smith, no; R. Smith, no.

### PENNSYLVANIA
**Democrats**—Borski, yes; Coyne, yes; Edgar, yes; Foglietta, yes; Gaydos, xxx; Gray, yes; Kanjorski, yes; Kolter, yes; Kostmayer, yes; Murphy, yes; Murtha, yes; Walgren, yes; Yatron, yes.
**Republicans**—Clinger, yes; Coughlin, yes; Gekas, yes; Goodling, yes; McDade, xxx; Ridge, yes; Ritter, no; Schulze, yes; Shuster, no; Walker, yes.

### RHODE ISLAND
**Democrat**—St Germain, yes.
**Republican**—Schneider, xxx.

## SOUTH CAROLINA

**Democrats**—Derrick, xxx; Spratt, yes; Tallon, yes.
**Republicans**—Campbell, xxx; Hartnett, xxx; Spence, no.

## SOUTH DAKOTA

**Democrat**—Daschle, yes.

## TENNESSEE

**Democrats**—Boner, yes; Cooper, yes; Ford, yes; Gordon, yes; Jones, yes; Lloyd, yes.
**Republicans**—Duncan, yes; Quillen, no; Sundquist, no.

## TEXAS

**Democrats**—Andrews, yes; Brooks, yes; Bryant, yes; Bustamante, yes; Chapman, yes; Coleman, yes; del la Garza, yes; Frost, yes; Gonzalez, yes; R. Hall, xxx; Leath, yes; Leland, yes; Ortiz, yes; Pickle, yes; Stenholm, no; Wilson, yes; Wright, yes.
**Republicans**—Archer, no; Armey, no; Bartlett, no; Barton, no; Boutler, no; Combest, no; DeLay, no; Fields, no; Loeffler, no; Sweeney, no.

## UTAH

**Republicans**—Hansen, no; Monson, no; Nielson, no.

## VERMONT

**Republican**—Jeffords, yes.

## VIRGINIA

**Democrats**—Boucher, yes; Daniel, no; Olin, yes; Sisisky, yes.
**Republicans**—Bateman, yes; Bliley, yes; Parris, no; Slaughter, no; Whitehurst, yes; Wolf, yes.

## WASHINGTON

**Democrats**—Bonker, xxx; Dicks, yes; Foley, yes; Lowry, yes; Swift, yes.
**Republicans**—Chandler, yes; Miller, yes; Morrison, yes.

## WEST VIRGINIA

**Democrats**—Mollohan, yes; Rahall, yes; Staggers, yes; Wise, yes.

## WISCONSIN

**Democrats**—Aspin, yes; Kastenmeier, yes; Kleczka, yes; Moody, yes; Obey, yes.
**Republicans**—Gunderson, yes; Petri, yes; Roth, no; Sensenbrenner, yes.

## WYOMING

**Republican**—Cheney, no.

SEPT. 30

# Senate, 78 to 21, Overrides Reagan's Veto and Imposes Sanctions on South Africa

**By STEVEN V. ROBERTS**

**W**ASHINGTON, Oct. 2—The Senate voted today to override President Reagan's veto of legislation imposing stiff economic sanctions on South Africa. In doing so it rejected his pleas for support as he prepares to meet Mikhail S. Gorbachev, the Soviet leader, in Iceland.

The vote was 78 to 21, or 12 votes more than the two-thirds vote necessary to override. Since the House also voted to rebuff the President earlier this week, the sanctions bill became law as soon as the Senate voted to override the President's veto.

The vote today capped a two-year effort by opponents of apartheid to force the Reagan Administration into exerting more pressure on the Pretoria government to change its policies of racial separation. The legislation will ban all new investment by Americans in South African businesses, prohibit the importation of such products as steel and coal from South Africa, and will cancel landing rights in the United States for South African airlines.

Many of the provisions of the law take effect immediately, while others will be gradually introduced over the next few months. For example, the import of iron, steel and agricultural products is banned immediately, while a similar ban on uranium, coal and textiles will take effect in 90 days. The ban on new investments takes effect in 45 days, and the law directs Mr. Reagan to stop all flights within 10 days.

Senator Richard G. Lugar, the Indiana Republican who heads the Foreign Relations Committee and was the chief sponsor of the measure, appealed in emotional terms to Pretoria to heed the action taken by Congress.

"As a friend of that government we are saying wake up!" he said.

After the vote, Senator Edward M. Kennedy, Democrat of Massachusetts, said, "The Senate's action today expressed the best ideals of the American people. The message to countries all over the world is, the United States will lead, and we're proud to lead."

OCT. 3

---

Following is the roll-call vote by which the Senate overrode President Reagan's veto of the bill imposing economic sanctions on South Africa. The 78 votes were 11 more than required.

### FOR OVERRIDING VETO—78

#### Democrats—47

| | | |
|---|---|---|
| Baucus, Mont. | Glenn, Ohio | Melcher, Mont. |
| Bentsen, Tex. | Gore, Tenn. | Metzenbaum, Ohio |
| Biden, Del. | Harkin, Iowa | |
| Bingaman, N.M. | Hart, Colo. | Mitchell, Me. |
| Boren, Okla. | Heflin, Ala. | Moynihan, N.Y. |
| Bradley, N.J. | Hollings, S.C. | Nunn, Ga. |
| Bumpers, Ark. | Inouye, Hawaii | Poli, R.I. |
| Burdick, N.D. | Johnston, La. | Proxmire, Wis. |
| Byrd, W.Va. | Kennedy, Mass. | Pryor, Ark. |
| Chiles, Fla. | Kerry, Mass. | Riegle, Mich. |
| Cranston, Calif. | Lautenberg, N.J. | Rockefeller, W. Va. |
| DeConcini, Ariz. | Leahy, Vt. | Sarbanes, Md. |
| Dixon, Ill. | Levin, Mich. | Sesser, Tenn. |
| Dodd, Conn. | Long, La. | Simon, Ill. |
| Eagleton, Mo. | Matsunaga, Hawaii | Stennis, Miss. |
| Exon, Neb. | | Zorinsky, Neb. |
| Ford, Ky. | | |

#### Republicans—31

| | | |
|---|---|---|
| Abdnor, S.D. | Gorton, Wash. | Murkowski, Alaska |
| Andrews, N.D. | Grassley, Iowa | |
| Boschwitz, Minn. | Hatfield, Ore. | Packwood, Ore. |
| | Hawkins, Fla. | |
| Chafee, R.I. | Heinz, Pa. | Quayle, Ind. |
| Cohen, Me. | Kassebaum, Kan. | Roth, Del. |
| D'Amato, N.Y. | | Spector, Pa. |
| Danforth, Mo. | Kasten, Wis. | Stafford, Vt. |
| Domenici, N.M. | Lugar, Ind. | Trible, Va. |
| Durenberger, Minn. | Mathias, Md. | Warner, Va. |
| | Mattingly, Ga. | Weicker, Conn. |
| Evans, Wash. | McConnell, Ky. | Wilson, Calif. |

### AGAINST OVERRIDING VETO—21

#### Republicans—21

| | | |
|---|---|---|
| Armstrong, Colo. | Hecht, Nev. | Rudman, N.H. |
| | Helms, N.C. | Simpson, Wyo. |
| Cochran, Miss. | Humphrey, N.H. | Stevens, Alaska |
| Denton, Ala. | Laxaft, Nev. | |
| Dole, Kan. | McClure, Idaho | Symms, Idaho |
| Goldwater, Ariz. | Nickles, Okla. | Thurmond, S.C. |
| Gramm, Tex. | Pressler, S.D. | Wallop, Wyo. |
| Hatch, Utah | | |

#### Not Voting—1

Garn, Utah

OCT. 3

---

# Kasparov Makes a Key Move, and the Fans Sense a Victory

**By SERGE SCHMEMANN**

MOSCOW, Oct. 4—As 800 people watched in tense silence in the Leningrad hall, the referee in the world chess championship today opened a move sealed by Gary Kasparov in a game adjourned the night before.

Then, when the move—a knight's attack on the king—was announced, the crowd exploded in a standing ovation, aware that Kasparov was guaranteed a victory in the game and, barring a near miracle, retention of his championship.

The challenger, Anatoly Karpov, struggled for 11 more moves in the slender hope Kasparov would commit a gross blunder, but both the champion and the audience knew that there was no escape.

Faced with an inevitable checkmate, Karpov resigned the game, the 22d in his bid to regain the title he lost to Kasparov a year ago. The 24-game rematch began July 28 in London and moved to Leningrad on Sept. 5.

OCT. 5

## Moves in the Critical Game
### QUEEN'S GAMBIT DECLINED

| White<br>Kasparov | Black<br>Karpov | White<br>Kasparov | Black<br>Karpov |
|---|---|---|---|
| 1. P-Q4 | N-KB3 | 24. Q-K3 | P-N5 |
| 2. P-QB4 | P-K3 | 25. N-K4 | PxP |
| 3. N-KB3 | P-Q4 | 26. NxBch | NxN |
| 4. N-B3 | B-K2 | 27. PxP | N-Q4 |
| 5. B-N5 | P-KR3 | 28. BxN | PxB |
| 6. BxN | BxB | 29. N-K5 | Q-Q1 |
| 7. P-K3 | O-O | 30. Q-KB3 | R-R3 |
| 8. R-B1 | P-B3 | 31. R-QB1 | K-R2 |
| 9. B-Q3 | N-Q2 | 32. Q-R3 | R-N3 |
| 10. O-O | PxP | 33. R-B8 | Q-Q3 |
| 11. BxP | P-K4 | 34. Q-KN3 | P-R5 |
| 12. P-KR3 | PxP | 35. R-R8 | Q-K3 |
| 13. PxP | N-N3 | 36. RxP | Q-B4 |
| 14. B-N3 | B-B4 | 37. R-R7 | R-N8ch |
| 15. R-K1 | P-QR4 | 38. K-R2 | R-QB8 |
| 16. P-R3 | R-K1 | 39. R-N7 | R-B7 |
| 17. RxRch | QxR | 40. P-B3 | R-Q7 |
| 18. Q-Q2 | N-Q2 | 41. N-Q7 | RxP |
| 19. Q-B4 | B-N3 | 42. N-B8ch | K-R3 |
| 20. P-KR4 | Q-Q1 | 43. R-N4 | R-QB5 |
| 21. N-R4 | P-R4 | 44. RxR | PxR |
| 22. R-K1 | P-N4 | 45. Q-Q6 | P-B6 |
| 23. N-B3 | Q-N1 | 46. Q-Q4 | Resigns |

OCT. 5

## Iranian Oil Minister in Key OPEC Role

**By JOHN TAGLIABUE**

GENEVA, Oct. 9—The seven-year-old war between Iran and Iraq is becoming an increasingly intrusive issue for the Organization of Petroleum Exporting Countries. As a result, the Iranian oil minister, Gholam Reza Aghazadeh, has been cast in the role of a major power broker within the organization.

Mr. Aghazadeh, unlike debonair ministers from the wealthy Arab countries of the Persian Gulf, is often seen in a scruffy gray beard and trimless gray suit without a necktie.

He is the linchpin of a three-nation bloc—Iran, Algeria and Libya. These countries share radical politics, large populations and high dependence on oil revenues, making them forceful proponents of higher prices.

His bold compromise at OPEC's last meeting, held here in August, paved the way for a production accord that lifted prices 30 percent.

At the August meeting, OPEC agreed to limit the output of 12 of its 13 members from Sept. 1 to Oct. 31 to 14.8 million barrels a day in an attempt to bolster prices by removing excess supplies from the market. OCT. 10

## How producers currently rank

Average crude oil production for January to August, in thousands of barrels a day.

| | |
|---|---:|
| Soviet Union | 12,228 |
| United States | 8,826 |
| **Saudi Arabia** | **4,847** |
| North Sea | 3,564 |
| China | 2,500 |
| Mexico | 2,418 |
| Iran | 2,012 |
| Venezuela* | 1,723 |
| Iraq | 1,695 |
| Nigeria* | 1,546 |
| United Arab Emirates | 1,438 |
|   Abu Dhabi | 1,023 |
|   Dubai | 350 |
|   Sharjah* | 65 |
| Kuwait | 1,370 |
| Indonesia* | 1,364 |
| Libya | 1,052 |
| Algeria | 601 |
| Oman | 552 |
| Qatar | 351 |
| Neutral Zone | 304 |
| Ecuador | 293 |
| Gabon | 164 |
| Others | 7,120 |
| Other East Europe | 440 |
| Total OPEC | 18,760 |
| Total world | 60,337 |

*Includes condensates: about 50,000 barrels a day for Nigeria; 60,000 for Sharjah; 140,000 for Venezuela, and 125,000 for Indonesia.

Source: *Petroleum Intelligence Weekly*

OCT. 10

## The Road Ahead; Each Side Blames Other for Failure at Reykjavík, but Meeting May Still Yield Success

**By BERNARD GWERTZMAN**

WASHINGTON, Oct. 13—The inability of President Reagan and Mikhail S. Gorbachev to attain tangible results at the Reykjavík meeting has left Soviet-American relations in a quandary, in the view of foreign policy experts within and outside the Government.

The Russians and the Americans could end up going their own ways for the remainder of the Reagan term, blaming each other—as they have started to do already—for allowing a package of arms control agreements to slip through their hands. And each in coming days will undoubtedly seek to portray the meeting in Iceland as a success for its side and a defeat for the other.

Soviet spokesmen are saying that Mr. Gorbachev was able to show that he had a stronger commitment to total arms control than did Mr. Reagan. Mr. Reagan and his spokesmen, meanwhile, are trying to persuade Americans and allies that the meeting was not a setback for American interests.

Patrick J. Buchanan, the White House communications director, stung by suggestions in some Washington quarters that Mr. Reagan mishandled the summit meeting, said today, "I think when the President of the United States says no to a nonnegotiable demand by the Secretary General of the Soviet Union that he give up the strategic defense of the United States, I don't think that's a failure."  OCT. 14

## Arms Control: What Might Have Been

The following are the tentative understandings that were reached before the impasse over "Star Wars" brought an end to the Iceland talks.

**Medium-range missiles.** The two leaders reached verbal agreement on banning all such missiles from Europe. Each side would have been allowed to have 100 warheads on medium-range missiles, with the American missiles stationed in the United States and the Soviet missiles in Soviet Asia. They also agreed on steps toward verification, on freezing shorter-range missiles pending further negotiations, and on the duration of such an interim accord.

**Nuclear testing.** The two sides agreed to an American plan to begin a phased accord, starting with verification of existing treaties and working toward an ultimate cessation of tests, as sought by the Russians.

**Strategic offensive nuclear forces.** The two sides agreed to limit each side's nuclear launchers, missiles and bombers to 1,600, and the number of warheads to 6,000. The Russians also agreed to an American plan to abolish all ballistic missiles over 10 years.

**Non-arms issues.** There was an agreed statement dealing with such questions as reuniting separated families and on emigration. There also were instructions drafted encouraging progress on several Soviet-American areas of possible cooperation.

OCT. 14

## Arms talks: a glossary

There are many specialized terms in the language of the nuclear arms talks. These are a few of those terms.

**Ballistic missile.** This missile, powered by a rocket engine, travels outside of the atmosphere for part of its flight.

**Conventional forces.** Forces capable of carrying out warfare without the use of nuclear weapons. Also distinguished from insurgency forces.

**Cruise missile.** A low-flying missile that looks like a flying torpedo, it is powered by an air-breathing engine and is armed with either nuclear or nonnuclear warheads. The current generation of cruise missiles, which are subsonic, can be launched from the ground (GLCMs), sea (SLCMs) or air (ALCMs).

**Reentry vehicle (RV).** The part of a ballistic missile that reenters the earth's atmosphere carrying the nuclear warhead.

**Intercontinental ballistic missile (ICBM).** A land-based missile that has a range of more than about 3,400 miles, including the Soviet SS-18 or the American Minuteman.

**Intermediate-range nuclear forces (INF).** Sometimes called theater nuclear forces (TNF). Missiles and aircraft with a range of less than 3,400 miles, including the Soviet SS-20 and the American Pershing 2 and ground-launched cruise missile. Intermediate-range bombers include the Soviet Backfire bomber—which is included in the American Geneva proposal as a strategic bomber—and the American B-111 bomber.

**Multiple independently targetable reentry vehicle (MIRV).** One of several reentry vehicles carried by a single ballistic missile that can be directed at separate targets. Missiles with MIRVs employ a dispensing mechanism, called a postboost vehicle, with devices that direct the reentry vehicles and their warheads to the various target points.

**Submarine-launched ballistic missile (SLBM).** A ballistic missile launched from a submarine.

**Strategic.** A term used to describe nuclear weapons that have range considered intercontinental, or more than 3,400 miles.

**Tactical.** Tactical weapons are short-range systems used on the battlefield.

**Throw weight.** The amount of weight a missile can carry to its target.

**Verification.** The process of determining whether a party is adhering to the terms of an agreement. Means of verification include surveillance satellites.

OCT. 26

# G.M. Plans to Sell South Africa Unit to a Local Group

By JOHN HOLUSHA

DETROIT, Oct. 20—The General Motors Corporation, the largest American company doing business in South Africa, said today that it would withdraw from South Africa by selling its operations there to a group of investors led by local G.M. managers.

Roger B. Smith, chairman of G.M., said in a statement that the company was pulling out because it had been losing money in South Africa and because little progress had been made in ending apartheid. However, the company will continue to sell automotive components to its former subsidiary.

The automotive giant, which in the past has argued that the jobs it provides by staying in South Africa bring economic benefits to all races, has been a leader among American companies doing business there. Its shift was hailed by leaders of groups seeking corporate divestment from that country.

"This is a tremendously significant decision," said Timothy Smith, director of the Interfaith Center on Corporate Responsibility. "Business will understand the symbolism of the action, and we expect to see the trickle of companies leaving to turn into a flood." He added that the G.M. decision was an indication that pressure from shareholder groups to eliminate South African investments was having an effect. "The fact is, G.M. was facing pressure from some significant investors." For G.M., the decision to pull out now, rather than at some other time, seems to reflect a combination of factors, including the continuing losses in South Africa and the increasing divestment pressure.

OCT. 21

## Pulling out
U.S. companies that have totally divested their South African operations so far in 1986.[1]

| Company Selling Unit | Nationality of Unit's Buyer |
|---|---|
| Applied Power | Liechtenstein |
| Ashland Oil | Netherlands |
| Ashland Oil[2] | Japan |
| Baxter Travenol | South Africa |
| Bell & Howell | South Africa |
| CBS | South Africa |
| Cooper Industries | South Africa |
| Delaware North | South Africa |
| Eaton | South Africa |
| Fairchild Industries | United States[3] |

| Company<br>Selling Unit | Nationality of<br>Unit's Buyer |
|---|---|
| GTE | South Africa |
| General Electric | South Africa |
| General Signal | South Africa |
| MacMillan | South Africa |
| Manpower[2] | Britain |
| Pennwalt | South Africa |
| Phillips Petroleum | West Germany |
| Rohm & Haas | South Africa |
| Scovill | United States[4] |
| Scovill | United States[5] |
| W. R. Stamler | (Liquidated) |
| Stanley Works | South Africa |
| VF Corporation | South Africa |

[1]Companies that have announced their intention to divest are Coca-Cola, Diamond Shamrock, General Motors, Marriott, Procter & Gamble and SPS Technology.
[2]Disinvestment in South Africa was part of a worldwide divestiture.
[3]Buyer: Eyedentify Inc.
[4]Buyer: Parker-Hannifin
[5]Buyer: Arvin Industries
Source: Investor Responsibility Research Center

OCT. 21

## The largest employers

Ten biggest U.S. employers in South Africa, as of September 1986.

| Company | Number<br>of<br>Employees | Percent<br>of '84<br>Sales from<br>South Africa |
|---|---|---|
| Mobile Corporation | 3,182 | N.A. |
| General Motors<br>Corporation[1] | 3,056 | 0.4% |
| USG Corporation | 2,631 | N.A. |
| Goodyear Tire and<br>Rubber Company | 2,471 | N.A. |
| Caltex Petroleum<br>Corporation[2] | 2,186 | N.A. |
| R. J. R. Nabisco | 2,084 | 0.22% |
| Allegheny Corporation | 2,025 | N.A. |
| I.B.M. Corporation | 1,550 | Less than 1% |
| Johnson & Johnson | 1,389 | Less than 1% |
| United Technologies<br>Corporation | 1,261 | 0.3% |

[1]Has announced intention to withdraw. Current work force is estimated at 2,800.
[2]Owned by Chevron Corp. and Texaco Inc.
N.A. Not available
Source: Investor Responsibility Research Center

OCT. 21

# Moscow Expels 5 and Bars U.S. Use of 260 Soviet Aides

By SERGE SCHMEMANN

MOSCOW, Oct. 22—Striking in another round of the diplomatic expulsions, the Soviet Union said today that five more staff members of the United States Embassy would have to leave and that all 260 Soviet employees of the embassy would be withdrawn.

The Soviet government further imposed restrictions on the number of Americans who could be stationed in the embassy for temporary duty and on the number of foreign house guests invited by American diplomats.

Gennadi I. Gerasimov, the Foreign Ministry spokesman, in announcing the latest expulsions, said other steps would be taken if the United States continued its "discriminatory practices" toward Soviet missions.

The Soviet steps were ordered after the United States expelled 5 Soviet diplomats and, in addition, ordered 50 others to leave to equalize the staffs of the two countries at 251 each.

In a televised speech today about his meeting in Iceland with President Reagan, Mikhail S. Gorbachev said that the expulsions by the United States after so important an event appeared "wild to normal people."

"We do not intend to allow such an outrage," he said. In Washington, the White House reacted to the Gorbachev speech by saying that the two sides seemed in accord on the need for arms control.

The United States seemed relieved that Moscow had expelled only five Americans in the latest retaliation.

State Department officials said they were weighing whether to call a truce or respond in kind.

Officials said that all Soviet diplomats suspected of being major spies were expected to leave as a result of the expulsions. OCT. 23

## U.S.-Soviet Sparring: A Year of Ousters

**March 7**—The United States tells the Soviet Union that it must reduce the size of the Soviet, Ukrainian and Byelorussian missions to the United Nations from 275 to 170 over two years, with the first cut of 25 by Oct. 1. The American announcement asserts that the Soviet Union is using the mission for spying.

**Aug. 23**—Gennadi F. Zakharov, a physicist who is a Soviet employee of the United Nations, is arrested in New York on espionage charges.

**Aug. 30**—Nicholas S. Daniloff, correspondent for *U.S. News & World Report*, is arrested in Moscow on espionage charges.

**Sept. 12**—Mr. Zakharov and Mr. Daniloff are freed from prison in the custody of their embassies.

**Sept. 12**—The chief Soviet delegate to the United Nations, Aleksandr M. Belonogov, says the Soviet Union has no plans to comply with the Oct. 1 deadline to remove 25 personnel, asserting that the order is illegal.

**Sept. 17**—The State Department, angered over the continued detention of Mr. Daniloff in Moscow and upset over the Soviet delegate's statement, presents a list of 25 who must leave the United States by Oct. 1 in compliance with the deadline. The United States also tells the Russians that if they retaliate, the United States will move to bring the Soviet and American Embassies to parity.

**Sept. 17**—The Russians protest, saying the United States has no right to make such an order.

**Sept. 29**—Mr. Daniloff is allowed to leave the Soviet Union.

**Sept. 30**—Mr. Zakharov is allowed to leave the United States after pleading no contest to spying charges. Secretary of State George P. Shultz announces a two-week grace period for compliance with the expulsion order.

**Oct. 11–12**—President Reagan and Mikhail S. Gorbachev, the Soviet leader, meet in Reykjavík, Iceland. The expulsion order is not discussed.

**Oct. 13**—The Soviet Union is given another week to comply with the expulsion order.

**Oct. 15**—The last of the 25 Soviet diplomats leave the United States.

**Oct. 19**—The Soviet Union expels 5 American diplomats, apparently in retaliation for the ouster of the 25 Soviet diplomats.

**Oct. 21**—The United States expels 5 Soviet diplomats in retaliation and says 50 more must leave to bring the size of the American and Soviet diplomatic delegations to parity. This must be done by Nov. 1, Washington says.

**Oct. 22**—The Soviet Union expels another five Americans, again apparently in retaliation. It says that to have true parity 260 Soviet nationals who work at the American Embassy in Moscow will stop working there.

OCT. 23

## NATO Nervously Contemplates a Conventional Forces Gap

By JAMES M. MARKHAM

BRUSSELS—For years, West European politicians have ritually urged the superpowers to strive for a world freed from the terror of nuclear weapons. Yet when Ronald Reagan and Mikhail S. Gorbachev boldly explored that prospect in Iceland, a number of the United States's allies became very nervous. However terrifying, American nuclear weapons have become symbols of a commitment to the defense of Western Europe—and a cheap way of compensating for the superiority in ground forces that the Warsaw Pact holds over NATO.

After Reykjavík, a new debate on the balance of conventional forces seemed likely within the Atlantic alliance. Although the explusions of diplomats by Moscow and Washington dominated the headlines last week, the prevailing assumption at NATO headquarters here was that Mr. Reagan and Mr. Gorbachev had broken so much ground at Reykjavík that eventually the superpowers would reach possibly momentous arms reduction accords. But one of the first questions being raised was what would be done about Europe's central front, where the forces of the North Atlantic Treaty Organization and the Warsaw Pact face each other.

It is widely agreed that the Warsaw Pact enjoys a numerical edge over the forces in NATO's integrated command. But one of the most significant developments of the last few years has been France's quiet operational realignment with the alliance. A pivotal assumption today is that French forces would join the rest of NATO in case of a Soviet ground attack in Europe. With French troops, NATO actually has a slight manpower edge—1,034,000 to 975,000—in the region running from the English Channel to the eastern frontiers of Poland.

Yet the Soviet pool of potential reinforcements is far greater than that of those who could arrive by air and sea from the United States and Britain to turn back a land assault. And, in keeping with Soviet military doctrine, which calls for quickly seizing the offensive in a European war, the Warsaw Pact has a considerable advantage in tanks, armored personnel carriers, artillery and helicopters. In a war, this advantage would presumably be exploited to try to achieve a stunning breakthrough in West Germany, possibly on the lightly defended north German plain. OCT. 26

## The face-off

NATO and Warsaw Pact conventional forces in Europe (1985–1986 estimates)

|  | NATO | Warsaw Pact |
|---|---|---|
| Aircraft (including fighters, interceptors and group attack craft) | 3,218 | 5,736 |
| Main battle tanks | 20,333 | 52,600 |
| Artillery | 9,414 | 30,500 |
| Antitank guns and missile launchers | 2,590 | 7,902 |
| Antiaircraft guns | 5,654 | 4,506 |
| Surface-to-surface missile launchers | 365 | 1,570 |
| Surface-to-air missiles | 880 | 5,808 |
| Division equivalents* | 33 | 78 1/3 |
| Troops deployed in Europe (excluding naval) | 2,088,000 | 2,685,000 |

*Warsaw Pact divisions normally have fewer members than many NATO divisions but have more tanks and artillery and thus represent similar combat power.
Source: International Institute for Strategic Studies

OCT. 26

## Prayers for Peace

On October 27, representatives of 12 major faiths gathered in Assisi at the invitation of the Pope, to pray for peace. The Vatican provided these excerpts from their prayers:

**Buddhist**—May all beings everywhere, plagued with sufferings of body and mind, obtain an ocean of happiness and joy.

**Hindu**—May God protect us; may He nourish us. May we work together with energy. May our studies be fruitful. May we love each other and live in peace.

**Jainist**—Peace and universal brotherhood is the essence of the gospel preached by all the enlightened ones of the past and of the future.

**Moslem**—And the servants of the Most Gracious are those who walk on the earth in humility, and when the ignorant address them, they say, "Peace."

**Shinto**—Although the people living across the ocean surrounding us, I believe, are all our brothers, why are there constant troubles in this world? Why do winds and waves rise in the ocean surrounding us? I only earnestly wish that the wind will soon puff away all the clouds which are hanging over the tops of the mountains.

**African Animist**—Almighty God, the Great Thumb we cannot evade to tie any knot, the Roaring Thunder that splits mighty trees, the All-Seeing Lord up on high who sees even the footprints of an antelope on a rock mass here on earth: You are the one who does not hesitate to respond to our call. You are the cornerstone of peace.

**American Indian**—In smoking the pipe, I invite my family to smoke with me and you, my friends, to pray with me in thanksgiving for this day and for world peace. I will pray that we all may commit ourselves to pray and to work for peace within our families, our tribes and our nations. I pray for all our brothers and sisters walking our mother earth.

**Jewish**—Our God in heaven, the Lord of Peace will have compassion and mercy upon us and upon all the peoples of the earth who implore his mercy and his compassion, asking for peace, seeking peace.

**Christian**—I say to you that hear, love your enemies, do good to those who hate you, bless those who curse you, pray for those who abuse you. To him who strikes you on the cheek, offer the other also; and from him who takes away your cloak do not withhold your coat as well. Give to everyone who begs from you; and of him who takes away your goods do not ask them again. And as you wish that men would do to you, do so to them.

Oct. 28

## How OPEC has fared under quota agreement

Effect on oil revenues and production since oil prices hit bottom in July.

| Country | Revenue (millions of U.S. dollars) | | Production (millions of barrels/day) | | |
|---|---|---|---|---|---|
| | Sept. | % Change From July | Sept. | % Change From July | Quota |
| Saudi Arabia | $1,481 | +9% | 4.5 | −21% | 4.353 |
| Iran[1] | 381 | 0 | 1.5 | −32 | 2.3 |
| Iraq | 549 | +58 | 1.8 | 0 | 2.1[2] |
| Kuwait | 286 | −7 | 0.9 | −44 | 0.9 |
| Neutral Zone[3] | 137 | +61 | 0.36 | −10 | — |
| U.A.E. | 418 | +23 | 1.265 | −19 | 0.95 |
| Qatar | 89 | +9 | 0.28 | −30 | 0.28 |
| **Mideast OPEC** | **3,341** | **+15** | **10.605** | **−22** | **10.883** |
| Venezuela | 415 | +21 | 1.67 | −7 | 1.555 |
| Nigeria | 451 | +21 | 1.3 | −16 | 1.3 |
| Libya | 349 | +30 | 0.99 | −14 | 0.99 |
| Indonesia | 300 | +32 | 1.3 | −3 | 1.189 |
| Algeria | 150 | +53 | 0.6 | −0 | 0.663 |
| Gabon | 40 | +25 | 0.137 | −19 | 0.137 |
| Ecuador | 53 | −5 | 0.225 | −25 | 0.183 |
| **Total OPEC** | **$5,099** | **+19%** | **16.827** | **−18%** | **16.9** |

[1] Production decline largely due to war with Iraq.
[2] Not an official quota.
[3] Area whose resources are shared equally by Saudia Arabia and Kuwait.

Sources: *Petroleum Intelligence Weekly;* Petroleum Finance Co.

Oct. 31

## Saudis Seek OPEC Price Meeting: Oil Markets Respond with Rally

**By PETER T. KILBORN**

WASHINGTON, Oct. 30—Saudi Arabia's acting oil minister, Hisham Nazer, called today for an urgent meeting of OPEC's three-member price committee only hours after he had succeeded Sheik Ahmed Zaki Yamani.

The purpose of the meeting, the Saudi Arabian Embassy here said, would be to begin the process of raising the price of oil to at least $18 a barrel. Regardless of any decision by the price committee—consisting of the oil ministers of Libya, Ecuador and Kuwait—no major change in policy could be made without the consent of all 13 OPEC members.

In response to the announcement, however, oil prices surged today on very heavy trading. On the New York Mercantile Exchange, for example, the price of one important futures contract for oil rose $1.31 a barrel, to $15.04, on record volume. Heating oil and gasoline prices also jumped, although many analysts said petroleum prices would eventually fall because there is still too much oil on the market.

OCT. 31

### The numbers from Moscow

After years of withholding data on social and economic conditions, the Soviet Union released several key indicators last week. Here is how they compare with those of the United States.

**Birth rate per 1,000 residents**

|      | Soviet Union | United States |
|------|--------------|---------------|
| 1983 | 19.8         | 15.5          |
| 1984 | 19.6         | 15.5          |
| 1985 | 19.4         | 15.7*         |

**Infant mortality rate per 1,000 births**

|      | Soviet Union | United States |
|------|--------------|---------------|
| 1983 | 25.3         | 11.2          |
| 1984 | 25.9         | 10.8          |
| 1985 | 26.0         | 10.6*         |

*provisional

**Total grain harvests**
(in millions of metric tons)

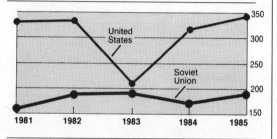

Sources: Soviet statistical yearbooks and newspapers; National Center for Health Statistics; Department of Agriculture

NOV. 2

## American is Freed After 18 Months as Beirut Captive

**By JOHN KIFNER**

LARNACA, Cyprus, Nov. 3—David P. Jacobsen, an American held hostage in Lebanon for nearly 18 months, was released Sunday and stopped here briefly today on his way to West Germany.

Islamic Holy War, the pro-Iranian Moslem fundamentalist group that had held Mr. Jacobsen, did not say specifically why it released him. It said the United States had made moves that could lead to the release of other captives, but it gave no details.

Two United States Navy helicopters arrived in Larnaca this morning from Beirut, about 100 miles east of here, carrying Mr. Jacobsen and Terry Waite, the Archbishop of Canterbury's special envoy.

"Good morning, it's a tremendous pleasure to be here," Mr. Jacobsen told reporters waiting at the airport. "I feel great, absolutely great. Would anyone like to challenge me to a six-mile jog around the airport?"

His face appeared somewhat lined, but he seemed rested and healthy. His beard was flecked with gray, and he wore what appeared to be new clothes: maroon slacks and a maroon sweater with navy blue and tan stripes.

Nov. 3

## Americans Still Missing in Beirut

**Edward Austin Tracy**
A self-described world traveler, poet and author of children's books. 56 years old from South Burlington, Vt. Reported kidnapped in West Beirut on Oct. 21. Accused by his abductors, the Revolutionary Justice Organization, of being a spy for Israel and the United States. A resident of Lebanon for several years. Speaks Arabic and has a certificate from Al Azhar University in Cairo documenting his conversion to Islam. Has lived abroad for the last 21 years and is said to have traveled to Iran, Iraq, Australia, Italy, Ethiopia, the Canary Islands and Trinidad, as well as Lebanon.

**Joseph James Cicippio**
Controller at the American University of Beirut and its hospital. 56 years old from Norristown, Pa. Kidnapped Sept. 12 on his way to work from his apartment in the faculty building. His wife, Elaham Ghandour, a Lebanese Moslem, works for the United States Embassy. His wife appealed to President Reagan in October to intervene on behalf of the hostages held in Lebanon, as the President did for Nicholas S. Daniloff, the American reporter who was charged with spying but was later freed by Moscow.

**Frank Herbert Reed**
Director of the private Lebanese International School. 53 years old from Malden, Mass. Kidnapped in West Beirut on Sept. 9. His wife, Sahmiyeh, is Syrian, and they have a 5-year-old son. Mrs. Reed joined Mrs. Cicippio in the plea to Mr. Reagan, broadcast over Lebanese state television.

**Thomas M. Sutherland**
Dean of agriculture at the American University of Beirut. 55 years old from Fort Collins, Colo. Seized by gunmen on the highway to Beirut's international airport on June 9, 1985. His wife, Jean, continues to teach at the university and recently offered to serve as mediator between the Reagan Administration and the Islamic Holy War group to win the release of her husband and the other American hostages.

**Terry A. Anderson**
Chief Middle East correspondent for The Associated Press. 39 years old from Batavia, N.Y. Kidnapped by gunmen on his way home on March 16, 1985. His wife, Mikki, and their daughter, Gabrielle, had left Beirut earlier for security reasons. Joined in November 1985 with Mr. Sutherland, David P. Jacobsen and the Rev. Lawrence M. Jenco, who was set free last July, in calling on President Reagan to "have mercy" and negotiate with their kidnappers. His sister, Peggy Say, who actively campaigned for the release of the hostages, offered in October to go to Beirut and meet the kidnappers.

**William Buckley**
A political officer at the United States Embassy in Beirut. 58 years old from Medford, Mass. Abducted by gunmen outside his home in West Beirut on March 16, 1984. Islamic Holy War said on Oct. 4, 1985, that it had killed Mr. Buckley in retaliation for the Israeli air raid on the Palestine Liberation Organization headquarters in Tunisia. Kidnappers later made public photographs of what they said was the American hostage's body, but the body has not been recovered and United States officials have not confirmed his death.

# Reagan Confirms Iran Got Arms Aid

**By BERNARD WEINRAUB**

WASHINGTON, Nov. 12—In a meeting with congressional leaders, President Reagan today for the first time personally acknowledged sending military supplies to Iran, according to Administration officials. He also defended the action as necessary for establishing ties to moderate elements there, they added.

The officials said the meeting occurred after Mr. Reagan unexpectedly summoned key congressional leaders to the White House to respond to increasing demands by legislators for an explanation of the Administration's reversal of its policy ruling out any deals for the release of American hostages.

The officials said Mr. Reagan told the group of four senators and House members that he saw some hope that the current secret negotiations with Iran would lead to the release of two more hostages.

In acknowledging the Administration's involvement in supplying arms to Iran, Mr. Reagan argued that the United States had undertaken clandestine contacts with the Teheran government because some factions in Iran were viewed, in the words of one participant at the meeting as "traditionalists or non-radicals who have a greater interest in U.S. ties."

Under sharp questioning from the legislators about Washington's involvement in arms shipments to Iran, Mr. Reagan said, in essence, that these were necessary to establish closer ties and to improve prospects for the release of some of the American hostages held in Lebanon, an Administration official said.

"We would be at fault if Khomeini died and we had not made any preparations for contacts with a future regime," said one Administration official, paraphrasing what Mr. Reagan said at the meeting. "The arms were necessary for that." He was referring to Ayatollah Ruhollah Khomeini, the paramount Iranian leader, who is strongly anti-American. The official added that the arms supplies for Iran did not constitute "ransom" for American hostages held in Lebanon by a pro-Iranian group. NOV. 13

## Timing of Shipments to Iran and of Hostage Releases

In the left-hand column are dates on which three reported shipments of American military equipment to Iran are said to have been made. On the right are dates on which American hostages have been taken and released in Beirut.

**March 16, 1984.** William Buckley, a political officer at the United States Embassy in Beirut, is kidnapped. In October 1985, Islamic Holy War says it has killed Mr. Buckley; no body is ever found.

**July 8, 1984.** The Rev. Benjamin Weir, a Presbyterian missionary in Lebanon, is kidnapped.

**Dec. 3, 1984.** Peter Kilburn, a librarian at the American University of Beirut, fails to report for work. After his captors say they have killed him in April 1986, his body is found in Beirut.

**Jan. 8, 1985.** The Rev. Lawrence Martin Jenco, a Roman Catholic priest and head of the Beirut office of Catholic Relief Services, is kidnapped.

**March 16, 1985.** Terry A. Anderson, chief Middle East correspondent for The Associated Press, is kidnapped.

**May 28, 1985.** David P. Jacobsen, director of the American University Hospital, is kidnapped.

**Sept. 14, 1985.** A plane that had carried one shipment to Iran is believed to have left Iran after making delivery.

**June 9, 1985.** Thomas M. Sutherland, dean of agriculture at the American University, is kidnapped.

**Sept. 14, 1985.** Mr. Weir is released.

**July 3–4, 1986.** Another shipment to Iran is believed to have been made.

**July 26, 1986.** Father Jenco is released.

**Sept. 9, 1986.** Frank Herbert Reed, director of the private Lebanese International School, is kidnapped.

**Sept. 12, 1986.** Joseph James Cicippio, controller at the American

**Late October 1986.** Yet another shipment to Iran is believed to have been made.

University of Beirut and its hospital, is kidnapped.

**Oct. 21, 1986.** Edward Austin Tracy, a self-described world traveler, poet and author of children's books, is kidnapped.

**Nov. 2, 1986.** Mr. Jacobsen is released, after the third shipment to Iran.

Nov. 13

# Manila and the Insurgents Agree to 60-day Truce Starting Dec. 10

By BARBARA CROSSETTE

MANILA, Nov. 26—Communist rebels and the government of President Corazon C. Aquino agreed today to a 60-day cease-fire.

The cease-fire, to begin Dec. 10, is the first formal cessation of hostilities in nearly 18 years of guerrilla war.

The pact, which could open the way to comprehensive peace talks, has the backing of the Philippine armed forces, according to a statement from the Deputy Chief of Staff. Military leaders were briefed on the draft agreement today by two government negotiators, Agriculture Minister Ramon V. Mitra and Teofisto Guingona, head of the Commission on Audits.

"Definitely, the military will support the decision taken by the panel," the Deputy Chief of Staff, Gen. Eduardo Ermita, said.

Both sides said tonight that the agreement would be signed here Thursday, the birthday of Mrs. Aquino's late husband, the onetime opposition leader Benigno S. Aquino, Jr., in the Club Filipino, where she took the oath of office in February.

The agreement comes as President Aquino is overhauling her government after asking for the resignation of her cabinet on Sunday. The presidential press office said today that the new cabinet lineup would be announced Friday.

The cease-fire agreement, which includes safety and immunity guarantees for Communist negotiators, leaves some other difficult questions yet to be resolved.

According to the negotiators for the Communist side, who held a news conference tonight, there has been no agreement, for example, on whether forced levies or "taxation" by rebel armies are an "act of hostility."

The Communist negotiators, Saturnino Ocampo and Antonio Zumel of the National Democratic Front, say they also intend in future talks to raise demands for the end of United States military aid to the Philippines and the "dismantling" or "removal" of American bases in the country.

Nov. 27

## Philippine Communists: Two Decades of Combat

**1965**—Election of President Ferdinand E. Marcos.

**Dec. 26, 1968**—Jose Maria Sison founds a new Communist Party of the Philippines (CPP), backed by China. (An earlier Communist insurgency, the Hukbalahap movement, had been mostly crushed by 1954.) Three months later, Bernabe Buscayno launches the CPP's military arm, the New People's Army, with 60 men and 36 rifles. (By November 1986 it has more than 23,000 members and an arsenal of more than 11,000 weapons, according to the Philippine army.)

**August 1972**—The imposition of martial law. Many Filipinos go to prison.

**Oct. 1, 1974**—Chinese-backed Communists now underground, building up their army.

**Aug. 26, 1976**—Bernabe Buscayno (Commander Dante) captured. (He was released in 1986 by President Corazon C. Aquino, along with Mr. Sison, who had also been jailed under martial law. They have now formed a new leftist party, the Partido ng Bayan, or People's Party. The official Communist Party is still illegal.)

**Aug. 21, 1983**—The assassination at Manila International Airport of the opposition figure Benigno S. Aquino, Jr.

**May 1984**—National legislative elections. Opposition members win 59 of 183 seats; could have won more if many potential candidates and voters had not boycotted the polls.

**Feb. 7, 1986**—"Snap" elections called by President Marcos to reaffirm his power end in anarchy as it becomes clear Mr. Marcos has tampered with election results that many believe would have given the victory to the ticket of Corazon C. Aquino and Salvador H. Laurel.

**Feb. 26, 1986**—Mr. Marcos flees the country after losing the support of the armed forces under Gen. Fidel V. Ramos and his defense minister, Juan Ponce Enrile.

**Aug. 5, 1986**—Aquino government opens cease-fire talks with Communists, asks for 30-day truce. Communists' National Democratic Front rejects the 30-day period and breaks off talks in September after the arrest of a Communist leader, Rodolfo Salas.

**Nov. 10, 1986**—Cease-fire talks resume after President Aquino tells her negotiators she wants an agreement by the end of the month.

**Nov. 12, 1986**—Rolando Olalia, a left-wing labor leader, is slain; the Communists again break off talks and say they will not resume negotiations until his killer is found.

**Nov. 23, 1986**—President Aquino, in the same speech in which she announces the resignation of Defense Minister Juan Ponce Enrile, gives the left until Nov. 30 to agree to a cease-fire; if they do not, she will break off the talks and step up military operations.

**Nov. 25, 1986**—The Communists come back to the negotiating table.

Nov. 27

## The Contras' Cash Flow: Five Up and Down Years

**December 1981** Administration officials tell House and Senate intelligence committees about President Reagan's secret decision to channel money and arms through the Central Intelligence Agency to the Nicaraguan rebels.

**December 1982** Congress approves a resolution that leaves the Administration free to continue supporting the rebels so long as the stated purpose is not to overthrow the government or to provoke a Nicaraguan-Honduran war.

During the period of covert financing, $80 million to $90 million is channeled to the Nicaraguan rebels through the Central Intelligence Agency. The two groups that receive most of the funds are the Nicaraguan Democratic Force (FDN) and the Democratic Revolutionary Alliance (ARDE).

**November 1983** Congress votes to finance the rebels openly, approving a $24 million spending ceiling on the aid.

**March 1984** Congress rejects a request from President Reagan for an additional $21 million for the contras because of the Central Intelligence Agency's involvement in the mining of several Nicaraguan harbors.

**October 1984** Congress adopts a compromise that bars the President from providing further aid to the rebels until after February 1985 and then only if both houses of Congress agree.

**June 1985** Congress agrees to resume aid to the rebels and approves $27 million in "humanitarian aid." It authorizes only one role for the C.I.A.—providing advice and intelligence information.

**October 1986** Congress approves $70 million in military aid and $30 million in nonmilitary aid for the contras. The funds are to be distributed among the United Nicaraguan Opposition (UNO), the Southern Opposition Bloc (BOS), and the Indian force known as Misurata.

Attorney General Edwin Meese 3d announces on Nov. 25, 1986, that $10 million to $30 million has been secretly diverted to the rebel forces since January.

Nov. 27

## Who Said What and When

In the weeks since the disclosure of shipments of United States arms to Iran, a handful of top officials have tried to put the crisis to rest through public statements. Here are some of the statements in the unfolding of a crisis for the Administration.

**President Reagan / Nov. 13**—"The charge has been made that the United States has shipped weapons to Iran as ransom payment for the release of American hostages in Lebanon, that the United States undercut its allies and secretly violated American policy against trafficking with terrorists. . . . Those charges are utterly false. The United States has not made concessions to those who hold our people captive in Lebanon. . . . I authorized the transfer of small amounts of defensive weapons and spare parts for defensive systems to Iran."

**Donald T. Regan, White House chief of staff / Nov. 14**—"I don't take kindly to this criticism by people who have not examined my record. How much more experience do you have to have in foreign policy than I do to believe you are qualified. . . . Some of us are like a shovel brigade that follow a parade down Main Street cleaning up. . . . We have never authorized, never allowed, never condoned large shipments by anyone, by Far Easterners, Mideasterners, Europeans, Israelis or anyone. We do not want large amounts of arms being shipped to either Iran or Iraq."

**George P. Shultz, Secretary of State / Nov. 16**— Asked if he believed more arms shipments should be sent to Iran: "Under the circumstances of Iran's war with Iraq, its pursuit of terrorism, its association with those holding our hostages, I would certainly say, as far as I'm concerned, no." Asked if he had the authority to speak for the entire Administration, he replied, "No."

**Robert C. McFarlane, former national security adviser / Nov. 16**—Sending "modest levels of arms" was a "reasonable price to pay" for developing a working relationship with moderate elements in Iran.

**John M. Poindexter, White House national security adviser / Nov. 16**—"We are very anxious to discuss in great detail with the appropriate congressional committees under the appropriate circumstances. . . . I'm basically an optimist, as the President is, and we will keep working on getting the hostages free."

**George P. Shultz / Nov. 17**—"There is a lot about what transpired that I don't know about."

**President Reagan / Nov. 17**—He says he has "absolutely no plans" to send more arms to Iran.

**President Reagan / Nov. 19**—"I weighed their views, I considered the risks of failure and the rewards of success, and I decided to proceed, and the responsibility for the decision and the operation is mine and mine alone. . . . I don't feel that I have anything to defend about at all."

**Robert C. McFarlane / Nov. 20**—"It was not kept from the Secretary of State. I'm somewhat surprised at the portrayal that it was. I told him repeatedly and often of every item that went on in this enterprise. . . . However well meaning and defensible our purposes were, to the extent that the introduction of arms transfers into the process has led to understandable turmoil that can have a very damaging effect on the ability of our country to lead, it was a mistake."

**Donald T. Regan / Nov. 20**—Speaking of Mr. McFarlane: "Let's not forget whose idea this was. It was Bud's idea. When you give lousy advice, you get lousy results."

**George P. Shultz / Nov. 21**—"There were discussions, and I participated in two of them. They were full-scale discussions."

**President Reagan / Nov. 24**—"I am not firing anybody. . . . I am not going to lie about that, I did not make a mistake."

**President Reagan / Nov. 25**—"Although not directly involved, Vice Admiral John Poindexter has asked to be relieved of his assignment as assistant to the President for national security affairs. . . . Lieutenant Colonel Oliver North has been relieved of his duties on the National Security staff. . . . I am deeply troubled that the implementation of a policy aimed at revolving a truly tragic situation in the Middle East has resulted in such controversy. As I've stated previously, I believe our policy goals toward Iran were well founded. However, the information brought to my attention yesterday convinced me that in one aspect, implementation of that policy was seriously flawed."

**Edwin Meese 3d, Attorney General / Nov. 25**— "What is involved is that in the course of the arms transfers, which involved the United States providing the arms to Israel, and Israel in turn transferring the arms—in effect selling the arms—to representatives of Iran, certain monies which were received in the transaction between representatives of Israel and representatives of Iran were taken and made available to the forces in Central America which are opposing the Sandinista government there."

Nov. 28

# Meese, Citing Possible Crime, Asks a Special Prosecutor; Carlucci Is Named for N.S.C.

By BERNARD WEINRAUB

WASHINGTON, Dec. 2—Saying that illegal acts may have been committed in the diversion of millions of dollars to Nicaraguan rebels from United States arms sales to Iran, the Administration said today that it was requesting an independent prosecutor to look into the case. President Reagan, in announcing the request for a special counsel in a four-minute televised speech, also said he was appointing a former deputy director of the Central Intelligence Agency, Frank C. Carlucci, as his national security adviser.

Mr. Carlucci, whose appointment received bipartisan support in Congress, will succeed Vice Adm. John M. Poindexter, who resigned last week in the furor over the clandestine diversion of aid.

Moments after Mr. Reagan spoke, Attorney General Edwin Meese 3d said, "We think that we have a statutory basis to believe that a Federal law may have been violated."

"There may have been people who are in a position in government who may have violated it," he said.

He added that the independent counsel would seek to determine "if there is any criminality whatsoever involved" in the case.

Mr. Reagan, who is facing bipartisan congressional pressure, said in his midday speech that the Justice Department had "turned up reasonable grounds" to seek the appointment of an independent counsel.

The President said he had "immediately urged" Mr. Meese "to apply in court here in Washington for the appointment of an independent counsel."

"If illegal acts were undertaken, those who did so will be brought to justice," Mr. Reagan said, speaking somberly from the Oval Office.

Mr. Meese said later, in a news conference at the Justice Department, "We are proceeding to make that application."

He said the application "will be broad enough to give an independent counsel the opportunity to look into all aspects of possible violations of Federal statutes and anything dealing with either the Iran transfer of arms or the transfer of funds to the contras," as the Nicaraguan rebels are known.  DEC. 3

## Prosecutors and Counsels: Those Who Have Served

In May 1973, during the height of the Watergate scandal, Attorney General Elliott L. Richardson set up an office of the special prosecutor to investigate the burglary of the Watergate offices and other cases related to the 1972 election.

**Archibald Cox:** The first special prosecutor, he was dismissed in October 1973, after five months on the job, on orders from President Nixon.

**Leon Jaworski:** Mr. Cox's successor. He made the Nixon tapes public. Several of President Nixon's aides, including H. R. Haldeman, John D. Ehrlichman and John N. Mitchell, were convicted of conspiracy to obstruct justice and other offenses.

**Henry S. Ruth, Jr.:** Succeeded Mr. Jaworski in October 1974, served until October 1975.

**Charles F. C. Ruff:** Held the position part-time while teaching at Georgetown University law school, until the office was closed in May 1977.

The 1978 Ethics in Government Act established the procedure under which special prosecutors are appointed. Amendments in 1982 changed the title of the post to independent counsel and extended the law for five years.

**Arthur H. Christy:** Appointed in 1979 to review the allegations that Hamilton Jordan, chief of staff in the Carter White House, had used cocaine. Mr. Jordan was cleared in 1980.

**Gerald J. Gallinghouse:** Appointed in 1980 to look into the allegations that Tim Kraft, President Carter's national campaign manager, had used drugs. Mr. Kraft was cleared in early 1981.

**Leon Silverman:** Appointed in December 1981 to look into the allegations that Raymond J. Donovan, Secretary of Labor, was involved in corrupt practices. The independent counsel reported in June and September 1982 that there was "insufficient credible evidence" against Mr. Donovan, but Mr. Silverman said the allegations remained "disturbing." Mr. Donovan is now on trial in State Supreme Court in the Bronx on fraud charges.

**Jacob A. Stein:** Appointed in April 1984 to review allegations concerning omissions on the financial disclosure forms of Edwin Meese 3d and various other financial transactions. In September 1984 Mr. Meese was cleared of any wrongdoing.

**James C. McKay:** Appointed in April 1986 to investigate whether a former Assistant Attorney General,

Theodore B. Olson, gave false testimony about the withholding of Environmental Protection Agency documents from congressional investigators. Mr. McKay resigned shortly thereafter to avoid appearance of conflict of interest. His law firm had been involved in a related case.

**Alexia Morrison:** Appointed in May 1986 to succeed Mr. McKay. The investigation of Mr. Olson is proceeding.

**Whitney North Seymour, Jr.:** Appointed in May 1986 after months of public discussion over the conflict of interest charges against Michael K. Deaver, a former White House aide who resigned in May 1985. The investigation is still open.

DEC. 3

## Arms and the Hostages: 2 Years of Secret Deals

These are some of the events figuring in the controversy over the secret sale of American arms to Iran and the diversion of profits to help the Nicaraguan rebels. The shaded areas indicate events that occurred behind the scenes.

### 1984

**March 16** William Buckley, a political officer at the United States Embassy in Beirut, later identified as the C.I.A. station chief, is kidnapped by pro-Iranian Moslem militants.

**July 8** The Rev. Benjamin Weir, a Presbyterian missionary, is kidnapped.

**November** Manucher Ghorbanifar, an Iranian exile, raises the issue of ransoming hostages in meeting in Hamburg with Iranian officials and Theodore C. Shackley, a former C.I.A. agent, who relays the proposal to Washington.

**Dec. 3** Peter Kilburn, a librarian at the American University of Beirut, is kidnapped.

### 1985

**Jan. 8** The Rev. Lawrence Martin Jenco, a Roman Catholic priest, is kidnapped.

**February** Mr. Ghorbanifar renews the proposal to trade arms for hostages.

**March 16** Terry A. Anderson, chief Middle East correspondent for The Associated Press, is kidnapped.

**May** President Reagan, concerned about the fate of the American hostages in Lebanon, asks Prime Minister Shimon Peres of Israel for help in winning their release. At about the same time, Mr. Ghorbanifar, under pressure from Iran to find arms in the West, makes contact with a Saudi businessman, Adnan M. Khashoggi, who introduces him to Israelis. Mr. Peres asks Al Schwimmer, a friend and arms dealer, to help free Mr. Buckley and the other hostages. Mr. Schwimmer enlists Yaacov Nimrodi, another Israeli arms dealer. They later get in touch with Mr. Ghorbanifar, apparently with the help of Mr. Khashoggi. A C.I.A. official suggests in a memo the possibility of selling arms to Iran as a way of blunting Soviet moves in the region. This is put into a proposal by two National Security Council staff members, but the idea goes nowhere.

**May 28** David P. Jacobsen, director of the American University hospital in Beirut, is kidnapped.

**June 9** Thomas M. Sutherland, dean of agriculture at the American University in Beirut, is kidnapped.

**July 8** In a speech denouncing the hijacking of a T.W.A. jetliner, President Reagan says, "Let me make it plain to the assassins in Beirut and their accomplices that America will never make concessions to terrorists."

**Late July** David Kimche, Director General of the Israeli Foreign Ministry, comes to Washington and tells Robert C. McFarlane, the national security adviser, that Iranian moderates want to make contact with the United States. In a follow-up meeting, he says that if the opening to Iran is to prove productive, the United States should agree to send arms to Iran, using Israelis as the intermediaries. He also says that this could lead to the release of all American hostages. Israel needs to know, however, whether the President would approve of such a sale by Israel, and whether it would agree to replenish Israeli stocks.

**Aug. 6** President Reagan listens to senior advisers, almost all of whom oppose arms to Iran. Mr. McFarlane says the President gives oral approval to the Israeli sale of arms and promises to replenish the stocks. Israel is told by Mr. McFarlane that the President approves. But Donald T. Regan, the White House chief of staff, asserts later that the President opposed such a sale and only acquiesced in it once it happened.

**Late August** First shipment of 100 TOW antitank missiles is sent with Israeli help and without a waiver of the American embargo on all arms sales to Iran. President Reagan is informed after the fact, Attorney General Edwin Meese 3d says later. But Mr. McFarlane says the President gave oral approval.

**Early September** Second shipment of 408 TOW missiles is sent to Iran by Israel.

**Sept. 14** Mr. Weir is released in Beirut, but there is no sign of the release of other hostages.

**Oct. 4** A pro-Iranian terrorist group says it has killed Mr. Buckley, but his body is not recovered.

**Nov. 22–23** Another arms shipment is sent but is returned; Iranians say the arms were obsolete. The C.I.A. was involved because the Israeli plane carrying the arms was in Portugal and the arms had to be transferred to another plane. Lieut. Col. Oliver L. North of the National Security Council staff tells the C.I.A. that the plane carried only oil-drilling equipment, when it actually carried equipment for the Hawk anti-aircraft missile.

**Dec. 4** Mr. McFarlane resigns as national security adviser as of the end of the year. Vice Adm. John M. Poindexter is appointed to succeed Mr. McFarlane in January.

**Dec. 6** Mr. Reagan meets with senior advisers, who urge him to stop selling arms to Iran because it has deteriorated into an arms-for-hostages undertaking, with only one hostage freed.

**Dec. 8** Mr. McFarlane tells Mr. Kimche and Mr. Ghorbanifar in London that the United States will no longer countenance arms shipments to Iran.

**Late December** Amiram Nir, an Israeli counterterrorism official, comes to Washington and says the Iranians have promised to free all hostages in exchange for more arms.

## 1986

**Jan. 7** At a White House meeting between the President and his top aides, Admiral Poindexter persuades Mr. Reagan to resume arms sales to the Iranians, arguing that it is the only way to gain the release of American hostages.

**Jan. 17** President Reagan signs a classified intelligence finding authorizing arms shipments to Iran. Weapons are later withdrawn by the C.I.A. from Pentagon stocks.

**Late February** The November 1985 shipment of arms to Iran is returned to Israel, and another arms shipment of Hawk missiles is sold to Iran. Mr. Khashoggi helps finance the deal.

**May 6** The State Department says, "The United States will make no concessions to terrorists." Secretary of State George P. Shultz later says Admiral Poindexter and William J. Casey, the Director of Central Intelligence, told him that no more arms were being supplied to Iran.

**May 15** A new $15 million loan for arms shipment to Iran is arranged by Mr. Khashoggi and two Canadian investors.

**May 28** Mr. McFarlane, Colonel North and others secretly travel to Teheran aboard a cargo plane carrying military spare parts. When he learns that no hostages have been freed, Mr. McFarlane cancels two other scheduled planeloads of weapons.

**May 31–June 1** Mr. McFarlane says Colonel North told him that some proceeds from Iran arms deals are going to Nicaraguan rebels.

**July 3–4** Another shipment of arms labeled as medical supplies arrives in Iran.

**July 26** Father Jenco is released.

**September** Mr. McFarlane makes a second trip to Teheran with another 23 tons of arms.

**Sept. 9** Frank Herbert Reed, director of the Lebanese International School in West Beirut, is kidnapped.

**Sept. 12** Joseph James Cicippio, controller at the American University in Beirut, is kidnapped.

**Oct. 5** A C-123 cargo plane carrying arms to the rebels is shot down over Nicaragua. Eugene Hasenfus, the sole survivor, is taken captive. Mr. Casey asks Colonel North if the C.I.A. was involved.

**Oct. 21** Edwin Austin Tracy, a poet and author of children's books, is kidnapped in West Beirut.

**Late October** The final known shipment of arms is sent to Iran.

**Oct. 30** The Justice Department asks the F.B.I. to delay its investigation into private schemes to aid Nicaraguan rebels because it might jeopardize negotiations to free the hostages.

**Nov. 2** Mr. Jacobsen is released.

**Nov. 3** A Lebanese weekly magazine, Al Shiraa, discloses that the United States sent Iran spare parts and ammunition after a secret visit to Teheran in early September by Mr. McFarlane.

**Nov. 4** The Speaker of the Iranian Parliament, Hojatolislam Hashemi Rafsanjani, says Mr. McFarlane and four other Americans visited Iran on a secret mission.

**Nov. 13** In a speech from the Oval Office, Mr. Reagan defends his "secret diplomatic initiative to Iran" and says he authorized the transfer of "small amounts of defensive weapons and spare parts."

**Nov. 25** President Reagan announces that Admiral Poindexter has resigned and that Colonel North has been dismissed. Attorney General Meese reports the diversion of money from arms sales to Iran to the Nicaraguan rebels.

DEC. 25

## OPEC, in Oil Output Cut, to Lift Barrel Price to $18

**By STEVE LOHR**

GENEVA, Dec. 20—After days of acrimonious deliberations, the accord reached at dawn today by the Organization of Petroleum Exporting Countries—to cut oil production and to raise prices quickly to $18 a barrel—was in line with previous reports from private ministerial sessions.

The reports from last week's sessions drove open-market oil prices up by roughly $2 a barrel, to more than $16 a barrel. But the production cuts of more than 7 percent for the first six months of next year exclude Iraq.

The Iraqi exclusion underlines the degree to which OPEC decisions are influenced by the six-year war between Iran and Iraq. It also raises doubts about whether the agreement to trim output will be sufficient to defend a price of $18 a barrel.

While expressing optimism, oil ministers admitted that the pact would face a testing period, as oil traders and companies will be seeing whether OPEC's production discipline holds.

"Basically, it's a good agreement," said Ali Khalifa al-Sabah, Kuwait's oil minister. "But over the next month or so, the market will be trying the agreement very, very hard."

In recent years, the 13-nation group's accords have often come unstuck as some countries cut prices or overproduced to increase national revenues.

DEC. 21

### OPEC's New Production Ceilings

Comparison of existing quotas with those agreed upon yesterday for the first six months of 1987, in thousands of barrels a day. Quotas are being cut by an average of nearly 5 percent; actual production, which has exceeded the current quotas, is to be reduced by more than 7 percent. Figures at right indicate potential production capacity.

|  | Current Quota | New Quota | Output Capacity |
|---|---|---|---|
| Saudi Arabia | 4,353 | 4,133 | 8,800 |
| Iran | 2,317 | 2,255 | 3,000 |
| Iraq[1] | — | — | 2,000 |
| United Arab Emirates | 950 | 902 | 2,125 |
| Kuwait | 999 | 948 | 2,300 |
| Qatar | 300 | 285 | 500 |
| **Mideast OPEC** | **8,919** | **8,523** | **18,725** |
| Venezuela | 1,574 | 1,495 | 2,500 |
| Nigeria | 1,304 | 1,238 | 1,800 |
| Indonesia | 1,193 | 1,133 | 1,700 |
| Libya | 999 | 948 | 1,500 |
| Algeria | 669 | 635 | 800 |
| Ecuador | 221 | 210 | 300 |
| Gabon | 160 | 152 | 200 |
| **Total OPEC** | **15,039**[2] | **14,334**[3] | **27,525** |

[1]Excluded from quotas, but agreement among 12 other OPEC members assumes Iraq's production will be 1.466 million barrels a day during the first half of 1987. Iraq production is now estimated at between 1.6 million and 1.7 million barrels.
[2]Total output, including Iraq, is estimated to be more than 17 million barrels.
[3]Total output, including Iraq, would be 15.8 million barrels under new accord.
Source for capacity figures: *Petroleum Intelligence Weekly*.

DEC. 21

### Political Prisoners: The Sakharov List

On December 23 Andrei D. Sakharov, the Soviet dissident, was allowed to return to Moscow after six years of exile in Gorky. In an interview on December 27, he said his physical infirmity and desire to resume his work in physics would prevent him from acting as the "leader or head" of dissent in the Soviet Union. "I am not the leader of an army," he said.

But he said he would continue to seek "the liberation of prisoners of conscience."

"There are many of them; it would be impossible to name them all," he said. "I would like to mention the names and plight of a few of them."

These are the prisoners he named:

**Genrikh O. Altunyan,** 53 years old, an engineer and radio technician from Kharkov, who was arrested in 1969 for anti-Soviet activities after he signed a human rights appeal to the United Nations. He was arrested again in 1980 and sent to a labor camp in connection with his human rights activism.

**Vladimir Gershuni,** editor of an underground literary publication in the late 1970s and later a contributor to the bulletin of a group that attempted to organize an independent labor union. A friend in Moscow said today that he had been sent to a psychiatric hospital.

**Sergei Khodorovich,** manager of a fund to aid political prisoners that was established by Alexander Solzhenitsyn, the writer, before his deportation from the Soviet Union in 1973. Mr. Khodorovich is serving a term in a labor camp. Dr. Sakharov said he had been held for 89 days in solitary confinement.

**Anatoly Koryagin,** 48, a psychiatrist who began serving a 12-year term in 1981. He was sentenced for anti-Soviet propaganda after he said that Soviet psychiatry was being used for political purposes. He is reported to be in grave condition in a prison in Chistopol, in the Tatar Republic of European Russia, where Anatoly T. Marchenko died earlier this month.

**Merab Kostava,** 47, a Georgian music critic who joined a group to monitor Soviet compliance with 1975 Helsinki accords on human rights. He was sentenced in May 1978 to three years in labor camp and two years in exile, and twice had his sentence extended.

**Mart Niklus,** an Estonian ornithologist, who has been in prison since 1981. He was active in an Estonian nationalist movement and in January 1980 signed a letter protesting Soviet intervention in Afghanistan.

**Yuri Shikhanovich,** of Moscow, who was arrested in 1983 for his role as editor of the *Chronicle of Current Events,* an underground publication.

**Aleksei Smirnov,** another editor of the *Chronicle,* who was arrested in 1982 and sentenced to six years of labor camp and four years of exile. Mr. Smirnov, 36, is the grandson of Aleksei Kosterin, a veteran of the Bolshevik Revolution who was active in the dissident movement until his death in 1968.

**Serafim Yevsyukov,** a former airline navigator for Aeroflot, who applied to emigrate in 1978, but was turned down, lost his job and was periodically detained.

DEC. 28

# Demographics Put Strain on Soviet Ethnic Seams

By BILL KELLER

MOSCOW—The official Soviet publishing agency prints textbooks in 52 languages to serve the disparate minorities of the Soviet Union. The state radio broadcasts in 67 languages. Flip on the state-run television here, and the show may be a Georgian comedy or Uzbek folk dancing.

But Moscow's affection for ethnic diversity has its limits, as the Republic of Kazakhstan was sternly reminded last week. A few days after students—apparently angered that Moscow had replaced a longtime Kazakh party chief with an ethnic Russian—took to the streets and burned cars in the Republic's capital, Alma-Ata, the newly installed leader in the Kazakh Republic began to assert himself.

The new party boss, Gennadi V. Kolbin, called for "urgent measures," presumably including a major personnel shakeup—to root out unhealthy "nationalist" tendencies and instill in the populace a spirit of "internationalism." Mikhail Solomentsev, the member of the ruling Politburo responsible for party discipline, joined in the tongue-lashing.

It was a pointed reminder that after 70 years the central authority in Moscow has failed to obliterate the strong identities of the many peoples who make up the empire. Demographers count more than 100 nationalities in this country that many Westerners often casually think of as "Russia." And because the highest birth rates are in the Moslem belt of Kazakhstan and Central Asia, the Soviet leader, Mikhail S. Gorbachev, may very well be in power long enough to see the Russians become a numerical minority in their own country. Demographers forecast that before the end of the century the Russians will fall below 50 percent of the population.

The rioting in Alma-Ata was just the most dramatic recent reminder of the stresses this diversity puts on central authority. This year alone, in the increasingly frank Soviet press there have been veiled hints of racial disturbances between Russians and the ethnic Yakuts in Siberia, attacks on the Ministry of Education in the Republic of Byelorussia for giving priority to the Russian language in schools and demands for more attention to writers who work in the Ukrainian language.

In Uzbekistan and Tadzhikstan, party leaders recently decried the rising influence of Islam and the tendency of local Communist leaders to "compromise" with it by remaining secretly active in their mosques.   DEC. 28

## The Soviet Union's population
(in millions, based on 1979 census)

| Total population | 262.0 |
|---|---|
| Russians | 137.4 |
| Ukrainians | 42.4 |
| Uzbeks | 12.5 |
| Byelorussians | 9.5 |
| Kazakhs | 6.6 |
| Tatars | 6.3 |
| Azerbaijanis | 5.5 |
| Armenians | 4.1 |
| Georgians | 3.6 |
| Moldavians | 3.0 |
| Lithuanians | 2.9 |
| Total population | 262.0 |
| Tadzhiks | 2.9 |
| Turkomans | 2.0 |
| Germans | 1.9 |
| Kirghiz | 1.9 |
| Jews | 1.8 |
| Chuvash | 1.8 |
| Latvians | 1.4 |
| Bashkir | 1.4 |
| Mordva | 1.2 |
| Poles | 1.2 |
| Estonians | 1.0 |

DEC. 28

# PART 2
# National

NYT/KEITH MEYERS

### Ricky Nelson, the singer, and 6 others were killed Dec. 31 when his DC-3 plane crashed in flames near De Kalb, Tex.

The other victims were identified by the Texas Department of Public Safety as Helen Blair, 27, Mr. Nelson's fiancée; Bobby Neal, 38; Patrick Woodward, 35; Rick Intzfield, 22; Andy Chappin, 30; and Clark Russell, 35.

Mr. Nelson was born Eric Hilliard Nelson May 8, 1940, in Teaneck, N.J., the younger son of Ozzie and Harriet Nelson.

JAN. 1

### Victims of an air crash in the Antarctic

Ben Callis, 33, Key West, Fla.; Paul R. Cox, 59, teacher, Brooklyn; James C. Howell, 43, teacher, Yellow Springs, Ohio; James M. Jasper, 56, librarian, Oxnard, Calif.; Irving Lambrecht, 63, retired, Los Angeles; Tim Lang, 33, petroleum manager, Carmichael, Calif.; Walther P. Michael, 72, teacher, Columbus, Ohio; and Wayne Riddle, 61, engineer, Buchanan, Mich.

JAN. 2

## Inmates in West Virginia Release Last 7 Hostages, Ending Uprising

By WILLIAM K. STEVENS

MOUNDSVILLE, W.Va., Jan. 3—Inmates who took over the West Virginia Penitentiary released their seven remaining hostages today and returned control of the prison to the state.

Three prisoners were killed in the uprising. Gov. Arch A. Moore, Jr., said he believed some inmates had set up kangaroo courts to decide "who they were going to destroy." He said that there would be no amnesty for the killers and that they would be prosecuted fully where murder cases could be established.

But he said there would be no "retaliation" against inmates for the takeover.

There were also reports that after an agreement ending the inmates' occupation was signed Thursday, bands of prisoners rampaged through the penitentiary, destroying as much as they could.

Mr. Moore, who said he deliberately stayed away from the scene while negotiations to end the occupation continued, escorted the last seven hostages out of the 120-year-old prison, a structure resembling a medieval fortress.

One or two at a time, they left the prison by the South Gate and stepped into ambulances to be taken to a hospital for observation. Governor Moore said six hostages the inmates released Thursday showed bruises and other signs of being "roughed up" but that the seven released today were unharmed. Whatever ill-treatment of hostages occurred took place in the early part of the takeover, he said.

He added that hostages were blindfolded at some times during their captivity and were frequently moved inside the prison.

Most hostages released today were in prison clothing and barefoot. One appeared to limp. When asked by distant, shouting reporters how they were, most answered "fine," "great," or "fantastic." One grinned and raised his arms in a gesture of triumph.

The seven hostages were a food service employee, William Henderson, and six guards, Roger Johnson, Mike Smith, John Wilson, William Wright, Leslie Howearth and Robert Willis.

JAN. 2

### Other Prison Riots

**November 1927**—Folsom Prison, Calif. Nine prisoners and three hostage guards were killed after pitched battles between prisoners and the National Guard.

**Oct. 3, 1929**—Colorado State Prison. Seven guards were slain and five convicts committed suicide after an escape attempt was aborted.

**Dec. 11, 1929**—Auburn State Prison, Auburn, N.Y. Eight prisoners and the chief keeper were slain. The warden, held hostage, was rescued by state troopers.

**April 21, 1930**—Ohio State Penitentiary, Columbus, Ohio. Rioting prisoners set a fire that killed 317 other inmates who were locked in their cells.

**May 2–4, 1946**—Alcatraz. Two guards and three inmates were killed in a riot that units of the marines helped quell after landing on the island in San Francisco Bay.

**Aug. 21, 1968**—Ohio State Penitentiary, Columbus, Ohio. Five convicts were shot to death when 500 National Guardsmen and the police charged through a hole blasted in the prison wall to quell a riot by 350 prisoners, who were protesting "sadistic guards," among other things.

**Sept. 9–13, 1971**—Attica Correctional Facility, Attica, N.Y. Thirty-one prisoners and nine guards and civilian employees held as hostages were killed as nearly 1,500 state troopers, sheriff's deputies and prison guards stormed the prison to put down an insurrection of 1,200 inmates. Another inmate and another guard who were injured died later. Twenty-eight other hostages were rescued.

**Feb. 2–3, 1980**—New Mexico State Penitentiary, Santa Fe, N.M. Rioting by some 400 inmates left 33 inmates dead. In addition, 90 inmates were injured along with 12 guards who were held hostage. The outbreak ended when more than 250 state police and National Guardsmen recaptured the prison without firing a shot.

**Aug. 29–30, 1983**—Conner Correctional Center, Hominy, Okla. Hundreds of National Guardsmen, police officers and prison officials herded more than 700 manacled inmates away from the prison after a riot left one convict dead, 22 people injured and five prison buildings heavily damaged. The riot was touched off in a dining hall by inmates who had not been fed their evening meal.

JAN. 4

## Major Business Holdings of the Mormon Church

Many of the church's properties are controlled by an umbrella company, the Deseret Management Corporation.

Among the major Mormon interests are the following.

**Insurance**
The Beneficial Life Insurance Company
The Continental Western Life Insurance Company
The Western American Life Insurance Company
The Utah Home Fire Insurance Company

**Television stations**
KSL-TV, Salt Lake City (CBS affiliate)
KIRO-TV, Seattle (CBS affiliate)

**Radio stations**
KSL-AM, Salt Lake City
KIRO-AM/KSEA-FM, Seattle
WRFM, New York
WCLR-FM, Chicago
KOIT-AM/FM, San Francisco
KBIG-FM, Los Angeles
KAAM-AM/KAFM-FM, Dallas
KMBZ-AM/KMBR-FM, Kansas City, Mo.

All of the stations are operated by the Bonneville International Corporation, a church subsidiary, which also owns the Bonneville Satellite Corporation, the Bonneville Entertainment Corporation and Bonneville Productions Inc., along with other smaller operating divisions.

**Publishing**
The Deseret News
The Deseret Press
The Deseret Book Company
Brigham Young University Press

**Agribusiness**
Along with several food-processing plants, the church has vast agricultural acreage, mostly held by:
U.I. Group, Utah (the church is majority stockholder)
Deseret Ranch of Canada
Elberta Farm, Utah
Deseret Farms of California
Deseret Land and Livestock, Utah
Deseret Farms of Texas
Deseret Ranch of Florida
Tempieview Farms, New Zealand

**Commercial Real Estate**
The church's commercial properties, as well as much of its assets in agribusiness, are held by two divisions, Zions Securities and the Beneficial Development Company. These include about 60 acres in downtown Salt Lake City and a number of buildings on this property.

Among other church assets are more than 50 percent of the stock of the Zion Cooperative Mercantile Institution, a retail chain that owns nine department stores in Utah; the Northland Business Park, being developed by the Beneficial Development Company on part of the church's 4,400 acres near Kansas City, and the Polynesian Cultural Center, a theme park.

JAN. 12

## Weapons of Choice: Crime by Crime

|         | Crime victims (in thousands) | Any weapon | Guns  | Knives | Other weapons | Type not known |
|---------|------------------------------|------------|-------|--------|---------------|----------------|
| Total   | 65,343                       | 36.7%      | 12.7% | 10.8%  | 13.3%         | 1.8%           |
| Rape    | 1,738                        | 26.5       | 9.5   | 11.9   | 4.7           | 1.2            |
| Robbery | 12,248                       | 49.1       | 20.0  | 18.2   | 11.6          | 2.4            |
| Assault | 51,358                       | 34.2       | 11.0  | 9.0    | 14.0          | 1.7            |

Source: U.S. Department of Justice

JAN. 12

## Weapons of Choice: Crime by Crime

Almost 37 percent of the 65.3 million rapes, robberies and assaults that took place in the United States between 1973 and 1982 involved the use of guns, knives or other weapons, the Justice Department reported last week. About one-third of the weapons were guns.

JAN. 12

## Some Milestones of the Auto Age

Here are some high points in the 100-odd years that got the automobile from there to here:

**1884:** In France, a patent is issued for a gas engine to drive the Delamare-Deboutteville steam car.

**1886:** On Jan. 29, the world's first practical motorcar is patented in Germany by Carl Benz.

**1894:** Rudolph Diesel exhibits the first working "rational heat engine" in Germany.

**1897:** Ransom E. Olds builds his first car. A successful steam car is assembled by the Stanley brothers, Francis and Freeland.

**1898:** In New York, the first independent auto dealer opens his shop. The next year, the first mechanic opens his garage, also in New York.

**1900:** The first national automobile show is held at Madison Square Garden. In addition, New York issues the country's first driver's license to Harold J. Birnie.

**1903:** Using $28,000 in cash, Henry Ford forms the Ford Motor Company.

**1904:** The five Studebaker brothers, former makers of Conestoga wagons, produce their first car.

**1905:** In St. Louis—and for the first time—an automobile is reported stolen.

**1907:** Vanderbilt Motor Parkway, privately owned and the nation's first major highway, opens on Long Island.

**1908:** William Crapo Durant organizes General Motors, absorbing Buick, Oakland and Oldsmobile.

**1912:** Redlands, Calif., paints white lines on the middle of the streets.

**1913:** Henry Ford creates the first moving production line at his Highland Park plant in Michigan.

**1914:** Work begins on the Lincoln Highway, the first transcontinental road. A stop sign is erected in Detroit, and Cleveland puts up a traffic light.

**1916:** President Wilson signs the Federal Aid Road Act, providing money for a network of American highways.

**1917:** Ford opens its River Rouge plant, the largest industrial complex on earth, with ore going in one side and automobiles coming out the other.

**1921:** Royce Hailey opens a "Pig Stand" in Dallas, the first drive-in restaurant. Lincoln cars are introduced.

**1924:** Walter P. Chrysler, a former general manager of General Motors, produces the first car to bear his name.

**1927:** The New York show introduces chrome trim, and Lockheed develops hydraulic brakes. On May 21, Ford produces its last Model T, number 15,007,033.

**1928:** The car radio is an innovation, and Chrysler takes over the Dodge Brothers operation.

**1935:** Oklahoma City installs the first parking meter.

**1938:** Buick has a better idea: the first turn signal.

**1947:** Henry Kaiser meets Joe Frazer and a new automotive entry bearing their names is born.

**1953:** Michelin invents the radial tire. Chevrolet introduces the Corvette, with the first plastic body.

**1954:** Studebaker and Packard merge their failing fortunes. Nash and Hudson form American Motors.

**1959:** Earle MacPherson, a G.M. engineer, sees his major suspension improvement, the MacPherson strut, appear for the first time on a British Ford.

**1963:** Studebaker ends its production in the United States.

**1964:** On April 17, Ford unveils its instantly popular Mustang, a car that spawns the "pony car" movement to small and powerful sport models.

**1966:** The Government creates a Department of Transportation.

**1970:** Congress passes the Clean Air Act.

**1973:** Arab producers put a ban on exports of oil to the United States. The following year, a 55 m.p.h. speed limit is imposed to conserve fuel.

**1978:** Volkswagen begins production in the United States.

**1984:** New York becomes the first state to require drivers, front-seat passengers and children under the age of 10 to wear seat belts. France celebrates the centennial of the automobile.

**1984:** The rest of the world observes the "real" centennial, marking the patent awarded to Carl Benz.

JAN. 26

## Cuts required by the budget-balancing law
(in millions of dollars)

### By agency

|  |  |
|---|---|
| Agriculture | $ 1,263.7 |
| Commerce | 68.2 |
| Military | 5,126.1 |
| Other military* | 497.0 |
| Education | 170.9 |
| Energy | 333.7 |
| Health and Human Services | 1,036.2 |
| Housing and Urban Development | 32.7 |
| Interior | 202.1 |
| Justice | 143.1 |
| Labor | 171.6 |
| State | 99.7 |
| Transportation | 373.4 |
| Treasury | 373.6 |

### By agency

|  |  |
|---|---|
| E.P.A. | 48.5 |
| General Services Administration | 15.2 |
| NASA | 223.2 |
| Office of Personnel Management | 597.0 |
| Small Business Administration | 37.2 |
| Veterans Administration | 196.5 |
| Legislative Branch | 62.1 |
| Judiciary | 37.8 |
| Executive Office of the President | 4.1 |
| Funds appropriated to the President | 268.8 |
| Other independent agencies | 317.6 |
| TOTAL | $11,700.0 |

### Military breakdown†

### By agency

|  |  |
|---|---|
| Operation and maintenance | $ 2,936 |
| Research, development, testing and evaluation | 915 |
| Procurement | 864 |
| Travel for military personnel | 226 |
| Military family housing | 74 |
| Military construction | 66 |
| Revolving and management funds | −44 |
| TOTAL | $ 5,126 |

*Civil functions of the Defense Department, such as the Army Corps of Engineers
†Numbers, in millions, are rounded. Table does not include anticipated savings in atomic energy defense activities or savings that result from omission of the 1986 cost-of-living increase for military retirees. Total cuts in military programs, including these items, are $5.85 billion.
*Sources: Congressional Budget Office, Office of Management and Budget

JAN. 15

# The Shuttle Explodes

By WILLIAM J. BROAD

CAPE CANAVERAL, Fla., Jan. 28—The space shuttle *Challenger* exploded in a ball of fire shortly after it left the launching pad today, and all seven astronauts on board were lost.

The worst accident in the history of the American space program, it was witnessed by thousands of spectators who watched in wonder, then horror, as the ship blew apart high in the air.

Flaming debris rained down on the Atlantic Ocean for an hour after the explosion, which occurred just after 11:39 A.M. It kept rescue teams from reaching the area where the craft would have fallen into the sea, about 18 miles offshore.

It seemed impossible that anyone could have lived through the terrific explosion 10 miles in the sky, and officials said this afternoon that there was no evidence to indicate that the five men and two women aboard had survived.

There were no clues to the cause of the accident. The space agency offered no immediate explanations, and said it was suspending all shuttle flights indefinitely while it conducted an inquiry. Officials discounted speculation that cold weather at Cape Canaveral or an accident several days ago that slightly damaged insulation on the external fuel tank might have been a factor.

Americans who had grown used to the idea of men and women soaring into space reacted with shock to the disaster, the first time United States astronauts had died in flight. President Reagan canceled the State of the Union Message that had been scheduled for tonight, expressing sympathy for the families of the crew but vowing that the nation's exploration of space would continue.

Killed in the explosion were the mission commander, Francis R. (Dick) Scobee; the pilot, Comdr. Michael J. Smith of the Navy; Dr. Judith A. Resnik; Dr. Ronald E. McNair; Lieut. Col. Ellison S. Onizuka of the Air Force; Gregory B. Jarvis, and Christa McAuliffe.

Mrs. McAuliffe, a high school teacher from Concord, N.H., was to have been the first ordinary citizen in space.

The *Challenger* lifted off flawlessly this morning, after three days of delays, for what was to have been the 25th mission of the reusable shuttle fleet that was intended to make space travel commonplace. The ship rose for about a minute on a column of smoke and fire from its five engines.

Suddenly, without warning, it erupted in a ball of flame.

The shuttle was about 10 miles above the earth, in the critical seconds, when the two solid-fuel rocket boosters are firing as well as the shuttle's main engines. There was some discrepancy about the exact time of the blast: The National Aeronautics and Space Administration said they lost radio contact with the craft 74 seconds into the flight, plus or minus five seconds.

Two large white streamers raced away from the blast, followed by a rain of debris that etched white contrails in the cloudless sky and then slowly headed toward the cold waters of the nearby Atlantic.

The eerie beauty of the orange fireball and billowing white trails against the blue confused many onlookers, many of whom did not at first seem aware that the aerial display was a sign that something had gone terribly wrong.

There were few sobs, moans or shouts among the thousands of tourists, reporters and space agency officials gathered on an unusually cold Florida day to celebrate the lift-off, just a stunned silence as they began to realize that the *Challenger* had vanished.

Among the people watching were Mrs. McAuliffe's two children, her husband and her parents and hundreds of students, teachers and friends from Concord.

"Things started flying around and spinning around and I heard some ohs and ahs, and at that moment I knew something was wrong," said Brian Ballard, the editor of *The Crimson Review* at Concord High School. "I felt sick to my stomach. I still feel sick to my stomach."

At an outdoor news conference held here this afternoon, Jesse W. Moore, the head of the shuttle program at NASA, said: "I regret to report that, based on very preliminary searches of the ocean where the *Challenger* impacted this morning, these searches have not revealed any evidence that the crew of *Challenger* survived." Behind him, in the distance, the American flag waved at half staff.

Coast Guard ships were in the area of impact tonight and planned to stay all night, with airplanes set to comb the area at first light for debris that could provide clues to the catastrophe. Some material from the shattered craft was reported to be washing ashore on Florida beaches tonight, mostly the small heat-shielding tiles that protect the shuttle as it passes through the earth's atmosphere.

Films of the explosion showed a parachute drifting toward the sea, apparently one that would have lowered one of the huge reusable booster rockets after its fuel was spent.

Pending an investigation, Mr. Moore said at the news conference this afternoon, hardware, photographs, computer tapes, ground support equipment and notes taken by members of the launching team would be impounded.

The three days of delays and a tight annual launching schedule did not force a premature launching, Mr. Moore said in answer to a reporter's question.

"There was no pressure to get this particular launch up," he said. "We have always maintained that flight safety was a top priority in the program."

Several hours after the accident, Mr. Moore announced the appointment of an interim review team, assigned to preserve and identify flight data from the mission, pending the appointment of a formal investigating committee.

The members of the interim panel are Richard G. Smith, the director of the Kennedy Space Center; Arnold Aldridge, the manager of the National Space Transportation System, Johnson Space Center; William Lucas, director of the Marshall Space Flight Center; Walt Williams, a NASA consultant, and James C. Harrington, the director of Spacelab, who will serve as executive secretary.

A NASA spokesman said a formal panel could be appointed as soon as Wednesday by Dr. William R. Graham, the director of the space agency.

All American manned space launchings were stopped for more than a year and a half after the worst previous American space accident, in January 1967, when three astronauts were killed in a fire in an Apollo capsule on the launching pad.

This year's schedule was to have been the most ambitious in the history of the shuttle program, with 15 flights planned. For the *Challenger,* the workhorse of the nation's shuttle fleet, this was to have been the 10th mission.

Today's launching had been delayed three times in three days by bad weather. The *Challenger* was to have launched two satellites and Mrs. McAuliffe was to have broadcast two lessons from space to millions of students around the country.

All day long, well after the explosion, the large mission clocks scattered about the Kennedy Space Center continued to run, ticking off the minutes and seconds of a flight that had long ago ended.

Long before lift-off this morning, skies over the Kennedy Space Center were clear and cold, reporters and tourists shivering in leather gloves, knit hats and down coats as temperatures hovered in the low 20s.

Icicles formed as ground equipment

sprayed water on the launching pad, a precaution against fire.

At 9:07 A.M., after the astronauts were seated in the shuttle, wearing gloves because the interior was so cold, ground controllers broke into a round of applause as the shuttle's door, whose handle caused problems yesterday, which was closed.

"Good morning, Christa, hope we go today," said ground control as the New Hampshire schoolteacher settled into the spaceplane.

"Good morning," she replied, "I hope so, too." Those are her last known words.

The lift-off, originally scheduled for 9:38 A.M., was delayed two hours by problems on the ground caused first by a failed fire-protection device and then by ice on the shuttle's ground support structure.

The launching was the first from pad 39-B, which had recently undergone a $150 million overhaul. It had last been used for a manned launching in the 1970s.

Just before lift-off, *Challenger*'s external fuel tank held 500,000 gallons of liquid hydrogen and oxygen, which are kept separate because they are highly volatile when mixed. The fuel is used in the shuttle's three main engines.

At 11:38 A.M. the shuttle rose gracefully off the launching pad, heading into the sky. The shuttle's main engines, after being cut back slightly just after lift-off, a normal procedure, were pushed ahead to full power as the shuttle approached maximum dynamic pressure when it broke through the sound barrier.

"*Challenger*, go with throttle up," said James D. Wetherbee of Mission Control in Houston at about 11:39 A.M.

"Roger," replied the commander, Mr. Scobee, "go with throttle up."

Those were the last words to be heard on the ground from the winged spaceplane and her crew of seven.

As the explosion occurred, Stephen A. Nesbitt of Mission Control in Houston, apparently looking at his notes and not the explosion on his television monitor, noted that the shuttle's velocity was "2,900 feet per second, altitude 9 nautical miles, downrange distance 7 nautical miles." That is a speed of about 1,977 miles an hour, a height of about 10 statute miles and a distance down range of about 8 miles.

The first official word of the disaster came from Mr. Nesbitt of Mission Control, who reported "a major malfunction." He added that communications with the ship had failed 1 minute 14 seconds into the flight.

"We have no downlink," he said, referring to communications from the *Challenger*. "We have a report from the flight dynamics officer that the vehicle has exploded."

His voice cracked. "The flight director confirms that," he continued. "We're checking with the recovery forces to see what can be done at this point."

In the sky above the Kennedy Space Center, the shuttle's two solid-fuel rocket boosters sailed into the distance.

The explosion, later viewed in slow-motion televised replays taken by cameras equipped with telescopic lenses, showed what appeared to be the start of a small fire at the base of the huge external fuel tank, followed by the quick separation of the solid rockets. A huge fireball then engulfed the shuttle as the external tank exploded.

At the news conference, Mr. Moore would not speculate on the cause of the disaster.

The estimated point of impact for debris was 18 to 20 miles off the Florida coast, according to space agency officials.

"The search and rescue teams were delayed getting into the area because of debris continuing to fall from very high altitudes, for almost an hour after ascent," said Mr. Nesbitt of Mission Control in Houston.

Speaking at 1 P.M. in Florida, Lieut. Col. Robert W. Nicholson, Jr., a spokesman for the rescue operation, which is run by the Defense Department, said range safety radars near the Kennedy Space Center detected debris falling for nearly an hour after the explosion. "Anything that went into the area would have been endangered," he said in an interview.

In addition, the explosion of the huge fuel supply would have created a cloud of toxic vapors. NASA officials said tonight that the hazardous gases presented no danger to land, but the Coast Guard was advising boats and ships to avoid the area.

In an interview last year, Tommy Holloway, the chief of the flight director office at the Johnson Space Center in Houston, talked about the possibility of a shuttle crash at sea.

"This airplane is not a good ditcher," he said. "It will float OK if it doesn't break apart, and we have hatches we can blow off the top. But the orbiter lands fast, at 190 knots. You come in and stop in 100 yards so so. You decelerate like gangbusters, and anything in the payload bay comes forward. We don't expect a very good day if it comes to that."

On board *Challenger* was the world's largest privately owned communication satellite, the $100-million Tracking and Data Relay Satellite, which with its rocket boosters weighed 37,636 pounds.

This morning, water froze on the shuttle service structure, used for fire-fighting equipment and for emergency showers that technicians would use if they were exposed to fuel. The takeoff was delayed because space agency officials feared that during the first critical seconds of launching, icicles might fly off the service structure and damage the delicate heat-resistant tiles on the shuttle, which are crucial for the vehicle's reentry through the earth's atmosphere.                    JAN. 29

---

### The *Challenger* Astronauts
Francis R. Scobee, commander
Michael J. Smith, pilot
Judith A. Resnik, electrical engineer
Ellison S. Onizuka, engineer
Ronald E. McNair, physicist
Gregory B. Jarvis, electrical engineer
Christa McAuliffe, teacher

JAN. 29

## Planned Shuttle Schedule for 1986

The shuttle program was suspended by NASA until investigations into the destruction of *Challenger* are complete.

**March 6** The orbiter *Columbia*
Nine days with crew of seven, including three astronomers. Payload: Telescopes to study Halley's comet; experiment to gather data on the extent of electroosmosis; experiment to measure the earth's radius, two student experiments.

**May 15** *Challenger*
Four days with crew of four. Payload: *Ulysses* spacecraft to study the sun by way of Jupiter; experiment to investigate the properties of the heliosphere, the sun and its environment.

**May 20** *Atlantis*
Four days with crew of four. Payload: *Galileo* probe to investigate Jupiter's atmosphere and satellites.

**June 24** *Columbia*
Seven days with crew of seven, including Pratiwi Sudarmono of Indonesia and Nigel Wood of Britain. Payload: Three communication satellites—*Palapa* (Indonesia), *Westar* (Western Union Telegraph Communications), *Skynet* (United Kingdom).

**Mid-July** *Discovery*
First flight from the military launching complex at Vandenberg Air Force Base in California. Crew of seven, including Air Force Under Secretary Edward Aldridge. Payload: Classified military equipment.

**July 26** *Challenger*
Five days with crew of six. Payload: Shuttle tracking satellite; project to study production of pharmaceuticals on a large scale.

**Aug. 20** *Atlantis*
Five days with crew of five. Payload: Space telescope, the most powerful in orbit, to study the edge of the universe.

**Sept. 4** *Columbia*
Secret Department of Defense mission.

**Sept. 27** *Challenger*
Five days with crew of seven, including an Indian and the first journalist to fly in space. Mission: To deploy communication satellite for India; to retrieve an experiment package put in orbit in 1984 to study the effects of space on various materials.

**Oct. 30** *Atlantis*
Seven days with crew of seven. Mission: To observe

the stars and universe through powerful space telescope deployed in August.

**Nov. 6** *Columbia*
Seven days in orbit; size of crew undecided. Payload: Two communication satellites and a science laboratory.

**Dec. 6** *Challenger*
Secret military mission.

JAN. 31

# President Names 12-Member Panel in Shuttle Inquiry

**By GERALD M. BOYD**

**W**ASHINGTON, Feb. 3—President Reagan appointed a 12-member independent commission today to take responsibility for investigating the cause of the explosion of the space shuttle *Challenger*.

It is time, Mr. Reagan said, to take a "hard look" at the disaster that killed the seven members of the *Challenger* crew last Tuesday.

The panel, the Presidential Commission on the Space Shuttle *Challenger* Accident, will take over responsibility for examining the accident, replacing the board already convened by the National Aeronautics and Space Administration as the official investigative body.

William R. Graham, Acting Administrator of the space agency, who attended a White House meeting where Mr. Reagan announced he was creating the panel, said the launching of future shuttles would be suspended until the commission completed its investigation. The group is to report to the President and the NASA Administrator within 120 days.

The commission, drawn mainly from scientific, educational and business circles, is headed by William P. Rogers, a former Attorney General and former Secretary of State.

Neil A. Armstrong, the former astronaut, who was the first person on the moon, will be vice chairman.

FEB. 4

## Members of Presidential Commission to Investigate the Explosion of the Space Shuttle *Challenger*

William P. Rogers, former Secretary of State and a senior partner in the New York City law firm of Rogers & Wells, chairman.

Neil A. Armstrong, former astronaut and the first man to land on the moon, now chairman of Computing Technologies for Aviation, Inc., of Charlottesville, Va.

Brig. Gen. Charles (Chuck) Yeager, U.S.A.F., retired, a former test pilot and member of the National Commission on Space.

Dr. Sally K. Ride, an astronaut who was the first American woman in space.

Dr. Albert D. Wheelon, a physicist and senior vice president of the Hughes Aircraft Company who is also a member of the President's Foreign Intelligence Advisory Board.

Robert W. Rummel, former vice president of Trans World Airlines and aerospace engineer who heads Robert W. Rummell Associates, a Mesa, Ariz., concern.

Dr. Arthur B. C. Walker, Jr., professor of applied physics at Stanford University.

Richard P. Feynman, professor of theoretical physics at the California Institute of Technology, Pasadena.

Eugene E. Covert, professor of aeronautics at the Massachusetts Institute of Technology, Cambridge, and a NASA consultant on rocket engines.

Robert B. Hotz, former editor of *Aviation Week* and *Space Technology* magazine.

David C. Acheson, a former senior vice president and general counsel of the Communications Satellite Corporation and a Washington lawyer in the firm of Drinker, Biddle & Reath.

Maj. Gen. Donald J. Kutyna, U.S.A.F., director of space systems and command, control and communications.

FEB. 4

## Military Budget Is Met with Skepticism

By BILL KELLER

WASHINGTON, Feb 5—President Reagan's proposed Pentagon budget was greeted with derision today by congressional Democrats, who said the request was unrealistic, and with skepticism by some budget analysts who said it appeared to understate the likely amount of military spending.

The President requested $311.6 billion, an increase of 11.9 percent, in new appropriations for the Defense Department in the fiscal year 1987. That compares with $278.4 billion in the fiscal year 1986, which began October 1.

Defense Secretary Caspar W. Weinberger, presenting the military budget to the Senate Armed Service Committee, was told by Democrats that there was no chance Congress would approve his requested increase of 12 percent next year in new spending for the Defense Department and 42 percent over the next five years.

Senator Sam Nunn of Georgia, the senior Democrat on the panel, who is an influential moderate on military issues, said that "the very best case" the Pentagon can expect is a 3-percent or 4-percent annual increase to keep pace with inflation over the next three to five years.

Mr. Nunn said that Mr. Weinberger's request, which comes to $320.3 billion in military programs when nuclear weapons programs at the Energy Department are counted, "may very well be in tune with the threat and the need, but it is not in tune with what is going to happen, even under the best of circumstances."

FEB. 6

### Billion-dollar weapons

Weapons programs in the Pentagon's proposed 1987 budget that would cost $1 billion or more.

| | |
|---|---|
| Strategic Defense Initiative | $4.8 |
| F-16 Falcon Air Force fighter plane | 3.9 |
| F/A-18 Hornet Navy fighter plane | 3.5 |
| Trident II submarine-launched ballistic missile | 3.1 |
| DDG-51 destroyer | 2.6 |
| SSN-688 attack submarine | 2.4 |
| F-15 Eagle Air Force fighter planes | 2.3 |
| M-1 tank | 2.2 |
| CG-47 Aegis cruiser | 2.1 |
| C-5B Galaxy transport plane | 2.0 |
| MX missile | 1.8 |
| Trident nuclear-missile submarine | 1.7 |
| Midgetman ballistic missile | 1.4 |
| AH-64 attack helicopter | 1.4 |
| Bradley fighting vehicle (armored troop carrier) | 1.2 |
| Patriot surface-to-air missile | 1.1 |

Amounts for classified programs, such as the Stealth aircraft, are not available. Rounded figures in billions.
Source: Defense Department

FEB. 6

### The Final Minute of the *Challenger* Official Data Released by NASA

- **6.6 seconds to launching.** Start of *Challenger*'s main engines.
- **0.0.** Solid fuel booster rockets ignite.
- **0.0587.** Lift-off.
- **0.445.** First evidence of black smoke near joint of right booster.
- **2.147.** Black smoke extends halfway across booster.
- **7.724.** Roll maneuver begins.
- **12-13.** Last visual indication of black smoke.
- **20.084.** Main engines begin throttle down to 94 percent.
- **21.124.** Roll maneuver completed.
- **36.084.** Main engines begin throttle down to 65 percent.

**40.0.** Vehicle responds to wind.
**52.084.** Main engines begin throttle up to 104 percent.
**58.774.** First indication of smoke on the side of the right booster in front of the external tank's aft attachment point, down and away from orbiter.
**59.0.** Maximum dynamic pressure.
**59.249.** Well-defined intense plume on side of right booster, down and away from orbiter.
**60.164.** Start of difference in chamber pressures of the two boosters.
**60.6.** Evidence of flame from right booster, down and away from orbiter.
**66.174.** Bright spot on right booster in plume, down and away from orbiter. Bright spots begin to appear on top side near orbiter.
**66.625.** Bright sustained glow on right booster on top side near orbiter.
**67.684.** Pressure change in oxygen inlet to orbiter's main engines.
**73.044.** Right booster chamber pressure lower than left booster's pressure.
**73.175.** Sudden cloud beside external tank.
**73.200-1.** Flash from region between orbiter and external tank's liquid hydrogen tank.
**73.226.** Explosion near booster forward attachment point.
**73.326.** Increased intensity of white flash in region of external tank's liquid oxygen tank.
**73.534.** No. 1 main engine on the orbiter shuts down because of intense heat in fuel pump.
**73.621.** Last data from orbiter.
**109.604.** Right booster destroyed by remote control.
**110.266.** Left booster destroyed by remote control.

FEB. 15

# Education Chief Lauds State of Schools in U.S.

**By ROBIN TONER**

WASHINGTON, Feb. 20—Secretary of Education William J. Bennett sketched a glowing portrait of American public schools today in his department's annual state-by-state review of public education. As high school drop-out rates decline, he said, college entrance examination scores are climbing.

"Some have said we can't have both excellence and equity in our schools," said Mr. Bennett. "Clearly, raising standards and expectations for everyone means everyone benefits."

Mr. Bennett's review was criticized by the National Education Association as unduly optimistic, and by some state education officials as incomplete and lending itself to misleading interpretations.

The review found that graduation rates rose from 1982 to 1984 in 39 states and that average scores on the two most widely used college entrance exams increased in 35 states in the last three years.

Mr. Bennett said the rising test scores showed that "the movement to raise academic achievement standards and restore discipline is showing results." And, he said, the decline in the drop-out rate shows that such gains are not coming at the expense of underprivileged students.

Mr. Bennett's report came three years after a bipartisan Federal commission called for significant upgrading of American education at all levels. That report, "A Nation at Risk," was considered a catalyst in the movement to raise educational standards. Mr. Bennett, arguing that this push was realizing results, said political leaders, educators, parents and children were "to be congratulated." MARCH 1

## Graduation rates state by state
Percent of public school students who graduated from high school each year.

|  | 1982 | 1984 |  | 1982 | 1984 |
|---|---|---|---|---|---|
| Minn. | 88.2% | 89.3% | Ill. | 76.1 | 74.5 |
| Neb. | 81.9 | 86.3 | Mass. | 76.4 | 74.3 |
| N.D. | 83.9 | 86.3 | Ore. | 72.4 | 73.9 |
| Iowa | 84.1 | 86.0 | Hawaii | 74.9 | 73.2 |
| S.D. | 82.7 | 85.5 | Okla. | 70.8 | 73.1 |

|       | 1982 | 1984 |        | 1982  | 1984  |
|-------|------|------|--------|-------|-------|
| Wis.  | 83.1 | 84.5 | W.Va.  | 65.3  | 73.1  |
| Vt.   | 79.6 | 83.1 | Mich.  | 71.6  | 72.2  |
| Mont. | 78.7 | 82.1 | Del.   | 74.7  | 71.1  |
| Kan.  | 80.7 | 81.7 | N.M.   | 69.4  | 71.0  |
| Ohio  | 77.5 | 80.0 | Tenn.  | 67.8  | 70.5  |
| Conn. | 70.6 | 79.1 | N.C.   | 67.1  | 69.3  |
| Utah  | 75.0 | 78.7 | R.I.   | 72.2  | 68.7  |
| Md.   | 74.8 | 77.8 | Ky.    | 65.9  | 68.4  |
| N.J.  | 76.5 | 77.7 | Nev.   | 64.8  | 66.5  |
| Me.   | 72.1 | 77.2 | Ariz.  | 63.4  | 64.6  |
| Pa.   | 76.0 | 77.2 | Tex.   | 63.6  | 64.6  |
| Ind.  | 71.7 | 77.0 | S.C.   | 62.6  | 64.5  |
| Mo.   | 74.2 | 76.2 | Calif. | 60.1  | 63.2  |
| Wyo.  | 72.4 | 76.0 | Ga.    | 65.0  | 63.1  |
| Idaho | 74.4 | 75.8 | Miss.  | 61.3  | 62.4  |
| Colo. | 70.9 | 75.4 | Fla.   | 60.2  | 62.2  |
| Ark.  | 73.4 | 75.2 | N.Y.   | 63.4  | 62.2  |
| N.H.  | 77.0 | 75.2 | Ala.   | 63.4  | 62.1  |
| Wash. | 76.1 | 75.1 | La.    | 61.5  | 56.7  |
| Alaska| 64.3 | 74.7 | D.C.   | 56.9  | 55.2  |
| Va.   | 73.8 | 74.7 | U.S.   | 69.7% | 70.9% |

The figures were calculated by dividing the number of graduates by the number of ninth-graders enrolled four years earlier and were adjusted for moves between states.

Source: Department of Education

FEB. 21

# Study by U.S. Department of Education Reports on Best Ways of Teaching

**By EDWARD B. FISKE**

In a step likely to provoke new debate on the Federal role in American education, the Department of Education is to give President Reagan a list of 41 findings about "what works" in public schools.

The list, to be presented Tuesday, begins with the assertion that "what parents do to help their children" is more important to academic success than "how well-off the family is."

The department embraces phonics, which stresses the relationship between spoken sounds and printed letters, as the best method of teaching reading, and it says the most effective schools focus on core academic subjects such as mathematics, assign lots of homework, have students memorize and emphasize the teaching of history.

The findings are contained in a 66-page booklet entitled "What Works: Research about Teaching and Learning." The first of 100,000 copies will be presented to the President at a ceremony in the East Room by William J. Bennett, the Secretary of Education.

In an interview yesterday, Mr. Bennett described the report as an effort to "tell the American public what we know about how to teach." He said providing such information was "the first and fundamental responsibility of the Federal Government in the field of education."

Mr. Bennett said care had been taken to avoid controversial policy issues and to endorse only those conclusions on which there was "broad and consistent" agreement. He said, "We asked ourselves: What can we say about teaching that is true, useful and important?"

Nevertheless, the list of findings has already drawn mixed reviews from educators. Frank L. Smith, chairman of the department of educational administration at the Teachers College of Columbia University, who reviewed an early copy, said the choices in the document presumed a "specific behavioral view of teaching" that many educators did not accept.

MARCH 1

## What Works in the Schools

How the Education Department describes sound education in its report "What Works."

### Curriculum of the Home

Parents are their children's first and most influential teachers. What parents do to help their children learn is more important to academic success than how well-off the family is.

### Early Writing

Children who are encouraged to draw and scribble "stories" at an early age will later learn to compose more easily, more effectively, and with greater confidence than children who aren't encouraged.

### Phonics

Children get a better start in reading if they are taught phonics. Learning phonics helps them to understand the relationship between letters and sounds and to "break the code" that links the words they hear with the words they see in print.

### Science Experiments

Children learn science best when they are able to do experiments, so they can witness "science in action."

### Learning Mathematics

Children in early grades learn mathematics more effectively when they use physical objects in their lessons.

### Homework Quantity

Student achievement rises significantly when teachers regularly assign homework and students conscientiously do it.

### Assessment

Frequent and systematic monitoring of students' progress helps students, parents, teachers, administrators and policymakers identify strengths and weaknesses in learning and instruction.

### Effective Schools

The most important characteristics of effective schools are strong instructional leadership, a safe and orderly climate, school-wide emphasis on basic skills, high teacher expectations for student achievement and continuous assessment of pupil progress.

### Teacher Supervision

Teachers welcome professional suggestions about improving their work, but they rarely receive them.

### History

Skimpy requirements and declining enrollments in history classes are contributing to a decline in students' knowledge of the past.

### Foreign Language

The best way to learn a foreign language in school is to start early and to study it intensively over many years.

### Preparation for Work

Business leaders report that students with solid basic skills and positive work attitudes are more likely to find and keep jobs than students with vocational skills alone.

MARCH 1

## Where the gasoline goes

| | Population (in thousands) | Gasoline use per capita, 1983 (in gallons) |
|---|---|---|
| Wyoming | 514 | 603 |
| Oklahoma | 3,298 | 537 |
| Nevada | 891 | 521 |
| Texas | 15,724 | 516 |
| Montana | 817 | 513 |
| New Mexico | 1,399 | 512 |
| Delaware | 606 | 499 |
| Georgia | 5,732 | 496 |
| Missouri | 4,970 | 488 |
| North Dakota | 680 | 483 |
| Kansas | 2,425 | 480 |
| Tennessee | 4,685 | 478 |
| Louisiana | 4,438 | 472 |
| Arkansas | 2,328 | 468 |
| Arizona | 2,963 | 464 |
| South Dakota | 700 | 462 |
| Alabama | 3,959 | 458 |
| North Carolina | 6,082 | 458 |
| South Carolina | 3,264 | 458 |
| Kentucky | 3,714 | 454 |
| Iowa | 2,905 | 453 |
| Florida | 10,680 | 450 |
| Minnesota | 4,144 | 446 |
| Virginia | 5,550 | 446 |
| Colorado | 3,139 | 442 |
| Nebraska | 1,597 | 442 |
| Vermont | 525 | 441 |

|  | Population (in thousands) | Gasoline use per capita, 1983 (in gallons) |
|---|---|---|
| Maine | 1,146 | 438 |
| Oregon | 2,662 | 436 |
| Indiana | 5,479 | 435 |
| New Jersey | 7,468 | 433 |
| Washington | 4,300 | 432 |
| Maryland | 4,304 | 431 |
| Mississippi | 2,587 | 431 |
| California | 25,174 | 424 |
| Idaho | 989 | 423 |
| Ohio | 10,746 | 413 |
| New Hampshire | 959 | 411 |
| Connecticut | 3,138 | 407 |
| Utah | 1,619 | 407 |
| Wisconsin | 4,751 | 402 |
| West Virginia | 1,965 | 396 |
| Michigan | 9,069 | 390 |
| Massachusetts | 5,767 | 383 |
| Illinois | 11,486 | 383 |
| Alaska | 479 | 380 |
| Pennsylvania | 11,895 | 360 |
| Rhode Island | 955 | 359 |
| New York | 17,667 | 297 |
| Hawaii | 1,023 | 293 |
| District of Columbia | 623 | 268 |

Source: Highway Users Federation

MARCH 2

## Closing the gap*
Black male wages as a percent of white male wages

| Years of experience | 1940 | 1950 | 1960 | 1970 | 1980 |
|---|---|---|---|---|---|
| 1–5 | 46.7 | 61.8 | 60.2 | 75.1 | 84.2 |
| 6–10 | 47.5 | 61.0 | 59.1 | 70.1 | 76.6 |
| 11–15 | 44.4 | 58.3 | 59.4 | 66.2 | 73.5 |
| 16–20 | 44.4 | 56.6 | 58.4 | 62.8 | 71.2 |
| 21–25 | 42.3 | 54.1 | 57.6 | 62.7 | 67.8 |
| 26–30 | 41.7 | 53.2 | 56.2 | 60.6 | 66.9 |
| 31–35 | 40.2 | 50.3 | 53.8 | 60.0 | 66.5 |
| 36–40 | 39.8 | 46.9 | 55.9 | 60.3 | 68.5 |
| All men | 43.3 | 55.2 | 57.5 | 64.4 | 72.6 |

*The economic gap between black men and whites narrowed sharply between 1940 and 1980, according to an analysis released by the Rand Corporation last week. The study, based on census data, ascribed the gains chiefly to better education, which led to better-paying jobs, and black migration to Northern cities. It found that black families did not share in the economic gains of black working men, particularly during the 1970s, because an increasing number of black families were headed by women.

MARCH 2

## Medal of Liberty

Twelve prominent Americans, 11 men and 1 woman, all of whom rose from immigrant beginnings, were selected yesterday as the first recipients of the Medal of Liberty, to be presented at the Statue of Liberty centennial celebration this summer.

The winners included Irving Berlin, the composer, from Russia; Dr. Kenneth B. Clark, the psychologist, from Jamaica; Franklin R. Chang-Diaz, the astronaut, from Costa Rica; Hannah Holborn Gray, president of the University of Chicago and former acting president of Yale University, from Germany; Bob Hope, the entertainer, from England; and Henry A. Kissinger, the former Secretary of State, from Germany.

Also named were I. M. Pei, the architect, from China; Itzhak Perlman, the violinist, from Israel; James B. Reston, the Pulitzer Prize–winning journalist and *New York Times* columnist, from Scotland; Dr. Albert B. Sabin, the physician who developed the oral polio vaccine, from the Soviet Union; Dr. An Wang, the founder and chairman of the board of Wang Labs Inc., from China; and Elie Wiesel, the author and chronicler of the Holocaust, from Rumania.

MARCH 2

## U.S. Releasing Lists of Hospitals with Abnormal Mortality Rates

**By JOEL BRINKLEY**

WASHINGTON, March 11—The Health and Human Services Department is preparing to release lists of the nation's hospitals that have mortality rates significantly higher or lower than the national average, the first such lists ever compiled.

The lists, provided to *The New York Times* and scheduled for general release on Wednesday, indicate that more than twice as many patients died at certain hospitals than would have been expected under national norms.

The lists were derived using case records from 10.7 million patients treated in 1984 whose bills were paid by Medicare, the Government program that assists the elderly and the disabled in paying their hospital costs. Nearly all the nation's hospitals treat Medicare patients, who make up almost half of all hospital patients.

Several New York hospitals were identified as having higher-than-average mortality rates for elderly Medicare patients.

But Federal officials warned that the statistics were suggestive, not conclusive. They said that perhaps half the hospitals shown might have acceptable explanations for their abnormal death rates among Medicare patients that had nothing to do with the quality of the medical care.

"This is not meant to point an accusing finger," said Dr. Henry R. Desmarais, Acting Administrator of the Health Care Financing Administration, which compiled the list. The list was intended to help state medical review agencies identify hospitals with problems, he said. "It is not a report card on the nation's hospitals," he added.

Even with that warning, releasing the data brought protests from the medical profession. "It's the dumbest thing I've ever seen H.H.S. do," said Jack Owen, executive vice president of the American Hospital Association. "It's utter folly," said Frederick Graefe, counsel for the American Protestant Health Association.

But consumer groups lauded the move, calling it one of the most significant changes in Federal policy for health-care consumers in decades. Whether or not the statistics are valid, they said, releasing the material is an important precedent.

"We've been waiting for this for a long time," said Dr. Sidney Wolfe, head of the Public Citizens Health Research Group, which lobbies for fuller disclosure of information on doctors and hospitals. "We're not worried about misuse of the data; people are too bright to do that."

MARCH 12

### Hospitals with death rates for Medicare patients *below* government forecasts

| | Patients | Actual Death Rate | Forecast Death Rate |
|---|---|---|---|
| **California** | | | |
| St. Helena Hospital & Health Center, Deer Park | 2,302 | 2.6% | 4.6% |
| Grossmont District Hospital, La Mesa | 6,261 | 3.0 | 4.9 |
| Mills Memorial Hospital, San Mateo | 3,992 | 5.1 | 7.0 |

# NATIONAL

| | Patients | Actual Death Rate | Forecast Death Rate |
|---|---:|---:|---:|
| **Connecticut** | | | |
| New Milford Hospital, New Milford | 1,187 | 1.7 | 5.0 |
| **District of Columbia** | | | |
| Georgetown University Hospital, Washington | 2,219 | 1.9 | 5.4 |
| Sibley Memorial Hospital, Washington | 2,777 | 2.9 | 4.8 |
| **Florida** | | | |
| Doctors' Hospital, Coral Gables | 3,590 | 1.1 | 4.0 |
| Holmes County Hospital, Bonifay | 535 | 5.2 | 9.7 |
| John F. Kennedy Memorial Hospital, Atlantis | 6,626 | 3.6 | 4.8 |
| Baptist Regional Health Services, Pensacola | 4,944 | 4.7 | 6.1 |
| St. Luke's Hospital, Jacksonville | 2,606 | 2.6 | 4.9 |
| Memorial Hospital, Ormond Beach | 3,772 | 5.3 | 6.9 |
| Memorial Medical Center of Jacksonville | 4,001 | 3.5 | 5.1 |
| **Georgia** | | | |
| Baldwin County Hospital, Milledgeville | 1,610 | 5.2 | 7.7 |
| Clayton General Hospital, Clayton | 2,955 | 3.1 | 4.9 |
| **Hawaii** | | | |
| G. N. Wilcox Memorial Hospital and Health Center, Lihue | 940 | 3.5 | 7.3 |
| **Illinois** | | | |
| University of Chicago Hospitals & Clinics, Chicago | 3,888 | 4.1 | 6.0 |
| Northern Illinois Medical Center, McHenry | 1,795 | 4.3 | 6.7 |
| Cook County Hospital, Chicago | 3,343 | 1.9 | 5.5 |
| **Iowa** | | | |
| Muscatine General Hospital, Muscatine | 1,060 | 2.6 | 5.7 |
| Boone County Hospital, Boone | 1,190 | 2.1 | 4.9 |
| Mercy Hospital, Iowa City | 2,999 | 1.2 | 3.5 |
| Mary Greeley Medical Center, Ames | 2,711 | 1.4 | 4.2 |
| Mercy Hospital, Davenport | 2,592 | 2.2 | 4.9 |
| Sartori Memorial Hospital, Cedar Falls | 847 | 1.9 | 5.2 |
| St. Luke's Methodist Hospital, Cedar Rapids | 5,025 | 1.5 | 3.8 |
| University of Iowa Hospitals and Clinics, Iowa City | 6,199 | 1.7 | 3.7 |
| St. Joseph Mercy Hospital, Mason City | 3,729 | 1.7 | 3.6 |
| St. Francis Hospital, Waterloo | 1,922 | 1.2 | 4.3 |
| Mercy Health Center, Dubuque | 3,537 | 1.9 | 4.8 |
| Mercy Hospital, Cedar Rapids | 3,843 | 2.4 | 4.6 |
| Iowa Methodist Medical Center, Des Moines | 5,969 | 1.8 | 4.3 |
| Mercy Hospital Medical Center, Des Moines | 6,405 | 2.1 | 4.1 |
| Broadlawns Medical Center, Des Moines | 766 | 0.4 | 3.9 |
| Des Moines General Hospital, Des Moines | 2,685 | 1.6 | 4.7 |
| **Kansas** | | | |
| University of Kansas Medical Center, Kansas City | 3,484 | 3.4 | 5.0 |
| St. Francis Regional Medical Center, Wichita | 8,340 | 3.7 | 4.9 |
| **Kentucky** | | | |
| King's Daughters' Hospital, Ashland | 3,367 | 4.9 | 6.7 |
| Methodist Hospital of Kentucky, Pikeville | 2,518 | 4.2 | 6.1 |
| Owen County Memorial Hospital, Owenton | 512 | 5.3 | 10.2 |

|  | Patients | Actual Death Rate | Forecast Death Rate |
|---|---:|---:|---:|
| **Louisiana** | | | |
| Feliciana Medical Center, Clinton | 656 | 4.1 | 8.1 |
| La Salle General Hospital, Jena | 1,339 | 2.8 | 6.0 |
| **Maryland** | | | |
| Physicians' Memorial Hospital, La Plata | 978 | 0.4 | 4.4 |
| Maryland General Hospital, Baltimore | 2,328 | 1.8 | 5.0 |
| Provident Hospital, Baltimore | 1,264 | 3.5 | 7.9 |
| Greater Baltimore Medical Center, Baltimore | 3,690 | 2.7 | 4.2 |
| **Massachusetts** | | | |
| Mount Auburn Hospital, Cambridge | 3,408 | 4.9 | 6.7 |
| Union Hospital, Lynn | 2,352 | 2.5 | 5.9 |
| Carney Hospital, Boston | 4,178 | 5.3 | 7.2 |
| Hunt Memorial Hospital, Danvers | 1,208 | 2.4 | 5.6 |
| Marlborough Hospital, Marlborough | 1,876 | 5.3 | 7.6 |
| Charlton Memorial Hospital, Fall River | 5,174 | 6.4 | 8.2 |
| Sancta Maria Hospital, Cambridge | 1,899 | 1.5 | 5.6 |
| Glover Memorial Hospital, Needham | 1,320 | 0.5 | 4.6 |
| Boston City Hospital, Boston | 1,538 | 0.2 | 5.9 |
| Milton Hospital, Milton | 2,312 | 4.2 | 6.5 |
| Faulkner Hospital, Boston | 3,417 | 5.1 | 7.7 |
| Hahnemann Hospital, Boston | 862 | 2.8 | 6.0 |
| Falmouth Hospital, Falmouth | 1,764 | 5.7 | 7.9 |
| **Michigan** | | | |
| McLaren General Hospital, Flint | 4,586 | 5.4 | 6.8 |
| Grand View Hospital, Ironwood | 1,020 | 3.9 | 7.7 |
| Chelsea Community Hospital | 986 | 4.2 | 7.7 |
| **Minnesota** | | | |
| Regina Memorial Hospital, Hastings | 569 | 4.6 | 8.4 |
| St. Paul–Ramsey Medical Center, St. Paul | 3,677 | 5.1 | 6.7 |
| **Mississippi** | | | |
| Greenwood Leflore Hospital, Greenwood | 4,229 | 1.5 | 2.9 |
| Jeff Anderson Regional Medical Center, Meridian | 3,065 | 5.0 | 7.4 |
| **Missouri** | | | |
| Jewish Hospital of St. Louis, St. Louis | 7,167 | 4.4 | 5.5 |
| Pemiscot County Memorial Hospital, Hayti | 1,250 | 5.8 | 8.6 |
| **Montana** | | | |
| Missoula Community Hospital, Missoula | 1,232 | 1.7 | 4.3 |
| **New Jersey** | | | |
| Deborah Heart and Lung Center, Browns Mills | 1,702 | 3.8 | 5.9 |
| **New York** | | | |
| Presbyterian Hospital in New York, New York | 9,646 | 6.4 | 7.4 |
| St. Jerome Hospital, Batavia | 1,608 | 6.7 | 9.0 |
| Roosevelt Hospital, New York | 4,104 | 5.9 | 8.4 |
| Montefiore Medical Center, the Bronx | 13,227 | 6.2 | 7.1 |
| New York Eye and Ear Infirmary, New York | 5,689 | 0.0 | 2.1 |

# NATIONAL

| | Patients | Actual Death Rate | Forecast Death Rate |
|---|---|---|---|
| Beth Israel Medical Center, New York | 6,230 | 2.5 | 6.2 |
| Glens Falls Hospital, Glens Falls | 5,970 | 5.7 | 7.0 |
| New York University Medical Center, New York | 6,755 | 4.4 | 6.5 |
| Champlain Valley Physicians Hospital Medical Center, Plattsburgh | 4,662 | 6.0 | 7.9 |
| Medical Arts Center Hospital, New York | 462 | 2.6 | 8.2 |
| Strong Memorial Hospital Rochester University, Rochester | 5,379 | 6.0 | 7.5 |
| Julia L. Butterfield Memorial Hospital, Cold Spring | 512 | 4.9 | 9.2 |
| Prospect Hospital, Bronx | 851 | 1.8 | 5.0 |
| Tompkins Community Hospital, Ithaca | 2,284 | 3.7 | 7.1 |
| Roswell Park Memorial Institute, Buffalo | 2,176 | 5.1 | 6.9 |
| Hospital for Joint Diseases, New York | 1,352 | 0.0 | 2.6 |
| Joint Diseases North General Hospital, New York | 869 | 3.5 | 7.0 |
| United Health Services, Johnson City | 8,995 | 5.5 | 6.8 |
| **North Carolina** | | | |
| Hoots Memorial Hospital, Yadkinville | 574 | 3.1 | 7.7 |
| Scotland Memorial Hospital, Laurinburg | 1,212 | 4.5 | 7.1 |
| Morehead Memorial Hospital, Eden | 1,264 | 2.1 | 5.3 |
| Frye Regional Medical Center, Hickory | 2,036 | 2.0 | 5.1 |
| **Ohio** | | | |
| Mercy Hospital of Hamilton | 3,804 | 3.5 | 5.4 |
| Mercy Medical Center, Springfield | 3,085 | 4.8 | 6.6 |
| Blanchard Valley Hospital, Findlay | 2,759 | 4.3 | 6.4 |
| Fostoria City Hospital, Fostoria | 929 | 4.1 | 7.2 |
| City Hospital, Bellaire | 1,326 | 3.9 | 6.5 |
| **Oregon** | | | |
| Sacred Heart General Hospital, Eugene | 5,809 | 1.4 | 4.0 |
| **Pennsylvania** | | | |
| Geisinger Medical Center, Danville | 6,911 | 1.5 | 3.8 |
| North Penn Hospital, Lansdale | 1,999 | 3.0 | 5.1 |
| Evangelical Community Hospital, Lewisburg | 2,399 | 3.0 | 5.3 |
| Chestnut Hill Hospital, Philadelphia | 3,221 | 4.3 | 6.3 |
| Franklin Regional Medical Center, Franklin | 4,026 | 3.6 | 5.0 |
| Lancaster General Hospital, Lancaster | 7,034 | 4.6 | 6.0 |
| Hospital of the University of Pennsylvania, Philadelphia | 5,447 | 3.4 | 5.1 |
| Suburban General Hospital, Norristown | 1,733 | 1.7 | 4.6 |
| Mercy Catholic Medical Center, Darby | 5,935 | 5.2 | 6.4 |
| Haverford Community Hospital, Havertown | 1,258 | 3.5 | 6.7 |
| Abington Memorial Hospital, Abington | 6,645 | 5.2 | 6.4 |
| Hanover General Hospital, Hanover | 2,178 | 3.7 | 6.6 |
| Episcopal Hospital, Philadelphia | 2,398 | 3.2 | 5.3 |
| Milton S. Hershey Medical Center, Hershey | 3,300 | 4.3 | 6.1 |
| St. Mary Hospital, Langhorne | 2,127 | 3.2 | 6.0 |
| **Rhode Island** | | | |
| Westerly Hospital, Westerly | 1,976 | 5.5 | 7.9 |
| **South Carolina** | | | |
| Medical University Hospital, Charleston | 2,649 | 2.4 | 4.2 |
| North Trident Regional Hospital, Charleston | 2,901 | 2.6 | 5.2 |

|  | Patients | Actual Death Rate | Forecast Death Rate |
|---|---|---|---|
| **Tennessee** | | | |
| Maury County Hospital, Columbia | 3,757 | 2.6 | 4.6 |
| **Texas** | | | |
| St. Paul Hospital, Dallas | 4,652 | 2.4 | 4.6 |
| Memorial Hospital, Lufkin | 2,970 | 0.2 | 3.4 |
| Rosewood General Hospital, Houston | 1,445 | 4.1 | 7.8 |
| Richardson Medical Center, Richardson | 969 | 2.7 | 6.2 |
| Spring Branch Memorial Hospital, Houston | 1,287 | 0.6 | 3.3 |
| Valley Community Hospital, Brownsville | 854 | 0.8 | 4.0 |
| **Virginia** | | | |
| University of Virginia Hospital and Children's Rehabilitation, Charlottesville | 5,368 | 3.3 | 4.9 |
| Grundy Hospital, Grundy | 923 | 2.4 | 5.8 |
| **West Virginia** | | | |
| Bluefield Community Hospital, Bluefield | 3,877 | 0.9 | 3.1 |

## Hospitals with death rates for Medicare patients *above* government forecasts

|  | Patients | Actual Death Rate | Forecast Death Rate |
|---|---|---|---|
| **Alabama** | | | |
| Lloyd Noland Hospital, Fairfield | 2,569 | 7.5% | 5.5% |
| **Arizona** | | | |
| Maricopa Medical Center, Phoenix | 2,076 | 8.1 | 6.0 |
| Community Hospital Medical Center, Phoenix | 462 | 7.1 | 2.7 |
| **California** | | | |
| Mercy Hospital of Sacramento, Sacramento | 5,216 | 6.1 | 4.6 |
| Oroville Hospital, Oroville | 2,137 | 6.7 | 4.6 |
| Greater Bakersfield Memorial Hospital, Bakersfield | 2,305 | 8.1 | 4.9 |
| Santa Clara Valley Medical Center, San Jose | 1,633 | 9.1 | 5.7 |
| Samuel Merritt Hospital, Oakland | 4,660 | 6.0 | 4.2 |
| Mercy Hospital and Medical Center, San Diego | 7,070 | 5.7 | 4.5 |
| Brookside Hospital, San Pablo | 2,707 | 6.9 | 4.6 |
| St. Francis Medical Center, Lynwood | 4,827 | 7.3 | 5.7 |
| Palomar Memorial Hospital, Escondido | 5,096 | 7.3 | 5.3 |
| Tri-City Hospital, Oceanside | 5,946 | 6.5 | 4.6 |
| City of Hope National Medical Center, Duarte | 1,439 | 8.1 | 5.4 |
| Long Beach Community Hospital, Long Beach | 3,439 | 6.9 | 5.1 |
| Valley Medical Center of Fresno, Fresno | 2,401 | 9.5 | 7.2 |
| Granada Hills Community Hospital, Granada Hills | 2,236 | 8.3 | 5.3 |
| Pomona Valley Community Hospital, Pomona | 4,579 | 6.8 | 5.2 |
| San Bernardino County Medical Center, San Bernardino | 913 | 11.1 | 6.7 |
| Redlands Community Hospital, Redlands | 3,339 | 7.7 | 6.1 |

|  | Patients | Actual Death Rate | Forecast Death Rate |
|---|---|---|---|
| Riverside General Hospital–University Medical Center, Riverside | 1,293 | 9.3 | 6.3 |
| Downey Community Hospital, Downey | 2,990 | 8.2 | 6.0 |
| Eden Hospital, Castro Valley | 2,628 | 7.1 | 5.3 |
| Mt. Diablo Hospital Medical Center, Concord | 3,843 | 6.3 | 4.9 |
| Barlow Hospital, Los Angeles | 131 | 18.3 | 4.0 |
| **Connecticut** | | | |
| Hartford Hospital, Hartford | 10,051 | 7.2 | 5.9 |
| Norwalk Hospital, Norwalk | 4,254 | 7.4 | 5.9 |
| **Florida** | | | |
| Orlando Regional Medical Center | 7,722 | 5.9 | 4.5 |
| Bayfront Medical Center, St. Petersburg | 4,492 | 7.7 | 5.5 |
| North Broward Medical Center, Pompano Beach | 6,742 | 6.2 | 4.6 |
| Palm Beach Gardens Medical Center, Palm Beach Gardens | 2,737 | 7.5 | 5.1 |
| Humana Hospital Cypress, Pompano Beach | 2,880 | 5.6 | 3.7 |
| **Georgia** | | | |
| Medical Center, Columbus | 2,901 | 7.0 | 5.1 |
| **Illinois** | | | |
| Lutheran Hospital, Moline | 2,795 | 8.7 | 6.1 |
| Little Company of Mary Hospital, Evergreen Park | 4,967 | 6.8 | 5.4 |
| St. Elizabeth's Hospital, Belleville | 5,847 | 6.6 | 5.2 |
| Oak Forest Hospital of Cook County, Oak Forest | 798 | 26.0 | 9.0 |
| **Indiana** | | | |
| Union Hospital, Terre Haute | 5,175 | 7.5 | 5.6 |
| Methodist Hospital of Indiana, Indianapolis | 8,698 | 6.3 | 5.0 |
| Broadway Methodist, Merrillville | 2,894 | 8.4 | 5.9 |
| **Iowa** | | | |
| Davenport Osteopathic Hospital, Davenport | 782 | 9.6 | 5.9 |
| **Kansas** | | | |
| Greeley County Hospital, Tribune | 91 | 20.9 | 10.0 |
| Holton City Hospital, Holton | 177 | 12.4 | 5.4 |
| **Kentucky** | | | |
| Western Baptist Hospital, Paducah | 4,272 | 6.6 | 5.2 |
| **Louisiana** | | | |
| Huey P. Long Memorial Hospital, Pineville | 524 | 9.4 | 5.3 |
| Humana Hospital, Springhill | 1,262 | 7.1 | 4.2 |
| Louisiana State University Hospital, Shreveport | 2,487 | 8.5 | 6.3 |
| Humana Hospital, Oakdale | 908 | 6.2 | 3.0 |
| Pendleton Memorial Methodist Hospital, New Orleans | 2,251 | 6.9 | 4.8 |
| River Parishes Medical Center, Laplace | 745 | 10.2 | 4.6 |
| **Maryland** | | | |
| Lutheran Hospital of Maryland, Baltimore | 1,768 | 10.5 | 7.5 |
| **Massachusetts** | | | |
| Haverhill Mun-Hale Hospital | 2,020 | 9.1 | 6.4 |
| Bay State Medical Center, Springfield | 8,709 | 8.6 | 7.4 |
| Soldiers' Home in Holyoke | 91 | 19.8 | 8.8 |

|  | Patients | Actual Death Rate | Forecast Death Rate |
|---|---|---|---|
| **Michigan** | | | |
| Doctors' Hospital, Detroit | 720 | 14.2 | 7.3 |
| Hurley Medical Center, Flint | 3,127 | 7.8 | 5.7 |
| Riverside Osteopathic Hospital, Trenton | 1,941 | 8.9 | 6.4 |
| Oakland General Hospital Osteopathic, Madison Heights | 2,106 | 8.5 | 5.5 |
| Southwest Detroit Hospital, Detroit | 1,397 | 9.8 | 6.1 |
| **Minnesota** | | | |
| St. Joseph's Hospital, St. Paul | 2,592 | 7.8 | 4.9 |
| St. John's Hospital, St. Paul | 2,282 | 7.4 | 5.3 |
| **Mississippi** | | | |
| Delta Medical Center, Greenville | 1,951 | 9.4 | 5.8 |
| **Missouri** | | | |
| Lakeside Hospital, Kansas City | 961 | 7.4 | 4.4 |
| Bethesda General Hospital, St. Louis | 1,328 | 5.9 | 3.4 |
| North Kansas City Memorial Hospital, North Kansas City | 3,493 | 6.5 | 4.6 |
| St. Louis City Hospital, St. Louis | 1,171 | 12.3 | 9.4 |
| **Nebraska** | | | |
| West Nebraska General Hospital, Scottsbluff | 2,978 | 5.9 | 3.8 |
| Memorial Hospital, Aurora | 513 | 9.9 | 3.3 |
| **Nevada** | | | |
| Humana Hospital Sunrise, Las Vegas | 6,768 | 6.0 | 4.9 |
| Southern Nevada Memorial Hospital, Las Vegas | 2,650 | 7.8 | 5.6 |
| Adelson Hospice, Las Vegas | 169 | 87.6 | 22.5 |
| **New Jersey** | | | |
| Newark Beth Israel Medical Center, Newark | 4,146 | 8.0 | 6.3 |
| Cooper Hospital–University Medical Center, Camden | 3,851 | 10.1 | 6.3 |
| Christ Hospital, Jersey City | 3,486 | 9.3 | 7.4 |
| St. Joseph's Hospital & Medical Center, Paterson | 5,536 | 9.2 | 7.1 |
| Millville Hospital, Millville | 1,697 | 8.7 | 5.7 |
| Community Memorial Hospital, Toms River | 7,797 | 9.0 | 7.8 |
| St. Francis Hospital, Jersey City | 2,637 | 9.0 | 7.2 |
| Zurbrugg Memorial Hospital, Willingboro | 2,365 | 8.1 | 5.9 |
| Muhlenberg Hospital, Plainfield | 3,996 | 8.0 | 6.5 |
| St. Peter's Medical Center, New Brunswick | 4,199 | 8.4 | 7.0 |
| Jersey Shore Medical Center, Neptune | 5,720 | 9.7 | 8.1 |
| Jersey City Medical Center, Jersey City | 1,782 | 11.3 | 8.1 |
| Monmouth Medical Center, Long Branch | 4,668 | 9.5 | 6.8 |
| Kennedy Memorial Hospitals University Medical Center, Stratford | 5,847 | 8.9 | 6.8 |
| **New York** | | | |
| Peninsula Hospital Center, Far Rockaway | 3,818 | 12.5 | 9.7 |
| Bronx-Lebanon Hospital Center, Bronx | 2,681 | 6.5 | 8.4 |
| Nassau County Medical Center, East Meadow | 3,825 | 14.7 | 9.7 |
| Southside Hospital, Bay Shore | 4,383 | 10.7 | 8.4 |
| St. Peter's Hospital, Albany | 4,916 | 10.9 | 8.9 |
| Lincoln Medical Mental Health Center, Bronx | 1,743 | 13.0 | 10.0 |
| North Shore University Hospital, Manhasset | 6,084 | 10.2 | 8.7 |
| Yonkers General Hospital, Yonkers | 2,884 | 9.2 | 7.4 |

|  | Patients | Actual Death Rate | Forecast Death Rate |
|---|---:|---:|---:|
| Bronx Municipal Hospital Center, Bronx | 4,256 | 12.2 | 7.9 |
| City Hospital Center at Elmhurst, Flushing | 3,451 | 16.7 | 14.1 |
| St. Joseph's Hospital Health Center, Syracuse | 5,499 | 10.3 | 8.8 |
| Little Falls Hospital, Little Falls | 1,563 | 8.6 | 6.2 |
| Ellis Hospital, Schenectady | 5,154 | 8.1 | 6.6 |
| House of the Good Samaritan, Watertown | 2,585 | 9.1 | 6.9 |
| Community Hospital at Glen Cove, Glen Cove | 3,145 | 10.1 | 8.0 |
| New Rochelle Hospital Medical Center, New Rochelle | 4,318 | 9.2 | 7.5 |
| Flushing Hospital and Medical Center, Flushing | 4,170 | 12.4 | 9.5 |
| Maimonides Medical Center, Brooklyn | 7,213 | 9.2 | 7.8 |
| Kings County Hospital Center, Brooklyn | 2,285 | 14.5 | 10.5 |
| Queens Hospital Center, Jamaica | 2,741 | 12.7 | 10.2 |
| Harlem Hospital Center, New York | 2,479 | 15.0 | 9.9 |
| Osteopathic Hospital, Flushing | 2,961 | 13.9 | 10.1 |
| Good Samaritan Hospital, West Islip | 4,759 | 10.6 | 9.2 |
| St. Vincent's Hospital & Medical Center, New York | 5,760 | 8.9 | 7.3 |
| Lake Shore Hospital, Irving | 697 | 10.8 | 6.8 |
| Parsons Hospital, Flushing | 1,549 | 13.8 | 9.0 |
| Smithtown General Hospital, Smithtown | 2,639 | 10.7 | 8.3 |
| Pelham Bay General Hospital, Bronx | 2,043 | 10.6 | 8.1 |
| St. Johns Episcopal Hospital, Garden City | 5,692 | 9.0 | 7.7 |
| Interfaith Medical Center, Brooklyn | 2,876 | 12.7 | 8.5 |
| **North Carolina** | | | |
| Forsyth Memorial Hospital, Winston-Salem | 8,988 | 7.5 | 6.3 |
| Granville Hospital, Oxford | 617 | 10.2 | 6.3 |
| Huntersville Hospital, Huntersville | 125 | 19.2 | 8.3 |
| **Ohio** | | | |
| Bethesda North Hospital, Cincinnati | 8,188 | 7.3 | 6.1 |
| **Oklahoma** | | | |
| Grand Valley Hospital, Pryor | 1,240 | 7.3 | 4.2 |
| South Community Hospital, Oklahoma City | 4,535 | 5.8 | 4.2 |
| **Pennsylvania** | | | |
| St. Agnes Medical Center, Philadelphia | 2,487 | 7.6 | 5.5 |
| Hahnemann University Hospital, Philadelphia | 4,662 | 5.8 | 4.5 |
| **Tennessee** | | | |
| Methodist Hospital–Central Unit, Memphis | 14,615 | 5.8 | 4.9 |
| Regional Medical Center at Memphis, Memphis | 1,578 | 11.1 | 8.2 |
| **Texas** | | | |
| Dallas County Hospital District, Dallas | 3,559 | 7.7 | 5.6 |
| R. E. Thomason General Hospital, El Paso | 720 | 10.0 | 6.4 |
| Southeast Baptist Hospital, San Antonio | 12,123 | 5.9 | 5.0 |
| Hermann Hospital, Houston | 4,647 | 6.5 | 4.8 |
| St. Mary Hospital, Port Arthur | 3,217 | 9.0 | 4.5 |
| Mesquite Physicians Hospital, Mesquite | 996 | 9.7 | 6.3 |
| Hopkins County Memorial Hospital, Sulphur Springs | 1,787 | 7.8 | 5.2 |
| Harris County Hospital District, Houston | 1,376 | 11.2 | 8.2 |
| Southwest Osteopathic Hospital, Amarillo | 566 | 10.1 | 5.8 |

|  | Patients | Actual Death Rate | Forecast Death Rate |
|---|---|---|---|
| **Virginia** | | | |
| St. Luke's Hospital, Richmond | 2,404 | 6.3 | 4.4 |
| King's Daughters' Hospital, Staunton | 2,396 | 7.6 | 5.4 |
| Riverside Hospital, Newport News | 4,868 | 7.0 | 5.3 |
| **Washington** | | | |
| Swedish Hospital Medical Center, Seattle | 8,778 | 5.3 | 4.0 |
| Shorewood Osteopathic Hospital, Seattle | 266 | 10.2 | 4.4 |
| **Wisconsin** | | | |
| St. Mary's Hospital, Milwaukee | 2,965 | 9.0 | 6.1 |
| Mount Sinai Medical Center, Milwaukee | 3,778 | 7.3 | 5.3 |
| St. Joseph's Hospital, Milwaukee | 5,605 | 8.8 | 7.3 |
| **Wyoming** | | | |
| Memorial Hospital of Natrona County, Casper | 1,891 | 7.0 | 4.5 |

MARCH 12

# Archives of Business: The Triangle Shirtwaist Fire

By TAMAR LEWIN

Seventy-five years ago this Tuesday, the Triangle Shirtwaist Company, east of Washington Square Park in New York City, went up in flames, killing 146 workers and sparking a nationwide crusade for safer working conditions.

The fire started just after 4:30 P.M., when the 500 young women who sewed the popular shirtwaist-style cotton blouses were getting ready to leave for the day. Fueled by scraps of material stored under the sewing machines, the flames spread in minutes from the 8th floor to engulf the 9th and 10th floors.

The panicked workers, mostly 16- to 23-year-old Italian and Jewish immigrants, rushed to escape, but the fire doors had been locked to keep them from leaving the building with stolen goods. And although the two elevator operators made 20 trips up and down, most of the young women were trapped.

Some scrambled to the sole fire escape. When it collapsed under their weight, they plunged to the pavement. When the elevators stopped running, dozens more workers, inside the building, jumped into the elevator shaft, trying to escape to safety by grabbing the cable.

Fire engines arrived quickly, but their ladders could not reach the ledges where the workers awaited rescue. Many of the women, their clothes and hair aflame, leaped from the building, crashing to their death on the sidewalk below. Their bodies soon littered the pavements. In a half hour, it was all over.

The Triangle fire, still thought to be the worst industrial tragedy in New York history, aroused the city's wrath—and, as word spread, that of horrified workers throughout the nation. It was a turning point in the early fight to eliminate tenement sweatshops and to upgrade workplace safety with fire drills, fire escapes and multiple staircases.

The two owners of the Triangle factory, Isaac Harris and Max Blanck, were indicted for manslaughter in mid-April 1911, under a New York State law providing that factory doors "shall be so constructed as to open outwardly, where practicable, and shall not be locked, bolted or fastened during working hours." But when the case went to trial, the jury acquitted the two "shirtwaist kings"—in part, say historians, because of the judge's narrow charge to the jury.

The lessons of the fire were not lost, though. In June 1911, the New York State Legislature created a Factory Investigating Commission, which sent inspectors into the tenements, factories and workshops of the time. Shocked by their reports, the commission passed 36 laws in three years, reforming everything from fire regulations to working hours for women and children.

"There are a lot of laws on the books now that weren't there 75 years ago for the workers at the Triangle company," said Larry Cary, president of the New York State Labor History Association. "But with the new growth of sweatshops among the illegal alien population, another Triangle fire is just waiting to happen."

And the issue of workplace safety, then and now, goes far beyond fire: Every day, workers at factories, construction sites, and even comfortable office buildings, are subjected to dangerous conditions, hazardous materials, and unhealthy practices, ranging from the simple trench cave-ins that killed scores of workers last year to the toxic substances that eventually cause cancer and debilitating diseases in thousands of workers.

Despite the 1970 creation of the Occupational Safety and Health Administration—and the passage of dozens of new laws and regulations on everything from mine safety to the labeling of hazardous substances—thousands of workers still die on the job every year, and millions more are injured. The National Safety Council estimates that on-the-job accidents cost the nation $34.6 billion in 1985.

Indeed, after several years of improvement, the problem seems to have worsened in the last two years. According to the Department of Labor's most recent data, workplace fatalities rose to 3,740 in 1984 from 3,100 in the previous year, while occupational injuries and illnesses climbed to 5.4 million from 4.85 million.

While some say the worsening statistics are due to the expanding economy—more workers on the job mean more injuries—other experts say that OSHA is at least partly to blame for those numbers. Since the Reagan Administration came into office, these critics say, OSHA enforcement has been sporadic at best, with full-scale inspections, until recently, only at plants whose accident rates are worse than average. The agency, which had 1,328 inspectors in the fiscal year 1980, was down to 1,086 in 1985. Over the same period, the number of inspections in response to complaints plummeted 46 percent, to 8,651. And the total penalties proposed dropped 44 percent, to $8.6 million.

Patrick Tyson, acting head of OSHA, defends the agency's record. "Overall, I think we are a very effective body," he said. "The total number of inspections hasn't gone down, and the inspections we are making are better targeted than ever before. The policy of only checking records at the safer plants is one that was suggested by career staff as a way of increasing our efficiency. As a practical matter, we place less emphasis on penalties."

OSHA has all but ceased referring safety violations to the Justice Department for criminal prosecution. In the last two years of the Carter Administration, a total of 15 cases were formally referred for criminal action; in the five years of the Reagan Administration, only 9 cases were referred. Mr. Tyson says the agency is simply trying to refer only those cases that can actually be won.

Local prosecutors, however, are pursuing more criminal cases in the occupational safety field than ever before. Some enforcement offices have even established special units to investigate criminal charges against companies—and in some cases, individual executives and managers—that carelessly endanger the lives of workers. MARCH 23

## The record by industry

Occupational injury and illness incidence rates per 100 full-time workers in 1984

|  |  |
|---|---|
| Lumber, Wood | 19.6 |
| Food | 16.7 |
| Fabricated Metals | 16.1 |
| Construction | 15.5 |
| Furniture, Fixtures | 15.3 |
| Rubber | 13.6 |
| Stone, Glass | 13.6 |
| Primary Metals | 13.3 |
| Agriculture | 12.0 |
| Non-electric Machinery | 10.7 |
| Manufacturing Average | 10.6 |
| Misc. Manufacturing | 10.5 |
| Leather Products | 10.5 |
| Paper | 10.4 |
| Mining | 9.7 |
| Transportation Equip. | 9.3 |
| Public Utilities | 8.8 |
| Textile Mills | 8.0 |
| Private Sector Average | 8.0 |
| Tobacco | 7.7 |
| Wholesale, Retail | 7.4 |
| Electric Equipment | 6.8 |
| Apparel | 6.7 |
| Printing | 6.5 |
| Instruments | 5.4 |
| Chemicals | 5.3 |
| Services | 5.2 |
| Petroleum | 5.1 |
| Finance, Insurance | 1.9 |

Source: Bureau of Labor Statistics

**MARCH 23**

## Congress: I'll Scratch Your PAC if You'll Scratch Mine

**By MARTIN TOLCHIN**

WASHINGTON, March 25—The dramatic growth of political action committees owes much to those who sought to fight fire with fire.

Known as PACs, these fund-raising vehicles were invented by organized labor in the 1930s, to the dismay of the business community, which then followed suit and outdid the unions in their ability to raise money and influence political campaigns.

The growing influence of both labor and business PACs on both the electoral and legislative processes has been a matter of concern to many members of Congress, some of whom have followed suit and created their own PACs in an effort to exert additional influence upon their colleagues. Congressional PACs contributed more than $9 million to the 1984 congressional campaigns, and Federal Election Commission officials say there are now at least 23 of them.

Critics contend that these congressional PACs, begun in the late 1970s and grown especially prosperous in recent years, are distorting the congressional process by making some legislators financially beholden to others and by extending the influence of PACs into hitherto sacrosanct cloakrooms, closed congressional caucuses and committee meetings and even onto the floor of the House and Senate.

**MARCH 26**

## The Committees and the Money

WASHINGTON, March 25—Following are major congressional political action committees and, unless otherwise specified, the amount they raised in 1984, the latest year for which figures are available from the Federal Elections Commission:

**13th C.D. Committee:** Representative Stephen J. Solarz, Democrat of Brooklyn, $68,588.
**24th Congressional District of California PAC:** Representative Henry A. Waxman, Democrat, $223,376.
**America's Small Business PAC:** Representative Andy Ireland, Republican of Florida, $14,308.
**California for America:** Senator Pete Wilson, Republican, $145,279.
**Campaign America:** Senator Bob Dole, Republican of Kansas, $1,272,817.
**Campaign for Prosperity:** Representative Jack F. Kemp, Republican of New York, $2,179,573.
**Chicago Campaign Committee:** Representative Dan Rostenkowski, Democrat of Illinois, $138,486.
**Citizens for a Competitive America:** Senator Ernest F. Hollings, Democrat of South Carolina, $53,367.
**Committee for a Democratic Consensus:** Senator Alan Cranston, Democrat of California, $112,546.
**Committee for a Progressive Congress:** Representative David R. Obey, Democrat of Wisconsin, $30,628 since 1985.
**Conservative Democratic PAC:** Representative Charles W. Stenholm, Democrat of Texas, $41,624.
**Democratic Candidate Fund:** The House Speaker, Thomas P. O'Neill, Jr., Democrat of Massachusetts, $117,654.
**Effective Government Committee:** Representative Richard A. Gephardt, Democrat of Missouri, $261,546 since 1985.
**Fund for a Democratic Majority:** Senator Edward M. Kennedy, Democrat of Massachusetts, $3,556,016.
**Fund for a Republican Majority:** Senator Ted Stevens, Republican of Alaska, $112,184.
**Fund for the Future Committee:** Senator John C. Danforth, Republican of Missouri, $141,419.
**House Leadership Fund:** Representative Thomas S. Foley, Democrat of Washington, $61,612.
**Independent Action:** Representative Morris K. Udall, Democrat of Arizona, $917,931.
**Majority Congress Committee:** Representative Jim Wright, Democrat of Texas, $332,264.
**National Council on Public Policy:** Senator John Glenn, Democrat of Ohio, $106,480.
**Salute America Committee:** Representative Vin Weber, Republican of Minnesota, $25,495 since 1985.
**The Democracy Fund:** Senator Paul Simon, Democrat of Illinois, $168,485 since 1985.
**Valley Education Fund:** Representative Tony Coelho, Democrat of California, $31,250.

MARCH 26

## Budget-Balancing Amendment Fails

On March 25 the Senate barely defeated a proposed constitutional amendment intended to require a balanced federal budget. The vote was 66 in favor and 34 opposed, one vote short of the two-thirds majority required to pass a constitutional amendment.

The result was a defeat for the Republican Senate leadership and for President Reagan, who sought the adoption of the amendment.

Senators of both parties said approval in December, 1985, of a statute designed to get the federal budget in balance—sponsored by Senators Phil Gramm of Texas and Warren B. Rudman of New Hampshire, both Republicans, and Ernest F. Hollings of South Carolina, a Democrat—reduced the pressure on Senators to vote for the constitutional amendment.

The roll-call vote follows:

### FOR AMENDMENT—66

#### Democrats—23

| | | |
|---|---|---|
| Bentsen, Tex. | Gore, Tenn. | Pell, R.I. |
| Bingaman, N.M. | Harkin, Iowa | Proxmire, Wis. |
| Boren, Okla. | Heflin, Ala. | Pryor, Ark. |
| Chiles, Fla. | Hollings, S.C. | Sasser, Tenn. |
| DeConcini, Ariz. | Johnston, La. | Simon, Ill. |
| Dixon, Ill. | Long, La. | Stennis, Miss. |
| Exon, Neb. | Melcher, Mont. | Zorinsky, Neb. |
| Ford, Ky. | Nunn, Ga. | |

#### Republicans—43

| | | |
|---|---|---|
| Abdnor, S.D. | Gramm, Tex. | Packwood, Ore. |
| Andrews, N.D. | Grassley, Iowa | |
| Armstrong, Colo. | Hatch, Utah | Pressler, S.D. |
| | Hawkins, Fla. | Quayle, Ind. |
| Boschwitz, Minn. | Hecht, Nev. | Roth, Del. |
| | Helms, N.C. | Rudman, N.H. |
| Cochran, Miss. | Humphrey, N.H. | Simpson, Wyo. |
| D'Amato, N.Y. | Kasten, Wis. | Specter, Pa. |
| Danforth, Mo. | Laxalt, Nev. | Stevens, Alaska |
| Denton, Ala. | Lugar, Ind. | |
| Dole, Kan. | Mattingly, Ga. | Symms, Idaho |
| Domenici, N.M. | McClure, Idaho | Thurmond, S.C. |
| Durenberger, Minn. | McConnell, Ky. | Trible, Va. |
| | Murkowski, Alaska | Wallop, Wyo. |
| East, N.C. | | Warner, Va. |
| Garn, Utah | Nickles, Okla. | Wilson, Calif. |
| Goldwater, Ariz. | | |

### AGAINST AMENDMENT—34

#### Democrats—24

| | | |
|---|---|---|
| Baucus, Mont. | Bradley, N.J. | Burdick, N.D. |
| Biden, Del. | Bumpers, Ark. | Byrd, W. Va. |

**AGAINST AMENDMENT—34**

**Democrats—24**

Cranston, Calif.
Dodd, Conn.
Eagleton, Mo.
Glenn, Ohio
Hart, Colo.
Inouye, Hawaii
Kennedy, Mass.
Kerry, Mass.

Lautenberg, N.J.
Leahy, Vt.
Levin, Mich.
Matsunaga, Hawaii
Metzenbaum, Ohio

Mitchell, Me.
Moynihan, N.Y.
Riegle, Mich.
Rockefeller, W. Va.
Sarbanes, Md.

**Republicans—10**

Chafee, R.I.
Cohen, Me.
Evans, Wash.
Gorton, Wash.

Hatfield, Ore.
Heinz, Pa.
Kassebaum, Kan.

Mathias, Md.
Stafford, Vt.
Weicker, Conn.

MARCH 26

## Seven Asteroids Are Named for Crew of the Space Shuttle

Seven recently discovered asteroids were named yesterday for the seven astronauts who died in the explosion of the space shuttle *Challenger*.

The asteroids, which were discovered by the Lowell Observatory in Flagstaff, Ariz., from 1980 to 1984, are believed to be from 5 to 10 miles in diameter.

The Central Bureau for Astronomical Telegrams of the International Astronomical Union yesterday notified observatories around the world of the new names. The bureau is at the Smithsonian Astrophysical Observatory in Cambridge, Mass.

According to Dr. Brian G. Marsden, its director, most of the seven asteroids are orbiting the sun in the asteroid belt between the orbits of Mars and Jupiter. But one, designated McAuliffe, is an Amor-type asteroid that comes well inside the orbit of Mars in its closest approaches to the sun.

The asteroid names that have been assigned are these:

No. 3350 for Francis R. Scobee, spacecraft commander.
No. 3351 for Comdr. Michael J. Smith of the Navy, pilot.
No. 3352 for S. Christa Corrigan McAuliffe, teacher-observer.
No. 3353 for Gregory B. Jarvis, payload specialist.
No. 3354 for Dr. Ronald E. McNair, physicist.
No. 3355 for Lieut. Col. Ellison S. Onizuka of the Air Force, mission specialist.
No. 3356 for Dr. Judith A. Resnik, mission specialist.

MARCH 27

## Figures in New York City Corruption Inquiries

Eight more people were indicted on charges of corruption last week as New York City and Federal investigators continued their inquiries into almost a dozen areas of municipal government.

Those areas include contracts between private debt-collection companies and the Parking Violations Bureau and other city agencies; the Taxi and Limousine Commission; the granting of franchises to cable television companies; the awarding of lucrative court appointments in Queens, and possible political corruption in the Bronx and Queens Democratic organizations.

The following people have been named thus far in indictments or in criminal complaints filed in court:

**Donald R. Manes**
*Former Queens Borough President and Queens Democratic Leader*
Named by United States Attorney for Manhattan as unindicted co-racketeer in charges involving bribery and extortion at the Parking Violations Bureau, and as a recipient of bribes paid by contractors for the agency. Named by Manhattan District Attorney as having corruptly used his influence to persuade the Board of Estimate to approve a $22.7-million contract to Citisource Inc. for a hand-held computer for traffic-ticketing agents. Committed suicide March 13.

**Stanley M. Friedman**
*Chairman, Executive committee of the Bronx Democratic County Committee; director, Citisource Inc.*
Indicted March 27 by a Manhattan grand jury on charges of conspiracy, securities fraud, grand larceny, forgery, tampering with public records, bribery and receiving bribes relating to the sale of stock in Citisource Inc. and its procurement of a city contract.

**Goeffrey G. Lindenauer**
*Former deputy director, Parking Violations Bureau*
Pleaded guilty March 10 to Federal charges of racketeering and mail fraud as part of an agreement with United States Attorney for Manhattan and Manhattan District Attorney to provide information and testify against others in Parking Violations Bureau bribery-extortion scandal and cases involving the granting of a city contract to Citisource Inc.

**Lester N. Shafran**
*Former director, Parking Violations Bureau*
Indicted March 26 by a Federal grand jury on charges of racketeering, racketeering conspiracy and mail fraud. Also charged with receiving bribes from System-

atic Recovery Services, a collection agency doing business with the Parking Violations Bureau.

**Michael J. Lazar**
*Real estate developer; former City Transportation Administrator*
Indicted March 26 by a Federal grand jury on charges of racketeering, racketeering conspiracy and mail fraud. Charges stem from the payment of bribes to Geoffrey G. Lindenauer, former director of the Parking Violations Bureau, to obtain contracts for Datacom Systems Corporation, for whom Mr. Lazar was a lawyer.

**Robert R. Richards**
*Former president, Citisource Inc.*
Indicted March 27 by a Manhattan grand jury on charges of conspiracy, securities fraud, grand larceny, forgery and tampering with public records in connection with the sale of stock in Citisource and procurement of its contract with the Parking Violations Bureau. Pleaded guilty to four counts of violations of business law, conspiracy and grand larceny. Cooperating with District Attorney's office.

**Marvin B. Kaplan**
*Chairman, Citisource Inc.*
Indicted March 27 by a Manhattan grand jury on charges of conspiracy, securities fraud, grand larceny, forgery, tampering with public records and bribery in connection with the sale of stock in Citisource and procurement of its city contract.

**Albert J. Kaplan**
*Director, Citisource Inc.*
Indicted March 27 by a Manhattan grand jury on charges of conspiracy, securities fraud, grand larceny, forgery, tampering with public records in connection with the sale of stock in Citisource and procurement of its city contract.

**Marvin H. Kushnick**
*Chief financial officer, Citisource Inc.*
Indicted March 27 by a Manhattan grand jury on charges of conspiracy, securities fraud, grand larceny, forgery and tampering with public records in connection with the sale of stock in Citisource and procurement of its city contract.

**E. Martin Solomon**
*Vice president, Citisource Inc.*
Indicted March 27 by a Manhattan grand jury with conspiracy, securities fraud, grand larceny, forgery and tampering with public records in connection with the sale of stock in Citisource and procurement of its city contract.

**Marvin Bergman**
*Lawyer; former law partner of Donald R. Manes*
Arrested March 26 by the United States Attorney for Manhattan on a criminal complaint of receiving bribes and splitting the proceeds with Donald R. Manes and Geoffrey G. Lindenauer to secure contracts from the Parking Violations Bureau for Aid Associates, a collection agency.

**Allen Scott**
*Vice president, Datacom Systems Corporation*
Arrested March 26 by the United States Attorney for Manhattan on a criminal complaint of extorting money from a private towing company in return for giving the towing company business relating to a contract Datacom held with the Parking Violations Bureau.

**Sheldon Chevlowe**
*Former New York City marshal*
Named by United States Attorney for Manhattan as unindicted co-racketeer and collector and transmitter of bribes in scheme involving Parking Violations Bureau. Died May 1983.

MARCH 30

## Wedlock and separation*

Americans were about twice as likely to marry as to divorce last year, according to new data from the National Center for Health Statistics. Compared with the previous year, the marriage rate had declined a bit, and the divorce rate had increased.

|      | Marriage rate** | Divorce rate** |
|------|-----------------|----------------|
| 1975 | 10.0            | 4.8            |
| 1976 | 9.9             | 5.0            |
| 1977 | 9.9             | 5.0            |
| 1978 | 10.3            | 5.1            |
| 1979 | 10.4            | 5.3            |
| 1980 | 10.6            | 5.2            |
| 1981 | 10.6            | 5.3            |
| 1982 | 10.6            | 5.0            |
| 1983 | 10.5**          | 4.9            |
| 1984 | 10.5**          | 4.9**          |
| 1985 | 10.2**          | 5.0**          |

*Number of marriages and divorces per 1,000 population
**Provisional data

MARCH 30

# South African Divestment Pressed; Leaders Aim to Widen College Drive

By GENE I. MAEROFF

BOSTON, April 4—College students observed a National Divestment Protest Day today, aimed at getting trustees to discontinue investments in South Africa, and their leaders are hoping the movement will be a springboard to involvement in other issues.

Today's protests, timed to coincide with the 18th anniversary of the assassination of the Rev. Dr. Martin Luther King, Jr., were part of a campaign that has become the biggest campus issue since the end of the Vietnam War.

Educators who saw student activism unfold in the 1960s think the circumstances were different and that the current protests are not likely to gather the same momentum. Among the many colleges that have not divested themselves, including seven of the eight Ivy League schools, are trustees who maintain that they can be more effective in helping blacks in South Africa by owning stock in companies that do business there.

But some students feel that the opposition to the racial separation policy of South Africa could be a first step toward building a movement to confront such concerns as American involvement in Central America, domestic race relations, environmental control and nuclear disarmament.

"Branching out to deal with other issues may mean losing the support of some students involved only because of their concern about South Africa, but to limit the movement to only one issue is to miss the point," said Scott Nova, a 20-year-old junior from Greenwich, Conn., who is active in the divestiture campaign at Dartmouth College.

Alyson Cole of Scarsdale, N.Y., a senior at Smith College who was involved in a sit-in over divestiture last month, agrees: "The reason why an issue like South Africa is winning support is because it is so blatant, but it is about imperialism and racism and that is what Central America is about, too."

Educators maintain that despite such efforts to widen the movement a repetition of the 1960s is unlikely because universities have experience in coping with protests, and students are compelled by the economy to think more about the future. Furthermore, the experts say there was an unusual confluence of events in the 1960s and the impact of the military draft in producing activism cannot be overlooked.

"I don't think apartheid will be the issue that triggers a bigger movement," said Alan E. Guskin, president of Antioch University in Ohio, who was a participant in the 1960s protests. "Students today are worried about their future, which they weren't in the 1960s, and that has a calming effect. Also, a lot of university administrators made errors in the 60s that they won't make again."

## Colleges That Have Got Rid of Stocks

According to the Africa Fund, an educational and humanitarian organization based in New York, the following colleges and universities have divested themselves since 1977 of all stocks in corporations doing business in South Africa.

**1986**
Bates College
Clark University
University of Minnesota Foundation
Roosevelt University
Seattle University

**1985**
Arizona State University
Barnard College
California State University, Northridge
Columbia University
Evergreen State College
Hartford Seminary

University of Iowa
Iowa State University
University of Louisville
University of Miami
University of Minnesota
Mount Holyoke College
State University of New York
State University of New York, Stonybrook Foundation
Ohio State University
University of Rhode Island Foundation
Rutgers University
Temple University
University of Vermont
Fairfield University
University of Kentucky
Sarah Lawrence College
Teacher's College, New York
Western Washington University

**1984**
Wayne State University
City University of New York

**1983**
Western Michigan University

**1982**
University of Maine

**1981**
Lutheran School of Theology

**1980**
Michigan State University

**1978**
Antioch College
Howard University
Ohio University
University of Wisconsin

**1977**
Hampshire College
University of Massachusetts

APRIL 5

# House Passes Bill Easing Controls on Sale of Guns

BY LINDA GREENHOUSE

WASHINGTON, April 10—The House of Representatives today approved a bill making it easier to buy, sell and transport firearms across state lines, but supporters of gun control succeeded in preserving the Federal ban on the interstate sale of pistols.

The dual actions came after an impassioned lobbying campaign, which continued until the end and enabled each side to claim a victory.

If the bill becomes law it will bring the first significant changes in Federal gun control since the Gun Control Act of 1968 was passed in the wake of the assassinations of the Rev. Dr. Martin Luther King, Jr., and Senator Robert F. Kennedy.

The bill would end that law's ban on interstate sales and transportation by individuals of rifles and shotguns, would diminish Federal record-keeping requirements on all guns for dealers and would allow owners to take unloaded firearms across state lines, accomplishing many of the objectives of the National Rifle Association.

In voting 233 to 184 to keep the existing ban on the sale of pistols across state lines, the House rejected a provision supported by the rifle association that would have permitted such sales if the gun dealer and the customer met face to face and if the sale met local requirements as to both the dealer's and the customer's place of residence. A bill passed by the Senate did include that provision.

APRIL 11

## House Roll Call on Guns

On April 10 the House voted, 286 to 136, to ease many restrictions on sales of guns imposed by the Gun Control Act of 1968. The key vote to do this was on an amendment proposed by Representative Harold Volkmer, Democrat of Missouri. One hundred twenty-eight Democrats and 158 Republicans voted for the Volkmer proposal and 118 Democrats and 18 Republicans voted against it. In the roll call below, in addition to "yes" and "no" votes, "xxx" indicates not voting and "present" indicates that the representative was in the House at the time of the voting but did not vote either yes or no. The roll call:

### ALABAMA
**Democrats**—Bevill, yes; Erdreich, yes; Flippo, yes; Nichols, xxx; Shelby, yes
**Republicans**—Callahan, yes; Dickinson, yes.

### ALASKA
**Republican**—Young, yes.

### ARIZONA
**Democrat**—Udall, yes.
**Republicans**—Kolbe, yes; McCain, yes; Rudd, yes; Stump, yes.

### ARKANSAS
**Democrats**—Alexander, yes; Anthony, yes; Robinson, yes.
**Republican**—Hammerschmidt, yes.

### CALIFORNIA
**Democrats**—Anderson, yes; Bates, no; Bellenson, no; Berman, no; Bosco, yes; Boxer, no; Brown, no; Burton, no; Coelho, yes; Dellums, no; Dixon, no; Dymally, no; Edwards, no; Fazio, no; Hawkins, no; Lantos, no; Lehman, yes; Levine, no; Martinez, no; Matsui, no; Miller, no; Mineta, no; Panetta, no; Roybal, no; Stark, no; Torres, no; Waxman, no.
**Republicans**—Badham, yes; Chappie, yes; Dannemeyer, yes; Dornan, yes; Dreier, yes; Fiedler, yes; Hunter, yes; Lagomarsino, yes; Lewis, yes; Lowery, yes; Lungren, yes; McCandless, yes; Moorhead, yes; Packard, yes; Pashayan, yes; Shumway, yes; Thomas, yes; Zschau, yes.

### COLORADO
**Democrats**—Schroeder, no; Wirth, yes.
**Republicans**—Brown, yes; Kramer, yes; Schaefer, yes; Strang, yes.

### CONNECTICUT
**Democrats**—Gejdenson, no; Kennelly, no; Morrison, no.
**Republicans**—Johnson, yes; McKinney, no; Rowland, yes.

### DELAWARE
**Democrat**—Carper, no.

### FLORIDA
**Democrats**—Bennett, no; Chappell, yes; Fascell, no; Fuqua, yes; Gibbons, no; Hutto, yes; Lehman, no; MacKay, yes; Mica, no; Nelson, yes; Pepper, no; Smith, no.
**Republicans**—Bilirakis, yes; Ireland, xxx; Lewis, yes; Mack, yes; McCollum, yes; Shaw, yes; Young, yes.

### GEORGIA
**Democrats**—Barnard, yes; Darden, yes; Fowler, yes; Hatcher, yes; Jenkins, yes; Ray, yes; Rowland, yes; Thomas, yes.
**Republicans**—Gingrich, yes; Swindall, yes.

### HAWAII
**Democrats**—Akaka, no; Heftel, xxx.

### IDAHO
**Democrat**—Stallings, yes.
**Republican**—Craig, yes.

### ILLINOIS
**Democrats**—Annunzio, no; Bruce, yes; Collins, no; Durbin, no; Evans, no; Gray, yes; Hayes, no, Lipinski, no; Price, yes; Rostenkowski, no; Russo, no; Savage, no; Yates, no.
**Republicans**—Crane, yes; Fawell, no; Grotberg, xxx; Hyde, yes; Madigan, yes; Martin, yes; Michael, yes; O'Brien, xxx; Porter, no.

### INDIANA
**Democrats**—Hamilton, yes; Jacobs, no; McCloskey, yes; Sharp, yes; Visciosky, no.
**Republicans**—Burton, yes; Coats, yes; Hiler, yes; Hillis, no; Myers, yes.

### IOWA
**Democrats**—Bedell, no; Smith, yes.
**Republicans**—Evans, yes; Leach, yes; Lightfoot, yes; Tauke, yes.

### KANSAS
**Democrats**—Glickman, yes; Slattery, yes.
**Republicans**—Meyers, yes; Roberts, yes; Whittaker, yes.

### KENTUCKY
**Democrats**—Hubbard, yes; Mazzoli, no; Natcher, yes; Perkins, yes.
**Republicans**—Hopkins, yes; Rogers, yes; Snyder, yes.

### LOUISIANA
**Democrats**—Boggs, xxx; Breaux, yes; Huckaby, yes; Long, yes; Roemer, yes; Tauzin, yes.
**Republicans**—Livingston, yes; Moore, yes.

### MAINE
**Republicans**—McKernan, yes; Snowe, yes.

### MARYLAND
**Democrats**—Barnes, no; Byron, yes; Dyson, yes; Hoyer, no; Mikulski, no; Mitchell, no.
**Republicans**—Bentley, yes; Holt, yes.

### MASSACHUSETTS
**Democrats**—Atkins, no; Boland, no; Donnelly, no; Early, no; Frank, no; Markey, no; Mavroules, no; Moakley, no; O'Neill, xxx (by tradition, the House Speaker seldom votes); Studds, no.
**Republican**—Conte, no.

### MICHIGAN
**Democrats**—Bonior, no; Carr, yes; Conyers, no; Crockett, no; Dingell, yes; Ford, yes; Hertel, no; Kildee, no; Levin, no; Traxler, yes; Wolpe, no.
**Republicans**—Broomfield, no; Davis, yes; Henry, no; Pursell, no; Schuette, yes; Siljander, yes; Vander Jagt, yes.

### MINNESOTA
**Democrats**—Oberstar, yes; Penny, yes; Sabo, no; Sikorski, yes; Vento, no.
**Republicans**—Frenzel, yes; Stangeland, yes; Weber, yes.

### MISSISSIPPI
**Democrats**—Dowdy, yes; Montgomery, yes; Whitten, yes.
**Republicans**—Franklin, yes; Lott, yes.

### MISSOURI
**Democrats**—Clay, no; Gephardt, xxx; Skelton, yes; Volkmer, yes; Wheat, no; Young, yes.
**Republicans**—Coleman, yes; Emerson, yes; Taylor, yes.

### MONTANA
**Democrat**—Williams, yes
**Republican**—Marlenee, yes.

### NEBRASKA
**Republicans**—Bereuter, yes; Daub, yes; Smith, yes.

### NEVADA
**Democrat**—Reid, yes.
**Republican**—Vucanovich, yes.

### NEW HAMPSHIRE
**Republicans**—Gregg, yes; Smith, yes.

### NEW JERSEY
**Democrats**—Dwyer, no; Florio, no; Guarini, no; Howard, no; Hughes, no; Rodino, no; Roe, no; Torricelli, no.
**Republicans**—Courter, yes; Gallo, yes; Rinaldo, no; Roukema, no; Saxton, yes; Smith, yes.

### NEW MEXICO
**Democrat**—Richardson, yes.
**Republicans**—Lujan, xxx; Skeen, yes.

### NEW YORK
**Democrats**—Ackerman, no; Addabbo, xxx; Biaggi, no; Downey, no; Garcia, no; LaFalce, no; Lundine, yes; Manton, no; McHugh, no; Mrazek, no; Nowak, no; Owens, no; Rangel, no; Scheuer, no; Schumer, no; Solarz, no; Stratton, no; Towns, no; Weiss, no.
**Republicans**—Boehlert, yes; Carney, yes; DioGuardi, no; Eckert, yes; Fish, yes; Gilman, yes; Green, no; Horton, yes; Kemp, yes; Lent, yes; Martin, yes; McGrath, yes; Molinari, yes; Solomon, yes; Wortley, yes.

### NORTH CAROLINA
**Democrats**—Hefner, yes; Jones, yes; Neal, yes; Rose, yes; Valentine, yes; Whitley, yes.
**Republicans**—Broyhill, yes; Cobey, yes; Coble, yes; Hendon, yes; McMillan, yes.

### NORTH DAKOTA
**Democrat**—Dorgan, yes.

### OHIO
**Democrats**—Applegate, yes; Eckart, yes; Feighan, no; Hall, no; Kaptur, no; Luken, yes; Oakar, no; Pease, yes; Seiberling, no; Stokes, xxx; Traficant, no.
**Republicans**—DeWine, yes; Gradison, no; Kasich, yes; Kindness, yes; Latta, yes; McEwen, yes; Miller, yes; Oxley, yes; Regula, yes; Wylie, no.

### OKLAHOMA
**Democrats**—English, yes; Jones, yes; McCurdy, yes; Synar, yes; Watkins, yes.
**Republican**—Edwards, yes.

### OREGON
**Democrats**—AuCoin, yes; Weaver, yes; Wyden, yes.
**Republicans**—D. Smith, yes; R. Smith, yes.

### PENNSYLVANIA
**Democrats**—Borski, no; Coyne, no; Edgar, no; Foglietta, no; Gaydos, yes; Gray, no; Kanjorski, yes;

Kolter, yes; Kostmayer, yes; Murphy, yes; Murtha, yes; Walgren, no; Yatron, yes.

**Republicans**—Clinger, yes; Coughlin, no; Gekas, yes; Goodling, yes; McDade, yes; Ridge, yes; Ritter, yes; Schulze, xxx; Shuster, yes; Walker, yes.

### RHODE ISLAND

**Democrat**—St Germain, no.
**Republican**—Schneider, no.

### SOUTH CAROLINA

**Democrats**—Derrick, yes; Spratt, yes; Tallon, yes.
**Republicans**—Campbell, yes; Hartnett, yes; Spence, yes.

### SOUTH DAKOTA

**Democrat**—Daschle, yes.

### TENNESSEE

**Democrats**—Boner, yes; Cooper, yes; Ford, yes; Gordon, yes; Jones, yes; Lloyd, yes.
**Republicans**—Duncan, yes; Quillen, yes; Sundquist, yes.

### TEXAS

**Democrats**—Andrews, yes; Brooks, yes; Bryant, yes; Bustamante, yes; Chapman, yes; Coleman, yes; de la Garza, yes; Frost, no; Gonzalez, no; R. Hall, yes; Leath, yes; Leland, no; Ortiz, yes; Pickle, yes; Stenholm, yes; Wilson, yes; Wright, no.
**Republicans**—Archer, yes; Armey, yes; Bartlett, yes; Barton, yes; Boulter, xxx; Combest, yes; DeLay, yes; Fields, yes; Loeffler, yes; Sweeney, yes.

### UTAH

**Republicans**—Hansen, yes; Monson, yes; Nielson, yes.

### VERMONT

**Republican**—Jeffords, yes.

### VIRGINIA

**Democrats**—Boucher, yes; Daniel, yes; Olin, yes; Sisisky, yes.
**Republicans**—Bateman, yes; Bliley, yes; Parris, yes; Slaughter, yes; Whitehurst, no; Wolf, yes.

### WASHINGTON

**Democrats**—Bonker, yes; Dicks, yes; Foley, yes; Lowry, no; Swift, yes.
**Republicans**—Chandler, yes; Miller, no; Morrison, yes.

### WEST VIRGINIA

**Democrats**—Mollohan, yes; Rahall, yes; Staggers, yes; Wise, yes.

### WISCONSIN

**Democrats**—Aspin, yes; Kastenmeier, no; Kleczka, yes; Moody, yes; Obey, yes.
**Republicans**—Gunderson, yes; Petri, yes; Roth, yes; Sensenbrenner, yes.

### WYOMING

**Republican**—Cheney, yes.

APRIL 10

# Annual Meetings: Surge of Social Issues

By BARNABY J. FEDER

The annual meeting season moves into full swing this week, and this year there is a surge in the number of shareholder-sponsored resolutions calling for social and political action.

There are 137 such motions this year, compared with 83 last year, according to estimates of the Council on Economic Priorities, a nonprofit, New York–based research organization that monitors corporate social policies.

Much of the activity centers on demands that companies either withdraw from South Africa or increase their opposition to that country's racially discriminatory apartheid system. This year, public pension funds are introducing a number of such motions, which have traditionally been sponsored by church groups.

"The major difference this year is the big presence of the pension funds pushing companies to sign the Sullivan Principles," said Steven Lydenberg, an official at the council, referring to guidelines on corporate behavior in South Africa devised by the Rev. Leon Sullivan of Philadelphia.

"The shareholder resolution is increasingly useful as a tool because a number of institutional investors are taking them seriously," said Timothy Smith, executive director of the Interfaith Center on Corporate Responsibility, an affiliate of the National Council of Churches that has coordinated church-sponsored resolutions.   APRIL 15

## Social issues up for vote
Various shareholder resolutions to be considered at upcoming annual meetings.*

| Resolution | Corporations Considering Adoption | Date of Annual Meeting |
|---|---|---|
| Withdraw from South Africa | American Home Products | April 28 |
| | Eastman Kodak | May 14 |
| | Exxon | May 15 |
| | I.B.M. | April 28 |
| | Mobil | May 8 |
| | Newmont Mining | May 6 |
| | Schlumberger | May 6 |
| | Timken | April 15 |
| Sign Sullivan Principles | Chicago Pneumatic Tool | May 13 |
| | Diamond Shamrock | April 17 |
| | Hughes Tool | April 23 |
| | Lubrizol | April 28 |
| | Pizza Inn | May 29 |
| | U.S. Steel | May 5 |
| | Wynn's International | April 23 |
| Halt loans to South Africa | BankAmerica | April 29 |
| | Chase Manhattan | April 15 |
| | Irving Bank | April 17 |
| | Manufacturers Hanover | April 18 |
| | J.P. Morgan | April 9 |
| Provide data or revise bank policies on third world debt | BankAmerica | April 29 |
| | Bankers Trust | April 15 |
| | Chemical Bank | April 22 |
| | Citicorp | April 15 |
| | NCNB | April 23 |
| Report on or halt operations of nuclear power plants and handling of nuclear waste | Carolina Power & Light | May 21 |
| | General Electric | April 23 |
| | Santa Fe–Southern Pacific | April 22 |
| | Union Electric | April 22 |
| Provide information about or set cutbacks in company's involvement in nation's space weapons program | Eastman Kodak | May 14 |
| | Ford | May 8 |
| | McDonnell Douglas | April 21 |
| | Raytheon | May 28 |
| | United Technologies | April 28 |

*As of April 1986

Source: Investor Responsibility Research Center

APRIL 15

## Trials of Reputed Mob Figures

All trials, unless otherwise noted, are being held in Federal District Court in Manhattan.

### Concluded

**Gambino Family**
Six reputed members of the Gambino crime family were convicted March 5 in a long trial that focused on an international car-theft ring. Two of the defendants were also found guilty of killing two people who had threatened to expose the ring. The reputed boss of the group, Paul Castellano, was the main defendant in the trial until his murder on Dec. 16.

**Matthew Ianniello**
Matthew (Matty the Horse) Ianniello, the reputed top "captain" in the Genovese crime family, was convicted with his business partner and seven associates on Dec. 30. The racketeering case concerned the skimming of more than $2 million from bars and restaurants secretly controlled by the Ianniello group.

**Gambino Family**
In State Supreme Court in Queens on March 25, Justice Ann B. Dufficy dismissed assault and robbery charges against John Gotti and a friend, Frank Colletta, a day after the complainant in the case, Romual Piecyk, testified he could not identify them as his assailants.

### Under way

**"Pizza Connection"**
A trial of 22 men involves charges that the defendants operated a major international Mafia drug ring. The ring is accused of using a network of pizzerias to conceal drug dealing and money laundering. The two main defendants are Gaetano Badalamenti, an admitted former chief of the Mafia in Sicily, and Salvatore Catalano, accused of being a leader of the Bonanno crime family in New York. The trial, which began with jury selection last Sept. 30, is expected to continue for several more months.

**Carmine Persico**
Mr. Persico, who is the reputed boss of the Colombo crime family, and eight others accused of being leaders, members and associates of his are charged with labor racketeering in the construction industry. The main racketeering charges include extortion, bribery and loan sharking. The trial began on Oct. 15 and could end in about a month or so.

**Matthew Ianniello**
Jury selection was completed and opening statements began yesterday in which Mr. Ianniello, Benjamin Cohen and several others are accused of racketeering, fraud and extortion involving private companies that collect garbage.

**John Gotti**
Jury selection continued yesterday in Federal court in Brooklyn in the racketeering trial of John Gotti, the reputed head of the Gambino family, and six others. The process is expected to continue the rest of the week. Bruce Cutler, Mr. Gotti's attorney, made a motion to postpone the case because of the publicity surrounding the case, especially publicity about the killing of Frank DeCicco, reputed to be Mr. Gotti's underboss. Judge Eugene H. Nickerson has not issued a ruling.

### Future

**Gambino Family**
Additional trials of reputed Gambino crime family members are expected soon in a series of related cases that began with the car-theft ring. The original racketeering indictment, which named Mr. Castellano and 20 others, included more than two dozen murders, extortion, jury tampering and mob control of the now-defunct Westchester Premier Theater. Judge Kevin Thomas Duffy divided the indictment into a series of trials.

**Mafia "Commission"**
Nine men charged with participating in a ruling "commission" of Mafia leaders are to go on trial for racketeering Sept. 8. Mr. Castellano was to be a defendant in that trial. The remaining defendants include the reputed bosses of the four other crime families in the metropolitan area.

**Anthony Salerno**
One of the reputed bosses, Anthony (Fat Tony) Salerno of the Genovese crime family, also faces trial with 14 men accused of being members and business associates of his group. The extensive charges include labor racketeering, construction bid-rigging, extortion, gambling and murder conspiracies. That indictment was filed last month, and the trial is not expected to begin until after the commission trial, which could go into next year.

**Phillip Rastelli**
On Wednesday, jury selection is expected to start before Judge Charles P. Sifton in the racketeering trial of Phillip Rastelli, the reputed boss of the Bonanno crime family, and 12 codefendants.

APRIL 15

# Awards for Heroism

On April 26 the Carnegie Hero Fund Commission honored 16 people from ten states and Canada who risked their lives to save others, including a 14-year-old Louisiana boy who swam through rapids to save a friend.

D. Robert Young of Forest Hill, La., at 14 the youngest of those honored by the commission founded by Andrew Carnegie in 1904, saved Velma Messer, a friend in a canoe that overturned in the Buffalo River near Saint Joe, Ark., on May 26, 1985.

Three of those honored died in their efforts. Either the heroes themselves or their next of kin were awarded a bronze medal and $2,500.

These were the others who were honored:

FLORES, Bertha, 30, of Calexico, Calif., an employee at a home for adolescent girls in Brawley, Calif., who helped two residents escape when fire broke out. She died while attempting to rescue her 5-month-old son, Victor, from the building. The infant also died.

GRAVES, Samuel M., Sr., 60, of Fairfield, Ala., who died after trying to save a child from a burning mobile home in Brighton, Ala., on Jan. 5, 1985.

PEPIN, Tomas R., 33, of New Britain, Conn., who died trying to save a woman from drowning in a stream near Matunuck, R.I., on Sept. 8, 1985. Both were carried by the current into the Atlantic Ocean. The woman survived.

PERSON, Edward F., 31, a farmer from Moultonboro, N.H., who helped a state police officer struggling with a prisoner over her gun. The prisoner escaped but later committed suicide.

BRAYBOY, Mary Elizabeth, 44, of Baton Rouge, La., who prevented an enraged office worker from shooting two co-workers in Carville, La., on March 29, 1984.

COCHRAN, Kerry E., 30, of Parkersburg, W.Va., who rescued a truck driver from his burning rig near Knightstown, Ind., on Feb. 20, 1985.

DUNCAN, Gloria, 27, of Fort St. James, British Columbia, who saved a woman from being stabbed to death along a rural road near Pinchi, British Columbia, on May 14, 1984.

GAIN, Kurt Lee, 18, of Seldovia, Alaska, who saved two boys from drowning in a lake in Anchorage, Alaska, on Sept. 8, 1984.

HARPER, Oscar E., 42, of Athens, Ga., who saved a 4-year-old neighbor boy from being shot to death by a man who had just killed the child's mother at their home on Sept. 7, 1985.

HOBAN, James L. 3d, 33, of Bear, Del., who saved a man from drowning in the Atlantic near Chincoteague, Va., on July 7, 1985.

JACKSON, Kenneth Levi, 30, of Cape Breton Island, Nova Scotia, who dove into the Georges River in Nova Scotia to save a woman from drowning.

PACHECO, Robert, 40, of Westport, Mass., who saved a man from being struck by a falling crane in Jersey City on Jan. 18, 1984.

SENA, Anthony T., 19, of San Bernardino, Calif., who tried to save a woman from being stabbed to death in the convenience store where he worked in San Bernardino on April 14, 1984. The woman later died.

WHOLEY, Neal T., 19, of West Hartford, Conn., who saved a 13-year-old girl from drowning in the Connecticut River near Rocky Hill, Conn., on June 28, 1985.

WOODHOUSE, John, 22, of Edmonton, Alberta, who rescued a man from a burning car in Edmonton on Feb. 3, 1985.

APRIL 27

# The Court, Capital Punishment and 'Death Qualified' Juries

By STUART TAYLOR

**W**ASHINGTON, May 11—The main thrust of the Supreme Court's constitutional rulings on the death penalty since 1972 has been to require special procedures to prevent the arbitrary, biased or erroneous imposition of the ultimate sanction. "Death is different," the Court said in 1976. Last week, however, the Court upheld another kind of special procedure unique to capital cases—one that, by screening out committed opponents of the death penalty, may produce juries more likely to vote for conviction. The decision was a major defeat for opponents of the penalty. It illustrates the tension between the aspirations of justices in the Court's moderate center to guard against unfairness and their increasingly dominant desire not to place undue burdens on states that want to execute vicious killers.

It was the capriciousness of the use of the punishment—against a small percentage of convicted murderers and rapists, not always in the most egregious cases—that led the Court to strike down all death penalty laws in 1972. Four years later, it upheld new state death penalty laws but only when they included special sentencing procedures with safeguards more elaborate than those required in any other kind of case.

Last week's decision, however, appeared to reflect the Court's reluctance to impose yet another procedural requirement on the 33 states in which juries play a role in capital sentencing, especially a requirement that several hundred death row inmates could argue had been violated in their cases.

The Court was rejecting one of the last remaining broad, systemic attacks on capital punishment at a time when 1,714 convicts were on death row, an all-time high. Some officials hope the decision will speed the pace of executions—there have been 6 so far this year and 56 since the Court's 1976 decisions.

MAY 11

## A death row logbook

| | Number of executions | Convict's race | | | Victim's race | |
|---|---|---|---|---|---|---|
| | | White | Black | Other | White | Black |
| 1977 | 1 | 1 | 0 | 0 | 1 | 0 |
| 1978 | 0 | 0 | 0 | 0 | 0 | 0 |
| 1979 | 2 | 2 | 0 | 0 | 2 | 0 |
| 1980 | 0 | 0 | 0 | 0 | 0 | 0 |
| 1981 | 1 | 1 | 0 | 0 | 4 | 0 |
| 1982 | 2 | 1 | 1 | 0 | 2 | 0 |
| 1983 | 5 | 4 | 1 | 0 | 5 | 1 |
| 1984 | 21 | 14 | 7 | 0 | 21 | 2 |
| 1985 | 18 | 9 | 7 | 2 | 20 | 9 |
| 1986 | 6 | 3 | 3 | 0 | 8 | 0 |
| Total | 56 | 35 | 19 | 2 | 63 | 12 |

MAY 11

# Academy of Sciences Picks Members

## Academy of Sciences Picks Members

WASHINGTON, May 11—The National Academy of Sciences, the private organization of scientists and engineers who act as official advisers to the Federal Government on matters of science and technology, has elected new members.

Following is a list of the new members, with their affiliations at the time of their nominations:

AURBACH, Gerald D., chief of metabolic diseases, National Institutes of Health, Bethesda, Md.

AXELROD, Robert, professor of political science and public policy, Berkeley.

BIZZI, Emilio, professor of brain sciences and human behavior, Massachusetts Institute of Technology, Cambridge.

BROWN, Walter Lyons, head of department of radiation physics research, A.T.&T. Bell Laboratories, Murray Hill, N.J.

CARBON, John, professor of biochemistry, department of biological science, University of California, Santa Barbara.

CHAMBERLIN, Michael J., professor of biochemistry, University of California, Berkeley.

COE, Michael D., professor of anthropology, Yale University, and curator of anthropology, Peabody Museum of Natural History, New Haven, Conn.

DANISHEFSKY, Samuel, professor of chemistry, Yale University.

DAUGHADAY, William H., professor of medicine, Washington University School of Medicine, St. Louis, Mo.

DERVAN, Peter B., professor of chemistry, California Institute of Technology, Pasadena.

DE VAUCOVLEURS, Gerard H., professor of astronomy, University of Texas, Austin.

DUESBERG, Peter H., professor, department of molecular biology, University of California, Berkeley.

EFRON, Bradley, professor, department of statistics, Stanford University, Stanford, Calif.

EHRLICH, Gert, professor of metallurgy and research professor, Coordinated Science Laboratory, University of Illinois, Urbana.

ENGLESBERG, Ellis, professor of microbiology, University of California, Santa Barbara.

FRAKE, Charles O., professor, department of anthropology, Stanford University.

GELLERT, Martin F., chief, section on metabolic enzymes, laboratory of molecular biology, National Institute of Arthritis, Diabetes, Digestive, and Kidney Diseases, National Institutes of Health.

GOLDBERGER, Arthur S., professor of economics, University of Wisconsin, Madison.

GOODMAN, Major M., professor, crop science, statistics, genetics and botany, North Carolina State University, Raleigh.

GROSS, David J., professor of physics, Princeton University, Massachusetts Institute of Technology.

HELLWARTH, Robert W., George Pfleger Professor of Electrical Engineering and professor of physics, University of Southern California, Los Angeles.

HERSKOWITZ, Ira, professor and vice chairman, department of biochemistry and biophysics, School of Medicine, University of California, San Francisco.

HILLE, Bertil, professor of physiology and biophysics, School of Medicine, University of Washington, Seattle.

JACKSON, Marion L., Franklin Hiram King Professor of Soil Science, University of Wisconsin, Madison.

KAN, Yuet Wai, professor, department of medicine, laboratory medicine, and biochemistry and biophysics, University of California, San Francisco.

KAUFMAN, Seymour, chief, laboratory of neurochemistry, National Institute of Mental Health, Bethesda.

KIEFFER, Susan W., geologist, United States Geological Survey, Flagstaff, Ariz.

KLEPPNER, Daniel, professor of physics, Massachusetts Institute of Technology.

KNOBIL, Ernst, H. Wayne Hightower Professor of the Medical Sciences and director, laboratory for neuroendocrinology, University of Texas Medical School, Houston.

LERMAN, Leonard S., director of diagnostics, Genetics Institute, Cambridge, Mass.

LETSINGER, Robert L., professor of chemistry, Northwestern University, Evanston, Ill.

LLINAS, Rodolfo, professor and chairman, department of physiology and biophysics, New York University School of Medicine, New York City.

MAJERUS, Philip W., professor of medicine and biochemistry, Washington University, School of Medicine.

MATTHEWS, Brian W., professor of physics, University of Oregon, Eugene.

McDONALD, Frank B., chief scientist, NASA headquarters, Washington.

MICHL, Josef, professor of chemistry, University of Utah, Salt Lake City.

MOLL, John L., director of integrated circuit structures research, the Hewlett-Packard Corporation, Palo Alto, Calif.

MOORE, C. Bradley, professor of chemistry, University of California, Berkeley.

MUSGRAVE, Richard A., adjunct professor of economics, University of California, Santa Cruz.
OGREN, William L., research leader, photosynthesis research unit, University of Illinois, Urbana.
PAINE, Robert T., professor of zoology, University of Washington, Seattle.
PENMAN, Sheldon, professor of biology, Massachusetts Institute of Technology.
RICHARDSON, Robert C., professor of physics, Cornell University, Ithaca, N.Y.
RUSSELL, Liane B., section head, mammalian genetics and teratology, biology division, Oak Ridge National Laboratory, Oak Ridge, Tenn.
RYAN, Clarence A., Jr., professor of chemistry, Washington State University, Pullman.
SCHRAMM, David N., professor, astronomy and astrophysics center, University of Chicago.
SEED, H. Bolton, professor of civil engineering, University of California, Berkeley.
SIBLEY, Charles G., William Robertson Coe Professor of Ornithology, Yale University.
SMITH, Joseph V., Louis Block Professor of Physical Sciences, University of Chicago.
SOLOVAY, Robert M., professor, department of mathematics, University of California, Berkeley.
STERNBERG, Shlomo Z., professor, department of mathematics, Harvard University.
TODARO, George J., scientific director, Oncogen, Seattle.
TURCOTTE, Donald L., department of geological sciences, Cornell University.
UHLENBECK, Karen K., professor, department of mathematics, University of Chicago.
UNGER, Roger H., professor of internal medicine, University of Texas Southwestern Medical School, Dallas.
WALLACH, Hans, professor emeritus of psychology, Swarthmore College, Swarthmore, Pa.
WANG, James C., professor, department of biochemistry and microbiology, Harvard University.
WEINTRAUB, Harold M., member, department of genetics, Fred Hutchinson Cancer Research Center, Seattle, Wash.

In addition, the academy announced the election of 15 distinguished scientists from 9 countries as foreign associates of the academy. Their election brings the total of academy foreign associates to 238.

Foreign associates are nonvoting members with citizenship outside the United States. Members and foreign associates are elected in recognition of their distinguished and continuing achievements in original research.

Following are the newly elected foreign associates:
CHARPAK, Georges, senior scientist, CERN, Geneva (France).
CLARK, J. Desmond, professor of anthropology, University of California, Berkeley (Britain).
FENG, T. P., professor and director, Institute of Physiology, Academia Sinica, Shanghai.
GEHRING, Walter J., professor, department of cell biology, Biozentrum, University of Basel, Switzerland.
HIRZENBRUCH, Friedrich, professor, University of Bonn, West Germany.
HSU, Kenneth Jinghua, professor of geology, Swiss Federal Institute of Technology, Zurich.
HUMPHREY, John Herbert, professor of immunology, Royal Postgraduate Medical School, London, United Kingdom.
IVERSON, Leslie L., director, Neuroscience Research Centre, Merck Sharp and Dohme Research Laboratories, Harlow, Essex, Britain.
KORNBERG, Hans Leo, Sir William Dunn Professor of Biochemistry, University of Cambridge, Britain.
MUTT, Viktor, professor of biochemistry, Karolinska Institute, Stockholm, Sweden.
POPPER, Karl Raimund, Sr., Fellow of the Royal Society, London.
REIG, Osvaldo A., professor, University of Buenos Aires.
SEATON, Michael J., professor, University College, London.
TONEGAWA, Susumu, professor, Center for Cancer Research and department of biology, Massachusetts Institute of Technology, Massachusetts Institute of Technology, Cambridge (Japan).
VAN MONTAGU, Marc C. E., associate professor in genetics and codirector, laboratory of genetics, State University of Ghent, Belgium; professor and director, laboratory for genetical virology, Free University, Brussels.

MAY 12

# Winners of the Medal of Freedom, the nation's highest civilian award, presented by President Reagan in Washington on May 12

Walter H. Annenberg, former ambassador to Great Britain and former publisher of *The Philadelphia Inquirer*, *The Daily Racing Form*, *TV Guide* and *Seventeen*.
Earl Blaik, head coach of the Army football team from 1941 to 1958.
Senator Barry Goldwater, the conservative Republican from Arizona, who was his party's 1964 candidate for president and is ending a 30-year

career in the Senate this year.

Helen Hayes, the actress.

General Matthew B. Ridgway, former supreme Allied commander in Europe and Army Chief of Staff.

Vermont Royster, retired editor and columnist of *The Wall Street Journal.*

Dr. Albert B. Sabin, developer of the oral polio vaccine.

MAY 13

# 1987 Budget Plan with Military Cut Approved in House

**By JONATHAN FUERBRINGER**

WASHINGTON, May 15—The House of Representatives today approved a 1987 budget plan that sets up a confrontation with President Reagan and the Senate over military spending.

The House plan, like the one approved by the Senate, also collides with the President's opposition to sizable revenue increases.

The House plan was approved on a party-line vote of 245 to 179, despite a last-minute plea by Mr. Reagan against the military cut it proposed, which he called "a breach of faith with our common duty to protect this nation." Only 17 Republicans voted yes, and 19 Democrats voted no. The Republican-controlled Senate gave overwhelming bipartisan approval to its plan two weeks ago.

The House plan sets spending at $994.3 billion and reduces the deficit to $137.1 billion in the fiscal year 1987, which starts Oct. 1. That figure is $7 billion below the Senate's $144 billion deficit, the ceiling set by the new budget-balancing law.

The plan reduces the military budget below this year's level, cutting the President's proposal by $35 billion, $16 billion more than the Senate cut. But both chambers' plans include $13.2 billion in new revenues, $7.3 billion more than the President proposed. Neither plan specifies how the revenue would be raised, but some form of tax increase is considered likely. Mr. Reagan would raise revenue through measures that he does not consider tax increases.

The House cuts in domestic programs of $7.65 billion are almost $3 billion less than the Senate and almost $15 billion less than the President sought.

The vote in the House ends the first chapter of the budget process under the new budget-balancing law, which threatens automatic spending cuts if Congress and the White House do not act to reduce the deficit to specified annual ceilings.

The House and the Senate now go to conference to try to work out their differences on the military budget, on which House leaders say they are willing to move toward the Senate's higher figure, and on domestic spending cuts, where the differences are more over what is cut, not how much.

While revenue increases in the two chambers' plans are the same, House leaders want presidential support before raising $4.7 billion of the $13.2 billion.

MAY 16

## House Roll Call Approving $994 Billion Budget

On May 15 the House voted 245 to 179 to approve a budget of $994 billion for the fiscal year beginning Oct. 1. Two hundred twenty-eight Democrats and 17 Republicans voted yes to approve the measure, and 19 Democrats and 160 republicans voted no. There is one vacancy in the 435-member House. An "xxx" indicates that a representative did not vote. The roll call:

### ALABAMA

**Democrats**—Bevill, yes; Erdreich, yes; Flippo, yes; Nichols, yes; Shelby, yes.

**Republicans**—Callahan, no; Dickinson, no.

### ALASKA

**Republican**—Young, no.

### ARIZONA
**Democrat**—Udall, yes.
**Republicans**—Kolbe, no; McCain, no; Rudd, no; Stump, no.

### ARKANSAS
**Democrats**—Alexander, yes; Anthony, yes; Robinson, yes.
**Republican**—Hammerschmidt, no.

### CALIFORNIA
**Democrats**—Anderson, yes; Bates, yes; Bellenson, yes; Berman, yes; Bosco, yes; Boxer, yes; Brown, yes; Burton, yes; Coelho, yes; Dellums, yes; Dixon, yes; Dymally, yes; Edwards, yes; Fazio, yes; Hawkins, yes; Lantos, yes; Lehman, yes; Levine, yes; Martinez, yes; Matsui, yes; Miller, yes; Mineta, yes; Panetta, yes; Roybal, yes; Stark, no; Torres, yes; Waxman, yes.
**Republicans**—Badham, no; Chapple, no; Dannemeyer, no; Dornan, no; Dreler, no; Fiedler, no; Hunter, no; Lagomarsino, no; Lewis, no; Lowery, no; Lungren, no; McCandless, no; Moorhead, no; Packard, no; Pashayan, no; Shumway, no; Thomas, no; Zschau, no.

### COLORADO
**Democrats**—Schroeder, yes; Wirth, no.
**Republicans**—Brown, no; Kramer, no; Schaefer, no; Strang, no.

### CONNECTICUT
**Democrats**—Gejdenson, yes; Kennelly, yes; Morrison, yes.
**Republicans**—Johnson, no; McKinney, yes; Rowland, no.

### DELAWARE
**Democrat**—Carper, yes.

### FLORIDA
**Democrats**—Bennett, no; Chappell, yes; Fascell, yes; Fuqua, yes; Gibbons, yes; Hutto, no; Lehman, yes; MacKay, yes; Mica, yes; Nelson, yes; Pepper, yes; Smith, yes.
**Republicans**—Bilirakis, no; Ireland, no; Lewis, no; Mack, no; McCollum, no; Shaw, no; Young, no.

### GEORGIA
**Democrats**—Barnard, yes; Darden, yes; Fowler, yes; Hatcher, yes; Jenkins, yes; Ray, yes; Rowland, yes; Thomas, yes.
**Republicans**—Gingrich, no; Swindall, no.

### HAWAII
**Democrats**—Akaka, yes; Heftel, xxx.

### IDAHO
**Democrat**—Stallings, no.
**Republican**—Craig, no.

### ILLINOIS
**Democrats**—Annunzio, yes; Bruce, yes; Collins, yes; Durbin, yes; Evans, yes; Gray, yes; Hayes, yes; Lipinski, yes; Price, yes; Rostenkowski, yes; Russo, yes; Savage, yes; Yates, no.
**Republicans**—Crane, no; Fawell, no; Grotberg, xxx; Hyde, no; Madigan, no; Martin, no; Michel, no; O'Brien, yes; Porter, no.

### INDIANA
**Democrats**—Hamilton, yes; Jacobs, yes; McCloskey, no; Sharp, yes; Visclosky, yes.
**Republicans**—Burton, no; Coats, no; Hiller, no; Hillis, no; Myers, no.

### IOWA
**Democrats**—Bedell, yes; Smith, yes.
**Republicans**—Evans, no; Leach, no; Lightfoot, no; Tauke, no.

### KANSAS
**Democrats**—Glickman, yes; Slattery, yes.
**Republicans**—Meyers, no; Roberts, no; Whittaker, no.

### KENTUCKY
**Democrats**—Hubbard, yes; Mazzoll, yes; Natcher, yes; Perkins, yes.
**Republicans**—Hopkins, no; Rogers, no; Snyder, no.

### LOUISIANA
**Democrats**—Boggs, yes; Breaux, yes; Huckaby, yes; Long, yes; Roemer, yes; Tauzin, yes.
**Republicans**—Livingston, no; Moore, no.

### MAINE
**Republicans**—McKernan, no; Snowe, no.

### MARYLAND
**Democrats**—Barnes, yes; Byron, no; Dyson, no; Hoyer, yes; Mikulski, yes; Mitchell, yes.
**Republicans**—Bentley, no; Holt, no.

### MASSACHUSETTS
**Democrats**—Atkins, yes; Boland, yes; Donnelly, yes; Early, yes; Frank, yes; Markey, yes; Mavroules, yes; Moakley, yes; O'Neill, xxx; Studds, yes.
**Republican**—Conte, yes.

### MICHIGAN
**Democrats**—Bonior, yes; Carr, no; Conyers, yes;

Crockett, yes; Dingell, yes; Ford, yes; Hertel, yes; Kildee, yes; Levin, yes; Traxler, yes; Wolpe, yes.

**Republicans**—Broomfield, no; Davis, yes; Henry, no; Pursell, no; Schuette, no; Siljander, no; Vander Jagt, no.

### MINNESOTA

**Democrats**—Oberstar, yes; Penny, yes; Sabo, yes; Sikorski, yes; Vento, yes.

**Republicans**—Frenzel, no; Stangeland, yes; Weber, yes.

### MISSISSIPPI

**Democrats**—Dowdy, yes; Montgomery, yes; Whitten, yes.

**Republicans**—Franklin, xxx; Lott, no.

### MISSOURI

**Democrats**—Clay, yes; Gephardt, yes; Skelton, yes; Volkmer, yes; Wheat, yes; Young, yes.

**Republicans**—Coleman, no; Emerson, no; Taylor, no.

### MONTANA

**Democrat**—Williams, yes.
**Republican**—Marlenee, no.

### NEBRASKA

**Republicans**—Bereuter, yes; Daub, no; Smith, no.

### NEVADA

**Democrat**—Reid, no.
**Republican**—Vucanovich, no.

### NEW HAMPSHIRE

**Republicans**—Gregg, no; Smith, no.

### NEW JERSEY

**Democrats**—Dwyer, yes; Florio, yes; Guarini, yes; Howard, yes; Hughes, yes; Rodino, yes; Roe, yes; Torricelli, yes.

**Republicans**—Courter, no; Gallo, no; Rinaldo, yes; Roukema, no; Saxton, no; Smith, yes.

### NEW MEXICO

**Democrat**—Richardson, yes.
**Republicans**—Lujan, xxx; Skeen, no.

### NEW YORK

**Democrats**—Ackerman, yes; Biaggi, xxx; Downey, yes; Garcia, yes; LaFalce, yes; Lundine, yes; Manton, yes; McHugh, yes; Mrazek, no; Nowak, yes; Owens, yes; Rangel, yes; Scheuer, xxx; Schumer, yes; Solarz, no; Stratton, yes; Towns, yes; Weiss, yes.

**Republicans**—Boehlert, no; Carney, no; DioGuardi, no; Eckert, no; Fish, no; Gilman, yes; Green, no; Horton, yes; Kemp, no; Lent, no; Martin, no; McGrath, no; Molinari, no; Solomon, no; Wortley, no.

### NORTH CAROLINA

**Democrats**—Hefner, yes; Jones, yes; Neal, yes; Rose, yes; Valentine, yes; Whitley, yes.

**Republicans**—Broyhill, no; Cobey, no; Coble, no; Hendon, xxx; McMillan, no.

### NORTH DAKOTA

**Democrat**—Dorgan, yes.

### OHIO

**Democrats**—Applegate, yes; Eckart, yes; Feighan, yes; Hall, yes; Kaptur, yes; Luken, yes; Oakar, yes; Pease, yes; Seiberling, yes; Stokes, yes; Traficant, yes.

**Republicans**—DeWine, no; Gradison, no; Kasich, no; Kindness, no; Latta, no; McEwen, no; Miller, no; Oxley, no; Regula, no; Wylie, no.

### OKLAHOMA

**Democrats**—English, no; Jones, yes; McCurdy, no; Synar, yes; Watkins, yes.

**Republican**—Edwards, no.

### OREGON

**Democrats**—AuCoin, yes; Weaver, yes; Wyden, yes.

**Republicans**—D. Smith, no; R. Smith, no.

### PENNSYLVANIA

**Democrats**—Borski, yes; Coyne, yes; Edgar, yes; Foglietta, yes; Gaydos, yes; Gray, yes; Kanjorski, yes; Kolter, yes; Kostmayer, yes; Murphy, yes; Murtha, yes; Walgren, yes; Yatron, yes.

**Republicans**—Clinger, no; Coughlin, yes; Gekas, no; Goodling, xxx; McDade, no; Ridge, no; Ritter, no; Schulze, no; Shuster, no; Walker, no.

### RHODE ISLAND

**Democrat**—St Germain, yes.
**Republican**—Schneider, yes.

### SOUTH CAROLINA

**Democrats**—Derrick, yes; Spratt, yes; Tallon, yes.
**Republicans**—Campbell, no; Hartnett, no; Spence, no.

### SOUTH DAKOTA

**Democrat**—Daschle, yes.

### TENNESSEE

**Democrats**—Boner, no; Cooper, yes; Ford, yes; Gordon, yes; Jones, yes; Lloyd, no.

**Republicans**—Duncan, no; Quillen, no; Sundquist, no.

### TEXAS

**Democrats**—Andrews, yes; Brooks, yes; Bryant, yes; Bustamante, yes; Chapman, yes; Coleman, no; de la Garza, yes; Frost, yes; Gonzalez, yes; Hall, no; Leath, yes; Leland, yes; Ortiz, yes; Pickle, yes; Stenholm, yes; Wilson, yes; Wright, yes.

**Republicans**—Archer, no; Armey, no; Bartlett, no; Barton, no; Boulter, no; Combest, no; DeLav, no; Fields, no; Loeffler, no; Sweeney, no.

### UTAH

**Republicans**—Hansen, no; Monson, no; Nielson, no.

### VERMONT

**Republican**—Jeffords, yes.

### VIRGINIA

**Democrats**—Boucher, yes; Daniel, yes; Olin, yes; Sisisky, yes.

**Republicans**—Bateman, no; Bliley, yes; Parris, no; Slaughter, no; Whitehurst, no; Wolf, no.

### WASHINGTON

**Democrats**—Bonker, yes; Dicks, yes; Foley, yes; Lowry, yes; Swift, xxx.

**Republicans**—Chandler, no; Miller, yes; Morrison, yes.

### WEST VIRGINIA

**Democrats**—Mollohan, yes; Rahall, yes; Staggers, yes; Wise, yes.

### WISCONSIN

**Democrats**—Aspin, yes; Kastenmeier, yes; Kleczka, yes; Moody, yes; Obey, yes.

**Republicans**—Gunderson, no; Petri, no; Roth, no; Sensenbrenner, no.

### WYOMING

**Republican**—Cheney, no.

MAY 16

# Management Cited as Key to Safety at U.S. Nuclear Reactors

By STUART DIAMOND

WASHINGTON, May 22—Members of the Nuclear Regulatory Commission today listed the best and worst nuclear power plants in the United States and said the differences were mainly a result of management, not equipment or design.

Their comments, at a congressional hearing on nuclear safety, follow concern both in Congress and the agency about hundreds of continuing problems at American nuclear plants involving safety system failures spurred by errors in operation, maintenance and management. The problems have taken on added significance since the Chernobyl reactor disaster in the Soviet Union, many nuclear experts say.

The five members of the commission said it was too early to make detailed comparisons between American plants and the Chernobyl reactor.

In response to questions by Representative Edward J. Markey, Democrat of Massachusetts, who ran the hearing, the commissioners listed 32 reactors at 19 plants.

"Management is the fundamental aspect of safety," said James K. Asselstine, a member of the commission. "There is a wide diversity in management performance among the plants and we don't regulate management very well."

## Best and Worst Nuclear Power Plants in the U.S.

**Best—15**

Duke Power Company, William McGuire 1 and 2 in Cornelius, N.C.
Duke Power Company, Oconee 1, 2 and 3 in Seneca, S.C.
Duke Power Company, Catawba 1 in Clover, S.C.
Northeast Utilities, Millstone 1, 2 and 3 in Waterford, Conn.
Alabama Power Company, Joseph M. Farley 1 and 2, Houston County, Ala.
Northern States Power Company, Monticello in Monticello, Minn.
Northern States Power Company, Prairie Island 1 and 2 in Red Wing, Minn.
Wisconsin Electric Power Company, Kewaunee, Carlton Township, Wis.

**Worst—17**

Tennessee Valley Authority, Sequoyah 1 and 2, Daisy, Tenn.
Tennessee Valley Authority, Browns Ferry 1, 2 and 3 in Decatur, Ala.
Sacramento Municipal Utility District, Rancho Seco, Clay Station, Calif.
Public Service Company of Colorado, Fort St. Vrain, Platteville, Colo.
Boston Edison Company, Pilgrim 1, Plymouth, Mass.
Indiana and Michigan Electric Company, Donald C. Cook 1 and 2, Bridgman, Mich.
Commonwealth Edison Company, LaSalle 1 and 2, Seneca, Ill.
Florida Power and Light Company, Turkey Point 3 and 4, Turkey Point, Fla.
Toledo Edison Company, Davis-Besse 1, Oak Harbor, Ohio
Detroit Edison Company, Fermi 2, Lagoona Beach, Mich.
Jersey Central Power and Light Company, Oyster Creek, Lacey Township, N.J.

MAY 23

# How Chernobyl Alters the Nuclear Equation

By STUART DIAMOND

The Soviet nuclear plant disaster at Chernobyl is casting a deepening shadow over reactors in the United States. Already, politicians and critics concerned about the ability to evacuate people in a major accident are taking steps to delay the operation of some of the 15 nuclear plants that are complete or nearly complete but not yet licensed for full power. Those plants, whose total investment is about $50 billion, include Shoreham on Long Island, Seabrook in New Hampshire and Commanche Peak in Texas.

Many experts insist that American reactors have more safety features than Soviet units.

## Hanging in the balance
U.S. nuclear plants proposed for operation soon

| Plant | Location | Utility | Percent completed | Full-power operation date |
|---|---|---|---|---|
| Beaver Valley 2 | Shippingport, Pa. | Duquesne Light | 94 | Late 1987 |
| Braidwood 1 | Braidwood, Ill. | Commonwealth Edison | 95 | May 1987 |
| Byron 2 | Byron, Ill. | Commonwealth Edison | 93 | May 1987 |
| Clinton 1 | Clinton, Ill. | Illinois Power | 100 | Nov. 1986 |
| Commanche Peak | Somervell County, Texas | Texas Utilities | 99 | Uncertain |
| Hope Creek 1 | Lower Alloways Township, N.J. | Public Service Electric and Gas | 100 | Dec. 1986 |
| Nine Mile 2 | Scriba, N.Y. | Niagara Mohawk | 98 | Spring 1987 |
| Palo Verde 3 | Wintersburg, Ariz. | Arizona Public Service | 99 | Fall 1987 |
| Perry 1 | North Perry, Ohio | Cleveland Electric | 100 | July 1986 |
| Seabrook 1 | Seabrook, N.H. | Public Service/N.H. | 99 | Uncertain |
| Shearon Harris 1 | New Hill, N.C. | Carolina Power and Light | 96 | Dec. 1986 |
| Shoreham | Shoreham, N.Y. | Long Island Lighting | 100 | Uncertain |
| South Texas 1 | Matagorda County, Texas | Houston Lighting and Power | 90 | Dec. 1987 |
| Vogtle 1 | Waynesboro, Ga. | Georgia Power | 94 | June 1987 |
| Watts Bar 1 | Spring City, Tenn. | Tennessee Valley Authority | 100 | Uncertain |

Sources: Individual utilities

MAY 25

These include an airtight structure to contain steam pressure and radiation, and multiple emergency cooling systems. But information brought to light last week challenges some of that reasoning. The Soviet reactor was found to have more safety features than first thought, including heavy walls for shielding, a huge water pool to reduce steam pressure and valves to seal in radiation. Also, a congressional subcommittee, headed by Edward J. Markey, a Massachusetts Democrat, released Nuclear Regulatory Commission documents showing that bad management and human error sometimes render safety features useless, a conclusion similar to findings after the Three Mile Island accident in 1979.                MAY 25

## New White House Fellows for 1986–87

On May 24, President Reagan announced the selection of 11 people as 1986–87 White House Fellows. They are:

PAUL GIGOT, 30 years old, editorial page editor of *The Asian Wall Street Journal*, Hong Kong.

KRISTINE A. LANGDON, 28, an associate with McKinsey & Company, Boston.

Maj. WILLIAM J. LENNOX of the Army, 36, a student at the Army Command and General Staff College in Fort Leavenworth, Kan.

MEREDITH A. NEIZER, 29, a transportation analyst with the Exxon International Company, Florham Park, N.J.

Capt. VICKI A. O'MEARA of the Army, 29, assistant to the general counsel at the Pentagon.

Maj. MICHAEL R. REOPEL of the Army, 33, assistant professor of social sciences at the United States Military Academy, West Point, N.Y.

Maj. MICHAEL C. RYAN of the Army, 36, a student at the College of Naval Command and Staff, Newport, R.I.

THOMAS A. SAPONAS, 37, research and development manager for the Hewlett-Packard Company, Colorado Springs.

ROBERT G. SCHWETJE, 37, vice president for personnel of Valleylab Inc., Boulder, Colo.

Maj. WILLIAM L. WEBB of the Army, 35, associate professor of social sciences at the United States Military Academy.

DIANE C. YU, 34, commissioner of the Alameda Superior Court, Oakland, Calif.

MAY 25

## Agricultural chemicals subject to a special E.P.A. safety review

Chemicals used primarily in agriculture that are undergoing a special review by the Environmental Protection Agency because they may pose threats to humans or wildlife

| Name | Trade Name | Primary Use | Major U.S. Manufacturers | Reason for Review | Status of Review |
|---|---|---|---|---|---|
| Alachlor | Lasso | Weed killer used on corn, soybeans, peanuts | Monsanto | Suspected carcinogen | Proposed decision due Aug. 1986 |
| Aldicarb | Temik | Worm killer used on peanuts, potatoes, citrus | Union Carbide | Suspected of acute toxicity | Proposed decision due July 1986 |
| Amitrole | Amitrol, Weedazole | Non-crop weed killer | Union Carbide, American Cyanamid and Aceto* | Suspected carcinogen | Proposed decision due in by Sept. 1987 |
| Cadmium | Kromad; Cadminate | Fungicide used on golf courses | Mallinckrodt, W. A. Cleory | Suspected of causing cancer, birth defects, fetal death | Proposed decision due in 1986 |

| Name | Trade Name | Primary Use | Major U.S. Manufacturers | Reason for Review | Status of Review |
|---|---|---|---|---|---|
| Captafol | Difolatan, Folcit | Fungicide used on apples, citrus, potatoes, tomatoes | Chevron | Suspected carcinogen | Proposed decision pending |
| Captan | Captan | Fungicide used on many crops | Stauffer, Chevron | Suspected carcinogen | Final decision due by Sept. 1987 |
| Cyanazine | Bladex | Weed killer used on corn, sorghum, cotton, wheat | Shell | Suspected of causing birth defects | Proposed decision due July 1986 |
| Daminozide | Alar | Plant growth regulator used on apples and other crops | Uniroyal** | Suspected carcinogen | Final decision awaiting restudy by manufacturer |
| Dicofol | Kelthane | Miticide used on citrus crops | Rohm & Haas, others | Harmful ecological effects | Final decision requires cuts in DDT-type compounds to 0.1% |
| Dinocap | Karathane | Fungicide used on apples | Rohm & Haas | Suspected of causing birth defects | Proposed decision due in 1986 |
| Inorganic Arsenicals | Many | Weed killer, insecticide, drying agent | Many | Suspected of causing cancer, birth defects, fetal death | Proposed decision due by Sept. 1987 |
| Linuron | Lorox | Herbicide used on fruits and vegetables | DuPont, others | Suspected carcinogen | Proposed decision due by Sept. 1987 |
| Pentachlorophenol | Penta | Weed killer used on lawns | Vulcan | Suspected of causing cancer, birth defects, fetal death | Final decision due in 1986 |
| Triphenylten Hydroxide | TPTH, Du-ter | Fungicide used on potatoes, peanuts, sugar beets | M & T Chemicals | Suspected of causing birth defects | Proposed decision due in 1986 |
| 2,4,5-Trichlorophenol | TCP | Microbiocide and slimicide used in water cooling towers | Many | Suspected of causing cancer, fetal death | Final decision due in 1986 |

*No U.S. manufacturer—the companies are the primary importers
**Chemical division sold to Avery International May 14, 1986.

Source: Environmental Protection Agency

# Reagan Is as Intent as Ever on Making Over the Courts

**By PHILIP SHENON**

**W**ASHINGTON—Many Democrats concede that a number of judges who took their places on the Federal bench during Ronald Reagan's first four years are perhaps too conservative, but by any measure are first-rate legal scholars. The roster of these well-regarded first-term nominees includes such judges as Robert H. Bork, recruited from the Yale Law School, and Richard A. Posner and Antonin Scalia, formerly of the University of Chicago faculty.

But a sizable chorus of critics, not all of them Democrats, are saying that the quality of judicial nominees, and especially those submitted for Federal appeals courts, has declined markedly in President Reagan's second term. And, along the way, Democratic members of the Senate, which passes on selections for the Federal courts, have begun raising sharper questions about nominees they regard as unqualified or underqualified.

Democrats say the perception that some recent candidates have been at best marginally qualified for judicial robes, a view supported in many instances by a screening panel of the American Bar Association, has provided them with ammunition for a broader attack on what they regard as the White House's effort to reshape the Federal judiciary.

"The word is out to the Administration that we will demand quality," said Senator Paul Simon, Democrat of Illinois. The Senator is a leading opponent of Daniel A. Manion, an Indiana lawyer who has been nominated to fill a vacancy on the Chicago-based Court of Appeals for the Seventh Circuit.

Last month, the Judiciary Committee forwarded Mr. Manion's name to the full Senate without recommendation. It was the first time the panel had denied its approval to a Reagan judicial nominee. The Justice Department said last week that the attacks on Mr. Manion were "baseless," but some officials acknowledged that without a substantial lobbying campaign he could become the Administration's first judicial nominee to be rejected.

Administration spokesmen have argued that the bar association ratings unfairly penalize many qualified candidates, particularly those who are young and thus have less courtroom experience. In any event, troubled nominations are hardly peculiar to Mr. Reagan. Jimmy Carter nominated three judges who received "unqualified" ratings from the bar association; so far, there have been none in the Reagan Administration. JUNE 1

## Choices for the bench
The appeals court appointments of Presidents Reagan, Carter, Ford, Nixon and Johnson.

|  | Reagan (second term) | Reagan (first term) | Carter | Ford | Nixon | Johnson |
|---|---|---|---|---|---|---|
| **Number of appointees** | 28* | 31 | 56 | 12 | 45 | 40 |
| Men | 25 | 30 | 45 | 12 | 45 | 39 |
|  | 89.2% | 96.8% | 80.4% | 100 % | 100 % | 97.5% |
| Women | 3 | 1 | 11 | 0 | 0 | 1 |
|  | 10.8% | 3.2% | 19.6% |  |  | 2.5% |

|  | Reagan (second term) | Reagan (first term) | Carter | Ford | Nixon | Johnson |
|---|---|---|---|---|---|---|
| **Race** | | | | | | |
| White | 28<br>100 % | 29<br>93.5% | 44<br>78.6% | 12<br>100 % | 44<br>97.8% | 38<br>95.0% |
| Black | 0 | 1<br>3.2% | 9<br>16.1% | 0 | 0 | 2<br>5.0% |
| Hispanic | 0 | 1<br>3.2% | 2<br>3.6% | 0 | 0 | 0 |
| Asian | 0 | 0 | 1<br>1.8% | 0 | 1<br>2.2% | 0 |
| **Experience** | | | | | | |
| Judicial | 12<br>43.0% | 22<br>70.9% | 30<br>53.6% | 9<br>75.0% | 26<br>57.8% | 26<br>65.0% |
| Prosecutorial | 7<br>25.0% | 6<br>19.3% | 18<br>32.1% | 3<br>25.0% | 21<br>46.7% | 19<br>47.5% |
| Neither | 15<br>53.6% | 8<br>25.8% | 21<br>37.5% | 3<br>25.0% | 8<br>17.8% | 8<br>20.0% |
| **Occupation** | | | | | | |
| Politics or government | 1<br>3.6% | 1<br>3.2% | 0 | 1<br>8.3% | 2<br>4.4% | 4<br>10.0% |
| Judiciary | 11<br>39.3% | 19<br>61.3% | 26<br>46.4% | 9<br>75.0% | 24<br>53.3% | 23<br>57.5% |
| Law | 10<br>35.7% | 6<br>19.2% | 18<br>32.3% | 2<br>16.6% | 15<br>33.3% | 12<br>30.0% |
| Teaching | 5<br>17.9% | 5<br>16.1% | 8<br>14.3% | 0 | 1<br>2.2% | 1<br>2.5% |
| Other | 1<br>3.6% | 0 | 1<br>1.8% | 0 | 3<br>6.7% | 0 |
| **American Bar Association Rating** | | | | | | |
| Exceptionally well qualified | 3<br>10.7% | 7<br>22.6% | 9<br>16.1% | 2<br>16.7% | 7<br>15.6% | 11<br>27.5% |
| Well qualified | 11<br>39.3% | 13<br>41.9% | 33<br>58.9% | 5<br>41.7% | 26<br>57.8% | 19<br>47.5% |
| Qualified | 14<br>50.0% | 11<br>35.5% | 14<br>25.0% | 4<br>33.3% | 12<br>26.7% | 8<br>20.0% |
| Not qualified | 0 | 0 | 0 | 1<br>8.3% | 0 | 1 |
| No report requested | 0 | 0 | 0 | 0 | 0 | 1<br>2.5% |

|  | Reagan (second term) | Reagan (first term) | Carter | Ford | Nixon | Johnson |
|---|---|---|---|---|---|---|
| **Party Affiliation** | | | | | | |
| Democratic | 0 | 0 | 46<br>82.1% | 1<br>8.3% | 1<br>6.7% | 38<br>95.0% |
| Republican | 27<br>96.4% | 31<br>100 % | 4<br>7.1% | 11<br>91.7% | 42<br>93.3% | 2<br>5.0% |
| Independent | 1<br>3.6% | 0 | 6<br>10.7% | 0 | 0 | 0 |

*Includes 3 nominees

Source: Professor Sheldon Goldman, University of Massachusettes

JUNE 1

## 3 States in Region Show Job Growth

A new study of employment in the 1980s shows that although the West and South are still leading the rest of the nation in job gains, some older industrial states are moving far ahead of others in their regions.

The study also showed that New York surpassed Florida last year in the net number of jobs gained, to rank second only to California, still by far the national leader in employment growth. New Jersey and Connecticut also had substantial job gains.

JUNE 5

### Jobs: A state-by-state tally
Number gained or lost, in thousands, from January 1985 to January 1986.

| Calif. | 333.0 | Ore. | 23.6 |
|---|---|---|---|
| N.Y. | 167.6 | Miss. | 23.4 |
| Fla. | 166.1 | Colo. | 23.0 |
| Ohio | 155.8 | Utah | 20.2 |
| Tex. | 135.8 | Nev. | 18.2 |
| Va. | 122.0 | Me. | 16.1 |
| Pa. | 106.0 | Iowa | 14.1 |
| Ga. | 105.5 | N.M. | 14.0 |
| Mich. | 100.0 | D.C. | 13.4 |
| N.J. | 87.0 | Vt. | 12.6 |
| N.C. | 80.7 | Del. | 11.3 |
| Ind. | 74.0 | Hawaii | 9.9 |
| Tenn. | 73.9 | Kan. | 9.9 |
| Ariz. | 73.9 | W.Va. | 8.8 |
| Mass. | 62.2 | Idaho | 7.1 |
| Wash. | 62.1 | Neb. | 5.4 |
| Mo. | 55.9 | Alaska | 4.0 |
| Md. | 54.7 | R.I. | 2.5 |
| S.C. | 46.0 | Mont. | 0.7 |
| Conn. | 38.9 | Wyo. | 0.7 |
| Ala. | 35.7 | S.D. | −1.1 |
| Ky. | 35.5 | N.D. | −1.6 |
| Ark. | 33.8 | Ill. | −1.7 |
| Wis. | 32.0 | Okla. | −9.6 |
| Minn. | 31.7 | La. | −10.5 |
| N.H. | 27.3 | | |

Source: Bureau of Labor Statistics

JUNE 5

## From John Jay to Warren Earl Burger: The 15 Chief Justices

**John Jay**
Born: Dec. 12, 1745, in New York City. Died: May 17, 1829, in Bedford, N.Y.
College: King's College (Columbia).
Appointed: By Washington in 1789.
Resigned: 1795.

**John Rutledge**
Born: September 1739, Charleston, S.C. Died: June 21, 1800, in Charleston.
Law school: Inns of Court, London.
Appointed: Pro tem by Washington in 1795 for less than one year. Served as Associate Justice.

**Oliver Ellsworth**
Born: April 29, 1745, in Windsor, Conn. Died: Nov. 26, 1807, in Windsor.
College: Princeton.
Appointed: By Washington in 1796. Resigned: 1800.

**John Marshall**
Born: Sept. 24, 1755, Germantown, Va. Died: July 6, 1835, Philadelphia, Pa.
Law school: William and Mary.
Appointed: By Adams in 1801. Died in office.

**Roger Brooke Taney**
Born: March 17, 1777, in Calvert County, Md. Died: Oct. 12, 1864, in Washington, D.C.
College: Dickinson.
Appointed: By Jackson in 1835, confirmed in 1836. Died in office.

**Salmon Portland Chase**
Born: Jan. 13, 1808, in Cornish, N.H. Died: May 7, 1873, in New York City.
College: Dartmouth.
Appointed: By Lincoln in 1864. Died in office.

**Morrison Remick Waite**
Born: Nov. 29, 1816, in Lyme, Conn. Died: March 23, 1888, in Washington, D.C.
College: Yale.
Appointed: By Grant in 1874. Died in office.

**Melville Weston Fuller**
Born: Feb. 11, 1833, in Augusta, Me. Died: July 4, 1910, in Sorrento, Me.
College: Bowdoin. Law school: Harvard.
Appointed: By Cleveland in 1888. Died in office.

**Edward Douglas White**
Born: Nov. 3, 1845, in Parish of Lafourche, La. Died: May 19, 1921, in Washington, D.C.
Colleges: Mount St. Mary's, Georgetown.
Appointed: By Taft in 1910. Died in office. Served as Associate Justice.

**William Howard Taft**
Born: Sept. 15, 1857, in Cincinnati, Ohio. Died: March 8, 1930, in Washington, D.C.
College: Yale. Law school: Cincinnati.
Appointed: By Harding in 1921. Resigned: 1930. Was President of the United States.

**Charles Evans Hughes**
Born: April 11, 1862, in Glens Falls, N.Y. Died: Aug. 27, 1948, in Osterville, Mass.
Colleges: Madison (Colgate), Brown. Law school: Columbia.
Appointed: By Hoover in 1930. Resigned: 1941. Served as Associate Justice.

**Harlan Fiske Stone**
Born: Oct. 11, 1872, in Chesterfield, N.H. Died: April 22, 1946, in Washington, D.C.
College: Amherst. Law schools: Columbia, Amherst.
Appointed: By Roosevelt in 1941. Died in office. Served as Associate Justice.

**Frederick Moore Vinson**
Born: Jan. 22, 1890, in Louisa, Ky. Died: Sept. 8, 1953, in Washington, D.C.
College: Centre. Law school: Centre.
Appointed: By Truman in 1946. Died in office.

**Earl Warren**
Born: March 19, 1891, in Los Angeles, Calif. Died: July 9, 1974, in Washington, D.C.
College: University of California. Law school: University of California.
Appointed: By Eisenhower in 1953, confirmed in 1954. Resigned: 1969.

**Warren Earl Burger**
Born: Sept. 17, 1907, in St. Paul, Minn.
College: University of Minnesota. Law school: St. Paul (Mitchell)
Appointed: By Nixon in 1969.

Source: "Guide to the U.S. Supreme Court," © 1979 by Congressional Quarterly Inc.

JUNE 16

## Cleaner water

Percent of selected cities' sewage flow meeting Federal standards established in Clean Water Act of 1977

|  | 1976 | 1980 |
|---|---|---|
| Boston | 4 | 2 |
| Chicago | 8 | 100 |
| Detroit | 1 | 99 |
| Jersey City | 1 | 4 |
| Los Angeles | 12 | 16 |
| Minneapolis | 3 | 99 |
| New York | 7 | 64 |
| Newark | 8 | 79 |
| Pittsburgh | 87 | 98 |
| Washington | 26 | 100 |

Source: Water Pollution Control Federation

JUNE 22

## Budget Accord: Programs Congress Saved

WASHINGTON, June 27—The congressional budget resolution approved early today retains 43 of 45 programs that President Reagan sought to end or significantly reduce, according to Pete V. Domenici, chairman of the Senate Budget Committee.

The resolution envisions the eventual end of Federal financing of Conrail and general revenue sharing. The resolution assumes the end of Conrail through its sale to the private sector. It also assumes that general revenue sharing will be halted Sept. 30.

However, the resolution would allow revenue sharing to continue if the House and Senate reapproved the program, appropriated money for it after approving offsetting spending cuts or revenue increases, and got presidential agreement for each of these steps, an outcome that is considered unlikely.

Following are the programs to be retained, according to Senator Domenici:
Export-Import Bank direct loans
Overseas Private Investment Corporation insurance programs
Advanced communications technology satellite
Rural Electrification Administration subsidies
Weatherization assistance programs
Environmental Protection Agency sewage treatment grants
Soil conservation programs
Landsat Sea grant and coastal zone management
Department of Agriculture Extension Service
Temporary emergency food and shelter
Federal crop insurance program
Trade adjustment assistance to firms
U.S. Travel and Tourism Administration
Postal subsidy
Rural housing loans
Small Business Administration
Section 202 housing
Amtrak
Interstate Commerce Commission
Washington Metro transit system
Maritime cargo preference expansion
Appalachian Regional Commission
Economic Development Administration
Urban Development Action Grants
Rental housing development grants
Section 312 rehabilitation loan fund
Section 108 loan guarantee program
Rural development program
Small Business Administration disaster loans
Community service block grants
Impact aid for school districts (Part B)
Library programs
Small higher education programs
State student incentive grants
College housing loans
Public Health Service health profession subsidies

Federal Emergency Management Agency supplemental food and shelter
Section 8 moderate rehabilitation
Rural housing grants
Legal Services Corporation
Grants for local juvenile delinquency programs
Public debt reimbursement to Federal Reserve Banks

JUNE 28

# 87 Chosen for Mayor's Liberty Medals

**By GEORGE JAMES**

Eighty-seven prominent people representing about 50 countries have been named to receive liberty medals from New York City Mayor Koch, who had criticized the selection of 12 prominent Americans by Liberty Weekend organizers as not representative enough of the ethnic groups that have immigrated to America.

The selection last March by the Statue of Liberty–Ellis Island Foundation of 12 naturalized citizens who have become leaders in their fields immediately created a controversy for not encompassing such major groups as the Irish, Italians and Poles.

The Mayor's list, to be officially released today, includes people from those groups and Greeks, Swedes, Hungarians and other ethnic groups that arrived in large numbers, as well as smaller immigrant groups, such as Cambodians and Panamanians.

The list represents a potpourri of occupations and professions from the worlds of the arts, entertainment, business, finance, labor, publishing, medicine, sports, religion and others.

These are the award winners:

Toshiko Akiyoshi, Japan, musician.
Licia Albanese, Italy, opera singer.
Theoni V. Aldredge, Greece, costume designer.
Daniel R. Alonso, Argentina, pathologist.
Karl G. Andren, Finland, entertainer.
Paul Anka, Canada, entertainer.
Claudio Arrau, Chile, pianist.
Isaac Asimov, Soviet Union, scientist and writer.
David Bar-Illan, Israel, pianist.
Mikhail Baryshnikov, Soviet Union, dancer.
Odon Betanzos, Spain, poet and critic.
Zbigniew Brzezinski, Poland, political scientist.
Khalid M. H. Butt, Pakistan, surgeon and professor.
Bernard Castro, Italy, businessman.
Christo, Bulgaria, artist.
Alistair Cooke, England, broadcaster and cultural historian.
Celia Cruz, Cuba, singer.
Peter Davies, Wales, professor and research scientist.
Willem de Kooning, Netherlands, artist.
Oscar de la Renta, Dominican Republic, fashion designer.
Kenan T. Erim, Turkey, professor.
Patrick Ewing, Jamaica, basketball player.
James C. Finlay, Ireland, educator.
Geraldine Fitzgerald, Ireland, actress.
Milos Forman, Czechoslovakia, film director.
Yvette Francis, Jamaica, scientist.
Uta Hagen, West Germany, actress.
Geoffrey Holder, Trinidad, choreographer and director.
John Houseman, Rumania, actor.
Archbishop Iakovos, Greece, religious leader.
Iman, Somalia, model and actress.
Leo Jung, Czechoslovakia, rabbi.
Elia Kazan, Greece, director and writer.
Francoise Kourilsky, France, actress and director.
Paul C. Kovi, Hungary, restaurateur.
Nicholas S. H. Krawciw, Ukraine, brigadier general.
John E. Lawe, Ireland, labor leader.
Wassily Leontief, Soviet Union, economist.

Tom G. Margittai, Hungary, restaurateur.
Peter Martins, Denmark, dancer and choreographer.
Ved Mehta, India, writer.
Zubin Mehta, India, conductor.
Gian Carlo Menotti, Italy, composer and director.
Zinka Milanov, Yugoslavia, opera singer.
Bert N. Mitchell, Jamaica, businessman and accountant.
Archbishop Torkom Manoogian, Armenia, religious leader.
Rupert Murdoch, Australia, publisher.
Andre Muzac, Haiti, surgeon.
Antonio Navarro, Cuba, engineer, corporate manager and writer.
Juan Negrin, Jr., Spain, doctor.
Louise Nevelson, Soviet Union, sculptor.
Mike Nichols, West Germany, stage and film director.
Jarmila Novotna, Czechoslovakia, opera singer.
Michael Olatunji, Nigeria, musician.
Claes Oldenberg, Sweden, artist.
Patrick A. Ongley, New Zealand, scientist.
Cely Carillo Onrubia, Philippines, actress-singer.
Maureen O'Hara, Ireland, actress.
Peter Ottley, Grenada, labor leader.
Nam June Paik, Korea, artist.
Dith Pran, Cambodia, photographer.
Anthony Quinn, Mexico, actor.
Jose Quintero, Panama, theater director.
I. I. Rabi, Austria, physicist.
Edward D. Re, Italy, judge.
Cleveland Robinson, Jamaica, labor leader.
Felix G. Rohatyn, Austria, banker.
A. M. Rosenthal, Canada, executive editor of *The New York Times*.
Archbishop Philip Saliba, Lebanon, religious leader.
Mongo Santamaria, Cuba, musician.
Tadeuscz Sendzimir, Poland, inventor-metallurgist.
Isaac Bashevis Singer, Poland, writer.
Elliot Skinner, Trinidad, anthropologist.
Felicien M. Steichen, Luxembourg, surgeon.
Lucia Suarez, Argentina, producer.
Jessica Tandy, England, actress.
Robert B. Thomson, Scotland, baseball player.
Pauline Trigere, France, designer.
Gerald Tsai, Jr., China, investor.
Liv Ullmann, Norway, actress.
Jorge Velasquez, Panama, jockey.
Diane Von Furstenberg, Belgium, fashion designer.
John Weitz, Germany, fashion designer.
Ruth Westheimer, Germany, psychosexual therapist.
C. N. Yang, China, physicist.
Franco Zeffirelli, Italy, director.
Mortimer B. Zuckerman, Canada, publisher.

JUNE 26

## Evolution of the budget

Budget figures for the fiscal year 1987 as proposed by President Reagan, originally approved by the Senate and House, and the House-Senate compromise.*

|  | Reagan | Senate | House | Compromise |
|---|---|---|---|---|
| Total spending | 1,010.3 | 1,001.2 | 994.2 | 995.0 |
| Revenues | 849.9 | 857.2 | 857.2 | 852.4 |
| Deficit | 160.4 | 144.0 | 137.1 | 142.6 |
| **Military** | | | | |
| Budget authority | 320.3 | 301.0 | 285.0 | 292.2 |
| Outlays | 296.7 | 282.0 | 276.2 | 279.2 |

|  | Reagan | Senate | House | Compromise |
|---|---|---|---|---|
| **Nonmilitary outlays** | | | | |
| International affairs | 16.5 | 14.2 | 13.8 | 14.0 |
| Science and space | 9.1 | 9.1 | 8.8 | 8.9 |
| Energy | 4.4 | 4.6 | 4.9 | 3.5 |
| Natural resources | 12.1 | 12.6 | 12.3 | 12.6 |
| Agriculture | 22.4 | 23.5 | 23.6 | 23.5 |
| Housing and business credit | 3.0 | 3.5 | 2.2 | 2.1 |
| Transportation | 25.6 | 27.8 | 25.5 | 25.9 |
| Community development | 6.3 | 7.2 | 7.0 | 7.0 |
| Education and social services | 27.5 | 30.6 | 30.6 | 30.6 |
| Health | 35.1 | 38.3 | 38.4 | 38.3 |
| Medicare | 70.6 | 72.8 | 73.4 | 73.3 |
| Income security | 119.5 | 121.5 | 121.4 | 121.8 |
| Social security | 211.7 | 209.4 | 209.4 | 209.4 |
| Veterans benefits | 26.5 | 26.5 | 26.7 | 26.6 |
| Justice | 7.1 | 7.2 | 7.2 | 7.2 |
| General government | 6.2 | 5.4 | 5.7 | 5.5 |
| Government assistance | 1.8 | 2.8 | 2.7 | 2.8 |
| Interest on national debt | 144.8 | 143.9 | 143.5 | 143.7 |
| Allowances | 0.8 | 0.5 | 0.6 | −0.1 |
| Undistributed offset receipts | −36.9 | −42.1 | −39.2 | −40.3 |

*Figures are outlays, except when otherwise stated, and are in billions of dollars. Numbers have been rounded.

Source: Congressional Budget Office

JUNE 28

# The Lead Sailing Ships

*Some have sailed halfway around the world. Others have come from around the corner. The 22 majestic ships in the vanguard of Friday's Parade of Sail—with their lore and echo of the past—represent nations from Indonesia to Uruguay.*

**1.**
***Eagle***
**United States**

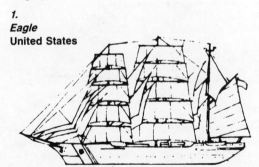

**2.**
***Danmark***
**Denmark**

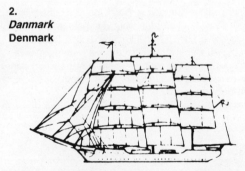

**1.** The host vessel, this white, steel-hulled bark—America's most famous tall ship—was built in 1936 in Hitler's Germany as a school ship. The United States acquired her as a war reparation and commissioned her for the training of Coast Guard cadets. The top of her three steel decks is covered with teak. Her figurehead is a golden eagle. Crew, 220; length, 295 feet; mast height, 147 feet.

**2.** This white, steel-hulled and full-rigged training ship, built in 1932, visited the 1939 New York World's Fair and was in Florida when Denmark was overrun by Germany. During the war, the Coast Guard used her for training, leading to the decision to acquire the *Eagle*, after the *Danmark* sailed home. Her figurehead is a gilded sea god. Crew, 99; length, 253 feet; mast height, 131 feet.

**3.**
*Christian Radich*
**Norway**

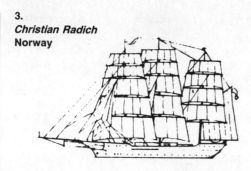

**3.** [Pronounced RAH-dik.] Built in 1937 as a Norwegian merchant marine training ship, she visited the 1939 World's Fair. Germany confiscated her in 1940 and used her as a floating barracks. After the war, she was found sunk and rebuilt. This full-rigged ship has a white steel hull and a figurehead of a young woman in a long blue dress. Crew, 85; length, 241 feet; mast height, 121 feet.

**4.**
*Libertad*
**Argentina**

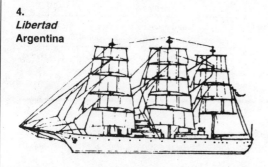

**4.** This full-rigged training vessel of the Argentine Navy, built in 1956, is one of the world's largest and fastest sailing ships. She has a white steel hull, a flush deck with a pilothouse forward of the main mast, a wide bridge and a funnel for engine exhaust between her main- and mizzenmasts. Crew, 277; length, 345 feet; mast height, 131 feet.

**5.**
*Belem*
**France**

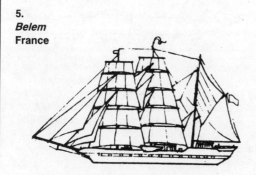

**5.** This steel-hulled bark, the largest of the French sail-training vessels, started out 90 years ago hauling cocoa beans and sugar. From 1913, when the Duke of Westminster made her into a yacht, until 1951, when she became a school ship, she stayed in private use. The French foundation that owns her completed her restoration last year. Crew, 70; length, 173 feet; mast height, 113 feet.

**6.**
*Zenobe Gramme*
**Belgium**

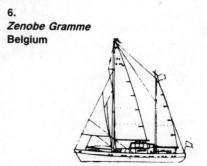

**6.** This Bermuda ketch, built in 1961, was designed for scientific research and is used for training and research by the Belgian Navy. She has a white hull of wood, a cabin house between her main and mizzenmasts and no bowsprit. Crew, 18; length, 95 feet, mast height, 108 feet.

**7.**
*Bluenose 2*
**Canada**

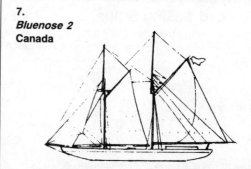

**7.** This two-masted, wood-hulled schooner is typical of the fleet that fished the Grand Banks from ports in New England and Canada until the 1930s. Built in 1963, she is a replica of Canada's most famous sailing vessel, the *Bluenose*, a famed racing ship. Owned by the Province of Nova Scotia, she is a goodwill ambassador for Canada. Crew, 14; length, 143 feet; mast height, 84 feet.

**8.**
*Esmeralda*
**Chile**

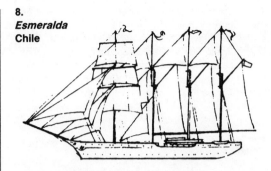

**8.** This four-masted barkentine has stirred controversy over her reputed use for torturing prisoners after the coup by Gen. Augusto Pinochet in 1973. A fire in 1946 delayed her launching, and the Chilean Navy bought her in 1954. Though a training craft, she is armed with four guns. Her steel hull is white and her figurehead is an Andes condor. Crew, 338; length, 370 feet; mast height, 159 feet.

**9.**
*Gloria*
**Colombia**

**9.** A three-masted bark, she was built in 1968 in Bilbao, Spain, the smallest and oldest of four sister ships that include the *Guayas*, the *Simón Bolívar* and the *Cuauhtemoc*. She is the sail-training vessel of the Colombian Naval Academy in Cartagena. The *Gloria* has a white steel hull, an enclosed pilothouse and a winged figurehead. Crew, 120; length, 249 feet; mast height, 131 feet.

**10.**
*Guayas*
**Ecuador**

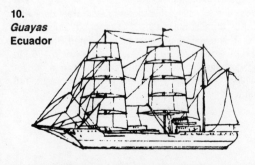

**10.** This three-masted bark, a sister ship of the *Gloria*, was built in 1977 in Bilbao. She can be spotted by her figurehead, a large condor. She has a white steel hull and twin 750-horsepower diesel engines, and is the sail-training vessel of the Ecuadorean Naval Academy in Guayaquil. Crew, 147; length, 258 feet; mast height, 125 feet.

**11.**
*Dewa Ruci*
**Indonesia**

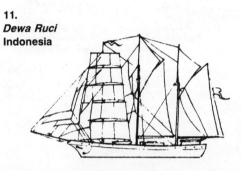

**11.** [Pronounced day-wah-ROO-chi.] The training ship of the Indonesian Naval Academy, this barkentine is named after an Indonesian epic sea god. Built in West Germany in 1952, her steel hull is gray with a white stripe. She carries a flag with stripes of red and white and a banner with an image of the garuda, Indonesia's legendary eagle. Crew, 146; length, 191 feet; mast height, 115 feet.

**12.**
*Galaxy*
**Israel**

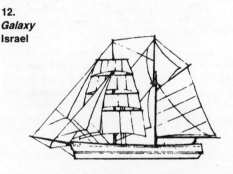

**12.** This privately owned brigantine cruises out of Eilat, on the Red Sea. Built in 1960 in Portugal, where she was a fishing trawler, she was rebuilt in 1983–84. Her floors are African hardwood, her paneling mahogany and her deck iroka. While not a Government ship, her blue wooden hull and white sails announce the national colors of Israel. Crew, 8; length, 120 feet; mast height, 87 feet.

**13.**
*Amerigo Vespucci*
**Italy**

**13.** This full-rigged ship, built in 1931, is prized for her elegant interior. She is one of the largest vessels in Op Sail and, at 50 feet, the widest. Her design is that of an 18th-century ship that had two gun decks, but her hull is steel and she carries no guns. She is the sail-training ship of the Italian Naval Academy in Livorno. Crew, 157; length, 331 feet; mast height, 135 feet.

**14.**
*Cuauhtemoc*
**Mexico**

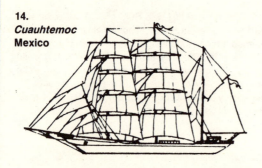

**14.** [Pronounced coo-OUT-ay-mock.] This three-masted white steel bark, built in 1982 in Spain—the newest of the Government-sponsored sail-training vessels—was named for the last Aztec emperor, who resisted Cortés and was eventually put to death by the Spanish. Crew, 199; length, 297 feet; mast height, 155 feet.

**15.**
*Soriandet*
**Norway**

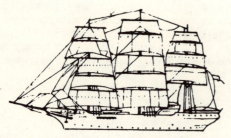

**15.** [Pronounced Seur-lahn-det.] Curved and decorated boards sweep back from the bow on either side of this full-rigged steel ship, which was built in 1927. During World War II, she was seized by the Germans. These days, she is maintained by a nonprofit foundation in the city of Kristiansand. Crew, 86; length, 216 feet; mast height, 115 feet.

**16.**
*Shabab Oman*
**Oman**

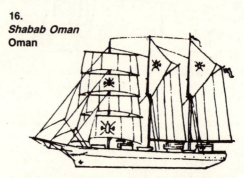

**16.** This wooden training vessel in the Sultan's navy, built in 1971 in Scotland as a topsail schooner, went under Omani colors in 1977 and received its current name, which means "Youth of Oman." Last year she was converted to a three-masted barkentine. Her 102-day voyage from Oman is one of the longest undertaken to this event. Crew, 51; length, 177 feet; mast height, 105 feet.

**17.**
*Sagres 2*
**Portugal**

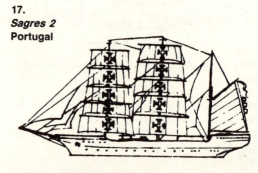

**17.** Easily identified by the large red crosses on her main- and foresails, this three-masted steel bark was built by the Germans in 1937. Damaged during World War II, she was taken over by the United States and then passed on to the Brazilians. She went in 1962 to the Portuguese, who, like the Brazilians, use her for training. Crew, 200; length, 294 feet; mast height, 148 feet.

**18.**
*Juan Sebastian de Elcano*
**Spain**

**18.** Named for the 16th-century commander of the lone galleon that returned from Magellan's expedition, this four-masted topsail schooner has been a training ship for the Spanish Navy for most of her 59 years. She has circumnavigated the globe six times. Crew, 343; length, 351 feet; mast height, 160 feet.

**19.**
*Capitan Miranda*
**Uruguay**

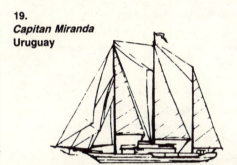

**19.** This three-masted schooner was built in Cádiz, Spain, in 1930 as a sailing cargo carrier. But after World War II, she operated as a power vessel with her rig removed. In the 1960s she was a hydrographic research vessel for the Uruguayan Navy. And in 1978 she became, once again, a sailing ship. Crew, 91; length, 179 feet; mast height, 120 feet.

**20.**
*Simón Bolivar*
**Venezuela**

**20.** Named for the hero of South America's fight for independence from Spain, this three-masted bark, built in 1980, has a figurehead symbolizing Liberty: draped in Bolívar's flag, she holds in her right hand the sword of liberation. The navy training vessel has black gunports painted onto her white hull of steel. Crew, 170; length, 270 feet; mast height, 120 feet.

**21.**
*Gazela of Philadelphia*
**United States**

**21.** Believed to be the oldest and largest wood-hulled square-rigger still putting out to sea, this three-masted barkentine was built in Portugal in 1883 with timber said to have planted by Prince Henry the Navigator. She is owned by the Penn's Landing Corporation and maintained by the Philadelphia Ship Preservation Guild. Crew, 30; length, 186 feet; mast height, 100 feet.

**22.**
*Elissa*
**United States**

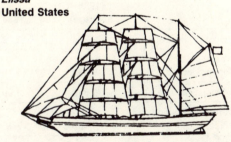

**22.** Built in 1877 in Aberdeen, Scotland, this bark, which has a gray band along the top of her white iron hull, has been, among other things, a cargo ship and a smuggler. She has traded under five different flags—British, Norwegian, Swedish, Finnish and Greek. She is now in the care of the Galveston Historical Society in Texas. Crew, 65; length, 150 feet; mast height, 103 feet.

# Risks of Being on Uncle Sam's Crew

By JONATHAN FUERBRINGER

WASHINGTON, July 6—In 1984, 6,688 Federal employees were bitten by dogs. An additional 2,642 employees were injured by bites of other animals and insects.

Dogs are a special hazard of the letter carrier, and dog bites are unique to the Federal Government as a major injury cause. They rank fifth on the list of work-related injuries and illnesses that befall Federal civilian employees, according to a new report. Other bites rank 10th.

Falls (24,949); materials handling (24,608); slipping, twisting or tripping (18,781); and striking against objects (13,640) are the first four problems on the list.

After dog bites come flying particles (5,244), falling objects (5,143), vehicles (4,173), dust and gases (3,667), bites by other animals and insects, and violence (1,992).

The new report, by the Labor Department's Occupational Safety and Health Administration, covers the causes of injury and illness related to work for the calendar year 1984. It also details rates of injuries for the fiscal years 1984 and 1985.   JULY 7

## Uncle Sam's crew

The agencies hurting the most (rate of work-related injury or illness per 100 employees)

|  | Number of workers (1985 average) | 1985 | 1984 |
| --- | --- | --- | --- |
| Architect of the Capitol | 2,294 | 14.17 | 13.22 |
| Panama Canal Commission | 8,339 | 9.07 | 8.19 |
| U.S. Postal Service | 733,856 | 8.32 | 8.90 |
| Government Printing Office | 5,488 | 8.05 | 7.15 |
| Soldiers' and Airmen's Home | 1,052 | 7.70 | 6.60 |
| Department of Interior | 76,172 | 7.44 | 7.30 |
| Tennessee Valley Authority | 33,215 | 7.31 | 7.58 |
| Smithsonian Institution | 3,958 | 7.20 | 9.10 |
| Department of Agriculture | 115,421 | 6.60 | 5.63 |
| Veterans Administration | 244,716 | 6.21 | 6.66 |

Source: Occupational Safety and Health Administration

JULY 7

## Liberty Aftermath

Figures compiled by official agencies participating in the four-day Liberty Weekend include the following:

**People**
Many millions; no official count.

**Ships**
255 sailing ships, 350 Coast Guard vessels, 33 warships (July 4 Op Sail)

**Boats**
30,000 pleasure craft (July 4)

**Boating Troubles**
1,800 calls (Coast Guard and police harbor unit)
179 boaters removed from crafts or water

**Police**
15,000 assigned for July 4 celebration

**Police Barriers**
5,778

**Police Overtime**
$4.26 million

**Medical Emergencies**
410 people treated, 178 taken to hospitals

**Food Sold**
1 million cans of beer and soda (Harbor Festival)

**Food Spoiled**
$3,700 of chocolate mousse (Harbor Festival)

**Campers**
400 in 142 tents (Flushing Meadows–Corona Park, Queens)
500 in 175 recreational vehicles (South Beach, Staten Island)

**Garbage**
250 cubic yards (collected after July 5 Central Park concert)

JULY 7

## Student Cocaine Use Remains Up as Use of Other Drugs Drops

By RICHARD HALLORAN

WASHINGTON, July 7—Cocaine use has remained high among high school and college students while the illicit use of marijuana, the most prevalent drug used, dropped from 1980 to 1984 and leveled off in 1985, according to a survey made public today.

The National Institute on Drug Abuse here, which financed the survey, and the Institute for Social Research at the University of Michigan in Ann Arbor, which conducted it, reported that 30 percent of all college students will have used cocaine at least once by the end of their fourth year in college.

The illicit use of many other drugs fell by half over the period from 1980 to 1985, the survey reported.

Dr. Lloyd D. Johnston, a director of the study, said in a statement: "The drug epidemic largely originated on the nation's campuses in the late 1960s, so it is significant to see evidence that it is receding on those same campuses.

"The most serious current problem clearly is the fact that cocaine use remains at peak levels in this population. This is also true among high school students and young adults generally, not just college students."

JULY 8

### Declining drug use on campus
Percentage of college students who had used the drugs below at least once during the year.

| Drug | 1980 | 1981 | 1982 | 1983 | 1984 | 1985 |
|---|---|---|---|---|---|---|
| Marijuana | 51% | 51% | 45% | 45% | 41% | 42% |
| Cocaine | 17 | 16 | 17 | 17 | 16 | 17 |
| Amphetamines | 22 | 22 | 21 | 17 | 16 | 12 |
| Tranquilizers | 7 | 5 | 5 | 5 | 4 | 4 |
| Opiates* | 5 | 4 | 4 | 4 | 4 | 2 |
| LSD | 6 | 5 | 6 | 4 | 4 | 2 |
| Methaqualone | 7 | 7 | 7 | 3 | 3 | 1 |
| Barbiturates | 3 | 3 | 3 | 2 | 2 | 1 |
| Heroin | 0† | 0† | 0† | 0† | 0† | 0† |
| Alcohol | 91 | 93 | 92 | 92 | 90 | 92 |

*Other than heroin.
†Less than one half of one percent.
Source: Institute for Social Research, University of Michigan

JULY 8

## High Court's 1985–86 Term: Mixed Results for President

By STUART TAYLOR, Jr.

WASHINGTON, July 10—In the Supreme Court term that ended Monday, President Reagan won a significant reaffirmation of presidential primacy in executing the laws, but he suffered a series of major defeats on issues at the heart of his social agenda.

The most notable aspect of the term was the Reagan Administration's boldness in urging its views of the law upon the Court, perhaps more aggressively than any predecessor in the past 50 years.

The Court responded by rejecting the Administration's advice, firmly and sometimes testily, in major decisions on abortion, affirmative action, minority voting rights, rules designed to require medical care for infants with severe disabilities, and other issues.

The Administration did achieve several victories, the most notable of which was the Court's decision last Monday striking down the central provision of the new budget-balancing law as an encroachment on presidential authority.

But that ruling represented a cautious extension of a decade-long trend strengthening the President against Congress, rather than a broad endorsement of this Administration's distinctive views on the separation of powers.

In general, the Court steered a moderate course through a docket laden with an unusual number of politically charged issues, shifting from left to right of center from one issue to the next as Warren E. Burger, who is retiring, ended 17 years as Chief Justice.

In major decisions that did not involve the Administration, the Court ruled for the first time that the Constitution bars severe forms of partisan gerrymandering and that it does not protect private homosexual relations between consenting adults.   JULY 11

## Who Lined Up with Whom

Justices William J. Brennan, Jr., and William H. Rehnquist, intellectual leaders of the Supreme Court, voted on opposite sides in 74 of the 147 cases decided by signed opinions this past session. The following is a breakdown of how frequently the other justices sided with Justice Brennan or Justice Rehnquist in those cases.

**WILLIAM J. BRENNAN, JR.,** 80 years old. Liberal. Wrote major decisions approving limited use of racial preferences to cure job discrimination. Joined in reaffirming constitutional abortion rights and in dissent from decision that Constitution does not bar prosecution of homosexuals for sodomy. Dissented from opinions limiting First Amendment protection for commercial advertisements and adult theaters showing sexually explicit films.

**THURGOOD MARSHALL,** 78 years old. Voted with Brennan 91 percent of the time.

**HARRY A. BLACKMUN,** 77 years old. Voted with Brennan 74 percent of the time.

**JOHN PAUL STEVENS,** 66 years old. Voted with Brennan 62 percent of the time.

**LEWIS F. POWELL, JR.,** 78 years old. Voted with Rehnquist 73 percent of the time.

**BYRON R. WHITE,** 69 years old. Voted with Rehnquist 76 percent of the time.

**SANDRA DAY O'CONNOR,** 56 years old. Voted with Rehnquist 77 percent of the time.

**CHIEF JUSTICE WARREN E. BURGER,** 78 years old. Voted with Rehnquist 86 percent of the time.

**WILLIAM H. REHNQUIST,** 61 years old. Conservative. Voted that Constitution does not protect private homosexual relations or women seeking abortions. Wrote dissents against use of affirmative action preferences to cure job discrimination against minorities. Wrote decisions limiting First Amendment protection for commercial speech and adult theaters.

JULY 11

## July 4 Cleanup Makes History

**By JOYCE PURNICK**

Liberty Weekend's revelers generated so much trash that the four-day event has entered the Garbage Hall of Fame.

According to the Sanitation Department, the celebration joined the Top 5 list of all-time great garbage generators, bumping the former No. 5, the ticker-tape parade for the Iranian hostages on Jan. 30, 1981.

That celebration produced 1,262 tons of trash; Liberty Weekend produced 2,079. However, it took four days to do so.

The others on the list managed to dirty things up in one or two days. Sometimes in a few hours.

No. 1, what Albert W. O'Leary, the author of the Sanitation Department's news release, called the "all-time granddaddy trash generator" in the city's history, was the celebration of V-J Day in 1945. On Aug. 14 and 15, 5,438 tons of trash were collected.

Second on the list was a ticker-tape parade honoring the astronaut John Glenn on March 1, 1962. That produced 3,474 tons of garbage. Next were a parade on April 20, 1951, for Gen. Douglas MacArthur, which yielded 3,249 tons of trash, and a May 22, 1963, ticker-tape parade for Maj. Gordon Cooper, the astronaut. That produced 2,900 tons of trash.

Not all cities know how dirty they are, but

New York does because city sanitation trucks are weighed at every disposal site, Mr. O'Leary said.

Preparing for the weekend, and the cleanup afterward, cost $1.05 million, the Sanitation Department has estimated.   JULY 12

## Impeachment of U.S. Judge Passes House

**By PHILIP SHENON**

WASHINGTON, July 22—The House of Representatives impeached a Federal official for the first time in 50 years today, charging a judge from Nevada with tax evasion and bringing "disrepute" on the Federal judiciary.

The 406-to-0 vote, in effect an indictment, opens the way for a Senate trial of the 69-year-old judge, Harry E. Claiborne of Las Vegas. He is serving a two-year Federal sentence for tax evasion but has refused to resign and continues to collect his $78,000 salary at the Maxwell Air Force Base stockade in Montgomery, Ala.   JULY 23

Below is a list of all previous cases sent to the Senate for trial after impeachment by the House.

William Blount, Senator from Tennessee, charges dismissed in 1799.

John Pickering, Federal judge in New Hampshire, removed from office in 1804 after charges of irregular judicial procedures, loose morals and drunkenness.

Samuel Chase, Associate Justice of the Supreme Court, acquitted in 1805.

James Peck, Federal judge in Missouri, acquitted in 1831.

West Humphreys, Federal judge in Tennessee, removed from office in 1862 for advocating secession and accepting office as a Confederate judge.

Andrew Johnson, President of the United States, acquitted in 1868.

Mark H. Delahay, Federal judge in Kansas, resigned in 1873 before Senate trial, charged with misconduct in office and intoxication.

William Belknap, Secretary of War, acquitted in 1876.

Charles Swayne, Federal judge in Florida, acquitted in 1905.

Robert Archbald, Associate judge of the United States Commerce Court, removed from office 1913, charged with using improper influence and accepting favors from litigants.

George English, Federal judge in Illinois, resigned in 1926 before Senate trial began, charged with partiality, tyranny and oppression.

Harold Louderback, Federal judge in California, acquitted in 1933.

Halsted Ritter, Federal judge in Florida, removed from office in 1936, charged with filing false tax returns.

JULY 23

## San Francisco Outstrips Philadelphia in Size

On July 29 the Census Bureau reported that San Francisco had replaced Philadelphia as the nation's fourth-largest urban area, behind New York, Los Angeles and Chicago.

Its population estimates for 1985 also showed that the Washington, D.C., area had slipped from eighth to tenth, passed by Houston and Dallas.

Of the 281 metropolitan statistical areas in the nation, the fastest-growing one was Naples, Fla. Its population increased by 36 percent from 1980 to 1985, to 116,900 people, moving from 264th to 235th in the rankings.

Among metropolitan areas with more than a million people, Phoenix grew fastest. Its population increased by 22.4 percent to 1,846,600. It moved from twenty-fourth to twenty-first place.

The San Francisco metropolitan area grew

by 8.2 percent in the five years, enabling it to pass the Philadelphia area, which grew by only 1.7 percent.  JULY 30

## Big-city rankings

Metropolitan statistical areas, their estimated population in 1985, current Census Bureau rank and 1980 rank. A metropolitan statistical area is a Federal designation for a central city and its surrounding communities.

| Area | Population | '80 rank |
|---|---|---|
| 1. New York | 17,931,100 | 1 |
| 2. Los Angeles | 12,738,200 | 2 |
| 3. Chicago | 8,085,200 | 3 |
| 4. San Francisco | 5,809,300 | 5 |
| 5. Philadelphia | 5,776,500 | 4 |
| 6. Detroit | 4,581,200 | 6 |
| 7. Boston | 4,051,400 | 7 |
| 8. Houston | 3,623,300 | 9 |
| 9. Dallas | 3,511,600 | 10 |
| 10. Washington | 3,489,500 | 8 |
| 11. Miami | 2,878,300 | 12 |
| 12. Cleveland | 2,776,400 | 11 |
| 13. Atlanta | 2,471,700 | 16 |
| 14. St. Louis | 2,412,400 | 14 |
| 15. Pittsburgh | 2,337,400 | 13 |
| 16. Minneapolis | 2,262,400 | 17 |
| 17. Baltimore | 2,252,800 | 15 |
| 18. Seattle | 2,247,400 | 18 |
| 19. San Diego | 2,132,700 | 19 |
| 20. Tampa | 1,868,700 | 22 |
| 21. Phoenix | 1,846,600 | 24 |
| 22. Denver | 1,827,100 | 21 |
| 23. Cincinnati | 1,679,900 | 20 |
| 24. Milwaukee | 1,550,300 | 23 |
| 25. Kansas City | 1,493,900 | 25 |

JULY 30

# Spending for Health Care in 1985 Rose at Lowest Rate in Two Decades

**By ROBERT PEAR**

WASHINGTON, July 29—Total spending for health care in the United States rose 8.9 percent last year, the lowest rate of increase in two decades, the Federal Government reported today.

Health care spending totaled $425 billion, or an average of $1,721 for every person in the country in 1985, the report said. Health-related activities accounted for 10.7 percent of the nation's total output of goods and services, the highest proportion of the gross national product to date, it said.

Benefit payments under the Government's two main health programs increased faster than overall health spending. Medicare payments to the elderly and disabled rose 12.2 percent, to $70.5 billion in 1985, while Medicaid payments to people with low incomes rose 9.4 percent, to $39.8 billion, according to the report by the Department of Health and Human Services.

The lower rate of increase in spending for health care was almost entirely a result of lower growth of medical prices, not to any reduction in the use of health services, the Government said. "The United States is not consuming any less health care goods and services than before, either in total or per capita," it added.

While the rate of increase waned, the price of medical care continued to rise at more than twice the overall inflation rate.

The 8.9 percent increase in health care spending last year followed increases of 9.2 percent in 1984 and 10.4 percent in 1983, 12.8 percent in 1982 and 15.7 percent in 1981, the biggest jump for a single year. Before 1984, the last year with a single-digit increase was 1965, when health care spending rose 9.3 percent to a total of $41.9 billion. That was the year in which Congress created Medicare and Medicaid.   JULY 30

### The cost of health care
National health expenditures in billions of current dollars, not adjusted for inflation, and as a percentage of the gross national product.

| Year | Spending (Billions) | % of G.N.P. |
|---|---|---|
| 1985 | 425.0 | 10.7 |
| 1984 | 390.2 | 10.3 |
| 1983 | 357.2 | 10.5 |
| 1982 | 323.6 | 10.2 |
| 1981 | 287.0 | 9.4 |
| 1980 | 248.1 | 9.1 |
| 1979 | 214.7 | 8.6 |
| 1978 | 189.7 | 8.4 |
| 1977 | 169.9 | 8.5 |
| 1976 | 150.8 | 8.5 |
| 1975 | 132.7 | 8.3 |
| 1974 | 116.1 | 7.9 |
| 1973 | 103.4 | 7.6 |
| 1972 | 94.0 | 7.7 |
| 1971 | 83.5 | 7.6 |
| 1970 | 75.0 | 7.4 |
| 1969 | 65.6 | 6.8 |
| 1968 | 58.2 | 6.5 |
| 1967 | 51.5 | 6.3 |
| 1966 | 46.3 | 6.0 |
| 1965 | 41.9 | 5.9 |

Source: Department of Health and Human Services

JULY 30

## "In" and "Out" Degrees

The latest figures from the United States Department of Education on undergraduate fields of study confirm that today's college students are keeping their eyes glued to the job market. Business and management, which ranked behind education and the social sciences in the number of degrees awarded in 1974, surged ahead by 1984. Other large gainers were computer and information science, communications and engineering—degrees that can immediately result in jobs. Losers were traditional liberal arts specialties such as education, literature, language study, philosophy and religion.   AUG. 3

### Bachelor's degrees conferred by institutions of higher education

| Program areas | 1973–74 | 1983–84 | % change* |
|---|---|---|---|
| Business and Management | 131,766 | 230,031 | 75 |
| Communications | 16,250 | 38,586 | 137 |
| Computer and Info Sciences | 4,756 | 32,172 | 576 |
| Education | 185,225 | 92,382 | −50 |
| Engineering | 42,840 | 75,732 | 77 |
| Foreign Languages | 18,840 | 9,479 | −50 |
| Health Sciences | 41,394 | 64,338 | 55 |
| English | 55,469 | 33,739 | −39 |
| Library and Archival Sciences | 1,164 | 255 | −78 |
| Life Sciences | 48,340 | 38,640 | −20 |
| Mathematics | 21,635 | 13,211 | −39 |
| Philosophy and Religion | 9,444 | 6,435 | −32 |
| Physical Sciences | 21,178 | 23,671 | 12 |
| Psychology | 51,821 | 39,872 | −23 |
| Social Sciences | 150,298 | 93,212 | −38 |

*Minus sign indicates declines.
Source: Center for Statistics, U.S. Department of Education

AUG. 3

# House Backs Veto of Bill to Curtail Imported Textiles

**By STEVEN V. ROBERTS**

**W**ASHINGTON, Aug. 6—The House of Representatives voted today to uphold President Reagan's veto of a bill that would have placed strict limits on imports of textiles from 12 countries, most of them in Asia.

The vote was 276 to 149, or eight votes short of the two-thirds margin needed to override a veto. The final tally followed geographical lines more than partisan lines, as 205 Democrats and 71 Republicans opposed the President. Forty-three Democrats and 106 Republicans backed Mr. Reagan's position.

The President had denounced the measure as dangerous protectionist legislation that would disrupt international trade and provoke foreign retaliation against American exporting industries. He worked hard against the bill in recent days, calling individual lawmakers to ask for their support.

The President's trade representative, Clayton K. Yeutter, called the vote a "gratifying victory" and added, "I do believe firmly that we would have had sheer chaos in international trade if this bill had become law."

But the large vote against the President showed that the nation's trade deficit, now growing at a rate of $170 billion a year, has become a major economic and political issue in many areas of the country. Democrats say they will use the issue in the fall election campaign, arguing that the Reagan Administration has failed to stem the loss of jobs to foreign competition in many basic industries.

AUG. 7

## House Roll Call on Trade Bill Veto

On August 6 the House failed to override President Reagan's veto of a bill cutting textile and apparel imports. The vote was 276 in favor of overriding (yes in roll call below) to 149 opposed (no below). That was eight votes less than the two-thirds majority required to override a veto when 425 members voted. There are three vacancies in the House and seven members voted present. While 205 Democrats and 71 Republicans voted to override, 43 Democrats and 106 Republicans voted against overriding the veto:

This was the roll-call vote:

### ALABAMA
**Democrats**—Bevill, yes; Erdreich, yes; Flippo, yes; Nichols, yes; Shelby, yes.
**Republicans**—Callahan, yes; Dickinson, yes.

### ALASKA
**Republican**—Young, no.

### ARIZONA
**Democrat**—Udall, yes.
**Republicans**—Kolbe, no; McCain, no; Rudd, no; Stump, no.

### ARKANSAS
**Democrats**—Alexander, yes; Anthony, yes; Robinson, yes.
**Republican**—Hammerschmidt, yes.

### CALIFORNIA
**Democrats**—Anderson, no; Bates, yes; Beilenson, no; Berman, no; Bosco, yes; Boxer, yes; Brown, yes; Burton, yes; Coelho, yes; Dellums, yes; Dixon, yes; Dymally, yes; Edwards, yes; Fazio, yes; Hawkins, yes; Lantos, yes; Lehman, yes; Levine, no; Martinez, yes; Matsui, no; Miller, no; Mineta, no; Panetta, no; Roybal, yes; Stark, no; Torres, yes; Waxman, no.
**Republicans**—Badham, no; Chappie, no; Dannemeyer, no; Dornan, no; Dreier, no; Fiedler, no; Hunter, yes; Lagomarsino, no; Lewis, no; Lowery, no; Lungren, no; McCandless, no; Moorhead, no; Packard, no; Pashayan, yes; Shumway, no; Thomas, yes; Zschau, no.

### COLORADO
**Democrats**—Schroeder, yes; Wirth, no.
**Republicans**—Brown, no; Kramer, no; Schaefer, no; Strang, no.

### CONNECTICUT
**Democrats**—Geldenson, yes; Kennelly, yes; Morrison, yes.

**Republicans**—Johnson, no; McKinney, yes; Rowland, no.

### DELAWARE
**Democrat**—Carper, yes.

### FLORIDA
**Democrats**—Bennett, no; Chappell, yes; Fascell, yes; Fuqua, yes; Gibbons, no; Hutto, yes; Lehman, yes; MacKay, no; Mica, no; Nelson, no; Pepper, xxx; Smith, yes.
**Republicans**—Bilirakis, yes; Ireland, no; Lewis, no; Mack, no; McCollum, no; Shaw, no; Young, no.

### GEORGIA
**Democrats**—Barnard, yes; Darden, yes; Fowler, yes; Hatcher, yes; Jenkins, yes; Ray, yes; Rowland, yes; Thomas, yes.
**Republicans**—Gingrich, yes; Swindall, yes.

### HAWAII
**Democrat**—Akaka, no.

### IDAHO
**Democrat**—Stallings, no.
**Republican**—Craig, no.

### ILLINOIS
**Democrats**—Annunzio, yes; Bruce, yes; Collins, yes; Durbin, yes; Evans, yes; Gray, yes; Hayes, yes; Lipinski, yes; Price, yes; Rostenkowski, no; Russo, yes; Savage, yes; Yates, yes.
**Republicans**—Crane, no; Fawell, no; Grotberg, xxx; Hyde, no; Madigan, no; Martin, no; Michel, no; Porter, no.

### INDIANA
**Democrats**—Hamilton, no; Jacobs, yes; McCloskey, yes; Sharp, yes; Visclosky, yes.
**Republicans**—Burton, no; Coats, no; Hiler, no; Hillis, yes; Myers, no.

### IOWA
**Democrats**—Bedell, present; Smith, no.
**Republicans**—Evans, no; Leach, no; Lightfoot, no; Tauke, no.

### KANSAS
**Democrats**—Glickman, no; Slattery, no.
**Republicans**—Meyers, no; Roberts, no; Whittaker, no.

### KENTUCKY
**Democrats**—Hubbard, yes; Mazzoli, no; Natcher, yes; Perkins, yes.
**Republicans**—Hopkins, yes; Rogers, yes; Snyder, no.

### LOUISIANA
**Democrats**—Boggs, yes; Breaux, yes; Huckaby, yes; Long, xxx; Roemer, yes; Tauzin, yes.
**Republicans**—Livingston, no; Moore, xxx.

### MAINE
**Republicans**—McKernan, yes; Snowe, yes.

### MARYLAND
**Democrats**—Barnes, yes; Byron, yes; Dyson, yes; Hoyer, yes; Mikulski, yes; Mitchell, yes.
**Republicans**—Bentley, yes; Holt, no.

### MASSACHUSETTS
**Democrats**—Atkins, yes; Boland, yes; Donnelly, yes; Early, yes; Frank, yes; Markey, yes; Mavroules, yes; Moakley, yes; O'Neill, yes (by tradition, the Speaker of the House seldom votes); Studds, yes.
**Republican**—Conte, yes.

### MICHIGAN
**Democrats**—Bonior, yes; Carr, yes; Conyers, yes; Crockett, yes; Dingell, yes; Ford, yes; Hertel, yes; Kildee, yes; Levin, yes; Traxler, yes; Wolpe, yes.
**Republicans**—Broomfield, no; Davis, yes; Henry, yes; Pursell, no; Schuette, yes; Siljander, xxx; Vander Jagt, no.

### MINNESOTA
**Democrats**—Oberstar, yes; Penny, no; Sabo, yes; Sikorski, yes; Vento, yes.
**Republicans**—Frenzel, no; Stangeland, no; Weber, no.

### MISSISSIPPI
**Democrats**—Dowdy, yes; Montgomery, yes; Whitten, yes.
**Republicans**—Franklin, yes; Lott, yes.

### MISSOURI
**Democrats**—Clay, yes; Gephardt, yes; Skelton, yes; Volkmer, yes; Wheat, yes; Young, yes.
**Republicans**—Coleman, yes; Emerson, yes; Taylor, yes.

### MONTANA
**Democrat**—Williams, yes.
**Republican**—Marlenee, no.

### NEBRASKA
**Republicans**—Bereuter, no; Daub, no; Smith, no.

### NEVADA
**Democrat**—Reid, yes.
**Republican**—Vucanovich, no.

### NEW HAMPSHIRE
**Republicans**—Gregg, yes; Smith, yes.

### NEW JERSEY
**Democrats**—Dwyer, yes; Florio, yes; Guarini, yes; Howard, yes; Hughes, yes; Rodino, yes; Roe, yes; Torricelli, yes.
**Republicans**—Courter, no; Gallo, no; Rinaldo, yes; Roukema, yes; Saxton, no; Smith, yes.

### NEW MEXICO
**Democrat**—Richardson, yes.
**Republicans**—Lujan, no; Skeen, yes.

### NEW YORK
**Democrats**—Ackerman, yes; Biaggi, yes; Downey, no; Garcia, yes; LaFalce, no; Lundine, yes; Manton, yes; McHugh, no; Mrazek, yes; Nowak, yes; Owens, yes; Rangel, yes; Scheuer, yes; Schumer, no; Solarz, no; Stratton, yes; Towns, yes; Waldon, yes; Weiss, yes.
**Republicans**—Boehlert, yes; Carney, no; DioGuardi, yes; Eckert, no; Fish, yes; Gilman, yes; Green, no; Horton, yes; Kemp, no; Lent, no; Martin, yes; McGrath, yes; Molinari, yes; Solomon, yes; Wortley, no.

### NORTH CAROLINA
**Democrats**—Hefner, yes; Jones, yes; Neal, yes; Rose, yes; Valentine, yes; Whitley, yes.
**Republicans**—Cobey, yes; Coble, yes; Hendon, yes; McMillan, yes.

### NORTH DAKOTA
**Democrat**—Dorgan, no.

### OHIO
**Democrats**—Applegate, yes; Eckart, yes; Feighan, yes; Hall, yes; Kaptur, yes; Luken, no; Oakar, yes; Pease, no; Seiberling, no; Stokes, yes; Traficant, yes.
**Republicans**—DeWine, no; Gradison, no; Kasich, no; Kindness, yes; Latta, no; McEwen, no; Miller, yes; Oxley, no; Regula, yes; Wylie, no.

### OKLAHOMA
**Democrats**—English, yes; Jones, yes; McCurdy, yes; Synar, yes; Watkins, yes.
**Republican**—Edwards, no.

### OREGON
**Democrats**—AuCoin, no; Weaver, yes; Wyden, no.
**Republicans**—D. Smith, yes; R. Smith, no.

### PENNSYLVANIA
**Democrats**—Borski, yes; Coyne, yes; Edgar, yes; Foglietta, yes; Gaydos, yes; Gray, yes; Kanjorski, yes; Kolter, yes; Kostmayer, yes; Murphy, yes; Murtha, yes; Walgren, yes; Yatron, yes.
**Republicans**—Clinger, yes; Coughlin, yes; Gekas, no; Goodling, yes; McDade, yes; Ridge, yes; Ritter, yes; Schulze, yes; Shuster, yes; Walker, no.

### RHODE ISLAND
**Democrat**—St Germain, yes.
**Republican**—Schneider, yes.

### SOUTH CAROLINA
**Democrats**—Derrick, yes; Spratt, yes; Tallon, yes.
**Republicans**—Campbell, yes; Hartnett, yes; Spence, yes.

### SOUTH DAKOTA
**Democrat**—Daschle, no.

### TENNESSEE
**Democrats**—Boner, yes; Cooper, yes; Ford, yes; Gordon, yes; Jones, yes; Lloyd, yes.
**Republicans**—Duncan, yes; Quillen, yes; Sundquist, yes.

### TEXAS
**Democrats**—Andrews, yes; Brooks, yes; Bryant, yes; Bustamante, yes; Chapman, yes; Coleman, yes; de la Garza, yes; Frost, yes; Gonzalez, yes; R. Hall, yes; Leath, yes; Leland, yes; Ortiz, yes; Pickle, no; Stenholm, yes; Wilson, yes; Wright, yes.
**Republicans**—Archer, no; Armey, no; Bartlett, no; Barton, no; Boulter, no; Combest, yes; DeLay, no; Fields, no; Loeffler, yes; Sweeney, yes.

### UTAH
**Republicans**—Hansen, no; Monson, no; Nielson, no.

### VERMONT
**Republican**—Jeffords, yes.

### VIRGINIA
**Democrats**—Boucher, yes; Daniel, yes; Olin, yes; Sisisky, yes.
**Republicans**—Bateman, no; Bliley, yes; Parris, yes; Slaughter, yes; Whitehurst, no; Wolf, no.

### WASHINGTON
**Democrats**—Bonker, no; Dicks, no; Foley, present; Lowry, no; Swift, no.
**Republicans**—Chandler, no; Miller, no; Morrison, no.

### WEST VIRGINIA
**Democrats**—Mollohan, yes; Rahall, yes; Staggers, yes; Wise, yes.

### WISCONSIN
**Democrats**—Aspin, yes; Kastenmeier, yes; Kleczka, no; Moody, yes; Obey, yes.

**Republicans**—Gunderson, yes; Petri, no; Roth, no; Sensenbrenner, no.

**WYOMING**

**Republican**—Cheney, no.

AUG. 7

# Reagan Undergoes Urinary Tests and Reports "Everything's Fine"

**By BERNARD WEINRAUB**

WASHINGTON, Aug. 9—President Reagan underwent a two-hour urological examination at the Bethesda Naval Medical Center today and declared afterward, "Everything's normal, everything's fine."

A moment later the White House physician, Dr. T. Burton Smith, issued a statement saying: "The examination revealed no abnormalities or evidence of tumor or any other disease. No further urological examinations are planned."

The statement appeared to end a spate of concern and speculation about Mr. Reagan's health after the disclosure Friday that he had canceled a weekend trip to the presidential retreat at Camp David, Md., to undergo the examination today. White House officials said they did not know if Mr. Reagan was experiencing any symptoms that made him decide to have the examination.

Mr. Reagan, who is 75 years old, appeared to move more slowly than usual as he left the hospital this afternoon with his wife, Nancy. They climbed aboard a United States Marine helicopter for the 15-minute flight to the White House.

"Everything's unchanged since 1982," Mr. Reagan said after arriving on the White House lawn.

AUG. 10

## Reagan Health Problems: A Variety over the Years

WASHINGTON, Aug. 8—Following is a chronology of President Reagan's medical problems and treatments:

**1967**—An operation, described as a transurethral prostatectomy, was performed to correct an anatomical abnormality of the neck portion of Mr. Reagan's urinary bladder and to remove about 30 "seedlike prostatic stones." The operation was done because Mr. Reagan had suffered a series of urinary tract infections. It was Mr. Reagan's most serious medical problem before he became President.

**1971**—Mr. Reagan, who has suffered from allergies since he was 29 years old, began receiving regular allergy shots.

**March 30, 1981**—After a speaking engagement at a hotel in Washington, Mr. Reagan was shot in an assassination attempt. A bullet passed close to his heart. The President had immediate surgery to remove the bullet and his rapid recovery was considered unusual by physicians.

**April 1, 1982**—Mr. Reagan underwent tests because of recently experienced discomfort in his urinary tract. Antibiotics were administered, the symptoms disappeared and no further medical treatment was required.

**Sept. 9, 1983**—Mr. Reagan began to wear a custom-designed hearing aid in public in his right ear. His hearing problems stem from the 1930s, when a .38-caliber pistol was fired near his right ear while filming a motion picture.

**May 18, 1984**—In a routine medical examination, a portion of a polyp was removed from the President's intestine and determined to be benign. This polyp was 4 millimeters in size and 40 centimeters from the end of the anal canal. No further surgery was scheduled to remove the rest of the growth. The White House called it "a normal development in the intestinal tract" and said it caused "no undue anxiety" in Mr. Reagan or his aides.

**March 8, 1985**—Doctors discovered a noncancerous or benign growth in the President's colon. It was described as a "small inflammatory pseudo-polyp."

**July 12, 1985**—Mr. Reagan underwent a polypectomy for the removal of the polyp found in the medical examination on March 8. In the surgery, a second and larger polyp was discovered in a procedure called a colonoscopy, which involves using an instrument to examine visually the full length of the colon.

**July 13, 1985**—Mr. Reagan underwent major abdominal surgery to remove what was believed to be a precancerous polyp in his colon and estimated to be five centimeters in diameter. Although the surgery was considered a success, two days later it was announced that the polyp was cancerous. The polyp had been removed from the large intestine and had been confined within the muscle of the bowel wall, with no apparent spread. Some experts believed there was a greater than 50 percent chance that the President would not suffer a recurrence of his cancer; others said his chances were far better than that.

**July 30, 1985**—Skin cancer known as basal cell carcinoma was detected in a pimple on Mr. Reagan's nose and removed. This cancer is usually associated with overexposure to the sun. Basal cell carcinomas are not regarded as a serious health problem because they rarely spread or kill.

**Oct. 10, 1985**—Skin cancer cells were removed from Mr. Reagan's nose in a "minor operation." The cancer was described as being of the basal cell variety, and doctors said it remained from his bout with cancerous cells on his nose in July.

**Jan. 17, 1986**—In a scheduled examination, the President had three small polyps removed from his colon, each from one to two millimeters in size. The same day it was determined that the polyps were "clinically benign." The examination was part of the normal routine after cancer surgery.

**June 20, 1986**—Doctors removed two small polyps from Mr. Reagan's colon in a scheduled examination. This examination was also part of the normal routine after abdominal surgery for colon cancer. Both polyps were benign.

AUG. 9

# G.O.P. Senators Seen with Big Cash Advantage

By STEVEN V. ROBERTS

WASHINGTON, Aug. 10—With less than three months remaining until the fall elections, most incumbent Republican senators have a large advantage in campaign funds over their Democratic challengers. This means the Democrats are facing an uphill struggle in their fight to regain control of the Senate after six years of Republican rule.

Money seldom guarantees victory in politics, and Democratic leaders still predict that they will gain a majority in the November elections. But they concede that the Republicans' overwhelming lead in the fund-raising sweepstakes gives the incumbents a crucial advantage in many states where races are now considered close.

Senator George J. Mitchell of Maine, chairman of the Democratic Senatorial Campaign Committee, says that, given the money situation, it is "something of a miracle" that the Democrats are still able to mount a challenge for control of the Senate. "They've got 100 factors in their favor," he said of the Republicans. "The first 99 are money and the last one is Reagan's personality."

Fred Wertheimer, president of Common Cause, a public affairs lobbying group that monitors campaign spending, added: "The money imbalance is potentially a major factor, particularly when it comes to close races."

Mr. Mitchell noted that Republicans had won 13 of the last 15 Senate elections that were decided by four points or less. "They just can pour that money in, almost without limit," he said.

AUG. 11

## Candidates with cash

List of Senate candidates (incumbents in capital letters) with cash on hand as reported to the Federal Election Commission as of June 30. Where the nomination is not yet settled, the candidate with the greatest cash-on-hand total is listed. Advantage indicates how much more one has on hand than the other.

| State | Name | Cash on hand | Cash-on-hand advantage |
|---|---|---|---|
| Ala. | DENTON (R) | $652,540 | $545,968 |
|  | Shelby (D) | 106,572 |  |
| Alaska | MURKOWSKI (R) | 420,025 | 392,570 |
|  | Olds (D) | 27,455 |  |
| Ariz. | McCain (R) | 504,635 | 501,987 |
|  | Kimball (D) | 2,648 |  |
| Ark. | BUMPERS (D) | 706,241 | 636,636 |
|  | Hutchinson (R) | 69,605 |  |
| Calif. | CRANSTON (D) | 1,416,556 | 971,755 |
|  | Zschau (R) | 444,801 |  |
| Colo. | Wirth (D) | 209,631 | 42,273 |
|  | Kramer (R) | 166,358 |  |
| Conn. | DODD (D) | 842,582 | 781,295 |
|  | Eddy (R) | 61,287 |  |
| Fla. | Graham (D) | 1,589,351 | 760,465 |
|  | HAWKINS (R) | 828,886 |  |
| Ga. | MATTINGLY (R) | 829,959 | 223,216 |
|  | Fowler (D) | 606,743 |  |
| Hawaii | INOUYE (D) | 752,905 | 737,932 |
|  | Hutchinson (R) | 14,973 |  |
| Idaho | SYMMS (R) | 963,820 | 727,205 |
|  | Evans (D) | 234,615 |  |
| Ill. | DIXON (D) | 847,925 | 813,466 |
|  | Koehler (R) | 34,459 |  |
| Ind. | QUAYLE (R) | 683,810 | 671,731 |
|  | Long (D) | 12,079 |  |
| Iowa | GRASSLEY (R) | 1,262,827 | 1,259,519 |
|  | Roehrick (D) | 3,308 |  |
| Kan. | DOLE (R) | 2,141,466 | 2,140,715 |
|  | Ringer (D) | 751 |  |
| Ky. | FORD (D) | 582,355 | 569,864 |
|  | Andrews (R) | 12,491 |  |
| La. | Moore (R) | 1,123,954 | 840,928 |
|  | Breaux (D) | 283,026 |  |
| Md. | Mikulski (D) | 420,355 | 356,999 |
|  | Sullivan (R) | 63,356 |  |
| Mo. | Bond (R) | 1,386,496 | 820,031 |
|  | Woods (D) | 566,465 |  |

| State | Name | Cash on hand | Cash-on-hand advantage |
|---|---|---|---|
| Nev. | Reid (D) | 503,554 | 118,357 |
| | Santini (R) | 385,197 | |
| N.H. | RUDMAN (R) | 390,731 | 355,211 |
| | Peabody (D) | 35,520 | |
| N.Y. | D'AMATO (R) | 3,200,951 | 2,423,082 |
| | Dyson (D) | 777,869 | |
| N.C.* | BROYHILL (R) | 270,627 | 213,342 |
| | Sanford (D) | 57,285 | |
| N.D. | ANDREWS (R) | 660,487 | 597,992 |
| | Conrad (D) | 62,495 | |
| Ohio | GLENN (D) | 476,987 | 453,842 |
| | Kindness (R) | 23,145 | |
| Okla. | NICKLES (R) | 1,954,261 | 1,029,670 |
| | Jones (D) | 924,591 | |
| Ore. | PACKWOOD (R) | 2,163,424 | 2,161,300 |
| | Weaver (D) | 2,124 | |
| Pa. | SPECTER (R) | 1,735,553 | 1,629,597 |
| | Edgar (D) | 105,956 | |
| S.C. | HOLLINGS (D) | 892,624 | 880,804 |
| | McMaster (R) | 11,820 | |
| S.D. | Daschle (D) | 230,982 | 141,485 |
| | ABDNOR (R) | 89,497 | |
| Utah | GARN (R) | 393,022 | 392,924 |
| | Oliver (D) | 98 | |
| Vt. | LEAHY (D) | 598,472 | 561,642 |
| | Snelling (R) | 36,830 | |
| Wash. | GORTON (R) | 821,140 | 746,758 |
| | Adams (D) | 74,382 | |
| Wis. | KASTEN (R) | 1,205,793 | 1,134,053 |
| | Garvey (D) | 71,740 | |

*Senator Broyhill was appointed July 3 to complete the term of the late Senator East.

Source: Common Cause, from Federal Election Commission records

AUG. 11

## The Devastating Effects of Heat and Drought

The rains that washed over much of the South and the Middle Atlantic states last weekend, and the lower temperatures they ushered in, brought a measure of encouragement to those scorched regions last week. So did the House of Representatives's passage, by a vote of 418 to 0, of a $530-million farm relief package similar to one approved earlier by the Senate. The congressional measures, coupled with a Reagan Administration assistance program, estimated at well over $1 billion, that went into effect a week ago Friday, would provide grain, feed, cash and other forms of aid to tens of thousands of farmers in a 10-state region stretching from Alabama to Pennsylvania. The degree to which farmers have already been hurt by months of high temperatures and scant rainfall is apparent from the accompanying tables, in which all figures are estimates. Meteorologists say it will take weeks of rain to end the drought. But for the next few days, at least, they are predicting that the weather in most of the affected region will be dry.

## Effect in key states
### Alabama

|  | Production as percent of U.S. total, 1985 | Percent of yield lost, 1986 | Amount of loss (millions of dollars) |
|---|---|---|---|
| Broiler chickens | 12.5 | 20 | $137 |
| Corn | 0.3 | 50 | 100 |
| Cotton | n.a. | 30 | 60 |
| Eggs | 4.1 | 25 | 50 |
| Hay | 1.0 | 67 | 5 |
| Pasture | 0.5 | 25–90 | n.a. |
| Peanuts | 14.5 | 50 | 84 |
| Soybeans | 1.3 | 50 | 95 |
| Wheat | 0.5 | 85 | 43 |

### Georgia

|  | Production as percent of U.S. total, 1985 | Percent of yield lost, 1986 | Amount of loss (millions of dollars) |
|---|---|---|---|
| Broiler chickens | 14.9 | 13 | $4 |
| Corn | 0.9 | 48 | 84 |
| Cotton | n.a. | 51 | 36 |
| Eggs | 6.3 | 16 | 2 |
| Hay | 0.8 | 79 | 34 |
| Peanuts | 46.6 | 28 | 145 |
| Pecans | n.a. | 50 | 36 |
| Soybeans | 1.8 | 71 | 128 |
| Tobacco | 5.3 | 29 | 37 |
| Wheat | 1.1 | 57 | n.a. |

### North Carolina

|  | Production as percent of U.S. total, 1985 | Percent of yield lost, 1986 | Amount of loss (millions of dollars) |
|---|---|---|---|
| Broiler chickens | 10.0 | 5 | $15 |
| Corn | 1.4 | 23 | 82 |
| Eggs | 4.8 | 5 | 12 |
| Hay | 0.5 | 50 | 25 |
| Pasture | 0.3 | 90 | 20 |
| Peanuts | 10.9 | 10 | 11 |
| Soybeans | 1.9 | 11 | 37 |
| Tobacco | 36.0 | 10 | 75 |
| Vegetables | n.a. | 15 | 22 |

### Maryland*

|  | Production as percent of U.S. total, 1985 | Percent of yield lost, 1986 | Amount of loss (millions of dollars) |
|---|---|---|---|
| Corn | 0.8 | 20–75 | $58 |
| Hay | 0.4 | 30–80 | 8 |
| Pasture | 0.1 | 45–90 | n.a. |

|  | Production as percent of U.S. total, 1985 | Percent of yield lost, 1986 | Amount of loss (millions of dollars) |
|---|---|---|---|
| Soybeans | 0.6 | 25–80 | 11 |
| Tobacco | 1.8 | 25–50 | 16 |
| Wheat | 0.3 | 15–50 | n.a. |

*Does not include data from every county.

## Delaware

|  | Production as percent of U.S. total, 1985 | Percent of yield lost, 1986 | Amount of loss (millions of dollars) |
|---|---|---|---|
| Broiler chickens | 4.4 | 0.5 | $1 |
| Corn | 0.2 | 42 | 12 |
| Hay | n.a. | 50 | 2 |
| Pasture | n.a. | 80 | 1 |
| Soybeans | 0.3 | 30 | 11 |
| Wheat | 0.1 | 28 | 1 |

## South Carolina

|  | Production as percent of U.S. total, 1985 | Percent of yield lost, 1986 | Amount of loss (millions of dollars) |
|---|---|---|---|
| Corn | 0.5 | 60 | $41 |
| Cotton | n.a. | 41 | 18 |
| Hay | 0.3 | 75 | 27 |
| Peanuts | 0.8 | 40 | 3 |
| Soybeans | 1.2 | 40 | 40 |
| Wheat | 0.5 | 16 | 4 |
| Tobacco | 6.4 | 8 | 10 |

Sources: Alabama Agricultural Stabilization and Conservation Service; Clemson University; County Emergency Board of Maryland; Delaware State Emergency Board; Georgia Farm Bureau; North Carolina Department of Agriculture; U.S. Department of Agriculture.

AUGUST 10

# V.A. Reports "Errors" in Dozens of Deaths After Heart Surgery

By JOEL BRINKLEY

WASHINGTON, Aug. 12—An internal audit of Veterans Administration hospitals found "preventable" medical errors in the cases of a large number of patients who died after heart surgery, a House subcommittee disclosed at a hearing today.

In the recent audit of cardiac care units at 21 Veterans Administration hospitals with higher than average mortality rates, inspectors studied the cases of 134 patients who died after surgery.

They found that more than half the incidents that apparently caused the deaths were "classified as being preventable" errors, according to a report by the Veterans Administration's Inspector General's Office, which was discussed at the hearing.

"That's a lot of patients who might have survived surgery if these errors had not been made," said Representative Ted Weiss, the Manhattan Democrat who is chairman of the Intergovernmental Relations and Human Resources Subcommittee, which held the hearing.

The Veterans Administration's director of surgical services, Dr. Robert A. Laning, at first professed not to be familiar with the report, but then said, "Those are just opinions."

AUG. 13

## Study of veterans' hospitals

The first column in the chart below shows the total number of operations done in the fiscal years 1983 and 1984 for the 52 highest risk surgical procedures. Other minor surgical procedures were not counted. The second number is the percent of patients who died. The third number shows the number of open-heart surgery cases performed in the fiscal year 1985 and the percent of those patients who died. Some Veterans Administration hospitals do not have open-heart surgery units.

Hospitals performing fewer than 100 surgical procedures in 1983–84 are not shown.

| Hosp location | Total number surgical cases | % Died | Open heart surgical cases | % Died |
|---|---|---|---|---|
| Minneapolis | 2,295 | 4.4 | 239 | 5.0 |
| Dallas | 2,251 | 5.5 | 140 | 5.0 |
| Houston | 2,185 | 6.0 | 252 | 4.8 |
| Hines, Ill. | 2,098 | 5.8 | 205 | 6.3 |
| Little Rock, Ark. | 2,064 | 7.0 | 295 | 4.1 |
| Long Beach, Calif. | 1,906 | 6.0 | 33 | 18.2 |
| San Antonio | 1,905 | 3.7 | 200 | 5.5 |
| Birmingham, Ala. | 1,838 | 4.6 | 379 | 3.4 |
| Nashville | 1,747 | 6.0 | 152 | 2.0 |
| Durham, N.C. | 1,736 | 6.7 | 134 | 6.0 |
| W. Los Angeles–Wadsworth, Calif. | 1,728 | 5.0 | 183 | 7.1 |
| Tampa, Fla. | 1,715 | 6.3 | 76 | 2.6 |
| Buffalo | 1,713 | 7.1 | 144 | 8.3 |
| Gainesville, Fla. | 1,659 | 4.3 | 127 | 0.8 |
| Memphis | 1,621 | 4.4 | 131 | 8.4 |
| Portland, Ore. | 1,616 | 4.7 | 159 | 1.3 |
| Milwaukee | 1,613 | 3.7 | — | — |
| Richmond | 1,558 | 4.2 | 254 | 5.1 |
| Cleveland | 1,532 | 8.0 | 153 | 4.6 |
| St. Louis | 1,509 | 7.6 | 20 | 5.0* |
| Denver | 1,497 | 6.9 | 109 | 9.2 |
| Boston | 1,430 | 5.7 | — | — |
| East Orange, N.J. | 1,395 | 8.5 | 75 | 5.3 |
| Lexington, Ky. | 1,394 | 5.7 | 75 | 10.7 |
| Indianapolis | 1,389 | 4.8 | 136 | 2.9* |
| Oklahoma City | 1,382 | 5.6 | 116 | 6.0 |
| San Diego | 1,382 | 3.2 | 175 | 4.0 |
| Atlanta | 1,352 | 3.8 | 55 | 5.5* |
| Ann Arbor, Mich. | 1,304 | 3.6 | 101 | 6.9 |
| Chicago-Westside, Ill. | 1,299 | 6.3 | 152 | 5.3 |
| New York | 1,282 | 4.5 | 134 | 4.5 |
| Columbia, Mo. | 1,271 | 4.6 | 108 | 4.6 |
| Pittsburgh–University Dr. | 1,261 | 6.6 | 90 | 5.6 |
| Iowa City | 1,260 | 4.3 | 29 | 6.9* |
| Brooklyn | 1,258 | 7.2 | 97 | 4.1 |
| Phoenix | 1,244 | 4.8 | — | — |
| Augusta, Ga. | 1,241 | 6.2 | 127 | 8.7 |
| Jackson, Miss. | 1,230 | 5.0 | — | — |
| Kansas City, Mo. | 1,218 | 5.6 | 70 | 5.7* |
| Miami | 1,212 | 7.3 | 81 | 3.7 |
| Temple, Tex. | 1,190 | 6.1 | — | — |
| San Juan, P.R. | 1,188 | 5.9 | 66 | 10.6 |
| Madison, Wis. | 1,178 | 3.5 | 106 | 2.8 |
| New Orleans | 1,173 | 6.1 | 86 | 3.5 |
| Asheville, N.C. | 1,169 | 3.8 | 190 | 1.1 |
| Philadelphia | 1,165 | 4.9 | — | — |
| Salt Lake City | 1,144 | 4.6 | 91 | 5.6 |
| Washington | 1,123 | 4.7 | 13 | 0.0 |
| Loma Linda, Calif. | 1,113 | 6.0 | — | — |
| San Francisco | 1,107 | 4.2 | 93 | 6.5 |
| Palo Alto, Calif. | 1,080 | 2.7 | 204 | 3.9 |
| Seattle | 1,065 | 5.8 | 95 | 3.2* |
| Albuquerque | 1,063 | 6.5 | 107 | 4.7 |
| Cincinnati | 1,059 | 4.1 | — | — |
| Bay Pines, Fla. | 1,030 | 5.0 | — | — |
| Tucson, Ariz. | 1,003 | 4.4 | 87 | 2.3* |
| Martinez, Calif. | 995 | 5.0 | — | — |
| Columbia, S.C. | 947 | 6.1 | — | — |
| Charleston, S.C. | 937 | 5.5 | 127 | 2.4 |
| Albany | 934 | 7.4 | — | — |
| Bronx | 922 | 7.5 | — | — |
| Omaha | 861 | 6.4 | — | — |
| Louisville, Ky. | 852 | 5.9 | — | — |
| West Haven, Conn. | 847 | 4.8 | 84 | 4.8 |
| Northport, L.I. | 818 | 6.1 | — | — |
| Shreveport, La. | 792 | 6.3 | — | — |
| Syracuse | 720 | 6.5 | — | — |
| Des Moines | 709 | 6.6 | — | — |
| Allen Park, Mich. | 679 | 7.1 | — | — |
| Chicago Lakeside, Ill. | 674 | 5.3 | — | — |
| Sepulveda, Calif. | 674 | 4.5 | — | — |
| Dayton, Ohio | 659 | 6.8 | — | — |
| Mountain Home, Tenn. | 657 | 8.8 | — | — |
| White River Junction, Vt. | 616 | 4.2 | — | — |
| Salem, Va. | 599 | 6.5 | — | — |
| Baltimore | 583 | 7.5 | — | — |
| Hampton, Va. | 578 | 4.5 | — | — |
| Brockton, Mass. | 563 | 4.1 | — | — |
| Wilkes-Barre, Pa. | 531 | 5.3 | — | — |
| Wilmington, Del. | 512 | 4.7 | — | — |
| West Roxbury, Mass. | 503 | 5.8 | 209 | 4.8 |
| Danville, Ill. | 496 | 5.8 | — | — |
| Newington, Conn. | 476 | 6.5 | — | — |
| Providence, R.I. | 456 | 6.8 | — | — |
| Reno | 455 | 2.6 | — | — |
| Fayetteville, N.C. | 450 | 4.4 | — | — |
| Sioux Falls, S.D. | 444 | 5.9 | — | — |
| Huntington, W.Va. | 431 | 5.6 | — | — |

| Hosp location | Total number surgical cases | % Died | Open heart surgical cases | % Died |
| --- | --- | --- | --- | --- |
| Muskogee, Okla. | 425 | 6.8 | — | — |
| Lake City, Fla. | 419 | 3.8 | — | — |
| Alexandria, La. | 413 | 5.1 | — | — |
| Togus, Me. | 395 | 4.3 | — | — |
| Biloxi, Miss. | 394 | 6.6 | — | — |
| Fargo, N.D. | 382 | 5.5 | — | — |
| Fresno, Calif. | 375 | 5.1 | — | — |
| Martinsburg, W.Va. | 363 | 3.9 | — | — |
| Spokane, Wash. | 353 | 5.4 | — | — |
| North Chicago, Ill. | 342 | 6.4 | — | — |
| Castle Point, N.Y. | 331 | 4.8 | — | — |
| Wichita, Kan. | 318 | 5.3 | — | — |
| Lincoln, Neb. | 299 | 7.0 | — | — |
| Iron Mountain, Mich. | 294 | 5.1 | — | — |
| Topeka, Kan. | 294 | 4.1 | — | — |
| Clarksburg, W.Va. | 283 | 5.3 | — | — |
| Tuskegee, Ala. | 280 | 4.3 | — | — |
| Boise, Idaho | 278 | 4.0 | — | — |
| Manchester, N.H. | 272 | 5.9 | — | — |
| Amarillo, Tex. | 270 | 3.3 | — | — |
| Beckley, W.Va. | 269 | 9.3 | — | — |
| Salisbury, N.C. | 248 | 7.7 | — | — |
| Erie, Pa. | 239 | 2.9 | — | — |
| Fayetteville, Ark. | 235 | 6.0 | — | — |
| Roseburg, Ore. | 228 | 2.6 | — | — |
| Livermore, Calif. | 226 | 2.7 | — | — |
| Poplar Bluff, Mo. | 200 | 8.0 | — | — |
| Fort Meade, S.D. | 189 | 3.2 | — | — |
| Big Spring, Tex. | 185 | 8.6 | — | — |
| Fort Harrison, Mont. | 185 | 2.7 | — | — |
| Dublin, Ga. | 183 | 4.9 | — | — |
| Lebanon, Pa. | 180 | 4.4 | — | — |
| Grand Junction, Colo. | 175 | 4.6 | — | — |
| Saginaw, Mich. | 172 | 2.3 | — | — |
| Prescott, Ariz. | 167 | 3.0 | — | — |
| Fort Wayne, Ind. | 161 | 5.0 | — | — |
| Leavenworth, Kan. | 156 | 3.2 | — | — |
| Marion, Ill. | 149 | 8.1 | — | — |
| Hot Springs, S.D. | 123 | 5.7 | — | — |
| Altoona, Pa. | 118 | 6.8 | — | — |
| Grand Island, Neb. | 116 | 5.2 | — | — |
| Kerrville, Tex. | 114 | 7.0 | — | — |

*Open heart surgery performed in affiliated university hospital.

AUG. 13

# Mail Carrier Kills 14 in Post Office, Then Himself

**By PETER APPLEBOME**

EDMOND, Okla., Aug. 20—A mail carrier in trouble with his supervisors opened fire in a crowded post office here early this morning, killing 14 workers and injuring 7 others before killing himself with a bullet in the head.

The police said the carrier, Patrick Henry Sherrill, of Oklahoma City, burst into the rambling one-story post office here about 6:45 A.M., pulled at least three pistols from a mail pouch and, without a word, started shooting at his fellow employees.

"He was in the center of the room with two .45s, blazing away," said Larry J. Vercelli, a postal union supervisor who talked with some of the employees after they had fled when the shooting began.

The police said one worker was shot in the parking lot behind the five-year-old brick post office. The police said they believed Mr. Sherrill shot the worker before entering the building and then tried to lock the back doors before unleashing his barrage on approximately 100 workers sorting mail and preparing for the day's deliveries.

Police SWAT teams found Mr. Sherrill and 14 fellow employees shot to death when they entered the post office about 8:30 A.M. after trying in vain to talk to the gunman. Seven others were treated at nearby hospitals for bullet wounds; two of the wounded were listed in critical condition. They were being treated at Edmond Memorial Hospital here and at Mercy Health Center in Oklahoma City.

It was the nation's worst shooting since July 18, 1984, when 21 people, including the gunman, died at a McDonald's restaurant in San Ysidro, Calif.

Here is a list of the dead and injured in the shootings today at the Edmond Post Office, as released by the police. Patrick H. Sherrill, 44 years old, of Oklahoma City, killed himself after the shootings.

**The dead**
Patricia Chambers, 41, of Wellston.
Judy Denney, 39, of Edmond.
Rick Esser, 38, of Bethany.
Patricia Gabbard, 47, of Oklahoma City.
Bill Miller, 30, of Piedmont.
Kenneth Morey, 49, of Guthrie.
Jonna Gragert Hamilton, 30, of Moore.
Patty Husband, 49, of Oklahoma City.
Betty Jarred, 34, of Oklahoma City.
Lee Phillips, 42, of Choctaw.
Jerry Pyle, 51, of Edmond.
Mike Rockne, 33, of Edmond.
Tom Shader, 31, of Bethany.
Patti Welch, 27, of Oklahoma City.

**The injured:**
William Nimmo, 40, of Edmond, critical condition.
Judith Walker, 40, of Edmond, critical condition.
Gene Bray, 54, of Edmond, serious condition.
Steven Vick, 24, of Oklahoma City, fair condition.
Eva Joyce Ingram, 45, fair condition.
Michael Bigler, 36, treated and released.

AUG. 21

# Two Planes Collide near Los Angeles

**By JUDITH CUMMINGS**

CERRITOS, Calif., Aug. 31—An Aeromexico jetliner approaching the Los Angeles International Airport collided with a small private plane today, raining destruction on a quiet residential neighborhood as bodies and fiery debris hurtled to the ground.

At least 67 people were killed, and it appeared that the toll would climb with casualties on the ground. Inspector Rob Smith of the Los Angeles County Fire Department said deaths of "two or three" people on the ground had been confirmed so far by the County Coroner's Office. He said that the identities had not been established.

No one aboard the airplanes survived. A spokesman for Aeromexico said 64 passengers and crew members were aboard Flight 498, a DC-9 that originated in Mexico City and made stops in Guadalajara, the resort town of Loreto, and Tijuana on its way to Los Angeles.

The Federal Aviation Administration said the other aircraft was a single-engine Piper Cherokee with three people aboard.

Ten houses were demolished and seven damaged when the airliner plunged to the ground, ripping a swath through a neat suburban subdivision.

At least nine people on the ground were injured including three who suffered first- and second-degree burns, and three firefighters. Officials said all the injuries were minor.

"We saw the two planes, but what we could really see was the tail on the big plane," said Beverly Lolley, a Cerritos homemaker. "It just came straight down, just like a movie, it just descended right on its nose. My friend said, 'Oh, my God, we're going to be killed.'"

SEPT. 1

## Collision Victims

Aeromexico released the following list of passengers aboard its Flight 498 on September 1:

**Passengers**
AVILA, Andrea (child), Mexican, Mexico City.
AVILA, Andres (child), Mexican, Mexico City.
BARRERO, Carmen, Mexican, Rosemead, Calif.
BASYE, Thomas, U.S., (no hometown).
BOOKER, Byron, U.S., Huntington Beach, Calif.
CARO, Aurea G., U.S., Los Angeles.
CORELIA, Mark, U.S., La Mirada, Calif.
CORELIA, Frank, U.S., La Mirada, Calif.
CROSNO, Robert, U.S., LaVerne, Calif.
CROSNO, Howard, U.S., Yucaipa, Calif.
ECHEVERRI, Juan, Colombian, Medellin, Colombia.
ESPINOZA, Clemente, Mexican, Mexico City.
FERRUFINO, Iris, U.S., Bayshore, N.Y.
FERRUFINO, Israel, Salvadoran, Bayshore, N.Y.
GARCIA, Paul, U.S., Los Angeles.
GARCIA, Linda, U.S., Los Angeles.

GONZALEZ, Dinorah, Mexican, Navojoa, Sonora, Mexico.
GUTIERREZ, Hector, Mexican, South Gate, Calif.
GUTIERREZ, Teresa, Mexican, South Gate, Calif.
GUZMAN, Manuel, U.S., Hesperia, Calif.
GUZMAN, Robert, U.S., Norwalk, Calif.
GUZMAN, Joe, U.S., Norwalk, Calif.
HENDRICK, Wendy, U.S., Lomita, Calif.
HENDRICK, Sharon, U.S., Lomita, Calif.
HARMELING, Sherryl Ann, U.S., San Francisco.
HUERTA, Gregorio, U.S., Norwalk, Calif.
KAPTOWSKY, Robert, U.S., Santa Monica, Calif.
KNIGHT, Rutilia, Mexican, Saugus, Calif.
KNIGHT, Patricia, (child) Mexican, Saugus, Calif.
KNIGHT, Elizabeth, (child) Mexican, Saugus, Calif.
LEANOS, Raul, Mexican, San Jose, Calif.
LEANOS, Elva, Mexican, San Jose, Calif.
LOPEZ, Carlos, Mexican, Navojoa, Sonora, Mexico.
LOPEZ, Guadalupe, Mexican, Navojoa, Sonora, Mexico.
LOPEZ, Carlos (child), Mexican, Navojoa, Sonora, Mexico.
NAVIS, Gloria, U.S., Los Angeles.
NAVIS, Raymond, U.S., Los Angeles.
OJEDA, Rosa Maria, Mexican, Mexico City.
PENA, Oscar, Mexican, Los Angeles.
PENA, Maria, Mexican, Los Angeles.
PENA, Maria Cristina (child), Mexican, Los Angeles.
PENA, Elizabeth, U.S., Los Angeles.
REYES, Jesus, Mexican, Queretaro, Mexico.
RUSH, Donald, U.S., Rockville Centre, N.Y.
RUSH, Frederick, U.S., Rockville Centre, N.Y.
STEIN, Sandy, U.S., San Antonio, Texas.
STEIN, Stanley, U.S., San Antonio, Texas.
SICAIROS, George, U.S., Whittier, Calif.
SICAIROS, Diana, U.S., Whittier, Calif.
SICAIROS, George (child), U.S., Whittier, Calif.
SICAIROS, Gabriel (child), U.S., Whittier, Calif.
VENTURA, Jaime, U.S., Lynwood, Calif.
WALSH, Richard, U.S., Los Angeles.
WINLACK, Donald, U.S., Bakersfield, Calif.
WINLACK, Georgia, U.S., Bakersfield, Calif.
WONG, Donald, U.S., West Covina, Calif.
WONG, Jason (child), U.S., West Covina, Calif.
WONG, Stefan (child), U.S., West Covina, Calif.

**The Crew**
VALDES PROM, Capt. Arturo, Mexico City.
VALENCIA, Hector, copilot, Mexico City.
TRILLO LOPEZ, Patricia, Mexico City.
LAVILLA BALLESTEROS, Laura E., Mexico City.
DIAZ HERNANDEZ, Rosalia, Mexico City.
SANCHEZ, Alma Gabriela, Mexico City.

SEPT. 2

## Air Collisions: Terror Aloft

Previous major international and domestic air collisions include these:

**Aug. 15, 1979**—Two medium-range Aeroflot Tupolev-134 airliners collided in midair over Dneprodzerzhinsk in the Ukraine, with a reported loss of 173 lives, including a soccer team on its way to a game in Tashkent.

**Sept. 25, 1978**—A Pacific Southwest Airlines Boeing 727 collided with a single-engine Cessna 172 over San Diego. All 135 passengers on the jet and the two in the Cessna were killed. Seven people on the ground also died when the wreckage plunged to earth.

**March 27, 1977**—In the world's worst air disaster, 574 people were killed when two Boeing 747 airliners, a KLM Royal Dutch Airlines plane and a Pan American Airways jet, collided and exploded on a runway at airport at Santa Cruz de Tenerife in the Canary Islands.

**Sept. 10, 1976**—A British Airways Trident and a chartered Yugoslav Inex-Adria DC-9 collided at 33,000 feet near Zagreb, Yugoslavia, killing all 176 people aboard.

**July 30, 1971**—A Japanese F-86 jet fighter and an All Nippon Airways 727 jet collided near Morioka in northern Japan, killing 162 people.

**Sept. 9, 1969**—An Allegheny Airlines DC-9 collided with a student pilot's plane over Shelbyville, Ind., killing 83 people.

**Dec. 16, 1960**—A United Airlines DC-8 jet and a Trans World Airlines Super-Constellation collided over Staten Island, killing 134 people.

**June 30, 1956**—A T.W.A. Super-Constellation and a United Airlines DC-7 flying a similar route east from Los Angeles slammed into each other over the Grand Canyon in a thunderstorm, killing all 128 people aboard.

SEPT. 1

# An Airborne Disaster Revives Old Questions

**By ROBERT LINDSEY**

CERRITOS, CALIF.—Amid the bodies, gutted homes and wreckage in a middle-class neighborhood devastated last week when a Mexican airliner and a single-engine private aircraft collided overhead was the logbook, faithfully kept up to date, of the smaller plane's pilot.

It showed that William C. Kramer, a retired metals company executive, had logged 231.1 hours in the air between the day in January 1980 when he obtained his pilot's license and the moment he took off on his final flight. "That," said John Lauber of the National Transportation Safety Board, "is a relatively low level of experience," especially considering it was accumulated over a period of more than five years.

The collision between an Aeromexico DC-9 and Mr. Kramer's Piper PA-28 has renewed questions about aviation safety that are likely to be raised in Congress during coming months. Among them is how safe the nation's air traffic control system is five years after President Reagan fired thousands of experienced controllers because of what he called an illegal strike.

Another question is whether new restrictions should be placed on the movements of small aircraft around major airports. That is, should the nation do more to protect passengers of commercial jets and people on the ground from mistakes by relatively inexperienced pilots?

It will be months before the National Transportation Safety Board issues a report assessing blame for the collision. It is still uncertain whether Mr. Kramer had a minor heart attack before the disaster. But according to Mr. Lauber the early evidence points to one inescapable conclusion: Mr. Kramer, like an errant driver going the wrong way on a one-way street, had strayed into airspace where he did not belong.                    SEPT. 7

## Disaster aloft

Major midair collisions over the United States*

| Year | Carrier or plane | Location | Total fatalities |
|------|------------------|----------|------------------|
| 1956 | United DC-7; TWA Lockheed Constellation | Grand Canyon | 128 |
| 1958 | United DC-7; Air Force F-100F | Las Vegas, Nev. | 49 |
| 1958 | Capital Viscount; National Guard T-33 | Brunswick, Md. | 12 |
| 1960 | United DC-8; T.W.A. Lockheed Super-Constellation | New York City | 140 |
| 1967 | T.W.A. DC-9; Beechcraft Baron | Urbana, Ohio | 26 |
| 1967 | Piedmont Boeing 727; Cessna | Hendersonville, N.C. | 82 |
| 1969 | Allegheny DC-9; Piper | Fairland, Ind. | 84 |
| 1971 | Hughes Airwest DC-9; Marine Corps F-4B | Duarte, Calif. | 50 |
| 1972 | North Central Convair 340; Air Wisconsin De Havilland DHC-6 | Appleton, Wis. | 13 |
| 1978 | Pacific Southwest Boeing 727; Cessna | San Diego | 151 |
| 1984 | Wings West Beech C-99; Rockwell Commander | San Luis Obispo, Calif. | 19 |
| 1986 | Helicopter; De Havilland DHC-6 | Grand Canyon | 25 |
| 1986 | Aeromexico DC-9; Piper | Cerritos, Calif. | 85–87** |

*Collisions involving commercial aircraft that resulted in 10 or more fatalities
**preliminary count

Source: National Transportation Safety Board

SEPT. 7

# $8.2 Million Raised by Bush Committee

By RICHARD L. BERKE

WASHINGTON, Sept. 6—Vice President Bush's political action committee raised $8.2 million in the 18-month period ended June 30, several times what any other prospective presidential candidate raised, according to figures made public today by the Federal Election Commission.

Mr. Bush's committee, the Fund for America's Future, spent $5.3 million in the period, $506,274 of which went to candidates running for the House and Senate this year, the figures show.

Political action committees, which raise and spend money to influence elections, have played a growing role in campaign financing, with corporate, labor and trade PACs historically collecting the most contributions. The figures show, for example, that the Realtors PAC has maintained the lead in contributions to Federal candidates.

But a more recent development is the proliferation of PACs set up by possible presidential candidates, who under Federal law are not allowed to directly use the funds for their personal campaigns. In the 18-month period, such committees collected contributions at the high levels previously reserved for the noncandidate PACs.

Mr. Bush has "redefined the presidential fund-raising game," said one expert, Michael Malbin, a professor at the University of Maryland who is a resident scholar at the American Enterprise Institute. He added: "I don't think any other candidate has hit $3 million before at this stage in an election cycle. It's a striking new development."

Mr. Bush established the Fund for America's Future in May 1985 with the stated purpose of raising money to help elect Republicans to Congress this year. But campaign financing experts say this and other committees are actually support systems for future presidential races.   SEPT. 7

## Growth in PAC collecting and spending

These figures show the political action committees that contributed the most money to Federal candidates over the 18 months from Jan. 1, 1985, to June 30, and the top money raisers in the same period among the so-called nonconnected political action committees, which are generally noncorporate and nontrade groups working in the interests of a certain candidate or cause.

**The Big Contributors**

| | |
|---|---|
| 1. Realtors Political Action Committee | $1,387,429 |
| 2. National Education Association PAC | 1,034,220 |
| 3. Build PAC of the National Association of Home Builders | 949,772 |
| 4. American Medical Association PAC | 869,098 |
| 5. Committee on Letter Carriers Political Education | 839,255 |
| 6. Association of Trial Lawyers PAC | 803,600 |
| 7. Seafarers Political Activity Donation | 768,956 |
| 8. National Association of Life Underwriters PAC | 737,317 |
| 9. U.A.W.-V-C.A.P. (United Auto Workers) | 711,470 |
| 10. Democratic Republican Independent Voter Education Committee (Teamsters) | 709,426 |
| 11. Machinists Nonpartisan Political League | 637,500 |
| 12. Active Ballot Club (United Food and Commercial Workers International Union) | 622,510 |
| 13. Airline Pilots Association PAC | 594,500 |
| 14. National Association of Retired Federal Employees PAC | 580,755 |
| 15. Transportation Political Education League (United Transportation Union) | 554,109 |

**The Big Money Raisers**

| | |
|---|---|
| 1. Fund for America's Future (Vice President Bush) | $8,249,387 |
| 2. National Congressional Club (Jesse Helms's associates) | 8,099,908 |
| 3. National Conservative Political Action Committee | 7,738,709 |
| 4. Auto Dealers for Free Trade PAC | 2,742,554 |
| 5. Campaign for Prosperity (Jack Kemp) | 2,260,577 |
| 6. Fund for a Conservative Majority (conservatives) | 2,176,332 |
| 7. Citizens for the Republic (President Reagan) | 2,019,098 |
| 8. Voter Guide (bipartisan California group) | 1,947,267 |
| 9. Fund for a Democratic Majority (Edward M. Kennedy) | 1,942,751 |
| 10. Campaign America (Bob Dole) | 1,874,449 |
| 11. National Committee for an Effective Congress (liberal Democrats) | 1,604,050 |
| 12. National PAC (Israeli interests) | 1,453,446 |
| 13. Republican Majority Fund (Howard H. Baker, Jr.) | 1,241,517 |
| 14. National Committee to Preserve Social Security PAC | 1,118,757 |
| 15. Council for a Livable World (antinuclear, environmental) | 990,094 |

Source: Federal Election Commission

SEPT. 7

# Funds and Jobs Are Pledged to Boston Students

By FOX BUTTERFIELD

BOSTON, Sept. 9—Leading Boston businesses have organized a $6 million program that will guarantee financial aid to all graduates of the city's public high schools who get into college and then provide jobs for them when they finish their education.

The complex program also includes activities to improve education. It has aroused interest in other cities and several foreign countries.

"This is an incentive for public high school students from the inner city to go to college and stay in it," said Edward E. Phillips, chairman of the New England Mutual Life Insurance Company. The company donated $1 million for an endowment to provide financial aid for those entering college, and Mr. Phillips has helped to raise much of the rest of the funds from 40 companies in Boston.

In addition, more than 350 companies have pledged to help provide jobs to the graduates. Among the other companies that have contributed large grants are the Bank of Boston, $1.5 million; the John Hancock Insurance Company, $1 million; the Bank of New England; and a number of prominent law firms, real estate developers and retail stores.

The major contributors to the Access permanent endowment, as of Wednesday, were the following:
Bank of Boston
Bank of New England
Beal Companies
Blue Cross/Blue Shield of Massachusetts
Boston Edison
Boston Five Cents Savings Bank
Boston Gas Company
Boston Foundation
The Boston Globe
Cabot, Cabot & Forbes
The Congress Group
Coopers & Lybrand
Digital Equipment
Gaston Snow & Ely Bartlett
Goodwin, Procter & Hoar
Hale & Dorr
Filene's
Gillette Company
Hill, Holiday, Connors, Cosmopulos Inc.

Houghton Mifflin Company
Immobilaire New England
John Hancock
Jordan Marsh
Liberty Mutual
The New England
New England Telephone
Palmer & Dodge
Polaroid
Ropes & Gray
Ryan, Elliot
Shawmut Bank
State Street Bank
Stop & Shop
   Other Access contributors are these:
Arthur Anderson & Company
Red Auerbach Fund
Bank of Boston
The Beacon Companies
Blue Shield of Mass Inc.
Boston Edison Foundation
Boston Pipe & Fitting Company Inc.
Cablevision Corporation of Boston
Cabot Corporation Foundation Inc.
Career School Expo
Central Cooperative Bank
F. H. Chase Inc.
Cipriani Advertising Inc.
Codman & Shurtleff Inc.
Contemporary Multi-Service
Corcoran Construction Company
Darkhorse Inc.
Delta Elevator Service Corporation
Dynagraf Inc.
Estech Management Company Inc.
Eaton Vance Corporation
Evans Medical Foundation Inc.
Joseph and Clara Ford Foundation
General Ship Corporation
Carol and Avram Goldberg Fund
Goodwin, Procter & Hoar
Gilbert Hood, Jr., Charitable Trust
Ellen Gilman Trust
Houghton Mifflin
IBM Corporation
Ingalls Associates Inc.

John Hancock Company
Honeywell
Jordan Marsh Company
Leggat Company
Liberty Mutual Insurance Company
Loomis, Sayles & Company
Marr Companies
Mohoney & Wright Ins. Agency
Marshalls
Merchants Cooperative Bank
Mintz, Levin, Cohn, Ferris
Mutual Bank Foundation
New England Board of Higher Education
Ogden Food Service
Otis & Ahearn Real Estate
Joseph Perini Memorial Foundation
Polaroid Foundation
Provident Bank for Savings
Sydney and Esther Rabb Family Fund
Raytheon Company
Saunders Hotels Company Inc.
Maurice H. Saval Company
Shawmut Bank of Boston.
Skidmore, Owings & Merrill
State Street Bank & Trust Company
Stop & Shop Foundation
Strive Endowment
Sunlife of Canada
Terrace Motel
The New England
The Skill Bureau Inc.
Two Oliver Inc.
Union Warren Savings Bank
Warren Publishing Company
S. D. Warren Company Weiner's Antique Shop
Zayre Corporation

SEPT. 10 AND 14

## 69 Ex-political Prisoners in Cuba Fly to a Joyous Welcome in U.S.

By JON NORDHEIMER

MIAMI, Sept. 15—With prayers of thanksgiving and deliverance, 69 former political prisoners from Cuba and about 40 members of their families arrived in the United States today.

Some of those who helped organize the move hoped the release of these people might signal a break in the immigration impasse between Washington and Havana.

A joyous throng of family members and old comrades of the prisoners greeted them with cheers, shouts and tears in Miami following a morning flight from Havana.

There were supposed to be 70 prisoners on the chartered plane, but one, Juan Gomez Blanco, died in a Havana hospital Sunday night, just hours before he was scheduled to board the flight. He had been released from a Cuban prison Thursday. Another, Jose Sanchez Pruna, collapsed in Miami at sprawling Tropical Park, where the prisoners were taken to meet friends and relatives.

Many of the former prisoners had been in prisons in Cuba for more than 20 years. Some, like Carmello Garcia Estevez, had been jailed shortly after Fidel Castro triumphantly marched into Havana to seize power on Jan. 1, 1959.

About half of the entourage aboard the plane remained in Miami to begin picking up their lives, while the rest boarded commercial flights to New York, Chicago, Los Angeles and a number of other cities where relatives awaited them. The United States Catholic Conference, the social-action arm of the nation's Roman Catholic bishops, had worked to arrange the release of the prisoners and their relocation here.      SEPT. 16

### Released from Cuba

This list of persons released by Cuba was provided by the Immigration and Naturalization Service:

ACOSTA Cabos, J.
ACOSTA Hernández, I.
AGUIAR Amirez, L.
ALONSO Valdez, M.
ALVAREZ González, R.
ALVAREZ Torres, M.
ARMS Estezez, C.
ARZOLA Guirado, R.
ARZOLA Perdomo, R.
BANOS Bacallao, N.
BARBON Fuentes, J.
BARO Miranda, O.
CABRERA Torres, Y.
CACERES Izquierdo, G.
CAPOTE Bernal, B.
CASANOVA Crespo, G.
CASTILLO Pérez, D.
CASUSAS Toledo, G.
COIRA Alvarez, M.
COLON Soca, A.
CONTINO García
CONTINO Marcia, M.
CONTINO Mayor, A.
CORCHO Valdes, M.
DE LA CABA Betancourt, C.
DELGADO Alvarez, J.
DELGADO Fernández, O.
DIAZ Martínez, J.
DOCINA Molina, H.
ESCALONA Avila, I.
ESPINOSA Coca, L.
ESPINOSA Prieres
FALCON Herrera, A.
FARRARAS García, R.
FERNANDEZ García, R.
FERRA Mulet, J.
FLORES Franqui, J.
GARCIA Estevez, C.
GARCIA Ledo, J.
GARCIA Molina, J.
GARCIA Pérez, I.
GARCIA Rojas, F.
GONZALEZ Herrera, R.
GONZALEZ Lorente, L.
GONZALEZ Ruiz, M.
GRAU Alsina, R.
GUTIERREZ, V.
HECHAVARRIA Granda, F.
HERNANDEZ, García A.
HERNANDEZ Hernández, A.
HERNANDEZ Verdecia, J.
ILLA Fernández, O.
IZQUIERDO Dáz, J.
JUNCO Benavides, J.
LA ROSA Luis, A.
LEDO, C.
LEDO, J.
LOIS Lizazo, C.
LOPEZ Fernández, P.
LORIGA Gómez, A.
MARCEAL Manuel, A.
MARQUEZ Batesta, T.
MARTINEZ Damas, C.
MARTINEZ, E.
MARTINEZ Hernández, Y.
MARTINEZ Hernández, J.
MONTES DE OCA Rodríguez, E.
MORA Rosal, E.
MORALES Mena, F.
NUNEZ Trujillo, D.
OLIVA Plutarco, R.
ORTIZ Curado, J.
ORTIZ Girado, J.
ORTIZ Tabio
PALACIOS Martinez, J.
PAULA Valdes, S.
PENA Cuzx, M.
PENA Valdez, P.
PIREZ González, A.
PIREZ Guerra, L.
PIREZ Rafael, L.
PRADO Fernández, A.
PRIERES Rodríguez, M.
RAMIREZ Bientz
RENONDO Cross, E.
RENONDO Trujillo, E.
RENONDO Trujillo, E.
RENONDO Trujillo
REYES Gómez, C.

RIVERA Barrios, R.
RIVERO Mondejar, J.
RIVERO Moreno, F.
RODRIGUEZ Barrientos, S.
RODRIGUEZ Delgado, J.
RODRIGUEZ García, J.
RODRIGUEZ García, R.
RODRIGUEZ Martínez, J.
RODRIGUEZ Mayo, J.
RODRIGUEZ Vega, F.
RUIZ Hernández, J.
SALAS Ledo, B.
SANCHEZ Pruna, J.
SOCA Domínguez, J.
SUAREZ Espinosa, D.
TAMAYO Francisco, S.
TEJERA Aguiar, S.
TEJERA Milian, S.
TORRES Martínez, J.
TORREZ Delgado
TRUJILLO González, M.
VARELA Mayo, R.

SEPT. 16

# Senate, 65 to 33, Votes to Confirm Rehnquist as 16th Chief Justice

By LINDA GREENHOUSE

WASHINGTON, Sept. 17—The Senate tonight confirmed William Hubbs Rehnquist as the 16th Chief Justice of the United States and Antonin Scalia to succeed him as an Associate Justice.

The vote on Justice Rehnquist was 65 to 33. The vote on Judge Scalia, now a judge on the United States Court of Appeals for the District of Columbia, was 98 to 0. Senator Jake Garn, the Utah Republican who is recovering from surgery, was absent, as was Senator Barry Goldwater, Republican of Arizona.

Forty-nine Republicans and 16 Democrats voted for Justice Rehnquist, with 31 Democrats and 2 Republicans voting against him.

Justice Rehnquist and Judge Scalia are to be sworn in next week, in time for the Court's next session, which begins Oct. 6.

Justice Rehnquist succeeds Warren E. Burger, who announced in June that he wanted to retire after 17 years as Chief Justice in order to spend all his time planning the celebration of the bicentennial of the Constitution. That event takes place one year from today.

Justice Rehnquist received more negative votes than any other Justice who has been confirmed to the High Court. The previous high number of negative votes, 26, was shared by three Justices: Mahlon Pitney, confirmed as an Associate Justice in 1912 by a vote of 50 to 26; Charles Evans Hughes, confirmed as Chief Justice in 1930 by a vote of 52 to 26; and Mr. Rehnquist himself, confirmed as an Associate Justice in 1971 by a vote of 68 to 26.

The vote tonight followed a bruising debate that began with four days of hearings before the Senate Judiciary Committee in midsummer and grew in intensity as the nomination reached the Senate floor.    SEPT. 18

## Vote on Chief Justice Rehnquist

This is the roll-call vote by which the Senate agreed to the confirmation of Associate Justice William H. Rehnquist to be Chief Justice of the United States:

### FOR CONFIRMATION—65

#### Democrats—16

Bentsen, Tex.
Boren, Okla.
Bumpers, Ark.
Chiles, Fla.
DeConcini, Ariz.
Dixon, Ill.
Ford, Ky.
Heflin, Ala.
Hollings, S.C.
Johnston, La.
Long, La.
Nunn, Ga.
Proxmire, Wis.
Pryor, Ark.
Stennis, Miss.
Zorinsky, Neb.

#### Republicans—49

Abdnor, S.D.
Andrews, N.D.
Armstrong, Colo.
Boschwitz, Minn.
Broyhill, N.C.
Chafee, R.I.
Cochran, Miss.
Cohen, Me.
D'Amato, N.Y.
Danforth, Mo.
Denton, Ala.
Dole, Kan.
Domenici, N.M.
Durenberger, Minn.
Evans, Wash.
Gorton, Wash.
Gramm, Tex.
Grassley, Iowa
Hatch, Utah
Hatfield, Ore.
Hawkins, Fla.
Hecht, Nev.
Heinz, Pa.
Helms, N.C.
Humphrey, N.H.
Kassebaum, Kan.
Kasten, Wis.
Laxalt, Nev.
Lugar, Ind.
Mattingly, Ga.
McClure, Idaho
McConnell, Ky.
Murkowski, Alaska
Nickles, Okla.
Packwood, Ore.
Pressler, S.D.
Quayle, Ind.
Roth, Del.
Rudman, N.H.
Simpson, Wyo.
Specter, Pa.
Stafford, Vt.
Stevens, Alaska
Symms, Idaho
Thurmond, S.C.
Trible, Va.
Wallop, Wyo.
Warner, Va.
Wilson, Calif.

**AGAINST CONFIRMATION—33**

**Democrats—31**

| | | |
|---|---|---|
| Baucus, Mont. | Harkin, Iowa | Metzenbaum, Ohio |
| Biden, Del. | Hart, Colo. | |
| Bingaman, N.M. | Inouye, Hawaii | Mitchell, Me. |
| Bradley, N.J. | Kennedy, Mass. | Moynihan, N.Y. |
| Burdick, N.D. | Kerry, Mass. | Pell, R.I. |
| Byrd, W.Va. | Lautenberg, N.J. | Riegle, Mich. |
| Cranston, Calif. | | Rockefeller, W.Va. |
| Dodd, Conn. | Leahy, Vt. | |
| Eagleton, Mo. | Levin, Mich. | Sarbanes, Md. |
| Exon, Neb. | Matsunaga, Hawaii | Sasser, Tenn. |
| Glenn, Ohio | | Simon, Ill. |
| Gore, Tenn. | Melcher, Mont. | |

**Republicans—2**

Mathias, Md.  Weicker, Conn.

SEPT. 18

# Harvard's Endowment Loses First Place to Texas

**By PETER APPLEBOME**

**H**OUSTON, Sept. 17—The endowment managed by University of Texas System has passed Harvard's to become the largest of any educational enterprise in the United States, according to an annual survey by the National Association of College and University Business Officers.

The survey marked the first time on record that Harvard's total endowment has been surpassed, but officials at both universities were quick to point out that there was little ground for comparison between the two endowments.

Funds under the management of the University of Texas System provide for the 14-member system, Texas A&M University and two other colleges in the A&M System. The Texas institutions enroll about 160,000 students; Harvard's endowment supports a system of about 16,000 students. By state law, much of the Texas endowment is restricted to paying interest on construction bonds.

In the state's oil boom, some of the money was used to pay for programs and hire faculty that helped the schools make conspicuous bids for educational excellence. The money was often described then as "a margin of excellence" that would catapult them into the first rank of American universities.

Now, while Harvard is celebrating its 350th anniversary, universities in Texas are attempting to deal with the financial shocks caused by falling oil prices. The state legislature is considering steep cuts in educational funding to deal with a budget deficit that is now projected to be $2.8 billion.

"It's a little untimely for us," said Michael Patrick, executive vice chancellor for asset management for the University of Texas System. "I don't know that we're helped by anything that suggests we're awash in money. Less than 10 percent of the resources for the U.T. system come from the endowment."

SEPT. 18

## Endowments: The 10 richest schools

Total university endowment at the end of each school year, in millions.*

| 1985 | | 1984 | |
|---|---|---|---|
| U. of Texas | $2,927.2 | Harvard | $2,486.3 |
| Harvard | 2,694.8 | U. of Texas | 2,273.3 |
| Princeton | 1,519.2 | Princeton | 1,287.9 |
| Yale | 1,308.7 | Yale | 1,060.7 |
| Stanford | 1,083.9 | Stanford | 944.0 |
| Columbia | 978.6 | Columbia | 855.2 |
| M.I.T. | 770.2 | M.I.T. | 645.6 |
| U. of California | 716.8 | U. of Rochester | 588.3 |
| Chicago | 640.8 | U. of California | 559.4 |
| Washington U., Mo. | 622.1 | Chicago | 517.1 |

*Survey by the National Association of College and University Business Officers

Source: *The Chronicle of Higher Education.*

SEPT. 18

## Cutting into National Forests

**By PHILIP SHABECOFF**

WASHINGTON—The People of Puerto Rico know the 30,000-acre Caribbean National Forest as *el Yunque*, the Anvil. It is the only tropical rain forest in the national forest system, and environmentalists and scientists have protested angrily against a recently unveiled Forest Service plan calling for more than one fifth of its acreage to be harvested for timber over the next 45 years.

Francisco Javier Blanco, executive director of the Puerto Rican Conservation Trust, predicted that such a harvest in the fragile ecosystem would cause "serious environmental problems," altering rainfall patterns and wiping out endangered species, such as the Puerto Rican parrot. The only reason for the plan, he charged, is the Reagan Administration's policy of increasing timber production from national forests.

Terry Tenold, the Forest Service planning officer in Puerto Rico, said that only areas cut in the past for charcoal would be harvested, and that the wood was needed for the Puerto Rican economy.

The Forest Service is under fire for many similar recently published plans, all required by the National Forest Management Act of 1976. The plans often call for sharply increased timber harvests, new roads into virgin areas and expanded grazing, mining and oil drilling activity.   SEPT. 28

### Big woods
States with largest National Forest areas

|  | National Forests as percent of state area | Total acres (in millions) |
|---|---|---|
| Idaho | 39 | 20 |
| Oregon | 27 | 16 |
| Colorado | 21 | 14 |
| Washington | 21 | 9 |
| California | 20 | 20 |
| Montana | 18 | 17 |
| Arizona | 15 | 11 |
| Utah | 15 | 8 |
| Wyoming | 14 | 9 |
| New Mexico | 12 | 9 |

*Source:* U.S. Forest Service

SEPT. 28

## Teamsters Bolster Campaign Coffers

**By RICHARD L. BERKE**

WASHINGTON, Oct. 12—In a major strategic shift for the nation's largest labor union, the International Brotherhood of Teamsters has made raising funds for political campaigns a top priority to bolster its influence.

The union's political action committee amassed 10 times more funds for contributions to candidates in a recent 18-month period than it had four years earlier.

Historically, the teamsters' political action committee has raised less than several other funds affiliated with organized labor, including funds with smaller memberships.

But the teamster fund ranked first among political action committees affiliated with labor in money collected and spent in the 18-month election cycle that ended June 30.

The teamster fund—called Democrat, Republican Independent Voter Education—raised $2.8 million and spent $1.4 million in that period, according to the Federal Election Commission. By contrast, in a parallel period ending June 30, 1982, the committee raised $280,000 and spent nearly $218,000, according to commission figures.

In the 18-month period that ended June 30, the fund, known as DRIVE, for its initials, contributed $643,626 to Democrats and $118,420 to Republicans running for the Senate or House of Representatives. Those contributions are relatively modest, given the amount the fund has on hand, because many of the committee's contributions were made late in the cycle or went to local races and have not been recorded by the commission, according to teamster officials.

The shift from limited fund-raising at local levels to a more centralized, national approach is part of an effort by the teamsters to maintain political clout at a time when the influence of organized labor is widely regarded as waning. The union says its membership is about 1.8 million, down from a high of 2.3 million in the late 1970s.  OCT. 13

## Growth of the Teamsters' PAC fund

**Top 20 Labor PAC's in Money Raised**
Figures are for the 18-month period ending June 30, 1986.

| | |
|---|---|
| 1. International Brotherhood of Teamsters | $2,806,109 |
| 2. National Education Association | 2,344,868 |
| 3. United Auto Workers of America | 1,951,004 |
| 4. National Association of Letter Carriers | 1,751,273 |
| 5. United Transportation Union | 1,507,526 |
| 6. Marine Engineers Beneficial Association Political Action Fund | 1,499,022 |
| 7. American Federation of State, County & Municipal Employees | 1,461,776 |
| 8. Machinists Non-Partisan Political League | 1,451,115 |
| 9. Communications Workers of America | 1,423,760 |
| 10. United Food & Commercial Workers International | 1,216,288 |
| 11. International Brotherhood of Electrical Workers | 1,192,124 |
| 12. International Longshoremen's Association | 1,150,279 |
| 13. Seafarers International Union | 1,002,910 |
| 14. Sheet Metal Workers International | 1,000,638 |
| 15. Air Line Pilots Association International | 946,419 |
| 16. American Federation of Teachers | 936,400 |
| 17. Marine Engineers Beneficial Association Retirees Group Fund | 866,811 |
| 18. Carpenters Legislative Improvement Committee | 822,367 |
| 19. American Postal Workers Union | 781,602 |
| 20. United Steelworkers of America | 710,801 |

Source: Federal Election Commission

**Teamster Money Raised and Spent**
Figures are political action committee totals, in millions of dollars, for the 18-month period ending July 1.

| | Raised | Spent |
|---|---|---|
| 1980 | .195 | .192 |
| 1982 | .280 | .217 |
| 1984 | 1.032 | .438 |
| 1986 | 2.80 | 1.44 |

OCT. 13

## 80 Named as Recipients of Ellis Island Awards

Eighty Americans from 42 ethnic groups were named yesterday as recipients of the Ellis Island Medal of Honor by the Statue of Liberty–Ellis Island Foundation.

The medals will be presented to the recipients, all either naturalized or native Americans, at a ceremony Oct. 27 on Ellis Island. That is the day before the 100th anniversary of the dedication of the Statue of Liberty, the final event of the 1986 Liberty Centennial observances.

The announcement of the awards was made at a news conference in a midtown restaurant by the president of the foundation, William F. May, and the chairman of the New York Statue of Liberty Centennial Commission, William D. Fugazy.

Honorary medals will also be presented to John Cardinal O'Connor; Lee A. Iacocca, chairman of the foundation; and Mr. May.

Mr. Fugazy said the medal was thought up in June, after the foundation's naming of 12 naturalized Americans for the Medal of Liberty had produced an outcry. Critics of the award noted then that not even such major ethnic groups as the Irish, Italians and Poles were represented among the 12.

At the end of June, Mayor Koch reacted to the protests by naming 87 prominent Americans of foreign ancestry to receive the 1986 Mayor's Libery Award. Some of those honored by the Mayor are also on the Ellis Island list.

Those named yesterday were selected from more than 15,000 nominations. The winners, a mixture of prominent and relatively unknown citizens, were screened by the National Ethnic Coalition of Organizations, which was selected for the work by the foundation.

These are the winners, by ancestry and present or former profession or occupation:

Muhammad Ali, African-American, boxer
Charles Allen, English, broker
Michel C. Bergerac, French, businessman
Dr. C. Kazys Bobelis, Lithuanian, surgeon
Victor Borge, Danish, entertainer
Joe Bowen, Welsh, contractor
John Brademas, Greek, educator
Zbigniew Brzezinski, Polish, educator
Anita Bryant, Native American, entertainer
Curtis L. Carlson, Swedish, executive
Cesar Chavez, Mexican, labor leader
Mildred Imach Cleghorn, Native American, activist
Claudette Colbert, French, actress
Walter Cronkite, Dutch, journalist
Edward J. DeBartolo, Italian, developer
John Denver, German, singer
Joe DiMaggio, Italian, baseball player
Lev. E. Dobriansky, Ukrainian, diplomat
Senator Christopher J. Dodd, Irish, politician
Kirk Douglas, Russian, actor
Alex Esclamato, Philippine, publisher
Archbishop Patrick P. Flores, Mexican, cleric
Erik J. Friis, Norwegian, activist
A. Bartlett Giamatti, Italian, educator
Roberto C. Goizueta, Cuban, executive
Dr. Vartan Gregorian, Armenian, librarian
Jon Hanson, Austrian, developer
Helen Hayes, Irish, actress
John F. Henning, Irish, labor leader
Benjamin Hooks, African-American, activist
Dolores Reade Hope, Irish, philanthropist
K. P. Hwang, Korean, executive
Archbishop Iakovos, Greek, cleric
Daniel K. Inouye, Japanese-American, politician
Tyyni Kalervo, Finnish, restaurateur
Dr. George S. Kanahele, Hawaiian-American, educator
Dr. Har Gobind Khorana, Asian-Indian, educator
Coretta Scott King, African-American, activist
John W. Kluge, German, executive
John Cardinal Krol, Polish, cleric
Former Senator Frank Lausche, Yugoslav, politician
Jean MacArthur, English, philanthropist
The Rev. Douglas Lachlan MacLean, Scottish, theologian
Dr. Herbert P. MacNeal, Scottish, physician
Archbishop Torkom Manoogian, Armenian, cleric
Aloysius A. Mazewski, Polish, activist
Dr. Matthew Mestrovic, Croatian, activist
Carlos Montoya, Spanish, guitarist
Prof. Gabriel Nahas, French, pharmacologist
Martina Navratilova, Czechoslovak, athlete
Michael Novak, Slovak, writer
Jacqueline Kennedy Onassis, French, editor
Arnold Palmer, Scottish, athlete
Milan Panic, Yugoslav, executive
Dr. Antonia Pantoja, Puerto Rican, social worker
Rosa Parks, African-American, activist
Gregory Peck, English, actor
John Petlica, Czechoslovak, broadcaster
Milton Petrie, Russian, philanthropist
Orville Prestholdt, Norwegian, Government official
Claire Quintal, Canadian, educator
Louise Rodrigues, Portuguese, teacher
Peter Rona, Hungarian, banker
Mirielle Rostad, Belgian, nurse
Paul Sanchez, Puerto Rican, labor leader
Domenick S. Scaglione, Italian, banker
Prof. Leo Schelbert, Swiss, educator
The Rev. Wallace R. Schulz, German, cleric
Dr. Glenn T. Seaborg, Swedish, scientist
Elsbeth M. Seewald, German, activist
Alexander Spanos, Greek, executive
Arthur Ochs Sulzberger, German, publisher
Dr. Zoltan Szaz, Hungarian, lobbyist
James Tamer, Lebanese, activist
Donald J. Trump, German, developer
Dr. Andrew Udvardy, Hungarian, activist
Barbara Walters, Rumanian, broadcaster
Andy Williams, Welsh, singer
Dr. Vera von Wiren-Garczynski, Russian, educator
Prof. Chien-Shung Wu, Chinese, physicist

OCT. 16

# Weary Lawmakers Put Final Touches on Hectic Session

By STEVEN V. ROBERTS

WASHINGTON, Oct. 18—An exhausted 99th Congress completed its business and adjourned tonight, and the lawmakers eagerly headed home for a final stretch of campaigning before the November elections.

In reviewing the last two years, congressional leaders maintained that they had written a solid record of legislative achievement highlighted by major revisions of the nation's tax regulations, immigration laws and budget procedures.

However, the leaders conceded, it was also a congressional session that had missed most of its deadlines, lapsed frequently into partisan fighting, and sometimes approached paralysis before ending at 9:31 P.M. As a result, the lawmakers failed to make a significant impact on reducing the huge Federal budget deficit, which will be the principal issue facing the 100th Congress when it convenes in January.

Representative Dan Rostenkowski, the Illinois Democrat who heads the House Ways and Means Committee, offered this epitaph for the 99th Congress: "It's been tough, but it's been productive."

The Senate majority leader, Bob Dole, said today: "We leave behind a record of unusual accomplishment." However, he added, the narrow six-vote margin held by Senate Republicans, plus the intense political maneuvering for control of the next Senate, had limited his flexibility. "It hasn't been easy," the Republican leader from Kansas admitted. As they ended their work, many lawmakers expressed frustration at the way Congress had spent so much of the last two years thwarted by a combination of inefficient procedures and independent lawmakers determined to use those procedures for maximum leverage on the legislative process.

Capitol Hill is a place these days where every faction seems to think time is on its side, and as Representative Leon E. Panetta, a California Democrat, noted, the 99th Congress "scored most of its points in overtime," the final two weeks after the original adjournment target of October 3.   OCT. 19

## The 99th Congress: Its 1986 Record

Following are the major actions of the 99th Congress, second session:

**The Courts:** President Reagan's nominations for the Supreme Court passed Senate muster. William H. Rehnquist was confirmed on a 65-to-33 vote, after a somewhat bitter committee debate, to replace Warren E. Burger as Chief Justice. Antonin Scalia was confirmed unanimously to be Associate Justice. Vice President Bush cast the tie-breaking vote for Daniel A. Manion's nomination to the Federal appellate bench. And, for the first time in 50 years, the Senate removed a Federal judge, convicting Harry E. Claiborne, imprisoned for tax evasion, on three impeachment counts voted by the House.

**Income Tax:** After long behind-the-scenes negotiations over the most comprehensive changes in the Federal income tax system since World War II, Congress passed the Tax Reform Act of 1986, consolidating 15 tax brackets into two and eliminating many tax breaks. Sixty percent of Americans are expected to pay lower taxes, 25 percent the same and 15 percent more.

**South Africa:** In a major rebuff to the President's foreign policy, Congress overrode his veto of economic sanctions against South Africa. Among other things, the legislation bans all new investment by Americans in South African businesses and prohibits key imports from South Africa.

**The Environment:** Congress expanded the national program to clean up toxic waste sites. The $9 billion, five-year program, with five times more money than previously authorized, will be financed largely by new taxes, including one on corporate earnings. Congress also approved, although a veto is possible, legislation to strengthen the Clean Water Act and provide money for building sewage treatment plants.

**Water Projects:** The first major legislation to finance water projects in 15 years was approved, and beneficiaries are to help pay for them. The $16.3 billion program includes many projects for the New York metropolitan area, such as dredging New York Harbor.

**Gun Control:** Federal laws on gun control were softened in legislation making it easier to buy, sell and transport firearms across state lines.

**Immigration:** To curtail the influx of illegal aliens, Congress approved the most sweeping changes in immigration law in at least two decades. The legislation would prohibit the hiring of illegal aliens and would offer legal status to those who have lived here continuously since before Jan. 1, 1982.

**Drugs:** Responding to the emotional issue of illegal drug use, Congress substantially increased penalties for Federal drug crimes and provided $1.7 billion for enforcement, education and treatment programs.

**The Military:** The most sweeping reorganization of the military command structure in a generation was approved. The reorganization strengthens the role of the Chairman of the Joint Chiefs of Staff, making him the President's principal military adviser, and gives new authority to field commanders. Congress approved $3.5 billion for the Strategic Defense Initiative; the President had asked $5.34 billion for the antimissile plan. The Pentagon budget was set at $290 billion, for the smallest increase of the Reagan Administration.

**The Deficit:** Congress met the deficit ceiling set by the budget-balancing law with a package of accounting maneuvers and sales of Federal assets, including Conrail.

**Convention Against Genocide:** Thirty-seven years after it was first submitted by President Truman, Congress approved a United Nations convention declaring genocide an international crime and obliging the nations that adhere to the convention to punish those who commit genocide.

**Embassy Security:** Security at overseas embassies was bolstered with legislation authorizing $2.4 billion over the next five years.

**Contra Aid:** Congress authorized $100 million in aid to the rebels in Nicaragua, supporting one key aspect of the President's foreign policy. Congress allowed for $70 million in military aid and $30 million in humanitarian aid to be released in three installments if the President determined that negotiations could not solve that country's civil war. A five-member commission would have to certify his assessment for the aid to be released.

**National Flower:** Congress declared the rose to be the national floral emblem.

OCT. 19

## Congress, Winding Up Work, Votes Sweeping Aliens Bill

**By ROBERT PEAR**

WASHINGTON, Oct. 17—As it moved toward adjournment, Congress today gave final approval to a landmark immigration bill.

By a vote of 63 to 24, the Senate agreed to the compromise bill, clearing the measure for action by President Reagan. The bill would prohibit the hiring of illegal aliens and offer legal status, or amnesty, to millions of illegal aliens who have lived in this country continuously since before Jan. 1, 1982.

The chief sponsor of the legislation, Senator Alan K. Simpson, Republican of Wyoming, said President Reagan "awaits this bill and has agreed to sign it." Mr. Reagan proposed similar legislation in 1981 to tighten control of the borders and to curtail the influx of illegal aliens.

The bill approved today, the Immigration Reform and Control Act of 1986, marks a historic change in American immigration policy. Under current law, illegal aliens may be deported, but it is generally not illegal for employers to hire them. Under the bill passed today, employers who hired illegal aliens would be subject to civil penalties ranging from $250 to $10,000 for each such alien.

OCT. 18

## Senate Roll Call on Immigration Bill

Following is the roll-call vote of the Senate on passage of the immigration bill:

### FOR THE BILL—63

#### Democrats—34

| | | |
|---|---|---|
| Baucus, Mont. | Gore, Tenn. | Metzenbaum, Ohio |
| Bentsen, Tex. | Harkin, Iowa | Moynihan, N.Y. |
| Biden, Del. | Hart, Colo. | Nunn, Ga. |
| Bingaman, N.M. | Hollings, S.C. | Pell, R.I. |
| Bradley, N.J. | Johnston, La. | Proxmire, Wis. |
| Burdick, N.D. | Kerry, Mass. | Pryor, Ark. |
| Byrd, W.Va. | Lautenberg, N.J. | Rockefeller, W.Va. |
| Chiles, Fla. | Levin, Mich. | Sarbanes, Md. |
| Cranston, Calif. | Long, La. | Sasser, Tenn. |
| Dixon, Ill. | Matsunaga, Hawaii | Simon, Ill. |
| Dodd, Conn. | Melcher, Mont. | |
| Eagleton, Mo. | | |
| Exon, Neb. | | |

#### Republicans—29

| | | |
|---|---|---|
| Andrews, N.D. | Hawkins, Fla. | Simpson, Wyo. |
| Boschwitz, Minn. | Heinz, Pa. | Specter, Pa. |
| Chafee, R.I. | Kassebaum, Kan. | Stafford, Vt. |
| D'Amato, N.Y. | Kasten, Wis. | Stevens, Alaska |
| Danforth, Mo. | Lugar, Ind. | Thurmond, S.C. |
| Dole, Kan. | Mattingly, Ga. | Trible, Va. |
| Durenberger, Minn. | McConnell, Ky. | Wallop, Wyo. |
| | Packwood, Ore. | Warner, Va. |
| Grassley, Iowa | Quayle, Ind. | Weicker, Conn. |
| Hatfield, Ore. | Roth, Del. | Wilson, Calif. |

### AGAINST THE BILL—24

#### Democrats—8

| | | |
|---|---|---|
| Bumpers, Ark. | Inouye, Hawaii | Riegle, Mich. |
| Ford, Ky. | Kennedy, Mass. | Zorinsky, Neb. |
| Heflin, Ala. | Mitchell, Me. | |

#### Republicans—16

| | | |
|---|---|---|
| Abdnor, S.D. | Domenici, N.M. | Humphrey, N.H. |
| Armstrong, Colo. | Garn, Utah | McClure, Idaho |
| | Gramm, Tex. | |
| Cochran, Miss. | Hatch, Utah | Nickles, Okla. |
| Cohen, Me. | Hecht, Nev. | Pressler, S.D. |
| Denton, Ala. | Helms, N.C. | Rudman, N.H. |

Oct. 18

## Prices up by 0.3% Bringing Increase in Social Security

By ROBERT D. HERSHEY, Jr.

**W**ASHINGTON, Oct. 23—The Commerce Department today reported a modest rise of three-tenths of 1 percent in inflation for September. The latest figures, in turn, will mean a 1.3 percent increase in Social Security and related benefits for more than 37 million Americans.

The higher benefits, tied directly to the rise in the Consumer Price Index for Urban Wage Earners and Clerical Workers between the third quarters of 1985 and 1986, take effect Jan. 1. The average Social Security retirement payment will rise $6 a month, to $488, the smallest increase by far since these benefits were tied to inflation in 1975.

In addition, today's report fixed the maximum wage subject to Social Security tax at $43,800 for 1987, up from $42,000 this year.

Oct. 24

### Social Security's inflation raises

Annual percentage increases in benefits since Social Security was linked to the Consumer Price Index.

| | | | |
|---|---|---|---|
| 1975 | 8.0 | 1981 | 11.2 |
| 1976 | 6.4 | 1982 | 7.4 |
| 1977 | 5.9 | 1983 | 3.5 |
| 1978 | 6.5 | 1984 | 3.5 |
| 1979 | 9.9 | 1985 | 3.1 |
| 1980 | 14.3 | 1986 | 1.3 |

Source: Social Security Administration

### The changes effective in January

How Social Security payments will change for beneficiaries and taxpayers as of January next year.

|  | 1986 | 1987 |
|---|---|---|
| Average benefit received by a retired worker* | $482 | $488 |
| Maximum benefit for a worker who retires in 1986 at age 65 | $760 | $769** |
| Limit on amount a person receiving benefits can earn without losing any benefits: | | |
|   For persons under age 65 | $5,760 | $6,000 |
|   For persons aged 65 to 69 | $7,800 | $8,160 |
|   For persons aged 70 and older | No limit | No limit |
| For workers, the maximum amount of annual earnings subject to Social Security tax | $42,000 | $43,800 |

*Increase of 1.3% tied to the Consumer Price Index begins in Jan. 2 checks.
**Increase of 1.3% would equal $9.88, but because agency must round down, increase becomes $9.

Source: Social Security Administration

OCT. 24

# End of Forced Retirement Means a Lot—to a Few

**By KENNETH B. NOBLE**

**W**ASHINGTON—When Congress voted earlier this month to eliminate mandatory retirement for nearly all workers, supporters called it a legislative landmark that would bring striking changes to the workplace. And from the outpouring of congressional sentiment in favor of the bill, one would guess that the existing law was forcing armies of Americans out of the workplace at 70 years of age.

"Abolishing age discrimination will offer new hope to older workers who are desperate to maintain their independence and dignity," declared Representative Claude Pepper, a Florida Democrat and the chief sponsor of the bill, who at 86 is the oldest member of Congress. Senator Howard M. Metzenbaum, an Ohio Democrat, predicted a "tremendous impact."

"Literally hundreds of thousands of Americans will stand taller and breathe a sigh of relief," he said, "knowing that mandatory retirement isn't hovering over them."

Economists and labor experts, however, are less stirred. "It's not that big a deal," said John L. Palmer, an economist at the Urban Institute, a Washington research group. "There just aren't large numbers of people out there who want to work but can't."

A study by the Employee Benefit Research Institute, a nonprofit, nonpartisan Washington organization, found that abolishing mandatory retirement in 1985 would have added 77,000 workers at most—49,000 men and 28,000 women—to the labor force. About 1.1 million people older than 70 are already working, most of them part-time.

OCT. 26

### Americans at work

| Age group | Percentage of men employed full-time | Percentage of women employed full-time |
|---|---|---|
| 16 to 19 | 18.7 | 14.1 |
| 20 to 24 | 60.5 | 46.3 |
| 25 to 34 | 82.5 | 51.0 |
| 35 to 44 | 86.5 | 51.5 |
| 45 to 54 | 82.8 | 47.2 |
| 55 to 59 | 71.0 | 35.3 |
| 60 to 64 | 46.1 | 21.7 |
| 65 and older | 8.2 | 2.7 |

|  | Percentage of men employed full-time or part-time | Percentage of women employed full-time or part-time |
|---|---|---|
| 60 and 61 | 65.7 | 38.6 |
| 62 to 64 | 44.3 | 27.7 |
| 65 to 69 | 23.6 | 13.0 |
| 70 and older | 10.3 | 4.2 |

Source: Bureau of Labor Statistics

OCT. 26

# Adjusting the Speed Limit to Match Reality

**By REGINALD STUART**

WASHINGTON—In January 1974, with blocks-long lines at filling stations, the Federal Government imposed a top speed of 55 miles an hour nationwide. Not three months later, when shortages eased, surveys found that many people were driving somewhat faster than that.

Now 4 out of 10 drivers exceed the national speed limit. And with gasoline cheap again, Congress began talking seriously, for the first time since 1974, about letting states decide whether to bump the limit up to 65 miles an hour. But House and Senate conferees fought to a draw over how to balance the driving time a higher limit would save against the lives it would cost, how to weigh states' rights against Federal responsibilities.

Even though last weekend's failure to agree meant the death of a multi-billion-dollar transportation bill, regional and philosophical divisions ran so deep that both sides considered it a victory, if a hollow one. Safety advocates, most of them from the East, wanted time to build public support for retaining the 55-mile-an-hour limit. Western proponents of the higher limit saw a proposed compromise as a new infringement on states' rights.

Senator after senator decried the speed limit as a "ridiculous" Federal imposition before voting to permit states to raise it to 65 miles an hour on rural stretches of the interstate highway system. The proposal lost in the House by a relatively slim margin, 218 to 198. But in conference, the House would accept the higher limit only if the Government mandated strict enforcement of the speed limit and the use of seat belts in states that chose 65. Representative James J. Howard, Democrat of New Jersey, the principal opponent of raising the limit, said that without enforcement standards, interstate traffic would be going 75 miles an hour or more, and thousands of lives would be lost.

OCT. 26

### Breaking the limit

Percentage of vehicles exceeding 55 miles an hour (fiscal 1985)

| | | | |
|---|---|---|---|
| 56.4 | Arizona | 43.3 | Nebraska |
| 54.0 | Rhode Island | 43.1 | Alabama |
| 53.2 | Vermont | 43.1 | Washington |
| 50.4 | New Hampshire | 42.6 | Alaska |
| 49.9 | Nevada | 42.6 | Ohio |
| 49.8 | Michigan | 41.7 | Indiana |
| 49.7 | California | 41.5 | Utah |
| 49.7 | Maine | 40.7 | Georgia |
| 49.7 | North Dakota | 40.5 | Tennessee |
| 48.5 | Massachusetts | 40.2 | Arkansas |
| 47.7 | Missouri | 40.1 | Delaware |
| 47.7 | Wyoming | 39.2 | Minnesota |
| 47.6 | Florida | 39.1 | Iowa |
| 47.4 | New Mexico | 39.1 | South Dakota |
| 47.1 | Oregon | 37.8 | Idaho |
| 47.0 | Mississippi | 37.0 | Illinois |
| 46.8 | New Jersey | 36.8 | Connecticut |
| 46.6 | Montana | 36.8 | Pennsylvania |
| 46.5 | Colorado | 36.5 | South Carolina |
| 45.6 | New York | 34.2 | North Carolina |
| 45.5 | Louisiana | 32.3 | Kentucky |
| 45.3 | Texas | 31.1 | Hawaii |
| 44.3 | Oklahoma | 29.5 | Virginia |
| 44.0 | Kansas | 26.5 | West Virginia |
| 43.7 | Wisconsin | n.a. | Maryland |

Sources: Federal Highway Administration, National Highway Traffic Safety Administration

OCT. 26

## Medals for Heroism

On October 30 the Carnegie Hero Fund Commission honored 19 people from 12 states and one province in Canada. Four of them died trying to help others, according to the commission, which presented each of the heroes or their survivors with a $2,500 cash award and a medal.

Those honored were:

**James T. Hays,** 77 years old, of Hemphill, Tex., and his son, Benjamin Hays, 47, of Austin, Tex., who saved a truck driver whose gasoline tanker overturned and caught fire in Santo, Tex., on Nov. 11, 1984.

**Daniel Farling St. John,** 20, of Prineville, Ore., who died trying to save a man from a burning house on Aug. 4, 1985.

**Raymond Leonard Mills,** 15, of Syracuse, Utah, who died helping to save his 12-year-old brother from drowning in a pool in Plymouth, Utah, on July 2, 1985.

**Charles J. Messa,** 41, of Evergreen, Colo., who died after helping in the rescue of a boy and an unsuccessful attempt to rescue a drowning girl in Bear Creek Lake, Colo., on May 27, 1985.

**Michael R. Howell,** 38, of Vancouver, Wash., who saved a woman from drowning in the Spokane River in Spokane, Wash., on March 19, 1984.

**Darryl Lindsay Curran,** 33, of San Diego, Calif., who saved two boys from a burning car in Escondido, Calif., on Oct. 2, 1985.

**Michael L. Foreman,** 31, of Baltimore, who saved an infant boy from a knife assault by a man in Pittsburgh on Jan. 1, 1985.

**William D. Shoemaker,** 12, of Elkland, Mo., who saved a 12-year-old boy from drowning in a farm pond on July 2, 1985.

**Gregory Ysais, Jr.,** 36, of Mission Viejo, Calif., who saved a 5-year-old girl from a mountain lion at San Juan Capistrano, Calif., on March 23, 1985.

**Riley Christmas, Sr.,** 46, of Portsmouth, Va., who helped save a man from suffocation in a barge in Cambridge, Md., on Sept. 17, 1985.

**John B. Boyarski,** 41, of Burnaby, British Columbia, who saved a 15-year-old girl from a man armed with a gun in Vancouver, British Columbia, on Aug. 8, 1985.

**Patrick Doland,** 35, of Hollywood, Fla., who helped save a man from drowning at Boca Raton, Fla., on Sept. 10, 1985.

**Floyd L. Anderson,** 55, of Jacksonville, Ill., who prevented a possible explosion at a propane gas distribution installation on Jan. 23, 1985.

**Lawrence Weigand 3d,** 13, of Marcus Hook, Pa., who saved an 8-year-old girl from being struck by a car on July 16, 1985.

**Abel O. Garcia,** 26, of Corpus Christi, Tex., and **John Ray Wilson,** 27, of Lufkin, Tex., who helped save two boys from drowning at Freeport, Tex., on June 4, 1984. Mr. Wilson died in his attempt.

**Joseph Reid,** 18, of Jacksonville, Fla., who saved a man from a collapsing and burning house in Jesup, Ga., on Sept. 19, 1984.

**Alfred Lamere,** 64, of Aberdeen, Wash., who saved a boy from drowning on Aug. 27, 1985.

Nov. 2

# Elections: Democrats Gain Control of Senate, Drawing Votes of Reagan's Backers

By E. J. DIONNE, Jr.

The Democrats won control of the Senate yesterday, dealing a major blow to President Reagan, who had criss-crossed the country pleading for a Republican victory.

Sweeping through the South and picking up key farm states, the Democrats were guaranteed at least 54 seats in the new Senate. Bob Dole, the Senate Republican leader, said the Democrats could have won as many 55 seats.

The Democrats, who won in the face of an overwhelming Republican financial advantage, will take control of all committee chairmanships and gain the power to put a brake on Mr. Reagan's effort to reshape the nation's judiciary, including the Supreme Court.

They were also expected to clash with the President over military spending and arms control.

Republicans feared that the shift in the Senate could lead to stalemate on Mr. Reagan's programs.

"I think it's going to be a difficult period for the President," said Senator Paul Laxalt, Republican of Nevada, who is a close friend of Mr. Reagan. "This will be awkward." Mr. Reagan refused to comment on the outcome of the election when he left Los Angeles to return to Washington yesterday.

The Democrats defeated Republican incumbents in Alabama, Georgia, North Carolina, Florida, North Dakota and South Dakota. They took seats where Republicans had retired in Maryland and Nevada.

In California, Senator Alan Cranston, a Democrat, turned back a strong challenge from Representative Ed Zschau. In Colorado, Representative Timothy E. Wirth, a Democrat, won a narrow victory over Representative Ken Kramer. Mr. Wirth was defending the seat of Senator Gary Hart, who is retiring to run for the Democratic presidential nomination in 1988.

The Republicans picked up one seat from the Democrats in Missouri, where former Gov. Christopher Bond, defeated Lieut. Gov. Harriett Woods.

The Republicans were consoled by picking up at least six governorships.

In one of the most important Republican gains, Guy Hunt, a former judge, appeared to have defeated Lieut. Gov. Bill Baxley in a bitter race in Alabama, where the Democratic Party was sharply divided. Mr. Hunt was the first Republican to win the state's governorship since Reconstruction. Just before the election, State Attorney General Charles Graddick, a Democrat, who defeated Mr. Baxley in the primary but had his victory set aside by the state party, dropped his planned write-in campaign. This apparently helped Mr. Hunt.

The Democrats maintained their majority in the House of Representatives, and seemed likely to post an unusually small midterm gain of five to eight seats. Democrats now hold a 253-to-180-seat majority, with two vacancies.

In both North and South Dakota, more than a third of those polled listed farm problems, a central Democratic theme, as a key issue in the elections. In both states, these voters backed Democrats by a margin of 3 to 1.

Nov. 5

## Shifting balances in the house: How regional power has changed

After each census the 435 seats in the House of Representatives are redistributed by population, so that a fast-growing state like California has gained seats at the expense of more stable states like New York and Illinois. In these stylized maps, each state and region is sized in proportion to its numerical strength in the House 40 years ago and today.

|  | 1946 | 1986 |
|---|---|---|
| **West** | 34 | 63 |
| Alaska | 0 | 1 |
| California | 23 | 45 |
| Hawaii | 0 | 2 |
| Nevada | 1 | 2 |
| Oregon | 4 | 5 |
| Washington | 6 | 8 |
| **Mountains and plains** | 29 | 32 |
| Arizona | 2 | 5 |
| Colorado | 4 | 6 |
| Idaho | 2 | 2 |
| Kansas | 6 | 5 |
| Montana | 2 | 2 |
| Nebraska | 4 | 3 |
| New Mexico | 2 | 3 |
| North Dakota | 2 | 1 |
| South Dakota | 2 | 1 |
| Utah | 2 | 3 |
| Wyoming | 1 | 1 |
| **Midwest** | 117 | 103 |
| Illinois | 26 | 22 |
| Indiana | 11 | 10 |
| Iowa | 8 | 6 |
| Michigan | 17 | 18 |
| Minnesota | 9 | 8 |
| Missouri | 13 | 9 |
| Ohio | 23 | 21 |
| Wisconsin | 10 | 9 |

|  | 1946 | 1986 |
|---|---|---|
| **South** | **128** | **133** |
| Alabama | 9 | 7 |
| Arkansas | 7 | 4 |
| Florida | 6 | 19 |
| Georgia | 10 | 10 |
| Kentucky | 9 | 7 |
| Louisiana | 8 | 8 |
| Mississippi | 7 | 5 |
| North Carolina | 12 | 11 |
| Oklahoma | 8 | 6 |
| South Carolina | 6 | 6 |
| Tennessee | 10 | 9 |
| Texas | 21 | 27 |
| Virginia | 9 | 10 |
| West Virginia | 6 | 4 |
| **East** | **127** | **104** |
| Connecticut | 6 | 6 |
| Delaware | 1 | 1 |
| Maine | 3 | 2 |
| Maryland | 6 | 8 |
| Massachusetts | 14 | 11 |
| New Hampshire | 2 | 2 |
| New Jersey | 14 | 14 |
| New York | 45 | 34 |
| Pennsylvania | 33 | 23 |
| Rhode Island | 2 | 2 |
| Vermont | 1 | 1 |

Nov. 5

## The *New York Times*/CBS News Poll
### Probable voters and nonvoters: The similarities and differences

|  |  | Voters | Non-voters |
|---|---|---|---|
| **Party** | Democrat | 39% | 31% |
|  | Republican | 33 | 27 |
|  | Independent | 28 | 42 |
| **Philosophy** | Liberal | 16 | 19 |
|  | Moderate | 46 | 39 |
|  | Conservative | 33 | 33 |
| **Paying Attention to Campaign** | A lot | 25 | 10 |
|  | Some | 40 | 28 |
|  | Not much | 24 | 62 |
| **Sex** | Men | 48 | 46 |
|  | Women | 52 | 54 |
| **Age** | 18–29 years | 20 | 40 |
|  | 30–44 years | 27 | 28 |
|  | 45–64 years | 33 | 20 |
|  | 65 years and older | 20 | 12 |
| **Race** | White | 85 | 77 |
|  | Black | 10 | 14 |
|  | Hispanic | 4 | 7 |
|  | Other | 1 | 3 |
| **Education** | Less than high school | 20% | 26% |
|  | High school graduate | 43 | 46 |
|  | Some college | 18 | 17 |
|  | College graduate | 19 | 12 |
| **Family Income** | Less than $12,500 | 14 | 18 |
|  | $12,500–$24,999 | 30 | 36 |
|  | $25,000–$34,999 | 23 | 23 |
|  | $35,000–$49,999 | 19 | 16 |
|  | Over $50,000 | 14 | 7 |

Of the population, 29 percent say they are not registered to vote. Of that group, 41 percent say they have never voted, and 20 percent do not know when they last voted. These were the main reasons they gave for not being registered:

| | |
|---|---|
| Moved recently | 23% |
| No particular reason or forgot | 19% |
| Not interested in politics | 11% |
| Too busy | 9% |
| Voting is waste of time | 7% |

Based on 2,016 telephone interviews conducted by *The New York Times* and CBS News Oct. 24–28, weighted to reflect likelihood of voting.

Nov. 5

# Democrats Rejoice at 55–45 Senate Margin but Still Seek Agenda to Counter Reagan

**By E. J. DIONNE, Jr.**

The Democrats declared yesterday that their triumph in the elections Tuesday marked the end of an era of Republican ascendancy, but they confronted the most popular President in recent American history without a clearly defined mandate for a new political agenda.

The Democrats' victory in the Senate and their renewed majority in the House gave the party control over the nation's legislative machinery in the final two years of Ronald Reagan's presidency. The results of the election also substantially altered the shape of American politics leading into the 1988 elections, when both parties will seek new presidential nominees.

With an edge of 55 seats to 45 in the Senate, including sweeping gains in the South and a strong showing in usually Republican Western states, Democrats argued that the elections marked the end of Mr. Reagan's control over the national political debate and the limits of his hopes for creating a new and lasting Republican majority.

"We can say it all in four words: The Democrats are back," said Paul G. Kirk, Jr., the Democratic national chairman, recalling Mr. Reagan's successful slogan in the 1984 elections.

House Speaker Thomas P. O'Neill, Jr., who savored Democratic gains that came in his final year in public life, said, "If there was a Reagan Revolution, it's over."

Mr. Reagan conceded only partial defeat, citing a net gain of eight governorships for his party and relatively small Republican losses in the House of Representatives as "fairly good news." And, indeed, Democratic Senate gains in the South were offset by gains of governorships by the Republicans in Alabama, Florida, South Carolina and Texas.

But Mr. Reagan, who traveled 25,000 miles and campaigned in 22 states pleading for voters not to make him a "six-year President" by giving the Democrats control of the Senate, acknowledged that the result "is not the outcome we sought."

Often by the narrowest of margins, Democrats defeated seven incumbent Republican senators, four of them in the South. Not a single Democratic Senate incumbent was defeated. The Democrats took two additional seats from the Republicans, where incumbents had retired. Only one Democratic seat switched to Republican hands, that of Senator Thomas F. Eagleton of Missouri, who retired.

Of the 12 Republican senators swept into office with President Reagan in 1980, six were defeated. The seventh Republican incumbent to lose, James T. Broyhill of North Carolina, was the interim appointee for another Republican seat picked up in the Reagan sweep by Senator John P. East, who killed himself in June.

The Democrats' net gain of eight seats in the 100-member Senate was likely to be larger than their gains in the 435-member House, a historical curiosity. The Democrats were sure to gain five seats in the House. In three districts, the results were inconclusive.

Never in this century has a party lost as many or more seats at midterm in the Senate as in the House.

If Republicans win all three seats in which the outcome was disputed, the new House would be made up of 258 Democrats and 177 Republicans.

Having lost the struggle for the Senate, the most important battle of the election, Republicans sought to highlight their achievements: the eight new governorships, the narrow loss in the House and the remarkable closeness of the Senate contests.

William Greener, a Republican National Committee official, noted that if the Republicans had had just 50,000 more votes in five small states, the Republicans would have obtained a 50-50 Senate split and held the body with the vote of Vice President Bush. With almost all the votes counted, Democrats were winning about 23.9 million votes in the 34 Senate races, Republicans 23.1 million.

Nov. 6

## The *New York Times*/CBS News Poll Portrait of the electorate: the vote for house of representatives

| % of 1986 total | | 1982 | | 1984 | | 1986 | |
|---|---|---|---|---|---|---|---|
| | | Democrat | Republican | Democrat | Republican | Democrat | Republican |
| — | **TOTAL** | 57% | 43% | 51% | 49% | 52% | 48% |
| 48 | Men | 55 | 45 | 48 | 52 | 51 | 49 |
| 52 | Women | 58 | 42 | 54 | 46 | 54 | 46 |
| 87 | Whites | 54 | 46 | 46 | 54 | 49 | 51 |
| 8 | Blacks | 89 | 11 | 92 | 8 | 86 | 14 |
| 3 | Hispanics | 75 | 25 | 69 | 31 | 75 | 25 |
| 16 | 18–29 years old | 59 | 41 | 51 | 49 | 51 | 49 |
| 32 | 30–44 years old | 54 | 46 | 54 | 46 | 52 | 48 |
| 24 | 45–59 years old | 56 | 44 | 50 | 50 | 54 | 46 |
| 28 | 60 and older | 58 | 42 | 48 | 52 | 52 | 48 |
| 8 | Not a high school graduate | — | — | 60 | 40 | 57 | 43 |
| 32 | High school graduate | — | — | 51 | 49 | 55 | 45 |
| 29 | Some college | — | — | 49 | 51 | 50 | 50 |
| 31 | College graduate | — | — | 50 | 50 | 51 | 49 |
| 26 | From the East | 65 | 35 | 54 | 46 | 52 | 48 |
| 37 | From the Midwest | 49 | 51 | 50 | 50 | 53 | 47 |
| 12 | From the South | 59 | 41 | 52 | 48 | 56 | 44 |
| 25 | From the West | 53 | 47 | 48 | 52 | 51 | 49 |
| 47 | White Protestant | 43 | 57 | 38 | 62 | 43 | 57 |
| 32 | Catholic | 63 | 37 | 58 | 42 | 55 | 45 |
| 4 | Jewish | 82 | 18 | 70 | 30 | 70 | 30 |
| — | White born-again Christian | 46 | 54 | 35 | 65 | — | — |
| 8 | White Fundamentalist or Evangelical Christian | — | — | — | — | 31 | 69 |
| 15 | Under $12,500 in income | 73 | 27 | 63 | 37 | 56 | 44 |
| 26 | $12,500–$24,999 | 60 | 40 | 54 | 46 | 53 | 47 |
| 21 | $25,000–$34,999 | 56 | 44 | 50 | 50 | 52 | 48 |
| 21 | $35,000–$50,000 | 49 | 51 | 47 | 53 | 53 | 47 |
| 17 | Over $50,000 | 37 | 63 | 39 | 61 | 47 | 53 |
| 39 | Democrat | 90 | 10 | 86 | 14 | 81 | 19 |
| 34 | Republican | 12 | 88 | 13 | 87 | 20 | 80 |
| 25 | Independent | 51 | 49 | 48 | 52 | 52 | 48 |
| 16 | Liberal | 80 | 20 | 76 | 24 | 71 | 29 |
| 46 | Moderate | 60 | 40 | 57 | 43 | 58 | 42 |
| 34 | Conservative | 35 | 65 | 31 | 69 | 35 | 65 |
| — | Professional or white collar | 48 | 52 | — | — | — | — |

# NATIONAL

| % of 1986 total | | 1982 | | 1984 | | 1986 | |
|---|---|---|---|---|---|---|---|
| | | Democrat | Republican | Democrat | Republican | Democrat | Republican |
| 29 | Professional or manager | — | — | 48 | 52 | 50 | 50 |
| 14 | Other white collar worker | — | — | 53 | 47 | 54 | 46 |
| 14 | Blue collar worker | 64 | 36 | 58 | 42 | 55 | 45 |
| 2 | Agricultural worker | 55 | 45 | 26 | 74 | 56 | 44 |
| 13 | Homemaker | — | — | 48 | 52 | 50 | 50 |
| 2 | Full-time student | — | — | 59 | 41 | 57 | 43 |
| 11 | Government employee | — | — | 58 | 42 | 62 | 38 |
| 2 | Unemployed | 71 | 29 | 70 | 30 | 63 | 37 |
| 19 | Retired | 61 | 39 | 48 | 52 | 52 | 48 |
| 28 | Union household | 68 | 32 | 64 | 36 | 63 | 37 |
| 25 | Women employed outside home | 59 | 41 | 56 | 44 | 56 | 44 |
| 58 | Voted for Reagan | 31 | 69 | 21 | 79 | 35 | 65 |
| 30 | Voted for Carter or Mondale | 89 | 11 | 93 | 7 | 83 | 17 |
| 2 | First-time voter | — | — | 47 | 53 | 49 | 51 |
| 10 | Liberal Democrats | 93 | 7 | 92 | 8 | 85 | 15 |
| 19 | Moderate Democrats | 90 | 10 | 87 | 13 | 81 | 19 |
| 8 | Conservative Democrats | 86 | 14 | 75 | 25 | 73 | 27 |
| 2 | Liberal Republicans | 27 | 73 | 13 | 87 | 23 | 77 |
| 12 | Moderate Republicans | 14 | 86 | 15 | 85 | 25 | 75 |
| 18 | Conservative Republicans | 8 | 92 | 11 | 89 | 17 | 83 |
| 17 | Democratic men | 89 | 11 | 83 | 17 | 81 | 19 |
| 21 | Democratic women | 91 | 9 | 87 | 13 | 80 | 20 |
| 17 | Republican men | 12 | 88 | 14 | 86 | 19 | 81 |
| 16 | Republican women | 12 | 88 | 15 | 85 | 21 | 79 |
| 13 | Independent men | 51 | 49 | 46 | 54 | 51 | 49 |
| 12 | Independent women | 52 | 48 | 52 | 48 | 53 | 47 |
| 30 | White Democrats | 89 | 11 | 82 | 18 | 78 | 22 |
| 5 | Black Democrats | 97 | 3 | 98 | 2 | 94 | 6 |
| 43 | White men | 52 | 48 | 43 | 57 | 47 | 53 |
| 45 | White women | 55 | 45 | 49 | 51 | 50 | 50 |
| 4 | Black men | 82 | 18 | 90 | 10 | 84 | 16 |
| 4 | Black women | 94 | 6 | 94 | 6 | 88 | 12 |
| 8 | Men, 18–29 years old | 60 | 40 | 47 | 53 | 48 | 52 |
| 8 | Women, 18–29 years old | 58 | 42 | 56 | 44 | 54 | 46 |
| 15 | Men, 30–44 years old | 52 | 48 | 52 | 48 | 52 | 48 |
| 17 | Women, 30–44 years old | 57 | 43 | 56 | 44 | 52 | 48 |

| % of 1986 total | | 1982 | | 1984 | | 1986 | |
|---|---|---|---|---|---|---|---|
| | | Democrat | Republican | Democrat | Republican | Democrat | Republican |
| 11 | Men, 45–59 years old | 54 | 46 | 47 | 53 | 50 | 50 |
| 12 | Women, 45–59 years old | 58 | 42 | 52 | 48 | 58 | 42 |
| 14 | Men, 60 and older | 56 | 44 | 46 | 54 | 51 | 49 |
| 14 | Women, 60 and older | 60 | 40 | 51 | 49 | 53 | 47 |
| 73 | Married | 52 | 48 | 49 | 51 | 51 | 49 |
| 27 | Not married | 63 | 37 | 56 | 44 | 56 | 44 |
| 36 | Married men | 50 | 50 | 46 | 54 | 50 | 50 |
| 36 | Married women | 54 | 46 | 52 | 48 | 53 | 47 |
| 12 | Unmarried men | 61 | 39 | 53 | 47 | 54 | 46 |
| 15 | Unmarried women | 65 | 35 | 59 | 41 | 58 | 42 |
| 23 | Whites in the East | 63 | 37 | 50 | 50 | 48 | 52 |
| 2 | Blacks in the East | 90 | 10 | 93 | 7 | 87 | 13 |
| 33 | Whites in the Midwest | 46 | 54 | 45 | 55 | 50 | 50 |
| 3 | Blacks in the Midwest | 87 | 13 | 95 | 5 | 84 | 16 |
| 10 | Whites in the South | 55 | 45 | 45 | 55 | 50 | 50 |
| 1 | Blacks in the South | 93 | 7 | 92 | 8 | 93 | 7 |
| 21 | Whites in the West | 50 | 50 | 44 | 56 | 47 | 53 |
| 1 | Blacks in the West | Insufficient Data | | 84 | 16 | Insufficient Data | |
| 13 | Men in the East | 64 | 36 | 50 | 50 | 52 | 48 |
| 14 | Women in the East | 65 | 35 | 58 | 42 | 51 | 49 |
| 18 | Men in the Midwest | 45 | 55 | 48 | 52 | 50 | 50 |
| 19 | Women in the Midwest | 53 | 47 | 52 | 48 | 55 | 45 |
| 6 | Men in the South | 58 | 42 | 48 | 52 | 55 | 45 |
| 6 | Women in the South | 60 | 40 | 55 | 45 | 57 | 43 |
| 12 | Men in the West | 51 | 49 | 46 | 54 | 48 | 52 |
| 13 | Women in the West | 55 | 45 | 50 | 50 | 54 | 46 |
| 60 | Approve of Reagan | 26 | 74 | — | — | 36 | 64 |
| 35 | Disapprove of Reagan | 90 | 10 | — | — | 79 | 21 |

1986 data based on interviews 8,997 voters leaving polling places around the nation on November 4. 1984 data based on interviews with 9,174 voters, and 1982 data based on interviews with 7,855 voters. Those who did not answer or said they had no opinion are not shown. Dashes indicate that a question was not asked in a particular year. In 1982 only, occupation referred to head of household. Family income categories in 1982: under $10,000, $10,000–19,999, $20,000–29,999, $30,000–49,999 and $50,000 and over.

Nov. 6

## The Senate contests

| State | Candidates | Votes | % of Vote |
|---|---|---|---|
| ALABAMA | •Shelby, Dem | 603,862 | (50) |
| | Denton, GOP* | 592,202 | (50) |
| ALASKA | Olds, Dem | 67,259 | (45) |
| | •Murkowski, GOP* | 81,855 | (55) |
| ARIZONA | Kimball, Dem | 337,579 | (40) |
| | •McCain, GOP | 516,342 | (60) |
| ARKANSAS | •Bumpers, Dem* | 433,552 | (62) |
| | Hutchinson, GOP | 262,046 | (38) |
| CALIFORNIA | •Cranston, Dem* | 3,559,985 | (51) |
| | Zschau, GOP | 3,447,296 | (49) |
| COLORADO | •Wirth, Dem | 529,063 | (51) |
| | Kramer, GOP | 512,828 | (49) |
| CONNECTICUT | •Dodd, Dem* | 627,091 | (65) |
| | Eddy, GOP | 339,552 | (35) |
| FLORIDA | •Graham, Dem | 1,840,465 | (55) |
| | Hawkins, GOP* | 1,509,070 | (45) |
| GEORGIA | •Fowler, Dem | 622,850 | (51) |
| | Mattingly, GOP* | 599,738 | (49) |
| HAWAII | •Inouye, Dem* | 241,872 | (74) |
| | Hutchinson, GOP | 86,896 | (26) |
| IDAHO | Evans, Dem | 185,094 | (48) |
| | •Symms, GOP* | 196,908 | (52) |
| ILLINOIS | •Dixon, Dem* | 1,988,848 | (65) |
| | Koehler, GOP | 1,038,966 | (34) |
| INDIANA | Long, Dem | 591,504 | (39) |
| | •Quayle, GOP* | 928,948 | (61) |
| IOWA | Roehrick, Dem | 295,309 | (34) |
| | •Grassley, GOP* | 580,271 | (66) |
| KANSAS | MacDonald, Dem | 245,264 | (30) |
| | •Dole, GOP* | 575,131 | (70) |
| KENTUCKY | •Ford, Dem* | 500,325 | (74) |
| | Andrews, GOP | 173,098 | (26) |
| LOUISIANA | •Breaux, Dem | 723,306 | (53) |
| | Moore, GOP | 645,860 | (47) |
| MARYLAND | •Mikulski, Dem | 657,549 | (61) |
| | Chavez, GOP | 424,293 | (39) |
| MISSOURI | Woods, Dem | 698,210 | (47) |
| | •Bond, GOP | 776,790 | (53) |
| NEVADA | •Reid, Dem | 130,952 | (51) |
| | Santini, GOP | 116,606 | (45) |
| N.HAMPSHIRE | Peabody, Dem | 79,037 | (34) |
| | •Rudman, GOP* | 153,707 | (66) |
| NEW YORK | Green, Dem | 1,674,927 | (41) |
| | •D'Amato, GOP* | 2,366,789 | (58) |
| N.CAROLINA | •Sanford, Dem | 819,621 | (52) |
| | Broyhill, GOP* | 764,032 | (48) |
| NORTH DAKOTA | •Conrad, Dem | 143,791 | (51) |
| | Andrews, GOP* | 140,812 | (49) |
| OHIO | •Glenn, Dem* | 1,946,915 | (62) |
| | Kindness, GOP | 1,173,602 | (38) |
| OKLAHOMA | Jones, Dem | 382,591 | (45) |
| | •Nickles, GOP* | 458,502 | (55) |
| OREGON | Bauman, Dem | 354,895 | (37) |
| | •Packwood, GOP* | 616,464 | (63) |
| PENN. | Edgar, Dem | 1,438,498 | (43) |
| | •Specter, GOP* | 1,902,674 | (57) |
| S. CAROLINA | •Hollings, Dem* | 463,354 | (64) |
| | McMaster, GOP | 261,394 | (36) |
| SOUTH DAKOTA | •Daschle, Dem | 151,612 | (52) |
| | Abdnor, GOP* | 141,427 | (48) |
| UTAH | Oliver, Dem | 116,186 | (27) |
| | •Garn, GOP* | 314,133 | (73) |
| VERMONT | •Leahy, Dem* | 123,462 | (64) |
| | Snelling, GOP | 67,263 | (35) |
| WASHINGTON | •Adams, Dem | 613,521 | (51) |
| | Gorton, GOP* | 584,766 | (49) |
| WISCONSIN | Garvey, Dem | 701,861 | (48) |
| | •Kasten, GOP* | 753,302 | (52) |

An asterisk denotes the incumbent.
A dot denotes the winner.

## The races for governor

| State | Candidate | Votes | % of Vote |
|---|---|---|---|
| ALABAMA | Baxley, Dem | 532,007 | (43) |
| | •Hunt, GOP | 688,774 | (56) |
| ALASKA | •Cowper, Dem | 70,784 | (52) |
| | Sturgulewski, GOP | 64,414 | (48) |
| ARIZONA | Warner, Dem | 296,188 | (35) |
| | •Mecham, GOP | 340,106 | (40) |
| | Schulz, Ind | 221,883 | (26) |
| ARKANSAS | •Clinton, Dem* | 437,571 | (64) |
| | White, GOP | 247,499 | (36) |
| CALIFORNIA | Bradley, Dem | 2,715,490 | (38) |
| | •Deukmejian, GOP* | 4,388,558 | (62) |
| COLORADO | •Romer, Dem | 615,833 | (59) |
| | Strickland, GOP | 434,134 | (41) |
| CONNECTICUT | •O'Neill, Dem* | 573,819 | (59) |
| | Belaga, GOP | 405,490 | (41) |
| FLORIDA | Pajcic, Dem | 1,511,099 | (46) |
| | •Martinez, GOP | 1,796,064 | (54) |
| GEORGIA | •Harris, Dem* | 825,783 | (70) |
| | Davis, GOP | 345,696 | (30) |
| HAWAII | •Waihee, Dem | 173,655 | (52) |
| | Anderson, GOP | 160,460 | (48) |
| IDAHO | •Andrus, Dem | 193,367 | (50) |
| | Leroy, GOP* | 190,011 | (50) |
| ILLINOIS | •Thompson, GOP* | 1,633,194 | (57) |
| | Stevenson III, Sid | 1,224,626 | (43) |
| IOWA | Junkins, Dem | 430,138 | (48) |
| | •Branstad, GOP* | 465,995 | (52) |
| KANSAS | Docking, Dem | 403,098 | (48) |
| | •Hayden, GOP | 435,643 | (52) |
| MAINE | Tierney, Dem | 127,342 | (30) |
| | •McKernan, GOP | 166,694 | (40) |
| | Huber, Ind | 63,080 | (15) |
| | Menario, Ind | 62,789 | (15) |
| MARYLAND | •Schaefer, Dem | 886,575 | (82) |
| | Mooney, GOP | 189,184 | (18) |
| MASS. | •Dukakis, Dem* | 1,151,036 | (69) |
| | Karlotis, GOP | 522,049 | (31) |
| MICHIGAN | •Blanchard, Dem* | 1,618,445 | (69) |
| | Lucas, GOP | 742,911 | (31) |
| MINNESOTA | •Perpich, Dem* | 760,303 | (56) |
| | Ludeman, GOP | 591,271 | (44) |
| NEBRASKA | Boosalis, Dem | 262,302 | (47) |
| | •Orr, GOP | 294,521 | (53) |
| NEVADA | •Bryan, Dem* | 187,264 | (73) |
| | Cafferata, GOP | 65,081 | (25) |
| N.HAMPSHIRE | McEachern, Dem | 116,154 | (46) |
| | •Sununu, GOP* | 134,674 | (54) |
| NEW MEXICO | Powell, Dem | 179,855 | (47) |
| | •Carruthers, GOP | 203,746 | (53) |
| NEW YORK | •Cuomo, Dem* | 2,681,629 | (65) |
| | O'Rourke, GOP | 1,342,125 | (32) |
| OHIO | •Celeste, Dem* | 1,856,680 | (61) |
| | Rhodes, GOP | 1,208,243 | (39) |
| OKLAHOMA | Walters, Dem | 385,059 | (49) |
| | •Bellman, GOP | 406,293 | (51) |
| OREGON | •Goldschmidt, Dem | 519,964 | (53) |
| | Paulus, GOP | 464,399 | (47) |
| PENN. | •Casey, Dem | 1,705,034 | (51) |
| | Scranton III, GOP | 1,632,575 | (49) |
| RHODE ISLAND | Sundlun, Dem | 101,024 | (33) |
| | •DiPrete, GOP* | 203,500 | (67) |
| S.CAROLINA | Daniel, Dem | 356,895 | (48) |
| | •Campbell, GOP | 280,274 | (52) |
| SOUTH DAKOTA | Herseth, Dem | 140,568 | (48) |
| | •Mickelson, GOP | 150,415 | (52) |
| TENNESSEE | •McWherter, Dem | 657,426 | (54) |
| | Dunn, GOP | 552,900 | (46) |
| TEXAS | White, Dem* | 1,575,712 | (47) |
| | •Clements, GOP | 1,803,237 | (53) |
| VERMONT | •Kunin, Dem* | 92,178 | (47) |
| | Smith, GOP | 74,678 | (38) |
| | Sanders, Ind | 28,451 | (15) |
| WISCONSIN | Earl, Dem* | 703,036 | (47) |

|         |                    |         | % of Vote |
|---------|--------------------|---------|-----------|
|         | •Thompson, GOP     | 802,424 | (53)      |
| WYOMING | •Sullivan, Dem     | 88,861  | (54)      |
|         | Simpson, GOP       | 75,810  | (46)      |

An asterisk denotes the incumbent.
A dot denotes the winner.

Nov. 6

# Blacks Cast Pivotal Ballots in Four Key Senate Races, Data Show

By LENA WILLIAMS

Democrats owe their new majority in the Senate, at least in part, to the black vote.

The black vote was crucial in four of the eight states the Democrats took from Republicans to regain control of the Senate in Tuesday's elections, according to political analysts and reviews of the polls of voters.

In Alabama, North Carolina, Louisiana and California the black vote was so heavily Democratic, according to the polling data, that it helped to stanch a substantial flow of white votes to Republican candidates.

Without the black vote, in each of those key races the Republican candidate would have won, in some cases by a substantial margin, according to a CBS News poll of voters who had cast their ballots.

A case in point is North Carolina, where the Republican candidate, Senator James T. Broyhill, won 56 percent of the white vote, while his Democratic opponent, Terry Sanford, a former governor, received only 43 percent of the white vote. By comparison, Mr. Sanford received 88 percent of the black vote to Mr. Broyhill's 8 percent. The overall tally gave Mr. Sanford 51 percent of the vote, as against 48 percent for Mr. Broyhill.

In California, blacks overwhelmingly supported the incumbent senator, Alan Cranston, a Democrat. With 82 percent of the black vote, Mr. Cranston was able to fight off a stiff challenge from his Republican opponent, Representative Ed Zschau. Mr. Zschau won only 10 percent of the black vote. The reverse is true with regard to white voters, who gave Mr. Zschau 50 percent of the vote and Mr. Cranston 47 percent.

Another test came in Alabama, where Democrats had not had serious hopes of winning what some black leaders called a race between two staunch conservatives, both of whom opposed legislation declaring the birthday of the Rev. Dr. Martin Luther King, Jr., a national holiday. Senator Jeremiah Denton, a Republican, would have defeated the Democrat, Representative Richard C. Shelby, had it not been for the black vote, according to the polls.

Here again, blacks choose to go with the Democratic candidate, giving Mr. Shelby 88 percent of their vote against 7 percent for Mr. Denton.

"Our loyalty is pretty well documented," said Jerry Wilson, director of the Voter Education Project at the Southern Regional Council in Atlanta, Ga. "I believe our issues now warrant and deserve more of a response because we are the ones who elected these people to office. Without our vote they wouldn't be where they are today."

In Louisiana, Representative John B. Breaux, the Democrat, defeated Representative W. Henson Moore, the Republican, with 85 percent of the black vote to Mr. Moore's 12 percent. Mr. Moore received 60 percent of the white vote as against Mr. Breaux's 39 percent.

Black voters were also pivotal in helping Democrats maintain their majority in the House. In addition, 22 black representatives were elected, giving the House its largest number of black members in history.

The *New York Times*/CBS News poll of

8,997 voters leaving polling places showed that whites gave Republicans a 51-to-49 percent edge. But that was more than made up for by the 86-to-14 percent majority the Democrats won among blacks. While such data cannot pinpoint particular House races in which the black vote won for the Democrats, it is clear that it had impact.

In that race, Mike Espy became the first black to be elected to the House from his state since Reconstruction.     Nov. 6

### The black vote in 4 senate races

|  | Whites, others | Blacks |
|---|---|---|
| **Alabama** | | |
| Percent of total | 79% | 21% |
| Shelby (D) | 38 | 88 |
| Denton (R) | 61 | 7 |
| **Louisiana** | | |
| Percent of total | 69 | 29 |
| Breaux (D) | 39 | 85 |
| Moore (R) | 60 | 12 |
| **North Carolina** | | |
| Percent of total | 82 | 16 |
| Sanford (D) | 43 | 88 |
| Broyhill (R) | 56 | 8 |
| **California** | | |
| Percent of total | 90 | 9 |
| Cranston (D) | 47 | 82 |
| Zschau (R) | 50 | 10 |

Based on CBS News Polls conducted Tuesday in Alabama with 1,300 voters, in Louisiana with 1,158 voters, in North Carolina with 1,171 voters and in California with 2,544 voters.

# Alaska Found to Lead Nation in Total Spent on Education

A study by the National Education Association, released on Nov. 7, showed that the nation spent an average of $3,723 on each pupil in the 1985–86 school year and that the average teacher salary was $25,813.

Alaska, spending $8,349 per pupil and paying an average teacher salary of $41,480, was in first place in each category. Utah, with per-pupil expenditures of $2,297, was last in that category and South Dakota was lowest in teachers' salary, at $18,095.

The N.E.A. also calculated that there was an average of nearly 18 students per teacher nationally, combining secondary and elementary schools.

Here is the association's state-by-state listing of average teacher pay and spending per pupil in 1985–86:

| State | Pay | Rank | Spending | Rank |
|---|---|---|---|---|
| **New England** | | | | |
| Maine | 19,583 | 48 | 3,346 | 31 |
| New Hampshire | 20,263 | 47 | 3,114 | 36 |
| Vermont | 20,325 | 46 | 3,554 | 26 |
| Massachusetts | 26,800 | 12 | 4,642 | 8 |
| Rhode Island | 29,470 | 5 | 4,669 | 7 |
| Connecticut | 26,610 | 13 | 4,888 | 6 |
| **Middle Atlantic** | | | | |
| New York | 30,678 | 3 | 5,710 | 2 |
| New Jersey | 27,170 | 10 | 5,536 | 3 |
| Pennsylvania | 25,853 | 17 | 4,168 | 12 |
| **East North Central** | | | | |
| Ohio | 24,500 | 24 | 3,547 | 27 |
| Indiana | 24,274 | 25 | 3,159 | 33 |
| Illinois | 27,170 | 10 | 3,621 | 22 |
| Michigan | 30,168 | 4 | 3,782 | 18 |
| Wisconsin | 26,525 | 14 | 4,247 | 11 |

| State | Pay | Rank | Spending | Rank |
|---|---|---|---|---|
| **West North Central** | | | | |
| Minnesota | 27,360 | 7 | 3,982 | 15 |
| Iowa | 21,690 | 37 | 3,568 | 25 |
| Missouri | 21,974 | 35 | 3,155 | 34 |
| North Dakota | 20,816 | 43 | 3,059 | 37 |
| South Dakota | 18,095 | 51 | 2,967 | 39 |
| Nebraska | 20,939 | 42 | 3,285 | 32 |
| Kansas | 22,644 | 29 | 3,914 | 17 |
| **South Atlantic** | | | | |
| Delaware | 24,624 | 23 | 4,517 | 9 |
| Maryland | 27,186 | 9 | 4,349 | 10 |
| Dist. of Col. | 33,990 | 2 | 5,020 | 5 |
| Virginia | 23,382 | 26 | 3,594 | 24 |
| West Virginia | 20,627 | 44 | 2,821 | 44 |
| North Carolina | 22,795 | 28 | 3,366 | 30 |
| South Carolina | 21,570 | 38 | 2,920 | 41 |
| Georgia | 22,080 | 34 | 2,980 | 38 |
| Florida | 22,250 | 33 | 3,731 | 20 |
| **East South Central** | | | | |
| Kentucky | 20,940 | 41 | 2,853 | 42 |
| Tennessee | 21,800 | 36 | 2,533 | 48 |
| Alabama | 22,934 | 27 | 2,729 | 46 |
| Mississippi | 18,443 | 50 | 2,305 | 50 |
| **West South Central** | | | | |
| Arkansas | 19,538 | 49 | 2,642 | 47 |
| Louisiana | 20,460 | 45 | 3,124 | 35 |
| Oklahoma | 21,419 | 39 | 2,752 | 45 |
| Texas | 25,160 | 21 | 3,429 | 28 |
| **Mountain** | | | | |
| Montana | 22,482 | 31 | 3,947 | 16 |
| Idaho | 20,969 | 40 | 2,509 | 49 |
| Wyoming | 27,224 | 8 | 5,440 | 4 |
| Colorado | 25,892 | 16 | 4,042 | 14 |
| New Mexico | 22,644 | 29 | 3,402 | 29 |
| Arizona | 24,640 | 22 | 2,829 | 43 |
| Utah | 22,341 | 32 | 2,297 | 51 |
| Nevada | 25,610 | 20 | 2,932 | 40 |
| **Pacific** | | | | |
| Washington | 26,015 | 15 | 3,705 | 21 |
| Oregon | 25,788 | 19 | 4,123 | 13 |
| California | 29,132 | 6 | 3,608 | 23 |
| Alaska | 41,480 | 1 | 8,349 | 1 |
| Hawaii | 25,845 | 18 | 3,766 | 19 |

Nov. 8

## Doctorates conferred by institutions of higher learning

| Discipline | 1970–71 | 1983–84 | % change |
|---|---|---|---|
| Business Management | 807 | 869 | 8 |
| Communications | 145 | 215 | 48 |
| Computer & Info. Sciences | 128 | 251 | 96 |
| Education | 6,403 | 7,473 | 17 |
| Engineering | 3,637 | 2,979 | −18 |
| Foreign Languages | 781 | 462 | −41 |
| Health Sciences | 459 | 1,163 | 153 |
| Life Sciences | 3,645 | 3,437 | −6 |
| Mathematics | 1,199 | 695 | −42 |
| Philosophy & Religion | 554 | 442 | −20 |
| Physical Sciences | 4,390 | 3,306 | −25 |
| Psychology | 1,782 | 2,973 | 67 |
| Social Sciences | 3,659 | 2,911 | 20 |

Minus sign indicates decline
Source: U.S. Department of Education, National Center for Education Statistics

Nov. 9

# Blackboard Notes
# Who's Getting the Ph.D.s?

**By SALLY REED**

More and more, it's women and foreign students who are studying for doctorates.

According to the latest data from the United States Department of Education, women claimed 34 percent of the 33,209 doctorates awarded in 1983–84—or seven times their percentage 20 years before. Over all, the number of Ph.D.s is up substantially in psychology and down in math and the physical sciences, where industry is luring potential candidates with lucrative starting salaries.

Big percentage gains have been registered in emerging fields involving health, computers and communications. The decline in engineering is a major problem, and colleges have actively recruited foreign students to fill classes. Non-Americans were awarded 53 percent of the engineering Ph.D. degrees in 1983–84.

Nov. 9

## State Medical Boards Disciplined Record Number of Doctors in '85

### By JOEL BRINKLEY

WASHINGTON, Nov. 8—The state agencies that discipline physicians revoked a record number of licenses for incompetence or other problems last year, almost 60 percent more than in 1984, a new report shows.

The number of lesser disciplinary actions, such as license suspension or probation, increased dramatically as well. The increase appeared to be the largest ever in a single year, and larger than the increases for the previous four years combined.

The new statistics come after years of criticism that many state medical boards, the most important agencies in the nation's medical discipline network, failed to punish doctors who were drunk, incompetent or impaired, allowing them to continue practicing, possibly harming or killing patients.

In June a report by the inspector general of the Department of Health and Human Services said that the boards disciplined "strikingly few" incompetent doctors. This week, however, the inspector general, Richard P. Kusserow, said he was "very pleased" by the new figures, adding, "It looks like things are just beginning to come together for the boards."

This is occurring, he and other medical officials said, as local, state and Federal agencies have begun to focus more attention on medical incompetence, seeking to save both lives and money. Incompetent doctors add billions of dollars to the nation's health care bill, in expensive treatment needed to fix mistakes and in malpractice suit settlements.

The official figures are published by the Federation of State Medical Boards, which represents licensing agencies in the 50 states and the District of Columbia. The federation showed that medical boards nationwide revoked the licenses of 406 doctors last year, up 59.2 percent from 255 in 1984. The totals for the earlier 1980s were similar to the 1984 figure.

In addition, the licenses of 235 doctors were suspended, 491 other doctors were placed on probation and 976 received penalties of another sort, ranging from reprimands to restrictions of their practice.

New York's medical board revoked the licenses of 42 doctors, the largest number in the country and almost twice as many as in the previous year. New Jersey ordered 146 disciplinary actions of all sorts, the third highest overall total nationwide, behind California, which has almost four times as many doctors, and Florida in second place.

Based on the number of disciplinary actions for every 1,000 doctors, New Jersey was the ninth most active board in the nation last year. New York ranked 44th. Connecticut, which revoked no licenses while placing four doctors on probation, ranked 49th.

This year, as last, Nevada's was the most aggressive board, disciplining almost 2 out of every 100 doctors in the state. Alaska was the only state reporting no disciplinary actions.

Nov. 9

## Disciplining doctors: The state-by-state record

Figures for 1985 actions by state medical boards. Actions other than license revocations include license suspensions, probation, reprimands, fines and restrictions of practice.

| State | Number of doctors | Licenses revoked | Total number of actions | Actions per 1,000 doctors |
|---|---|---|---|---|
| 1. Nevada | 1,604 | 11 | 30 | 18.7 |
| 2. Arizona | 6,942 | 11 | 115 | 16.6 |
| 3. Utah | 3,025 | 5 | 43 | 14.2 |
| 4. Oklahoma | 4,866 | 6 | 46 | 9.5 |
| 5. Idaho | 1,331 | 1 | 12 | 9.0 |
| 6. Oregon | 5,764 | 2 | 51 | 8.8 |
| 7. Mississippi | 3,279 | 2 | 28 | 8.5 |
| 8. Georgia | 10,742 | 7 | 89 | 8.3 |
| 9. New Jersey | 18,313 | 17 | 146 | 8.0 |
| 10. Arkansas | 3,532 | 3 | 27 | 7.6 |
| 11. Kansas | 4,350 | 5 | 33 | 7.6 |
| 12. Missouri | 9,750 | 34 | 73 | 7.5 |
| 13. Virginia | 11,875 | 11 | 76 | 6.4 |
| 14. Iowa | 4,305 | 1 | 27 | 6.3 |
| 15. Indiana | 8,542 | 9 | 52 | 6.1 |
| 16. Florida | 26,566 | 15 | 153 | 5.8 |
| 17. Kentucky | 5,982 | 8 | 32 | 5.3 |
| 18. North Dakota | 1,130 | 0 | 6 | 5.3 |
| 19. Washington | 9,693 | 5 | 47 | 4.8 |
| 20. Texas | 28,254 | 28 | 134 | 4.7 |
| 21. South Carolina | 5,303 | 5 | 23 | 4.3 |
| 22. Louisiana | 8,312 | 3 | 35 | 4.2 |
| 23. Wisconsin | 8,969 | 8 | 37 | 4.1 |
| 24. Alabama | 6,090 | 3 | 24 | 3.9 |
| 25. Rhode Island | 2,385 | 5 | 9 | 3.8 |
| 26. Pennsylvania | 27,727 | 27 | 103 | 3.7 |
| 27. West Virginia | 3,319 | 3 | 12 | 3.6 |
| 28. Colorado | 6,879 | 0 | 23 | 3.3 |
| 29. Minnesota | 9,326 | 2 | 30 | 3.2 |
| 30. Ohio | 21,319 | 22 | 67 | 3.1 |
| 31. Maine | 2,232 | 4 | 7 | 3.1 |
| 32. New Mexico | 2,630 | 2 | 8 | 3.0 |
| 33. Illinois | 24,903 | 9 | 75 | 3.0 |
| 34. Tennessee | 8,982 | 5 | 27 | 3.0 |
| 35. California | 69,208 | 39 | 187 | 2.7 |
| 36. North Carolina | 11,347 | 11 | 30 | 2.6 |
| 37. Hawaii | 2,388 | 0 | 6 | 2.5 |
| 38. Washington, D.C. | 3,755 | 8 | 9 | 2.4 |
| 39. Montana | 1,276 | 0 | 3 | 2.4 |
| 40. Michigan | 17,206 | 10 | 38 | 2.2 |
| 41. Massachusetts | 19,242 | 15 | 29 | 1.5 |
| 42. Maryland | 14,491 | 0 | 20 | 1.4 |
| 43. Wyoming | 707 | 1 | 1 | 1.4 |

| State | Number of doctors | Licenses revoked | Total number of actions | Actions per 1,000 doctors |
|---|---|---|---|---|
| 44. New York | 56,392 | 42 | 75 | 1.3 |
| 45. South Dakota | 1,003 | 0 | 1 | 1.0 |
| 46. New Hampshire | 2,060 | 0 | 2 | 1.0 |
| 47. Delaware | 1,252 | 0 | 1 | 0.8 |
| 48. Vermont | 1,436 | 1 | 1 | 0.7 |
| 49. Connecticut | 9,544 | 0 | 4 | 0.4 |
| 50. Nebraska | 2,707 | 0 | 1 | 0.4 |
| 51. Alaska | 608 | 0 | 0 | 0.0 |

Source: The Federation of State Medical Boards, as reported by the individual state boards, and the American Medical Association

Nov. 9

# High Fees for Guest Lecturers Stir Argument at Carolina University

By WILLIAM E. SCHMIDT

COLUMBIA, S.C., Nov. 11—For officials at the University of South Carolina, it began as a matter of academic strategy: To gain national visibility, they would hire well-known public figures as lecturers and part-time teachers.

But in recent weeks James B. Holderman, the university's president, and a number of "distinguished visiting professors," including Jihan el-Sadat, the widow of the Egyptian leader, and Lyn Nofziger, a former top political aide to President Reagan, have found themselves at the center of an argument here.

As the result of a judge's ruling in a lawsuit, school officials disclosed last month that they had paid hundreds of thousands of dollars in salaries and expenses to a small group of visiting lecturers and professors.

In a state so hard up for money that public employees are facing a mandatory pay freeze, and where tuition for university students was raised twice in the last two years, the disclosures about the salaries to visiting lecturers have aroused anger on and off campus.

But officials at the university defend the payments and the practice as a boon to the university. They say it creates excitement on campus and helps draw private contributions.

In legal papers filed by the university, officials said most of the money came from a university account for the office of the president and was made up of appropriated funds.

The largest sum for visiting lecturers, about $313,000 in salary and expenses, was paid to Mrs. Sadat for three semesters during which she lectured to one class a week.

Mr. Nofziger and others, including Robert MacNeil and James Lehrer, the public television news commentators, and Howard Simons, former managing editor of *The Washington Post* and now curator of the Nieman Foundation at Harvard University, are receiving $30,000 to $45,000 each this semester to appear on campus one to three times a month as guest lecturers or part-time instructors.

And according to university records, Bill Cosby, the comedian, was given $25,000 last spring when he spoke at the university's commencement ceremonies, where he was also awarded an honorary degree as a doctor of humane letters. Mr. Cosby refused to discuss the matter, but university officials said Monday that he had returned his fee as an "anonymous" gift.

Jonathan Knight, associate secretary of the American Association of University Professors in Washington, said the group had no data on such salaries nationally, but he was surprised at the sums being paid at South Carolina and believed them to be unusually high. In addition, he explicitly condemned the practice of paying fees to commencement speakers who were also being given honorary degrees.

Mr. Knight said universities typically hire distinguished people as visiting professors as "a kind of calling card" for the school. "But what they are doing there strikes me as an absolute perversion of that kind of reasonable practice," he added.  Nov. 13

## Pursuing personalities

To gain national visibility, the University of South Carolina in Columbia has been hiring well-known public figures as lecturers, part-time teachers and consultants. In a state so pressed for money that public employees are facing a mandatory pay freeze, the high cost of cultivating such ties has stirred controversy. These are among the well-paid visitors:

| | Time spent on campus | Earnings |
|---|---|---|
| **Jihan el-Sadat,** widow of President Anwar el-Sadat of Egypt | One class a week for three semesters | $212,000* |
| **Lawrence S. Eagleburger,** former Under Secretary of State | Various guest appearances and special lectures, consulting | $75,000 a year |
| **Mursisaad el-Din,** former Egyptian cabinet member | Nearly every day for three semesters | $58,000 |
| **Howard Simons,** former managing editor, *The Washington Post* | Once a week | $45,000 a semester |
| **James Lehrer,** television news commentator | Twice a semester | $37,500 a semester |
| **Robert MacNeil,** television news commentator | Twice a semester | $37,500 a semester |
| **Lyn Nofziger,** former aide to President Reagan | Once a month | $30,000 a semester |
| **Bill Cosby,** entertainer | Delivery of commencement address | $25,000** |
| **Dena Kaye,** writer and daughter of Danny Kaye, the entertainer | Twice a semester | $25,000 a semester |
| **Henry A. Kissinger,** former Secretary of State | Two days | $25,000 |
| **Gayle Sayers,** former running back, Chicago Bears | Various consulting visits | $25,000 this semester |
| **Yoshio Okawara,** former Japanese Ambassador to the United States and Australia | Two visits | $12,500 a visit |
| **James Prior,** member of Parliament and chairman, General Electric Company of Britain | Four visits over three semesters | $12,500 a visit |
| **John C. West,** former Governor of South Carolina and U.S. Ambassador to Saudi Arabia | Ten visits a semester | $10,000 a semester |

*Plus $106,000 in expenses
**Plus earnings from concert on campus that night
Source: University of South Carolina

Nov. 16

# U.S. Jury Convicts Eight as Members of Mob Commission

**By ARNOLD H. LUBASCH**

All eight defendants in a dramatic 10-week racketeering trial were convicted yesterday of operating a "commission" that ruled the Mafia throughout the United States.

The Federal trial in Manhattan attained national significance as the first case to focus on the commission of top crime leaders, portrayed by the prosecution as "the board of directors" of the Mafia, or La Cosa Nostra.

"The verdict reached today has resulted in dismantling the ruling council of La Cosa Nostra," the United States Attorney, Rudolph W. Giuliani, said in a statement issued by his office in Manhattan.

Law-enforcement authorities said the verdicts would make it easier to fight racketeering. The Government has recently been making a major assault on the mob, and since last year has brought Mafia cases in Kansas City, Boston, New Jersey and Philadelphia, among other places.

At 12:20 P.M. in a crowded, tensely quiet courtroom of Federal District Court, the jury announced its verdict on the sixth day of deliberations, convicting all the defendants of all the charges against them.

Three defendants convicted as the bosses of crime families were Anthony (Fat Tony) Salerno of the Genovese group, Anthony (Tony Ducks) Corallo of the Lucchese group and Carmine (Junior) Persico of the Colombo group. Mr. Persico acted as his own lawyer. According to the 22-count indictment, the defendants conducted the affairs of "the commission of La Cosa Nostra" in a racketeering pattern that included murders, loan-sharking, labor payoffs and extensive extortion in the concrete industry in New York City.

As the guilty verdict was being announced, the defendants seemed stoic. But the jury's foreman brushed tears from her eyes after reading the long verdict, which took 20 minutes. Defense lawyers said the convictions would be appealed.

Judge Richard Owen set sentencing for Jan. 6, when each defendant faces up to 20 years in prison on the main racketeering charge and additional terms on related charges. Theoretically, for most of the defendants, the maximum sentence would be more than 300 years.

## The Convicted Mob Members

**Anthony (Fat Tony) Salerno,** 75 years old, boss of Genovese family, with 200 members and hundreds of associates based in Greenwich Village, East Harlem and on Brooklyn and Jersey waterfronts. Considered senior member of commission. Held other top family posts of consigliere and underboss. Had risen through ranks to become an influential captain. Previously convicted on Federal tax and gambling charges. Lives on estate in Rhinebeck, N.Y.

**Anthony (Tony Ducks) Corallo,** 73, boss of Lucchese family, with 110 members and unspecified number of associates based in Brooklyn and Bronx. Considered most powerful crime boss on Long Island. Longtime leader of his family. Reportedly began gangland career on Upper East Side as member of old East 107th Street gang. Previously convicted on charges of bribery of New York political figures during Lindsay administration and of extortion and narcotics. Lives in Oyster Bay Cove, L.I.

**Carmine (Junior) Persico,** 53, boss of Colombo family, with 115 members and at least 500 associates based in Brooklyn and Staten Island. Sentenced Monday to 39 years in prison on earlier racketeering conviction. Accused of carrying out first murder when 17 years old and of later committing or ordering several others. Spent many years in prison for hijacking, bribe conspiracy, extortion, labor racketeering, labor corruption, embezzlement, business shakedowns, loan-sharking, numbers running and narcotics. Lives in Brooklyn and has a farm in Saugerties, N. Y.

**Gennaro (Gerry Lang) Langella,** 47, acting boss and underboss of the Colombo family. Long a close associate of Persico, he helped run family while Persico was in prison. Sentenced Monday in other trial along with Persico, but to longer prison term—65 years. Also previously convicted on charges of robbery, obstruction of justice and racketeering. Lives in Brooklyn.

**Anthony (Bruno) Indelicato,** 38, captain in Bonanno family, with 195 members and 500 associates in New York, New Jersey, Pennsylvania, Arizona, Florida and California. Said to have been promoted to either "made" member or captain for participating in 1979 slaying of Bonanno boss, Carmine Galante. Father, Alphonse (Sonny Red) Indelicato, was Bonanno captain killed in power struggle in 1981 after taking part in Galante plot. Bruno Indelicato also said to have been targeted for killing. Previously convicted on weapons charge. Lives in lower Manhattan.

**Ralph Scopo,** 58, member, or soldier, of Colombo family. President of Cement Workers District Council from 1977 to 1984. Because of ill health, severed from racketeering trial that led to sentencing Monday of his superiors, Persico and Langella. Described as family's "principal operative" in extorting payoffs from companies in New York's concrete industry. Previously convicted of grand larceny and assault. Lives in Queens.

**Salvatore (Tom Mix) Santoro,** 72, underboss of Lucchese family. As member of gang said to be responsible for crimes on Brooklyn waterfront. Charged but not convicted of murder of shipyard foreman in 1945. Like his boss, Corallo, alumnus of old East 107th Street gang and associate in narcotics operations of Charles (Lucky) Luciano. Previously convicted on narcotics charges and sentenced to four years in prison in 1952. Lives in Bronx.

**Christopher (Christie Tick) Furnari,** 62, consigliere, or counselor, of the Lucchese family. Previously convicted on sodomy and assault charges. Lives on Staten Island.

Nov. 20

## Hailing a cab
Taxi service in selected cities

| | Number of licensed cabs | How number is determined | Starting fare (cost/miles) | Estimated cost of traveling two miles* |
|---|---|---|---|---|
| New York | 11,787 | Ceiling set in 1947 | $1.10 1/9 | $2.80 |
| Chicago | 4,600 | Ceiling set in 1945 | $1.00 1/5 | $2.80 |
| Houston | 1,923 | Ceiling adjusted annually | $1.40 1/5 | $3.11 |
| Dallas | 1,500 | Unlimited, but restricted to existing licensees | $1.35 1/10 | $3.20 |
| Philadelphia | 1,500 | Ceiling set in 1982 | $1.25 1/7 | $3.85 |
| Detroit | 1,310 | Ceiling set in 1945 | $0.90 1/9 | $2.60 |
| Los Angeles | 950 | Ceiling set in 1981 | $1.90 1/5 | $4.30 |
| San Diego | 899 | Ceiling set in 1983 | $1.17** | $4.37 |
| Phoenix | 500 | Free entry | $1.00** | $3.25 |
| San Antonio | 477 | Ceiling set in 1984 | $1.45 1/5 | $3.25 |

*Does not include waiting time, which increases fare.
**Average; fares and distances vary from one company to another.
Source: Manhattan Institute for Policy Research; International Taxicab Association

Nov. 23

# Outgoing Governor in New Mexico Bars the Execution of 5

**By ROBERT REINHOLD**

SANTA FE, N.M., Nov. 26—In a dramatic Thanksgiving Eve move to thwart his successor, Gov. Toney Anaya of New Mexico today commuted the death sentences of all five men awaiting execution in the state, saying the penalty was "inhumane, immoral and anti-God."

Lawyers said it was believed to be the first mass reprieve since Gov. Winthrop Rockefeller of Arkansas commuted the death sentences of all 15 inmates awaiting execution in 1970.

Today's action came just five weeks before the Democratic governor is to complete his four years in office, during which he stayed all pending executions. "My personal beliefs do not allow me to permit the execution of an individual in the name of the state," he said minutes after signing executive orders reducing the sentences to life imprisonment.

He added that to leave office without acting would assure the execution of one or more of the five men and "for me to simply walk away now will make me as much an accomplice as others who would participate in their execution."

His Republican successor, Garrey Carruthers, had campaigned heavily on the crime issue and had said, "The first thing I want to see on my desk after I'm elected governor is the paperwork necessary to restart the death penalty."

The five are:

William Wayne Gilbert, 37 years old, a former pilot in Vietnam, who was convicted of rape, kidnapping and first-degree murder of an Albuquerque woman. He was scheduled to die by lethal injection Jan. 16. He has been convicted of three other murders, including his wife's.

Richard Reynaldo Garcia, 31, serving time for robbery, jail escape and the murder of a prison guard. His execution date was Jan. 1.

Michael Anthony Guzman, 24, convicted of raping and murdering a coed at the University of New Mexico in 1981.

Joel Lee Compton, 33, convicted of murdering an Albuquerque policeman. He would be eligible for parole at 65.

Eddie Lee Adams, 24, convicted of the rape and strangulation murder of an 80-year-old Clovis, N. M., woman.

Mr. Anaya coupled his action with a call for greater aid to the victims of violent crime and for wider efforts to eliminate child abuse, racism and other root causes of crime.

The last person to be executed in New Mexico was David Cooper Nelson in 1960. Since the penalty was restored, seven have been sentenced to death, two reversed by the courts. Mr. Anaya reprieved the five others.

Nov. 27

# Do Mayors Have Comparable Worth?

**By BRUCE LAMBERT**

Mayor Edward Koch of New York City was dubbed the "Million-Dollar Mayor" when he said he could get 10 times his municipal salary—$110,000—in private business. Now some kind of raise appears probable, not only for Mr. Koch but also for other elected city officials, under a new system whereby a panel of outside compensation experts will make recommendations.

The prospect raises a hard-to-answer question: How much is a mayor worth?

Many people would shrink from the task of governing New York City, no matter how high the pay. Others might jump at the chance, regardless of salary.

Mr. Koch is not the nation's highest-paid mayor. That title, according to a United States Conference of Mayors survey this year, belongs to Detroit's Coleman A. Young, who earns $115,000. Paradoxically, at the bottom of the pay scale is the man recently rated the nation's best mayor in a *City & State* magazine poll of municipal finance experts. He is Henry G. Cisneros of San Antonio, the 10th biggest city in the country. His pay is $3,000 annually, plus $20 for each weekly City Council meeting, a total of $4,040. The full-time city manager makes $100,000. "Mayor Koch's salary is not out of line—there are certainly a number of mayors and managers in that range," said Michael W. Brown, the Conference of Mayors' spokesman.

"When you look at the scope of responsibility and stress factors, these salaries are not an exceptional amount of money," Mr. Brown added. DEC. 14

### Bringing home the bacon
What some mayors and city managers earn

| City | Mayor or city manager | Salary |
|---|---|---|
| Detroit | Coleman A. Young | $115,000 |
| Phoenix | Marvin Andrews | 112,000 |
| New York City | Edward I. Koch | 110,000 |
| San Francisco | Dianne Feinstein | 107,349 |
| Dallas | Richard Knight, Jr.* | 106,197 |
| Houston | Kathryn J. Whitmire | 104,978 |
| San Diego | John Lockwood | 100,000 |
| Los Angeles | Tom Bradley | 88,778 |
| Philadelphia | W. Wilson Goode | 70,000 |
| Chicago | Harold Washington | 60,000** |

*Acting city manager
**$80,000 in 1987

DEC. 14

# U.S. Panel Suggests Big Rise in Salaries for Senior Officials

**By KENNETH B. NOBLE**

WASHINGTON, Dec. 15—A presidential advisory commission today recommended substantial salary increases, some more than 80 percent, for Federal judges, members of Congress and executive branch officials. The panel also said it "feels strongly" that in return for higher salaries, members of Congress should be barred from getting honorariums and other earnings for speeches and public appearances, or the permitted amounts should be significantly reduced.

The recommendations, which will probably be revised by President Reagan and which Congress has the authority to reject with his assent, include a 60 percent raise for Federal district judges, to $130,000 a year. Members of Congress would make $135,000; they are now paid $77,400.

Saying that "financial compensation is becoming a strong negative factor" in attracting qualified people to top positions in the Government, the nine-member Commission on Executive, Legislative and Judicial Salaries concluded unanimously that "significant salary increases for top Federal officials are essential."

But Ralph Nader, the consumer activist, said today that he saw no urgent need for such raises. "It's basically the rich and powerful recommending huge increases to the powerful in government," Mr. Nader said. "Procedurally, it's a monstrosity. What you have here is a commission holding no public hearings, holding no news conference to answer questions, and then recommending to the President an outlandish figure so that he can cut it down to an outrageous figure." DEC. 16

## Proposed salary increases

| Executive Branch | Salary Jan. 1, '87 | Proposed salary |
|---|---|---|
| Vice President | $100,800 | $175,000 |
| Cabinet officers | 88,800 | 160,000 |
| Deputy secretaries of Cabinet departments, heads of offices and agencies | 77,400 | 135,000 |
| Under Secretaries of Cabinet departments, chairmen of regulatory commissions | 75,800 | 130,000 |
| Assistant Secretaries of Cabinet departments, regulatory commission members, Cabinet department general counsels | 74,500 | 120,000 |
| Directors of major bureaus of Cabinet departments | 70,800 | 110,000 |
| **Annual Cost of Proposed Increases** | | **$40,577,800** |

| Legislative Branch | Salary Jan. 1, '87 | Proposed salary |
|---|---|---|
| Speaker of the House | $100,800 | $175,000 |
| President pro tem, majority and minority leaders | 87,600 | 160,000 |
| Senators, representatives, four delegates to Congress, Resident Commissioner for Puerto Rico, Comptroller General | 77,400 | 135,000 |
| Director of Congressional Budget Office, Deputy Comptroller General, Librarian of Congress, Architect of the Capitol | 75,800 | 130,000 |
| Deputy Director of Congressional Budget Office, General Counsel | 74,500 | 120,000 |
| **Annual Cost of Proposed Increases** | | **$31,651,000** |

| Judicial Branch | Salary Jan. 1, '87 | Proposed salary |
|---|---|---|
| Chief Justice | $111,700 | $175,000 |
| Associate Justices | 107,200 | 165,000 |
| Judges, Circuit Courts of Appeal, Court of Military Appeals | 85,700 | 135,000 |
| Judges, District Courts, Court of International Trade, Tax Court | 81,100 | 130,000 |
| U.S. Court of Claims | 72,300 | 130,000 |
| **Annual Cost of Proposed Increases** | | **$77,600,200** |
| **TOTAL COST OF PROPOSED INCREASES** | | **$149,829,000** |

Source: Commission on Executive, Legislative and Judicial Salaries

DEC. 16

## Carnegie Panel Cites 24 Heroes

Bradley Hall, 17, who crawled 28 feet on his stomach through thick smoke to save Roland Winters, a muscular dystrophy victim threatened by a Christmas tree fire, was one of 24 people honored by the Carnegie Hero Fund Commission during Christmas week.

Besides the Anaheim teenager, who was not injured, the commission honored these people, five of whom gave their lives:

Lucille Moore, 75, of Columbus, Ohio, who died Nov. 7, 1985, after saving a neighbor from a fire.

Michael D. Croft, 40, an off-duty police officer from Cheektowaga, N.Y., who rescued an 84-year-old man from a fire March 10, 1986.

Phillip Andrew Wynne, 29, of Mobile, Ala., who rescued an 80-year-old woman from an assault in her home July 23, 1985.

Dennis G. Thomas, 30, of Port Huron, Mich., who saved a woman from drowning in the Black River on Jan. 23, 1986.

John Stratton, 25, of Lansdowne, Pa., who

carried a man to safety from a burning building Dec. 29, 1985.

Clayburn R. Marsh, 49, of Crosbyton, Tex., who rescued a woman who was almost electrocuted on Dec. 8, 1985.

Gregory A. Mellinger, 25, of Stevens, Pa., who saved a 65-year-old man who fell through ice while fishing on a lake March 10, 1986.

Steven Roy Edmonson, 31, of Manchester, Ga., who rescued two boys from a burning tractor-trailer on Dec. 17, 1985.

Joseph W. Schmider, 29, of Perkasie, Pa., who saved a woman and her daughter from a fire on Dec. 1, 1984.

Harold L. Shelton Jr., 28, of La Porte, Ind., who rescued a man from a fire in his home Aug. 26, 1985.

George J. Slatky, 48, of Hunlock Creek, Pa., who rescued a woman from a masked man armed with a knife who tried to pull her out of her car Jan. 21, 1986.

Charles B. McCracken, 30, of Tenino, Wash., who saved two girls and helped to save their mother from a burning pickup truck Oct. 26, 1985.

Richard G. Spillmann, 40, of Olympia, Wash., who helped Mr. McCracken.

David C. Ruble, 30, of Dreyfus, Ky., who rescued a 10-year-old girl from a burning house.

Robert Lee Thomas, 23, of San Antonio, who rescued a 15-year-old girl from an assault Feb. 27, 1986.

Rex A. Lewis, 30, of Hollister, Calif., who tried in vain to save a man from suffocation Oct. 19, 1984, after a power plant accident.

Michael DeWitt Puckett, 31, of Fresno, Calif., who helped save Mr. Lewis from suffocation.

Arthur J. Foucault, 61, of Orlando, Fla., who rescued a 1-year-old boy from burning on March 11, 1986.

Bret M. Lincoln, 25, of Blackstone, Mass., who helped to save a 13-year-old boy and tried to save a 10-year-old from drowning Jan. 27, 1986.

Ronald J. Mobley, 30, of Gypsy, W.Va., who died helping to save a 16-year-old girl from drowning Aug. 11, 1985.

Danny Cummings, 27, William R. Burns, 34, and Raymond R. Dawley, Jr., 37, all of Radcliff, Ky., who were killed by toxic gases while attempting to save a co-worker from suffocation at a waste treatment plant on July 5, 1985.

DEC. 26

## Some Also-Rans Must Keep Running for Years

By RICHARD L. BERKE

**W**ASHINGTON, Dec. 29—John B. Connally would probably just as soon forget the 1980 Republican precinct caucuses in Iowa, which marked the beginning of the end of his presidential bid.

But the proprietor of the Twin Torch Inn in Waterloo, Iowa, has not forgotten Mr. Connally. The former Texas governor's defunct campaign still owes the motel $1,634 for lodging its workers six years ago.

Rena Langenberg, who runs the inn, says she has initiated a new policy on the presidential campaign entourages that slog through her state every four years.

"We no longer accept anyone that has anything to do with campaigns," Ms. Langenberg said, "unless they pay in advance."

The money owed to the Twin Torch Inn is a minuscule part of the 1980 Connally campaign's total debt. According to the most recent Federal Election Commission figures, Mr. Connally owes $841,653.

The Texas Republican is not the only former candidate whose campaign committee is swimming in red ink. Although presidential aspirants are already building war chests for

1988, 10 contenders from the past still have debts to remind them of their failed tries at the White House.

Even the campaign committee of a former President, Jimmy Carter, still owes $676,197 from 1980.

The candidates' debts, large and small, are owed to banks, telephone companies, printing concerns, hotels and newspaper clipping services. Senator John Glenn's 1984 campaign owes $1.9 million plus interest to banks and $360 to the Kentucky Fried Chicken outlet in Manchester, N.H.

Soliciting contributions is considered a distasteful necessity of a political campaign. But continuing to raise money after the election to retire debts is even less desirable, particularly if the candidate was defeated. Because Federal law prohibits individuals from contributing more than $1,000 to a single presidential committee, a candidate cannot ask supporters who have already contributed that amount to help him pay off leftover debts after the election is over.

That is why it often takes years for presidential candidates to pay their debts. Many recall that it took more than 13 years to pay off the obligations of Hubert H. Humphrey's 1968 campaign.     DEC. 30

## Debts and Surpluses

| Presidential candidate, year | Receipts 1/1/85 to 9/30/86 | Cash on hand | Debts |
|---|---|---|---|
| John B. Anderson (Ind.) 1984 | $10,587 | $9,464 | $0 |
| Reubin Askew (D) 1984 | 25,508 | 0 | 0 |
| Jimmy Carter (D) 1980 | 52,706 | 1,880 | 676,197 |
| John B. Connally (R) 1980 | 101,150 | 198 | 841,653 |
| Alan Cranston (D) 1984 | 212,269 | 22,349 | 641,673 |
| Bob Dole (R) 1984 | 0 | 5,913 | 0 |
| John Glenn (D) 1984 | 416,102 | 7,777 | 2,838,733 |
| Gus Hall (Communist) 1984 | 23,985 | 4,723 | 48,166 |
| Gary Hart (D) 1984 | 1,973,059 | 0 | 2,423,228 |
| Ernest F. Hollings (D) 1984 | 9,198 | 3,160 | 10,049 |
| Jesse Jackson (D) 1984 | 348,558 | 1,940 | 67,548 |
| Edward M. Kennedy (D) 1984 | 10,279 | 36 | 83,386 |
| Lyndon LaRouche (D) 1984 | 1,115,229 | 190,347 | 2,604,907 |
| George McGovern (D) 1984 | 44,429 | 1,195 | 0 |
| Walter F. Mondale (D) 1984 | 3,245,292 | 317,163 | 0 |
| Richard M. Nixon (R) 1972 | 267 | 6,156 | 0 |
| Ronald Reagan (R) 1984 | 1,391,687 | 1,058,264 | 0 |
| Morris K. Udall (D) 1984 | 250 | 21 | 0 |

Source: Federal Election Commission reports

DEC. 30

## Florida Grows

On December 30 the Census Bureau announced that Florida moved past Illinois into fifth place in population in the United States in 1986.

The top six states in estimated population were:
California, 26,981,000
New York, 17,772,000
Texas, 16,682,000
Pennsylvania, 11,889,000
Florida, 11,675,000
Illinois, 11,553,000

DEC. 31

# PART 3
# Public Opinion

# President Highly Popular in Poll; No Ideological Shift Is Discerned

By R. W. APPLE, Jr.

President Reagan continues to be extremely popular with the American public, according to the latest *New York Times*/CBS News Poll, but there is no clear evidence that he has yet achieved the ideological realignment he has long sought.

Sixty-five percent, or about two thirds, of the 1,581 people interviewed said that they approved of the way Mr. Reagan was handling his job five full years after he took office. No president in the last half century has demonstrated quite that much staying power; at comparable stages of their incumbencies, Dwight D. Eisenhower had 60 percent of the public with him and Franklin D. Roosevelt had about the same.

On the eve of his State of the Union Message, which is to be delivered today, 39 percent of the public think most Americans are politically more conservative than they were five years ago, but 23 percent think they are more liberal. But on a range of ideological questions first asked about five years ago, no clear swing to the right has been discerned.

The economy remains a major preoccupation of the public and a major source of Mr. Reagan's strength. The survey, which was carried out by telephone Jan. 19 through 23, found that 52 percent approve of his handling of the nation's economy, as against 39 percent who do not, and that 39 percent consider their families' financial situation better today than it was a year ago, as against 16 percent who consider themselves worse off. The margin of sampling error was plus or minus three percentage points.

Asked what they thought was the biggest change in the United States in Mr. Reagan's time in office, more people by far mentioned improvement in the economy than anything else.

Mr. Reagan's decision to meet in Geneva with Mikhail S. Gorbachev, the Soviet leader, and the outcome of the meeting in late November appear to have had a considerable impact on Americans' view of East-West relations. Just before the summit conference, only 32 percent of the poll's respondents said they thought it would eventually produce "real arms control agreements." But now, even after the immediate postconference glow of favorable news coverage has faded, 41 percent of those questioned express optimism that the ongoing process will ultimately succeed.

The survey found that 53 percent of Americans think Mr. Reagan wants an arms control agreement badly enough to make real concessions to get it, that 37 percent think Mr. Gorbachev does, and that 28 percent think both of them do. In all three cases, the figures represent a considerably more optimistic view than that expressed to interviewers in early November, before the meeting.

But it is still the economy that has done the most to promote and maintain the President's strong standing. Very few people cited foreign policy matters when asked what they viewed as the biggest change in the United States since 1981; moreover, only 25 percent of those interviewed say the United States is more respected by other countries than it was five years ago, while 37 percent say it is less respected.

Mr. Reagan's popularity extends across most segments of American society as he begins his sixth year in the Oval Office. He has the approval of more than half of the public in all age groups, in all regions, in cities, towns, suburbs and urban areas, of all religious groups, of both sexes, of all levels of education and of all shades of political philosophy—conservative, moderate and liberal.    JAN. 26

# The *New York Times*/CBS News Poll
Shift to the Right: Perceptions and Realities

|  |  | As Reagan Era Began | | Now* |
|---|---|---|---|---|
|  |  | Date of Poll | Response (Percent) | Response (Percent) |
| Do you approve or disapprove of the way Ronald Reagan is handling his job as President? | Approve<br>Disapprove | 4/81 | 67<br>18 | 65<br>24 |
| How would you describe your views on most political matters? Generally, do you think of yourself as liberal, moderate or conservative? | Liberal<br>Moderate<br>Conservative | 1/81 | 16<br>40<br>37 | 21<br>38<br>36 |
| In the past five years, do you think your political views have become more liberal, or more conservative, or haven't they changed? | More liberal<br>More conservative<br>Haven't changed | (Not asked before) | | 16<br>24<br>53 |
| What's happened to the way Americans think about political issues in the last five years? Are they more liberal in their political thinking now, or more conservative, or hasn't there been much change? | More liberal<br>More conservative<br>Not much change | (Not asked before) | | 23<br>39<br>32 |
| Do you agree or disagree with the following statement? Protecting the environment is so important that requirements and standards cannot be too high, and continuing environmental improvements must be made regardless of cost. | Agree<br>Disagree | 9/81 | 45<br>42 | 66<br>27 |
| In your opinion, do you think that most people who receive money from welfare could get along without it if they tried, or do you think most of them really need this help? | Could do without<br>Really need help | 11/80 | 51<br>39 | 40<br>35 |
| There is an increase in the number of people living together without being married. Do you think this is okay, or is it something that's always wrong, or doesn't it matter much to you? | Okay<br>Always wrong<br>Doesn't matter | 4/81 | 27<br>43<br>27 | 22<br>43<br>31 |
| Do you approve or disapprove of this alternative for dealing with crime: allowing the police to stop and search anybody on suspicion? | Approve<br>Disapprove | 1/81** | 48<br>50 | 47<br>50 |
| There were many government programs created in the 1960s to try to improve the condition of poor people in this country. Do you think these programs generally made things better, made things worse, or didn't they have much impact one way or the other? | Made things better<br>Made things worse<br>Not much impact | 11/80 | 30<br>20<br>42 | 39<br>18<br>38 |

|  |  | Date of Poll | As Reagan Era Began Response (Percent) | Now* Response (Percent) |
| --- | --- | --- | --- | --- |
| Do you think that, in general, the Federal Government creates more problems than it solves, or do you think it solves more problems than it creates? | Creates more Solves more | 1/81 | 63 19 | 51 31 |
| How much of the time do you think you can trust the Government in Washington to do what is right—just about always, most of the time, or only some of the time? | Just about always Most of the time Some of the time Almost never (volunteered) | 10/80† | 2 23 69 4 | 5 37 54 1 |

*Current data based on 1,581 telephone interviews Jan. 19–23. Past data from *New York Times*/CBS News Polls unless otherwise indicated.
**Newsweek* Poll by Gallup.
†American National Election Study.

JAN. 28

## Poll Finds Children Remain Enthusiastic on Space Flight

**By ADAM CLYMER**

American children, although pained by the space shuttle explosion that killed a teacher who reminded them of one of their own, seem resiliently enthusiastic about the space program, according to a *New York Times*/CBS News Poll.

Two thirds of the children who were asked said they would like to travel in space, as against only half their parents. More children than adults want to go on sending civilians into space, the poll indicates, and even those children who say the accident has made them think worse of the shuttle program overwhelmingly favor continuing it.

Adult enthusiasm was also clear. Among the 1,120 adults interviewed, 80 percent said the shuttle program should continue, although only 46 percent said they would be willing to pay more in taxes if that proved necessary to keep it going.

Sixty-eight percent said an accident was bound to happen "sooner or later," and only 16 percent thought there was too much emphasis on manned rather than unmanned flights. For all adults, the margin of sampling error was plus or minus three percentage points.

Because of concern at the National Aeronautics and Space Administration and among experts on children that the explosion might have a deep impact on American children, *The Times* and CBS News interviewed 224 children 9 through 17 years old and asked 158 adults about children 5 through 8 years old. The telephone interviews were conducted Thursday and Friday, and the children were interviewed when parents agreed.

Three fourths of the parents said they had talked to their children about the accident, and three fifths of the children interviewed said their schools had had programs or discussions about the accident. Such steps, recommended by psychologists, might have affected the children's reactions. Several children said they felt better after such discussions.

For example, a 10-year-old Indiana girl said: "I felt very sad. I talked to my parents about it. It made me feel better to talk." A 13-year-old New York City girl said: "I was sad and shocked. We talked about it a lot in school and it helped." A 13-year-old Delaware girl said: "A prayer was led at a basketball game. I felt better."

About a fifth of the children said they thought worse of the shuttle program after the accident than they had before. But even that group overwhelmingly favored the program and said they wanted civilians included. A clear majority of them said they would take a trip in space if they could.

Among the children 9 through 17 years old, 39 percent said they had been upset a lot by the disaster, and 40 percent said they had been upset a little. The survey of children had a margin of sampling error of plus or minus seven percentage points.

Girls were more likely than boys to say they had been upset a lot. The older group, those 14 through 17, were more likely to say that than were those 9 through 13.

It was clear that the presence of the teacher, Christa McAuliffe, in the shuttle crew had heightened the impact of the accident. Many mentioned her directly, and 73 percent said they knew before the launching that a teacher was going into space. Sixty-nine percent of the children—63 percent of the boys and 74 percent of the girls—said Mrs. McAuliffe seemed like one of their own teachers.

These were some of the ways in which children described their reactions:

A 13-year-old Delaware girl said, "I didn't cry, but I was mad for her husband and children."

An 11-year-old Florida girl said, "I thought about the astronauts' kids."

A 9-year-old Pennsylvania boy said, "I felt bad because of the people who died and the kids left without a teacher."

A 15-year-old New York City girl said, "All the teacher's learning has been wasted."

The parents who spoke of the 5- to 8-year-olds in their households reported a lower level of distress. Thirty percent of them said those children were upset by the shuttle accident, and just over half said they thought it was because a teacher had been on the flight.

That lower level of distress could result from those children's having paid less attention to the accident.

Twenty-five percent of the parents of young children said they had watched the launching in school, as against 40 percent of the older children who said they had watched.

FEB. 2

## The *New York Times*/CBS News Poll*
Children and Space: Sorrow and Determination

| | | 9–13 years | 14–17 years | Boys | Girls | Total |
|---|---|---|---|---|---|---|
| *While you were in school Tuesday, did you watch the space shuttle launch on television?* | Yes | 49 | 31 | 39 | 43 | 41 |
| | No | 51 | 68 | 61 | 55 | 58 |
| *A lot of people are saying that school kids are very upset by the shuttle explosion and the fact that a teacher was killed. Were you upset? Were you upset a lot, or a little?* | Upset a lot | 30 | 52 | 34 | 46 | 40 |
| | Upset a little | 48 | 29 | 45 | 35 | 40 |
| | Not upset | 11 | 20 | 17 | 12 | 15 |
| *Before the accident, were you told in school or by your parents that a teacher was going into space?* | Yes | 76 | 69 | 74 | 72 | 73 |
| | No | 19 | 29 | 24 | 24 | 24 |
| *Did the teacher on the shuttle flight seem to you like one of your own teachers?* | Yes | 74 | 64 | 63 | 76 | 70 |
| | No | 23 | 30 | 32 | 21 | 26 |
| *After the space accident, was there a special talk or discussion or assembly about it at school?* | Yes | 68 | 53 | 55 | 68 | 62 |
| | No | 31 | 45 | 44 | 30 | 37 |

|  |  | 9–13 years | 14–17 years | Boys | Girls | Total |
| --- | --- | --- | --- | --- | --- | --- |
| If you had a chance when you're older to travel in outer space, would you go, or not? | Would | 66 | 61 | 72 | 56 | 64 |
|  | Would not | 27 | 32 | 22 | 37 | 29 |
| Think about how much it costs and how risky it can be to send people into space. Do you think we should keep using the space shuttle, or not? | Yes | 85 | 82 | 87 | 81 | 84 |
|  | No | 10 | 14 | 7 | 17 | 12 |
| Some people say that only astronauts should go into space because it is dangerous and there is not much room in the shuttle. Other people say that if teachers and reporters go, too, they can help explain the program to all of us. What do you think? Should it be just astronauts, or should other people go, too? | Astronauts only | 20 | 16 | 16 | 21 | 18 |
|  | Other people, too | 77 | 84 | 83 | 76 | 80 |

*Based on telephone interviews with 224 children aged 9–17 conducted Jan. 30–31.

FEB. 2

# Poll Finds Americans Divided on Reply to Terror

By DAVID K. SHIPLER

Most Americans believe the United States Government could be doing more to combat international terrorism, but they are divided and uncertain about the value of military action, a recent *New York Times*/CBS News Poll has shown.

Considerable concern about the surge in terrorism emerged from telephone interviews with 1,581 adults from Jan. 19 through 23, as 57 percent said that because of the danger of such attacks they would not want friends to travel abroad this year.

The poll revealed a sense of personal helplessness and a desire for greater government action. Fifty-two percent of those surveyed said they thought there was nothing that individuals could do to protect themselves against terrorism. The poll had a margin of sampling error of plus or minus 3 percentage points.

By a margin of 79 to 11 percent, those surveyed thought Western European countries could be doing more.

Only 38 percent expressed confidence that the United States Government was doing all it could to protect Americans, and 55 percent thought more could be done. Those who said the Government was not doing enough to protect Americans were most heavily represented among women, blacks, the poor, the less educated and people who disapproved of Mr. Reagan's performance.

But there was no agreement on what measures to take to reduce terrorism. Hardly any of those questioned said they believed less news coverage of terrorists would help. Most respondents focused on security, retaliation and punishment rather than attempts to address the grievances of certain groups and other root causes of the violence.   FEB. 9

## The *New York Times*/CBS News Poll*
Attitudes toward Terrorism

|  |  | Men | Women | Total |
|---|---|---|---|---|
| Is the United States government doing all it can to protect American citizens against terrorism, or should it be doing more? | Doing all it can<br>Should be doing more | 44%<br>51 | 33%<br>58 | 38%<br>55 |
| Do you think Western European countries are doing enough against terrorism, or should they be doing more? | Doing enough<br>Should be doing more | 12<br>81 | 10<br>78 | 11<br>79 |
| If the United States took military action against those responsible every time a terrorist attack affected Americans, do you think that would reduce terrorism, or would it only make things worse? | Would reduce terrorism<br>Only make things worse | 43<br>46 | 37<br>51 | 40<br>49 |
| If the United States made it a policy to take military action against a government it believes has trained or financed terrorists, do you think that would reduce terrorism, or would it only make things worse? | Would reduce terrorism<br>Only make things worse | 43<br>44 | 37<br>49 | 40<br>46 |
| Should the United States take the kind of military action you support even if some innocent people might be killed? | Yes<br>No<br>Not asked | 39<br>17<br>40 | 24<br>22<br>47 | 31<br>20<br>44 |
| Do you think that foreign governments are involved in the planning and financing of most terrorist acts? | Yes<br>No | 72<br>20 | 58<br>28 | 64<br>24 |
| If a friend were planning a trip abroad this year, would you suggest cancelling the trip because of terrorism, or not? | Yes<br>No<br>Depends on where (volunteered) | 51<br>36<br>11 | 63<br>27<br>8 | 57<br>31<br>9 |

*Based on 1,581 telephone interviews Jan. 19–23.

FEB. 9

# Government Trust: Less in West Europe Than U.S.

By E. J. DIONNE, Jr.

ROME, Feb. 15—Citizens of the leading Western European democracies trust their governments less than Americans trust theirs and are far less inclined to express pride in their countries, polls by *The New York Times* have found.

But the study also found sharp variations in national feelings of trust over the last decade and suggested that Americans place an extremely strong emphasis on national pride.

The findings emerged from polls carried out by *The Times* and CBS News in the United States and by Gallup International for *The Times* in five European countries.

According to the surveys taken in late 1985, 49 percent of Americans said they trusted the Government in Washington to do what is right "all or most of the time." The comparable figure in West Germany was 41 percent, and in France and Italy 33 percent.

In Britain and Spain, the figures were even lower, 30 percent and 29 percent, respectively.

For the United States, a telephone poll was

conducted and had a margin of sampling error of plus or minus 3 percentage points. In the European countries, face-to-face interviews were used, with a margin of sampling error of plus or minus 4 percentage points.

More startling were the findings when respondents were asked whether they were proud of their country.

In the United States, 87 percent said they were "very proud" to be an American. At the other extreme, only 21 percent of West Germans described themselves as "very proud" to be a German. And while only 1 percent of Americans said they were not very proud or not at all proud of their country, fully 32 percent of West Germans gave this response.

The other countries in Europe fell in between. Some 42 percent of the French, 44 percent of the Italians, 58 percent of the British and 65 percent of the Spaniards said they were "very proud" to be a citizen of their country.

FEB. 16

## Trust in Government*

*How much do you trust (the government/the government in Washington) to do what is right? Do you trust it just about always, most of the time, only some of the time, or almost never?*

|  | Great Britain | West Germany | France | Italy | Spain | United States |
|---|---|---|---|---|---|---|
| Almost always | 5 | 6 | 6 | 8 | 5 | 8 |
| Most of the time | 25 | 35 | 27 | 25 | 25 | 41 |
| Some of the time | 43 | 37 | 41 | 37 | 43 | 42 |
| Almost never | 25 | 18 | 19 | 26 | 25 | 7 |

*1985 figures for European countries come from a Gallup International poll conducted in October and November for *The New York Times*. U.S. figures are from a *New York Times*/CBS News poll, conducted November 6–10. Those who said they don't know or had no answer are not shown.

FEB. 16

# Abortion: One Issue That Seems to Defy a Yes or No

### By ADAM CLYMER

The political fight over abortion, which once provoked hopes and fears of a constitutional amendment and a government more concerned with and involved in the morality of its citizens, has settled into trench warfare. The troops still assemble regularly. Last month, 36,000 foes of abortion marched on the Supreme Court to protest the anniversary of its decision in *Roe* v. *Wade,* and next month the decision's supporters hope to gather as many or more of their partisans at the Lincoln Memorial.

But neither side hopes for recent triumphs, and a recent *New York Times* Poll suggests that a key reason for the shift in atmosphere is that Americans do not see abortion in anything like the clear, black-and-white terms discerned by activists on the issue.

In Washington, there is no longer an imminent prospect of a constitutional amendment forbidding or limiting abortions—a fact that represents a strategic success for the groups that call themselves pro-choice. President Reagan regularly renews his calls for an amendment, but it has become clear that he will not spend serious political capital on the fight.

Instead, for organizations such as Planned Parenthood or institutions such as the District of Columbia government, which advise or pay for abortions using funds from other sources, the battle is over Federal money for abortions themselves. And there the recent record is one of tactical victories for the groups that oppose abortion and call themselves pro-life.

Peter Gemma, head of the National Pro-Life Political Action Committee, agrees that in the last few years "there have been no dramatic gains" for his side. But he contends that more judges who oppose abortion are being appointed and that his allies have realistic hopes of "cutting off Federal appropriations for anyone who does consultation on abortions." On the other side, Ann F. Lewis, executive director of Americans for Democratic Action, is optimistic because she sees politicians competing for younger voters and concluding that a rigid anti-abortion stance is a sure way to discourage them.

But the *Times* Poll indicates two deeply felt conflicts in the public that make unlikely solid support for sweeping changes in either direction. First, 56 percent of the public said they did not approve of the present legal situation, with 40 percent saying they wanted abortion legal "only in such cases as saving the life of the mother, rape or incest," and 16 percent saying it should not be permitted at all. But only three fourths of them, or 41 percent of the population, said they wanted the Constitution amended to make their belief the law of the land. FEB. 23

## The *New York Times* Poll*
Attitudes toward Abortion

*Which of these statements comes closest to your opinion? Abortion is the same thing as murdering a child, OR abortion is not murder because a fetus isn't really a person?*

|  | Murder | Not murder |
|---|---|---|
| Total | 55 | 35 |
| Men | 49 | 43 |
| Women | 61 | 28 |
| Men under 45 years | 47 | 44 |
| Men 45 or older | 51 | 41 |
| Women under 45 years | 61 | 31 |
| Women 45 or older | 62 | 25 |
| Men with no college education | 52 | 39 |
| Men with at least some college | 42 | 49 |
| Women with no college education | 67 | 22 |
| Women with at least some college | 48 | 43 |

*Do you agree or disagree with the following statement? Abortion is sometimes the best course in a bad situation.*

|  | Agree | Disagree |
|---|---|---|
| Total | 66 | 26 |
| Men | 67 | 22 |
| Women | 65 | 30 |
| Men under 45 years | 69 | 24 |
| Men 45 or older | 65 | 19 |
| Women under 45 years | 65 | 33 |
| Women 45 or older | 65 | 27 |
| Men with no college education | 64 | 23 |
| Men with at least some college | 73 | 21 |
| Women with no college education | 61 | 32 |
| Women with at least some college | 72 | 25 |

*What do you think about abortion? Should it be legal as it is now, legal ONLY in such cases as saving the life of the mother, rape or incest, OR should it not be permitted at all?*

|  | Legal as is now | Legal only to save mother, rape or incest | Not permitted |
|---|---|---|---|
| Total | 40 | 40 | 16 |
| Men | 42 | 40 | 14 |
| Women | 38 | 41 | 18 |
| Men under 45 years | 46 | 40 | 11 |
| Men 45 or older | 36 | 40 | 19 |
| Women under 45 years | 44 | 39 | 15 |
| Women 45 or older | 31 | 43 | 21 |

|  | Legal as is now | Legal only to save mother, rape or incest | Not permitted |
|---|---|---|---|
| Men with no college education | 37 | 43 | 16 |
| Men with at least some college | 52 | 34 | 11 |
| Women with no college education | 31 | 42 | 22 |
| Women with at least some college | 54 | 37 | 7 |

*Based on 1,354 telephone interviews conducted December 14–18.

FEB. 23

# Surge in Sympathy for Farmer Found

**By WILLIAM ROBBINS**

KANSAS CITY, Mo., Feb. 24—Half the American public, persuaded that the country's farmers face serious economic problems, wants to see an increase in Federal spending to help them, the latest *New York Times*/CBS News Poll shows.

The support of 50 percent for more spending, up from 36 percent a year ago, was underlined when 55 percent of the public said they were willing to pay more taxes if an increase would help troubled farmers save their land. Only 12 percent favored a decrease in spending, down from 14 percent a year ago.

A key reason for those views, the poll of 1,174 adults suggests, is a deep reservoir of good will in the general public for their food producers who, as many see it, also nurture much of what is best in the American character.

Many also have more personal concerns. Thirty percent said they fear—mistakenly, according to leading agricultural economists—that widespread failures among small farms would lead to food shortages or rising costs. The poll, conducted by telephone last Wednesday and Thursday, has a margin of sampling error of plus or minus three percentage points. Fears of food shortages or rising costs are gen-

**The *New York Times*/CBS News Poll**
**On helping the farmer***

|  | Should increase federal spending on farm programs | Will pay more taxes to keep farmers from losing land | Government should help farmers more than others | Farm life is more honest and moral than elsewhere |
|---|---|---|---|---|
| TOTAL | 50% | 55% | 52% | 58% |
| Cities of over 500,000 people | 51 | 59 | 55 | 44 |
| Cities of 50,000–500,000 | 54 | 58 | 54 | 59 |
| Suburbs | 52 | 56 | 54 | 58 |
| Cities of 10,000–50,000 | 48 | 62 | 49 | 64 |
| Rural, less than 10,000 people | 41 | 47 | 45 | 59 |
| Men | 48 | 56 | 48 | 59 |
| Women | 52 | 54 | 55 | 56 |
| Northeast | 59 | 56 | 55 | 50 |
| Midwest | 45 | 56 | 52 | 61 |
| South | 48 | 53 | 54 | 62 |
| West | 49 | 57 | 45 | 54 |

*Based on 1,174 telephone interviews conducted Feb. 19 and 20.

FEB. 25

erally scoffed at by farm economists, who say that whatever happens to the small farmer, the land will be planted and that farming will remain a highly competitive business.

## Poll in Europe Finds Few Support a U.S. Military Reply to Terrorism

By E. J. DIONNE, Jr.

LONDON, March 8—People in France, Britain and West Germany say they believe American military action against international terrorism would only make the problem worse, even though they are dissatisfied with their own governments' handling of the problem, a *New York Times* Poll shows.

The survey found some support for joining American economic sanctions against Libya, something that the governments of all three countries have declined to do.

French respondents favored joining in the sanctions, 42 percent to 29 percent; West Germans were evenly divided, at 33 percent, and the British opposed the sanctions by a margin of 41 percent to 38 percent, a gap equal to the margin of sampling error of the British survey. In the West German survey, the margin of sampling error was also three points; in France it was four points.

In addition, less than half the respondents in the three countries said the United States was "overexcited" about terrorism. And most agreed, as President Reagan has argued, that Libya and the Palestine Liberation Organization had been involved in terrorist attacks.

The poll also found that no more than a fifth of those surveyed in any of the three nations said pressure on Israel to make concessions to the Palestinians would help to solve the problem.

The survey was conducted last month by *The Times* to measure Western Europeans' opinions on an issue that has irritated relations between their governments and Washington.

No survey was conducted in Italy, the site of many recent terrorist incidents, including an attack on Dec. 27 at a Rome airport, because it was not possible to get survey results in a timely fashion. In the countries polled, all interviewing was concluded before the assassination of Prime Minister Olof Palme of Sweden on Feb. 28.

One striking finding of the poll, coordinated for *The Times* by Market and Opinion Research International of London, was the extent to which purely domestic terrorism was considered a greater problem than terrorist acts linked to the Middle East. This finding was clearly connected to other opinions; in particular, people who said domestic terrorism was the greater problem tended to be less sympathetic to United States initiatives.

In Britain, which faces intermittent violence stemming from the conflict in Northern Ireland, an overwhelming majority of the 1,951 people interviewed—59 percent to 25 percent—considered domestic terrorism the greater danger. Northern Ireland itself was not included in the British survey.

In West Germany, domestic terrorism, most recently linked to the Red Army Faction, was seen as a greater threat than foreign terrorist groups by 41 percent to 35 percent among the 2,007 people interviewed.

Only in France was terrorism from abroad seen as the more serious problem, by a plurality of 43 percent to 38 percent of the sample of 994 adults. France has had terrorist attacks by extreme leftist groups and Basque and Corsican separatists, as well as by Middle Eastern and Armenian groups. MARCH 9

## The *New York Times* Poll*
European Views on Terrorism

| | | Great Britain | France | West Germany |
|---|---|---|---|---|
| On this card are a number of actions the government could take against international terrorism. Which of these do you think would help reduce international terrorism or don't you think any of them would help? Please mention all those actions you think might help. Any others? | Military action against terrorists | 29 | 22 | 22 |
| | Much stricter security at airports | 63 | 69 | 65 |
| | Military action against foreign governments that support terrorists | 15 | 16 | 12 |
| | Economic sanctions against governments that support terrorists | 34 | 48 | 39 |
| | Pressure on Israel to make concessions to the Palestinians | 16 | 20 | 15 |
| | None/Nothing the government can do | 9 | 7 | 5 |
| | DK/NA | 9 | 9 | 17 |
| If the United States took military action against those responsible every time a terrorist attack affected Americans, do you think this would reduce international terrorism or would it only make things worse? | Would reduce terrorism | 17 | 27 | 22 |
| | Make things worse | 64 | 44 | 45 |
| | Depends (volunteered) | 4 | | |
| Do you agree or disagree that the United States is getting overexcited about international terrorism? | Agree | 41 | 21 | 19 |
| | Disagree | 42 | 52 | 47 |

*Based on 1,951 face-to-face interviews in Britain February 8–12, 994 in France February 7–21 and 2,007 in West Germany February 1–10. European interviews coordinated by Market and Opinion Research International.

MARCH 9

## Most in Poll Say City Corruption Is Widespread and Hurts Services

By RICHARD J. MEISLIN

Most New York City residents perceive corruption as being widespread in the city government and believe that it has a considerable effect on the quality of the services the city provides, according to a *New York Times*/WCBS-TV News Poll.

A vast majority of those polled also said Mayor Koch should be held responsible for corruption around him, and more than half said they did not believe the Mayor's assertion that he was unaware that there was serious corruption in his administration.

Half of those questioned said, however, that they believed that the people around the Mayor, rather than Mr. Koch himself, were in charge of what goes on in the city government.

New Yorkers continue to view Mr. Koch himself as very honest, and approval of the overall job he is doing as Mayor, at 65 percent, remains near the highest levels he has attained in public polls, despite the municipal corruption scandal that has shaken his administration since January.

More than half of the 1,176 New York City residents interviewed by telephone Sunday and Monday said they believed that the city government could be run without corruption, rejecting the idea that corruption was just a part of the way things worked in the city. And 77 percent expressed confidence that Mr. Koch would take stronger actions to prevent future corruption in the city. The sampling error in the survey was plus or minus 3 percentage points.

The interviews were conducted nearly two months after the current allegations of corruption in New York City government began to come to light, and even as the first official to be indicted in the scandal—Geoffrey G. Lindenauer, the former deputy director of the city's Parking Violations Bureau—was negotiating to reduce his possible penalties in return for testimony against other officials.

About three quarters of those interviewed said corruption had an effect on the quality of the city services they used, with 35 percent saying it had a major impact and 39 percent saying it had some.

Many people had difficulty defining precisely how corruption had affected them, but of those who did, some spoke about their impression that money that would otherwise go into services such as transit was instead going to enrich city employees and contractors, and others spoke about a general decline in services, particularly transit.

MARCH 13

## The *New York Times*/WCBS-TV Poll*

*Do you think that corruption in government is a part of the way things work in New York City, or do you think the city government can be run without corruption?*

In the poll, 39 percent thought that corruption in government was part of the way things work in the city and 54 percent thought the city could be run without it.

| | | Corruption is how city works | City could work without corruption | Total |
|---|---|---|---|---|
| *How common do you think corruption is in New York City government—is it widespread, or is it limited to a few isolated incidents?* | Widespread | 66 | 58 | 61 |
| | Isolated incidents | 27 | 32 | 29 |
| | In between | 4 | 4 | 3 |
| *Do you think corruption in the city government has a major impact on the quality of the city services you use, some impact, or not much impact?* | Major impact | 40 | 33 | 35 |
| | Some impact | 38 | 41 | 39 |
| | Not much impact | 16 | 19 | 18 |
| *Mayor Koch has said that he was unaware that there was serious corruption in city government? Do you believe that, or not?* | Believe that | 29 | 43 | 38 |
| | Don't believe | 64 | 47 | 53 |
| *How much do you think Mayor Koch should be held responsible for corruption in the city government—a lot, some, or not much?* | A lot | 41 | 36 | 37 |
| | Some | 38 | 43 | 40 |
| | Not much | 16 | 17 | 17 |
| | All | 1 | 1 | 1 |
| | None | 2 | 1 | 2 |
| *Do you think Ed Koch will take stronger actions to prevent corruption in the future, or won't he do anything different?* | Will take action | 75 | 79 | 77 |
| | Nothing different | 18 | 15 | 16 |

*Based on 1,176 telephone interviews conducted March 9–10.

MARCH 13

# Poll Shows Confusion on Aid to Contras

**By DAVID K. SHIPLER**

Americans are uncertain about which side the United States is backing in Nicaragua and only one out of four supports President Reagan's request for $100 million in aid to the rebels who are trying to overthrow the Nicaraguan government, according to the latest *New York Times*/CBS News Poll.

With the approach of another key vote by the House of Representatives on the President's proposal, majorities of those polled accepted his argument that Nicaragua is a risk to American interests, but opposed his remedy of $100 million in aid.

Only 38 percent knew that Washington was supporting the guerrillas and not the government. That confusion extended to the nature of Nicaragua's government, which is aligned with the Soviet Union; just 20 percent said it was Communist, 19 percent said it was a right-wing dictatorship and 49 percent said they didn't know.

Nevertheless, after questions about the Reagan aid plan had been asked, a more defined image of Nicaragua seemed to emerge. Fifty-nine percent of the 1,601 adults interviewed by telephone from April 6 through 10 answered yes when asked if they thought the Nicaraguan government would provide the Soviet Union with military bases, and 56 percent agreed that Nicaragua constituted a threat to the security of other Central American countries. The survey's margin of sampling error was plus or minus three percentage points.

It therefore appeared that President Reagan had succeeded only partially in his efforts to sway the American public toward his views on Central America. There was concern, but it failed to translate into support for action by the United States. APRIL 15

## The *New York Times*/CBS News Poll*
Aid to the Contras: Ignorance and Opposition

| Which side does the U.S. Government support in Nicaragua—the current government, the people fighting the government, or haven't you been following this closely enough to say? | | Government | People fighting | Not following |
|---|---|---|---|---|
| | Republicans | 5 | 40 | 45 |
| | Democrats | 5 | 31 | 52 |
| | Independents | 3 | 43 | 44 |
| | Men | 5 | 52 | 34 |
| | Women | 3 | 25 | 59 |
| | 18–44 years old | 5 | 38 | 49 |
| | 45 and older | 4 | 38 | 46 |
| | High school graduate or less | 4 | 31 | 54 |
| | Some college or more | 5 | 52 | 34 |
| | Whites | 4 | 39 | 46 |
| | Blacks | 5 | 28 | 58 |
| | Northeast | 4 | 43 | 41 |
| | Midwest | 4 | 39 | 46 |
| | South | 5 | 31 | 53 |
| | West | 4 | 39 | 48 |

|  | Yes | No |
|---|---|---|
| Do you think the U.S. government should give $100 million in military and other aid to the contras trying to overthrow the government in Nicaragua? | | |
| Republicans | 36 | 51 |
| Democrats | 16 | 74 |
| Independents | 27 | 59 |
| Men | 35 | 56 |
| Women | 17 | 68 |
| 18–44 years old | 29 | 62 |
| 45 and older | 20 | 64 |
| High school graduate or less | 22 | 65 |
| Some college or more | 31 | 57 |
| Whites | 26 | 61 |
| Blacks | 16 | 74 |
| Northeast | 27 | 61 |
| Midwest | 22 | 67 |
| South | 27 | 59 |
| West | 24 | 64 |

|  |  | Yes | No |
|---|---|---|---|
| Which side does the U.S. government support in Nicaragua—the current government, the people fighting the government, or haven't you been following this closely enough to say? | Government | 29 | 58 |
|  | People fighting | 40 | 52 |
|  | Not following | 14 | 72 |
| Do you think the government of Nicaragua threatens the security of other Central American countries, or not? |  | 36 | 54 |
|  |  | 11 | 82 |
| Do you think Nicaragua will provide military bases for the Soviet Union? | Yes | 34 | 55 |
|  | No | 16 | 75 |
| Do you think its important to the security of the United States to eliminate communism from Latin America, or can communist governments exist in Latin America without threatening U.S. security? | Eliminate communism | 38 | 51 |
|  | Exist w/o threat | 13 | 79 |
| Are you afraid the United States will get involved in Nicaragua the way it did in Vietnam? | Yes | 17 | 73 |
|  | No | 43 | 44 |
| Do you approve or disapprove of the way Ronald Reagan is handling his job as President? | Approve | 35 | 52 |
|  | Disapprove | 8 | 84 |

*Based on 1,601 telephone interviews conducted April 6–10.

APRIL 15

# A Poll Finds 77% in U.S. Approve Raid on Libya

**By ADAM CLYMER**

The American people overwhelmingly support the bombing of Libya, despite widespread fears that it will lead to more international terrorism and even to war with that country, a *New York Times*/CBS News Poll shows. But a poll in Britain found very heavy disapproval.

The telephone survey of 704 Americans Tuesday night showed that 77 percent of the public approved of the bombing and 14 percent disapproved. Thirty percent thought it would reduce terrorism, but 43 percent thought it would lead to more.

The attack led to a huge surge in backing for President Reagan's handling of foreign policy. Last week 51 percent of the public approved; after Monday night's bombing the figure was 76 percent. His highest previous rating level was 56 percent just before the Geneva summit meeting.

Thirty percent said they thought the bombing would lead to war with Libya. But majorities of those who feared more terrorism or war still approved of the bombing. The margin of sampling error in the poll was plus or minus four percentage points.

But the British poll, taken for *The Times* of London, showed a very different reaction in the country from which F-111 bombers took off for the attack. There, only 29 percent said Mr. Reagan was right to order the bombing, and dissatisfaction with Prime Minister Margaret Thatcher's job performance reached a near-record 68 percent.

The poll, conducted Tuesday night and Wednesday, had a margin of sampling error of plus or minus four percentage points.

Twenty-eight percent of the 1,051 Britons interviewed in person by Market & Opinion Research International said they had only "a little confidence" that the United States would "deal wisely with the Libyan situation over the next few weeks," and 43 percent said they had "no confidence at all."   APRIL 17

## The Bombing of Libya: Americans For, British Against*

|  | Approve | Disapprove |
|---|---|---|
| Americans were asked: Do you approve or disapprove of United States jets bombing Libya? | 77% | 14% |

|  | Right | Wrong |
|---|---|---|
| British were asked: Do you think President Reagan was right or wrong to order the bombing of Libya in reaction to Libya's support given to terrorists? | 29% | 66% |

| A Breakdown for the U.S. | Approve | Disapprove |
|---|---|---|
| Men | 83% | 11% |
| Women | 71% | 17% |
| White | 80% | 12% |
| Black | 53% | 30% |

| Of those who think bombing will: | Approve | Disapprove |
|---|---|---|
| Reduce terrorism | 91% | 1% |
| Increase terrorism | 65% | 27% |
| Lead to war | 67% | 23% |
| Not lead to war | 87% | 8% |

*In the United States, 704 telephone interviews were conducted by *The New York Times* and CBS News the evening of April 15. In Britain, 1,051 in-person interviews were conducted by Market & Opinion Research International April 15–16.

APRIL 17

# Japanese Favor a Global Role, a Survey Finds

By CLYDE HABERMAN

TOKYO, May 2—Most Japanese believe their country has become a global power and that, as such, it should be playing a broader role in international affairs, according to a poll conducted by *The New York Times,* CBS News and the Tokyo Broadcasting System.

A majority of the Japanese surveyed, 55 percent, said they believed one of Japan's main obligations should be to provide more aid to poorer nations. According to the survey, 31 percent also felt their country's international responsibilities required it to work harder to reduce its large trade surpluses.

The findings thus suggest significant support for two basic themes struck repeatedly by the Japanese Government in recent years—that it must do something soon about growing trade imbalances and that it must increase economic assistance to poor nations.

But the Japanese, who were interviewed in person from April 4 through 6 in advance of the economic summit meeting, which starts Sunday, were far less receptive to the idea of increased military spending as another way of fulfilling global obligations. A stronger military is another stated priority of Prime Minister Yasuhiro Nakasone. But only 12 percent thought that Japan should assume a larger share of its own defense.

Americans polled by telephone from April 6 through 10 were slightly less inclined to view Japan as a world power, with 53 percent of the 1,601 respondents saying it was such a power "that should assume responsibilities to other countries," and 36 percent saying it was not. In Japan, 62 percent of the 1,415 respondents said their country was a world power and 31 percent said it was not. In each country the margin of sampling error was plus or minus three percentage points.    MAY 3

## The *New York Times*/CBS News/Tokyo Broadcasting System Poll*
Japan as World Power, Trade Partner

| | | United States | Japan |
|---|---|---|---|
| **United States:** *Do you think Japan has become a world power that should assume responsibilities to other countries, OR do you think Japan is not yet a world power?* | World power<br>Not world power | 53<br>36 | 62<br>31 |
| **Japan:** *Do you think Japan has become a world power that must carry out many responsibilities to other countries, or do you think Japan is not yet a world power that must carry out many international responsibilities?* | | | |
| **Japan:** *In that regard, what specially do you think Japan should do in order to carry out its international responsibilities. Pick as many as you think necessary from the following:* | a. It should take more of a share of its own defense.<br>b. It should spend more money on aid to developing countries.<br>c. It should accept more refugees from Southeast Asia.<br>d. It should make more of an effort to reduce its trade imbalance.<br>e. None | | 12<br><br>55<br><br>22<br><br><br>31<br>4 |

|  |  | United States | Japan |
|---|---|---|---|
| Who sells more goods to the other country? Does Japan sell more products to the United States or does the United States sell more products to Japan? (Japanese version asked if Japan exports more goods to the U.S. than Japan imports from the U.S.) | Japan sells more | 85 | 64 |
|  | U.S. sells more | 6 | 31 |
| How much do you think Japan's government now restricts the sale of American goods in Japan—a great deal, some, not much, or not at all? | A great deal | 33 | 20 |
|  | Some | 40 | 53 |
|  | Not much | 10 | 20 |
|  | Not at all | 3 | 2 |
| In general, do you think these restrictions by the Japanese government are fair or unfair to the United States? | Fair | 14 | 49 |
|  | Unfair | 53 | 23 |
| The United States Congress says it will put more restrictions on imports from Japan. Do you think they'll really do that, or do you think they're just saying that? | Will | 36 | 72 |
|  | Just saying | 52 | 21 |

*Based on 1,601 telephone interviews in the U.S. April 6–10 and 1,415 personal interviews in Japan April 4–6.

MAY 3

# How Americans Rate Big Business

**By ADAM CLYMER**

The American people do not think much of the honesty, sense of social responsibility or products of big business in this country, a *New York Times* Poll shows.

When asked whether ethical standards are higher in the Federal Government or in big corporations, 35 percent sided with the often-maligned Federal Government, compared to 24 percent who chose big corporations. Only 33 percent said big business does an excellent or a pretty good job at seeing to it that its executives behave legally and ethically. And 53 percent said white-collar crime in business is committed "very often." The margin of sampling error was plus or minus three percentage points.

In other areas, 38 percent of the public said big business does an excellent or pretty good job in contributing to the well-being of local communities, but 56 percent thought it does a poor or an "only fair" job. Big business got an even worse rating on keeping the environment clean. And a majority, 54 percent of the 1,099 adults interviewed by telephone from April 29 through May 1, agreed with the statement "American products are not made as well as they used to be," while 41 percent said products are as good or better—but people complain more now. One question spoke to the Horatio Alger story, so much a part of the traditional American dream: "Do you think it's as possible now as it was when you finished school to start out poor in this country, work hard in business and become rich?" Only 51 percent of the public said yes. JUNE 8

## New York Times Poll*
How Americans Rate Big Business

*Do you think it's as possible now as it was when you finished school to start out poor in this country, work hard in business and become rich?*

|  | Total | Men | Women | White | Black |
|---|---|---|---|---|---|
| Possible | 51 | 58 | 44 | 53 | 39 |
| Not possible | 41 | 34 | 47 | 39 | 52 |
| Depends/Still in school (volunteered) | 4 | 4 | 5 | 4 | 5 |
| DK/NA | 4 | 3 | 5 | 4 | 1 |

|  | 18–29 years old | 30–49 years old | 50 years and older |
|---|---|---|---|
| Possible | 53 | 49 | 50 |
| Not possible | 41 | 44 | 38 |
| Depends/Still in school (volunteered) | 4 | 3 | 6 |
| DK/NA | 3 | 3 | 6 |

*In general, do you think moral and ethical standards are higher in big corporations, or higher in the Federal Government?*

|  | Total | Men | Women | White | Black |
|---|---|---|---|---|---|
| Big corporations | 24 | 27 | 22 | 27 | 17 |
| Federal government | 35 | 38 | 32 | 31 | 57 |
| The same (volunteered) | 15 | 17 | 14 | 17 | 8 |
| DK/NA | 26 | 19 | 32 | 27 | 18 |

|  | Income less than $25,000 | $25,000–$35,000 | More than $35,000 |
|---|---|---|---|
| Big corporations | 21 | 23 | 32 |
| Federal government | 39 | 35 | 31 |
| The same (volunteered) | 12 | 19 | 20 |
| DK/NA | 28 | 24 | 17 |

*Based on 1,099 telephone interviews conducted April 29 through May 1.

JUNE 8

# New Restrictions on Immigration Gain Public Support, Poll Shows

**By ROBERT PEAR**

There is strong and growing public support for new restrictions on immigration despite widespread sympathy for both legal and illegal immigrants as individuals.

The latest *New York Times*/CBS News Poll shows that 49 percent of all adult Americans want immigration decreased, while 42 percent say it should be increased. When the last major immigration law was adopted in 1965, eliminating past racial quotas, 46 percent of the public in a Gallup Poll said that immigration levels should be kept the same or increased, while only 33 percent wanted them decreased.

The new telephone poll of 1,618 adults was

taken to assess public attitudes as the nation prepared to celebrate the centennial of the Statue of Liberty, a beacon for millions of immigrants. It found that Americans have contradictory, ambivalent feelings about immigration.

Even opponents of immigration said that their own neighborhoods would welcome immigrants. Paradoxically, 45 percent of the respondents said that new immigrants worked harder than native-born Americans, but 47 percent said that most ended up on welfare. Further, 49 percent of those interviewed said they believed that illegal immigration now exceeded legal immigration, which most experts dispute.

A third of the public said that immigrants took jobs away from Americans. But a larger group, slightly more than half of all people interviewed, said immigrants generally took jobs that Americans did not want. Hispanic people and residents of Western states were most likely to say that aliens took jobs Americans did not want.

Contrasting with the 49 percent who said they believed that most of the people who had recently moved to the United States were here illegally, 32 percent said that most of the recent immigrants were legal. The margin of sampling error in the June 19–23 telephone survey was plus or minus three percentage points.

JULY 1

## The *New York Times*/CBS News Poll
Views of Immigrants

| | | White | Black | Hispanic | Total |
|---|---|---|---|---|---|
| *Overall, would you say most recent immigrants to the United States contribute to this country, or do most of them cause problems?* | Contribute | 32 | 38 | 48 | 34 |
| | Cause problems | 46 | 41 | 33 | 44 |
| | Both | 7 | 4 | 7 | 7 |
| | Depends on origin | 2 | — | 3 | 2 |
| | DK/NA | 13 | 17 | 10 | 13 |
| *If some of today's new immigrants moved into your neighborhood, would they be welcomed, or not really welcomed?* | Welcomed | 67 | 77 | 68 | 68 |
| | Not welcomed | 19 | 10 | 18 | 18 |
| | Depends on origin | 8 | 9 | 8 | 8 |
| | DK/NA | 5 | 4 | 6 | 5 |
| *Do you think most of the people who have moved to the United States in the last few years are here legally, or are most of them here illegally?* | Legal | 33 | 27 | 28 | 32 |
| | Illegal | 47 | 59 | 56 | 49 |
| | Half and half | 6 | 5 | 8 | 6 |
| | DK/NA | 14 | 10 | 9 | 13 |
| *Do you think life in America is easier for immigrants today than it was for immigrants at the beginning of this century, or harder today than it was then, or do you think it's about the same?* | Easier | 47 | 55 | 37 | 47 |
| | Harder | 25 | 17 | 36 | 25 |
| | Same | 22 | 25 | 19 | 22 |
| | DK/NA | 7 | 3 | 7 | 6 |
| *Do you think immigrants coming to this country today mostly take jobs away from American citizens, or do they mostly take jobs Americans don't want?* | Take jobs away | 34 | 44 | 19 | 34 |
| | Take jobs Americans don't want | 52 | 42 | 67 | 34 |
| | Both | 10 | 11 | 6 | 9 |
| | DK/NA | 5 | 3 | 8 | 5 |

| | | White | Black | Hispanic | Total |
|---|---|---|---|---|---|
| Generally, do today's immigrants work harder than people born here, not as hard, or isn't there much difference? | Harder | 44 | 46 | 52 | 45 |
| | Not as hard | 9 | 5 | 9 | 8 |
| | Not much difference | 33 | 40 | 31 | 33 |
| | Depends | 6 | 1 | 4 | 5 |
| | DK/NA | 8 | 8 | 4 | 8 |
| Do you think most new immigrants end up on welfare, or not? | Yes | 47 | 48 | 41 | 47 |
| | No | 35 | 36 | 46 | 36 |
| | DK/NA | 17 | 16 | 14 | 17 |
| Do you think the Government should penalize employers who hire people who are here illegally? | Yes | 73 | 59 | 34 | 69 |
| | No | 17 | 26 | 49 | 20 |
| | Depends | 5 | 7 | 4 | 5 |
| | DK/NA | 5 | 8 | 13 | 5 |
| The law requires that illegal aliens be deported. Do you think an exception should be made for those who have lived here for several years without breaking any laws? | Yes, should | 55 | 65 | 79 | 58 |
| | No, should not | 33 | 27 | 14 | 32 |
| | Depends | 7 | 5 | 3 | 6 |
| | DK/NA | 5 | 3 | 4 | 5 |
| If the U.S. Border Patrol is unable to stop the flow of illegal aliens from Mexico to the United States, do you think we should use the Army to keep them out, or would this be too drastic a step? | Use Army | 35 | 27 | 13 | 34 |
| | Too drastic | 54 | 65 | 77 | 57 |
| | Depends | 4 | 2 | 1 | 3 |
| | DK/NA | 7 | 7 | 9 | 7 |
| Do you think special arrangements should be made for agriculture to bring in temporary workers from other countries to pick crops, or not? | Yes | 35 | 31 | 55 | 36 |
| | No | 46 | 41 | 33 | 44 |
| | DK/NA | 6 | 5 | 6 | 6 |
| In deciding who should be allowed to immigrate to the United States, who should get the greater preference—people whose skills will benefit this country the most, or people who will be helped the most by the economy and political freedom of the United States? | Benefit the U.S. | 48 | 54 | 52 | 50 |
| | Be helped by freedom of the U.S. | 28 | 32 | 32 | 28 |
| | Both | 10 | 4 | 9 | 9 |
| | DK/NA | 14 | 10 | 7 | 13 |

Based on 1,618 telephone interviews conducted June 19–23. People who called themselves whites or blacks of Hispanic origin are counted as Hispanic.

JULY 1

## The *New York Times*/CBS News Poll*
## More Opposition to Immigration

| | | 1965 | 1986 |
|---|---|---|---|
| Should immigration be kept at its present level, increased or decreased? | Increased | 8 | 7 |
| | Decreased | 33 | 49 |
| | Kept same | 39 | 35 |
| | DK/NA | 20 | 9 |

*Figures for 1986 are based on a *New York Times*/CBS News telephone survey of 1,618 people conducted June 19–23. The 1965 figures are from a Gallup Poll.

Breakdown of 1986 Figures

**People who say immigration should be:**

| | Increased | Kept at current level | Decreased |
|---|---|---|---|
| **Total** | 7% | 35% | 49% |
| Men | 7 | 34 | 51 |
| Women | 7 | 36 | 47 |
| White* | 5 | 34 | 52 |
| Black* | 11 | 41 | 39 |
| Hispanic | 25 | 36 | 31 |
| Resident of: | | | |
| Northeast | 8 | 44 | 38 |
| Middle West | 6 | 34 | 53 |
| South | 8 | 31 | 53 |
| West | 8 | 31 | 51 |
| Liberal | 8 | 36 | 48 |
| Moderate | 8 | 38 | 45 |
| Conservative | 5 | 31 | 57 |
| First ancestor arrived before 1776 | 6 | 35 | 50 |
| Born abroad or from family arriving in U.S. after 1941 | 17 | 46 | 29 |
| Consider themselves part of an ethnic group | 12 | 40 | 40 |
| Know recent immigrant well | 11 | 41 | 39 |
| Many recent immigrants in community, but don't know any well | 6 | 30 | 55 |
| Family Income: | | | |
| Under $12,500 | 8 | 25 | 55 |
| $12,500–$24,999 | 5 | 34 | 53 |
| $25,000–$34,999 | 6 | 36 | 51 |
| $35,000–$50,000 | 11 | 36 | 42 |
| Over $50,000 | 8 | 43 | 42 |
| Education: | | | |
| Less than high school diploma | 9 | 27 | 55 |
| High school graduate | 5 | 37 | 51 |
| Some college | 8 | 34 | 49 |
| College graduate | 10 | 44 | 35 |

*Excludes Americans of Hispanic descent.

JULY 1

# Opinion Narrows over High Court

**By ADAM CLYMER**

The American public is now about evenly split on whether the Supreme Court is too liberal or too conservative in its decisions, the latest *New York Times*/CBS News Poll shows.

The public is also closely divided on whether the Court is doing a good job, a view it clearly rejected in the late 1960s and early 1970s. Moreover, in two key areas, abortion and the rights of people accused of crimes, the public sided with the High Court and against its critics.

The survey of 1,618 adults was taken last month just after Chief Justice Warren E.

Burger announced his retirement and President Reagan announced plans to solidify the conservative forces on the Court with the nominations of Associate Justice William H. Rehnquist to be Chief Justice and Judge Antonin Scalia of the Court of Appeals for the District of Columbia to be an Associate Justice of the Supreme Court.

The June 19–23 telephone poll thus preceded the Court's decisions permitting states to outlaw sodomy and striking down the central provision of the budget-balancing law, but it appeared to show a long-term trend toward support of the Court. For example, the *Times*/CBS News Poll found that 7 percent of the public rated the Court excellent, 39 percent called it good, 41 percent graded it fair and 7 percent said it was poor. The difference between those who gave positive ratings of excellent and good and those who gave negative ratings of fair and poor did not exceed the poll's margin of sampling error of plus or minus three percentage points.

But in Gallup Poll measurements of the same question from 1968 through 1973, clear majorities of 51 to 54 percent rated the Court fair or poor.

When the public was asked in the *Times*/CBS News Poll if the Court, in general, was "too liberal or too conservative in its decisions," 34 percent said too liberal, 38 percent said too conservative and 10 percent said that it was about right.

In a Gallup Poll taken in July 1973, 35 percent said it was too liberal and only 26 percent said it was too conservative. Seventeen percent said it was about right.   JULY 13

### The *New York Times*/CBS News Poll Judging the Supreme Court

| | | 1963 | 1973 | 1986 |
|---|---|---|---|---|
| *In general, what kind of rating would you give the Supreme Court—excellent, good, fair, or poor?* | Excellent | 10 | 6 | 7 |
| | Good | 33 | 31 | 39 |
| | Fair | 26 | 36 | 41 |
| | Poor | 15 | 15 | 7 |
| | DK/NA | 16 | 12 | 6 |

The 1986 figures are based on 1,618 telephone interviews conducted June 19 to 23. The 1963 and 1973 figures are from Gallup polls.

JULY 13

## Public Found Ready to Sacrifice in Drug Fight

**By ADAM CLYMER**

Sharply rising concern over drugs has led two thirds of Americans to say they would pay more taxes to jail drug sellers, and three fourths of full-time workers to say they would be willing to take a drug test, The *New York Times*/CBS News poll shows.

Those were key specific findings as 13 percent of 1,210 adults interviewed by telephone from Aug. 18 through 21 called drugs the nation's most important problem, more than those who cited unemployment, fear of war, or other economic difficulties.

As attention to the issue has intensified, so has public concern; in an April survey, only 2 percent picked drugs as the nation's most important problem.

The findings come shortly before the House of Representatives is to vote Sept. 10 on a $2 billion to $3 billion Democratic antidrug program. The White House has also promised a new antidrug plan this fall. But the public indicated deep skepticism about politicians on this issue, with 60 percent saying most officials were making their proposals for publicity, and 24 percent saying most were sincere.

Even so, the public remained hopeful that solutions could be found. Fifty-one percent said illegal drug use could be reduced "a great deal" by drug tests in the workplace, and at least 40 percent each said the same thing of stiffer penalties for sellers, more educational programs and stiffer penalties for users. The poll had a margin of sampling error of plus or minus 3 percentage points.

One measure of the rising concern was a reversal of the trend toward tolerating marijuana use, with 57 percent saying possession of small amounts should be treated as a criminal offense. In 1977, a Gallup Poll showed only 41 percent felt that way. Antimarijuana sentiment had been stronger before that.

Moreover, there was clear concern about the implications of professional athletes using drugs and widespread agreement that television and movies glamorized drug use.

When asked to name a program or movie that did so, 11 percent cited "Miami Vice," a fast-paced police show that finished ninth in last season's ratings. Rick Citter, an NBC-TV broadcast standards official, said that must be a misperception, for "in every case drugs are not glamorized and are shown to be a very destructive habit." SEPT. 2

## New York Times/CBS News Poll
### Opinion About Drugs: The Generation Gap

| | 18–44 years | 45 & older | Total |
|---|---|---|---|
| What do you think is the most important problem facing this country today? (Percentage who volunteered "drugs.") | 11 | 16 | 13 |
| What do you think is the most important problem facing the community you live in? (Percentage who volunteered "drugs.") | 15 | 11 | 13 |
| Which of these statements comes closest to what you think: Increased drug use means that there has been a fundamental breakdown in American morals, OR increased drug use is a serious problem but it doesn't mean our morals have broken down? | | | |
|   Fundamental breakdown | 44 | 60 | 50 |
|   Not moral breakdown | 52 | 28 | 42 |
|   DK/NA | 1 | 2 | 1 |
| Do you happen to know of any specific place in the community where you live where illegal drugs are sold, or know of any person who sells them? | | | |
|   Yes | 28 | 10 | 20 |
|   No | 71 | 87 | 77 |
|   DK/NA | 2 | 3 | 2 |
| How effective do you think each of these proposals would be in reducing illegal drug use in this country. Would it reduce illegal drug use a great deal, reduce it a little, or wouldn't it have any real effect? (Percentage who said "a great deal.") | | | |
|   Requiring drug testing in the workplace | 50 | 53 | 51 |
|   Stiffer penalties for persons caught selling drugs | 39 | 63 | 48 |
|   More educational programs about drug abuse | 46 | 44 | 45 |
|   Stiffer penalties for persons caught using drugs | 37 | 49 | 42 |
|   Having the U.S. military make raids into other countries to destroy drugs produced there | 36 | 35 | 35 |
|   More drug treatment programs | 30 | 32 | 31 |
|   Having celebrities come out against drugs | 23 | 28 | 26 |

|  | 18–44 years | 45 & older | Total |
|---|---|---|---|
| *Would you favor a policy that would require workers in general to be tested to determine whether they have used illegal drugs recently, OR would that be an unfair invasion of privacy?* | | | |
| Favor testing | 39 | 53 | 44 |
| Invasion of privacy | 53 | 32 | 44 |
| DK/NA | 3 | 8 | 5 |
| *If your employer wanted to test all employees to determine if they had used illegal drugs recently, would you be willing to be tested, OR would that be an unfair invasion of your privacy?* | | | |
| Willing | 69 | 85 | 72 |
| Invasion of privacy | 25 | 12 | 22 |
| DK/NA | 2 | 2 | 2 |
| *Who do you think is more responsible for the drug problem in our country today—the person who sells illegal drugs or the person who uses illegal drugs?* | | | |
| Sellers | 54 | 66 | 59 |
| Users | 30 | 17 | 25 |
| Both (volunteered) | 14 | 14 | 14 |
| DK/NA | 2 | 3 | 2 |
| *Do you think possession of small amounts of marijuana should or should not be treated as a criminal offense?* | | | |
| Yes | 54 | 61 | 57 |
| No | 43 | 26 | 36 |
| DK/NA | 2 | 14 | 7 |
| *Do you think that movies and television shows encourage illegal drug use in general by making it appear to be glamorous?* | | | |
| Yes | 62 | 65 | 63 |
| No | 32 | 23 | 28 |
| DK/NA | | | |
| IF YES: What movie or television program has done this? (Percentage who volunteered "Miami Vice.") | 14 | 6 | 11 |
| *Which is a more serious problem in this country today—illegal drug use or alcohol abuse?* | | | |
| Illegal drug use | 39 | 46 | 42 |
| Alcohol abuse | 39 | 21 | 32 |
| Both equal | 20 | 28 | 24 |
| DK/NA | 2 | 4 | 3 |

SEPT. 2

## New York Times/CBS News Poll Support for Drug Testing

"If your employer wanted to test all employees to determine if they had used illegal drugs recently, would you be willing to be tested, or would that be an unfair invasion of your privacy?"

| Percentage willing to be tested: | |
|---|---|
| TOTAL | 72% |
| Factory | 71% |
| Office | 73% |

| Percentage willing to be tested: | |
|---|---|
| 45–64 years old | 84% |
| 30–44 | 70% |
| 18–29 | 67% |

Based on telephone interviews with the 669 full-time workers in the sample of 1,210 polled Aug. 18–21.

SEPT. 2

## Summit Aftermath: Poll Shows Arms Control Optimism and Support for Reagan

**By ADAM CLYMER**

The American public's initial reaction to the Reykjavík summit meeting is quite supportive of President Reagan and very optimistic about the future of arms control, a *New York Times*/CBS News poll shows.

But there was no indication in the survey that this support had translated into advantages for Republicans in the November elections. Voting preferences among the 767 Americans interviewed by telephone Oct. 14 and on the morning of Oct. 15 were unchanged from the views of those same respondents two weeks earlier.

Public reactions may deepen or swerve as the issue is debated, but the survey suggested that Mr. Reagan had, at the least, put his stamp on the first impressions in the mind of an American public that rarely focuses intently on foreign-policy issues.

The poll was conducted as Administration officials, after President Reagan's nationally broadcast speech Monday night, have been offering their view of events through dozens of newspaper and television interviews in what they describe as one of their most intense public relations campaigns.

Yesterday, continuing that effort, Secretary of State George P. Shultz visited The New York Times, and Richard B. Wirthlin, Mr. Reagan's poll taker, said overall approval of Mr. Reagan's handling of his job had jumped from 64 percent among 1,000 people interviewed Oct. 9 and 10 to 73 percent among 500 interviewed on Oct. 14.

In the *Times*/CBS News Poll, 44 percent said the blame for the failure of the meeting to produce an arms-control agreement rested on Mikhail S. Gorbachev, the Soviet leader, and only 17 percent blamed Mr. Reagan. Eleven percent blamed both, 4 percent neither and the rest had no opinion. The poll had a margin of sampling error or plus or minus 4 percentage points.

Moreover, only 20 percent said the President "should have given up the Strategic Defense Initiative—'Star Wars'—in order to get Gorbachev to agree to a big reduction in Soviet and U.S. nuclear weapons," while 68 percent sided with Mr. Reagan and said he should not.

The most striking single comparison with past surveys emerged from the answers to the question: "Even though no agreement was reached at the Iceland summit, do you think that meeting will eventually lead to real arms-control agreements, or not?"

Fifty-seven percent said such agreements would result, and 31 percent said they would not.

OCT. 16

### *New York Times*/CBS News Poll
### Summit Failure: Who Is More to Blame?

| Who is more to blame for not reaching an arms control agreement at the Iceland summit meeting—Ronald Reagan or Mikhail Gorbachev? | | |
|---|---|---|
| | Reagan | 17% |
| | Gorbachev | 44 |
| | Both | 11 |
| | Neither | 4 |
| | DK/NA | 25 |

Based on telephone interviews with 767 people on Oct. 14 and 15.

OCT. 16

## New York Times/CBS News Poll Reagan and the Russians

| | | Approve | Disapprove | Don't know |
|---|---|---|---|---|
| Do you approve or disapprove of the way Ronald Reagan is handling relations with the Soviet Union? | April 1981 | 58% | 20% | 23% |
| | September 1981 | 62 | 19 | 19 |
| | January 1982 | 54 | 31 | 15 |
| | January 1983 | 45 | 32 | 23 |
| | January 1985 | 60 | 26 | 13 |
| | September 1986 | 61 | 26 | 13 |
| | October 1986 | 72 | 20 | 8 |

| | | Yes | No | Don't know |
|---|---|---|---|---|
| Even though no agreement was reached at the Iceland summit, do you think that meeting will eventually lead to real arms control agreements, or not? | November 1985* | 32% | 55% | 13% |
| | January 1986* | 41 | 47 | 11 |
| | October 1986 | 57 | 31 | 12 |

*Questions referred to Geneva summit.

OCT. 16

## New York Times/CBS News Poll Choosing Between Candidates for the House

### Which Party?

"If the 1986 elections for the U.S. House of Representatives were being held today, would you vote for the Republican candidate or the Democratic candidate in your district?"

| | |
|---|---|
| Democratic | 43% |
| Republican | 39% |
| Don't know or other answer | 18% |

### What Factor Is Most Important?

"Sometimes people decide to vote for a candidate for the U.S. House of Representatives because of national issues. Sometimes, it's because of local or state issues. Sometimes it's because of the candidate's political party. And sometimes it's because of the candidate's character or experience. This year, what will make the biggest difference in how you vote—a national issue, a local or state issue, the candidate's political party, or the candidate's character or experience?" Democratic and Republican breakdowns refer to how respondent would vote.

**Character/Experience 40.9%**
| | |
|---|---|
| Democratic | 16.5% |
| Republican | 16.2% |
| Other | 8.2% |

**State and local issues 23.0%**
| | |
|---|---|
| Democratic | 9.9% |
| Republican | 8.8% |
| Other | 4.3% |

**National issues 19.9%**
| | |
|---|---|
| Democratic | 8.2% |
| Republican | 8.1% |
| Other | 3.6% |

**Party 8.4%**
| | |
|---|---|
| Democratic | 4.1% |
| Republican | 4.3% |

**No answer 7.4%**
| | |
|---|---|
| Democratic | 3.9% |
| Republican | 2.0% |
| Other | 1.5% |

Based on telephone interviews with 1,062 registered voters conducted Sept. 28–Oct. 1., weighted to reflect likelihood of voting.

OCT. 7

### New York Times/CBS News Poll
### Issues Affecting House Races

*Which of these five issues will matter to you most in deciding how you will vote for Congress—is it competition from foreign goods, OR controlling Federal spending, OR the Strategic Defense Initiative (which some people call Star Wars), OR the economy, OR illegal drugs, OR will none of these issues matter more than the others?*

|  | Total | Percent Voting for Republican | Percent Voting for Democrat |
|---|---|---|---|
| Economy | 25% | 38 | 55 |
| Controlling Federal Spending | 14 | 60 | 34 |
| Illegal Drugs | 13 | 41 | 51 |
| Strategic Defense Initiative | 12 | 60 | 36 |
| Competition from Foreign Goods | 7 | 41 | 55 |
| None of These | 18 | 54 | 42 |
| Combination (volunteered) | 10 | 33 | 50 |
| DK/NA | 2 | 30 | 54 |

Based on telephone interviews of 1,409 registered voters Oct. 24–28, weighted to reflect likelihood of voting. Don't know and combination responses are not included.

OCT. 31

## Mexican Pessimism Is Found in Survey

**By WILLIAM STOCKTON**

MEXICO CITY, Nov. 12—More than half of all Mexicans believe that Mexico's economic troubles are so profound that the country will never recover, a *New York Times* Poll has found.

A portrait of the Mexican people's deep pessimism about their country's economic plight emerges from the poll, conducted Oct. 28 to Nov. 4.

It reveals a nation lacking confidence about its future, longing for political change, deeply suspicious of the government's motives and questioning its leaders' ability to manage the country's affairs.

At the same time, Mexicans are not blaming their president, Miguel de la Madrid. Half of those polled said he was doing a good job, a finding that some Mexican scholars interpret as a reflection of the authoritarian nature of the country's political system.

The most striking finding in the face-to-face poll of 1,576 people is the belief that Mexico will never return to the economic boom of the 1960s and 1970s.

Asked when they thought Mexico would resolve its economic crisis, 54 percent said never. Only 15 percent said the problems might be resolved in a decade or less.

Overall, 78 percent named various economic matters as the country's biggest problem. In contrast, 12 percent named poor government or political corruption as the most serious concern.

The survey, which had a margin of sampling error of plus or minus 4 percentage points, was one of the most thorough ever conducted in Mexico, a difficult nation for polling because a third of its population lives in communities of fewer than 2,500 people, many of them in remote areas. The poll surveyed people in communities of more than 2,500, but was supplemented by a special sampling of 299 people in communities of 1,000 to 2,500. Their views were found to be almost identical to those in the regular sample.

Almost two thirds of those polled said the political system should be changed so that candidates of other parties would win elections more often. So deep is this feeling that even half of the supporters of the ruling party said the system should be changed.

NOV. 16

## The *New York Times* Poll
## Mexicans on Mexico

*What do you think is the main problem that you have in Mexico today?*

| | |
|---|---|
| Inflation/low salaries | 53% |
| Foreign debt | 16% |
| Poor government and political corruption | 12% |
| Unemployment | 8% |
| Drugs, vice, crime | 3% |
| Overpopulation | 2% |
| Other problems | 7% |

*How would you rate the condition of the national economy?*

| | |
|---|---|
| Very good | — |
| Good | 11% |
| Bad | 53% |
| Very bad | 35% |

*And how would you rate your own economic situation?*

| | |
|---|---|
| Very good | 1% |
| Good | 41% |
| Bad | 48% |
| Very bad | 11% |

*When do you believe Mexico will emerge from the economic crisis?*

| | |
|---|---|
| In less than five years | 3% |
| Between 5 and 10 years | 12% |
| In more than 10 years | 30% |
| Never | 54% |

*Do you approve or disapprove of the way Miguel de la Madrid has handled his job as President?*

| | |
|---|---|
| Approve | 53% |
| Disapprove | 46% |

*How frequently do you think the federal government does what is right?*

| | |
|---|---|
| Nearly always | 6% |
| Most of the time | 15% |
| Only some of the time | 60% |
| Almost never | 18% |

In-person interviews conducted Oct. 28 through Nov. 4 with 1,576 people.

Nov. 16

## Mexicans, in a Poll, Say They Consider U.S. to Be a Friend

### By WILLIAM STOCKTON

MEXICO CITY, Nov. 16—Although relations between the governments of Mexico and the United States have been strained in recent months, a large majority of Mexicans consider the United States to be a friend and look with envy toward its democratic system of government and strong economy.

But a poll conducted throughout Mexico by *The New York Times* found that the Mexicans, a proud and nationalistic people, consider their way of life and moral and social values to be far superior to those of people in the United States. They are alarmed by what they are being told by their leaders and the Mexican press about drug abuse in the United States, and they do not believe the United States is doing enough to curb it. But they are concerned about drug abuse and trafficking in Mexico, too, and 67 percent want the Mexican government to do more to stop it.

The poll makes it clear that Mexicans do not like the overall tone of United States foreign policy and definitely disapprove of United States efforts to topple the Sandinista government in Nicaragua, even though they feel that Nicaragua threatens the security of Central America.

Nov. 17

## The *New York Times* Poll
## The View from Mexico: Attitudes About the U.S.

*What do you consider to be the best thing about the United States?*

| | |
|---|---|
| Democracy, system of government | 16% |
| No inflation | 14% |

| | |
|---|---:|
| Employment, jobs | 12% |
| Technology | 7% |
| Government cares about people | 5% |
| Other | 21% |
| No answer | 25% |

*What do you think is worst about the U.S.?*

| | |
|---|---:|
| Drug addiction and trafficking | 20% |
| Nuclear arms | 12% |
| Intervention in other countries | 9% |
| Crime, violence and racism | 9% |
| Keeping Mexicans from working in the United States | 8% |
| Other foreign policy | 8% |
| No answer | 24% |

*Is your opinion of the government of the United States favorable or unfavorable, or don't you know enough about it to have an opinion?*

| | |
|---|---:|
| Favorable | 48% |
| Unfavorable | 27% |
| No opinion | 25% |

*How would you describe the relations between Mexico and the United States?*

| | |
|---|---:|
| Very friendly | 7% |
| Friendly | 59% |
| Unfriendly | 30% |
| Very unfriendly | 3% |

*How serious a problem do you think the use of illegal drugs like heroin and cocaine is in the U.S.?*

| | |
|---|---:|
| Very serious | 83% |
| Serious | 15% |
| Minor | 1% |
| Not a problem | 1% |

*How serious a problem do you think the use of illegal drugs like heroin and cocaine is in Mexico?*

| | |
|---|---:|
| Very serious | 54% |
| Serious | 31% |
| Minor | 14% |
| Not a problem | 1% |

*Should the government of Mexico do more to stop the export of drugs to the United States, do less, or do about what it is doing now?*

| | |
|---|---:|
| More | 67% |
| Less | 9% |
| Same as now | 24% |

In-person interviews conducted Oct. 28 through Nov. 4 with 1,576 people.

# Poll Rating Dives; 46% Approve Reagan's Work, down 21 Points

**By RICHARD J. MEISLIN**

President Reagan's overall public approval rating has plunged to 46 percent, from 67 percent a month ago, amid deep public concern over his Administration's arms deal with Iran and the funneling of funds to Nicaraguan rebels, according to a *New York Times*/CBS News Poll.

The decline is the sharpest one-month drop ever recorded by a public opinion poll in measuring approval of presidential job performance, according to Andrew Kohut, president of the Gallup Organization. Presidential approval polling began in 1936.

The poll, conducted Sunday, Nov. 30, found that a majority of Americans believe that the Reagan Administration is "covering up" the facts of its arms deal with Iran and that the incident is at least as serious as the Watergate affair, which toppled the Administration of Richard M. Nixon in 1974.

A majority of the 687 adults questioned by telephone nationwide also said they believed that the President and senior Administration officials knew that money from the sale of arms to Iran was being used to aid the contras, as the Nicaraguan rebels are known. This is despite repeated public assertions by Mr. Reagan and top members of his Administration in recent days that they had been unaware of the matter.

The poll marks the first time that approval of Mr. Reagan's job performance has fallen below 50 percent since the economic recession of 1982 and its immediate aftermath in early 1983, when his ratings hovered in the 41 to 49 percent range.

While he is still widely viewed as a strong

leader of high honesty and integrity, public confidence in the President's ability to deal with an international crisis has declined sharply. A wide majority of those questioned said they had greater trust in Congress than in Mr. Reagan to make correct decisions on foreign policy.  DEC. 2

### Rating Reagan's Performance

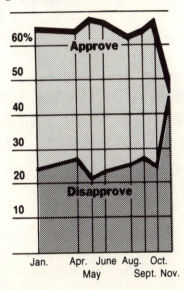

November figure based on 687 phone interviews in a *New York Times*/CBS News poll conducted Nov. 30.

DEC. 2

# Analyzing the Drop in Reagan's Ratings

**By ADAM CLYMER**

It used to take a lot longer for Presidents to lose as much support as Ronald Reagan lost last month. But just as it had been a public opinion phenomenon that his level of approval remained solid for three years, even when people said they disliked his policies, his sudden decline also broke polling records.

The latest *New York Times*/CBS News poll showed that while 67 percent approved of his handling of his job at the end of October, a month later only 46 percent did. In other words, one American in five changed his mind about the President in the wake of the Iran arms disclosures. The rating was the lowest accorded Mr. Reagan since 1982, when the Administration's plans to change Social Security benefits became a campaign issue.

Franklin D. Roosevelt, in whose Administration George Gallup started asking about presidential job performance, never lost that much support. Harry S Truman did, but it took three months at the end of 1945. Richard M. Nixon did it in four months in 1973; Gerald R. Ford lost 21 points in six weeks before and after his pardon of Mr. Nixon in September 1974. No one else has had such a loss in less than six months.

In fact, foreign policy setbacks often help, rather than hurt, a President. Pearl Harbor, for example, boosted Mr. Roosevelt from 72 percent to 84 percent approval, and the Communist invasion of South Korea raised Mr. Truman from 37 percent to 46 percent. The seizure of the United States Embassy in Teheran produced 19 points for Jimmy Carter.

In those and similar cases, the President could rally the nation by showing determination to fight back against a foreign enemy. Here that course seems precluded: The President is in trouble in part because his Administration was trying to be nice to a foreign enemy, and one that he campaigned against in 1980. Only 16 percent of the public in the *Times*/CBS News poll said they approved of "selling arms to Iran in order to get American hostages in Lebanon released."

There is more to Mr. Reagan's sudden decline. Some of it seems to be caused by the differences in his circumstances and his predecessors'. News makes a quicker, deeper impact than it did 20 years ago. And some of Mr.

Reagan's difficulty seems to be caused by his political characteristics, his strengths as well as his weaknesses.

Peter D. Hart, a Democratic polltaker, saw a series of circumstances as crucial. He cited the failure to get an arms agreement at Reykjavík, the crash in Nicaragua of the arms plane supplying the contras and November's election reversals as elements weakening the foundation of support for Mr. Reagan. And, he noted, "a lot of information got out very quickly, and the public paid attention." Because of memories of Watergate, Mr. Hart said, "they thought they had experienced it before."

A Republican, Linda Divall of American Viewpoint, thought the damage was deep because it hit at two areas of carefully assembled strength: this Administration's credibility in foreign affairs and the increasing trust in government that it has nurtured in six years in office.

The three analysts also focused attention on Mr. Reagan himself, as the poll did when it found only 37 percent of the public confident of his "ability to deal wisely with a difficult international crisis," and 37 percent who said he was "really in charge of what goes on in his Administration." Moreover, 53 percent of the 687 people polled by telephone on Nov. 30 said the President "knew that money from the Iranian arms sales was going to help the contras in Nicaragua"—which he denies.

Martin Wattenberg, an associate professor of political science at the University of California at Irvine, pulled these arguments and findings together in saying: "He's had disasters before—the recession, Lebanon—but you couldn't trace these to his personal faults. But this one you can, because he's 'not in charge.' It's putting emphasis on the negatives that have been there all along." Moreover, Ms. Divall and Mr. Hart agreed, the Iran crisis revolves around one of Mr. Reagan's singular strengths. Far more than most politicians, he had always been credited with honesty. Mr. Hart said he seemed to be a "straight shooter." To Ms. Divall, the image was one of being "very genuine and very open."

Now that keystone of political strength has been not so much directly contradicted, for Mr. Reagan is still rated as having more honesty and integrity than most people in public life, but called into question. Not only did two thirds of the public see his Administration as trying to cover up, but there is the 53 percent who say he knew about the money for the contras all along.    DEC. 7

# The White House Crisis New Poll Shows 47% Hold View Reagan Is Lying

By GERALD M. BOYD

About half the public says that President Reagan is "lying" when he asserts that he had no knowledge that funds from the sale of arms to Iran were being diverted to Nicaraguan insurgents, according to the latest *New York Times*/CBS News poll.

Besides that blow to Mr. Reagan's credibility, the poll showed that his job approval rating had not rebounded despite a series of recent moves by the President. Forty-seven percent said they approved of the job Mr. Reagan was doing, a statistically insignificant difference from the 46 percent who approved in a survey one week ago that showed a 21-point drop in his approval rating.

The latest poll, conducted by telephone among 1,036 adults on Dec. 7 and 8, showed that the public regarded how the Administration handled the facts of the case as the "worst" aspect of the secret dealings. Fewer respondents were concerned about the deci-

## Reagan: Generally trusted . . .

*Do you think Ronald Reagan has more honesty and integrity than most people in public life?*

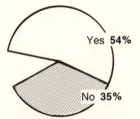

Yes 54%
No 35%

## . . . but not on Iran arms sales

*Ronald Reagan has said he did not know that the money from the Iranian arms sales was going to help the contras who are fighting against the government in Nicaragua. Do you think he was telling the truth or was he lying when he said that?*

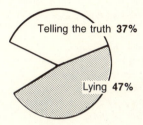

Telling the truth 37%
Lying 47%

Based on 1,036 telephone interviews in a *New York Times*/CBS News poll conducted Dec. 7–8.

DEC. 10

sion to sell arms to Iran and even fewer about providing funds to the Nicaraguan insurgents.

The survey results indicated for the first time that the disclosures about the secret dealings could make it more difficult for the Republican presidential candidate in 1988. In a *Times*/CBS News poll in October, before such disclosures began, 33 percent of the registered voters who were surveyed said that they would probably vote for a Republican candidate, while 32 percent preferred a Democrat. In the latest poll, 39 percent backed a Democrat and 27 percent a Republican.

DEC. 10

## *New York Times*/CBS News Poll
## The Iran Controversy: Registering Dissatisfaction

| | | Total | Liberal | Moderate | Conservative |
|---|---|---|---|---|---|
| Do you approve or disapprove of the way Ronald Reagan is handling his job as President? | Approve | 47% | 47% | 46% | 53% |
| | Disapprove | 42 | 45 | 45 | 36 |
| | DK/NA | 11 | 9 | 9 | 11 |
| Do you approve or disapprove of the way Ronald Reagan is handling the whole issue of Iranian arms sales and the contras? | Approve | 20% | 20% | 20% | 24% |
| | Disapprove | 61 | 69 | 64 | 56 |
| | Only Iran | 1 | — | 1 | 1 |
| | Only contras | 1 | — | 1 | 1 |
| | DK/NA | 18 | 10 | 14 | 18 |
| In your opinion, which of these three things is the worst? Is it selling arms to Iran, OR is it using the money to help the contras in Nicaragua, OR is it how the Administration has handled the facts about it? | Selling arms to Iran | 26% | 24% | 25% | 24% |
| | Using the money to help the contras | 7 | 10 | 8 | 6 |
| | How the Administration has handled the facts | 51 | 58 | 54 | 48 |
| | All three | 2 | 2 | 1 | 4 |
| | Arms and Administration | 1 | 1 | 2 | 1 |
| | Arms and contras | 1 | 1 | 1 | — |
| | Contras and Administration | — | 5 | 1 | 14 |
| | DK/NA | 11 | | 8 | |

|  |  | Total | Liberal | Moderate | Conservative |
|---|---|---|---|---|---|
| Ronald Reagan said his Administration would cooperate fully with the investigation into the Iranian arms sales and the contras. Do you think Reagan has seen to it that his Administration is cooperating as much as he said it would, or not? | Yes | 38% | 40% | 38% | 39% |
|  | No | 45 | 48 | 47 | 43 |
|  | Depends | 4 | 4 | 4 | 5 |
|  | DK/NA | 12 | 8 | 10 | 13 |
| Do you think the Reagan Administration will be prevented from accomplishing its goals in the next two years because of all the time it will have to spend on the issue, or not? | Yes | 55% | 59% | 62% | 51% |
|  | No | 30 | 31 | 26 | 35 |
|  | DK/NA | 15 | 10 | 12 | 14 |

Percentages based on 1,036 telephone interviews conducted Dec. 7–8.

DEC. 10

## New York Times/CBS Sports Poll On America's Team

Here's what the fans said when asked what their favorite National Football League team was.

|  | 1/84* | 12/84 | 12/86 |  | 1/84* | 12/84 | 12/86 |
|---|---|---|---|---|---|---|---|
| Atlanta | 2% | 1% | 1% | Minnesota | 2 | 2 | 3 |
| Buffalo | 1 | 1 | 1 | New England | 1 | 1 | 3 |
| Chicago | 3 | 4 | 12 | New Orleans | 2 | 1 | 1 |
| Cincinnati | 2 | 1 | 2 | Giants | 1 | 5 | 7 |
| Cleveland | 1 | 1 | 4 | Jets | 1 | 1 | 3 |
| Dallas | 17 | 18 | 12 | Philadelphia | 1 | 1 | 2 |
| Denver | 1 | 1 | 2 | Pittsburgh | 8 | 5 | 5 |
| Detroit | 3 | 2 | 2 | San Diego | 1 | 2 | 1 |
| Green Bay | 2 | 3 | 2 | San Francisco | 4 | 5 | 6 |
| Houston | § | § | † | St. Louis | 1 | 2 | † |
| Indianapolis | 1 | § | 1 | Seattle | 3 | 4 | 1 |
| Kansas City | 1 | † | 1 | Tampa Bay | 1 | † | § |
| Raiders | 5 | 9 | 4 | Washington | 13 | 6 | 6 |
| Rams | 1 | 1 | 2 |  |  |  |  |
| Miami | 4 | 11 | 7 |  |  |  |  |

*CBS Sports Poll (Percentages based on respondents who said they were interested in sports).
†Less than one percent.
§Not chosen by anyone.
Based on a poll of 608 fans conducted by telephone Dec. 14 and 15. Margin of sampling error 3 percentage points or less.

DEC. 21

# PART 4
# Business and Industry

NYT/FRED CONRAD

## Firm Zeros in on Car Trends

**By JOHN HOLUSHA**

**W**ESTLAKE VILLAGE, Calif.—Like to tinker with cars? If so, you are four times more likely to buy a pickup truck than someone who never looks under the hood.

Drive only because you have to? That makes you almost twice as likely to own an imported car than someone who regards a twisting road as a driving challenge.

These insights are part of what makes J. D. Power & Associates one of the best-known voices in automotive research. As an independent market research firm, the Power organization has attracted attention both because of its concentration on the automotive market and because of its rankings on new-car quality and consumer satisfaction with the auto companies. Its insights into car-buying habits are drawn from a study on the subject that looks into hundreds of personality quirks.

Unlike most auto research, which remains largely in the hands of the companies that have paid for it, Power's conclusions are published in a monthly newsletter, the Power Report on Automotive Marketing, which is widely quoted.

Not everyone agrees with Power's findings, of course. Jose Dedeurwaerder, the president of the American Motors Corporation, has criticized the consumer satisfaction ratings, which usually put A.M.C. near the bottom of the heap.

JAN. 21

### Car Buyer Categories

Car buyers fall into six basic categories, according to a survey done by J. D. Power & Associates in early 1985. Below are the categories, along with the percentage and types of cars they buy.

| Category | Percentage | Description | Make |
|---|---|---|---|
| Autophiles | 24% | Know a lot about cars and enjoy working on them. | Dodge, Pontiac |
| Sensible-centrists | 20% | Prize practicality. | Volvo, A.M.C. |
| Comfort-seekers | 17% | Favor options and luxury models. | Jaguar, Mercedes, Lincoln |
| Auto-cynics | 14% | View cars as appliances. | Porsche |
| Necessity-drivers | 13% | Prefer an alternative way of traveling. | A.M.C. |
| Auto-phobes | 12% | Care most about safety | Oldsmobile, Mercury |

Source: J. D. Power & Associates

JAN. 21

## Eastern's Battle over Wages

**By AGIS SALPUKAS**

**M**IAMI SPRINGS, Fla., Jan. 21—Wayne A. Yeoman, the senior vice president of finance at Eastern Airlines, earlier this week pointed to a chart of figures that showed the airline's operating expenses not much higher than other carriers, including low-cost ones—except for wages.

Those costs at Eastern are two to four times higher than at airlines such as People Express, Continental and Southwest, another chart showed.

The question often asked, he said at a press briefing at the carrier's headquarters here, was could the airline do better by trying to reduce costs in other areas besides labor. "It simply can't be done," he said, since Eastern was already competitive in its other costs.

To union leaders such as Charles F. Bryan, the president of District 100 of the International Association of Machinist and Aerospace Workers, the litany is familiar. "That's what they have been saying for the past 10 years," he said in an interview.

Eastern's top executives believe, however, that only deep permanent cuts in its labor costs can now make the carrier viable.

They argue that they had no choice but to take the risky course announced on Monday of imposing a contract on Eastern's flight attendants' union that contains permanent wage cuts, provides for longer working hours and furloughs 1,010 of 7,200 attendants by Feb. 4. The airline contends that service will not be hurt by the cutbacks, either on its Boston–New York–Washington shuttle or other routes. "One reason we were able to do this," said Joe Scott, an Eastern spokesman in Miami, "was that we could do it and still keep service operating at present levels."

JAN. 22

### Airline costs, for labor and other items

Costs per seat mile, in terms of salary, wages, and benefits, Jan.–Sept. 1985, in cents per mile.

| | |
|---|---|
| Delta | 3.44 |
| Eastern | 3.21 |
| United | 3.04 |
| American | 2.87 |
| Piedmont | 2.85 |
| Western | 2.26 |
| Southwest | 1.74 |
| Continental | 1.33 |
| People Express | 0.68 |

Costs per seat mile, including other operating expenses, outside of labor, Jan.–Sept. 1985, in cents per mile.

| | |
|---|---|
| Piedmont | 4.91 |
| Eastern | 4.74 |
| Delta | 4.70 |
| United | 4.63 |
| American | 4.51 |
| Western | 4.30 |
| Continental | 4.29 |
| Southwest | 3.85 |
| People Express | 3.46 |

JAN. 22

# Ford and Chrysler Finish Strong Year

**By JOHN HOLUSHA**

DETROIT, Feb. 13—The American automobile industry wrapped up the second-most-profitable year in its history today, as the Ford Motor Company reported 1985 earnings of $2.52 billion and the Chrysler Corporation reported $1.64 billion.

Added to the $4 billion reported earlier by the General Motors Corporation, it brought the Big Three's total profit for the year to $8.16 billion—a sum exceeded only by the $9.8 billion the industry earned in 1984.

The Ford and Chrysler yearly figures were somewhat crimped by their respective fourth-quarter results: Chrysler posted a big decline over the comparable 1984 period; Ford's earnings were virtually a rerun of its 1984 quarter.

Most industry analysts say the auto companies will be hard pressed to match the performance of the last two years in the future, as new entrants and added production capacity

## Auto makers: Higher sales, but lower earnings
1985 results for Big Three auto makers

| Company | Earnings (billions of dollars) | % Chg. from 1984 | Sales (billions of dollars) | % Chg. from 1984 | Output (millions of units) | % Chg. from 1984 |
|---|---|---|---|---|---|---|
| General Motors | $4 | −11 | $ 96.3 | 15 | 6.4 | 13.4 |
| Ford | 2.5 | −14 | 52.7 | 1 | 2.8 | −3.7 |
| Chrysler | 1.6 | −33 | 21.3 | 9 | 1.5 | 1.3 |
| TOTAL | 8.1 | −17.3 | 170.3 | 9.3 | 10.7 | 5.9 |

Source: Ward's Automotive Reports

FEB. 14

make the American car market more competitive.

"Capacity is going to increase by close to 20 percent over the next few years, and that has negative implications for profits," commented Jean-Claude Gruet, an analyst with Salomon Brothers Inc.

"Sales are likely to be down in 1986 compared to 1985, but even if they are flat, imports are going to take another 400,000 units out of the hide of the domestic producers," said Maryann N. Keller, an analyst with Vilas-Fischer Associates.  FEB. 14

## Pain reliever market
Shares of total over-the-counter analgesic sales in the U.S.

| Product | Market Share 1983 | Market Share 1985 |
|---|---|---|
| ASPIRIN | | |
| Anacin | 15% | 8% |
| Excedrin | 8% | 7% |
| Bayer | 10% | 7% |
| Bufferin | 8% | 6% |
| Other | 20% | 18% |
| Total | 61% | 46% |

| Product | Market Share 1983 | Market Share 1985 |
|---|---|---|
| IBUPROFEN | | |
| Advil | 0% | 6% |
| Nuprin | 0% | 3% |
| Total | 0% | 9% |
| ACETAMINOPHEN | | |
| Tylenol | 30% | 35% |
| Anacin 3 | 5% | 4% |
| Panadol | 2% | 2% |
| Datril | 2% | 1% |
| Other | 0% | 3% |
| Total | 39% | 45% |

Source: Paine Webber

FEB. 18

## Changing airline picture
Future ranking of top 10 airline companies, reflecting acquisitions, using 1985 revenue passenger miles

| | | Revenue Passenger Miles (in billions) | Previous Rank |
|---|---|---|---|
| 1. | Texas Air | 50.9 | |
| | Eastern* | 33.1 | 3 |
| | Continental | 16.4 | 8 |
| | New York Air | 1.4 | 22 |

## BUSINESS AND INDUSTRY

|   | Revenue Passenger Miles (in billions) | Previous Rank |
|---|---|---|
| 2. United | 48.0 | |
| United | 41.5 | 2 |
| Pan Am Pacific | 6.5 | |
| 3. American | 44.1 | 1 |
| 4. Northwest | 33.0 | |
| Northwest | 22.3 | 7 |
| Republic* | 10.7 | 10 |
| 5. TWA | 32.0 | 4 |
| 6. Delta | 30.1 | 5 |

|   | Revenue Passenger Miles (in billions) | Previous Rank |
|---|---|---|
| 7. Pan Am | 20.6 | 6 |
| 8. People Express | 15.5 | |
| People Express | 11.0 | 9 |
| Frontier | 4.5 | 15 |
| 9. Western | 10.4 | 11 |
| 10. US Air | 9.7 | 12 |

*Proposed purchase   Source: Airline Economics Inc.

FEB. 25

## Litigation against directors: cases and costs rising

|   | 1974 | 1984 | Percent Change |
|---|---|---|---|
| Percent of companies reporting one or more claims against directors and officers | 7.1 | 18.6 | 162 |
| Number of claims per 100 responding companies | 9.8 | 35.0 | 257 |
| Percentage of claims with payment over $1 million | 4.8 | 8.3 | 73 |
| Average defense cost per claim | $181,500 | $ 461,000 | 154 |
| Average payment to a claimant | $385,000 | $ 583,000 | 51 |
| Average total cost per claim | $566,500 | $1,044,000 | 84 |

Source: Surveys by the Wyatt Company

MARCH 7

## Where Saturn fits in lineup with rivals
A price list in current dollars of certain base-model autos, ranked by overall length in inches

|   | Price | Length |
|---|---|---|
| Yugo | $3,990 | 139.0 |
| Chevrolet Sprint | 5,390 | 141.1 |
| Chevrolet Spectrum | 6,658 | 155.9 |
| Toyota Tercel | 5,598 | 158.7 |
| Hyundai Excel | 4,995 | 161.0 |
| **Saturn*** | — | **162.4** |

|   | Price | Length |
|---|---|---|
| Ford Escort | 6,327 | 163.9 |
| Plymouth Horizon | 6,209 | 164.8 |
| Volkswagen Jetta | 8,150 | 171.7 |
| Chevrolet Cavalier | 6,706 | 172.3 |
| Pontiac Grand Am | 8,549 | 177.5 |
| Chevrolet Celebrity | 8,735 | 188.3 |

*As proposed for production by 1990.

APRIL 7

## Dollars for diplomas

One of the reasons college seniors can feel better this spring is that starting salaries for college graduates are up "significantly." That's the word from the 1986 Endicott Report, an annual survey conducted at Northwestern University of the hiring plans of 230 major companies. The average starting salary will be $21,060, up 6.5 percent over last year's $19,764. The report also predicts job offerings will rise by 2 percent. Following are salary figures for popular fields of activity.

### Starting Salaries for College Graduates

| Bachelor's Degrees | 1985 | 1986 | % Rise |
|---|---|---|---|
| Accounting | $20,388 | $21,216 | 4.1 |
| Business Administration | 20,676 | 21,324 | 3.1 |
| Chemistry | 23,400 | 24,264 | 3.7 |
| Computer | 25,572 | 26,172 | 2.3 |
| Economics or Finance | 20,520 | 22,284 | 8.6 |
| Engineering | 27,624 | 28,512 | 3.2 |
| Liberal Arts | 19,764 | 21,060 | 6.5 |
| Mathematics or Statistics | 23,532 | 23,976 | 1.9 |
| Sales-Marketing | 19,872 | 20,688 | 4.1 |

| Master's Degrees | 1985 | 1986 | % Rise |
|---|---|---|---|
| Accounting | 24,696 | 25,968 | 5.2 |
| Engineering | 32,100 | 33,288 | 3.7 |
| MBA with Nontechnical BA | 30,000 | 31,548 | 5.2 |
| MBA with Technical BS | 27,732 | 28,944 | 4.4 |
| Other Technical Fields | 31,512 | 33,168 | 5.3 |

Source: 1986 Endicott Report, Northwestern University

APRIL 13

## Director Insurance Drying Up

### By TAMAR LEWIN

When the Armada Corporation lost its directors' and officers' insurance earlier this year, causing 8 of the 10 members of the board to resign, the Detroit-based manufacturer of alloys and exhaust systems set a special requirement for the replacement candidates: they could not be too rich.

The company reasoned that if the directors were sued, and had to pay damages out of their personal assets, Armada could afford to indemnify them only if they did not have many assets.

Armada is not the only company having insurance problems these days. Because of increased litigation, larger court awards and a rapidly shrinking pool of available insurance, many companies can no longer find, or afford, insurance for their directors and officers.

Without insurance coverage, executives and board members may be held personally liable for paying damages to shareholders and others who are harmed by corporate actions.

When no insurer will provide coverage, many companies, including the BankAmerica Corporation, have found ways to provide their own, either through a captive subsidiary or by creating an insurance consortium with several companies. Such arrangements, however, put extra pressure on the directors when faced with a tough decision such as the one BankAmerica's directors confronted in Sanford I. Weill's proposal this week to become the chief executive officer.   MARCH 7

## Lowest Charge Rates Sought

A list of 51 banks that charge interest rates of less than 18 percent for Visa and Mastercard credit purchases, compiled by Representative Charles E. Schumer, Democrat of New York

### Northeast
Apple Bank for Savings (Manhattan): 15.8%, $20, grace period 30 days.
Bank of New England (Boston): 16.8%, annual fee $21, 25 days.
Bank Leumi (Manhattan): 16.8%, $20, 25 days.
Connecticut Society for Savings (Wethersfield, Conn.): 14.9%, $20, no grace period.
Crossland Savings Bank (Brooklyn): 16.8%, $20, 28 days.
Dollar Drydock (Jericho, L.I.): 16.8%, $20, 25 days.
First National Bank of Boston: 17.04%, $21, 30 days.
Manufacturers Hanover (Hicksville, L.I.): 17.8%, $20, 25 days.

Rhode Island Hospital Trust National Bank (Providence, R.I.): 17.8%, $15, 30 days.
Shawmut Bank of Boston: 16.98%, $24, no grace period.
Shawmut, Worcester City Bank (East Longmeadow, Mass.): 16.98%, $24, no grace period.
State Street Bank (Quincy, Mass.): 16.5%, $25, 25 days.

**Middle Atlantic**
Atlantic Financial Savings and Loan (Bala Cynwyd, Pa.): 16.9%, $15, no grace period.
Bank of New York (Newark, Del.): 16.98%, $18, 7 days.
Chevy Chase Savings and Loan (Chevy Chase, Md.): 14%, $16, 30 days.
Corestates Bank of Delaware (Wilmington, Del.): 17.9%, $18, 25 days.
Dreyfus Corporation (Newark, Del.): 16.98%, $18, 30 days.
Maryland National Bank (Newark, Del.): 17.9%, $18, 30 days.
Philadelphia Society for Savings (Millsboro, Del.): 15.07%, $18, 30 days.
Pittsburgh National Bank: 17%, $18, 30 days.
Provident Bank of Maryland (Baltimore): 17.8%, $18, 21 days.
Provident National Bank (Philadelphia): 17%, $18, no grace period.

**Southeast**
Bank of Virginia (Richmond): 17.4%, $30, 30 days.
Dominion Bank (Vienna, Va.): 10.5%, $15, 25 days (regional customers only).
Mechanics and Farmers Bank (Salem, N.C.): 14%, $18, 30 days.
Republic National Bank of Miami: 17%, $20, 20 days.
Southeast Bank (Miami): 16.5%, $48, 30 days.

**Middle West**
Comerica Midwest (Toledo, Ohio): 16.9%, $30 (rebated), no grace period.
First National Bank of Cleveland: 16.2%, $18, 25 days.
First National Bank of Lincolnshire (Lincolnshire, Ill.): 18% for under $2,500; 16% for up to $10,000; 15% for over $10,000; $20; 25 days.
Gem Savings Bank (Dayton, Ohio): 15%, $20, 15 days (residents of Ohio, Kentucky and Indiana only).
National City Bank (Cleveland): 16.2%, $18, 5 days (Ohio residents only).
Security Savings Bank (Jackson, Mich.): 14.9%, $12, no grace period.

**South Central**
Banc Texas (Dallas): 14.5%, no annual fee, no grace period.
Broadway National Bank (San Antonio): 14%, no annual fee, no grace period.
Cullen Center Bank and Trust Co. (San Antonio): 14.1%, no annual fee, no grace period.
First Commercial Bank (Little Rock, Ark.): 12.5%, $18, no grace period (Arkansas residents only).
Interfirst Bank of Dallas: 14.1%, no annual fee, no grace period.
National Bank of Fort Sam Houston (San Antonio): 14.58%, no annual fee, no grace period.
Republic Bank (Dallas): 14.5%, no annual fee, no grace period.
Simmons First National Bank (Pine Bluff, Ark.): 12%, $22.50, 25 days.
Texas American Bank (Fort Worth): 14.5%, no annual fee, no grace period.
Union National Bank (Little Rock, Ark.): 12%, $20, no grace period.

**Northwest**
Northwest Bank/Seattle Trust and Savings (Seattle): 15%, $18, 16 to 18 days.
People's Bank (Seattle): 15%, $18, 25 days (residents of Washington, Idaho and Oregon).
Puget Sound National Bank (Tacoma, Wash.): 15%, $18, no grace period.
Rainier National Bank (Seattle): 15%, $18, 25 days (Western U.S. only).
Seattle First: 15%, $18, 25 days.

**West**
Continental Bank and Trust (Salt Lake City): 16.58%, $20, 25 days.
Security Pacific Bank (Los Angeles): 17.4%, $45, 25 days.
Working Assets Visa (San Francisco): 17.5%, $22, 25 days.

APRIL 22

# Black-Owned Concerns Reflected '85 Economy

**By JONATHAN P. HICKS**

The nation's 100 biggest black-owned companies generally reflected the pattern of the economy as a whole in 1985, with construction and media companies showing strong sales results, and energy and manufacturing concerns reporting more lackluster performances.

### The largest black-owned businesses in 1985

| 1985 Rank | 1984 Rank | Company | Main business | 1985 Sales* |
|---|---|---|---|---|
| 1 | 1 | Johnson Publishing Co.<br>Chicago | Publishing, cosmetics, broadcasting and television production | $154,860 |
| 2 | 2 | Motown Industries<br>Los Angeles | Entertainment | 149,029 |
| 3 | 3 | H. J. Russell Construction<br>Atlanta | Construction, development, communications | 118,000 |
| 4 | — | Philadelphia Coca-Cola Bottling Co.<br>Philadelphia | Soft-drink bottling | 102,000 |
| 5 | 5 | Soft Sheen Products<br>Chicago | Hair-care products | 85,000 |
| 6 | 7 | G & M Oil Co.<br>Baltimore | Petroleum products | 61,853 |
| 7 | — | Interstate Landscaping Co.<br>Harrisburg, Ill. | General contracting | 61,000 |
| 8 | — | TLC Group<br>New York | Paper sewing patterns | 60,000 |
| 9 | 10 | Systems and Applied Sciences Corp.<br>Vienna, Va. | Computer and electronic data systems | 58,000 |
| 10 | 6 | Wardoco Inc.<br>New Haven, Conn. | Commercial fuel oils | 49,505 |

*In thousands of dollars, as of Dec. 31, 1985.

Source: *Black Enterprise*

MAY 7

But there were some notable exceptions, according to the 14th annual survey on the companies, published by *Black Enterprise* magazine. Black-owned companies that sold computer and electronic data services generally showed strong results last year, while such concerns in the general economy were less robust, the survey found. The survey results were published in the June issue of *Black Enterprise*.

In all, sales for the nation's top 100 black-owned companies surged 14.8 percent in 1985, to $2.94 billion, from $2.56 billion in 1984. That compares with a 2.8-percent growth rate in sales of the Fortune 500 companies. The black-owned companies, nearly all of which are privately held, do not report net income.

## Ad Agency Mergers Changing the Business

**By RICHARD W. STEVENSON**

Madison Avenue, the symbolic if not actual home of the advertising world, is going through its most dramatic change since the business began a century ago.

Agencies are being bought and sold at a pace never before seen. In the process, huge advertising and marketing service companies, dubbed "mega-agencies," that dwarf the size of traditional agencies are being created.

Just yesterday, the Saatchi & Saatchi Company of London announced that it had agreed to acquire Ted Bates Worldwide for $450 million, the biggest merger yet.

The acquisition would make Saatchi & Saatchi the largest agency in the world, wresting that title away from an as-yet unnamed combination of three other major concerns—BBDO International, the Doyle Dane Bernbach Group and Needham Harper Worldwide—that was announced only two weeks ago.

The consolidation into fewer and bigger agencies reflects converging trends and business problems, according to advertising executives. Among them are the increasing desire of companies to have their ad agencies provide services in major markets around the world, the need for more financial and management stability in a notoriously volatile industry, and the need of publicly owned agencies to grow even in a sluggish business environment.

"These mergers are definitely not being done from the bottom up: How can we better serve our clients?" said Alan J. Gottesman, an analyst at L. F. Rothschild, Unterberg, Towbin Inc. "They are being done from the top down: How can we better manage our business?"   MAY 13

## The New Advertising Empires

Top five U.S. agency super groups according to worldwide billings in 1985.

| Agency<br>Major subsidiary<br>networks* | World billings<br>in millions | U.S. billings<br>in millions |
|---|---|---|
| **Saatchi & Saatchi Co. P.L.C.*** <br> Ted Bates Worldwide <br> Backer & Spielvogel <br> DFS-Dorland Worldwide** | $7,632.4 | $4,652.1 |
| **BBDO/DDB/Needham** <br> BBDO International <br> Doyle Dane Bernbach Group <br> Needham Harper Worldwide | 5,016.9 | 3,743.1 |
| **Interpublic Group** <br> McCann-Erickson Worldwide <br> SSC&B: Lintas Worldwide | 4,827.9 | 2,351.9 |
| **JWT Group** <br> J. Walter Thompson Co. | 3,817.4 | 2,365.8 |
| **Young & Rubicam** <br> Wunderman, Ricotta & Kline <br> Sudler & Hennessey | 3,575.3 | 2,272.0 |

*Including acquisition of Ted Bates Worldwide announced May 12, 1986.
**Previously Dancer Fitzgerald Sample and Dorland Advertising.   Source: *Advertising Age*

## Saatchi & Saatchi's Major Acquisitions

Price represents down payment, in millions of dollars.

| Date | Company | Type of business | Price |
|---|---|---|---|
| 1976 | Garland Compton Holdings | Advertising | —* |
| 1981 | Dorland Advertising | Advertising | $ 3.0 |
| 1982 | Compton Communications | Advertising | 27.9 |
| 1983 | McCaffrey & McCall | Advertising | 10.0 |
| 1984 | The Hay Group | Consulting | 100.0 |
|  | Yankelovich, Skelly & White | Market research | 12.0 |
| 1985 | The Rowland Co. | Public relations | 10.0 |
|  | Howard Marlboro Group | Sales promotion | 14.0 |
|  | Siegel & Gale | Corporate identification | 2.0 |
|  | Kleid Co. | Direct marketing | 4.0 |

| Date | Company | Type of business | Price |
|---|---|---|---|
| 1986 | Dancer Fitzgerald Sample | Advertising | 75.0 |
| | Backer & Spielvogel | Advertising | 50.0 |
| | **Ted Bates Worldwide** | **Advertising** | **450.0**\*\* |

\*Operations merged  
\*\*Full price  
Source: Saatchi & Saatchi Co.

MAY 13

## Gannett's "Triple Crown" Bidding Feat

LOUISVILLE, Ky., May 19—Allen H. Neuharth, chairman of the Gannett Company, said today that acquiring the daily newspapers in this city of the Kentucky Derby was the last step in "winning the Triple Crown."

He was delightedly referring to Gannett's success over the last year in outbidding other communications companies for three newspaper prizes: *The Des Moines Register, The Detroit News* and now *The Courier-Journal* and *The Louisville Times.*

Under the aggressive direction of Mr. Neuharth, dressed today in his signature colors of black and gray, Gannett has become the nation's largest newspaper group. It owns more daily papers, representing more daily circulation, than any other chain. The new additions bring Gannett's newspaper holdings to 93 dailies, including *USA Today.* Their circulation totals more than six million.

Gannett also owns the largest outdoor advertising company in North America; *USA Weekend*, a Sunday newspaper magazine formerly known as *Family Weekly*, and eight television stations. Soon it will acquire its 16th radio station.

For 1985 the company reported operating revenues of $2.2 billion, with pretax earnings of $485 million, despite what analysts estimate was a loss of about $85 million at *USA Today.* In the last 10 years Gannett's revenues and profits have grown more than fourfold. Its present stock price of $79 represents about 22 times the annual earnings per share.

## Gannett: Continuing to expand
Recent major acquisitions made by Gannett Co., Inc.

| Acquisition | Date | Price of deal |
|---|---|---|
| *The Oakland Tribune**<br>*The Cincinnatti Enquirer*<br>Six television stations | June 7, '79 | $370 million |
| *The Gainesville Times*, Ga.<br>Poultry & Egg News<br>*The Knoxville Journal*<br>*El Diario-La Prensa*<br>*Norwich Bulletin*, Conn. | March 31, '81<br><br>June 2, '81<br>Aug. 25, '81<br>Nov. 17, '81 | $80 million combined total |
| *Jackson Daily News*, Miss.<br>*Hattiesburg American*, Miss.<br>*Madison County Herald*, Miss.<br>*Clarion-Ledger*, Canton, Miss. | May 28, '82 | $110 million |
| WTCN-TV, Minneapolis (now WUSA-TV) | April 13, '83 | $75 million |

| Acquisition | Date | Price of deal |
|---|---|---|
| WLVI-TV, Boston | June 23, '83 | $42 million |
| KKBQ-AM and FM, Houston | Dec. 3, '84 | $35 million |
| *Family Weekly* magazine (now *USA WEEKEND*) | Mar. 29, '85 | $38 million |
| *The Des Moines Register* *The Jackson Sun* | July 1, '85 | $195 million |
| *Detroit Evening News* along with five television stations, two radio stations, smaller newspapers plus some weeklies.** | Feb. 18, '86 | $717 million combined total |
| *The Louisville Courier-Journal* *The Louisville Times* | closes in mid-July | $300 million |

*Sold in 1983
**(3 TV stations, and 2 radio stations immediately sold, for about $200 million.)

MAY 20

# Henley's Historic Offering

By KENNETH N. GILPIN

It started as a collection of companies that another company wanted to cast off. Yesterday, it took its place in corporate history as making the biggest initial public stock offering in the American securities market, a deal that grew and grew to more than $1 billion.

Institutional and individual investors yesterday snapped up $1.2 billion worth of stock in The Henley Group Inc., a collection of 38 diverse companies spun off by the Allied-Signal Corporation under Michael D. Dingman, who at the time was president of Allied-Signal.

Securities analysts said the enthusiastic response to the stock, which was priced at $21.25 a share, had as much to do with Henley's management as with the nature of its assets, which amount to more than $5.3 billion. Mr. Dingman, 54 years old, is a proven deal maker who was chairman and chief executive of the Wheelabrator-Frye Corporation before it was taken over by the Signal Companies in 1983, and then president of Signal before it was acquired by the Allied Corporation in 1985.

MAY 21

## Largest public offerings

The Henley offering, along with the ten largest initial public offerings in the U.S., in millions of dollars.

| Amount raised | Name | Date released |
|---|---|---|
| $1,187.0 | The Henley Group | May 20, 1986 |
| 855.0 | First Australian Prime Fund | April 17, 1986 |
| 824.0 | Fireman's Fund | Oct. 24, 1985 |
| 750.0 | Rockefeller Center Properties | Sept. 12, 1985 |
| 657.9 | Ford Motor Co. | Jan. 18, 1956 |
| 374.4 | Philadelphia Savings Fund Society | April 14, 1983 |
| 292.9 | California Federal | March 29, 1983 |

| Amount raised | Name | Date released |
|---|---|---|
| 292.3 | Morgan Stanley | March 21, 1986 |
| 278.9* | British Telecommunications | Dec. 3, 1984 |
| 243.6 | Glendale Federal | Oct. 5, 1983 |
| 240.0 | The Merrill Lynch Convertible Securities Fund | July 25, 1985 |

*Sold in U.S.    Source: New Issues, Ft. Lauderdale, Fla.

MAY 21

# When the Tax Rules Don't Quite Fit

By DAVID E. ROSENBAUM

WASHINGTON, June 8—The tax bill before the Senate this week is one of the most sweeping pieces of legislation Congress has considered in years. A 1,489-page opus, it would completely overhaul the Federal income tax system and affect the taxes paid by nearly every person and company in America.

Tax rates would be dramatically lowered under the bill, hundreds of loopholes would be plugged, six million poor people would be removed from the tax rolls altogether and dozens of profitable corporations that pay little or no tax now would be subjected to a minimum tax.

Not all the elements, however, are so cosmic in nature. Buried within the bill, which weighs well over five pounds, are about 175 items known as transition rules, special provisions that exempt particular companies, communities and individuals from specific conditions that would otherwise apply.

The transition rules are written in such Delphic prose that, in most cases, no one can interpret them except the author, the taxpayer involved and the auditors at the Internal Revenue Service.

For example, one rule would give a Rochester company, Praxis Biologics Inc., an exemption from an extra tax that would otherwise be imposed on royalties it earns from selling vaccines to pharmaceutical companies. This is how the rule is described in the bill: "In the case of a taxpayer which was incorporated on Feb. 17, 1983, and the five largest shareholders of which are doctors of medicine, any royalties of such taxpayer from products resulting from medical research shall be treated in the same manner as royalties from computer software are treated."

A staff member who worked on the transition rules said he did not know why they were written in such an obscure way except that "it's always been done that way."    JUNE 9

## Who the Winners Are

WASHINGTON, June 8—In response to requests from several senators, Senator Bob Packwood released a list of the beneficiaries of transition rules in the Senate tax overhaul bill. It was merely a list of names, with no explanation of who the Senate sponsor was or what rule was being applied. For the record, following are the beneficiaries:

Agri-Beef
Air Products
Albany City Center
Alcoa
Allegheny Electric Co-op
Aloha Tower Development Program
Applied Energy Services
Archibald Power
Arrowhead Springs
Arrowhead Stadium
Atlanta Stadium
Atlanta Underground Project
Avon
Ball Corporation Pollution Control
Baltimore Gas and Electric
Baltimore Stadium
Bangor solid waste
Barbara Jordan 2d
Bayonne Co-generation
Bayside Center

Ben Tillman Redevelopment Project
Big Horn Co-generation
Bond pooling
Bonneville Power Authority
Brooklyn Union Gas
Buffalo Stadium
Cable television
Cafeteria plans
Cajun II coal-fired generating unit
Capital District Energy Center
Cellular telephones
CF Industries ammonia plants
Channel
Chester Solid Waste Association
Church pension plans
Cimarron Coal Company
CMC/Colt
Co-generation projects
Commercial National Bank
Continental Airlines
Control Data
Cox Enterprises
Dade County Aviation Notes
Dallas Rapid Transit
Delaware Power and Light
Delta Air Lines
Diamond Star Project
Dineh Power Plant
Downtown Denver Retail Project
Duke Power Pollution Control Project
Dulles Rapid Transit
Eastbank Wastewater Treatment
Facility Enesco
Federal Express Satellites
Fiber-optic communications
Florida solid waste projects
Frankfort Arsenal
General Development
General Mills
General Motors special tool
Gilberton Power Company
Grand Gulf Nuclear Plant
Great Northern Nakoosa Pulp Mill
Greenbriar Leasing
Harborplace
Hawaii Multifamily Housing Project
Hayber Development
Hellsgate Hydroelectric
Hennepin County Solid Waste Project
Hot Springs National Park
Houston Astrodome
Hydroelectric power
Isle of Wight Sports Facility
Jacksonville Landing
Kansas independent colleges

Kern River pipeline
Keyser Power
Kiel Auditorium
Lake Superior Paper
Laundry detergent plants
Life insurance companies
Long Lake Energy Corporation
Louisiana ESOPs
Manhattan, Kan., Urban Development Action Grant projects
Manville Corporation
M.C.A.
M.C.I.
Mid-Columbia River Power Project
Minneapolis Convention Center
Minneapolis Retail Complex Mishoe Towers
Mississippi Chemical
Missouri Urban Development Action Grant projects
Mojave pipeline projects
Montana hydroelectric/co-generation projects
Mount Vernon Mills
Multimedia
Murphy Oil
National Parks Historic Sites
Navy ships
Navy yard
New England/Hydro Quebec
New Hampshire post office building
New Orleans Convention Center
New Orleans Riverwalk
New York Metropolitan Transit Authority
New York Power Authority
New York State Electric and Gas
North Pier Terminal
North Sea Development
Northwest Orient Airlines
Ocean State Power
Offshore vessels
Old Town Parking Garage/Heliport
Orange County Tourist Development
Outlet building/garage
Owings Mills Town Center
Pacific-Texas Pipeline
Pan Am World Airways
Pennzoil
PERC rules
Personal holding companies
Philadelphia Airport Hotel
Philadelphia Electric
Philadelphia Trash-to-Steam
Phillips Petroleum
Phoenix Sports Complex
Physicians Mutual Insurance
Pioneer Place Parking Garage
Pitt, Temple and Lincoln

Point Arguello
Poplar Hill
Portland Convention Center
Portland Urban Renewal
P.P.G.
Providence Convention Center/Parking
Quonset Power
Railroad grading and tunnel bores
RCA Satellites
Rialto Tire Burning Plant
River Front University
Science Park River Place
St. Louis convention center
St. Louis stadium
San Diego/North County Recovery Project
Semass
Solid waste projects
Sonat
South Bellridge Co-generation
South Carolina Medical University Project
South Pointe
Steel companies
Strawberry Square
Superdome
Sverdrup
Supplier service contracts
Temple Eastex Co-generation
Texaco
Texas City Co-generation
The Tides
Tiffany Lanes
Times Square Redevelopment
Toyota plant
United Telecom
University of Delaware
Unocal
Upper Pontalbo apartments
Valleyview Project
Viacom
Vidalia Hydroelectric Facility
Walt Disney enterprises
Wood energy projects

JUNE 9

# For Drivers, the Fun Is Back

**By JOHN HOLUSHA**

BREA, Calif.—"Are you having fun yet?" That is what advertisements along the West and Gulf coasts of the country are asking sales prospects as they promote the Suzuki Samurai, a small, four-wheel-drive Jeep-like vehicle that was introduced into the American market late last year.

"We are presenting it as an enjoyable alternative to the small car," said N. Douglas Mazza, the vice president of sales and marketing for Suzuki, which is best known in this country for its motorcycles. "A lot of small cars are boring. We're telling people that they can have a four-wheel-drive convertible for under $7,000."

The Suzuki vehicle, which went on sale in November in California, Florida and Georgia, is the latest entry in a growing segment of the American car market known as sports utility vehicles. Although most vehicles in this category are officially classified as trucks, most are being used as everyday noncommercial transportation by drivers who want something other than a conventional sedan.

With its Range-Rover model, Land-Rover-Leyland International Holdings of London recently entered the market, which is dominated by the domestic companies. The American Motors Corporation's Jeep models are among the best-known four-wheel-drive vehicles, which also include the General Motors Corporation's Blazer models, the Ford Motor Company's Broncos and the Chrysler Corporation's Ramcharger.

JUNE 17

## Most popular vehicles

Best-selling sports utility vehicles in 1985, and suggested retail price for four-wheel-drive models.

| Model | Number sold |
|---|---|
| **Chevrolet S-10 Blazer** $10,698 | 187,234 |
| **Ford Bronco II** $11,501 | 104,934 |
| **Jeep Cherokee** $11,474 | 89,432 |
| **Chevrolet Suburban** $12,456 | 58,906 |
| **Ford Bronco** $12,782 | 52,281 |

Source: Integrated Automotive Resources; *Buyer's Guide*

JUNE 17

# Oil Industry's Bulls Abandon Optimism

By LEE A. DANIELS

Early this year, when crude oil prices plunged from $27 to $12 a barrel and sent shock waves through the oil industry, George M. Keller, the plainspoken chairman of the Chevron Corporation, helped lead the industry's bullish countercharge.

Prices would not remain at depressed levels, he said repeatedly. They would rebound enough to average $20 a barrel for the year.

Now, however, Mr. Keller acknowledges that the industry bulls have lost their campaign, largely because of the continuing failure of the Organization of Petroleum Exporting Countries to curb its crude oil output.

The loss, he and other industry executives believe, will further tear the tattered fabric of the U.S. oil patch—forcing additional and sharper cuts in company exploration budgets for the year, dramatically shrinking domestic oil production and in years to come increasing the volume of crude oil imported from OPEC countries to worrisome levels.

Charles J. DiBona, the president of the American Petroleum Institute, an industry association, said that if $15-a-barrel prices persist through the 1980s, the combination of falling production and rising demand would likely force the United States to import more oil than it did in the peak year of 1979, when it brought in nine million barrels a day. Last year the United States imported five million barrels a day, 32 percent of its consumption.

United States oil companies have cut by 24 percent, on average, their planned 1986 capital spending—the majority of which is targeted for exploration and development—from 1985 levels, according to a recent survey by John S. Herold Inc., an oil industry consulting concern.

AUG. 4

## Tightening the pursestrings

How various segments of the U.S. oil industry have altered their capital spending plans, in millions of dollars.

| Changes by Industry Groups Group | Number of companies | Capital expenditures | | Percent change |
|---|---|---|---|---|
| | | 1985 | Est. 1986 | |
| Integrated | 19 | $43,833 | $33,740 | −23 |
| Producing | 27 | 1,535 | 969 | −37 |
| Gas pipeline | 9 | 3,609 | 2,353 | −35 |
| Contract drilling | 3 | 178 | 91 | −49 |
| Service and supply | 13 | 756 | 690 | −9 |
| **Total** | **71** | **$49,911** | **$37,843** | **−24** |

**Changes by Companies**

| Leading integrated companies | Reported spending 1985 | Original budget 1986 | Current budget 1986 | Percent change from 1985 |
|---|---|---|---|---|
| Amerada Hess | $699 | — | $365 | −50 |
| Amoco | 5,303 | 5,000 | 3,500 | −34 |
| Atlantic Richfield | 3,600 | 3,000 | 2,000 | −44 |
| Chevron | 4,035 | 5,000 | 3,500 | −13 |
| Exxon | 10,800 | 10,000 | 8,000 | −26 |
| Mobil | 3,478 | 4,100 | 3,000 | −14 |
| Occidental Petroleum | 1,152 | 1,200 | 1,100 | −5 |
| Pennzoil | 590 | N.A. | 358 | −39 |
| Phillips | 1,088 | 1,400 | 1,000 | −9 |
| Shell Oil | 4,400 | N.A. | 3,900 | −11 |
| Standard Oil | 2,800 | 2,500 | 2,000 | −29 |
| Sun | 1,600 | 1,560 | 1,260 | −21 |
| Tenneco | 1,725 | N.A. | 1,300 | −25 |
| Unocal | 1,707 | 1,500 | 1,219 | −29 |

N.A. Not available

Source: John S. Herold Inc.

AUG. 4

# Bipartisan Leaders Predict Passage of Tax Bill in Fall; President Hails Agreement

By DAVID E. ROSENBAUM

WASHINGTON, Aug. 17—Leading congressional advocates and opponents of the historic tax revision bill that House and Senate negotiators approved Saturday night said today that the measure would almost certainly be enacted this fall but not without further struggle.

The bill would bring about the most comprehensive restructuring of the Federal income tax law since World War II. Its reverberations would be felt in the finances of nearly every household and business, and throughout the nation's economy.

The bill would lower the top tax rate for individuals, now 50 percent, to 28 percent. And the top tax rate for corporations, now 46 percent, would become 34 percent. Each of the new rates is one percentage point higher than it was in the version of the bill that the Senate passed in June.

The legislation also eliminates or restricts many deductions and other tax preferences. It would raise business taxes by about $120 billion over five years and reduce the taxes paid by individuals by a like amount. AUG. 18

### Highlights of the Tax Bill

**Tax Cuts:** Three quarters of the 100 million filers would get cuts averaging 6.1 percent. Six million lower-income couples and individuals would pay no tax, but 20 million filers would pay more. Individuals would get $120 billion in cuts over the next five years.

**Brackets:** In 1988, only two basic brackets would remain: 15 percent for joint filers with income under $29,750, and 28 percent above that figure. A third, marginal, rate of 33 percent would apply to some portion of high incomes, beginning at $71,900 for joint filers. This would be phased in by having five tax rates for 1987, ranging from 11 to 38.5 percent. Many high-income persons face tax increases next year.

**Corporate Rates:** Top rate reduced to 34 percent from 46 percent, but corporations would owe an additional $120 billion in taxes over the next five years.

**Standard Deduction:** Increased to $3,000 from $2,480 for single taxpayers; to $5,000 from $3,670 for joint filers; and to $4,400 from $2,480 for single heads of households.

**Personal Exemption:** Increased from $1,080 now to $1,900 in 1987, to $1,950 in 1988, to $2,000 in 1989, and indexed for inflation in subsequent years. Phased out for highest income people.

**Mortgage Interest:** Remains deductible for first and second homes. On home equity loans, the homeowner could deduct interest only if the proceeds go into home improvement, tuition or medical costs.

**Other Interest:** Eliminated as a deduction for auto, credit card and other consumer loans.

**State and Local Taxes:** Income and property taxes remain deductible; deductions for sales taxes would go.

**Capital Gains:** Long-term profits, now taxed at 20 percent or less, would be taxed at a top rate of 28 percent beginning next year.

**I.R.A.s:** Present law would apply for those not covered by company pensions and for individuals whose income is $25,000 or less and for joint filers whose income is $40,000 or less. Individuals earning $25,000 to $35,000 and couples earning $40,000 to $50,000 get a partial deduction. Couples earning over $50,000 and single people earning over $35,000 lose their deduction, but may still deposit up to $2,000 a year and earn interest tax free.

**Business Investment:** The investment tax credit is repealed effective last Jan. 1. Depreciation is somewhat less generous than present law. Tax breaks for some industries, including real estate, timber, defense, banking and insurance, are curbed. Oil and gas benefits are largely preserved.

**Business Entertaining:** The cost of meals and entertainment, now fully deductible, would be only 80 percent deductible.

Aug. 18

## How the Tax Bill Evolved

Following is a chronology of important events leading to the Senate and House conferees' agreement Saturday on tax-overhaul legislation:

**January 1977:** In the final days of the Ford Administration, Treasury Secretary William E. Simon introduces "Blueprints for Basic Tax Reform," which calls for a system with three tax brackets: 8, 25 and 38 percent.

**May 27, 1982:** Senator Bill Bradley, a New Jersey Democrat, and Representative Richard A. Gephardt, a Missouri Democrat, introduce a bill that would eliminate many deductions. It also calls for reducing the number of tax rates for individuals to three, replacing the rate range of 11 to 50 percent with a range of 14 to 28 percent. In addition, it proposes taxing corporate profits at a flat 30 percent rate, dumping the graduated tax and its 46 percent top rate. This bill follows many other tax-simplification proposals.

**Jan. 25, 1984:** President Reagan begins his drive to change the tax system by announcing in his State of the Union Message that he has asked the Treasury Department to study how to simplify and improve the fairness of the tax code.

**April 1984:** Senator Robert W. Kasten, Jr., of Wisconsin and Representative Jack F. Kemp of New York sponsor a Republican alternative to the Bradley-Gephardt bill. It would lower the top tax rate for individuals and businesses to 25 percent.

**Nov. 26, 1984:** The Treasury Department recommends a tax-simplification plan to President Reagan that would consolidate the 14 income tax brackets for individuals to 15, 25 and 35 percent, and cut the top rate for businesses to 33 from 46 percent.

**May 28, 1985:** President Reagan proposes legislation to eliminate many tax loopholes and deductions and transform an "un-American" tax system into one that is "clear, simple and fair for all." His proposal would reduce individual rates to 15, 25 and 35 percent and lower the top rate for corporations to 33 percent.

**Dec. 3, 1985:** The House Ways and Means Committee votes, 28 to 8, to send to the full House a bill that would consolidate the income tax rates for individuals to 15, 25, 35 and 38 percent; lower the top rate for corporations to 36 percent; and raise overall corporate taxes by $140 billion. On Dec. 17, the House—after a dramatic last-minute intervention by the President—passes the tax bill in a voice vote.

**May 7, 1986:** The Senate Finance Committee, which at one point appeared hopelessly at odds, passed what some experts said was an inspired bill, 20 to 0, that would consolidate the 14 income tax brackets for individuals to 15 percent and 27 percent, cut the top corporate rate to 33 percent and raise overall business taxes by $100 billion. On June 24, the Senate passes the bill 97 to 3.

**Aug. 12, 1986:** House and Senate conferees begin face-to-face negotiations, but the session ends in acrimony. Senator Bob Packwood, an Oregon Republican and chairman of the Senate Finance Committee, and Representative Dan Rostenkowski, Democrat of Illinois and chairman of the House Ways and Means Committee, begin meeting to try to fashion a compromise.

**Aug. 16, 1986:** House and Senate conferees approve the Packwood-Rostenkowski compromise. It would set individual tax rates at 15 and 28 percent, lower the top corporate rate to 34 percent and raise overall business taxes by about $120 billion.

AUG. 18

# The Hunts' Bid to Buy Time

By RICHARD W. STEVENSON

DALLAS, Sept. 1—When crashing oil prices forced the Placid Oil Company to default on a $1.2 billion loan last spring, the company's owners, the Hunt brothers of Dallas, were true to the brash gambling legacy of their father, H. L. Hunt: They told bankers that instead of paying them off, they wanted to sink more money into drilling for bigger-than-ever gushers.

What the Hunts saw as a sure thing, however, the banks saw as too big a gamble. The disagreement set off a chain of events, including the filing of bitter lawsuits, that led Placid, one of its subsidiaries and one of the Hunt family's core trusts to enter bankruptcy proceedings on Aug. 29.

The confrontation between Placid and its lenders provides a glimpse, pieced together from court documents and interviews with lawyers and bankers, into the workings of the secretive Hunt empire. It also underscores how, as the odds turned against them this year, the brothers—Nelson Bunker, W. Herbert and Lamar—followed the family tradition of raising the stakes.

In addition, advisers to the Hunts say the case raises questions about whether the banks acted too hastily, and to their own detriment, in demanding loan repayment, thus forcing Placid to seek protection from its creditors. For their part, the banks deny that they acted prematurely.

The pressure on the Hunts could get worse in the short run as the banks intensify their efforts to extract money from Placid and from the brothers' other business and personal holdings. In any event, the filings under Chapter 11 of the Federal Bankruptcy Code are signs of the deep financial distress within one of the nation's great family fortunes, once estimated at more than $6 billion.

The origins of the crisis date back to 1980, when Placid and the other cornerstone of the family wealth, the Penrod Drilling Company, borrowed almost $2 billion to rescue Bunker

### The largest creditors

Placid Oil Co. creditors holding the 10 largest uninsured claims, all trade debts except where noted.

| Creditor | Amount |
|---|---|
| Brown & Root | $3,646,053 |
| American International Underwriters* | $2,000,000 |
| Marathon Letorneau Co. | $1,411,706 |
| McDermott Inc. | $984,361 |
| Haman AKA Chain Trading Co. | $984,133 |
| Pumpkin Air Inc. | $673,624 |
| NL Baroid | $514,627 |
| Halliburton Services | $438,221 |
| R. J. Brown & Associates | $384,839 |
| Oceaneering International Inc. | $357,492 |

*Contingent unliquidated and disputed claims under self-insurance program.

SEPT. 2

and Herbert Hunt when the value of their huge silver investments plummeted. The loans were restructured during the next few years, and although the companies occasionally had difficulty making payments, they were up to date coming into this year.

Then came the oil price crash. With its cash flow drying up, Placid, on March 27, missed a $30 million principal payment to the consortium of 18 banks, led by Republicbank of Dallas. Placid still owed $773 million on the loan.

SEPT. 2

## What the Hunt family owns

| The children of H. L. Hunt and Lyda Bunker | Major Holdings |
|---|---|
| Margaret Hunt Hill | Margaret Hunt Trust Estate |
| Haroldson Lafayette Hunt 3d | Haroldson L. Hunt, Jr., Trust Estate |
| Caroline Hunt Schoellkopf | Caroline Hunt Trust Estate, Rosewood Corp., Rosewood Properties[1], Rosewood Hotels[1], Rosewood Resources[1] |
| Nelson Bunker Hunt | Nelson Bunker Hunt Trust Estate |
| William Herbert Hunt | William Herbert Hunt Trust Estate |
| Lamar Hunt | Lamar Hunt Trust Estate, Kansas City Chiefs |
| Owned together by:<br>Nelson Bunker Hunt<br>William Herbert Hunt<br>Lamar Hunt | Hunt Energy Corp., Hunt Properties Inc., Hunt International Petroleum Co., Penrod Drilling Co., Placid Oil Co., Placid Refining Co.[2], Placid International Oil Ltd.[2], Placid Investment Co.[2], Placid Building & Service Co.[2], Placid Chemical Co.[2] |
| **The children of H. L. Hunt and Frania Tye** | |
| Haroldina Lee Franch[3] | Assets unknown |
| **The family of H. L. Hunt and Ruth Ray** | |
| Owned together by:<br>Ruth Ray Hunt (mother)<br>Ray Lee Hunt<br>June Hunt<br>Helen Hunt Hendrix<br>Swanee Hunt | Hunt Consolidated Inc.[4], Hunt Oil Co., Hunt Investment Co., Hunt Consolidated Resources Corp., Woodbine Development Corp., Brooks Well Servicing Inc., Hunt Refining Corp., Union Life Insurance Co. of Arkansas, Yemen Hunt Oil Co., Hunt U.K. Ltd. |
| **Ray Lee Hunt** | Southwest Media Corp. |

[1] Subsidiaries of Rosewood Corp.
[2] Subsidiaries of Placid Oil Co.
[3] Only surviving child of four.
[4] Parent company

SEPT. 2

## Dayton Plans Sale of B. Dalton Chain

**By ISADORE BARMASH**

In a move reflecting soft demand for books and the sharp inroads made by discounters, the Dayton-Hudson Corporation said yesterday that it would sell B. Dalton, the nation's second-largest chain of bookstores.

With 777 outlets in 48 states, including 4 in New York City, B. Dalton had sales last year of $538 million, exceeded only by Waldenbooks at $565 million. But its earnings have slipped in recent years as it cut its margins to compete with discount stores, analysts said. And retail book sales have been flat generally this year, they added, because of the high prices of hardcover books and interest in new electronic products, particularly videotapes.

These factors combined to convince Dayton-Hudson, which founded the chain 20 years ago, to find a buyer, according to analysts and industry sources.

"I see the book business rapidly deteriorating for high-cost chains like Dalton," said one discount competitor, Robert Haft, president of the nine-year-old Crown Books, the fourth-biggest book chain. "They are in high-rent malls with the big department stores; we are in strip centers with supermarkets and drug stores and pay one quarter to one third their rents." He said that any buyer of B. Dalton will have to "invest at least twice as much more after buying the company to make it work right."

Oct. 1

## The best sellers

Rank based on 1985 store revenues, including nonbook items. Dollar figures are in millions. Rank in 1983 is in parentheses.

| | |
|---|---|
| 1 (2) Waldenbooks | $565 |
| 2 (1) B. Dalton | 538 |
| 3 (3) Barnes & Noble | 225 |
| 4 (4) Crown Books | 137 |
| 5 (5) Kroch's & Brentano's | 42 |
| 6 (6) Zondervan | 39 |
| 7 (8) Doubleday | 28 |
| 8 (7) Gateway | 27 |
| 9 (10) Coles* | 20 |
| 10 (9) Cokesbury | 20 |

*Canadian-based operation.
Revenues are for U.S. stores only.     Source: BP Report

Oct. 1

## Feeding Fido Is Big Business

**By PETER H. FRANK**

DALLAS, Oct. 3—Last year, an estimated $5.4 billion in pet food was sold in America, almost four times more than was spent on baby food. Grocery stores took in more money selling pet food than they did selling cereal, candy, soup or coffee.

But if pet food is a big industry, it is also lethargic, growing at only 2 to 3 percent annually. Expansion through marketing and new-product development can be slow and uncertain. Companies more and more must consider acquisitions to achieve significant growth.

When Quaker Oats outraced the Ralston Purina Company recently to acquire Anderson, Clayton & Company, it was said to be motivated more by that company's familiar

## The pet food market: Who's serving up what

| | Ralston Purina | Nestlé (Carnation) | Mars (Kal-Kan) | H. J. Heinz (Star-Kist) | Grand Met U.S.A. | Quaker Oats[1] | Anderson, Clayton (Gaines) |
|---|---|---|---|---|---|---|---|
| **Brands** In order of dollar sales | Dog Chow, Cat Chow, Tender Vittles, Purina 100, Chuck Wagon | Friskies, Mighty Dog, Come'N Get It, Chef's Blend, New Breed | Kal-Kan, Meal Time, Crave, Beef Bites, MPS | 9 Lives, Jerky Treats, Square Meal, Meaty Bones | Alpo, Alamo Brand, Liv-A-Snaps, Alpo Jerky, Tabby | Ken-L-Ration, Puss'n Boots Moist Meals, Snausages, Tender Chunks | Gravy Train, Cycle, Gaines Burgers, Dry Cycle, Top Choice |
| **Market Share '85** | 26.9% | 12.2% | 8.4% | 7.8% | 7.1% | 7.1% | 6.6% |
| **Pet Food Sales '85** In millions | $1,450.1 | $659.0 | $453.3 | $422.1 | $384.9 | $383.2 | $356.8 |

[1] In deal to acquire Anderson, Clayton. Sources: John C. Maxwell, Jr. *Advertising Age;* Dun and Bradstreet; pet food companies

OCT. 4

pet food labels—including Gaines Burgers, Top Choice and Cycle dog foods—than by its well-known food products for humans.

Quaker won the battle for Anderson, Clayton with an $805 million offer, or $66 a share, topping the $64-a-share bid made by Ralston. Ralston is by far the industry's largest seller of pet food, with 26.9 percent of the market in 1985. Quaker tied for No. 5, with a 7.1 percent share last year.

Without an acquisition, "you're lucky to gain a half of a point" of market share a year, said John C. Maxwell, Jr., an analyst with Furman Selz Mager Dietz & Birney Inc. in New York. He estimated that Anderson, Clayton's Gaines division had a 6.6 percent share last year, which will nearly double Quaker's market share. "They'll gain shelf space any way they can," he said. "This just pushes Quaker Oats into No. 2, but it still is very competitive."

"To have an opportunity to double your share is a major opportunity," said George J. Yapp, president of Quaker Oats's pet foods division. "Market share position has become fairly entrenched. To double your business from a share standpoint without an acquisition is a much longer-term prospect."

With 51.7 million dogs and 56.1 million cats owned in the United States, more than half of the households nationwide have at least one cat or dog, according to Lawrence E. Fisher, manager of MRCA Information Services in Stamford, Conn. In a study conducted for the Pet Food Institute, MRCA estimated that the dogs were owned in 38.7 percent of the country's homes, while 29.4 percent had cats.

OCT. 4

# Time Inc. Will Buy Textbook Publisher

**By GERALDINE FABRIKANT**

Time Inc., the nation's largest magazine publisher, said yesterday that it would acquire the company that helped teach millions of Americans how to read. In a $520 million deal, Time plans to acquire Scott, Foresman &

Company, the elementary and high school textbook publisher that for years produced the Dick and Jane readers.

Scott, Foresman is owned by the SFN Companies, which will also sell the South-Western Publishing Company, its other educational publishing business, to the International Thomson Organization of Canada for $270 million in cash.

For Time, the acquisition of Scott, Foresman marks a significant move into textbook publishing. Time already owns Little, Brown Company, which has a small position in college publishing but is primarily a trade book publisher.

For SFN, the total price for the two subsidiaries is almost double the $423 million paid to take the company private in February 1985 in a leveraged buyout.   OCT. 15

## The textbook market

How schoolbooks are selling . . . estimated sales, in millions of dollars.

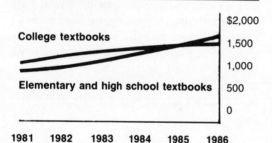

Source: *Book Industry Trends 1986*, by John P. Dessauer

. . . And who's leading the sales

| Elementary, High School Textbook Sellers | 1985 ($ millions) | 1984 ($ millions) | Percent Change |
|---|---|---|---|
| SFN Companies | $289.4 | 238.8 | +21.2% |
| Simon & Schuster (Educational) | 278.0 | 185.0 | +50.3 |
| Harcourt Brace Jovanovich | 221.4 | 175.8 | +25.9 |
| Houghton Mifflin Co. | 173.4 | 157.4 | +10.2 |
| Macmillan Inc. | 156.6 | 127.8 | +22.5 |

| College Textbook Sellers | | | |
|---|---|---|---|
| Simon & Schuster (Educational) | 181.3 | 175.0 | +3.6 % |
| McGraw-Hill Book Co. | 133.4 | 127.9 | +4.3 |
| **SFN Companies** | **82.1** | **79.2** | **+3.7** |
| CBS Publishing Group | 74.5 | 70.2 | +6.1 |
| John Wiley & Sons Inc. | 73.0 | 73.0 | 0 |

Source: *Educational Marketer*, August 1986, Knowledge Industry Publications

OCT. 15

# Head of CBS Quits Under Pressure

**By GERALDINE FABRIKANT**

After a tense, lengthy board meeting yesterday, Thomas H. Wyman, the embattled chairman and chief executive of CBS Inc., resigned as head of the communications giant, the company announced last night.

Mr. Wyman will be relieved of his role immediately, CBS said. Laurence A. Tisch, the company's largest shareholder and the chairman of the Loews Corporation, will become acting chief executive and chairman of a new management committee, to serve until a new chairman and chief executive are selected, the company said in a two-page statement.

In addition, William S. Paley, the 84-year-old founder of CBS and holder of 8.1 percent of the company's stock, will become acting chairman. Harold Brown, a board member and a former Defense Secretary, will head an executive search committee.

Mr. Paley said in a statement: "As founder of the company, I am delighted that Laurence Tisch will serve as acting C.E.O. during this transition. Larry has not only proven his extraordinary ability as a businessman and leader in the success of his own company, Loews, but, most important, he shares the values and principles that have guided CBS throughout the period of its growth. I respect and admire him, and look forward to working with him."
SEPT. 11

## A Board in Turmoil

Until yesterday, the makeup of the CBS Inc. board was as follows:

Thomas H. Wyman, age 56. Chairman of the board, president and chief executive.
William S. Paley, 84. Chairman of the executive committee; chairman of the board from 1946 until April 1983.
Michel C. Bergerac, 54. Private investor; ex-Revlon head.
Harold Brown, 58. Chairman of the Foreign Policy Institute at the School of Advanced International Studies of the Johns Hopkins University. A former Secretary of Defense.
Walter Cronkite, 69. Special correspondent for CBS News.
Roswell L. Gilpatric, 79. Retired presiding partner of Cravath, Swaine & Moore.
James R. Houghton, 49. Chairman of Corning Glass Works.
Newton N. Minow, 60. Law partner in Sidley & Austin.
Henry B. Schacht, 51. Chairman of Cummins Engine Company.
Edson W. Spenser, 59. Chairman of Honeywell Inc.
Franklin A. Thomas, 51. President of the Ford Foundation.
Laurence A. Tisch, 63. Chairman of Loews Corporation.
Marietta Tree, 68. A director of Llewelyn-Davies, Sahni Inc., a city planning firm.
James D. Wolfensohn, 52. President of James D. Wolfensohn Inc., advisory firm.

SEPT. 11

## 19 Months of Upheaval

Since the start of 1985, CBS has been in a state of flux. In fending off takeovers, it has undergone a complicated recapitalization that has had severe financial consequences. Following is a chronology of key events leading up to the change in executives at the broadcast company:

**January 1985:** Senator Jesse Helms helps to organize an effort by Fairness in Media, a group of conservative investors, to buy sufficient stock in CBS to change what the North Carolina Republican calls the "liberal bias" in coverage by CBS News of "political events, personages and views."

**Feb. 11, 1985:** Fairness in Media confirms that it is considering a proxy battle to get one or two seats on the 13-member CBS board.

**Feb. 13, 1985:** CBS files a suit in U.S. District Court to block the efforts of Fairness in Media, saying that the group's campaign was, in effect, political fund-raising, and that it made false statements to the Securities and Exchange Commission.

**Feb. 26, 1985:** CBS agrees to relinquish its list of shareholders to Fairness in Media after the group agrees to a number of conditions for its use, including the assurance that it would not be used for political fund-raising.

**March 1985:** Rumors begin to circulate on Wall Street that Ted Turner, the Atlanta broadcasting entrepreneur, plans to make a bid for CBS.

**March 13, 1985:** CBS's chairman, Thomas H. Wyman, tells a group of security analysts that there appears to be "no financial substance" behind reports that Ted Turner is planning a bid for the company.

**March 29, 1985:** Fairness in Media drops plans to conduct its proxy fight, saying that it did not have sufficient time to wage a full-scale effort.

**April 3, 1985:** Wall Street sources say that the General Electric Company discussed an arrangement to buy CBS in a friendly merger for about $150 a share, if the broadcasting company were to get a serious, unfriendly takeover offer. CBS denies the reports.

**April 18, 1985:** Ted Turner formally announces a bid to buy 67 percent of CBS with a package of stock in his Turner Broadcasting System, as well as bonds and other notes paying high interest. The view on Wall Street was that he stood only a slim chance of succeeding.

**April 22, 1985:** CBS directors unanimously reject the Turner bid.

**May 5, 1985:** The Gannett Company's chairman, Allen Neuharth, denies rumors that Gannett and Ted Turner are discussing a possible partnership in a takeover of CBS.

**July 3, 1986:** CBS announces a $954.8 million recapitalization plan in which it will buy back up to 21 percent of its stock. The heavy debt CBS assumes substantially increases the cost of acquiring the company.

**July 29, 1985:** The chairman of Loews Corporation, Laurence A. Tisch, says his company has purchased 9.9 percent of CBS common stock. Loews says it expects to tender its entire stake of 2.9 million shares to CBS under the broadcast company's buyback program.

**July 31, 1985:** Ted Turner suffers another setback when the Federal Communications Commission cancels a session of oral arguments on his bid.

**Aug. 27, 1985:** Turner Broadcasting formally tells the F.C.C. that it is withdrawing its application to take control of CBS.

**Oct. 17, 1985:** Laurence Tisch said Loews will buy up to 25 percent of CBS. He is invited to join the CBS board as a friendly director who, analysts say, could forestall a hostile takeover bid.

**March 25, 1986:** Oilman Marvin Davis says he offered to buy CBS for more than $160 a share, or $3.75 billion in cash, but was turned down.

**July 5, 1986:** CBS said it would trim 700 jobs in the broadcast group, leading some analysts to speculate that the austerity plan reflected the growing role played by Laurence Tisch.

**Sept. 10, 1986:** Thomas Wyman resigns as chairman and chief executive of CBS. Laurence Tisch becomes active chief executive and William E. Paley, the company's 86-year-old founder, becomes acting chairman.

SEPT. 11

# I.R.A.s to Lose Some Punch

By GARY KLOTT

WASHINGTON, Oct. 29—Individual Retirement Accounts, which became an American institution in a few short years, lose a lot of their allure under the new tax law. Millions of middle- and upper-income workers covered by a company pension plan will no longer be allowed to claim deductions for I.R.A. contributions.

By no means does this spell the end of I.R.A.'s. Couples with incomes below $50,000 and single individuals with incomes below $35,000 will still be able to claim a full or partial I.R.A. deduction—whether or not they are covered by an employer pension plan. And even those not eligible for a deduction may still find I.R.A.s of value in sheltering their retirement savings, although it will also focus increased attention on 401(k) employee retirement plans as a replacement.

In most instances, the benefits of 401(k) plans, offered by more and more companies since they were introduced in 1978 and for which it is estimated that more than 20 million people are currently eligible, surpass those of fully deductible I.R.A.s.

OCT. 30

# Mixed Bag for Small Business

By GARY KLOTT

WASHINGTON, Nov. 5—The Tax Reform Act of 1986 contains many changes that will have a fundamental impact on small businesses, from the "mom-and-pop"

## Comparing I.R.A.'s and other investments

Amounts accumulated, after taxes, if withdrawn in years shown by a taxpayer in the 28 percent tax bracket depositing the same amount annually in each investment.

### Impact on Persons Using I.R.A. for Retirement Savings Only

|  |  | Regular Savings 8% Yield | Deductible I.R.A. 8% Yield | Nondeductible I.R.A. 8% Yield | Municipal Bond 8% Yield |
|---|---|---|---|---|---|
| Annual Deposit* |  | $1,440 | $2,000 | $1,440 | $1,440 |
| Year Withdrawn | 5 | $9,984 | $10,564 | $10,025 | $10,044 |
|  | 10 | 21,289 | 23,970 | 21,693 | 21,559 |
|  | 15 | 36,247 | 43,667 | 37,891 | 36,968 |
|  | 20 | 56,038 | 72,609 | 60,746 | 57,590 |
|  | 30 | 116,875 | 177,618 | 140,384 | 122,114 |

### Impact on Persons Using I.R.A. as a Savings Account**

| Year Withdrawn | 5 | $9,984 | $9,097 | $9,833 | $10,044 |
|---|---|---|---|---|---|
|  | 10 | 21,289 | 20,640 | 20,880 | 21,559 |
|  | 14 | 32,911 | 33,669 | 32,449 | 33,517 |
|  | 19 | 51,625 | 56,745 | 51,800 | 52,971 |
|  | 20 | 56,038 | 62,524 | 56,509 | 57,590 |
|  | 30 | 116,875 | 152,949 | 127,086 | 122,114 |

*For valid comparisons, a full $2,000 contribution is made each year only to the deductible I.R.A. accounts. Deposits to other accounts are designated in after-tax dollars, that is $1,440 ($2,000 minus 28 percent tax).
**I.R.A. figures include impact of 10 percent penalty for premature withdrawal.

Source: Arthur Andersen & Company

Oct. 30

grocery store to the schoolteacher who designs dresses at home at night.

For many businesses, the new law is very much a mixed bag.

Many small businesses that are incorporated, for example, will discover inducements to change their legal form. And people with sideline businesses will be encouraged to show a profit to protect their future deductions.

Self-employed individuals get a new deduction for part of the cost of their health insurance premiums. And the new law doubles the amount of business equipment that can be written off immediately rather than depreciated over a period of years.

At the same time, depreciation deductions for cars used in business get scaled back, while home office deductions come under tighter restrictions. And individuals who carry on a sideline business will need to show profits more frequently if they want to continue to write off all their expenses.

The most significant feature of the new law is the reduction in tax rates. Sole proprietorships and partnerships will benefit from the drop in the top individual tax rates to 28 percent (33 percent for some high-income individuals), from 50 percent. Corporations will benefit from the drop in the top corporate rate to 34 percent, from 46 percent.

As under the old law, small businesses will pay lower graduated rates on part or all of their taxable income—15 percent on the first $50,000 and 25 percent on income between $50,000 and $75,000.

With the top individual rate dropping below the corporate rate for the first time, many tax advisers are urging their small-business clients to reorganize their business. The advice: Convert from a corporation to an "S corporation" to take advantage of the lower individual rate. An S corporation, named for a subchapter of the corporate tax code, is a form of business organization that combines the tax advantages of partnerships and the limited liability features of corporations.

Nov. 6

## The new tax law and write-offs for business

**Computer Depreciation**
Percent of cost that can be written off each year.

| Year | Old Law | New Law |
|---|---|---|
| 1 | 15% | 20% |
| 2 | 22 | 32 |
| 3 | 21 | 19 |
| 4 | 21 | 12 |
| 5 | 21 | 12 |
| 6 | — | 6 |

Nov. 6

**Business Car Depreciation**
Percent of cost that can be written off each year.

| Year | Old Law | New Law |
|---|---|---|
| 1 | 25% | 20% |
| 2 | 38 | 32 |
| 3 | 37 | 19 |
| 4 | — | 12 |
| 5 | — | 12 |
| 6 | — | 6 |

Nov. 6

**Limits on Car Depreciation**
Yearly limit on depreciation deductions for cars costing more than $12,800.

| Year | Old Law | New Law |
|---|---|---|
| 1 | $3,200 | $2,560 |
| 2 | 4,800 | 4,100 |
| 3 | 4,800 | 2,450 |
| 4 | 4,800 | 1,475 |
| —* | 4,800 | 1,475 |

*Subsequent years.    Source: Laventhol & Horwath

Nov. 6

## How corporate tax rates are graduated

| Taxable Income | Tax Rates Old Law | Tax Rates New Law[1] |
|---|---|---|
| $25,000 and under | 15% | 15% |
| $25,001 to $50,000 | 18 | 15 |
| $50,001 to $75,000 | 30 | 25 |
| $75,001 to $100,000 | 40 | 34 |
| More than $100,000 | 46[2] | 34[3] |

[1] For tax years beginning on or after July 1, 1987.
[2] An additional 5% tax up to $20,250 was imposed on corporate taxable income greater than $1 million. Corporations with taxable income of at least $1,405,000 paid a flat rate of 46%.
[3] An additional 5% tax up to $11,750 is imposed on corporate taxable income greater than $100,000, up to $335,000. Corporations with taxable income of at least $335,000 will thus pay a flat rate of 34%.

Source: Ernst & Whinney

Nov. 6

# G.M.'s Obsession with Size

### By JOHN HOLUSHA

DETROIT—"I have always believed in planning big, and I have always discovered after the fact that, if anything, we didn't plan big enough."—Alfred P. Sloan, Jr., *My Years with General Motors*.

No company anywhere has celebrated the virtues of sheer bigness more than the General Motors Corporation, the world's largest auto maker. It was a philosophy shaped and spelled out by Alfred P. Sloan, Jr., the company's legendary chairman, who fashioned a loose confederation of struggling car ventures into America's largest industrial enterprise—one that supplied a car for every taste and pocketbook. By 1962, General Motors made one out of every two cars sold in America.

Mr. Sloan stepped down as chief executive in 1946 and died in 1966, but he has yet to

### Measuring growth: How big three auto makers compare

| | Employees[1] | | | | | | Assembly Plants | | Market Share[2] | |
|---|---|---|---|---|---|---|---|---|---|---|
| | Worldwide | | Hourly U.S. | | Salaried U.S. | | | | | |
| | 1980 | 1985 | 1980 | 1985 | 1980 | 1985 | 1980 | 1986 | 1980 | 1985 |
| G.M. | 746,000 | 811,000 | 376,000 | 400,000 | 141,000 | 161,000 | 25 | 30[3] | 45.8% | 42.5% |
| Ford | 426,735 | 369,300 | 76,000 | 69,000 | 74,717 | 78,700 | 17 | 14 | 17.2% | 18.8% |
| Chrysler | 92,596 | 107,850 | 51,938 | 60,231 | 24,773 | 24,573 | 7 | 7 | 8.8% | 11.3% |

[1]Including subsidiaries.
[2]For cars sold in the United States.
[3]G.M. announced Thursday that it will close six of these final assembly plants.

Source: *Ward's Automotive Reports:* company reports

Nov. 8

relax his grip. His enormous success established a mindset that persists. Even as General Motors announced its decision this week to close 11 of its plants (and probably still more after that), the company's leaders insisted that it was not cutting capacity, but simply improving its ability to maintain its historic market leadership.

The question now is whether General Motors is going far enough, or whether it is clinging too long to an obsession with size and market share.

Both the Ford Motor Company and the Chrysler Corporation have already concluded that in today's car market, less is more. Both companies, under varying degrees of duress, have preceded G.M. in shutting plants and cutting employment to bring their size in line with what they could sell in bad times as well as good.

Chrysler, once on the edge of bankruptcy, slashed white-collar employment to 20,000 from 40,000, and is now the American car maker with the lowest cost per unit.

Ford, which has shrunk its employment steadily since 1979, is expected to earn $2.8 billion this year—some $200 million more than G.M. It would be the first time since Mr. Sloan's G.M. surged past Ford in 1924 that the No. 2 company has beaten G.M. on the bottom line.

But G.M. executives continue to say their strategy will pay off. Even as Japanese cars flooded into the American market in the 1980s, G.M. stood stubbornly in its quest for bigness and in trying to hold market share. The company commanded 45 percent of the market in the early 1980s, and that remained the company's target, albeit a costly one.

Nov. 8

## Military Spending Questioned

### By PAUL LEWIS

PARIS, Nov. 10—A spate of studies by economists in Europe and the United States is raising questions about the effect of military spending on the health of a country's civilian industry.

The studies are appearing at a time when governments on both sides of the Atlantic are reemphasizing their long-held view that large military expenditures, particularly for research, spur growth in the economy as a whole.

In a speech late last month, for example, President Reagan contended that his Strategic

## Military Spending and Industrial Performance

Countries spending more on military research have generally scored lower in economic competitiveness, a study by Lloyds Bank Review shows.

| Country | Defense research and development, as % of G.D.P. | | Civil research and development, as % of G.D.P. | | Competitiveness indicator* | |
|---|---|---|---|---|---|---|
| | 1979 | 1982 | 1979 | 1982 | 1979 | 1982 |
| Britain | 0.68% | 0.68% | 1.6% | 1.6% | 99.0 | 94.3 |
| United States | 0.58 | 0.72 | 1.8 | 2.0 | 100.3 | 99.7 |
| France | 0.50 | 0.38 | 1.4 | 1.6 | 103.5 | 100.2 |
| Sweden | 0.22 | 0.24 | 1.7 | 1.7 | 102.9 | 117.2 |
| West Germany | 0.13 | 0.11 | 2.2 | 2.5 | 111.3 | 128.9 |
| Japan | 0.01 | 0.01 | 2.3 | 2.5 | 110.3 | 138.3 |

*Competitiveness indicator represents excess of output over domestic absorption.

Nov. 11

Defense Initiative "could open whole new fields of technology" to the civilian sector, likening the anticipated benefits to the wealth of jobs and industries created by the space program. France's new conservative government has made much the same claim in defending its decision to increase funds for military research at nearly twice the rate as spending on civilian projects.

But three British economists, writing in the current issue of *Lloyds Bank Review*, say there appears to be an inverse relationship between high military spending and industrial performance throughout the Western world.

The economists—Mary Kaldor, Margaret Sharp and William Walker—note that Britain and the United States, which consistently spend more than other Western countries on military research, tend to score low in a gauge of economic competitiveness used by the Organization for Economic Cooperation and Development. In contrast, West Germany and Japan, which spend next to nothing on military research, have highly efficient industries as measured by the organization, whose members are 24 Western industrial countries.

Nov. 11

## Auto Industry Adjusting to a Painful New Reality

**By JOHN HOLUSHA**

DETROIT—General Motors produced another batch of bad news last week. Beset by slumping sales and determined not to return to the generous incentives that led to a whopping third-quarter loss, the automotive giant will temporarily cut production by as much as a third, idling more than 30,000 workers.

In addition, 11 facilities employing 29,000 workers will close permanently, starting next year. Although the critics of the closings ranged from labor leaders to H. Ross Perot, the recently ousted member of G.M.'s board, it was widely recognized that most of the plants were obsolete and due for replacement. Most auto industry analysts, and company officials themselves, predicted that this would be only the first and least painful round of shutdowns as G.M. adjusts to the new realities of the American car market.

The reason for this glum outlook is that the automotive market in the United States resembles a telephone-booth-stuffing contest: Everybody on the outside is trying to crowd in, and the ones already inside are being squeezed.

So-called "voluntary" restrictions have limited automotive imports from Japan for most of the decade. But the restrictions simply induced Japanese manufacturers to build assembly plants in this country. They also opened the way for new entrants, such as the Yugo from Yugoslavia and this year's import sensation, the Hyundai, which is made in Korea and whose base model sells for just $4,995.

DEC. 21

## Challenge from abroad
The manufacture of Japanese vehicles in North America

| Manufacturer | Location | First year of production | Vehicle production, Jan.–Nov., 1986 | Vehicle production at full capacity |
|---|---|---|---|---|
| **United States** | | | | |
| Honda | Marysville, Ohio | 1982 | 211,636 | 360,000 |
| Toyota* | Fremont, Calif. | 1984 | 178,080 | 250,000 |
| Nissan | Smyrna, Tenn. | 1983 | 156,490 | 240,000 |
| Mazda | Flat Rock, Mich. | 1987 | 0 | 240,000 |
| Mitsubishi** | Bloomington, Ill. | 1988 | 0 | 240,000 |
| Isuzu/Fuji | Lafayette, Ind. | 1989 | 0 | 120,000 |
| **Canada** | | | | |
| Honda | Barrie, Ontario | 1986 | 600 | 80,000 |
| Toyota | Cambridge, Ontario | 1988 | 0 | 50,000 |
| Suzuki/GM | Ingersoll, Ontario | 1988 | 0 | 50,000 |

*Joint venture with General Motors
**Joint venture with Chrysler

Sources: *Ward's Automotive International, Automotive News*

1987 and 1988 import models and country of manufacture

| | | | |
|---|---|---|---|
| Volkswagen Fox | Brazil | Mercury Tracer** | Mexico |
| Pontiac LeMans | Korea | Dodge Colt* | Thailand |
| Ford Festiva | Korea | Proton Saga | Malaysia |
| Mercury Tracer* | Taiwan | | |

*Sold in Canada
**Sold in U.S.

Source: Company reports

DEC. 21

# Paramount's Surprise Streak

**By GERALDINE FABRIKANT**

The Paramount Pictures Corporation is having a boffo year.

From *Pretty in Pink* in February to *Top Gun*, *Crocodile Dundee*, *Star Trek IV: The Voyage Home* and this month's *The Golden Child*, starring Eddie Murphy, Paramount has produced an almost unbroken string of hits. So far this year, its films are expected to account for as much as 21 percent of the industry's total box office gross, pulling in about $600 million, twice as much as its nearest competitors.

In the history of the film business, that is an extraordinary gap. "The studio will end up with a huge chunk of the top 10 films of the year," said Art Murphy, the film industry expert for *Variety*, the trade newspaper.

Paramount is not only the envy of its rivals, but the speed of its turnaround is bewildering some of Hollywood's most jaded executives, including its own.

After all, just two years ago, with the highly publicized departure of its top management, Barry Diller and Michael Eisner, the studio's fortunes seemed certain to diminish.

Though the performances of movie studios often run in cycles, Paramount's comeback has been rapid, particularly since the studio had a mere 1.5 percent of the box office gross last February before the release of *Pretty in Pink*, its hit movie about teenagers. "Usually a company starts a calendar year with some momentum from Christmas," Mr. Murphy said. "Paramount had none."  DEC. 22

## Paramount's marquee

Films released in 1986 by Paramount. Box office gross in thousands.

| Opening | Title | Type | Box office gross as of 12/18* |
|---|---|---|---|
| Feb. 7 | Lady Jane | Drama | $ 278 |
| Feb. 28 | Pretty in Pink | Drama | 40,500 |
| March 7 | 16 Days of Glory | Documentary | 84 |
| March 14 | Gung Ho | Comedy | 36,571 |
| March 27 | April Fool's Day | Horror | 12,948 |
| May 2 | Blue City | Action | 6,948 |
| May 9 | Fire With Fire | Love story | 4,636 |
| May 16 | Top Gun | Action | 168,500 |
| June 11 | Ferris Bueller's Day Off | Comedy | 70,400 |
| July 25 | Heartburn | Comedy | 25,314 |
| Aug. 1 | Friday the 13th, Part 6 | Sequel | 19,472 |
| Aug. 15 | The Whoopee Boys | Comedy | 445 |
| Sept. 26 | Crocodile Dundee | Adventure | 103,300 |
| Oct. 3 | Children of a Lesser God | Drama | 20,600 |
| Nov. 26 | Star Trek 4 | Sequel | 48,500 |
| Dec. 12 | The Golden Child | Action | 15,500 |

*Studio normally keeps about 50 percent of this figure.
Source: Entertainment Data Inc.; Paramount Pictures Corp.

DEC. 22

# PART 5
# Finance and Markets

NYT/MARILYN K. YEE

## The most severe drops in the Dow-Jones average*

The ten largest point drops for the Dow Jones Industrials, calculated from the previous day's close.

| Date | Decline |
|---|---|
| Jan. 8, 1986 | −39.10 |
| Oct. 28, 1929 | −38.33 |
| Oct. 25, 1982 | −36.33 |
| May 28, 1962 | −34.95 |
| Sept. 26, 1955 | −31.89 |
| Oct. 29, 1929 | −30.57 |
| Nov. 26, 1973 | −29.05 |
| Nov. 19, 1973 | −28.67 |
| Jan. 9, 1974 | −26.99 |
| Nov. 6, 1929 | −25.55 |

*In percentage terms, the Jan. 8, 1986, fall was a decline of 2.5 percent, not nearly as deep as the 12.8 percent drop of Oct. 28, 1929.   Source: Dow Jones

JAN. 9

## Wall Street firms, publicly and privately owned

Leading privately held investment banking firms ranked by amount of capital, in millions of dollars as of December 1984.

| | |
|---|---|
| Goldman, Sachs | $859 |
| Drexel Burnham Lambert | 561 |
| Stephens Inc. | 320 |
| Kidder, Peabody | 243 |
| Smith Barney | 207 |
| Spear, Leeds & Kellogg | 205 |
| Allen & Co. | 150 |
| John Nuveen & Co. | 119 |
| Neuberger & Berman | 106 |
| Dillon, Read | 66 |
| Brown Brothers Harriman | 62 |
| Lazard Frères & Co. | 30 |

Leading investment banking firms that have been acquired or gone public since 1981.

| | |
|---|---|
| Prudential-Bache Securities* | March '81 |
| Shearson Lehman Brothers* | June '81 |
| Dean Witter Reynolds* | Dec. '81 |
| Salomon Brothers* | March '82 |
| Rooney, Pace Group** | Oct. '83 |
| Jefferies Group** | Oct. '83 |
| L. F. Rothschild† | Sept. '85 |
| Bear, Stearns** | Oct. '85 |
| Alex. Brown & Sons† | Jan. '86 |
| Morgan Stanley† | Jan. '86 |

*Acquired
**Went public
†Public offering proposed
Source: Lipper Analytical Securities Corp.

JAN. 27

# Skepticism on Bank Earnings

**By ERIC N. BERG**

Continuing a winning streak begun early last year, most of the nation's major banks reported higher earnings per share in the fourth quarter of 1985. But, in a widening debate, there was considerable disagreement over the quality of those earnings and the prospect of maintaining them.

Of the nation's 15 banks with the greatest assets, 11 reported gains in per-share income. They achieved this, moreover, at a time when many were making significant provisions for loan losses and when their non-interest expenses—outlays for such things as salaries and real estate—were soaring.

While all of this capped a year in which most banks' stocks and earnings rose steadily, some Wall Street analysts voiced skepticism.

They said the results were often artificially inflated by extraordinary items, such as the sale of real estate or a change in the method of funding pension obligations.

In addition, many analysts said that with tumbling oil prices and with many loan portfolios of questionable quality, there is little reason to look for major improvements in banks' fortunes in 1986.

"Most banks will show mediocre earnings results this year," said Mark Biderman, an analyst at Oppenheimer & Company. "The oil situation just reinforces my view that 1986 will be a tough year for the banks." JAN. 30

## A roundup of fourth-quarter bank results

1985 fourth-quarter results for the nation's 15 largest bank holding companies

| Return on assets (Annualized return on each $100 of average total assets*) | | Return on equity (Annualized return on each $100 of average common equity*) | | Leverage (Primary capital as a percentage of total average assets) | | Change in earnings (Percentage change in per share net income from 1984 period*) | |
|---|---|---|---|---|---|---|---|
| J. P. Morgan | $ 1.01 | J. P. Morgan | $ 16.65 | Continental Illinois | 12.13% | Chase | +35.90% |
| Bankers Trust | 0.76 | Bankers Trust | 16.01 | J. P. Morgan | 8.06% | Mellon Bank Corp | +26.40% |
| First Interstate | 0.71 | Security Pacific | 15.51 | Wells Fargo | 7.63% | Wells Fargo | +13.54% |
| First Bank System | 0.71 | First Bank System | 15.01 | Mellon | 7.39% | First Bank System | +12.59% |
| Security Pacific | 0.69 | Continental Illinois | 14.46 | First Chicago | 7.34% | Bankers Trust | +12.00% |
| Bank of Boston | 0.65 | Chemical | 14.36 | Chemical | 7.20% | First Interstate | +11.40% |
| Chemical | 0.63 | Chase | 14.35 | Security Pacific | 7.08% | Chemical | +10.34% |
| Wells Fargo | 0.63 | Wells Fargo | 14.13 | Chase Manhattan | 7.04% | Continental Illinois | +8.30% |
| Chase Manhattan | 0.61 | First Interstate | 13.88 | Bank of Boston | 7.00% | Manufacturers Hanover | +7.50% |
| Mellon Bank Corp. | 0.56 | Citibank | 13.80 | First Bank System | 6.81% | Security Pacific | +3.70% |
| First Chicago | 0.54 | Manufacturers Hanover | 13.03 | Bankers Trust | 6.66% | First Chicago | +1.00% |
| Citibank | 0.52 | Bank of Boston | 12.78 | Manufacturers Hanover | 6.41% | J. P. Morgan | +0.00 |
| Manufacturers Hanover | 0.49 | First Chicago | 11.96 | Citibank | 6.40% | Citibank | −11.00% |
| Continental Illinois | 0.40 | Mellon Bank Corp. | 10.40 | First Interstate | 6.37% | Bank of Boston | −46.00% |
| BankAmerica | −0.65 | BankAmerica | −19.22 | BankAmerica | 6.34% | BankAmerica | −† |

*Returns and change in earnings are based on net income applicable to common stockholders.
**Cannot be computed, loss in current quarter.
†Not applicable, loss in quarter.

JAN. 30

# Size Less a Gauge of Banks' Success

By ERIC N. BERG

For the second consecutive year, many of the nation's largest banks have reported no growth or have shown only meager increases in assets. The trend, according to banking experts, is clear: Running a highly profitable bank is what bankers are striving for most, and size alone is no longer a measure of success.

"Size is just not as important as it used to be," said William E. Gibson, chief economist for Republicbank Dallas.

At Citicorp, Thomas E. Jones, the chief accounting officer, said: "It is absolutely not our ambition to be the biggest bank. We just want to be the most profitable."

Notwithstanding Mr. Jones's comment, Citicorp grew rapidly in 1985, to $173.6 billion in assets from $150.6 billion, a 15.3 percent increase that permitted it to continue as the largest banking organization in America. The No. 2–ranked BankAmerica Corporation, which has been disposing of many bad loans, was far off in the distance, with $118.5 billion in assets.

Significantly, though, most of Citicorp's growth came from new consumer loans; business loans were flat. Of 23 other big banks surveyed, 16 showed single-digit growth or a decline in assets, while the remaining seven grew at double-digit rates.

Even the banks that expanded most rapidly in 1985 and climbed in rank, such as the Bank of Boston Corporation, the NCNB Corporation of Charlotte, N.C., and Suntrust Banks of Atlanta, achieved their growth through acquisition rather than through booking fresh loans.

FEB. 4

## The 25 largest U.S. banking companies
United States bank holding companies ranked by total assets on Dec. 31, 1985

| | Headquarters | Total '85 Assets (billions) | Total '84 Assets (billions) | Percent Change |
|---|---|---|---|---|
| Citicorp | New York | $173.6 | $150.6 | 15.3 |
| BankAmerica | San Francisco | 118.5 | 117.7 | 0.7 |
| Chase Manhattan | New York | 87.7 | 86.9 | 0.9 |
| Manufacturers Hanover | New York | 76.5 | 75.7 | 1.0 |
| J.P. Morgan & Company | New York | 69.4 | 64.1 | 8.3 |
| Chemical New York | New York | 57.0 | 52.2 | 9.2 |
| Security Pacific | Los Angeles | 53.6 | 46.1 | 16.3 |
| Bankers Trust | New York | 50.6 | 45.2 | 12.0 |
| First Interstate | Los Angeles | 49.0 | 45.5 | 7.7 |
| First Chicago | Chicago | 38.9 | 39.6 | −1.8 |
| Mellon Bank Corp. | Pittsburgh | 33.4 | 30.6 | 9.2 |
| Continental Illinois | Chicago | 30.5 | 30.4 | 0.3 |

| | Headquarters | Total '85 Assets (billions) | Total '84 Assets (billions) | Percent Change |
|---|---|---|---|---|
| Wells Fargo | San Francisco | 29.4 | 28.2 | 4.3 |
| Bank of Boston | Boston | 28.3 | 22.1 | 28.1 |
| First Bank System | Minneapolis | 25.5 | 22.4 | 13.8 |
| Marine Midland | Buffalo | 23.4 | 22.1 | 5.9 |
| Republicbank | Dallas | 23.2 | 21.6 | 7.4 |
| Mcorp | Dallas | 22.6 | 20.7 | 9.2 |
| Interfirst | Dallas | 22.1 | 21.6 | 2.3 |
| Irving Bank Corp. | New York | 21.7 | 19.0 | 14.2 |
| Norwest Corporation | Minneapolis | 21.4 | 21.3 | 0.5 |
| Texas Commerce | Houston | 20.1 | 20.7 | −2.9 |
| NCNB | Charlotte, N.C. | 19.8 | 15.7 | 26.1 |
| Suntrust Banks | Atlanta | 19.4 | 15.8 | 22.8 |
| Crocker National | San Francisco | 19.2 | 22.3 | −14.0 |

FEB. 4

# Midwest Bank Focus: Growth

**By STEVEN GREENHOUSE**

CHICAGO, Feb. 14—Despite their past troubles, the First Chicago Corporation and Continental Illinois still are considered the only banking giants of the Middle West capable of competing head to head with the likes of Citibank. As barriers to interstate banking tumble in Illinois and nearby states, however, several regional banks are expected to join the big leagues through mergers.

"We're interested in building our bank into a megaregional organization, and we think others will want to do likewise," said John F. Fisher, senior vice president at Banc One of Columbus, Ohio, which has more than $10 billion in assets. "In the 1990s," he added, "we'll see some megaregionals getting together to form banks that will be competitive with Citibank and Chase Manhattan."

Banc One is already moving aggressively to expand into neighboring states. It has bought, or agreed to buy, four Indiana banks, a Kentucky bank and a Michigan bank. And the Ameritrust Corporation of Cleveland has moved boldly as well, having agreed to acquire the First Indiana Bankcorp in Elkhart, with more than $700 million in assets.

Some bank officials and analysts say the Middle West's new interstate banking laws will lead to a wave of mergers that will create a few new $20-billion banks.

But not everyone thinks the merger phenomenon will mushroom throughout the region. With problems in the Farm Belt and Rust Belt continuing to drag down the region's economy, many bank experts do not expect the Middle West to experience the bank merger mania that has swept through the Southeast and Southwest.

"In the Midwest, everyone is likely to be much more cautious than in other regions," said Paul M. Homan, executive vice president of the Continental Illinois Corporation, which, with $30.5 billion in assets, is the region's second-largest bank holding company. "We're not as attractive a banking market. The economic potential for some of the states here is not as bright as Florida or Arizona."

FEB. 17

## Comparing large midwest banks
The 10 largest Middle West banks, ranked by assets, in billions of dollars

| | |
|---|---|
| First Chicago Bank, Chicago | $38.9 |
| Continental Illinois, Chicago | $35.3 |
| First Bank System, Minneapolis | $25.5 |
| Norwest, Minneapolis | $21.5 |
| NBD Bancorp, Detroit | $16.7 |
| National City Corp., Cleveland | $12.5 |
| Banc One Corp., Columbus, Ohio | $10.8 |
| Comerica, Detroit | $ 9.8 |
| Harris Trust Chicago | $ 9.2 |
| Society Corp. Cleveland | $ 8.7 |

Source: Keefe, Bruyette & Woods

FEB. 17

## Dow surges 43.10 to 1,746.05
Where March 11 fits in record book (Top five daily point gains of the Dow Jones industrial average)

**Nov. 3, 1982**     **43.41**
Midterm election results viewed as mandate to keep interest rates declining to foster growth.

**March 11, 1986**     **43.10**
Wall Street enthusiastic over falling interest rates, including cuts in discount and prime rates.

**Aug. 17, 1982**     **38.81**
Salomon Brothers economist, Henry Kaufman, predicts further substantial interest rate declines.

**Oct. 6, 1982**     **37.07**
Rally in credit markets raises expectations interest rates will continue to fall.

**Nov. 30, 1982**     **36.43**
Renewed interest by institutional investors contributes to upturn fueled by dropping interest rates.

**Top five daily volume marks on the New York Stock Exchange, in millions of shares**

| | |
|---|---|
| Aug. 3, 1984 | 236.57 |
| Aug. 6, 1984 | 203.05 |
| Jan. 29, 1986 | 198.81 |
| Feb. 28, 1986 | 191.70 |
| **March 11, 1986** | **187.27** |

Source: New York Stock Exchange

MARCH 12

## Top 10 volume sessions
Trades on the New York Stock Exchange, in millions of shares

| Volume | Date | Dow Industrials Close | Dow Industrials Change |
|---|---|---|---|
| 236.6 | Aug. 3, 1984 | 1,202.08 | +36.00 |
| 210.3 | March 12, 1986 | 1,745.45 | −0.60 |
| 203.1 | Aug. 6, 1984 | 1,202.96 | +0.88 |
| 193.8 | Jan. 29, 1986 | 1,558.94 | +2.52 |
| 191.7 | Feb. 28, 1986 | 1,709.06 | −4.93 |
| 187.3 | March 11, 1986 | 1,746.05 | +43.10 |
| 186.9 | Oct. 19, 1984 | 1,225.93 | +0.55 |
| 181.8 | Feb. 27, 1986 | 1,713.99 | +17.09 |
| 181.0 | Dec. 5, 1985 | 1,482.91 | −1.49 |
| 180.3 | Jan. 8, 1986 | 1,526.61 | −39.10 |

Source: New York Stock Exchange

MARCH 13

## A quickening pace
Length of time between historic closes of Dow Jones industrial average

| Mark Surpassed | Date | Close | Time Since Previous Mark* |
|---|---|---|---|
| 100 | Jan. 12, 1906 | 100.25 | —** |
| 200 | Dec. 19, 1927 | 200.93 | 21Y, 11M, 7D |
| 300 | Dec. 31, 1928 | 300.00 | 1Y, 12D† |
| 400 | Dec. 29, 1954 | 401.97 | 25Y, 11M, 29D |
| 500 | March 12, 1956 | 500.24 | 1Y, 2M, 14D |
| 600 | Feb. 20, 1959 | 602.21 | 2Y, 11M, 8D |
| 700 | May 17, 1965 | 705.25 | 2Y, 2M, 25D |
| 800 | Feb. 28, 1964 | 800.14 | 2Y, 9M, 11D |
| 900 | Jan. 28, 1965 | 900.95 | 11M |
| 1,000 | Nov. 14, 1972 | 1,003.16 | 7Y, 9M, 17D |
| 1,100 | Feb. 24, 1983 | 1,121.81 | 10Y, 3M, 10D |
| 1,200 | April 26, 1983 | 1,209.46 | 2M, 2D |
| 1,300 | May 20, 1985 | 1,304.88 | 2Y, 24D |
| 1,400 | Nov. 6, 1985 | 1,403.44 | 5M, 16D |
| 1,500 | Dec. 11, 1985 | 1,511.70 | 1M, 5D |
| 1,600 | Feb. 6, 1986 | 1,600.69 | 1M, 26D |
| 1,700 | Feb. 27, 1986 | 1,713.99 | 21D |
| 1,800 | March 20, 1986 | 1,804.24 | 21D |

*In years, months and days
**Dow first calculated as 20-stock industrial average on Jan. 2, 1897. Closed at 40.74.
†Dow first calculated as 30-stock industrial average on Oct. 1, 1928. Closed at 240.01.

Source: Purcell, Graham & Co.

MARCH 21

## How Dow stocks have fared in 500-point rally
Ranking of 30 Dow Jones industrial stocks by percentage change from time Dow average last closed below 1,300 to when it first closed above 1,800

| Company | Close on 9/20/85 | Close on 3/20/86 | Point Change | Percentage Change |
|---|---|---|---|---|
| Union Carbide* | 17⅝ | 32⅛ | +14½ | +82.3 |
| American Express | 41⅞ | 68¼ | +26⅜ | +63.0 |
| Philip Morris** | 76¼ | 123½ | +47¼ | +62.0 |
| McDonald's† | 63⅛ | 97½ | +34⅜ | +54.5 |
| Merck | 108 | 166 | +58 | +53.7 |
| Owens-Illinois | 46½ | 70½ | +24 | +51.6 |
| Woolworth | 48 | 72 | +24 | +50.0 |
| United Technologies | 37⅜ | 53¼ | +15⅞ | +42.5 |
| 3M | 74¾ | 106⅜ | +31⅝ | +42.3 |
| Sears, Roebuck | 33¾ | 47½ | +13¾ | +40.7 |
| **Dow Jones average** | **1,297.94** | **1,804.24** | **+506.3** | **+39.0** |
| American Can | 55 | 76¼ | +21¼ | +38.6 |
| Eastman Kodak | 43¼ | 59½ | +16¼ | +37.6 |

| Company | Close on 9/20/85 | Close on 3/20/86 | Point Change | Percentage Change |
|---|---|---|---|---|
| Westinghouse Electric | 38 | 51 | +13 | +34.2 |
| Procter & Gamble | 57 | 76¼ | +19¼ | +33.8 |
| Du Pont | 56½ | 75¼ | +18¾ | +33.2 |
| General Electric | 58⅞ | 78⅜ | +19½ | +33.1 |
| Bethlehem Steel | 16¼ | 21⅜ | +5⅛ | +31.5 |
| Alcoa | 33¼ | 42¾ | +9½ | +28.6 |
| International Paper | 47¾ | 61⅛ | +13⅜ | +28.0 |
| General Motors | 67½ | 86 | +18½ | +27.4 |
| Inco | 13⅛ | 16½ | +3⅜ | +25.7 |
| Goodyear | 28 | 34⅝ | +6⅝ | +23.7 |
| Allied-Signal | 43⅜ | 52⅝ | +9¼ | +21.3 |
| I.B.M. | 126¾ | 150⅛ | +23⅜ | +18.4 |
| Navistar†† | 7¾ | 8¾ | +1 | +12.9 |
| Exxon | 49¾ | 55⅝ | +5⅞ | +11.8 |
| A.T.&T. | 21½ | 23 | +1½ | +7.0 |
| Chevron | 36¾ | 38 | +1¼ | +3.4 |
| Texaco | 35¼ | 29½ | −5¾ | −16.3 |
| U.S. Steel | 30¼ | 23⅝ | −6⅝ | −21.9 |

*Prices reflect a three-for-one split plus value of a right representing certain proceeds from planned sale of Carbide's consumer businesses.
**Replaced General Foods in Dow listing on Oct. 30, 1985
†Replaced American Brands in Dow listing on Oct. 30, 1985
††Traded as International Harvester before Feb. 20, 1986

MARCH 27

# Market and the Dow in Step

### By VARTANIG G. VARTAN

Since 1896, the Dow Jones industrial average has meant the stock market to most Americans, though professionals quibble that, in fact, it is a flawed gauge of market activity.

But in the bull market of the past six months, when the Dow gained a record 500 points, the market as a whole has followed right along.

The granddaddy of market averages, the Dow originally contained just 12 issues, including such now-forgotten names as the Distilling and Cattle Feeding Company.

Its current roster of 30 issues is dominated by big-name, old-line companies. For that reason, some critics say it is inherently flawed.

Nonetheless, "the Dow still means 'the market' to most investors, and money managers also keep harking back to it," said Raymond F. DeVoe, Jr., strategist for Legg Mason

Wood Walker Inc. "A key reason is its historical continuity. A lot of people remember when it first approached 1,000 in February 1966."

Last Thursday, the Dow Jones industrial average closed above 1,800 for the first time—at 1,804.24—capping a gain of 506.30 points, or 39 percent, since Sept. 20, the biggest six-month point advance in its history. Yesterday it closed at another record high, 1,810.70, up 32.20.

Up nearly 30 percent during the same six-month period were two broader measures of the market: the New York Stock Exchange's index of common stocks and Standard & Poor's 500-stock index.          MARCH 27

## Stocks' Rate-Propelled Surge

**By ERIC SCHMITT**

The sharp decline in interest rates sent the nation's stock markets soaring in the first quarter, producing the biggest percentage gain for the Dow Jones industrial average in more than a decade.

Conversely, sinking oil prices hobbled the stocks of oil and natural gas producers as well as oilfield service companies and equipment makers. For example, 9 of the 10 poorest performing stocks on the New York Stock Exchange in the quarter ended Monday were related to the beleaguered oil patch.

Of the 6,231 stocks tracked by Media General Financial Services, based in Richmond, 4,324 were up for the quarter, 1,580 were down and 327 were unchanged.

Plunging interest rates spurred the Dow to gain more than 270 points during the quarter. The average closed Monday at 1,818.61, up 17.6 percent from 1,546.67 at the beginning of the quarter, the biggest quarterly percentage gain since the first quarter of 1975.

The American Stock Exchange market-value index closed on Monday at 270.03, up 9.7 percent from 246.13 three months ago. The Nasdaq composite index of over-the-counter issues rose 15.3 percent during the quarter, to 374.72, from 324.93.

"The winners were clearly interest-sensitive companies," said Steven G. Einhorn, cochairman of the investment policy committee at Goldman, Sachs & Company.

He cited home builders, building material companies and manufacturers of mobile homes as among the "stellar performers." Lower mortgage rates have set off a boom in the housing market in recent months.

Mr. Einhorn also said that, while the sharp drop in oil prices spelled disaster for the stocks of oil producers, drillers and banks with large energy portfolios, many other companies benefited. Trucking companies and airlines, for instance, paid lower fuel bills and thus became more attractive issues.

Analysts said that the first-quarter performance was a continuation of the bullish pace of the fourth quarter of 1985.

"The basic fundamental that's driven the market is still in place," said John D. Connolly, investment strategist for Dean Witter Reynolds. "Rates are still going down, and as long as rates go down, bond prices go up and stock prices go up."          APRIL 2

## First-quarter gainers and losers on the O-T-C

Over-the-counter common stocks that showed the largest percentage gains and declines in 1986. Prices are adjusted for any splits, and listings include no stocks trading for less than $2 a share or fewer than 1,000 shares.

| Stock | March 31 Close | First Quarter Pct. Change | Comment |
| --- | --- | --- | --- |
| **Gainers** | | | |
| Vistar Film | 4 3/16 | +509.1 | Movie maker/distributor increases revenues. |
| Annandale Corp. | 2 5/8 | +500.0 | Financial consultant invests in successful undervalued companies. |
| Digitech | 3 3/8 | +414.3 | Communications equipment maker signs contract with Southwestern Bell. |
| Western Allenbee | 4 7/16 | +373.3 | Oil company joins Dutch concern in gold mining venture. |
| Chancellor Computer | 3 | +336.4 | Computer designer expands sales force. |
| Vega Biotch | 5 1/4 | +320.0 | Company announces joint agreement with Du Pont. |
| Hybridoma | 2 7/8 | +318.2 | Biotech company's long-range acquisition plan attracts investors. |
| Western World TV | 2 7/8 | +283.3 | TV production company to coproduce cartoons of the Incredible Hulk. |
| Cable Adv. | 2 3/16 | +275.0 | Cable TV ad broker acquires advertising sales companies. |
| Fertil-a-chron | 2 11/32 | +275.0 | Electronic fertility analyzer attracts biotech investors. |
| **Losers** | | | |
| Daisy Systems | 11 1/2 | −61.0 | Computer maker announces unexpected loss. |
| Bioassay | 2 1/2 | −60.8 | Reversal in biotech company's earnings projections. |
| Firstsouth | 11 1/2 | −57.4 | Arkansas bank posts a loss because of real estate lending. |
| Celina Fin. A | 2 | −55.6 | Life insurance company expects to take $14 million charge against earnings. |
| Orfa Corp. | 2 5/8 | −54.3 | Shareholders file suit against waste treatment company. |
| Neti Tech. | 3 7/8 | −49.2 | Canadian manufacturer |
| E. Hines Lumber | 11 1/2 | −48.9 | Company undergoes liquidation process. |
| Alaska Nat'l. Bank | 7 | −48.1 | Fairbanks bank posts loss. |
| BancOklahoma | 9 | −47.1 | Oklahoma bank posts loss from energy-related loans, cuts dividends. |
| North Atlantic Tech | 2 | −46.7 | Heat systems company hurt by lower energy prices. |

## First-quarter gainers and losers on the Amex

Amex-listed common stocks that showed the largest percentage gains and declines in 1986. Prices are adjusted for any splits, and listings include no stocks trading for less $2 a share or fewer than 1,000 shares.

| Stock | March 31 Close | First Quarter Pct. Change | Comment |
|---|---|---|---|
| **Gainers** | | | |
| Heritage Entertainment | 9½ | +261.9 | Distributor of Soviet films benefits from Reagan-Gorbachev meeting in 1985. |
| San Carlos Milling | 3¼ | +225.0 | Sugar cane miller attracts American investors after Marcos falls. |
| Oppenheimer Industries | 15½ | +188.4 | Ranchland developer has no explanation for stock runup. |
| Philippine Long D. Tel. | 5 | +166.7 | American investors flock to phone company after Aquino takes control. |
| Seligman Assoc. | 14½ | +152.2 | Home builder posts strong sales and earnings increases. |
| Hovnanian Enterpr.s | 26½ | +136.9 | Apartment builder announces 3-for-2 stock split. |
| Aloha | 24 | +118.2 | Airline holding company target of leveraged buyout from management. |
| Washington Homes | 20⅝ | +113.6 | Home builder announces 3-for-2 stock split. |
| Superior Care | 2⅛ | +112.5 | Supplier of home health-care services improves earnings. |
| Key Co. A | 6½ | +108.0 | Home builder profits from declining interest. |
| **Losers** | | | |
| NRM Energy | 4¼ | −65.3 | Energy company cuts quarterly dividend and posts loss. |
| Convest Energy | 4½ | −60.4 | Oil partnership's quarterly payments may be suspended. |
| American Royalty | 5 | −59.2 | Oil patch–related trust battered by energy slump. |
| Damson Energy A | 3⅛ | −55.4 | Oil, natural gas partnership cuts cash distribution. |
| Graham-McCormick | 2½ | −54.5 | Energy downturn hampers growth for oil properties manager. |
| Damson Energy B | 3¼ | −51.9 | Oil, natural gas partnership cuts cash distribution. |
| Saxon Oil Dev. | 3⅞ | −50.0 | Oil driller hurt by industry slide. |
| Energy Devel. | 6⅝ | −49.0 | Oil, natural gas producer is buffeted. |
| Summit Energy | 2¾ | −47.6 | Oil and natural gas exploration company. |
| Tex Amer. Energy | 2⅝ | −44.7 | Another troubled energy company. |

APRIL 2

## First-quarter gainers and losers on the N.Y.S.E.

N.Y.S.E.-listed common stocks that showed the largest percentage gains and declines in 1986. Prices are adjusted for any splits, and listings include no stocks, trading for less $2 a share or fewer than 1,000 shares.

| Stock | March 31 Close | First Quarter Pct. Change | Comment |
|---|---|---|---|
| **Gainers** | | | |
| L. E. Myers Grp. | 7⅞ | +231.6 | Bank lenders agree to restructuring of electrical systems supplier. |
| Marantz | 10½ | +200.0 | Stereo systems maker reports sharply higher sales in February. |
| Storage Technology | 4⅛ | +135.7 | Computer systems supplier cuts costs. |
| Banco Central SA | 21⅞ | +108.3 | Spain's largest bank benefits from weakened dollar. |
| Service Resources Corp. | 9¼ | +100.0 | Financial printer benefits from Wall Street activity. |
| General Homes Corp. | 11 | +87.2 | Houston-based home builder approves a merger. |
| MDC Holdings | 22 | +87.2 | Investor group acquires 17.5% of home builder. |
| Consumers Power | 13⅞ | +85.0 | Utility to convert nuclear power plant to natural gas. |
| Allied Products | 42⅝ | +80.4 | Machinery manufacturer has earnings turnaround. |
| Chicago Pn'matic Tool | 36½ | +80.2 | Air-powered tool maker subject of takeover bid by Danaher Corp. |
| **Losers** | | | |
| Smith International | 2¼ | −66.7 | Slump in oil prices sends oil drilling tool maker into Chapter 11. |
| Reading & Bates | 2⅜ | −51.3 | Offshore oil drilling company battered by cuts in exploration dollars. |
| Gearhart Industries | 3¾ | −50.8 | Energy downturn affects oilfield services company. |
| Entex Energy | 5½ | −50.6 | Houston-based natural gas utility. |
| Zapata Corp. | 4 | −47.5 | Sales fall for oil drilling equipment company. |
| First City Bancorp Texas | 6⅞ | −46.6 | Heavy portfolio of energy loans. |
| Texas Int'l. | 3⅛ | −45.7 | Oilfield services company hurt by price slide. |
| Kaneb Services | 3⅞ | −45.6 | Oil and natural gas producer. |
| Inexco Oil | 3⅛ | −44.4 | Oil and natural gas producer. |
| LAC Minerals Ltd. | 14⅝ | −43.8 | Canadian metals producer in court dispute over ownership of gold mine. |

APRIL 2

## How Mutual Funds Performed in First Quarter

Funds showing largest percentage gains and declines in net asset value from previous quarter, with income dividends and capital gains distributions reinvested

### Gainers

| | |
|---|---|
| Benham Target 2010 | +54.20 % |
| Fidelity Destiny II | +44.27 |
| Benham Target 2005 | +43.78 |
| First Investors U.S. Government Plus I | +41.58 |
| Fidelity Overseas | +38.52 |
| Strong Opportunity | +36.20 |
| Fidelity Select Savings and Loan | +33.37 |
| Zenith Fund Capital Growth | +32.74 |
| Benham Target 2000 | +31.28 |
| Rochester Growth Fund | +30.56 |

### Losers

| | |
|---|---|
| Strategic Capital Gains | −13.58 % |
| Fidelity Select Energy Services | −12.01 |
| First Investors Natural Resources | −10.86 |
| Fidelity Select Energy | −9.42 |
| Vanguard Special Energy | −8.07 |
| Financial Portfolio Energy | −8.05 |
| Putnam Energy Resources | −5.75 |
| Continental Option Income Plus | −4.73 |
| Strategic Silver | −4.48 |
| Venture Income Plus | −1.92 |

Source: Lipper Analytical Services

APRIL 4

# Bonds Spur Banking Profits

By ERIC N. BERG

Major commercial banks are clearly committed to becoming powerful contenders in the world of investment banking. Now that first-quarter results are out, the banks have shown just how tantalizing the business of Wall Street can be.

Of the 15 largest commercial banks, ranked by assets, 10 reported double-digit increases in per-share earnings for the quarter ended March 31. The average increase of all 15 was 14.1 percent, well above what many industrial corporations are reporting.

Of the 10 banks that showed higher earnings, the great bulk could be attributed to their capital gains on government bond portfolios, bond-trading income, commissions on foreign-exchange dealings and fees for giving financial advice. While banks have been pushing into these areas for years, their efforts have gained enormous momentum in recent months, as profitability in their traditional lending markets has dwindled.

The five banks whose results lagged had flat or lower earnings, reflecting poorly positioned investment portfolios, or serious loan problems.

Loan growth continued flat in the first quarter, profitability in big-time corporate lending remained dismal and loan losses rose sharply. As a result, analysts believe there is no end in sight to big banks' exodus from traditional lending and into investment banking. Only smaller banks around the country continue to focus heavily on lending.

"Basically, the multinational banks benefited from what I would describe as merchant banking businesses," said James G. Ehlen, Jr., a Goldman, Sachs & Company analyst.

MAY 1

# A roundup of first-quarter bank results

1986 first-quarter results for the nation's 15 largest bank holding companies.

| Return on assets (Annualized return on each $100 of average total assets.*) | | Return on equity (Annualized return on each $100 of average common equity.*) | | Leverage (Primary capital as a percentage of total average assets.) | | Change in earnings (Percentage change in per share net income from 1985 period.*) | |
|---|---|---|---|---|---|---|---|
| J. P. Morgan | $1.33 | J. P. Morgan | $22.08 | Wells Fargo | 8.96% | First Chicago | +55.9% |
| Bankers Trust | 0.89 | Bankers Trust | 18.90 | J. P. Morgan | 8.23% | Mellon Bank Corp. | +45.9% |
| Bank of Boston | 0.77 | Continental Illinois | 15.96 | Continental Illinois | 7.98% | J. P. Morgan | +42.1% |
| First Bank System | 0.75 | First Bank System | 15.80 | First Chicago | 7.67% | First Bank System | +25.2% |
| Mellon Bank Corp. | 0.71 | Bank of Boston | 15.29 | First Bank System | 7.40% | Bankers Trust | +20.0% |
| Security Pacific | 0.70 | Chemical | 15.19 | Mellon Bank Corp. | 7.11% | Wells Fargo | +15.4% |
| Wells Fargo | 0.68 | Citibank | 15.17 | Security Pacific | 7.10% | Chemical | +14.9% |
| Chase Manhattan | 0.67 | Security Pacific | 14.90 | Chemical | 7.07% | Bank of Boston | +12.0% |
| Chemical | 0.66 | Wells Fargo | 14.19 | Chase Manhattan | 7.00% | Chase Manhattan | +12.0% |
| First Interstate | 0.65 | Mellon Bank Corp. | 14.10 | Bank of Boston | 6.90% | Security Pacific | +11.0% |
| First Chicago | 0.60 | Chase Manhattan | 13.50 | Manufacturers Hanover | 6.68% | First Interstate | +8.9% |
| Citibank | 0.57 | First Interstate | 12.87 | First Interstate | 6.52% | Manufacturers Hanover | +6.5% |
| Manufacturers Hanover | 0.47 | First Chicago | 12.65 | Bankers Trust | 6.51% | Continental Illinois | 0.0% |
| Continental Illinois | 0.42 | Manufacturers Hanover | 12.19 | Citibank | 6.37% | Citibank | −7.0% |
| BankAmerica | 0.22 | BankAmerica | 4.92 | BankAmerica | 6.34% | BankAmerica | −50.8% |

*Returns and change in earnings are based on net income applicable to common stockholders.

MAY 1

## The changing capital position of top securities firms

Comparison of the 15 largest firms by capital at the end of 1979 and 1985, in millions of dollars.

| 1979 | | 1985 | |
|---|---|---|---|
| 1. Merrill Lynch & Company | $784.2 | 1. Merrill Lynch & Company | $2,646.9 |
| 2. Shearson Loeb Rhoades | 246.3 | 2. Salomon Brothers | 2,320.1 |
| 3. Paine Webber | 243.2 | 3. Shearson Lehman Brothers | 2,251.0 |
| 4. E. F. Hutton Group | 238.0 | 4. Dean Witter Financial Services | 1,365.3 |
| 5. Salomon Brothers | 228.7 | 5. Prudential-Bache Securities | 1,259.3 |
| 6. Dean Witter Reynolds | 186.1 | 6. Goldman, Sachs & Company* | 1,201.0 |
| 7. Goldman, Sachs & Company | 181.0 | 7. E. F. Hutton & Company | 1,143.4 |
| 8. Bache Halsey Stuart Shields | 178.7 | 8. First Boston | 1,042.3 |
| 9. Stephens Inc. | 145.1 | 9. Drexel Burnham Lambert Group | 949.3 |
| 10. First Boston | 127.2 | 10. Bear, Stearns & Company** | 811.0 |
| 11. Morgan Stanley & Company | 107.5 | 11. Paine Webber Group | 804.7 |
| 12. Drexel Burnham Lambert Group | 104.4 | 12. Donaldson, Lufkin & Jenrette | 479.0 |
| 13. Lehman Brothers Kuhn Loeb | 103.8 | 13. Van Kampen Merritt | 471.5 |
| 14. A. G. Becker-Warburg Paribas Becker | 100.5 | 14. Morgan Stanley & Company | 454.6 |
| 15. Kidder, Peabody & Company | 92.4 | 15. Kidder, Peabody & Co. | 391.9 |

*As of Nov. 30, 1985
**As of Jan. 31, 1986

Source: Securities Industry Association

MAY 5

## Trading cited by S.E.C.

Ten most profitable securities transactions that the Securities and Exchange Commission alleges were executed illegally by Dennis B. Levine.*

| Stock | Deal and Date Announced | Shares Purchased and Date** | Profit |
|---|---|---|---|
| Nabisco Brands | Merger talks with R. J. Reynolds, 5/30/85 | 150,000 5/6/85 | $2,694,421 |
| American Natural Resources Co. | Tender offer by Coastal Corp., 3/1/85 | 145,500 2/14/85 | 1,371,057 |
| Jewel Companies | Tender offer by American Stores Co., 6/1/84 | 75,000 3/22/84 | 1,206,275 |
| Houston Natural Gas | Merger offer by Internorth, 5/2/85 | 74,800 4/30/85 | 907,655 |
| McGraw Edison Co. | Leveraged buyout, 3/22/85 | 79,500 3/14/85 | 906,836 |
| Itek Corp. | Tender offer by Litton Industries, 1/17/83 | 50,000 11/12/82 | 805,035 |
| G. D. Searle & Co. | Searle family to sell stake, 9/28/84 | 60,000<br>278 call options 8/27/84 | 613,503<br>221,240 |

| Stock | Deal and Date Announced | Shares Purchased and Date** | Profit |
|---|---|---|---|
| RCA Corp. | Hertz Corp. unit sold, 9/23/83; CIT Financial to be sold, 9/26/83 | 25,000<br>800 call options 9/20/83 | 88,173<br>277,469 |
| Carter Hawley Hale Stores | Tender offer by the Limited, 4/2/84 | 34,000 3/22/84 | 222,148 |
| Criton Corp. | Tender offer by Dyson-Kissner-Moran Corp., 8/24/82 | 27,000 8/17/82 | 212,628 |

*Dates and profit figures are approximate.
**Common stock, unless otherwise indicated. Date represents date of first purchase.
Source: Complaint filed in U.S. District Court, Southern District of New York, by Securities and Exchange Commission against Dennis B. Levine.

# Salomon Brothers Still No. 1 Underwriter

In what was by far a record half for the issue of corporate securities, several Wall Street firms took the booming flow as an opportunity to leapfrog ahead in the closely watched rankings of underwriters.

Salomon Brothers clung to the top spot, with $28.7 billion of underwritings in the half, according to the Securities Data Company. An increased share of that total was accounted for by equity, rather than debt securities, the firm's traditional strength. And First Boston stayed in second, with $19.8 billion, according to the Securities Data figures.

But Drexel Burnham Lambert, which is slowly expanding beyond its stronghold in the low-grade, or "junk," bonds realm, leaped from fifth in 1985 to third in the first half, with $17.3 billion in underwritings. It was followed by Morgan Stanley & Company, which scooted up from sixth to fourth.   JULY 1

## Leading underwriters in the first half of 1986

Managing underwriters, ranked by dollar amount raised on new issues of taxable securities sold in the U.S. and worldwide, for the six months ended June 1986, with full credit given to lead manager.

**U.S.**

| | Amount underwritten ($ millions) | Issues managed |
|---|---|---|
| Salomon Brothers | 28,725 | 245 |
| First Boston | 19,825 | 235 |
| Drexel Burnham Lambert | 17,327 | 127 |
| Morgan Stanley | 15,736 | 136 |
| Goldman, Sachs | 14,930 | 138 |
| Merrill Lynch Capital Markets | 13,460 | 150 |
| Shearson Lehman Brothers | 7,311 | 109 |
| Kidder Peabody | 3,998 | 77 |
| Prudential-Bache | 2,268 | 27 |
| Paine Webber | 2,130 | 61 |

**Worldwide**

|  | Amount underwritten ($ millions) | Issues managed |
|---|---|---|
| Salomon Brothers | 33,264 | 277 |
| First Boston | 27,700 | 290 |
| Morgan Stanley | 19,189 | 170 |
| Drexel Burnham Lambert | 17,650 | 131 |
| Goldman, Sachs | 16,847 | 152 |
| Merrill Lynch Capital Markets | 16,758 | 175 |
| Shearson Lehman Brothers | 8,770 | 120 |
| Nomura Securities | 8,206 | 70 |
| Deutsche Bank | 7,581 | 48 |
| Daiwa Securities | 4,965 | 51 |

Source: Securities Data Company

JULY 1

# Stock Tally: A Familiar Look

**By ERIC SCHMITT**

Makers of a wide array of consumer goods—ranging from egg cartons to aspirins to shoes—and a new crop of merchandisers who rely on cable television to sell discounted products sparked the stock markets during the second quarter.

The roster of winners and losers between April 1 and June 30 had a familiar look. As in the previous two quarters, specialty retailers, apparel manufacturers, food companies and interest-sensitive issues bulled ahead. Energy concerns, computer makers and capital goods companies, except chemical and paper concerns, foundered.

Takeover stocks, however, were not nearly as evident among the top gainers as they were a year ago. Nor were there any rockets lit under the stocks of companies in sectors, such as technology and capital goods businesses, that would have flourished if the economy had grown as many analysts had predicted.

The boom in the consumer goods stocks, which are generally resistant to fluctuations in the economy, reinforced the belief that the economy had failed to catch fire. It also indicated that many investors were skeptical that important cyclical issues would turn the corner soon, analysts said.

Of the 6,240 stocks tracked by Media General Financial Services, based in Richmond, 3,313 were up for the quarter, 2,563 were down and 364 were unchanged.

Lower interest rates, while not fueling a meteoric rise in the Dow Jones industrial average as took place in the first quarter, helped the average advance more than 70 points during the quarter to close at a record high. The average briefly pierced the 1,900 barrier before closing Monday at 1,892.72, up 4.1 percent from 1,818.61 at the beginning of the quarter.

The American Stock Exchange market-value index closed Monday at 284.20, up 5.2 percent from 270.03 three months ago. The Nasdaq composite index of over-the-counter issues rose 8.2 percent, to a record 405.51, from 374.72.

Despite the growing investor interest in Nasdaq issues, whose six-month volume exceeded the 1985 level by 53 percent, analysts were generally disappointed in the markets' performances.

JULY 2

## Second-quarter gainers and losers on the N.Y.S.E.

N.Y.S.E.-listed common stocks that showed the largest percentage gains and declines in the second quarter of 1986. Prices are adjusted for any splits, and listings include no stocks trading for less $2 a share or fewer than 1,000 shares.

### Gainers

| Stock | June 30 close | 2nd-quarter pct. change | Comment |
|---|---|---|---|
| Amfesco Industries | 4⅛ | +153.8 | Footwear company in Chapter 11 cuts losses. |
| LLC Corporation | 4⅛ | +120.0 | Consumer products company to merge with Amalgamated Sugar. |
| Wayne-Gossard Corporation | 25 | +100.0 | Apparel company posts earnings turnaround from 1985. |
| Mobile Home Industries | 2⅜ | +90.0 | Mobile home maker emerges from Chapter 11, acquiring Opic Corp. |
| Gap Inc. | 87⅞ | +78.0 | Apparel company raises dividend, sells assets in pottery subsidiary. |
| Ponderosa Inc. | 25⅛ | +73.3 | Steakhouse chain posts seven-fold earnings increase. |
| Merabank Federal Savings Bank | 47⅝ | +65.3 | Arizona bank acquired by state's largest public utility. |
| Smith International Inc. | 3⅝ | +61.1 | Drilling company consolidates operations in filing for bankruptcy. |
| Craig Corporation | 17 | +60.0 | Photographic products company increases earnings. |
| Unifirst Corporation | 30¾ | +59.7 | Garment rental company buys Bishop Uniform Service. |

### Losers

| Stock | June 30 close | 2nd-quarter pct. change | Comment |
|---|---|---|---|
| Manville Corporation | 2¾ | −66.2 | Reorganization plan dilutes common stock. |
| Ideal Basic Industries | 2¼ | −53.8 | Cement maker sued by shareholders. |
| Financial Corporation of America | 8¾ | −48.5 | Thrift unit holding company fails to meet financial goals. |
| L.E. Myers Company | 4⅛ | −47.6 | Construction company's sales drop in 2nd quarter. |
| Mesabi Trust | 3½ | −46.2 | Iron ore company trust hobbled by slack demand from steel industry. |
| Sunshine Mining Company | 2⅞ | −43.9 | Declining silver and crude oil prices depress earnings. |
| Arrow Electronics Inc. | 9¼ | −43.1 | Components maker posts loss in first quarter. |
| LTV Corporation | 5⅛ | −42.3 | Steel maker faces huge losses because of downturn in industry. |
| Southeastern Public Service Company | 4⅛ | −42.1 | Victor Posner–controlled utility hurt by textile subsidiary. |

| | Losers | | |
|---|---|---|---|
| Gearhart Industries | 2¼ | −40.0 | Uncertainty over debt restructuring hurts stock of oil field services company. |

## Second quarter gainers and losers on the Amex

Amex-listed common stocks that showed the largest percentage gains and declines in the second quarter of 1986. Prices are adjusted for any splits, and listings include no stocks trading for less $2 a share or fewer than 1,000 shares.

| | | Gainers | |
|---|---|---|---|
| Stock | June 30 close | 2nd-quarter pct. change | Comment |
| Resorts International (class B) | 142½ | +165.1 | Death of casino operator's chairman opens potential for company buyout. |
| C. H. Masland & Company | 72½ | +123.1 | Carpet maker acquired by Burlington Industries. |
| Hinderliter Industries | 4½ | +100.0 | Oil field equipment company resumes preferred dividend. |
| Lee Pharmaceuticals | 30 | +96.7 | Nail care company improves earnings for second quarter. |
| International Banknote Company | 9¾ | +90.2 | Financial printer's hologram business booms. |
| Tempo Enterprises Inc. | 18¾ | +87.5 | Cable TV operator benefits from home shopping network. |
| Olla Industries | 71⅝ | +80.8 | Handbag maker switches to reinsurance business. |
| Bush Industries | 21⅛ | +79.8 | Electronics maker forecasts 2nd quarter earnings change. |
| Shopwell Inc. | 31 | +71.0 | A & P acquires Bronx-based supermarket chain. |
| Graphic Technology Inc. | 16⅝ | +68.4 | Maker of bar code shelf labels shows sales increases. |
| | | Losers | |
| ADI Electronics Inc. | 2½ | −53.5 | Components maker fails to find merger partner. |
| Inflight Services | 2⅞ | −51.5 | Airlines' film supplier posts writedown in 1st quarter |
| Winn Enterprises | 2⅜ | −45.7 | Dairy considers sale of some or all of its operations. |
| Helionetics Inc. | 2 | −38.5 | Electronic power equipment maker defaults on promissory note. |
| Ducommun Inc. | 20⅞ | −38.1 | Weak sales in semiconductor industry hurt electronic parts distributor. |
| CMI Corporation | 5⅛ | −37.9 | Institutional investors sell large holdings in construction equipment company. |
| Consolidated Oil and Gas | 2⅛ | −37.0 | Company may default on $1.3 million in debenture interest payments. |
| Damson Energy | 2 | −36.0 | Energy company's earnings hurt by drop in price of oil and natural gas. |

## Second-quarter O-T-C gainers and losers

O.T.C.-listed common stocks that showed the largest percentage gains and declines in the second quarter of 1986. Prices are adjusted for any splits, and listings include no stocks trading for less $2 a share or fewer than 1,000 shares.

### Gainers

| Stock | June 30 close | 2nd-quarter pct. change | Comment |
|---|---|---|---|
| Avery Inc. | 5⅝ | +400.0 | Coal holding company acquires Uniroyal's chemical business. |
| Interleukin-2 Inc. | 7⁵⁄₃₂ | +377.1 | Biomedical company researches cure for AIDS. |
| C.O.M.B. Company | 34 | +272.6 | Stock of video shopping company caught in industry's growth. |
| Radyne Corporation | 3⅝ | +262.5 | Satellite modem maker streamlines operations. |
| Olson Industries | 36 | +227.3 | Egg and hamburger carton maker posts record earnings in first quarter. |
| Toth Aluminum Corporation | 4¼ | +195.7 | Company introduces cheaper way to make aluminum byproducts. |
| Pharmacontrol Corporation | 18 | +182.4 | Liquid aspirin maker benefits from poisoned capsule scare. |
| Mills-Jennings Company | 10 | +158.1 | Slot machine maker has 2-for-1 stock split. |
| Stuart McGuire Company | 4½ | +157.1 | Mail-order business signs new contracts with large retailers. |
| Financial Benefit Group (class B) | 7 | +146.2 | Insurance holding company places 1.2 million shares in private offering. |

### Losers

| Stock | June 30 close | 2nd-quarter pct. change | Comment |
|---|---|---|---|
| Advanced Tobacco Products | 2¾ | −67.6 | Investors sell large holdings in smokeless tobacco company. |
| Westworld Community Healthcare | 4⅝ | −67.3 | Tighter Medicare payment policies squeeze company's earnings. |
| Spectran Corporation | 5¼ | −61.8 | Optic fiber maker's sales plunge in glutted market. |
| Silver Hart Mines | 3½ | −61.1 | Investors selling large blocks of Edmonton mining company's stock. |
| Endo Lase Inc. | 2⅞ | −56.6 | Investor seeks to oust executives of medical products concern. |
| Telecrafter Corporation | 4⅜ | −53.9 | Cable TV company reduces stake in information network. |
| Steiger Tractor Inc. | 2⅜ | −53.7 | Tractor company files for bankruptcy. |
| Machine Vision International | 2 | −52.9 | Robotics company projects 2nd quarter loss of more than $2.4 million. |
| Laser Photonics Inc. | 2⅛ | −50.0 | Industrial laser company fails to meet profit projections. |
| Jack Henry & Associates | 3⅝ | −50.0 | Earnings for new computer software company plunged. |

JULY 2

# Marketplace: How the Funds Did in Quarter

**By VARTANIG G. VARTAN**

The nation's two top-performing mutual funds in the second quarter had one thing in common: They rode to stardom chiefly on the soaring price of Home Shopping Network Inc., the "hottest" new issue of this year. Home Shopping, a cable television retailer, went public on May 13 at $18 a share and closed on June 30 at $95.375 on the American Stock Exchange.

"Home Shopping was the dramatic event for us," acknowledged G. Kenneth Heebner, portfolio manager of Zenith Fund–Capital Growth, a Boston-based fund that posted a total return of 38.28 percent for the latest three months. "That stock is 20 percent of our portfolio."

In Milwaukee, Richard Strong, co-portfolio manager of the Strong Opportunity Fund, said Home Shopping "represents our biggest position and our best winner." His fund, which began operations on Jan. 1, scored a total return of 31.79 percent for the second quarter.

A survey of 526 equity mutual funds by Lipper Analytical Services showed an average return—market appreciation plus reinvested dividends—of 5.15 percent. This compared with a 5.89 percent gain for Standard & Poor's 500-stock index.

In more specialized categories—Lipper monitors 1,008 funds of all types—the health care group turned in the top performance, with a return of 13.55 percent. This reflected the buoyant action of biotechnology issues. International funds that invest only in foreign stocks ranked second among the sectors, with a return of 8.78 percent. The falling value of the dollar against foreign currencies continued to help these funds.

Gold-oriented funds—down 8.03 percent on average—constituted the only sector that showed a negative return during the quarter.

The poorest performers were two funds investing almost exclusively in South African gold stocks. The Strategic Investments Fund fell 20.82 percent, while United Services Gold Shares dipped 18.83 percent. For all of last year, the same funds also ranked as the worst

## How mutual funds performed in second quarter

Funds showing largest percentage gains and declines in net asset value from previous quarter, with income dividends and capital gains distributions reinvested.

**Gainers**

| | |
|---|---|
| Zenith Fund–Capital Growth | +38.28% |
| Strong Opportunity | +31.79 |
| Baird Capital Development | +23.73 |
| Investors Research | +23.16 |
| Bull & Bear Special Equity | +22.05 |
| Twentieth Century Vista | +20.94 |
| Twentieth Century Gift | +18.62 |
| Equitec Siebel Aggressive | +18.61 |
| Pacific Horizon Aggressive Growth | +18.56 |
| Great Pacific Growth Fund | +18.20 |

**Losers**

| | |
|---|---|
| Strategic Investments | −20.82 |
| U.S. Gold Shares | −18.83 |
| American Heritage | −18.00 |
| First Investors Natural Resources | −16.32 |
| Sherman, Dean Fund | −14.96 |
| Franklin Gold Fund | −14.00 |
| Fidelity Select Precious Metals | −13.09 |
| Vanguard Special Gold | −12.01 |
| Strategic Silver | −11.24 |
| Industry Fund of America | −10.86 |
| Keystone Precious Metals | −10.73 |

Source: Lipper Analytical Services

JULY 7

performers in the fund industry, reflecting both a decline in the value of South Africa's currency, the rand, and a drop in the gold stocks themselves. JULY 7

# The Dilemma of Inside Trading

### By TAMAR LEWIN

*The Big Chill*, the hit movie that captured the spirit of the 1980s, was not a cops and robbers caper. But if you paid attention, you saw a crime in the making.

Kevin Kline, playing the head of Running Dog, a sneakers company, is out jogging with William Hurt when he gives his pal a tip. Running Dog, he confides, is about to be acquired, and Mr. Hurt can triple his money by buying its stock beforehand.

The crime in progress involves insider trading—exploiting advance knowledge of an important development to buy or sell stock before the public knows about it.

These days, with the drumbeat of criminal charges against a parade of Wall Street professionals, it sometimes seems that many have joined Mr. Kline in passing on inside information. And it is hard to dispute that what the Federal Government is uncovering—such as the scheme in which Dennis B. Levine, an investment banker, swapped secrets with other investment bankers and set up offshore bank accounts to hide his stock market profits—involves behavior that should be punished.

But increasingly, some experts are worried that the Securities and Exchange Commission's vigorous enforcement campaign may be stretching the securities laws too far. They say the commission may be distorting those laws by applying them to sins adequately covered by other statutes. And they also say that, once past the black-and-white instances of obvious wrongdoing, it becomes harder and harder to judge what is acceptable, either morally or legally, in routine Wall Street practice.

"From the behavior of the stock market, it seems that there are a lot of Kevin Klines out there," said John C. Coffee, Jr., who teaches securities and criminal law at the Columbia University School of Law. "It wouldn't usually be the head of the company passing on the tip, of course. Any major deal involves dozens of people, from the investment bankers to the lawyers to the printers. It can be very difficult to trace exactly who leaked the information to whom."

Indeed, signs are that insider trading has become epidemic. Almost invariably, the stock price of a company being acquired rises dramatically—and trading intensifies—in the days and weeks before a takeover is announced. JULY 21

## The insider cases in 1986

The criminal cases related to insider trading brought in 1986 by the U.S. Attorney's office in the Southern District of New York, as of July 18, 1986.

| Defendant | Title | Company | Sentence |
| --- | --- | --- | --- |
| Darius N. Keaton | Director | Sante Fe International | Jan. 16; indicted, awaiting trial |
| Krishan Taneja | Employee | Office of Manhattan Borough President | March 6; given six months imprisonment, $10,000 fine |
| Michael David | Attorney | Paul, Weiss | June 5; pleaded not guilty |
| Dennis B. Levine | Managing Director | Drexel Burnham | June 5; pleaded guilty, awaiting sentence |

| Defendant | Title | Company | Sentence |
|---|---|---|---|
| Robert Salisbury | Analyst | Drexel Burnham | June 5; pleaded guilty, awaiting sentence |
| Martin Shapiro | Stockbroker | Moseley, Hallgarten, Estabrook & Weeden | June 5; pleaded guilty, awaiting sentence |
| Daniel J. Silverman | Holder of account | Account with Moseley, Hallgarten, Estabrook & Weeden | June 5; pleaded guilty, awaiting sentence |
| Andrew Solomon | Analyst | Marcus Schloss | June 5; pleaded guilty, awaiting sentence |

Source: Office of U.S. Attorney, Southern District of New York

JULY 21

## Company News: Sumitomo of Japan Plans to Buy a Stake in Goldman, Sachs

**By JAMES STERNGOLD**

Goldman, Sachs & Company, a premier investment banking house and one of the last independent partnerships on Wall Street, announced yesterday that it was negotiating to sell a large stake to the Sumitomo Bank Ltd., Japan's—and the world's—third-largest bank.

The deal, if completed, would be a significant step by a Japanese financial institution into the American capital markets and an important symbolic jump in the globalization of financial markets.

It would also all but bring to a close an era when Wall Street was dominated by independent private firms entirely owned by their partners.

The huge amounts of capital required to compete in today's volatile global financial markets and the risks that securities houses face have forced nearly every other top firm to sell shares to the public or find a major financial partner.

The 117-year-old Goldman, Sachs, the sixth-largest Wall Street firm at the end of 1985 and the largest remaining partnership, now joins that list.

Sumitomo would pay $500 million to become a limited partner, giving it up to 12.5 percent of the investment bank's income, before taxes, by the end of 1988, according to Goldman, Sachs. Goldman, Sachs said it had $1.33 billion in capital at the end of May. A Goldman, Sachs official said that, at least initially, Sumitomo would own less than 12.5 percent of the partnership and that Sumitomo would have no voting rights or role in management.

AUG. 7

## Sumitomo's high global rank . . .
U.S. and overseas banks listed by assets as of Dec. 31, 1985.

| Bank | Country | Assets ($ billions) | Employees |
|---|---|---|---|
| 1. Dai-ichi Kangyo Bank | Japan | $158.3 | 21,125 |
| 2. Fuji Bank | Japan | 142.7 | 15,836 |

| Bank | Country | Assets ($ billions) | Employees |
|---|---|---|---|
| 3. Sumitomo Bank | Japan | 135.9 | 14,486 |
| 4. Mitsubishi Bank | Japan | 133.5 | 15,075 |
| 5. Citibank | U.S. | 129.5 | 57,666 |
| 6. Banque Nationale de Paris | France | 123.8 | 59,924 |
| 7. Credit Agricole Mutuel | France | 123.6 | 74,091 |
| 8. Sanwa Bank | Japan | 123.5 | 15,766 |
| 9. Credit Lyonnais | France | 112.1 | 54,870 |
| 10. Norinchukin Bank | Japan | 106.3 | 3,261 |

Source: The American Banker

AUG. 7

# Banks' Non-loan Profits Ebb

By ERIC N. BERG

Earlier this year, the nation's big banks reported booming profits from foreign-exchange commissions, securities trading and surging values of bond portfolios. But such huge windfalls in areas outside of lending were unlikely to go on forever, and they did not. As a result, many banks have reported flat or reduced earnings for the second quarter.

Some banks, notably J. P. Morgan & Company's Morgan Guaranty Trust Company and the Bankers Trust Company, did continue to post healthy gains in earnings from investment banking. Analysts said they were impressed by the continued ability of such organizations to maintain and even increase earnings in a difficult banking environment.

By contrast, however, Citicorp, the Chemical New York Corporation and the Manufacturers Hanover Corporation all reported lower investment banking results. Like many Wall Street firms, these banks suffered from reduced trading profits and skimpier capital gains on bonds held for investment.  AUG. 8

## A roundup of second-quarter bank results

Second-quarter 1986 results for the nation's 15 largest bank holding companies.

| Return on assets | | Return on equity | | Loan quality | | Change in earnings | |
|---|---|---|---|---|---|---|---|
| Annualized return on each $100 of average total assets.* | | Annualized return on each $100 of average common equity.* | | Nonperforming assets as a percentage of total assets. | | Percentage change in per share net income from 1985 period. | |
| J. P. Morgan | $1.30 | J. P. Morgan | $20.99 | J. P. Morgan | 0.93 | First Chicago | +1,250.0 |
| Bankers Trust | 0.74 | Bankers Trust | 15.97 | Citicorp | 1.41 | J. P. Morgan | +47.4 |
| Wells Fargo | 0.72 | First Bank System | 15.94 | Bankers Trust | 1.50 | Bank of Boston | +21.0 |
| First Bank System | 0.72 | Security Pacific | 15.37 | Bank of Boston | 2.13 | First Bank System | +19.6 |

| Return on assets | | Return on equity | | Loan quality | | Change in earnings | |
|---|---|---|---|---|---|---|---|
| Annualized return on each $100 of average total assets.* | | Annualized return on each $100 of average common equity.* | | Nonperforming assets as a percentage of total assets. | | Percentage change in per share net income from 1985 period. | |
| Security Pacific | 0.71 | Bank of Boston | 15.08 | Chase Manhattan | 2.27 | Continental Illinois | +15.4 |
| Bank of Boston | 0.69 | Chemical | 14.18 | First Chicago | 2.35 | Chase Manhattan | +15.0 |
| First Interstate | 0.69 | Wells Fargo | 13.90 | Chemical Bank | 2.40 | Wells Fargo | +14.0 |
| Chemical | 0.63 | Chase Manhattan | 13.27 | Mellon National | 2.42 | Bankers Trust | +14.0 |
| First Chicago | 0.61 | First Interstate | 13.05 | First Interstate | 2.59 | First Interstate | +10.5 |
| Mellon National | 0.60 | First Chicago | 12.38 | Security Pacific | 2.61 | Security Pacific | +10.2 |
| Chase Manhattan | 0.59 | Citicorp | 12.38 | First Bank System | 2.64 | Manufacturers Hanover | +1.0 |
| Citicorp | 0.47 | Mellon National | 11.93 | Continental Illinois | 2.75 | Chemical Bank | −8.1 |
| Continental Illinois | 0.46 | Manufacturers Hanover | 11.16 | Manufacturers Hanover | 2.95 | Citicorp | −12.0 |
| Manufacturers Hanover | .43 | Continental Illinois | 8.51 | Wells Fargo | 2.95 | Mellon National | −23.7 |
| BankAmerica | N.M. | BankAmerica | N.M. | BankAmerica | 4.25 | BankAmerica | −82.0 |

*Returns and change in earnings are based on net income applicable to common stockholders

AUG. 8

# Changes on Canada's Wall Street

**By DOUGLAS MARTIN**

TORONTO, Aug. 11—With its partnerships, its old money and its easy arrogance, Bay Street, the hub of the Canadian securities industry here, is reminiscent of Wall Street a decade or two ago. But like Wall Street, Bay Street is changing its staid ways. "The game is over for the private club," said Austin Taylor, chairman of McLeod Young Weir Ltd., the country's fifth-biggest securities firm and a respected member of the old guard.

The government of the province of Ontario, which is home to most of the Canadian financial industry, has proposed loosening restraints, effective Jan. 1, on the ownership of investment houses by foreigners and financial institutions; one proposed change would allow Canada's five leading banks to buy up to 30 percent each of investment houses.

If the changes go into effect, Canadian houses—which sell stocks and bonds, manage underwritings and perform other functions identical to those of American dealers—will move much closer to deregulation. The idea is to allow firms to become large enough to compete with the big American and Japanese players in an increasingly global market.

Meanwhile, Bay Street itself is bracing for change. Many of the leading investment firms are shopping for merger partners. Some nine partnerships have sold shares publicly for the first time. The country's biggest house, Dominion Securities Pitfield Ltd., is said to be laying plans for a stock sale, as are Wood Gundy Inc. and the Gordon Capital Corporation.

**Individual stock performance**
(Changes in 10 of the 30 stocks in the Dow Jones industrial average from Aug. 12, 1982, to July 2, 1986, when the Dow average hit its record high. All prices are adjusted for splits, stock dividends and spinoffs.)

| Stock | Close 8/12/82 | Close 7/2/86 | Percent change | Dow Rank | Close 8/14/86 |
|---|---|---|---|---|---|
| Woolworth | 8.44 | 46.50 | **451.08** | 1 | 43.125 |
| Union Carbide | 14.08 | 57.13 | **305.66** | 2 | 21.875 |
| McDonald's | 20.37 | 75.63 | **271.31** | 5 | 65.50 |
| American Express | 17.87 | 62.00 | **246.89** | 6 | 62.00 |
| Sears | 18.13 | 48.38 | **166.90** | 11 | 44.50 |
| Exxon | 25.00 | 61.38 | **145.50** | 13 | 64.125 |
| I.B.M. | 62.25 | 149.50 | **140.16** | 15 | 134.25 |
| A.T.&T. | 46.47 | 110.64 | **138.08** | 16 | 23.50 |
| General Motors | 39.88 | 78.25 | **96.24** | 20 | 71.00 |
| Bethlehem Steel | 15.00 | 14.63 | **−2.50** | 30 | 8.50 |

Source: Purcell, Graham & Co.

AUG. 15

But the firms clearly have a way to go—and, as the continuing amalgamation of the United States investment industry suggests, they may have started too far behind and too late. Only a dozen of the approximately 90 Canadian houses have more than $10 million in equity. The industry's combined capital is just slightly over $800 million (United States). That is less than a fifth of the capital of the Nomura Securities Company of Japan, the world's biggest investment firm. And it is one third the capital of Salomon Brothers, the world's third-biggest firm. AUG. 12

## Canada's top firms

Canadian securities firms ranked by capital at the end of 1985, in millions of Canadian dollars.

| Firm | Capital |
|---|---|
| Dominion Securities Pitfield Ltd. | $130.1 |
| Wood Gundy Inc. | 115.9 |
| Gordon Capital Corp. | 115.1 |
| Burns Fry Ltd. | 79.2 |
| McLeod Young Weir Ltd.* | 73.4 |
| Richardson Greenshields of Canada Ltd. | 60.8 |
| Nesbitt Thomson Inc. | 56.0 |
| Merrill Lynch Canada Inc. | 50.4 |
| Midland Doherty Financial Corp. | 39.6 |
| Lèvesque, Beaubien Inc. | 25.0 |

*As of the end of September 1985.
Source: The Financial Post 500

AUG. 12

## The stock market's four-year climb

**Major stock averages**
(Changes in the major stock market indexes from the close of trading on Aug. 12, 1982, when the bear market ended, to the close on Aug. 14, 1986.)

| Index | Close on 8/12/82 | Close on 8/14/86 | Percent change | Record High Date |
|---|---|---|---|---|
| Dow Jones Industrials | 776.92 | 1,844.91 | 137.46 | 1,909.03 7/2/86 |
| Dow Jones Transportations | 292.12 | 754.00 | 158.11 | 830.84 3/31/86 |
| Dow Jones Utilities | 103.22* | 210.04 | 103.49 | 210.04 8/14/86 |
| S.&P. 500 | 102.42 | 246.25 | 140.43 | 252.70 7/2/86 |
| N.Y.S.E. Composite | 58.80 | 141.79 | 141.14 | 145.15 7/2/86 |
| Amex Market Value | 118.64 | 271.22 | 128.61 | 285.19 6/25/86 |
| Nasdaq Composite | 159.14 | 379.52 | 138.48 | 411.16 7/3/86 |

*Close on Aug. 13, 1982, when that index hit its low.

AUG. 15

# Turning to Europe for Equity

**By STEVE LOHR**

LONDON, Aug. 20—Large American companies have long viewed Europe's capital markets as fertile territory for the sale of their bonds. Now such names as Citicorp, Harcourt Brace Jovanovich, Black & Decker, Transamerica and Chesebrough-Pond's are finding they can raise equity capital there as well.

"Most American companies would have never considered a European issue a few years ago, but now it is a widely recognized option," said Kenneth Kermes, executive vice-president of finance for the Black & Decker Corporation.

The stock issues, dubbed Euroequities, are siblings to Eurobonds in that they tap the hoard of dollars held abroad. So far this year, 17 American companies and one Government agency, the Student Loan Marketing Association, have issued Euroequities, compared with two corporations and one agency in all of 1985. That brought in $3.21 billion of permanent capital in the first six months of this year, compared with $3.18 billion of Euroequity sales for all of 1985 and just $306 million in 1984.

Although the American companies offering Euroequities represent disparate industries, they do have several things in common. Typically, a Euroequity deal represents about 20 percent of a larger offering, with the remainder

## Largest american euroequity issues in 1986

| Date of euroequity issue* | Company | Number of shares (thousands) | Offer price per share | Proceeds ($ millions) |
|---|---|---|---|---|
| March 20 | Morgan Stanley & Co. | 1,600 | $56.50 | **$90.4** |
| May 19 | Henley Group Inc. | 4,000 | 21.25 | **85.0** |
| May 7 | Fireman's Fund Corp. | 1,600 | 41.50** | **66.4** |
| April 10 | H. F. Ahmanson & Co. | 1,000 | 63.375 | **63.4** |
| June 17 | Citicorp | 1,000 | 58.18 | **58.2** |
| May 7 | Bear, Stearns & Co. | 1,500 | 35.00 | **52.5** |
| July 14 | Student Loan Marketing Association | 1,000 | 51.125 | **51.1** |
| May 16 | Travelers Corp. | 1,000 | 49.25 | **49.3** |
| April 21 | Conagra Inc. | 1,000 | 48.00 | **48.0** |
| Feb. 26 | Chesebrough-Pond's Inc. | 1,150 | 40.50 | **46.6** |

*Through Aug. 1, 1986.
**With each share, purchaser also gets one warrant, and every two warrants are convertible to one share of stock at a price of $43.70.

Source: Credit Suisse First Boston Research

AUG. 21

sold in the United States. "Tombstone" ads that appear in the American business press, in fact, might list an American syndicate of investment bankers for four million shares of a deal and a separate syndicate list of London-based underwriters for one million shares. In contrast, Eurobond offerings typically stand by themselves without a simultaneous United States offering.

Another common characteristic, which Eurobonds also share, is that Euroequities are usually issued by companies whose markets are international. Selling the securities is easier because the names of the American companies often are familiar names to European investors.

AUG. 21

## The market's managers

Lead managers on Euroequity issues in the first six months of 1986, ranked by amount raised.

| Firm | Number of issues | Total raised ($ million) |
|---|---|---|
| Credit Suisse First Boston | 11 | $1,031.7 |
| Enskilda Securities | 2 | 380.6 |
| Morgan Stanley International | 6 | 320.8 |
| Swiss Bank Corporation International | 5 | 283.2 |
| Merrill Lynch Capital Markets | 3 | 243.6 |
| Deutsche Bank Capital Markets | 1 | 227.4 |
| Union Bank of Switzerland | 3 | 208.9 |
| S. G. Warburg Securities | 1 | 166.7 |
| Shearson Lehman Brothers International | 3 | 157.6 |
| Salomon Brothers International | 2 | 98.4 |

Source: *Euromoney*

AUG. 21

## Wide Use of Computers to Set Trading Pattern Contributed to Slide

By JOHN CRUDELE

The stock market's plunge this week was as much a product of computer technology and Wall Street inventiveness as it was a reflection of new worries over the economy.

Part of the market's decline clearly relates to emerging concerns on Wall Street over the failure of interest rates to come down further. High interest rates impose a drag on all economic activity, from the purchase of new homes and new cars to investment in factories and equipment, thus presaging a bleak period for the economy.

But at least as important, experts say, is the new order on Wall Street, where the combination of exotic financial markets and instruments and advanced computer capabilities has introduced a degree of uncertainty—and volatility—heretofore unknown.

Yesterday, the widely watched Dow Jones industrial average fell 34.17 points on record volume, on the heels of an 86.61-point drop Thursday, bringing the total decline for the week to 141.03 points, or 7.4 percent. Wall Street was shocked by the abruptness of it all.

"People in the business for a lot shorter period that I have been had to be amazed by the action," said 70-year-old Gene Jay Seagle, director of technical research for Gruntal Inc., a brokerage firm.

SEPT. 13

### The biggest postwar percentage declines
Ten largest one-day declines on a percentage basis in the Dow Jones industrial average since May 1945.

| Date | Percentage decline | Point decline | Reason |
|---|---|---|---|
| Sept. 26, 1955 | 6.54 | 31.89 | President Eisenhower's heart attack and its political implications. |
| May 28, 1962 | 5.71 | 34.95 | "Panic" selling, with little news to support it except steelmakers' attempt to raise prices and White House pressure against it. |
| Sept. 3, 1946 | 5.56 | 10.51 | Investor confidence generally undermined by slow production a year after the end of the war. |
| June 26, 1950 | 4.65 | 10.44 | Communist invasion of South Korea. |
| Sept. 11, 1986 | 4.61 | 86.61 | Investor concern about accelerating trend toward higher interest rates. |
| Sept. 9, 1946 | 4.41 | 7.93 | Gloomy labor situation. |
| Feb. 25, 1946 | 4.29 | 8.39 | Much gossip of poor first-quarter earnings and reduced dividends, together with confusion over the Government's price-wage policy. |
| Nov. 3, 1948 | 3.85 | 7.30 | Countrywide selling after President Harry S Truman upsets Thomas E. Dewey in reelection. |
| June 29, 1950 | 3.70 | 7.96 | Continued shock from news of war in Korea. |
| Oct. 25, 1982 | 3.52 | 36.33 | Disappointment over the Federal Reserve Board's failure to cut the discount rate. |

Source: Salomon Brothers Inc.

SEPT. 13

### The five busiest trading days

Trades on the New York Stock Exchange, in millions of shares.

| Volume | Date | Dow Industrials Close | Dow Change |
|---|---|---|---|
| 240.5 | Sept. 12, 1986 | 1,758.72 | −34.17 |
| 237.6 | Sept. 11, 1986 | 1,792.89 | −86.61 |
| 236.6 | Aug. 3, 1984 | 1,202.08 | +36.00 |
| 210.3 | March 12, 1986 | 1,745.45 | −0.60 |
| 203.1 | Aug. 6, 1984 | 1,202.96 | +0.88 |

Source: New York Stock Exchange

SEPT. 13

# The Yanks Muscle In on the City

By FRED R. BLEAKLEY

LONDON—When Robert Maxwell, the British newspaper baron and stock wheeler-dealer, unloaded a huge portfolio 10 days ago, he did not take the usual route of asking British brokers to peddle the stocks bit by bit. Instead, he invited three foreign investment houses to bid on the whole package, finally selling it to Goldman, Sachs International, the London arm of the American investment house, for nearly $300 million.

London's cozy world of stockbrokers and floor traders had never seen such risk taking. It was the largest single stock purchase in British history and Goldman, Sachs rushed to resell the shares before their prices could fall. There was awe that Goldman, Sachs would risk millions in losses for a profit that at best would be a thin one. "It was a successful transaction," was all that Robert M. Conway, Goldman's managing director, would say of the deal.

Goldman, Sachs isn't the only American high roller these days in The City, London's mile-square version of New York's Wall Street district. Last week, the financial community was buzzing with reports that Merrill Lynch, buying gilts, had lost between $18 million and $37 million when gilt prices suddenly plunged. Gilts are the British government's equivalent of United States Treasury securities. Merrill declined to comment on the reports, which appeared in British newspapers.

The talk of the financial community, in fact, is about the extraordinary risks that American investment houses are beginning to take as they aggressively try not only to gain a foothold in Britain's securities markets, but to dominate those markets as quickly as possible. The battle is not for big short-term profits. British stock and bond trading is only a fraction of what goes on in New York. And what profits there are must be shared with British firms as well as the European and Japanese houses that are also battling to be big players here—now that deregulation has arrived.

The American goal, instead, is to eventually gain big chunks of new business as London's still-tiny domestic securities markets finally expand and The City takes its seat as one of the three major trading centers in the emerging worldwide financial marketplace. "This is a test of who will be the players in the year 2000," says John M. Hennessy, chairman of the Credit-Suisse First Boston Corporation.

To be sure, London is already a major center even without the deregulation that is now opening up Britain's still-tiny securities markets. At roughly $90 billion a day, foreign currency trading here is nearly twice that of either Tokyo or New York. Dozens of international financial instruments trade in London's secondary markets, along with a bevy of commodities. And The City is the center of Eurobond trading, in which companies or governments float bond issues abroad—a practice that has mushroomed to $200 billion a year from $30 billion five years ago.

But London's stock, bond and gilt markets had been uninviting to outsiders. Stiff restrictions had discouraged foreign investors and even many in Britain. Now those restrictions are being rapidly phased out, with the most dramatic steps to be taken on Oct. 27—"Big Bang" Day. After that day, an electronic stock market will have come into existence, facilitating off-floor trading. A single firm, foreign or British, will be allowed to both trade stocks and also represent customers, functions now kept separate. The number of firms sanctioned by the Bank of England to trade in government gilts will have risen to 27—eight of them American—from three British houses. And fixed brokerage commissions will be eliminated, allowing the sort of stiff price competition that Wall Street has known since it ended fixed commissions on May 1, 1975—America's "May Day." SEPT. 28

## The buildup for the Big Bang

| American Company | London Employees 1984 | London Employees 1986 | Major British purchases | comments |
|---|---|---|---|---|
| Bankers Trust | 610 | 710 | None | A leader in introducing leveraged buyouts to British corporations |
| Chase Manhattan | 1,407 | 2,480 | Simon & Coates (stockbroker) Laurie, Millbank (stockbroker) | Using acquisitions to form the nucleus of British teams in equities and gilts |
| Citicorp | 1,350 | 2,100 | Vickers da Costa (stockbroker) Scrimgeour Kemp-Gee (stockbroker) Seccombe Marshall (money markets) | Plans a global link for equities research as part of its push into investment banking |
| Credit Suisse First Boston | 412 | 595 | None | Leader among Eurobond underwriters sees Big Bang as a crucial test for future world players |
| Drexel Burnham Lambert | 200 | 350 | None | Big in commodities but finding it tough to sell Europeans on junk bonds |
| Goldman, Sachs | 140 | 500 | None | Penetrated British merger business by helping British companies fend off raiders; willing to take big risks in equities |
| Merrill Lynch* | 1,000 | 1,700 | Giles & Caswell (gilt dealer) | Rejected costly acquisitions, determined to gain a big share in gilts |
| Morgan Guaranty | 1,350 | 1,350 | None | Took advantage of opportunity to become a gilt dealer but is staying out of the equities fray for now |
| Morgan Stanley | 124 | 600 | None | Won't compete in gilts; a developer of London's huge Canary Wharf real estate project |
| Salomon Brothers | 160 | 574 | None | New international headquarters establishes London as the nerve center of its global operations |

| American Company | London Employees 1984 | London Employees 1986 | Major British purchases | comments |
|---|---|---|---|---|
| Security Pacific | 347 | 1,500 | Hoare Govett (stockbroker) | Purchase of major British stockbroker establishes presence in equities and gilts |
| Shearson Lehman Brothers | 275 | 1,200 | L. Messel (stockbroker) | $20 million acquisition provides entrée to British institutional investors |

*Employees are for Merrill Lynch's Europe/Middle East division.

SEPT. 28

## Stocks Weakened in Quarter

By ERIC SCHMITT

Takeover and gold mining stocks, as well as a paint company that changed its stripes, a fish meal producer and a Philippine sugar miller, emerged as the big winners on Wall Street during the third quarter.

Between July 1 and Sept. 30, the fortunes of familiar market stalwarts such as retailers, utilities, tobacco companies and soft drink manufacturers waned. Despite the weak, though at times volatile, market, several cyclical stocks such as mining, papers, chemicals and energy managed to restore some of their former luster.

Of the 6,367 stocks tracked by Media General Financial Services, based in Richmond, 1,336 stocks were up for the quarter, 4,679 were down and 352 were unchanged.

The Big Board posted its first quarter-to-quarter decline in a year, partly because profit takers carved deeply into the Dow Jones industrial average. The average set a new record of 1,919.71 on Sept. 4, but then spiraled down and closed Sept. 30 at 1,767.58, down 6.6 percent from 1,892.72 at the beginning of the quarter. Yesterday the index closed at 1,782.90.

The American Stock Exchange market-value index closed Sept. 30 at 260.69, down 8.3 percent from 281.20 three months ago. The Nasdaq composite index of over-the-counter issues dropped 13.5 percent, to 350.67, from its record high of 405.51 at the end of the second period.

OCT. 2

### The Big Board's third-quarter gainers and losers

New York Stock Exchange common stocks that showed the largest percentage gains and declines in the third quarter of 1986. Prices are adjusted for splits, and listings exclude stocks trading for less than $2 a share or fewer than 1,000 shares.

| Stock | Sept. 30 close | 2d-quarter pct. change | Comment |
|---|---|---|---|
| **Gainers** | | | |
| Robertshaw Controls Co. | 84½ | +77.9 | Siebe P.L.C. buys thermostat manufacturer for $85 a share. |
| Freeport-McMoran Gold Co. | 13 | +73.3 | Mining company opens new mine in Nevada. |

| Stock | Sept. 30 close | 2d-quarter pct. change | Comment |
|---|---|---|---|
| | | **Gainers** | |
| Trans World Airlines | 25⅝ | +68.0 | Airline forecasts big 4th-quarter profit increase. |
| Beneficial Corp. | 77¾ | +67.2 | Financial services company up for sale. |
| Owens-Corning Fiberglas | 78¼ | +63.0 | Fiberglass products company adopts reorganization plan. |
| Newmont Gold Co. | 14⅞ | +60.8 | New mining company's income up as gold prices climb. |
| Ex-Cell-O Corp. | 77⅜ | +60.4 | Textron acquires diversified automotive parts company. |
| Benguet Corp. (Class B) | 5½ | +57.1 | Philippine mining company prospers from gold price rise. |
| Hammermill Paper Co. | 63¾ | +50.9 | International Paper buys paper company for $64.50 a share. |
| Gelco Corp. | 23⅜ | +49.6 | Coniston Partners bids for truck leasing services company. |
| | | **Losers** | |
| Floating Point Systems Inc. | 12½ | −67.0 | Computer company reports $2.9 million 3d-quarter loss. |
| LTV Corp. | 2⅛ | −58.5 | Oil and steel company files for Chapter 11 bankruptcy. |
| Marantz Co. | 3⅝ | −51.7 | Stereo components maker has another quarterly loss. |
| Bethlehem Steel Corp. | 7⅛ | −51.7 | Steelmaker's stock shaken by LTV bankruptcy. |
| LTV (Class AA) | 4⅛ | −51.5 | Oil and steel company files for Chapter 11 bankruptcy. |
| Cullinet Software Inc. | 6¾ | −47.6 | Computer maker blames big quarterly loss on soft market. |
| Wackenhut Corp. | 19¼ | −46.5 | Sales for security systems company fall as costs rise. |
| Zenith Labs Inc. | 8⅞ | −45.4 | Drug company recalls 33 drugs for Federal review. |
| Storage Technology Corp. | 2⅛ | −45.2 | Data storage equipment company in Chapter 11. |
| General Host Corp. | 13⅞ | −44.5 | Specialty retailer posts 2d-quarter loss of $5.3 million. |

OCT. 2

## Third-quarter gainers and losers on the Amex

Amex-listed common stocks that showed the largest percentage gains and declines in the third quarter of 1986. Prices are adjusted for splits, and listings exclude stocks trading for less than $2 a share or fewer than 1,000 shares.

| Stock | Sept. 30 close | 3d-quarter pct. change | Comment |
|---|---|---|---|
| | | **Gainers** | |
| San Carlos Milling Co. | 4¼ | +100.0 | Foreign investment interest helps Philippine sugar miller. |
| Servisco Inc. | 32½ | +100.0 | Service Control Corp. bids for garment rental company. |
| Philippine Long Distance Telephone | 11⅞ | +86.3 | Philippine utility benefits from foreign investment interest. |

| Stock | Sept. 30 close | 3d-quarter pct. change | Comment |
|---|---|---|---|
| **Gainers** | | | |
| Jet America Airlines | 4⅜ | +75.0 | Alaska Air acquires small regional carrier. |
| Swift Energy Co. | 4⅜ | +75.0 | Oil and gas exploration concern increases sale of partnerships. |
| Electronics Corp. of America | 51⅞ | +69.4 | Rockwell International buys electronics control company. |
| International Proteins Corp. | 5⅞ | +62.1 | Fish meal distributor buys Delaware real estate developer. |
| Interwest Corp. | 9⅝ | +60.4 | Investment company enters real estate market. |
| Hofmann Industries | 3¾ | +50.0 | Increased royalties from Postal Service mail carts raise steel tubing company's profits. |
| Echo Bay Mine Ltd. | 21¼ | +40.5 | Higher precious metals prices aid Canadian mining company. |
| **Losers** | | | |
| Lear Petroleum Partnership | 2 | −84.6 | French concern's unit buys troubled oil, gas partnership. |
| Saxon Oil Development Partnership | 2 | −51.5 | Oil and gas exploration company cuts dividend 80%. |
| Booth Inc. | 4 | −50.0 | Soft drink machine company's income falls 38% in June quarter. |
| Care Enterprises (Class B) | 3⅝ | −48.2 | Earnings diluted after nursing services company issues 2.5 million new shares. |
| Care Enterprises (Class A) | 3⅜ | −47.1 | Earnings diluted after nursing services company issues 2.5 million new shares. |
| International Banknote Co. | 5¼ | −46.2 | Volatile stock of securities printer drops in bear market. |
| Rockaway Corp. | 13 | −45.5 | Investors sell stock in postage meter distributor to avoid margin call. |
| Verit Industries | 9⅞ | −44.8 | Volatile market buffets consumer electronics maker. |
| Magnet Bank | 7¾ | −44.6 | Loan losses hurt West Virginia thrift unit. |
| Kit Manufacturing Co. | 5⅜ | −44.2 | Mobile-home maker records 38% lower quarterly profits. |

OCT. 2

## Third-quarter O-T-C gainers and losers

O.T.C.-listed common stocks that showed the largest percentage gains and declines in the third quarter of 1986. Prices are adjusted for splits, and listings exclude stocks trading for less than $2 a share or fewer than 1,000 shares.

| Stock | Sept. 30 close | 3d-quarter pct. change | Comment |
|---|---|---|---|
| **Gainers** | | | |
| Western Telecommunications (Class B) | 17½ | +288.6 | Stock conversion plan of microwave relay systems company is approved. |
| Metropolitan Consolidated Industries | 10¼ | +215.4 | Paint company changes to real estate concern. |
| Balchem Corp. (Class B) | 8⅝ | +97.1 | Chemicals company posts strong 2d-quarter earnings. |
| Telemation Inc. | 10¼ | +95.2 | Price Communications buys 56% of TV production company. |
| International Mobile Machines Corp. | 18⅜ | +88.5 | Mobile telephone company tests wireless phone system. |
| Colonial American Bankshares | 35½ | +79.7 | Central Fidelity offers stock for bank holding company. |
| Davidson Tisdale Mines Ltd. | 4³⁄₁₆ | +76.3 | Getty Resources buys into Canadian gold mining company. |
| Orange Free State Investment Trust | 31½ | +72.6 | Gold price rise helps South African gold mining company. |
| Welkom Gold Holdings Ltd. | 8³⁄₁₆ | +72.4 | Gold price rise helps South African mining company. |
| NEC Corp. | 77¾ | +69.5 | Japanese computer company seeks stake in Honeywell. |
| **Losers** | | | |
| Computer and Communications Technology Corp. | 3⅛ | −72.2 | Shareholders sue computer products company for stock manipulation. |
| Monoclonal Antibodies Inc. | 6¾ | −70.0 | Pregnancy test kit maker named in patent suit. |
| American Passage Marketing Corp. | 2½ | −69.2 | Expensive promotions crimp film processor's earnings. |
| All American Television | 4¾ | −67.2 | Television program distributor's stock fluctuates. |
| Philip Crosby Associates Inc. | 6½ | −66.9 | Manufacturing consultant sees lower 4th-quarter profits. |
| Admac Inc. | 3¾ | −65.9 | Delay in new products sales hurts maker of mining equipment. |
| Entre Computer | 2⅜ | −62.0 | Computer store chain takes a charge for asset revaluation. |

| Stock | June 30 close | 2nd-quarter pct. change | Comment |
|---|---|---|---|
| **Losers** | | | |
| Savers Inc. | 3⅜ | −61.3 | Arkansas thrift holding company has June quarter loss. |
| Freedom Savings and Loan | 3½ | −61.1 | Florida thrift unit forecasts $8 million 2d-quarter loss. |

OCT. 2

# BankAmerica Head Is Stepping Down

**By ANDREW POLLACK**

SAN FRANCISCO, Oct. 10—Samuel H. Armacost, whose tenure at the helm of the BankAmerica Corporation has been marked by turmoil and huge losses, will resign this weekend, the banking company announced today.

As Mr. Armacost's replacement, banking sources said, the board of directors is expected to name A. W. Clausen, the president of the World Bank until last June and the chief of BankAmerica until Mr. Armacost took over five years ago. The board is to meet on Sunday.

Industry sources said directors had forced Mr. Armacost's resignation as president and chief executive officer. The sources said the directors had become convinced that a change was needed to restore the health of the nation's second largest banking company and the confidence of customers and investors. Citicorp, based in New York, is the nation's largest banking institution.

BankAmerica, buffeted by rumors in recent weeks, is now the target of a takeover offer by First Interstate Bancorp of Los Angeles, a bank less than half its size.

Industry sources said the BankAmerica board had gradually become disenchanted with Mr. Armacost and that the bid from First Interstate, received last Friday, had tipped the scales.

Appointing a new chief could be a prime element in a plan to buy time and remain independent, some analysts contend. Others, however, argue that directors might want to consider the takeover and that they had dismissed the 47-year-old Mr. Armacost because he was adamantly opposed.

First Interstate declined to comment on what it would do now. The bank is expected to continue to press its bid, a stock transaction that First Interstate values at $18 a share, but which analysts value at closer to $15 a share.

BankAmerica's stock rose 62.5 cents today, to $14.875, on the New York Stock Exchange, after the news of Mr. Armacost's resignation.

OCT. 11

## The Armacost Years at BankAmerica

When Samuel H. Armacost took over the BankAmerica Corporation, the holding company that owns the Bank of America was the biggest and one of the most profitable banking organizations in the United States. But in the next six years, profits turned to losses and the bank dropped to No. 2 in size—far behind Citicorp. Following is a chronology of key events at BankAmerica since Mr. Armacost took over:

**Dec. 1, 1980:** Mr. Armacost is named president and chief executive officer.

**April 16, 1981:** Bank reports 19 percent drop in first-quarter profits.

**Jan. 19, 1982:** Bank says 1981 earnings fell 31 percent, to $445.4 million.

**Feb. 8, 1983:** Bank says 1982 earnings rose 1.4 percent, to $451.4 million.

**Nov. 15, 1984:** Comptroller of the Currency tells bank to sign a pledge that it will bolster its financial underpinnings.

**Jan. 27, 1985:** Bank confirms it suspended several employees and began an investigation into a $37 million loss. Disclosures in next week show bank acted as escrow agent and trustee for at least $27 million of notes purportedly backed by phony or inflated mortgages.

**April 2, 1985:** Bank says its insurer plans to cancel liability insurance for bank directors and officers.

**July 11, 1985:** Bank announces plans to cut staff by 1,500 to 2,500.

**July 18, 1985:** Bank reports a second-quarter loss of $338 million.

**Aug. 5, 1985:** Bank cuts dividend for first time in more than 50 years.

**Jan. 21, 1986:** Bank reports loss of $337 million for 1985 and eliminates quarterly dividends on common stock. Treasury Department imposes record $4.75 million civil penalty on the bank for failing to report 17,000 large cash deposits or transfers it believes may have been engineered by drug traffickers and other criminals to launder money.

**July 16, 1986:** Bank reports a quarterly loss of $640 million.

**Oct. 6, 1986:** Bank receives a formal takeover offer from First Interstate for about $2.78 billion.

**Oct. 10, 1986:** Mr. Armacost says he will resign.

OCT. 11

# Profit Pressure at Top Banks

By ERIC N. BERG

Many corporations cite the drowsy economy for their mediocre profits. The nation's biggest banks, however, largely have themselves to blame for another quarter of lackluster results.

In the three months ended Sept. 30, these giant institutions failed for the most part to offset continued declines in their core lending businesses with new areas of growth, analysts say.

At the same time, they let their costs climb at rates more appropriate for a highly inflationary economy. And they continued to pay the price for overly optimistic credit decisions made years ago in the farm, energy and real estate sectors. Loan writeoffs rose sharply.

The result was a disappointing quarter, in which the average increase in earnings per share for the most closely watched banks, the top seven, was only 3 percent. Bank stocks are also struggling, having fallen 20 percent since midyear in the case of a few big-city banks.

"It is just becoming very difficult to make money in banking," said Stephen Berman, the industry analyst at Nomura Securities. "I don't think banks are earning well, and I am concerned about their prospects."

Mr. Berman was referring to the largest banks. Significantly, the fortunes of the vast majority of banks in America have been rising as borrowing by consumers continued at a robust pace. Moreover, smaller corporations, without lending alternatives, remained loyal to local banks.

And even among the big banks, there were exceptions to the otherwise gloomy picture.

Wells Fargo & Company, which earlier this year acquired the Crocker National Corporation, showed it was possible to double in size without doubling expenses; Wells's net income rose to $77.4 million from $48.6 million a year earlier.

NOV. 5

## A roundup of third-quarter bank results

Third-quarter 1986 results for the nation's 15 largest bank holding companies.

### Return on Assets

*Annualized return on each $100 of average total assets.\**

| | |
|---|---|
| J. P. Morgan | $ 1.12 |
| Bank of Boston | 0.77 |
| Bankers Trust | 0.76 |
| First Bank System | 0.74 |
| First Chicago | 0.74 |
| Security Pacific | 0.70 |
| First Interstate | 0.70 |
| Wells Fargo | 0.67 |
| Chemical | 0.65 |
| Mellon National | 0.56 |
| Chase Manhattan | 0.55 |
| Citicorp | 0.49 |
| Manufacturers Hanover | 0.49 |
| Continental Illinois | 0.47 |
| BankAmerica | N.M. |

### Return on Equity

*Annualized return on each $100 of average common equity.\**

| | |
|---|---|
| J. P. Morgan | $ 17.85 |
| Bank of Boston | 17.24 |
| Bankers Trust | 16.21 |
| Security Pacific | 15.68 |
| First Bank System | 15.60 |
| Wells Fargo | 15.50 |
| First Chicago | 13.76 |
| Chemical | 13.74 |
| First Interstate Bank | 13.41 |
| Manufacturers Hanover | 12.35 |
| Citicorp | 12.33 |
| Chase Manhattan | 12.13 |
| Mellon National | 11.13 |
| Continental Illinois | 8.45 |
| BankAmerica | N.M. |

### Loan Quality

*Nonperforming assets as a percentage of total assets.\**

| | |
|---|---|
| J. P. Morgan | 0.89 |
| Citicorp | 1.51 |
| Bankers Trust | 1.68 |
| Bank of Boston | 1.99 |
| First Bank System | 2.00 |
| Mellon National | 2.14 |
| Chase Manhattan | 2.18 |
| First Chicago | 2.27 |
| Security Pacific | 2.38 |
| First Interstate | 2.53 |
| Chemical | 2.72 |
| Wells Fargo | 2.87 |
| Continental Illinois | 2.94 |
| Manufacturers Hanover | 3.13 |
| BankAmerica | 4.40 |

### Change in Earnings

*Percentage change in fully diluted earnings per share\**

| | |
|---|---|
| Wells Fargo | 27.36 |
| Bank of Boston | 25.89 |
| First Chicago | 19.23 |
| First Bank System | 17.69 |
| Continental Illinois | 15.38 |
| Bankers Trust | 11.68 |
| First Interstate | 11.18 |
| Security Pacific | 9.65 |

| Change in Earnings | |
|---|---:|
| Manufacturers Hanover | 9.05 |
| Mellon National | 7.88 |
| Chemical | 3.98 |
| Citibank | 1.88 |
| J. P. Morgan | −0.87 |
| Chase Manhattan | −8.93 |
| BankAmerica | −177.42 |

*Returns and change in earnings are based on net income applicable to common stockholders.
N.M. Not meaningful because of losses.

Nov. 5

# Can Salomon Brothers Learn to Love Junk Bonds?

**By JAMES STERNGOLD**

This is bonus season at Salomon Brothers, when department heads at Wall Street's largest investment bank gather behind closed doors to judge their staffs and parcel out millions of dollars in year-end checks.

Few firms on Wall Street are likely to be more generous with Christmas bonuses than Salomon Brothers, the most profitable publicly owned securities house in America. But despite Salomon's prosperity, uncertainty hangs in the air at its busy, unglamorous offices in lower Manhattan. For Salomon's top executives are locked in a wrenching debate over the firm's future—a debate that figured in the recent decision of Henry Kaufman, Salomon's chief economist and one of Wall Street's most influential voices, to resign from two key executive posts.

Mr. Kaufman and some others want their 76-year-old firm to stick closely to its traditional strength as Wall Street's leader in underwriting and in trading a broad range of creditworthy stocks and bonds—the classic role of the investment bank. But there is also great pressure for Salomon to leap into takeovers financed with low-quality, high-yield debt known as junk bonds. That would be a radically different business for the august firm.

Salomon Brothers has hardly any presence in the booming Wall Street business of financing takeovers with these junk bonds or with an investment bank's own capital. That activity, loosely referred to as merchant banking, is all the rage these days, and Salomon's top echelon seems on the brink of a decision to participate.

The man on whom the ultimate decision will rest is John H. Gutfreund, the low-keyed, cigar-puffing chairman and chief executive of Salomon Brothers and its holding company, Salomon Inc. Mr. Gutfreund, whose own background, like that of the firm, is in traditional securities trading, admits to being vexed.

"Do we want to reaffirm our mission or do we want to change our mission?" he says. "I'm not prepared to dismantle what got us where we are." But he adds that Salomon risks losing revenues and customers if it does not try to become a major adviser and financier to corporate raiders such as Ronald Perelman, T. Boone Pickens or Carl Icahn. Until recently, Salomon shied away from this new breed of entrepreneur, preferring to represent the blue-chip industrial companies that often are the raiders' targets.

Despite Mr. Gutfreund's cautiousness, his firm is preparing to commit chunks of its $2.2 billion in capital to finance corporate acquisitions or buyouts. It is a business that can produce big fees, but can tie up capital in "bridge" loans for weeks or months, until the money can be recovered through the sale of high-risk junk bonds. Currently, Salomon invests mostly in creditworthy securities, a low-margin business in which the securities must be bought and sold in huge volumes each day to build up big profits.

Nov. 16

### How Salomon Brothers may change its strategy
**It Is the Top Underwriter of Stocks and Bonds...**
*Ranked by total value of issues managed so far in 1986*

|  | Amount ($ billions) |
|---|---|
| Salomon Brothers | $42.8 |
| First Boston | 37.8 |
| Drexel Burnham | 27.1 |
| Morgan Stanley | 27.0 |
| Goldman, Sachs | 25.8 |
| Merrill Lynch | 24.9 |
| Shearson Lehman | 13.5 |
| Kidder, Peabody | 8.8 |
| Paine Webber | 4.3 |
| Prudential-Bache | 3.6 |

Source: IDD Information Services

### But It May Stake a Larger Claim in Junk Bonds...
*Ranked by total value of junk bond issues managed so far in 1986*

|  | Amount ($ billions) |
|---|---|
| Drexel Burnham | $15.0 |
| Merrill Lynch | 3.2 |
| Morgan Stanley | 3.0 |
| First Boston | 2.1 |
| Goldman, Sachs | 1.9 |
| Salomon Brothers | 1.7 |
| Shearson Lehman | 1.2 |
| Kidder, Peabody | 1.1 |
| Bear, Stearns | 1.0 |
| Donaldson, Lufkin | 0.7 |

Source: IDD Information Services

### And Use Them to Increase Its Acquisition Business
*Advisers ranked by value of publicly disclosed deals completed in 1985*

|  | Amount ($ billions) |
|---|---|
| Goldman, Sachs | $45.7 |
| First Boston | 42.2 |
| Morgan Stanley | 40.5 |
| Shearson Lehman | 19.5 |
| Salomon Brothers | 16.4 |
| Lazard Frères | 13.8 |
| Kidder, Peabody | 12.2 |
| Drexel Burnham | 12.2 |
| Merrill Lynch | 11.7 |
| Dillon, Read | 8.6 |

Source: *Mergers and Acquisitions* magazine.

Nov. 16

# Thrift Units Post Solid Profits

**By ERIC N. BERG**

In sharp contrast to the mediocre earnings being reported by the nation's biggest banks, profits at the largest savings and loan associations are booming.

Indeed, notwithstanding the fact that some 200 thrift units remain in dire financial condition, experts predict another upbeat year for the savings industry, with after-tax profits forecast at a record $6 billion.

"The politicians and regulators focus on the 10 percent of the industry that has slipped out of line, but the remaining 90 percent is doing extremely well," said Allan G. Bortel, the head of savings institution research at Shearson Lehman Brothers Inc.

The third quarter showed just how lucrative the savings and loan business can be. Of the nation's 15-largest publicly held savings institutions, 14 reported a return on equity—a basic measure of financial-institution profitability—exceeding 10 percent. Return on assets—another key gauge of corporate performance in the finance sector—exceeded a robust 1 percent at six institutions and was 0.80 percent or more at nine.

By comparison, of the 15 biggest commercial banks, only one, J. P. Morgan & Company, turned in a return on assets above 1 percent.

A number of factors explain why the big thrift units have been able to outperform the large banks.

Lower interest rates have helped both types of institutions, in the sense that borrowers now find it easier to make monthly payments. But while the lower rates have increased lending volume at savings institutions, volume remains sluggish at banks.

What is more, banks only recently began emphasizing loan selling, which generates fees, as a response to this sales sluggishness. Savings institutions, both to reduce their interest-rate exposure and to avoid the risk that borrowers might repay their loans early, have been selling their loans for years.  Nov. 28

## A roundup of third-quarter savings & loan results

Third-quarter 1986 results for the nation's 15 largest savings and loan institutions.

**Return on assets**
Annualized return on each $100 of average total assets.*

| | |
|---|---|
| Columbia Savings | $1.80 |
| Golden West Financial | 1.48 |
| Great Western Financial | 1.22 |
| H. F. Ahmanson | 1.13 |
| Crossland Savings | 1.09 |
| Home Federal | 0.97 |
| CalFed Inc. | 0.96 |
| Great American First | 0.87 |
| GlenFed Inc. | 0.73 |
| Imperial Corp. America | 0.70 |
| First Federal Michigan | 0.45 |
| CityFed Financial | 0.43 |
| Gibraltar Financial | 0.41 |
| Meritor Financial Group | 0.18 |
| Financial Corp. America | 0.15 |

**Return on equity**
Annualized return on each $100 of average common equity.*

| | |
|---|---|
| Columbia Savings | $34.01 |
| Imperial Corp. America | 31.47 |
| Golden West Financial | 30.68 |
| Great Western Financial | 20.98 |
| Great American First | 20.80 |
| H. F. Ahmanson | 20.14 |
| Gibraltar Financial | 18.36 |
| CalFed Inc. | 17.43 |
| Crossland Savings | 17.35 |
| GlenFed Inc. | 17.14 |
| Fin. Corp. America | 16.05 |
| First Federal Michigan | 14.10 |
| Home Fed. (San Diego) | 13.99 |
| CityFed Financial | 12.32 |
| Meritor Financial | 3.29 |

**Loan quality**
Scheduled items (or equiv.) as percentage of total assets.*

| | |
|---|---|
| First Federal Michigan | 0.31 |
| Columbia Savings | 0.51 |
| GlenFed Inc. | 0.64 |
| Home Fed. (San Diego) | 0.64 |

**Loan quality**
**Scheduled items (or equiv.) as percentage of total assets.***

| | |
|---|---|
| Golden West Financial | 0.72 |
| Great American First | 0.84 |
| Gibraltar Financial | 0.93 |
| CalFed Inc. | 1.06 |
| H. F. Ahmanson | 1.07 |
| Crossland Savings | 1.11 |
| Imperial Corp. | 1.28 |
| Meritor Financial | 1.39 |
| Great Western Financial | 1.89 |
| CityFed Financial | 2.27 |
| Fin. Corp. America | 5.19 |

**Change in earnings**
**Percentage change in fully diluted earnings per share.***

| | |
|---|---|
| Home Fed. (S.D.)† | 1,542.86 |
| GlenFed Inc. | 49.46 |
| Great American First | 40.58 |
| Great Western Financial | 29.03 |
| H. F. Ahmanson | 11.10 |
| Fin. Corp. America | 9.09 |
| CalFed Inc. | 6.06 |
| Gibraltar Financial | 4.35 |
| First Federal Michigan | 2.02 |
| Columbia Savings | 1.19 |
| Golden West Fin. | −16.76 |
| Meritor Financial | −24.14 |
| CityFed Financial | −31.82 |
| Crossland Savings | N.M. |
| Imperial Corp. | N.M. |

*Returns and change in earnings are based on net income applicable to common stockholders.
†Sharp rise due to depressed 1985 results.
N.M. Not meaningful because of losses.
Source: Shearson Lehman Brothers Savings Institutions Equity Research.

Nov. 28

# Stock Strength Predicted

**By JOHN CRUDELE**

On Aug. 13, 1982, with the nation stumbling out of a recession, the Federal Reserve Board used its vast powers over interest rates to try to bring the economy out of its slump, and in doing so touched off the Great Bull Market of the 1980s.

Four and a half years later, Wall Street is wondering whether the most successful millionaire maker of all time can continue to romp for at least one more year.

Even though corporate earnings did not live up to expectations this past year, Wall Street triumphed, thanks in large part to some heady first-half gains, spurred by lower interest rates on competing bond investments. The Dow Jones industrial average, which tracks the action of 30 of the nation's biggest stocks, rose 22.6 percent in 1986, far outpacing the broader indexes of the New York, American and over-the-counter stock markets.

The blue-chip Dow index even threatened to catapult through the vaunted 2,000 level during December, before pulling back. On Wednesday, Dec. 31, it closed at 1,895.95, not far off its record of 1,955.57 set Dec. 2.

To put those numbers in perspective, the Dow closed at just 788.05 on that Friday in August 1982 when the Federal Reserve cut the discount rate, which is the all-important rate it charges its member banks for loans. In the 52 months since then, in what has become by some measures the second best bull market in history both in terms of percentage gains and duration, investors have made an estimated $500 billion in paper profits from equities.

JAN. 2, 1987

## 1986 gainers and losers on the N.Y.S.E.

N.Y.S.E. listed common stocks that showed the largest percentage gains and declines in 1986. Prices are adjusted for splits, and listings exclude stocks trading for less than $2 a share or fewer than 1,000 shares.

| Stock | Dec. 31 close | % change from 1985 close | Comment |
|---|---|---|---|
| **Gainers** | | | |
| Service Resources | 15½ | +235.1 | Holding company for financial printer reports improved results. |
| Banco Central | 34¼ | +226.2 | Spain's largest bank helped by improving economy. |
| Patten Corporation | 16 | +220.0 | Vermont-based property developer shows strong profits. |
| Reebok International | 23⅜ | +152.7 | Maker of athletic footwear shows sharp profit rise. |
| Nord Resources | 21¼ | +150.0 | Rising profits projected for mining and processing company. |
| First Capital Holdings | 14⅞ | +147.9 | Financial services company shares boom in mutual funds. |
| Circuit City Stores | 30⅝ | +147.5 | Earnings on rise for retailers of consumer electronics. |
| Roper Corp. | 18⅜ | +133.3 | Earnings recovery for supplier to Sears, Roebuck. |
| Gap Inc. | 35¾ | +130.6 | New merchandising strategy for apparel retailer lifted profits. |
| L. E. Myers | 5⅜ | +126.3 | New investor acquires 6.6% of utility construction stock. |
| **Losers** | | | |
| First City Bancorp. | 3⅛ | −73.8 | Texas company suffers from depressed loan portfolio. |
| GCA Corp. | 2 | −73.3 | Equipment maker hit by recession in semiconductors. |
| Entex Energy | 3⅜ | −69.7 | Limited partnership suffers from weak energy sector. |
| Ensource Inc. | 6⅛ | −69.4 | Oil and gas explorer hit by declining energy prices. |
| Kaneb Services | 2¼ | −68.4 | Energy company expected to show loss for 1987. |
| Floating Point Systems | 11¼ | −68.3 | Weak capital spending eroded profits of computer maker. |
| Western Union | 4 | −67.7 | Telecommunications company is still losing money. |
| Tidewater Inc. | 4¼ | −66.0 | Owner of offshore fleet suffers from oversupply of oil and gas. |
| Royal International | 6⅛ | −64.2 | Retail optical chain shows depressed earnings. |
| Towle Manufacturing | 2⅜ | −64.2 | Silver and housewares concern filed for bankruptcy protection. |

JAN. 2, 1987

## 1986 gainers and losers on the Amex

Amex-listed common stocks that showed the largest percentage gains and declines in 1986. Prices are adjusted for splits, and listings exclude stocks trading for less than $2 a share or fewer than 1,000 shares.

| Stock | Dec. 31 close | % change from 1985 close | Comment |
|---|---|---|---|
| **Gainers** | | | |
| Philippine Long Distance | 12¾ | +580.0 | Net soars in positive political environment. |
| Lifetime Corp. | 3 | +200.0 | Health services concern aided by acquisitions. |
| Crown Crafts | 24 | +190.9 | Home furnishing concern's earnings quadruple. |
| Heritage Entertainment | 7⅜ | +181.0 | Film distributor raised funds for expansion. |
| Woodstream Corporation | 23⅞ | +165.3 | Sporting goods company's earnings jump. |
| Aloha Inc. | 28½ | +159.1 | Lower fuel costs and L.B.O. lift Hawaiian airline. |
| Lee Pharmaceuticals | 10⅝ | +157.6 | Profits soar for maker of false fingernails. |
| Hovnanian Enterprises | 18½ | +150.8 | Homebuilder buoyed by higher sales and prices. |
| Resorts International | 124 | +150.5 | New merchandising strategy for apparel retailer lifted profits. |
| Lazare Kaplan | 9⅝ | +148.4 | Diamond concern moves from loss to profits. |
| **Losers** | | | |
| Convest Energy Partners | 2¼ | −80.2 | Company, hit by lower energy prices, suspends dividend. |
| NRM Energy | 2⅞ | −76.5 | Concern is battered by oil and gas price weakness. |
| Sandy Corp. | 3¾ | −74.8 | Higher prices, lower margins hit training-program marketer. |
| Engineered System and Dev. | 4 | −71.9 | Weak market for floppy disks causes profit drop. |
| CMI Corp. | 2⅜ | −70.3 | Losses force suspension of energy conversion plant. |
| Conner Corp. | 5 | −69.9 | Mobile home manufacturer raises loss reserve. |
| Professional Care | 2½ | −69.2 | Company officials indicted in Medicaid fraud. |
| Alfin Fragrances | 8½ | −66.2 | F.D.A. seeks further proof on its skin-aging retardant. |
| Energy Development Partners | 4¾ | −63.5 | Energy price drop forces big write-down. |
| Prism Enterprises | 4 | −61.9 | Not available. |

Jan. 2, 1986

## Most active N.Y.S.E. issues in 1986

| Stock | Volume (millions of shares) | 1986 high | 1986 low | 1986 close | Change from 1985 |
|---|---|---|---|---|---|
| A.T.&T. | 528.7 | 27⅞ | 20⅞ | 25 | — |
| USX | 435.1 | 28¾ | 14½ | 21½ | −5⅛ |
| I.B.M. | 407.6 | 161⅞ | 119¼ | 120 | −35½ |
| Mobil | 262.7 | 40⅞ | 26¼ | 40⅛ | +9⅞ |
| Exxon | 241.3 | 74⅛ | 48⅜ | 70⅛ | +15 |
| Eastman Kodak | 240.4 | 70 | 45⅞ | 68⅝ | +18 |
| Phillips Petroleum | 227.6 | 12¾ | 8¼ | 11¾ | −⅜ |
| Goodyear | 225.4 | 50 | 29 | 41⅞ | +10⅝ |
| General Motors | 221.4 | 88⅝ | 65⅞ | 66 | −4⅜ |
| Navistar | 217.2 | 11⅝ | 4¾ | 4¾ | −3¾ |
| Sears | 210.1 | 50⅜ | 35⅞ | 39¾ | +¾ |
| Texaco | 206.5 | 37⅛ | 26 | 35⅞ | +5⅞ |
| American Express | 201.5 | 70⅛ | 50½ | 56⅝ | +3⅝ |
| Commonwealth Edison | 198.0 | 35¾ | 28⅝ | 33⅞ | +4½ |
| Bank-America | 197.9 | 18½ | 9½ | 14⅝ | −1 |

JAN. 2, 1987

## Most active Amex issues in 1986

| Stock | Volume (millions of shares) | 1986 high | 1986 low | 1986 close | Change from 1985 |
|---|---|---|---|---|---|
| Wickes Companies | 270.2 | 7 | 3¼ | 3½ | −1¼ |
| BAT Industries | 120.2 | 7 | 4½ | 6¹³⁄₁₆ | +2⁵⁄₁₅ |
| Wang Labs B | 108.1 | 21¾ | 10½ | 11⅝ | −8 |

| Stock | Volume (millions of shares) | 1986 high | 1986 low | 1986 close | Change from 1985 |
|---|---|---|---|---|---|
| Lorimar-Telepictures | 59.0 | 33⅜ | 15¼ | 16⅛ | † |
| Texas Air | 57.3 | 40⅞ | 14⅛ | 33¾ | +18¾ |
| AM International | 47.7 | 8⅝ | 4⅞ | 6⅜ | +⅜ |
| Echo Bay Mines | 43.5 | 24 | 13 | 23 | +9¾ |
| Horn & Hardart | 41.1 | 19¼ | 6½ | 12¼ | +4⅝ |
| First Australia Prime | 41.1 | 11¾ | 8 | 8⅓ | † |
| Amdahl | 39.8 | 25¾ | 13½ | 23⅜ | +8¾ |
| Hasbro | 36.5 | 30⅞ | 16½ | 19½ | +2⅛ |
| Home Group | 35.5 | 31½ | 17 | 21 | −3½ |
| TIE/Communications | 32.1 | 7⅛ | 2¾ | 3¼ | −3⅝ |
| Husky Oil Limited | 28.6 | 9 | 4⅞ | 8⅛ | +½ |
| Home Shopping Nwk | 27.5 | 44⅝ | 12⅝ | 37⅛ | — |

†Not applicable; new listing in 1986

JAN. 2, 1987

## Most active Nasdaq issues in 1986

| Stock | Volume (millions of shares) | 1986 high | 1986 low | 1986 close | Change from 1985 |
|---|---|---|---|---|---|
| MCI | 447.1 | 13¼ | 6 | 6¼ | −5 |
| Glaxo Holding | 276.7 | 17¾ | 10⅞ | 15⅜ | +4⅜ |
| Jaguar | 254.1 | 9¼ | 4⅝ | 7¹⁵⁄₁₆ | +3 |
| Apple Computer | 238.0 | 43⅞ | 21¾ | 40½ | +18½ |
| Intel | 192.5 | 32¼ | 16⅜ | 21 | −8¼ |

| Stock | Volume (millions of shares) | 1986 high | 1986 low | 1986 close | Change from 1985 |
|---|---|---|---|---|---|
| Seagate | 176.7 | 21 | 7⅛ | 19⅛ | +11⅞ |
| Henley Group | 130.0 | 24¼ | 17¼ | 22⅝ | — |
| Convergent Tech. | 121.9 | 14 | 4⅛ | 6 | −5⅞ |
| Intergraph Corp. | 121.4 | 40½ | 15¼ | 17 | −19¾ |
| THT Lyd | 117.3 | 8¾ | 1¼ | 2¹⁵⁄₁₆ | +1⁹⁄₁₆ |
| U.S. Health Care | 113.6 | 22⅞ | 11⅛ | 11⅝ | −8¾ |
| Tandon Corp. | 113.2 | 7⅞ | 1⅞ | 2⁵⁄₁₆ | −2⁹⁄₁₆ |
| HBO | 112.4 | 18¼ | 8½ | 9¼ | −9⅛ |
| DSC Communications | 106.1 | 12¾ | 5⅜ | 5¾ | −3¼ |
| Tandem Computers | 104.1 | 39½ | 19½ | 34¼ | +12 |

# Heavy Bond Demand

**By MICHAEL QUINT**

With bond yields falling to their lowest level in about nine years, corporate treasurers displayed an awesome appetite for borrowing in 1986. More than $200 billion of new bonds were issued, twice the record set in 1985.

And with bond rates expected to remain at those low levels, investment bankers predict that corporations will continue to flock—although in smaller numbers—to the market. Although many analysts forecast lower rates for early 1987, they acknowledge that the drop should not be as precipitous as the 2-percentage-point decline early last year, and some warn that rates might rise modestly late in 1987.

Analysts at Salomon Brothers estimate that new corporate bond issues, after subtracting bonds that are refinanced, might total about $84 billion in 1987, down slightly from the record $90.9 billion in 1986.

Apart from the activity stimulated by lower interest rates, a record $32.5 billion of high-yield "junk bond" financing was arranged last year. Although other Wall Street firms are devoting more resources to arranging sales of these bond issues, Drexel Burnham Lambert continues to dominate the market.

But even though Drexel's dominance of the junk bond market has elevated the firm into the ranks of the top 10 underwriters, its other underwriting activities fall short of the industry leaders. The First Boston Corporation, combined with Credit Suisse First Boston, its international affiliate, continues as the leading underwriter of debt securities, followed by Salomon Brothers, which is the largest firm in the American debt market.   JAN. 2, 1987

## Leading underwriters in 1986

Total corporate debt issued worldwide rose to $428.8 billion last year from $252.7 billion in 1985. More than half the total—$217.9 billion—was in the United States, up from $97.5 billion in 1985. The total amount handled by the 10 leading underwriters worldwide is shown in the first column. Full credit is given to the book, or lead, manager. Dollars in millions.

| Manager | Global | U.S.[1] | Mortgage[2] | Junk[3] |
|---|---|---|---|---|
| First Boston/ Credit Suisse | 60,712.3 | 39,840.1 | 12,093.4 | 1,541.9 |
| Salomon Brothers | 52,562.1 | 44,057.3 | 17,023.3 | 2,423.8 |
| Morgan Stanley | 36,109.9 | 26,786.0 | 3,804.5 | 2,480.2 |
| Merrill Lynch Cap. Mkts. | 31,165.0 | 24,243.8 | 7,592.3 | 3,174.8 |

| Manager | Global | U.S.[1] | Mortgage[2] | Junk[3] |
|---|---|---|---|---|
| Goldman, Sachs | 26,571.5 | 22,490.5 | 2,590.5 | 1,499.2 |
| Drexel Burnham Lambert | 25,454.2 | 21,877.5 | 1,365.7 | 14,587.8 |
| Shearson Lehman Bros. | 17,030.3 | 12,593.0 | 3,843.1 | 2,018.7 |
| Nomura Securities | 16,847.0 | 250.0 | n.a. | n.a. |
| Deutsche Bank | 12,076.1 | n.a. | n.a. | n.a. |
| Daiwa Securities | 10,795.6 | 125.0 | n.a. | n.a. |

[1]Nonconvertible debt issues.
[2]Not included in global total.
[3]Nonconvertible high yield bonds.

Source: IDD Information Services

JAN. 2, 1987

## The top deals of 1986

The 10 biggest deals announced and completed during the past year, in billions of dollars.

| Purchaser | Company purchased | Price |
|---|---|---|
| Kohlberg, Kravis & Roberts | Safeway Stores | $5.3 |
| Burroughs Corporation | Sperry Corporation | 4.4 |
| Occidental Petroleum | Midcon | 2.5 |
| May Department Stores | Associated Dry Goods | 2.4 |
| Ralston Purina | Union Carbide's battery division | 1.4 |
| Coca-Cola | JTL | 1.4 |
| JSC/MS Holdings | Container Corporation of America | 1.2 |
| Pontifex (Lockheed unit) | Sanders Associates | 1.2 |
| International Paper | Hammermill Paper | 1.1 |
| Wells Fargo | Crocker National | 1.1 |

Source: Mergers & Acquisitions magazine

JAN. 2, 1987

# Funds Trail Big Stock Gauges

**By VARTANIG G. VARTAN**

Investors stormed into mutual funds last year, but they probably would have been better off investing in a run-of-the-mill blue-chip stock. That is because the average stock mutual fund was left in the dust by the Standard & Poor's index of 500 leading stocks.

Even so, the roster of 568 general equity funds showed, on average, a healthy performance, producing a total return of 13.39 percent. But this lagged behind the leading market indicators, since the investment concentration during 1986 was on large-capitalization blue chips. The S.&P. 500-stock index had a total return, including dividends, of 18.71 percent, while the total return of the Dow average was 27.25 percent.

International funds, which invest only in foreign stocks, ranked as the best-performing sector of the mutual fund industry in 1986, with a total return averaging 53.25 percent. The internationals, which ranked second behind the health care funds in 1985, benefitted from the declining value of the dollar against foreign currencies.

Results for the fourth quarter, however, showed a change in leadership. "Capital appreciation funds and technology funds—relatively poor performers for the year as a whole—ranked among the best gainers," according to Michael Lipper, president of Lipper Analytical Services, which monitors the fund industry.

For the final quarter alone, top honors went to two small funds. First was the $4.3 million Delcap Fund 1, with a return of 17.36 percent. It was followed by 44 Wall Street Equity, with assets of $8.2 million, which was ahead 17.11 percent. Both are capital appreciation funds,

## How mutual funds have performed

Funds showing largest percentage changes in net asset value in 1986 from 1985, and in fourth quarter from previous quarter.*

### Annual changes

| Gainers | | Losers | |
|---|---|---|---|
| New England Zenith Capital Growth | +95.21% | 88 Fund | −30.54% |
| Merrill Lynch Pacific | +78.05 | American Heritage | −26.05 |
| Nomura Pacific Basin | +74.48 | Fidelity Select Electronics | −23.85 |
| Newport Far East | +73.26 | Bowser Growth | −22.89 |
| Financial Portfolio Pacific | +72.49 | Strategic Capital Gains | −21.39 |
| GT Pacific Growth | +70.04 | Dividend/Growth Laser, Advanced Technology | −21.16 |
| Fidelity Overseas | +69.25 | Steadman American Industry | −19.72 |
| BBK International | +61.97 | 44 Wall Street | −16.26 |
| T. Rowe Price International | +61.29 | Fidelity Select Energy Services | −15.75 |
| GT Japan Growth | +60.62 | First Investors Natural Resources | −14.85 |

### Quarterly changes

| Gainers | | Losers | |
|---|---|---|---|
| Delcap Fund I | +17.36% | Strategic Silver | −10.43% |
| 44 Wall Street Equity | +17.11 | Bowser Growth | −9.90 |
| First Investors U.S. Government Plus I | +14.86 | Rochester Convertible | −8.83 |
| Financial Portfolio Technology | +13.94 | Sherman Dean Fund | −8.57 |
| USAA Gold | +12.89 | Shield Aggressive Growth | −7.82 |
| Trustees Commingled International | +12.84 | American Capital Life Stock | −7.72 |
| Benham Target 2010 | +11.43 | Rochester Growth | −6.95 |
| Fidelity Select Computer | +11.00 | Wealth Monitors | −6.94 |
| Gintel Erisa | +10.83 | Fidelity Select Life Insurance | −6.77 |
| IDS Precious Metals | +10.41 | Strategic Capital Gains | −6.44 |

*Dividends, capital gains reinvested.

Source: Lipper Analytical Services Inc.

JAN. 7

which as small funds can rack up excellent performances by hitting it right on just a few stocks.

Similarly, the No. 1 performer for the full year, out of 950 funds of all types, was the $7-million-in-assets New England Zenith Capital Growth, with a gain of 95.21 percent. G. Kenneth Heebner, portfolio manager of the Boston-based fund, found a winner in Home Shopping Network, a new issue that rose sevenfold between May and December.

JAN. 7

# PART 6
# Sports

## Pro football's leading receivers

| | Catches | Years |
|---|---|---|
| Charlie Joiner | 716 | 17 |
| Charley Taylor | 649 | 13 |
| Don Maynard | 633 | 15 |
| Raymond Berry | 631 | 13 |
| Steve Largent | 627 | 10 |
| Harold Carmichael | 590 | 14 |
| Fred Biletnikoff | 589 | 14 |
| Harold Jackson | 579 | 16 |
| Lionel Taylor | 567 | 10 |
| Lance Alworth | 542 | 11 |
| Bobby Mitchell | 521 | 11 |
| Billy Howton | 503 | 12 |
| Ozzie Newsome | 502 | 8 |
| Cliff Branch | 501 | 14 |

JAN. 4

## The top five pro football postseason rushing performances in yards gained

248—Eric Dickerson, L.A. Rams, vs. Dallas, 1985 season.
206—Keith Lincoln, San Diego, vs. Boston, 1963.
202—Lawrence McCutcheon, L.A. Rams, vs. St. Louis, 1975.
202—Freeman McNeil, Jets, vs. Cincinnati, 1982.
196—Steve Van Buren, Philadelphia, vs. L.A. Rams, 1949.

JAN. 6

# Tip of the Mike to Broadcasting's Best

## Best football broadcasters

(in the judgment of Michael Goodwin, who writes the TV Sports column for *The Times*)

**Host: Bob Costas, NBC.** Only in his second year, Costas wins for his ability to do a little comedy, give the facts and dispense some insights, all while keeping matters moving painlessly forward.
**Ex-player: Ahmad Rashad, NBC.** Usually has something to say that is worth listening to.
**Parimutuel Clerk: Pete Axthelm, NBC.** He gets the nod in part for his spunk and friendly face and in part for his so-close-it-was-scary prediction that the Bears would beat the Giants, 23–0. (The final was 21–0.)
**Play-by-Play: Pat Summerall, CBS.** All-round pro, good voice, humor, enthusiasm, knowledge.
**Analyst: John Madden, CBS.** Summerall's partner, and together they are far and away the best in the business.

JAN. 14

## Baseball pay: How free agents fared

Free agents who had to sign with their 1985 clubs by midnight Wednesday or otherwise become ineligible to sign with them until May 1, 1986

| Name | Team | Contract Terms |
|---|---|---|
| Tony Bernazard | Cleveland | 2 years, $1.14 million. |
| Tom Brookens | Detroit | 2 years, $755,000. |
| Jamie Easterly | Cleveland | 2 years, $720,000. |
| Carlton Fisk | White Sox | 2 years, $1.75 million. |
| Kirk Gibson | Detroit | 3 years, $4 million. |
| Donnie Moore | California | 3 years, $3 million. |
| Joe Niekro | N.Y. Yankees | 3 years, $2.325 million. |
| Phil Niekro | N.Y. Yankees | 1 year, $250,000 ($350,000 if on opening-day roster). |
| Butch Wynegar | N.Y. Yankees | 3 years plus an option year, $2.2 million. |

## Baseball earnings in 1985

Average salaries by position in the major leagues for 1985. For the six field positions, players included played in 100 or more games; designated hitters played in 80 or more games; starting pitchers made 19 or more starts and relief pitchers made fewer than 10 starts and 25 or more relief appearances. The number in parentheses is the number of players used to determine salaries.

| Position | American League | National League | Major League Total |
|---|---|---|---|
| 1B | (13) $537,353 | (9) $960,027 | (22) $710,265 |
| 2B | (12) 488,542 | (12) 438,406 | (24) 463,474 |
| 3B | (12) 467,646 | (10) 563,467 | (22) 511,201 |
| SS | (13) 237,310 | (9) 656,401 | (22) 408,756 |
| C | (12) 445,253 | (9) 614,581 | (21) 532,771 |
| OF | (36) 585,712 | (29) 538,730 | (65) 564,751 |
| DH | (10) 709,865 | Not applicable | (10) 709,865 |
| SP | (55) 427,324 | (53) 475,803 | (108) 451,115 |
| RP | (61) 326,472 | (52) 345,744 | (113) 335,341 |

JAN. 10

# Super Bowl

In Super Bowl XX, the Chicago Bears (NFC) defeated the New England Patriots (AFC) by 46–10. Mike Ditka was the winning coach and Ray Berry the losing coach in the January 26 game, played in New Orleans before 73,818. Richard Dent was the most valuable player, and the winners received $36,000 each while the losers got $18,000.

Below are the results of earlier Super Bowls:

## Results: from I to XIX

| Result | Winning Coach | Losing Coach | Date and Site | Attendance | Most Valuable Player | Winning Share | Losing Share |
|---|---|---|---|---|---|---|---|
| Green Bay (NFL) 35, Kansas City (AFL) 10 | Vince Lombardi | Hank Stram | Jan. 15, 1967, Los Angeles | 61,946 | Bart Starr | $15,000 | $7,500 |
| Green Bay (NFL) 33, Oakland (AFL) 14 | Vince Lombardi | John Rauch | Jan. 14, 1968, Miami | 75,546 | Bart Starr | 15,000 | 7,500 |
| New York (AFL) 16, Baltimore (NFL) 7 | Weeb Ewbank | Don Shula | Jan. 12, 1969, Miami | 75,389 | Joe Namath | 15,000 | 7,500 |
| Kansas City (AFL) 23, Minnesota (NFL) 7 | Hank Stram | Bud Grant | Jan. 11, 1970, New Orleans | 80,562 | Len Dawson | 15,000 | 7,500 |
| Baltimore (AFC) 16, Dallas (NFC) 13 | Don McCafferty | Tom Landry | Jan. 17, 1971, Miami | 79,204 | Chuck Howley | 15,000 | 7,500 |
| Dallas (NFC) 24, Miami (AFC) 3 | Tom Landry | Don Shula | Jan. 16, 1972, New Orleans | 81,023 | Roger Staubach | 15,000 | 7,500 |
| Miami (AFC) 14, Washington (NFC) 7 | Don Shula | George Allen | Jan. 14, 1973, Los Angeles | 90,182 | Jake Scott | 15,000 | 7,500 |
| Miami (AFC) 24, Minnesota (NFC) 7 | Don Shula | Bud Grant | Jan. 13, 1974, Houston | 71,882 | Larry Csonka | 15,000 | 7,500 |

# SPORTS

| Result | Winning Coach | Losing Coach | Date and Site | Attendance | Most Valuable Player | Winning Share | Losing Share |
|---|---|---|---|---|---|---|---|
| Pittsburgh (AFC) 16, Minnesota (NFC) 7 | Chuck Noll | Bud Grant | Jan. 12, 1975, New Orleans | 80,997 | Franco Harris | 15,000 | 7,500 |
| Pittsburgh (AFC) 21, Dallas (NFC) 17 | Chuck Noll | Tom Landry | Jan. 18, 1976, Miami | 80,187 | Lynn Swann | 15,000 | 7,500 |
| Oakland (AFC) 32, Minnesota (NFC) 14 | John Madden | Bud Grant | Jan. 9, 1977, Pasadena, Calif. | 103,428 | Fred Biletnikoff | 15,000 | 7,500 |
| Dallas (NFC) 27, Denver (AFC) 10 | Tom Landry | Red Miller | Jan. 15, 1978, New Orleans | 75,804 | Harvey Martin and Randy White | 18,000 | 9,000 |
| Pittsburgh (AFC) 35, Dallas (NFC) 31 | Chuck Noll | Tom Landry | Jan. 21, 1979, Miami | 78,656 | Terry Bradshaw | 18,000 | 9,000 |
| Pittsburgh (AFC) 31, Los Angeles (NFC) 19 | Chuck Noll | Ray Malavasi | Jan. 20, 1980, Pasadena, Calif. | 103,985 | Terry Bradshaw | 18,000 | 9,000 |
| Oakland (AFC) 27, Philadelphia (NFC) 10 | Tom Flores | Dick Vermeil | Jan. 25, 1981, New Orleans | 75,500 | Jim Plunkett | 18,000 | 9,000 |
| San Francisco (NFC) 26, Cincinnati (AFC) 21 | Bill Walsh | Forrest Gregg | Jan. 24, 1982, Pontiac, Mich. | 81,270 | Joe Montana | 18,000 | 9,000 |
| Washington (NFC) 27, Miami (AFC) 17 | Joe Gibbs | Don Shula | Jan. 30, 1983, Pasadena, Calif. | 103,667 | John Riggins | 36,000 | 18,000 |
| Los Angeles (AFC) 38, Washington (NFC) 9 | Tom Flores | Joe Gibbs | Jan. 22, 1984, Tampa, Fla. | 72,920 | Marcus Allen | 36,000 | 18,000 |
| San Francisco (NFC) 38, Miami (AFC) 16 | Bill Walsh | Don Shula | Jan. 20, 1985, Palo Alto, Calif. | 84,059 | Joe Montana | 36,000 | 18,000 |

### New Members of Pro Football Hall of Fame

**Willie Lanier** Middle linebacker, Kansas City Chiefs, 11 seasons, 149 games. A ferocious tackler, he led an upset of Minnesota in Super Bowl IV. Career totals: 27 pass interceptions (2 returned for touchdowns) and 13 recoveries of opponents' fumbles.

**Paul Hornung** Running back and kicker, Green Bay Packers, 9 seasons, 104 games. In 1960 he scored 176 points, still a record. He kicked 190 of 194 extra points, 66 of 140 field goals, rushed for 3,711 yards and passed for 1,480.

**Ken Houston** Defensive back, Houston Oilers and Washington Redskins, 14 seasons, 196 games. He intercepted 49 passes and returned 9 for touchdowns, the latter a career record. In 1971 with the Oilers, he returned 4 interceptions for touchdowns, a feat matched only by Jim Kearney of Kansas City in 1972.

**Fran Tarkenton** Quarterback, Minnesota Vikings and New York Giants, 18 seasons, 246 games. Holds career passing records in attempts (6,467), completions (3,686), yards (47,003) and touchdowns (342).

**Doak Walker** Running back, defensive back, placekicker and kick-return man, Detroit Lions, 6 seasons, 67 games. He scored 534 points by kicking 183 of 191 extra points, 49 of 87 field goals, running for 12 touchdowns, catching 21 and returning a punt for another.

JAN. 29

## College Basketball '86

CHAPEL HILL, N.C.—Less than two minutes remained as Kenny Smith, the North Carolina guard, hurriedly drove downcourt, his team trailing by 5 points. The top-ranked Tar Heels had come back from a 13-point second-half deficit against a highly ranked Georgia Tech team drawing support from a wildly enthusiastic home crowd. Time was running out.

Yet the visitors from Chapel Hill remained oddly confident, as if they were in command.

Dean Smith, the North Carolina coach, left intact the three-guard lineup of Jeff Lebo, Steve Hale and Kenny Smith that had fueled the rally, instructing his players to force action defensively against a Yellow Jacket squad that had grown tentative trying to milk the clock.

Unmentioned but ever-present in the Carolina players' minds was a 25-season history peppered with great escapes by Smith's teams, including several this season and last, bolstered by hours of preparation so carefully calibrated that North Carolina players say they never encounter a game situation they haven't practiced before.

"They just believe if they do what they're told, they'll win," said Billy Cunningham, the former Philadelphia 76ers coach who played for Dean Smith two decades ago and now watches Smith's teams as a television commentator. "It's amazing, when you have the ability to believe in somebody or something that strongly, the confidence it produces."

Sure enough, during the final two minutes the Tar Heels forced a key turnover and outscored Tech 6–1 to send the game into overtime. They went on to win, 78–77. FEB. 9

### How Dean Smith of the University of North Carolina stands among college basketball coaches

Leading Division I Coaches
**By percentage** (minimum 10 head coaching seasons)

| | Seas. | W | L | Pct. |
|---|---|---|---|---|
| 1. Clair Bee | 21 | 410 | 86 | .827 |
| 2. Adolph Rupp | 41 | 875 | 190 | .822 |
| 3. Jerry Tarkanian* | 17 | 425 | 95 | .817 |
| 4. John Wooden | 29 | 667 | 161 | .806 |
| 5. Dean Smith* | 24 | 575 | 166 | .776 |
| 6. Phog Allen | 46 | 771 | 233 | .768 |

**By victories** (minimum 10 head coaching seasons)

| | | |
|---|---|---|
| 1. | Adolph Rupp | 875 |
| 2. | Phog Allen | 771 |
| 3. | Henry Iba | 767 |
| 4. | Ed Diddle | 759 |
| 5. | Ray Meyer | 724 |
| 6. | John Wooden | 667 |
| 7. | Marv Harshman | 642 |
| 8. | Cam Henderson | 611 |
| 9. | Slats Gill | 599 |
| 10. | Ralph Miller*† | 610 |
| 11. | Guy Lewis* | 588 |
| 12. | Dean Smith* | 575 |
| 13. | Paul Hinkle | 560 |
| 14. | Norm Sloan*† | 553 |
| 15. | Frank McGuire | 550 |

*Active coaches
†Records through Friday, Feb. 7

FEB. 9

# Richardson Is Banned as Tests Find Cocaine

### By SAM GOLDAPER

Michael Ray Richardson, the Nets' playmaking guard whose personal problems have undermined his splendid athletic talent, was banned from the National Basketball Association yesterday after testing positive for cocaine use.

A grim-faced David Stern, the league's commissioner, made the announcement at a midtown hotel after the league received the results of the drug test late Monday night. The commissioner called it "a tragic day for Michael Ray Richardson, nothing less than the destruction by cocaine of a once-flourishing career."

The action can be appealed after two years, and Richardson could be reinstated with the approval of the league and the National Basketball Players Association, the players' union.

Charles Grantham, Richardson's agent and the executive vice president of the player's union, said that his client had denied taking drugs.

"Michael said the tests were incorrect," Grantham said. "Sugar says he's clean, that he didn't use drugs." Grantham said that Richardson had already taken another test, and that it was not "within the realm of impossibility" that the first tests were wrong. "We'd like to have them verified. Too many things are inconclusive," he said.

The banning of Richardson was mandatory. Under the terms of a drug agreement negotiated between the N.B.A. and the players' union that was announced on Sept. 28, 1983, any player found using drugs three times would automatically be banned from the league.

Under the agreement, which carried an amnesty period until Dec. 31, 1983, for players who came forward and accepted treatment, the first time a player was found to be using drugs he would continue to receive his salary and would undergo treatment at his club's expense. A second offense would result in suspension without pay and further treatment, again at the club's expense. A third offense called for the player to be banned for life from the N.B.A.

Richardson, 30 years old, is the first active player to be banned under the agreement. John Drew, who is now playing in the Continental Basketball Association, was banned last fall, although he had already been released by the Utah Jazz. Drew appealed the ban, but the N.B.A. upheld it last month.

FEB. 26

## Richardson's ordeal is recounted

(The events leading up to the suspension of Michael Ray Richardson from the National Basketball Association)

**June 9, 1978**—The Knicks, picking fourth in the college draft, select Mike Richardson of the University of Montana. The Knick coach, Willis Reed, calls the 6-foot-5-inch guard "one of the best all-around guards in the nation."

**Oct. 22, 1982**—The Knicks trade Richardson and future considerations to the Golden State Warriors for Bernard King.

**Feb. 6, 1983**—The Nets send Mickey Johnson and Eric (Sleepy) Floyd to Golden State for Richardson.

**May 11, 1983**—Richardson checks into a treatment program at Fair Oaks Hospital in Summit, N.J.

**Aug. 12, 1983**—Richardson voluntarily enters a cocaine abuse rehabilitation program at the Hazeldon Foundation, a drug-treatment center outside Minneapolis.

**Sept. 28, 1983**—Richardson calls a news conference to announce that he is cured.

**Oct. 4, 1983**—Richardson disappears from the Nets preseason camp in Princeton, N.J.

**Oct. 7, 1983**—Richardson contacts the N.B.A. Players Association. The Nets' coach, Stan Albeck, informs the team that Richardson has suffered a relapse and is being prepared for a treatment program.

**Oct. 11, 1983**—Richardson is waived after disappearing for three days and refusing to enter a rehabilitation center.

**Oct. 12, 1983**—Richardson's agent, Pat Healy, files a grievance against the N.B.A. asking that Richardson be paid during rehabilitation and reinstated "if and when he completes the program."

**Oct. 14, 1983**—Richardson enters Regent Hospital, a psychiatric hospital in Manhattan, for treatment for his relapse of cocaine use.

**Nov. 1, 1983**—Richardson is released from Regent Hospital after two and a half weeks of treatment.

**Nov. 17, 1983**—Richardson's wife, Rene, is granted a divorce.

**Dec. 21, 1983**—The Nets agree to reinstate Richardson after a two-month suspension.

**Jan. 28, 1984**—Richardson marries Leah Burton.

**Spring 1985**—Richardson is named the league's Comeback Player of the Year.

**Sept. 3, 1985**—Richardson signs a four-year contract, guaranteed for the first three years, with an average annual salary of $725,000.

**Nov. 10, 1985**—Richardson misses a team flight from Newark to San Antonio, citing traffic problems. He arrives the next day, a few hours before game time.

**Dec. 27-28, 1985**—Following the team's Christmas party, Richardson visits a bar with Daryl Dawkins and Bobby Cattage, then disappears.

**Dec. 30, 1985**—Richardson contacts his agent, Charles Grantham.

**Dec. 31, 1985**—Grantham notifies Lewis Schaffel, the Nets' executive vice president, that Richardson has had a relapse. He is suspended without pay and subsequently enters a drug-treatment center in Pasadena, Calif.

**Jan. 20, 1986**—Richardson returns to the Nets.

**Feb. 10, 1986**—Richardson calls in sick and misses a team practice and a doctor's appointment. He is fined an undisclosed amount and suspended for one game.

**Feb. 11, 1986**—The league orders that Richardson be tested to determine if his disappearance was related to a drug relapse.

**Feb. 12, 1986**—The test results are negative, and Richardson joins the team in Cleveland.

**Feb. 20, 1986**—Richardson is arrested and charged with assault after trying to break into his Mahwah, N.J., home.

**Feb. 24, 1986**—Richardson tests positive for cocaine.

**Feb. 25, 1986**—Richardson is banned from the N.B.A.

FEB. 26

# Baseball Orders Suspension of 11 Drug Users

By MICHAEL GOODWIN

Baseball Commissioner Peter Ueberroth yesterday suspended for one year Keith

Hernandez of the Mets, Dale Berra of the Yankees and five other major league players for cocaine use. However, Mr. Ueberroth offered to lift the suspensions if the players agreed to certain conditions, including contributing 10 percent of their salaries this year to programs to combat drug abuse and submitting to drug tests for the remainder of their careers.

Four other players were suspended for 60 days, with the bans to be lifted if they give 5 percent of their salaries to drug programs and agree to testing.

The commissioner also said he would require 10 other players to undergo testing for the remainder of their careers because of past use of cocaine. These 10 are not to be penalized.

Any of the players involved who have positive tests for cocaine, marijuana, morphine or heroin would automatically be subject to the suspension, Mr. Ueberroth said. Similarly, those who refuse to be tested would be subject to the suspensions, which would be effective opening day. Those suspended would not be paid.

The one-year suspensions were handed out to those players who Mr. Ueberroth said had not only used drugs themselves but had also "in some fashion facilitated the distribution of drugs in baseball." He said these players had shared drugs with teammates and in some cases introduced players to drug dealers.

In addition to Mr. Hernandez and Mr. Berra, the players given one-year suspensions were Joaquín Andújar, Dave Parker, Jeff Leonard, Lonnie Smith and Enos Cabell.

MARCH 1

## Paying the price

Following are the amounts, representing 10 percent of the player's annual salary, that would have to be donated to a drug-abuse prevention facility or program by players disciplined by Commissioner Peter Ueberroth.

| Player | Team | Salary | Donation |
| --- | --- | --- | --- |
| Keith Hernandez | Mets | $1,350,000 | $135,000 |
| Joaquín Andújar | Oakland | 1,150,000 | 115,000 |
| Jeff Leonard | San Francisco | 900,000 | 90,000 |
| Dave Parker | Cincinnati | 875,000 | 87,500 |
| Lonnie Smith | Kansas City | 850,000 | 85,000 |
| Dale Berra | Yankees | 512,500 | 51,250 |
| Enos Cabell | Los Angeles | 450,000 | 45,000 |

Following are amounts, representing 5 percent of the annual salary, that would have to be donated.

| Lee Lacy | Baltimore | 600,000 | 30,000 |
| Claudell Washington | Atlanta | 600,000 | 30,000 |
| Al Holland | Yankees | 400,000 | 20,000 |
| Lary Sorensen | Chicago Cubs | 200,000 | 10,000* |

*Sorensen's contract has three different possible payments. He will get $200,000 if he is on an opening-day major league roster or $100,000 if he is in the minor leagues. If he is released in spring training, he would receive $50,000. His donation, if required from that payment, would be $2,500.

MARCH 1

### Steals in the N.B.A.

These are the 10 best single-game theft performances in league history:

| | |
|---|---|
| Larry Kenon, Spurs, vs. Kings, 1975–76 | 11 |
| Jerry West, Lakers, vs. Sonics, 1973–74 | 10 |
| L. Steele, Blazers, vs. Lakers, 1974–75 | 10 |
| Fred Brown, Sonics, vs. 76ers, 1976–77 | 10 |
| Gus Williams, Sonics, vs. Nets, 1977–78 | 10 |
| Eddie Jordan, Nets, vs. 76ers, 1978–79 | 10 |
| J. Moore, Spurs, vs. Pacers, 1984–85 | 10 |
| L. Lever, Nuggets, vs. Pacers, 1984–85 | 10 |
| C. Drexler, Blazers, vs. Bucks, 1985–86 | 10 |
| A. Robertson, Spurs, vs. Suns, 1985–86 | 10 |

MARCH 6

# For Yogi Berra, a Happy Return

### By IRA BERKOW

**K**ISSIMMEE, Fla.—In a period spanning a little more than 40 years. Yogi Berra has survived both D-Day and George Steinbrenner, and is alive and well and coaching in Kissimmee.

Lawrence Peter (Yogi) Berra is 60 years old and a long way from when he was 19 on June 6, 1944, and serving on a Navy landing craft at Normandy—"They called it the suicide squad," he said with a smile. And he is a long way from April 30, 1985, when, just 16 games into the season, Steinbrenner, the Yankees' principal owner and noted manager-dumper, dropped Berra as manager.

Berra rarely complains or backbites. All he said about his Steinbrenner past is, "I didn't get a fair shake."

Now, for the first time in his 40-year big-league baseball career, Berra wears neither the vertical blue pinstripes of the Yankees nor the Mets but the horizontal orange of the Houston Astros, who are limbering up for the season in this tourist haven that is close by Disney World.

"I'm happy to be in a baseball uniform," Berra said. "The only difference now is the stripes are goin' the other way." He seems relaxed and content as he enters the ball field on a recent warm, sunny afternoon before a spring training game.

"Yogi, Yogi, our Yogi," squeals a middle-aged female fan when she spots Berra entering the ballpark here. She is one of many who stand imploringly along the low wire-mesh fence that separates the spectators from the baseball folks in the Osceola County Stadium here. They wait and seek an autograph from this gnomic, knock-kneed, accommodating figure, this old, unlikely looking hero, the gold frames of his glasses sparkling in the sun, the sprigs of gray hair extending from beneath his blue baseball cap, his thick neck and wrists and hands browned by the sun, and, tucked under his left arm, a fungo bat with his familiar No. 8 inscribed on the handle.

"Can I get a picture of you with my kids, Yogi?" calls a man in a floppy tennis hat.

Berra pushes back the bill of his cap. When the picture is taken, Berra says to a companion, "Oh, oh, got my toothpick in my mouth."

"How's Elston Howard doin' these days?" someone asked, referring to Berra's former teammate.

"He died," said Berra, scribbling away.

"He was young," said the man.

"Yeah, he was," said Berra, taking another notepad.

Craig Reynolds, an infielder for the Astros, has joined Berra in signing autographs.

Someone hands Berra an old baseball card.

"Gee, I was young there," Berra said. Craig looks over, appearing incredulous at the youthful Berra pictured on the card. "What year was that?" he asked.

"About 1951," said Berra.

"I wasn't even *born* then," said Reynolds, who arrived on this planet in 1952.

MARCH 24

## Berra's 40 Years

"I don't know what else to do. I been doin' it since I was 14 years old."

**1946–1963:** Played for Yankees . . . 2116 Games . . . 358 HR . . . .285 Avg.

**1964:** Managed Yankees* . . . W 99 L 63 . . . Lost in World Series

**1965:** Played for Mets . . . 4 Games . . . 0 HR . . . .222 Avg.

**1965–71:** Coach for Mets

**1972–75:** Managed Mets** . . . 292–296 . . . Won Pennant in 1973.

**1976–1983:** Coach for Yankees

**1984–85:** Managed Yankees† . . . 93–85

**1986:** Coach for Astros

*Replaced after 1964 season.
**Replaced Aug. 5, 1975.
†Replaced April 30, 1985.

MARCH 24

## The 22 summers of Phil Niekro

| Year | W-L | SO | E.R.A. |
|---|---|---|---|
| 1964 | 0-0 | 8 | 4.80 |
| 1965 | 2-3 | 49 | 2.88 |
| 1966 | 4-3 | 17 | 4.14 |
| 1967 | 11-9 | 129 | 1.87 |
| 1968 | 14-12 | 140 | 2.59 |
| 1969 | 23-13 | 193 | 2.57 |
| 1970 | 12-18 | 168 | 4.27 |
| 1971 | 15-14 | 173 | 2.98 |
| 1972 | 16-12 | 164 | 3.06 |
| 1973 | 13-10 | 131 | 3.31 |
| 1974 | 20-13 | 195 | 2.38 |
| 1975 | 15-15 | 144 | 3.20 |
| 1976 | 17-11 | 173 | 3.29 |
| 1977 | 16-20 | 262 | 4.04 |
| 1978 | 19-18 | 248 | 2.88 |
| 1979 | 21-20 | 208 | 3.39 |
| 1980 | 15-18 | 176 | 3.63 |
| 1981 | 7-7 | 62 | 3.11 |
| 1982 | 17-4 | 144 | 3.61 |
| 1983 | 11-10 | 128 | 3.97 |
| 1984 | 16-8 | 136 | 3.09 |
| 1985 | 16-12 | 149 | 4.09 |
| Total | 300-250 | 3,197 | 3.23 |

Niekro played for the Braves in Milwaukee then Atlanta from 1964 through 1983; he played for the Yankees in 1984 and 1985.

MARCH 30

## N.C.A.A. championship basketball games

1939—Oregon 46, Ohio State 33.
1940—Indiana 60, Kansas 42.
1941—Wisconsin 39, Washington State 34.
1942—Stanford 53, Dartmouth 38.
1943—Wyoming 46, Georgetown 34.
1944—Utah 42, Dartmouth 40 (overtime).
1945—Oklahoma A & M 49, N.Y.U. 45.
1946—Oklahoma A & M 43, North Carolina 40.
1947—Holy Cross 58, Oklahoma 47.
1948—Kentucky 58, Baylor 42.
1949—Kentucky 46, Oklahoma State 36.
1950—C.C.N.Y. 71, Bradley 68.
1951—Kentucky 68, Kansas State 58.
1952—Kansas 80, St. John's 63.
1953—Indiana 69, Kansas 68.
1954—La Salle 92, Bradley 76.
1955—San Francisco 77, La Salle 63.
1956—San Francisco 83, Iowa 71.
1957—North Carolina 54, Kansas 53 (3 overtimes).
1958—Kentucky 84, Seattle 72.
1959—California 71, West Virginia 70.
1960—Ohio State 75, California 55.
1961—Cincinnati 70, Ohio State 65 (overtime).
1962—Cincinnati 71, Ohio State 59.

1963—Loyola, Ill. 60, Cincinnati 58 (overtime).
1964—U.C.L.A. 98, Duke 83.
1965—U.C.L.A. 91, Michigan 80.
1966—Texas Western 72, Kentucky 65.
1967—U.C.L.A. 79, Dayton 64.
1968—U.C.L.A. 78, North Carolina 55.
1969—U.C.L.A. 92, Purdue 72.
1970—U.C.L.A. 80, Jacksonville 69.
1971—U.C.L.A. 68, Villanova 62.
1972—U.C.L.A. 81, Florida State 76.
1973—U.C.L.A. 87, Memphis State 66.
1974—North Carolina St. 76, Marquette 64.
1975—U.C.L.A. 92, Kentucky 85.
1976—Indiana 86, Michigan 68.
1977—Marquette 67, North Carolina 59.
1978—Kentucky 94, Duke 88.
1979—Michigan State 75, Indiana State 64.
1980—Louisville 59, U.C.L.A. 54.
1981—Indiana 63, North Carolina 50.
1982—North Carolina 63, Georgetown 62.
1983—North Carolina St. 54, Houston 52.
1984—Georgetown 84, Houston 75.
1985—Villanova 66, Georgetown 64.
1986—Louisville 72, Duke 69.

MARCH 31 AND APRIL 1

## Positional leaders

The highest paid player at each position (all figures are based on base salary, pro-rated share of signing bonus and any other guaranteed money attributed to this year).

|  |  |  |
|---|---|---|
| First Base | Bob Horner, Atlanta | $1,800,000 |
| Second Base | Willie Randolph, Yankees | 1,050,000 |
| Shortstop | Ozzie Smith, St. Louis | 1,940,000 |
| Third Base | Mike Schmidt, Phil. | 1,936,333 |
| Left Field | Jim Rice, Boston | 2,080,000 |
| Center Field | Dale Murphy, Atlanta | 1,800,000 |
| Right Field | Dave Winfield, Yankees | 1,861,460 |
| Catcher | Gary Carter, Mets | 1,885,714 |
| D.H. | Andre Thornton, Clev. | 1,100,000 |
| Starting Pitcher | Fernando Valenzuela, L.A. | 1,600,000 |
| Relief Pitcher | Bruce Sutter, Atlanta | 1,729,167 |

APRIL 6

## Baseball salaries: The biggest raises

The 10 biggest raises from 1985 to 1986, some on new contracts, some within existing contracts.

| | '85 Salary | '86 Salary | Raise |
|---|---|---|---|
| 1. Jim Rice, Boston | $740,000 | $2,080,000 | $1,340,000 |
| 2. Don Mattingly, Yankees | 455,000 | 1,375,000 | 920,000 |
| 3. Dwight Gooden, Mets | 450,000 | 1,320,000 | 870,000 |
| 4. Bert Blyleven, Minnesota | 650,000 | 1,460,000 | 800,000 |
| 5. Orel Hershiser, L.A. | 212,000 | 1,000,000 | 788,000 |
| 6. Bret Saberhagen, K.C. | 160,000 | 925,000 | 765,000 |
| 7. Donnie Moore, California | 407,500 | 1,000,000 | 592,500 |
| 8. Jimmy Key, Toronto | 131,250 | 700,000 | 568,750 |
| 9. Keith Hernandez, Mets | 1,100,000 | 1,650,000 | 550,000 |
| 10. Charlie Leibrandt, K.C. | 225,000 | 770,000 | 545,000 |

# Computer Likes Mets, Dodgers, Yankees, Royals

The way the computer sees it, the Dodgers are a strong choice and the Yankees are the narrowest of favorites, with the Mets and the Royals somewhere in between.

Each winter Pete Palmer, co-author with John Thorn of "The Hidden Game of Baseball," runs last season's records through his computer and comes up with a set of predictions based on how players did in recent seasons, primarily the last three. His statistics assign different values to everything a batter does offensively, from singles to sacrifice flies, and calculates how many runs he adds to (or subtracts from) his team's total. Each pitcher is measured by how many earned runs fewer —or more—than the league average he allows, a statistic the Times has carried under the label "earned runs prevented" since 1984. Modest adjustments are then made, team by team, for such factors as unearned runs allowed.

The projected division standings, shown below, indicate tighter races and fewer total victories for division winners than usual. As Palmer explains, "The teams are actually closer on paper than they end up," with injuries and luck, good and bad, expanding the differences.

## National League East

|  | W | L | Pct. | GB |
|---|---|---|---|---|
| Mets | 91 | 71 | .562 |  |
| St. Louis | 85 | 77 | .525 | 6 |
| Chicago | 84 | 78 | .519 | 7 |
| Montreal | 83 | 79 | .512 | 8 |
| Philadelphia | 79 | 83 | .488 | 12 |
| Pittsburgh | 75 | 87 | .463 | 16 |

## National League West

| Los Angeles* | 91 | 71 | .562 |  |
|---|---|---|---|---|
| San Diego | 82 | 80 | .506 | 9 |
| Cincinnati | 79 | 83 | .488 | 12 |
| Houston | 78 | 84 | .481 | 13 |
| Atlanta | 77 | 85 | .475 | 14 |
| San Francisco | 68 | 94 | .420 | 23 |

*Computations made before Pedro Guerrero was hurt.

And these were the April 6 forecasts by Joseph Durso and Murray Chass of *The Times*, with Durso predicting the National League standings and Chass forecasting the American League outcome:

## American League East

| Yankees | 93 | 69 | .574 |  |
|---|---|---|---|---|
| Toronto | 92 | 70 | .568 | 1 |
| Baltimore | 90 | 72 | .556 | 3 |
| Detroit | 89 | 73 | .549 | 4 |
| Boston | 88 | 74 | .543 | 5 |
| Milwaukee | 72 | 90 | .444 | 22 |
| Cleveland | 68 | 94 | .420 | 26 |

## American League West

| Kansas City | 86 | 76 | .531 |  |
|---|---|---|---|---|
| Chicago | 79 | 83 | .488 | 7 |
| California | 78 | 84 | .481 | 8 |
| Minnesota | 77 | 85 | .475 | 9 |
| Oakland | 76 | 86 | .469 | 10 |
| Seattle | 75 | 87 | .463 | 11 |
| Texas | 71 | 91 | .438 | 15 |

APRIL 7

## Sub-2:10 marathons since 1984

| Time | Runner, Country | Finish | Date | Site |
|---|---|---|---|---|
| 2:07:12 | Carlos Lopes, Portugal | 1 | April 20, 1985 | Rotterdam |
| 2:07:13 | Steve Jones, Britain | 1 | Oct. 20, 1985 | Chicago |
| 2:08:05 | Jones, Britain | 1 | Oct. 21, 1984 | Chicago |
| 2:08:08 | Robleh Djama, Djibouti | 2 | Oct. 20, 1985 | Chicago |
| 2:08:09 | Ahmed Saleh, Djibouti | 1 | April 14, 1985 | Hiroshima |
| 2:08:10 | Juma Ikangaa, Tanzania | 1 | Feb. 9, 1986 | Tokyo |
| 2:08:15 | Takeyuka Nakayama, Japan | 2 | April 14, 1985 | Hiroshima |
| 2:08:16 | Jones, Britain | 1 | April 21, 1985 | London |
| 2:08:26 | Djama, Djibouti | 3 | April 14, 1985 | Hiroshima |
| 2:08:29 | Belayenh Densimo, Ethiopia | 2 | Feb. 9, 1986 | Tokyo |
| 2:08:34 | Charles Spedding, Britain | 2 | April 21, 1985 | London |
| 2:08:39 | Abebe Mekonen, Ethiopia | 3 | Feb. 9, 1986 | Tokyo |
| 2:08:43 | Nakayama, Japan | 4 | Feb. 9, 1986 | Tokyo |
| 2:08:48 | Rob de Castella, Australia | 3 | Oct. 20, 1985 | Chicago |
| 2:08:58 | Mark Plaatjes, South Africa | 1 | May 4, 1985 | Pt. Elizabeth |
| 2:09:03 | Michael Heilmann, E. Germany | 4 | April 14, 1985 | Hiroshima |
| 2:09:05 | Mekonen, Ethiopia | 5 | April 14, 1985 | Hiroshima |
| 2:09:06 | Lopes, Portugal | 2 | Oct. 21, 1984 | Chicago |
| 2:09:09 | de Castella, Australia | 3 | Oct. 21, 1984 | Chicago |
| 2:09:09 | Mekonen, Ethiopia | 1 | April 19, 1986 | Rotterdam |
| 2:09:14 | Jorg Peter, East Germany | 1 | July 20, 1984 | Potsdam |
| 2:09:15 | Densimo, Ethiopia | 2 | April 19, 1986 | Rotterdam |
| 2:09:16 | Allister Hutton, Britain | 3 | April 21, 1985 | London |
| 2:09:21 | Lopes, Portugal | 1 | Aug. 12, 1984 | Los Angeles |
| 2:09:23 | Christoph Herle, W. Germany | 4 | Apr. 21, 1985 | London |
| 2:09:30 | Heilmann, E. Germany | 2 | July 20, 1984 | Potsdam |
| 2:09:41 | Ernest Seleke, South Africa | 1 | Mar. 31, 1984 | Pt. Elizabeth |
| 2:09:43 | Henrik Jorgensen, Denmark | 5 | Apr. 21, 1985 | London |
| 2:09:51 | Masanari Shintaku, Japan | 1 | Dec. 1, 1985 | Fukuoka |
| 2:09:56 | John Treacy, Ireland | 2 | Aug. 12, 1984 | Los Angeles |
| 2:09:57 | Spedding, Britain | 1 | May 13, 1984 | London |
| 2:09:57 | Gianni Poli, Italy | 4 | Oct. 20, 1985 | Chicago |
| 2:09:58 | Spedding, Britain | 3 | Aug. 12, 1984 | Los Angeles |
| 2:09:58 | John Graham, Britain | 2 | April 14, 1985 | Rotterdam |

APRIL 20

## The first round

The first-round selections in the National Football League draft. There were only 27 picks because Cleveland chose Bernie Kosar in a supplemental draft.

| Team | Player | Position | School |
|---|---|---|---|
| 1. Tampa Bay | Bo Jackson | Running back | Auburn |
| 2. Atlanta | Tony Casillas | Nose tackle | Oklahoma |
| 3. Houston | Jim Everett | Quarterback | Purdue |
| 4. Indianapolis | Jon Hand | Defensive end | Alabama |
| 5. St. Louis | Anthony Bell | Linebacker | Michigan State |
| 6. New Orleans | Jim Dombrowski | Offensive tackle | Virginia |
| 7. Kansas City | Brian Jozwiak | Offensive tackle | W. Virginia |
| 8. San Diego | Leslie O'Neal | Defensive end | Okla. State |
| 9. Pittsburgh | John Rienstra | Guard | Temple |
| 10. Philadelphia | Keith Byars | Running back | Ohio State |
| 11. Cincinnati | Joe Kelly | Linebacker | Washington |
| 12. Detroit | Chuck Long | Quarterback | Iowa |
| 13. San Diego | James FitzPatrick | Offensive tackle | So. Cal. |
| 14. Minnesota | Gerald Robinson | Defensive end | Auburn |
| 15. Seattle | John Williams | Running back | Florida |
| 16. Buffalo | Ronnie Harmon | Running back | Iowa |
| 17. Atlanta | Tim Green | Linebacker | Syracuse |
| 18. Dallas | Mike Sherrard | Wide receiver | U.C.L.A. |
| 19. Giants | Eric Dorsey | Defensive end | Notre Dame |
| 20. Buffalo | Will Wolford | Offensive tackle | Vanderbilt |
| 21. Cincinnati | Tim McGee | Wide receiver | Tennessee |
| 22. Jets | Mike Haight | Offensive tackle | Iowa |
| 23. L.A. Rams | Mike Schad | Offensive tackle | Queen's Univ. |
| 24. L.A. Raiders | Bob Buczkowski | Defensive end | Pittsburgh |
| 25. Tampa Bay | Roderick Jones | Defensive back | S.M.U. |
| 26. New England | Reggie Dupard | Running back | S.M.U. |
| 27. Chicago | Neal Anderson | Running back | Florida |

APRIL 30

## The road to the Derby

Below are the graded stakes races for 3-year-olds leading to the Kentucky Derby on May 3. Grade I races are noted with an asterisk. Distances are in furlongs (one furlong is ⅛ mile); the Derby is 10 furlongs.

| Date | Race | Track | Distance | Winner | Time |
|---|---|---|---|---|---|
| Jan. 4 | Tropical Park Derby | Calder | 9 | Strong Performance | 1:54 ⅖ |
| Feb. 2 | El Camino Real Derby | Bay Meadows | 8½ | Snow Chief | 1:42 ⅗ |
| Feb. 5 | Hutcheson | Gulfstream | 7 | Papal Power | 1:23 ⅘ |
| Feb. 8 | San Vicente | Santa Anita | 7 | Grand Allegiance | 1:23 ⅕ |
| Feb. 17 | Fountain of Youth (1st Div.) | Gulfstream | 8½ | Ensign Rhythm | 1:46 ⅗ |
| Feb. 17 | Fountain of Youth (2d Div.) | Gulfstream | 8½ | My Prince Charming | 1:46 |
| Feb. 22 | San Rafael | Santa Anita | 7 | Variety Road | 1:35 ⅗ |
| March 1 | Florida Derby* | Gulfstream | 9 | Snow Chief | 1:51 ⅘ |
| March 8 | Swift | Aqueduct | 6 | Landing Plot | 1:11 ⅘ |
| March 15 | Tampa Bay Derby | Tampa Bay | 8½ | My Prince Charming | 1:46 ⅗ |
| March 16 | San Felipe* | Santa Anita | 8½ | Variety Road | 1:45 ⅖ |
| March 22 | Everglades | Hialeah | 8½ | Badger Land | 1:46 ⅕ |
| March 22 | Bay Shore (1st Div.) | Aqueduct | 7 | Zabaleta | 1:22 |
| March 22 | Bay Shore (2d Div.) | Aqueduct | 7 | Buck Aly | 1:23 ⅘ |
| March 22 | Jim Beam | Latonia | 8½ | Broad Brush | 1:44 ⅕ |
| March 23 | Louisiana Derby | Fair Grounds | 9 | Country Light | 1:50 ⅖ |
| April 5 | Flamingo* | Hialeah | 9 | Badger Land | 1:47 |
| April 5 | Gotham | Aqueduct | 8 | Mogambo | 1:34 ⅗ |
| April 6 | Santa Anita* Derby | Santa Anita | 9 | Snow Chief | 1:48 ⅗ |
| April 12 | Lexington* | Keeneland | 8½ | Wise Times | 1:44 ⅖ |
| April 19 | Wood Memorial* | Aqueduct | 9 | Broad Brush | 1:50 ⅗ |
| April 19 | Garden State Stakes | Garden State | 9 | Fobby Forbes | 1:51 |
| April 19 | Arkansas Derby* | Oaklawn | 9 | Rampage | 1:48 ⅕ |
| April 19 | California Derby | Golden Gate | 9 | Vernon Castle | 1:48 |
| April 24 | Blue Grass* | Keeneland | 9 | Bachelor Beau | 1:51 ⅕ |
| April 26 | Derby Trial | Churchill Downs | 8 | Savings | 1:35 ⅗ |
| May 3 | The Derby | Churchill Downs | 10 | Ferdinand | 2:02 ⅘ |

APRIL 30–MAY 3

## The top strikeout games
The best single-game strikeout performances since 1900.

| Name, team | Opponent | Date | IP | SO |
|---|---|---|---|---|
| Tom Cheney, Washington | Baltimore | Sept. 12, 1962 | 16 | 21 |
| Roger Clemens, Boston | Seattle | April 29, 1986 | 9 | 20 |
| Luis Tiant, Cleveland | Minnesota | July 3, 1968 | 10 | 19 |
| Steve Carlton, St. Louis | Mets | Sept. 15, 1969 | 9 | 19 |
| Tom Seaver, Mets | San Diego | April 22, 1970 | 9 | 19 |
| Nolan Ryan, California | Boston | June 14, 1974 | 12 | 19 |
| Nolan Ryan, California | Boston | Aug. 12, 1974 | 9 | 19 |
| Nolan Ryan, California | Detroit | Aug. 20, 1974 | 11 | 19 |
| Nolan Ryan, California | Toronto | June 8, 1977 | 10 | 19 |

MAY 1

# Player's Night to Remember Is No Night to Sleep

### By IRA BERKOW

BOSTON—At first, only the catcher's mitt was loud. Roger Clemens began cracking his swift fastball and cunning curves into Rich Gedman's thick glove, and the Seattle batters swung and missed and swung and missed.

Clemens struck out the side in the first inning, and quickly the fans on this cool New England night perked up. "It was a small crowd," Clemens would recall, "but it was a noisy one." And, as the game proceeded, every time he got two strikes on a batter, most of the crowd of 13,414 in Fenway Park Tuesday night was screaming.

"I wasn't sure what they were screaming about," Clemens said this afternoon, "until Nip came over to me." He meant Al Nipper, also a pitcher with the Red Sox. "He said, 'Man, Rocket, you got a chance for an all-time record.'"

It was the bottom of the eighth, and Nipper had just seen the Fenway Park scoreboard flash the information that Clemens had 18 strikeouts and was two short of breaking the major-league record.

Clemens struck out Spike Owens, swinging, to tie the record, and then got Phil Bradley, looking, for No. 20.

"I was pitching on all adrenaline at this time," said Clemens, "and challenging them. I was throwing the ball right down the heart of the plate." When the third baseman, Wade Boggs, came over to him after the Bradley strikeout and shook his hand, Clemens thought, "Hey, the game is over!"

Not yet. Ken Phelps, the next batter, was intent on not striking out for the fourth time in the game, and he succeeded. But all he could do was hit a ball weakly to the shortstop for the final out.

MAY 1

## Clemens's victims
The Seattle Mariners who struck out against Roger Clemens Tuesday night.

| First Inning | Second |
|---|---|
| Spike Owen | Jim Pressley |
| Phil Bradley | Ivan Calderon |
| Ken Phelps | |

| Third | Seventh |
|---|---|
| Dave Henderson | Bradley |
| | Phelps |
| **Fourth** | |
| Bradley | **Eighth** |
| Phelps | Calderon |
| Gorman Thomas | Henderson |
| **Fifth** | **Ninth** |
| Pressley | Owen |
| Calderon | Bradley |
| Danny Tartabull | |

MAY 1

**Sixth**

Henderson
Steve Yeager

## Making It Big

Of players with a minimum of 10 years in the majors, these are the only ones who came straight to the majors and stayed there:

Ethan Allen (1926–38)
Johnny Antonelli (1948–61)
Ernie Banks (1953–71)
Jack Barry (1908–19)
Frank Chance (1898–1914)
Jack Coombs (1906–20)
Bob Feller (1936–56)
Frank Frisch (1919–37)
Milt Gaston (1924–34)
Dick Groat (1953–67)
Jim Hunter (1965–79)
Al Kaline (1953–74)
Sandy Koufax (1955–66)
Ted Lyons (1923–46)
Danny MacFayden (1926–43)
Billy O'Dell (1954–67)
Mel Ott (1926–47)
Eddie Plank (1901–17)
Eppa Rixey (1912–33)
Carl Scheib (1943–54)
Dave Winfield (1973–present)
Ed Yost (1944–62)
Tom Zachary (1918–36)

MAY 11

## Making It Big: More for the List

To the Sports Editor:

Your listing of players under the title "Making It Big" (*The New York Times,* May 11) omitted a large number who also came straight to the major leagues and stayed for a minimum of 10 years. Three of those players are in the Hall of Fame (Chief Bender, Walter Johnson, George Sisler) and many of the others are not unknown to serious baseball fans. Some of the players on the first list, including Frank Chance, played in the minors after ending their careers in the major league. Of the players on the following list, only Sam Chapman didn't play in the minors after leaving the big leagues. Keeping the list to players beginning their careers after 1900, these are the additions:

Chief Bender (1903–15)
Sam Chapman (1938–51)
Pete Donohue (1921–31)
Joe Dugan (1917–29)
Bibb Falk (1920–31)
Grady Hatton (1946–56)
Walter Johnson (1907–27)
Sherry Magee (1904–19)
Lee (Buck) Ross (1936–45)
George Sisler (1915–30)
George Uhle (1919–34)
Guy (Doc) White (1901–13)
Cy Williams (1912–30)
Lawton (Whitey) Witt (1916–26)

And, if you exclude playing time in the Negro Leagues, as the inclusion of Ernie Banks suggests, then we must add Larry Doby (1947–59).

Before leaving this list and your earlier one, it is worth a moment to reflect on these observations: Of the 37 players on both lists, 13, or more than one-third, are in the Hall of Fame.

STEPHEN E. MILMAN
Wilton, Conn.

MAY 25

## Gooden vs. a list of legends

Dwight Gooden, who pitches for the Mets at Los Angeles tonight, had an earned-run average of 1.04 before Cincinnati nicked him for three runs in five innings last Sunday. Then it zipped to 1.42, suggesting just how tough it will be for Dr. K to cut into the list of modern history's single-season E.R.A. leaders, a roll that is dominated by legends from the dead-ball epoch and that has been cracked only once in the last 68 years. Here's the listing (minimum of one inning pitched for every game on the team's schedule):

| | |
|---|---|
| Dutch Leonard, 1914 Red Sox | 1.01 |
| Three Finger Brown, 1906 Cubs | 1.04 |
| Walter Johnson, 1913 Senators | 1.09 |
| Bob Gibson, 1968 Cardinals | 1.12 |
| Christy Mathewson, 1909 Giants | 1.14 |
| Jack Pfeister, 1907 Cubs | 1.15 |
| Addie Joss, 1908 Indians | 1.16 |
| Carl Lundgren, 1907 Cubs | 1.17 |
| Grover Alexander, 1915 Phillies | 1.22 |
| Cy Young, 1908 Red Sox | 1.26 |
| Ed Walsh, 1910 White Sox | 1.27 |
| Walter Johnson, 1918 Senators | 1.27 |
| Christy Mathewson, 1905 Giants | 1.27 |
| Jack Coombs, 1910 Athletics | 1.30 |
| Three Finger Brown, 1909 Cubs | 1.31 |

MAY 16

## Pivotal people

When Patrick Ewing was named the National Basketball Association's rookie of the year last week, he became the 12th center to win the award since its inception in 1953. Among the dozen, he ranks fifth in first-year scoring average but last in rebounding. The roll call, from most recent to most distant.

| | Pts. | Rebs. |
|---|---|---|
| Patrick Ewing, 1985–86 | 20.0 | 9.0 |
| Ralph Sampson, 1983–84 | 21.0 | 11.1 |
| Alvan Adams, 1975–76 | 19.0 | 9.1 |
| Bob McAdoo, 1972–73 | 18.0 | 9.1 |
| Dave Cowens, 1970–71 | 17.0 | 15.0 |
| K. Abdul-Jabbar, 1969–70 | 28.8 | 14.5 |
| Wes Unseld, 1968–69 | 13.8 | 18.2 |
| Willis Reed, 1964–65 | 19.5 | 14.7 |
| Jerry Lucas, 1963–64 | 17.7 | 17.4 |
| Walt Bellamy, 1961–62 | 31.6 | 19.0 |
| Wilt Chamberlain, 1959–60 | 37.6 | 27.0 |
| Ray Felix, 1953–54 | 17.6 | 13.3 |

MAY 27

# Robert Trent Jones Creates Golf Courses That Survive

### By PETER ALFANO

**M**ONTCLAIR, N.J.—The solitude was disturbed only by the familiar click-clack of cleated shoes on pavement and the clinking of silverware in the clubhouse restaurant, sounds indigenous to a golf course and compatible with the buzzing and chirping that nature does on the fairways. Among the games that people play, golf is more like shooting the rapids or mountain climbing than hitting a baseball or making a basket, for it focuses on overcoming a number of hazards, natural and manmade.

So weekend duffers and professionals alike have come to view golf not just as a game, but sometimes a matter of survival. And during the difficult moments when the ball is playing hide-and-seek in the tall grass or communing with the fish in a lake, golfers cannot easily be persuaded to appreciate esthetics.

At times like these, they are convinced that men such as Robert Trent Jones, who has built so many of these 18-hole picture postcard settings, and Mother Nature, who provides the raw materials, are equal partners in a conspiracy to embarrass them.

"Golf should be a fair test," Jones said. "If the average golfer shoots 90, he'll be comfortable. If he shoots 120, he'll want to give up the game. And I don't think the public wants to see the pros winning with scores of 19 under par."

It is the nature, though, of a frazzled golfer to be forgiving. How can anyone be angry at a golf course for very long? Or at the man who built it? There are few epithets spilled over lunch or at the 19th hole. As the story goes, the golfer who throws his clubs into the water in frustration invariably nearly drowns trying to save them.

Besides, as he walked through the crowded restaurant in the Montclair Golf Club on a summerlike day last week, Robert Trent Jones hardly looked the villain of the piece, someone who would conspire to keep golfers in the rough.

The most famous golf architect in the world is a short, cherubic-looking man with thin strands of silver hair and a grandfatherly demeanor. And even though he will be 80 years old on June 20, no one does it better. He was greeted warmly by club members and responded in kind, learning about matters of paramount importance: "How's your game?"

JUNE 1

### Jones's sweet 18

Robert Trent Jones's 18 favorite golf holes, all of which he built or redesigned.

| Hole | Course | Par |
|---|---|---|
| 16th | Augusta National, Augusta, Ga. | 3 |
| 4th | Baltusrol, lower course, Springfield, N.J. | 3 |
| 16th | Golden Horseshoe, Williamsburg, Va. | 3 |
| 3rd | Mauna Kea, Manuela, Hawaii | 3 |
| 9th | Point O'Woods, Benton Harbor, Mich. | 3 |
| 13th | Ballybunion Golf Club, Ireland | 4 |
| 18th | Congressional Country Club, Bethesda, Md. | 4 |
| 16th | Hazeltine National Golf Club, Chaska, Minn. | 4 |
| 16th | Oakland Hills, south course, Birmingham, Mich. | 4 |
| 17th | Oakmont, Oakmont, Pa. | 4 |
| 12th | Peachtree Golf Club, Atlanta, Ga. | 4 |
| 7th | Sotogrande Golf Club, Cádiz, Spain | 4 |
| 3rd | Troia Golf Club, Setubal, Portugal | 4 |
| 13th | Dorado Beach, Puerto Rico | 5 |
| 16th | Firestone Country Club, south course, Akron, Ohio | 5 |
| 13th | Oak Hill, Rochester, N.Y. | 5 |
| 13th | Palmetto Dunes, Hilton Head, S.C. | 5 |
| 1st | Spyglass Hill, Pebble Beach, Calif. | 5 |

JUNE 1

### Scouting

#### Who *Are* These Guys?

One day in 1971, Harry Walker, manager of the Houston Astros, summoned from the bullpen an untested rookie right-hander named Larry Yount, older brother of Robin Yount. While warming up on the mound for his debut, however, Yount pulled an arm muscle, marking the end of his major league career, in which he never threw an official pitch. He is the hurler on a "Don't Waste More Time on a Dream than You Have To" all-star team compiled by Steven Goldberg, professor of sociology at City College and baseball fanatic. The record books confirm that each of those on Professor Goldberg's team played exactly one game in the majors and did nothing else that shows up as a positive or negative statistic.

C—Bob Scherbarth, 1950 Red Sox
1B—Monte Pfyl, 1907 Giants
2B—Tom McDermott, 1885 Balt. (A.A.)
SS—Otto Neu, 1917 Browns
3B—John Karst, 1915 Dodgers
OF—Moonlight Graham, 1905 Giants
OF—Harvey Grubb, 1912 Indians
OF—Elmer Pence, 1922 White Sox

JUNE 3

## U.S. Open, Nicklaus Plays It His Way

**By DAVE ANDERSON**

SOUTHAMPTON, L.I., June 9—On the 3rd tee at Shinnecock Hills, the world's most famous 46-year-old golfer surveyed the thick trees and bushes down the left side of the 453-yard hole.

"That's jungle," Jack Nicklaus said. "Never hit a driver here. Hook it and you can forget it."

Instead, the man known as the Golden Bear hit his 3-wood. Soaring high, the ball floated slightly to the right and landed in the middle of the lush green fairway. With a smile, he quickly strode off the tee on this celebrated but up to now cloistered course where the 86th United States Open will begin Thursday.

"They'll be screaming about this course," Nicklaus was saying of the other Open golfers. "About how tough it is, about the rough, about everything. But 90 percent of those guys have never played a golf course this hard."

He has. And at one time or another, he has won on many of those hard courses. Over more than a quarter of a century, he has secured his stature as the best golfer in history by winning a record 20 major titles—the United States Open a record-sharing four times, the British Open three times, the Professional Golfers Association championship five times, the United States Amateur twice and, of course, the Masters a record six times, most recently two months ago.

If indeed 90 percent, or even 75 percent, of the 150 golfers in the Open have never played a course as difficult as Shinnecock Hills, it minimizes the number that Nicklaus has to beat.

"It's not that long, but it's a left-to-right course, most of the holes are designed that way," he said. "Craig Stadler should do well here. Bruce Lietzke, Lanny Wadkins, Tom Kite, they hit it left to right. It should be a good course for Seve Ballesteros and Bernhard Langer."

Shinnecock Hills should also be a good course for Nicklaus, especially in the glow of his theatrical triumph at the Augusta National.

"Winning the Masters," he said, "puts me into a position of making myself believe I can win here. My chances are probably better than a high percentage of the field because of the nature and the type of golf course Shinnecock is. Strength and length are not a tremendous factor here, but I've got to work on driving the ball better."

Every so often during this practice round, tee shots with his driver would sail far into the rough on the right.

"But by the time the Open starts, I should be all right," he said. "I will have played this course seven times."

Before the official practice rounds, scheduled to begin today, only a few touring pros had ever played Shinnecock Hills at all. Nicklaus played it for the first time last summer with three friends, shooting a par 70 with two birdies and two bogies. His first round recently occurred after he drove up alone in a white Cadillac from the Suffolk County airport in Westhampton, where his tan-and-brown jet called *Air Bear* had landed.

"The first couple," he said on the first tee to his impromptu gallery of about a dozen, "will be very scratchy."

He pushed his drive into the rough on the right. Another ball. Another push to the right. He pulled his third ball into the left rough. The fourth sailed straight, far down the fairway, and he would play that one.

"I'm trying to find some way not to hurt myself," he said. "That's always my concern when I step off an airplane."

Walking onto the green of the 394-yard 1st hole after a 9-iron approach from 125 yards, he glanced at Shinnecock's sand hills, which create the atmosphere of a Scottish or English linksland course.

"It's going to be a very British U.S. Open," he said. Throughout this practice round, his comments would tell more about how he would think his way around Shinnecock in the Open than how he would play his way around it. At the 408-yard 4th hole, he drove into the thick left rough. Turning to Greg Gagliardo, a Shinnecock caddie, he asked the distance to the pin.

"You've got 137 yards," the caddie said.

Nicklaus hit a 7-iron short of the green.

"Wrong club," he said. "Let me have a 6."

This time the ball soared high into the prevailing southwest wind off the nearby Atlantic Ocean and floated onto the green.

"The wind," he said, "comes through that chute where there are no bushes."

At the 535-yard 5th, his drive was down the left side into the grassy rough. Hitting another ball, he pushed it far to the right into the brown rough.

"That's the swing we're having trouble with," he said. "That's the one we've got to eliminate."

On the back tee of the 471-yard 6th, a par 4, he was unable to see the fairway, which slopes down toward a large pond about 80 yards in front of the green, the only water on the course.

"Aim for that V," his caddie said, "near the right of the treeline on the left."

Again he pushed his drive to the right, into the brown rough. Dissatisfied, he hit another drive into the middle of the fairway. From there, he put a 1-iron over the pond to the right of the green. Returning to his first ball, he floated a 5-iron from dry brown rough short of the green.

"But if you're in this," he said, staring now at thick green rough nearby, "you can't get it over the water."

When he arrived at his first ball, he frowned. It was buried in deep greenish-brown rough about 10 yards to the right of the humped green, which resembled the lower lip of a pouting child.

"Over a hump and down a hill," he said. "Can't do much with it."

He didn't. His ball barely landed on the green, then rolled back off. Another ball barely stayed on the green. On to the 188-yard 7th, where his 3-iron tee shot stopped on the grassy knoll above the sharply sloping green.

"You've got a neatsey chip," somebody said.

Nicklaus's shot rolled 15 feet below the cup. "Now I know what 'neatsey' means," he said.

Leaving the green, he turned and faced the wind, which was blowing at about 10 miles per hour from the nearby 3rd fairway.

"This green," he said, "will get very fast with the wind coming over the top of it."

His drive at the 367-yard 8th hopped into the left rough, barely visible a few feet away.

"This is the shot I've always wanted to learn, because you can't play it, nobody can play it," he said, then he smiled. "Years ago, we could hit a 3-iron out of there. And if you believe that, it'll snow tomorrow. The older you get, the better you used to be. Or the stronger."

His 8-iron was just short, but his second ball got to the green.

"The more wind," he said, "the less spin you want on the ball."

At the 9th hole, stretched to 447 yards by a new tee, Nicklaus didn't know where to aim his drive.

"The right chimney on the clubhouse," his caddie said. "That's the line."

Nicklaus obliged, then he hooked a 6-iron to the far left side of the green, which sits atop the small plateau near the clubhouse veranda.

"I'm trying," he said in annoyance, "to get more out of this club than I want to get out of it."

His second shot stopped about 20 feet below the cup in the back right corner of the green that slopes down sharply from back to front. After putting his two balls, he dropped a ball above the cup and barely touched it with his putter. Missing the cup, it rolled about 12 feet below the hole.

"It's a little quick, like the third at Seminole," he said. "They've watered it, too."

At the 409-yard 10th, his first tee shot skidded left into deep rough. His second landed in the rough to the right of where the fairway drops into a deep valley. He lofted a 6-iron onto the front of the green. His third ball from the tee had rolled down to the bottom of the valley, and he spun that up on the green. But after holing out both balls, he glanced back at the fairway.

"I think a 3-wood or a 1-iron is better off the tee," he said. "Driving to the bottom makes for an awkward second shot."

At the 158-yard 11th, which many Shinnecock members consider the most difficult hole on the course, he floated a 7-iron that spun back and to the right on the sloping green, stopping about 20 feet from the cup.

"This is the hole you don't want to be left," he said.

At the 472-yard 12th, he hit his best drive of the round.

"That's my old shot, my U.S. Open shot," he said. "I play so much better left to right. At the Masters I had to play right to left, but this is mostly a left-to-right course. That's why I like this golf course."

But on the 377-yard 13th, his tee shot drifted into the short rough.

"You really can't hit it too far left here," he said after hitting an 8-iron to the green. "The approach is better from the left."

Walking to his ball, Nicklaus noticed high thick weeds above the bunker to the left of the green.

"The U.S.G.A. will leave that and call it character," he said to H. Virgil Sherrill, a former Shinnecock president, who is the chairman of its Open committee. "That's what they did at Pebble Beach—left it like that and called it character."

At the 444-yard 14th, which doglegs to the right, he hit a 3-wood off the tee. His 6-iron from 185 yards bounced onto the front of the green. Dissatisfied, he hit another 6-iron that rolled about 15 feet beyond the cup. He carefully putted both balls.

"The green is faster this way," he said, meaning from the front.

After putting out on the 397-yard 15th, he did what he had done on every other green: select what he thought would be the four most likely pin positions during the Open's four rounds.

"One front right," he said. "Two over there on the left and one back right."

Trying for distance on the 544-yard 16th, Nicklaus again pushed his drive far into the right rough near the bushes.

"There it is again," he said, "50 yards right."

After a 5-iron and two putts at the 172-yard 17th, he pulled his drive on the 450-yard 18th into the left rough, just off the roller coaster fairway.

"You don't want to be here," he said. "This is about as thick a rough as I've seen on this golf course."

His 5-iron from 193 yards came up just short of the green, again in thick left rough. Using a sand wedge, he chipped weakly. Two more chips also were short of the cup.

"If it's thick," he said, "you've got to go after it, dummy."

And for all his triumphs, when the Open begins Thursday the Golden Bear will be going after what no golfer has ever achieved—a "grand slam" of winning the Masters, the United States Open, the British Open and the P. G. A. championship in the same year.

"I look at this Open," he was saying now, "as one of six Opens where I had a chance to get the second leg of the slam."

He achieved that only in 1972, winning the Masters and then the Open at Pebble Beach. In the British Open at Muirfield in Scotland a month later, his final-round 66 missed by a stroke from forcing an 18-hole playoff with Lee Trevino.

"But if I can win here," he was saying now, "I'd have a good chance in the British Open at Turnberry, and with the P. G. A. at Inverness, a shortish course, almost anybody can win. If you have a chance for the slam, you've got to go after it."

"The slam," somebody said, "must be in the back of your mind."

"The slam," Jack Nicklaus said sharply, "is in the front of my mind."   JUNE 9

## Jack Nicklaus's U.S. Open record

| Year | Site | Total | Finish | Strokes Behind | Relation to Par | Money |
|---|---|---|---|---|---|---|
| 1985 | Oakland Hills | missed cut | (76, 73) | | | |
| 1984 | Winged Foot | 289 | T21 | 13 | plus 9 | $6,575 |
| 1983 | Oakmont | 300 | T43 | 20 | plus 16 | 2,847 |
| 1982 | Pebble Beach | 284 | 2 | 2 | minus 4 | 34,506 |
| 1981 | Merion | 280 | T6 | 7 | even par | 9,920 |
| **1980** | **Baltusrol** | **272** | **1** | **—** | **minus 8** | **55,000** |
| 1979 | Inverness | 291 | 9 | 7 | plus 7 | 7,500 |
| 1978 | Cherry Hills | 289 | T6 | 4 | plus 5 | 7,548 |
| 1977 | Southern Hills | 285 | T10 | 7 | plus 5 | 4,100 |
| 1976 | Atlanta A.C. | 287 | T11 | 10 | plus 7 | 4,000 |
| 1975 | Medinah | 289 | T7 | 2 | plus 1 | 7,500 |
| 1974 | Winged Foot | 294 | T10 | 7 | plus 14 | 3,750 |
| 1973 | Oakmont | 282 | 4 | 3 | minus 2 | 9,000 |
| **1972** | **Pebble Beach** | **290** | **1** | **—** | **plus 2** | **30,000** |
| 1971* | Merion | 280 | 2 | — | even par | 15,000 |
| 1970 | Hazeltine | 304 | T51 | 23 | plus 16 | 900 |
| 1969 | Champions | 289 | T25 | 8 | plus 9 | 1,300 |
| 1968 | Oak Hill | 279 | 2 | 4 | minus 1 | 15,000 |
| **1967** | **Baltusrol** | **275** | **1** | **—** | **minus 5** | **30,000** |
| 1966 | Olympic | 285 | 3 | 7 | plus 5 | 14,000 |
| 1965 | Bellerive | 299 | T32 | 17 | plus 19 | 550 |
| 1964 | Congressional | 295 | T23 | 17 | plus 15 | 475 |
| 1963 | The Country Club | missed cut | (76, 77) | | | |
| **1962**\*\* | **Oakmont** | **283** | **1** | **—** | **minus 1** | **17,500** |
| 1961 | Oakland Hills | 284 | T4 | 3 | plus 4 | amateur |
| 1960 | Cherry Hills | 282 | 2 | 2 | minus 2 | amateur |
| 1959 | Winged Foot | missed cut | (77, 77) | | | |
| 1958 | Southern Hills | 304 | T41 | 19 | plus 24 | amateur |
| 1957 | Inverness | missed cut | (80, 80) | | | |

*Lost to Lee Trevino in playoff, 68 to 71.
\*\*Defeated Arnold Palmer in playoff, 71 to 74.

JUNE 9

### Familiar names in the Top 10
The leaders in finishing in the top 10 of the United States Open. Total in parentheses.

| | | | | | | | | | | | | | | | | | |
|---|---|---|---|---|---|---|---|---|---|---|---|---|---|---|---|---|---|
| **Jack Nicklaus (17)** | 1982 | 1981 | 1980 | 1979 | 1978 | 1977 | 1975 | 1974 | 1973 | 1972 | 1971 | 1968 | 1967 | 1966 | 1962 | 1961 | 1960 |
| | 2 | T6 | 1 | 9 | T6 | T10 | T7 | T10 | 4 | 1 | 2 | 2 | 1 | 3 | 1 | T4 | 2 |
| **Walter Hagen (16)** | 1935 | 1933 | 1932 | 1931 | 1928 | 1927 | 1926 | 1925 | 1924 | 1922 | 1921 | 1919 | 1916 | 1915 | 1914 | 1913 | |
| | 3 | T4 | 10 | T7 | 4 | 6 | 7 | T5 | T4 | 5 | 2 | 1 | 7 | T10 | 1 | T4 | |
| **Ben Hogan (15)** | 1960 | 1959 | 1958 | 1956 | 1955 | 1954 | 1953 | 1952 | 1951 | 1950 | 1948 | 1947 | 1946 | 1941 | 1940 | | |
| | T9 | T8 | T10 | T2 | 2 | T6 | 1 | 3 | 1 | 1 | 1 | T6 | T4 | T3 | T5 | | |
| **Arnold Palmer (13)** | 1975 | 1974 | 1973 | 1972 | 1969 | 1967 | 1966 | 1964 | 1963 | 1962 | 1960 | 1959 | 1956 | | | | |
| | T9 | T5 | T4 | 3 | T6 | 2 | 2 | T5 | 3 | 2 | 1 | T5 | 7 | | | | |
| **Sam Snead (12)** | 1968 | 1959 | 1957 | 1955 | 1953 | 1952 | 1951 | 1949 | 1948 | 1947 | 1939 | 1937 | | | | | |
| | T9 | T8 | T8 | T3 | 2 | T10 | T10 | T2 | 5 | 2 | 5 | 2 | | | | | |
| **Julius Boros (11)** | 1973 | 1965 | 1963 | 1960 | 1958 | 1957 | 1956 | 1955 | 1952 | 1951 | 1950 | | | | | | |
| | T7 | T4 | 1 | T3 | 3 | T4 | T2 | T5 | 1 | T4 | 9 | | | | | | |
| **Gary Player (9)** | 1979 | 1978 | 1977 | 1974 | 1965 | 1963 | 1962 | 1961 | 1958 | | | | | | | | |
| | T2 | T6 | T10 | T8 | 1 | T8 | T6 | T9 | 2 | | | | | | | | |

JUNE 9

# How Fast, How Far? No Limits in Sight

**By FRANK LITSKY**

How fast is fast? It depends on whom you listen to.

In one episode of a wonderful television series of yesteryear, Batman ran a 3-minute mile. And Robin, obviously the Boy Wonder, ran every step with him.

In another bit of television fantasy, the Six Million Dollar Man sprinted at 60 miles an hour. That works out to a 100-meter dash in 3.73 seconds.

Enough, already. The world record for the mile is Steve Cram's 3 minutes 46.32 seconds, much faster than anything Batman could really do without the Batmobile. Though the world record for 100 meters is 9.93 seconds, the people who run near that speed don't have bodies built in the laboratory that invented the Six Million Dollar Man.

Will anyone ever run a mile in 3 minutes? Not in our lifetime, but maybe in the 21st century. Will anyone ever run 100 meters in 3.73 seconds? Probably not in anyone's lifetime, but who can say?

There are no limits to how fast man can run or how high or how far he can jump or throw. The same holds true for women, especially because women's track and field is not nearly as developed as men's.

Sooner or later, the record breaking that has continued for the more than 120 years of recorded statistics will probably pause for a breath. But don't bet on it because no one has discovered limits to track-and-field performances.

After studying running records of the previous 50 years, three Cincinnati scientists, led by Dr. Henry W. Ryder, an internist, concluded that barriers were largely psychological rather than physiological.

The three men, writing in *Scientific American* in 1976, said that whatever the record, the body might be able to run faster if the mind accepted the record. The barriers, they said, were the existing records and the unwillingness of others to try to break them.

"There must be a physiological limit to human running speed," they said, "but it certainly has not yet materialized at any distance." Ten years later it still hasn't.

In the not-too-distant past, there were all kinds of barriers and ultimates—the 4-minute mile, the 60-foot shot put, the 7-foot high jump. Then, from 1954 to 1956, Roger Bannister ran a mile in 3 minutes 59.4 seconds, Charlie Dumas high-jumped 7 feet ½ inch and Parry O'Brien put the shot 60 feet 10 inches—and those barriers were gone.

Actually, those barriers were figures of convenience, nice round numbers that were little more than worthy goals. More was made of them than should have been.

The mile has long been the glamour race, and it retains a mystery and charm even though every other event in international competition is contested at metric distances.

From 1942 to 1945, Gunder Hagg and Arne Andersson of Sweden broke or equaled the world record for the mile three times each, usually by beating the other. They got it down to 4:01.3, and the 4-minute mile seemed imminent. But it did not come until May 6, 1954, when Roger Bannister, an English medical student, ran 3:59.4.

Bannister's feat so captivated the imagination that television and radio stations interrupted their live coverage of the Army-McCarthy hearings in Congress to rush the news to the American public. And for the next decade every subsequent sub-4-minute mile was acclaimed far and wide.

In 1967, Jim Dunaway published a 20-page booklet listing 128 races that had produced 242 sub-4-minute miles by 80 men. Stan Saplin, another track historian, said earlier this year that more than 450 men had run at least one sub-4-minute mile. (The closest a woman has come is 4:16.71 by Mary Decker Slaney last August.) Standards for the mile are higher now. Cram's world record for the mile is 13 seconds faster than Bannister's.

No one can know where any records will go, but it is fun to guess. The accompanying table gives guesses where world records will be in the year 2000. If you cannot conceive of a 3:39 mile, an 8-6 high jump, a 21-6 pole vault or a 31-foot long jump, just remember the story of Brutus Hamilton.

Hamilton was the celebrated track coach at the University of California. In 1934, to amuse his team, he attempted to determine the best performances that could ever be achieved. He had Finnish physicists prepare graphs on energy, expectancy and fatigue. He applied mathematical laws dealing with psychological compensation. Then he issued his list of "ultimates of human effort." He brashly predicted such obviously unattainable performances that the track world was astonished.

Soon Hamilton was astonished. Within months after his ultimates included a shot put of 57 feet 1 inch, Jack Torrance of Louisiana State University put the shot precisely 57 feet 1 inch.

In 1952, with his list of ultimates shattered, Hamilton compiled a new list. In 1962, with only two ultimates surviving, he compiled another new list. A year later, John Pennel's pole vault of 16 feet 6¾ inches and Adolph Plummer's time of 44.9 seconds for 440 yards had made two of Hamilton's newest ultimates obsolete.

These days, once-in-a-lifetime performances seem to come once a year. In 1984, an East German named Uwe Hohn threw the javelin 343 feet 10 inches, the entire length of a football field plus one and a half end zones. The sport's astounded hierarchy promptly legislated a new javelin that would travel less distance and thus not endanger spectators in the stands.

In 1985, Sergei Bubka of the Soviet Union pole vaulted 19 feet 8¼ inches, exactly 6 meters. The pole vault ultimate that Brutus Hamilton envisioned in 1934 was 15-1. Hamilton could not know that the bamboo poles of that era would be replaced by springy fiberglass that seemed to bend forever and take the vaulter for a ride.

New equipment is just one reason why performances keep getting better. Track shoes are lighter and better designed. Tracks, with their plasticlike surfaces, are faster and truer than the pockmarked dirt and clay ovals of the past.

There are more good athletes from more parts of the world.

Coaching is better. Athletes are bigger and stronger, and they know more about race tactics. They can study films of themselves and others, and they can benefit from computer analyses of their techniques.

Training methods and techniques are better. Athletes train harder and longer.

It is no wonder that records become fragile. Even Bob Beamon's long-jump record, probably the best in any track-and-field event, seems sure to fall.

In the 1968 Olympics, Beamon's astounding long jump of 29 feet 2½ inches was not only the first 29-foot jump but also the first over 28 feet. He was aided by the 1½-mile altitude of Mexico City because the thinner air meant less resistance to a flying body. He was also aided by a following wind reported at precisely 2 meters a second (4.473 miles an hour), the maximum allowed for record consideration. People on the field said the wind seemed much stronger.

Altitude or not, wind or not, Beamon put together a perfect jump. He did not come close to it again, never jumping farther than 27 feet 4¾ inches.

These days, Carl Lewis keeps getting close to the record but never quite reaches it. He will make his next attempt at this week's USA/Mobil national outdoor championships in Eugene, Ore. Excluding performances aided by excessive wind, there have been 22 outdoor and indoor jumps of 28 feet or longer. Beamon has only one of the 22. Lewis has 18, including jumps of 28-10¼ outdoors and indoors.

Lewis thinks he can break Beamon's record. So does Beamon.

"I never expected the record to last this long," said Beamon.

"I know I can break it," said Lewis. "But everything has to be right—the weather, the runway, the wind, the takeoff."

Lewis was speaking of one event. He could have been speaking of every event. As Fred Thompson, the highly successful coach of the Atoms Track Club women in Brooklyn and an assistant coach of the 1988 United States Olympic team, said, "I can't see one event where people can't break the world record."

One of the best of the women's world records is in the 800-meter run, which Jarmila Kratochvilova of Czechoslovakia ran in 1 minute 53.28 seconds in 1983.

"I've got a 13-year-old kid on my team who runs a good 800," said Thompson. "If I tell her to run 2:12 or 2:10, people say I'm going too fast with her. But the world record is 1:53, so if you run 2:15 you're not way ahead of anything."

In other words, says Thompson, you cannot run fast unless you run fast. In time, his 13-year-old prodigy may run fast enough to break the world record, and she will hold it until another young prodigy comes along.

All of which means that ultimates are guaranteed to survive—until they are broken.

JUNE 16

## How far? No limits in sight
Reaching for the limits

| Event | 1934 World Records | 1934 Hamilton Ultimates | 1952 Hamilton Ultimates | 1986 World Records | 2000 Ultimates* |
|---|---|---|---|---|---|
| 100 Meters | 10.3 | 10.6 | 10.6 | 9.93 | 9.80 |
| 200 Meters | 20.6 | 20.05 | 20.05 | 19.72 | 19.40 |
| 400 Meters | 46.2 | 46.2 | 45.6 | 43.86 | 42.80 |
| 800 Meters | 1:49.8 | 1:46.7 | 1:46.0 | 1:41.73 | 1:39.10 |
| 1,500 Meters | 3:48.8 | 3:44.78 | 3:42.0 | 3:29.46 | 3:23.00 |
| One Mile | 4:06.2 | 4:01.66 | 4:00.0 | 3:46.32 | 3:39.00 |
| 5,000 Meters | 14:17 | 14:02.36 | 13:50.0 | 13:00.40 | 12:42.00 |
| 10,000 Meters | 30:06.2 | 29:17.7 | 28:50.0 | 27:13.81 | 26:45.00 |
| 110-Meter Hurdles | 14.2 | 13.82 | 13:.4 | 12.93 | 12.80 |
| 400-Meter Hurdles | 50.6 | 50.4 | 50.4 | 47.02 | 46.40 |
| High Jump | 6-9⅛ | 6-11⅛ | 7-0 | 7-10¾ | 8-6 |
| Pole Vault | 14-4⅜ | 15-1 | 15-9 | 19-8¼ | 21-6 |
| Long Jump | 26-2⅛ | 27-4¾ | 27-4¾ | 29-2½ | 31-0 |
| Triple Jump | 51-7 | 54-0¼ | 54-0¼ | 58-11½ | 60-8 |
| Shot-Put | 53-1¾ | 57-1 | 60-0 | 74-2½ | 77-6 |
| Discus Throw | 171-11⅞ | 182-1⅜ | 190-0 | 235-9 | 260-0 |
| Hammer Throw | 189-6½ | 200-8¼ | 210-0 | 283-3 | 300-0 |
| Javelin Throw | 249-8½ | 256-10¼ | 265.0 | 343-10 | 350-0 |

*The Ultimates for the year 2000 are based on the estimates of Frank Litsky of *The New York Times*.

JUNE 16

## The first round of the N.B.A. Draft

| Team | Player | Position | School |
|---|---|---|---|
| 1. Cleveland | Brad Daugherty | Center-forward | N.C. |
| 2. Boston | Len Bias | Forward | Maryland |
| 3. Golden State | Chris Washburn | Center | North Carolina State |
| 4. Indiana | Chuck Person | Forward | Auburn |
| 5. Knicks | Kenny (Sky) Walker | Forward | Kentucky |
| 6. Phoenix | William Bedford | Center | Memphis State |
| 7. Dallas | Roy Tarpley | Forward | Michigan |
| 8. Cleveland | Ron Harper | Guard | Miami-Ohio |
| 9. Chicago | Brad Sellers | Forward | Ohio State |
| 10. San Antonio | Johnny Dawkins | Guard | Duke |
| 11. Detroit | John Salley | Center-forward | Georgia Tech |
| 12. Washington | John Williams | Forward | Louisiana State |
| 13. Nets | Dwayne Washington | Guard | Syracuse |

| Team | Player | Position | School |
|---|---|---|---|
| 14. Portland | Walter Berry | Forward | St. John's |
| 15. Utah | Dell Curry | Guard | Virginia Tech |
| 16. Denver | Maurice Martin | Guard | St. Joseph's, Pa. |
| 17. Sacramento | Harold Pressley | Forward | Villanova |
| 18. Denver | Mark Alarie | Forward | Duke |
| 19. Atlanta | Billy Thompson | Forward | Louisville |
| 20. Houston | Buck Johnson | Forward | Alabama |
| 21. Washington | Anthony Jones | Guard | Nevada–Las Vegas |
| 22. Milwaukee | Scott Skiles | Guard | Michigan State |
| 23. L.A. Lakers | Ken Barlow | Forward | Notre Dame |
| 24. Portland | Arvidas Sabonis | Forward | Soviet Union |

JUNE 18

## King of the road

Get tired of driving? Then consider Richard Petty, who's rolled up some 350,000 miles on the racetrack alone since joining the stock-car circuit in 1958. Petty's participation in the Miller American 400 at Brooklyn, Mich., last Sunday was the 1,000th race of his Nascar career, a record by far for any major circuit. These are the 10 busiest drivers in Nascar's 39-year history:

| | Races | Won |
|---|---|---|
| Richard Petty | 1,000 | *200 |
| Bobby Allison | 660 | 82 |
| Buddy Baker | 635 | 19 |
| J. D. McDuffie | 603 | 0 |
| James Hylton | 578 | 2 |
| David Pearson | 573 | 105 |
| Elmo Langley | 530 | 2 |
| David Marcis | 528 | 5 |
| Buck Baker | 526 | 46 |
| Cale Yarborough | 525 | 83 |

*Another record.

JUNE 18

## A Ladder Made of Iron

When Dale Murphy took the field in Atlanta against the Giants last night, he moved past Richie Ashburn into 11th place on the list of baseball's iron men. The next target for Murphy (and for Cal Ripken): Pete Rose, the only player with two consecutive-game streaks among history's top 20.

Lou Gehrig, 2,130
Everett Scott, 1,307
Steve Garvey, 1,207
Billy Williams, 1,117
Joe Sewell, 1,103
Stan Musial, 895
Eddie Yost, 829
Gus Suhr, 822
Nellie Fox, 798
Pete Rose, 745
Dale Murphy, 731*
Richie Ashburn, 730
Ernie Banks, 717
Pete Rose, 678

Cal Ripken, Jr., 677*
Earl Averill, 673**
Frank McCormick, 652
Sandy Alomar, 648
Eddie Brown, 618
Roy McMillan, 585

*Current as of July 1, 1986.

JULY 1

# Who Is Baseball's Best? Players Say Mattingly

### By CRAIG WOLFF

He has been a batting champion, his league's most valuable player, and now his contemporaries have affirmed what all the numbers and awards say about Don Mattingly. To the major league baseball players, Mattingly is the best in the game.

That was the chief finding of a *New York Times* poll conducted in the locker rooms of all 26 teams. The poll produced surprises and curiosities, but for the most part, celebrated the accomplishments of a group of young players who through magnificent performances have quickly risen to dominance in the game.

Dale Murphy of the Atlanta Braves, twice an m.v.p., was voted the best nonpitcher in the National League. Dwight Gooden, who won 24 games last season and lost just 4, and who is 10-3 this year, was selected the best pitcher in the National League, and Roger Clemens, who won 14 straight this season before finally losing, and who set a major league record when he struck out 20 batters in one game in late April, was named the American League's best pitcher.

These players will come together next week in Houston for the 57th All-Star Game in a tribute to youth. Murphy is the old man at 30. But Gooden is 21, Clemens 23 and Mattingly 25.

The biggest curiosity of all is that Mattingly, the Yankee first baseman, may not start for the American League All-Star team as voted by the fans; he trails Wally Joyner, the California Angels' home run–hitting rookie. It might be a surprise to the fans that Mattingly's teammate, Rickey Henderson, finished second over all in the voting for best player, but players recognize him as one of the game's best all-round athletes.

Mattingly won the acclaim of his peers in a poll conducted by the *Times* in 17 cities from June 21 through July 2. The 26 teams at any time maintain a roster of 24 players, and 417 players responded to the question: "Including pitchers, who is the best baseball player now active in the major leagues?" Mattingly, the smallish, quiet player from Evansville, Ind., who has been likened to a modern-day Lou Gehrig, attracted 56 votes, or 13 percent.

JULY 7

## The Players' Poll: Best in Each League

**American League Leaders**

| Non-pitcher | Total votes | % of votes |
|---|---|---|
| Don Mattingly, Yankees | 69 | 30 |
| R. Henderson, Yankees | 33 | 14 |
| Wade Boggs, Red Sox | 24 | 10 |
| George Brett, Royals | 19 | 8 |
| Eddie Murray, Orioles | 17 | 7 |
| Don't Know/No Answer | 23 | 10 |

| Starting pitcher | Total votes | % of votes |
|---|---|---|
| Roger Clemens, Red Sox | 204 | 89 |
| Mike Witt, Texas | 3 | 1 |
| Ron Guidry, Yankees | 3 | 1 |
| Don't Know/No Answer | 11 | 5 |

| Relief pitcher | Total votes | % of votes |
|---|---|---|
| Don Aase, Orioles | 142 | 62 |
| Dan Quisenberry, Royals | 19 | 8 |
| Mark Eichhorn, Blue Jays | 11 | 5 |
| Dave Righetti, Yankees | 11 | 5 |
| Don't Know/No Answer | 22 | 10 |

| Manager | Total votes | % of votes |
|---|---|---|
| Dick Howser, Royals | 37 | 16 |
| B. Valentine, Rangers | 33 | 14 |
| Earl Weaver, Orioles | 30 | 13 |
| Don't Know/No Answer | 47 | 20 |

## National League Leaders

| Non-pitcher | Total votes | % of votes |
|---|---|---|
| Dale Murphy, Braves | 49 | 26 |
| Tony Gwynn, Padres | 28 | 15 |
| Hubie Brooks, Expos | 18 | 10 |
| Tim Raines, Expos | 18 | 10 |
| Ryne Sandberg, Cubs | 18 | 10 |
| Don't Know/No Answer | 24 | 13 |

| Starting pitcher | Total votes | % of votes |
|---|---|---|
| Dwight Gooden, Mets | 85 | 45 |
| F. Valenzuela, Dodgers | 57 | 30 |
| Bob Knepper, Astros | 9 | 5 |
| Don't Know/No Answer | 16 | 9 |

| Relief pitcher | Total votes | % of votes |
|---|---|---|
| Jeff Reardon, Expos | 102 | 55 |
| Lee Smith, Cubs | 20 | 11 |
| Dave Smith, Expos | 14 | 7 |
| Rich Gossage, Padres | 7 | 4 |
| John Franco, Reds | 7 | 4 |
| Don't Know/No Answer | 17 | 9 |

| Manager | Total votes | % of votes |
|---|---|---|
| Whitey Herzog, Cardinals | 58 | 31 |
| Chuck Tanner, Braves | 34 | 18 |
| Roger Craig, Giants | 23 | 12 |
| Davey Johnson, Mets | 16 | 9 |
| Don't Know/No Answer | 29 | 16 |

## ... And best in both leagues

| Player | Team | Total votes | % of votes |
|---|---|---|---|
| Don Mattingly | Yankees | 56 | 13 |
| Rickey Henderson | Yankees | 42 | 10 |
| Dale Murphy | Braves | 40 | 10 |
| Eddie Murray | Orioles | 39 | 9 |
| Dwight Gooden | Mets | 38 | 9 |
| Roger Clemens | Red Sox | 33 | 8 |
| George Brett | Royals | 15 | 4 |
| Wade Boggs | Red Sox | 13 | 3 |
| Don't Know/No Answer | — | 72 | 17 |

Results based on questionnaires filled out by 417 players between June 21 and July 2.

JULY 7

## The players' All-Star teams

| | National League | American League |
|---|---|---|
| Starting pitcher | Dwight Gooden, Mets | Roger Clemens, Red Sox |
| Relief pitcher | Jeff Reardon, Expos | Don Aase, Orioles |
| Catcher | Gary Carter, Mets | Lance Parrish, Tigers |
| First baseman | Keith Hernandez, Mets | Don Mattingly, Yankees |
| Second baseman | Ryne Sandberg, Cubs | Lou Whitaker, Tigers |
| Shortstop | Hubie Brooks, Expos | Cal Ripken, Jr., Orioles |
| Outfielders | Dale Murphy, Braves | Rickey Henderson, Yankees |
| | Tim Raines, Expos | Kirby Puckett, Twins |
| | Tony Gwynn, Padres | Jim Rice, Red Sox |
| Designated hitter | | Don Baylor, Red Sox |
| Manager | Whitey Herzog, Cards | Dick Howser, Royals |

JULY 7

## All-Star Voting

Final fan balloting for the starting team for the 1986 All-Star Game, to be played July 15 at the Astrodome in Houston:

### AMERICAN LEAGUE

**Catcher**
1. Lance Parrish, Detroit, 1,049,080; 2. Jim Sundberg, Kansas City, 489,003; 3. Bob Boone, California, 392,881; 4. Rick Dempsey, Baltimore, 293,637; 5. Steve Yeager, 288,995; 6. Rich Gedman, Boston, 244,133; 7. Ernie Whitt, Toronto, 234,516; 8. Butch Wynegar, Yankees, 191,455.

**First Base**
1. Wally Joyner, California, 917,972; 2. Don Mattingly, Yankees, 783,846; 3. Eddie Murray, Baltimore, 455,133; 4. Steve Balboni, Kansas City, 313,450; 5. Willie Upshaw, 265,348; 6. Bill Buckner, Boston, 215,181; 7. Darrell Evans, Detroit, 211,687; 8. Kent Hrbek, Minnesota, 207,773.

### Second Base
1. Lou Whitaker, Detroit, 633,399; 2. Willie Randolph, Yankees, 526,714; 3. Frank White, Kansas City, 481,968; 4. Bobby Grich, California, 371,369; 5. Alan Wiggins, Baltimore, 323,756; 6. Damaso Garcia, Toronto, 301,859; 7. Julio Cruz, Chicago, 212,026; 8. Jim Gantner, Milwaukee, 174,909.

### Third Base
1. George Brett, Kansas City, 1,257,432; 2. Wade Boggs, Boston, 1,172,529; 3. Doug DeCinces, California, 250,366; 4. Rance Mulliniks, Toronto, 195,384; 5. Paul Molitor, Milwaukee, 163,478; 6. Mike Pagliarulo, Yankees, 148,278; 7. Darnell Coles, Detroit, 145,992; 8. Brook Jacoby, Cleveland, 117,595.

### Shortstop
1. Cal Ripken, Baltimore, 1,486,806; 2. Alan Trammell, Detroit, 391,117; 3. Tony Fernandez, Toronto, 381,284; 4. Angel Salazar, Kansas City, 257,696; 5. Dick Schofield, California, 248,354; 6. Alfredo Griffin, Oakland, 214,196; 7. Ozzie Guillen, Chicago, 191,338; 8. Ernest Riles, Milwaukee, 166,322.

### Outfield
1. Rickey Henderson, Yankees, 1,027,144; 2. Dave Winfield, Yankees, 895,550; 3. Kirby Puckett, Minnesota, 736,328; 4. Reggie Jackson, California, 719,139; 5. Jose Canseco, Oakland, 585,116; 6. Jim Rice, Boston, 515,320; 7. Robin Yount, Milwaukee, 410,922; 8. Kirk Gibson, Detroit, 399,693; 9. Jesse Barfield, Toronto, 394,039; 10. Willie Wilson, Kansas City, 387,054; 11. Fred Lynn, Baltimore, 358,570; 12. George Bell, Toronto, 343,740; 13. Carlton Fisk, Chicago, 309,560; 14. Lloyd Moseby, Toronto, 275,111; 15. Lonnie Smith, Kansas City, 271,920; 16. Harold Baines, Chicago, 270,984.

JULY 10

## All-Star Voting
Final fan balloting for starting team for the 1986 All-Star Game, to be played July 15, at the Astrodome in Houston:

#### NATIONAL LEAGUE

### Catcher
1. Gary Carter, Mets, 1,476,141; 2. Tony Pena, Pittsburgh, 486,972; 3. Terry Kennedy, San Diego, 421,754; 4. Mike Fitzgerald, Montreal, 375,185; 5. Jody Davis, Chicago, 368,027; 6. Mike Scioscia, Los Angeles, 345,319; 7. Mike Heath, St. Louis, 185,986; 8. Ozzie Virgil, Atlanta, 173,916.

### First Base
1. Keith Hernandez, Mets, 995,279; 2. Steve Garvey, San Diego, 858,032; 3. Pete Rose, Cincinnati, 442,504; 4. Andres Galarraga, Montreal, 397,314; 5. Jack Clark, St. Louis, 364,975; 6. Will Clark, San Francisco, 300,376; 7. Leon Durham, Chicago, 246,307; 8. Bob Horner, Atlanta, 240,064.

### Second Base
1. Ryne Sandberg, Chicago, 1,054,770; 2. Steve Sax, Los Angeles, 507,259; 3. Tommy Herr, St. Louis, 474,912; 4. Johnny Ray, Pittsburgh, 432,432; 5. Vance Law, Montreal, 408,616; 6. Tim Flannery, San Diego, 350,309; 7. Wally Backman, Mets, 285,911; 8. Bill Doran, Houston, 271,256.

### Third Base
1. Mike Schmidt, Philadelphia, 891,165; 2. Graig Nettles, San Diego, 644,620; 3. Tim Wallach, Montreal, 578,153; 4. Terry Pendleton, St. Louis, 342,735; 5. Chris Brown, San Francisco, 326,040; 6. Ron Cey, Chicago, 299,351; 7. Ken Oberkfell, Atlanta, 283,632; 8. Bill Madlock, Los Angeles, 266,987.

### Shortstop
1. Ozzie Smith, St. Louis, 1,379,870; 2. Hubie Brooks, Montreal, 924,992; 3. Garry Templeton, San Diego, 451,484; 4. Shawon Dunston, Chicago, 325,161; 5. Dave Concepcion, Cincinnati, 308,089; 6. Dickie Thon, Houston, 236,386; 7. Mariano Duncan, Los Angeles, 198,375; 8. Jose Uribe, San Francisco, 172,873.

### Outfield
1. Darryl Strawberry, Mets, 1,619,511; 2. Dale Murphy, Atlanta, 1,256,198; 3. Tony Gwynn, San Diego, 987,943; 4. Tim Raines, Montreal, 905,095; 5. Willie McGee, St. Louis, 710,443; 6. Dave Parker, Cincinnati, 624,374; 7. Vince Coleman, St. Louis, 597,540; 8. Andre Dawson, Montreal, 580,685; 9. Mike Marshall, Los Angeles, 393,407; 10. Kevin McReynolds, San Diego, 377,226; 11. Mitch Webster, Montreal, 363,144; 12. Jose Cruz, Houston, 345,808; 13. Chili Davis, San Francisco, 325,804; 14. Jeff Leonard, San Francisco, 286,206; 15. Keith Moreland, Chicago, 278,547; 16. George Foster, Mets, 265,871.

JULY 11

## Players of the Decade
These are the leading all-star vote-getters of the 1980s:

**AMERICAN LEAGUE**
George Brett, 12,982,579
Rod Carew, 10,523,128

Reggie Jackson, 8,731,982
Carlton Fisk, 8,716,103
Robin Yount, 7,384,794
Fred Lynn, 7,349,511
Jim Rice, 6,334,406
Lance Parrish, 6,020,037
Dave Winfield,* 5,953,466
Rickey Henderson, 5,197,144

**NATIONAL LEAGUE**
Mike Schmidt, 10,892,450
Gary Carter, 10,440,600
Steve Garvey, 9,563,017
Ozzie Smith, 8,232,064
Dale Murphy, 7,199,917
Pete Rose, 6,539,252
Andre Dawson, 6,466,741
Keith Hernandez, 6,330,828
Dave Concepcion, 6,319,341
Dave Parker, 5,850,605

*Received 1,681,043 votes with Padres (NL) in 1980, for overall total of 7,634,509.

JULY 15

# Clemens Is Perfect as American League Wins, 3–2

By MICHAEL MARTINEZ

HOUSTON, July 15—The pregame buildup had been about pitching, about Dwight Gooden and Roger Clemens and their memorable achievements as the two dominant pitchers in baseball. But Gooden was merely a footnote tonight, his work reduced to three innings and a home run that he permitted in the second inning. Clemens became the leading character in a game that came down to pitching and helped the American League to a 3–2 victory over the Nationals in the 57th All-Star Game.

Clemens—performing in the Astrodome, not far from where he grew up—was the winning pitcher and the most valuable player. Gooden was the loser.

The Boston Red Sox right-hander started and retired all nine batters he faced, and the American League held on after Charlie Hough gave up two runs in the bottom of the eighth.

And the evening included a climactic finish: Don Aase got Chris Brown to hit into a game-ending double play after the National League had runners at first and second with no outs.

"I know I took this game for real," said Dick Howser, the American League manager. "We've been in the back seat for so long." Clemens threw 25 pitches—21 of them for strikes—and then Ted Higuera retired the first four batters he faced before Darryl Strawberry lined a single to right in the fifth.

But the night was not theirs alone. Fernando Valenzuela of Los Angeles followed Gooden in the fourth and struck out the first five batters he faced. It was a feat that had been accomplished only once before in an All-Star Game: Carl Hubbell did it in 1934 when he struck out, in order, Babe Ruth, Lou Gehrig, Jimmie Foxx, Al Simmons and Joe Cronin. All five are in the Hall of Fame.

Valenzuela's victims were less formidable: Don Mattingly, Cal Ripken and Jesse Barfield in the fourth, then Lou Whitaker and Higuera to open the fifth. Higuera, who pitches for Milwaukee, had never gone to bat in a big league game before.

The National League finished with 12 strikeouts, tying an All-Star Game record, and the American League had seven. Gooden had two strikeouts, but they were his only worthy moments.

The Met right-hander, who was selected to start the game against Clemens, worked a scoreless first and had two outs in the second before Dave Winfield doubled to right and Whitaker hit an 0-and-2 pitch over the fence in right.

Frank White added a bases-empty homer as a pinch hitter for Whitaker in the seventh, and it was decisive. It came off Mike Scott, the Astros' pitcher.

The evening fell out of its orderly fashion,

however. Charlie Hough, the Texas knuckleball specialist, replaced Higuera in the seventh and the Nationals made a belated rally in the eighth. Hough was working with Rich Gedman, the Boston catcher, who had never before worked with a knuckleball pitcher. Hough gave Gedman an oversized glove, but their eighth inning was unpredictable.

Hough struck out three batters, but one of them, Hubie Brooks, reached base on a passed ball. Another, Chris Brown, went from second to third on a wild pitch and scored on the passed ball to Brooks. Dave Righetti, the Yankee reliever, came in and got Glenn Davis to hit a pop fly.  JULY 16

### Used wheels, mint condition

Having swiped 16 bases (in 22 attempts) already this year, Dave Lopes seems certain to become the most successful geriatric base stealer in modern major league history. According to research by Bill Dean of the Baseball Hall of Fame, these are the single-season pacesetters among all players at least 40 years old.

|  | Age | SB |
|---|---|---|
| Honus Wagner, 1914 Pirates | 40 | 23 |
| Willie Mays, 1971 Giants | 40 | 23 |
| Honus Wagner, 1915 Pirates | 41 | 22 |
| Ty Cobb, 1927 Athletics | 40 | 22 |
| Lou Brock, 1979 Cardinals | 40 | 21 |
| Dave Lopes, 1986 Cubs | 40 | 16 |
| Nap Lajoie, 1916 Athletics | 40 | 15 |
| Sam Rice, 1930 Senators | 40 | 13 |
| Dummy Hoy, 1902 Reds | 40 | 11 |
| Honus Wagner, 1916 Pirates | 42 | 11 |

JULY 17

## Specter of Award Follows Saberhagen

By MURRAY CHASS

Maybe Cy Young was never afflicted because he never won it, but Bret Saberhagen clearly is the latest victim of the curse of the Cy Young Award. Although the curse doesn't always strike, it can be devastating when it does. If Saberhagen is skeptical, he can seek the views of Rick Sutcliffe, John Denny, LaMarr Hoyt, Pete Vuckovich, Steve Stone and Randy Jones, among others.

Saberhagen won the American League Cy Young Award last season after leading Kansas City to postseason heaven with 20 victories and only 6 defeats. This season he is struggling with a 5–10 record and a 4.18 earned run average, compared with 2.87 last year.

His National League counterpart, Dwight Gooden of the Mets, isn't exactly struggling, though some observers suggest otherwise, but he has already lost as many games, four, as he did all last season. His 10-4 record entering last night's game in Houston, however, doesn't put him in the category with Saberhagen and other previous winners who were afflicted the following season with a poor record or a disabling injury.

Saberhagen finished the season 7-12, and Gooden was 17-6.  JULY 20

### Cy Young winners of last 15 years and their records the year after they won

**American League**
1985, Saberhagen, 20-6 to 5-10
1984, Hernandez, 32 saves to 31
1983, Hoyt, 24-10 to 13-18
1982, Vuckovich, 18-6 to 0-2
1981, Fingers, 28 saves to 29
1980, Stone, 25-7 to 4-7
1979, Flanagan, 23-9 to 16-13
1978, Guidry, 25-3 to 18-8
1977, Lyle, 26 saves to 9
1976, Palmer, 22-13 to 20-11
1975, Palmer, 23-11 to 22-13
1974, Hunter, 25-12 to 23-14
1973, Palmer, 22-9 to 7-12
1972, G. Perry, 24-16 to 19-19
1971, Blue, 24-8 to 6-10

**National League**
1985, Gooden, 24-4 to 10-4
1984, Sutcliffe, 16-1 to 8-8
1983, Denny, 19-6 to 7-7
1982, Carlton, 23-11 to 15-16
1981, Valenzuela, 13-7 to 19-13
1980, Carlton, 24-9 to 13-4
1979, Sutter, 37 saves to 28
1978, G. Perry, 21-6 to 12-11
1977, Carlton, 23-10 to 16-13
1976, Jones, 22-14 to 6-12
1975, Seaver, 22-9 to 14-11
1974, Marshall, 21 saves to 13
1973, Seaver, 19-10 to 11-11
1972, Carlton, 27-10 to 13-20
1971, Jenkins, 24-13 to 20-12

JULY 20

# Hitting Stride

When Don Baylor was hit by a pitch from José DeLeon of the Chicago White Sox on Monday night in Boston, it was the 23rd time this season that Baylor had reached first base the hard way—by absorbing the impact of a thrown baseball. Baylor is now one behind the American League's single-season record he shares with Bill Freehan of the Detroit Tigers and Norm Eberfeld of the Washington Senators. At age 37, Baylor is also creeping closer to the career record of 243 held by Ron Hunt, who also set the single-season record when he failed to get out of the way 50 times while playing for Montreal in 1971. The 10 batters hit most by pitches in their major league careers:

| Player, seasons | HBP |
|---|---|
| Ron Hunt, 1963–71 | 243 |
| Don Baylor, 1970–* | 215 |
| Frank Robinson, 1956–76 | 198 |
| Minnie Minoso, 1949–64** | 192 |
| Nellie Fox, 1947–65 | 142 |
| Art Fletcher, 1909–22 | 141 |
| Chet Lemon, 1975–* | 121 |
| Sherm Lollar, 1946–63 | 115 |
| Frank Crosetti, 1932–48 | 114 |
| Bill Freehan, 1961–76 | 114 |
| Buck Herzog, 1908–20 | 114 |

*Active.
**Also 5 games in 1976 and 1980.

AUG. 6

## Gordon White's Predicted Top 20 on College Football

1. Oklahoma
2. Michigan
3. Texas A&M
4. Miami
5. Alabama
6. U.C.L.A.
7. Penn State
8. Tennessee
9. Ohio State
10. Nebraska
11. Baylor
12. Clemson
13. L.S.U.
14. Arkansas
15. Michigan State
16. Arizona State
17. Maryland
18. Texas
19. Florida State
20. Florida

AUG. 20

# Mets a Baseball "Jewel" in Attendance, Revenue

**By JOSEPH DURSO**

The New York Mets are a glorious exception to major league baseball's prediction that its 26 teams will collectively lose $59 million this year.

Not only are the Mets so far ahead in first place in the National League East that they have been conceded its championship by their rivals, but they have dislodged the Yankees as the No. 1 draw in town and are driving toward the three million mark in home attendance, a level attained in past years only by the Los Angeles Dodgers.

In the fiscal year ended April 30—before most of this year's attendance came into play—the Mets' gate receipts rose nearly 50 percent, to $19.8 million. Last season, the Mets played before 2.7 million people in Shea Stadium, the largest season's attendance of any sports team in New York history.

The Mets' broadcasting revenue almost doubled, to $14.9 million in the last fiscal year from $8.2 million the previous year, and total revenue soared to $43.1 million from $27 million, producing a bottom line of $9.6 million in pretax income and $5 million in net income.

According to data being circulated by Dillon, Read & Company, the Mets apparently have become one of the most valuable assets of Doubleday & Company, which reportedly is being offered for sale by Nelson Doubleday, Jr., its president. AUG. 22

## A financial scorecard for the Mets

Income statement of the New York Mets baseball team, owned and operated by Doubleday & Co. For fiscal years ended April 30, in thousands of dollars.

|  | 1986 | 1985 | 1984 |
|---|---|---|---|
| **Revenues** | | | |
| Gate receipts | $19,889 | $13,100 | $8,329 |
| Scoreboard advertising | 1,253 | 1,242 | 1,023 |
| Broadcasting | 14,932 | 8,206 | 6,984 |
| Concession | 6,136 | 3,936 | 2,545 |
| Other operating | 619 | 292 | 210 |
| Restaurant | 293 | 207 | 221 |
| **Total revenues** | 43,122 | 26,983 | 19,313 |
| **Cost of sales** | | | |
| Major spring training | (373) | (389) | (369) |
| Major regular operating | (13,174) | (9,261) | (10,259) |
| Minor spring training | (259) | (271) | (239) |
| Minor regular operating | (4,057) | (3,774) | (3,453) |
| Shea Stadium operations | (4,372) | (3,640) | (2,742) |
| NYC rent and lease | (1,089) | (1,079) | (938) |
| **Gross profit** | 19,798 | 8,568 | 1,312 |
| **Operating expenses** | | | |
| Marketing | (1,872) | (1,607) | (1,270) |
| Ticket operation | (1,130) | (885) | (611) |
| Administrative salaries | (1,074) | (972) | (823) |
| Travel | (138) | (100) | (95) |
| Supplies | (248) | (214) | (138) |
| Insurance expenses | (1,418) | (848) | (563) |
| Office expenses | (942) | (766) | (826) |
| Professional fees | (190) | (150) | (182) |
| Payroll, excise and other taxes | (568) | (392) | (409) |
| Scoreboard | (400) | (400) | (400) |
| **Operating income** | 11,817 | 2,236 | (4,004) |
| Player disposition expense | 106 | (753) | (736) |
| Other income | (1,423) | (2,717) | (2,377) |
| Depreciation | (936) | (1,022) | (1,942) |
| **Pretax income** | 9,564 | (2,256) | (9,058) |

Note: Some columns may not add due to rounding.

AUG. 22

## Pro Football Forecast

These were the preseason predictions of the order of finish in the National Football League made by Michael Janofsky, who covers professional football for *The Times*:

National Football Conference

Eastern Division: Washington Redskins, New York Giants, Dallas Cowboys, St. Louis Cardinals, Philadelphia Eagles.

Central Division: Chicago Bears, Minnesota Vikings, Green Bay Packers, Detroit Lions, Tampa Bay Buccanneers.

Western Division: San Francisco 49ers, Los Angeles Rams, New Orleans Saints, Atlanta Falcons.

American Football Conference

Eastern Division: New England Patriots,

Miami Dolphins, New York Jets, Indianapolis Colts, Buffalo Bills.

Central Division: Cincinnati Bengals, Cleveland Browns, Houston Oilers, Pittsburgh Steelers.

Western Division: Denver Broncos, Los Angeles Raiders, Kansas City Chiefs, Seattle Seahawks, San Diego Chargers.   SEPT. 7

## N.F.L. final standings

### American Conference

| | W | L | T | Pct. | Points For | Agt. |
|---|---|---|---|---|---|---|
| **Eastern Division** | | | | | | |
| New England | 11 | 5 | 0 | .688 | 412 | 307 |
| Jets | 10 | 6 | 0 | .625 | 364 | 386 |
| Miami | 8 | 8 | 0 | .500 | 430 | 405 |
| Buffalo | 4 | 12 | 0 | .250 | 287 | 348 |
| Indianapolis | 3 | 13 | 0 | .188 | 229 | 400 |
| **Central Division** | | | | | | |
| Cleveland | 12 | 4 | 0 | .750 | 391 | 310 |
| Cincinnati | 10 | 6 | 0 | .625 | 409 | 394 |
| Pittsburgh | 6 | 10 | 0 | .375 | 307 | 336 |
| Houston | 5 | 11 | 0 | .313 | 274 | 329 |
| **Western Division** | | | | | | |
| Denver | 11 | 5 | 0 | .688 | 378 | 327 |
| Kansas City | 10 | 6 | 0 | .625 | 358 | 326 |
| Seattle | 10 | 6 | 0 | .625 | 366 | 293 |
| L.A. Raiders | 8 | 8 | 0 | .500 | 323 | 346 |
| San Diego | 4 | 12 | 0 | .250 | 335 | 396 |

### National Conference

| | W | L | T | Pct. | Points For | Agt. |
|---|---|---|---|---|---|---|
| **Eastern Division** | | | | | | |
| Giants | 14 | 2 | 0 | .875 | 371 | 236 |
| Washington | 12 | 4 | 0 | .750 | 368 | 296 |
| Dallas | 7 | 9 | 0 | .438 | 346 | 337 |
| Philadelphia | 5 | 10 | 1 | .344 | 256 | 312 |
| St. Louis | 4 | 11 | 1 | .281 | 218 | 351 |
| **Central Division** | | | | | | |
| Chicago | 14 | 2 | 0 | .875 | 352 | 187 |
| Minnesota | 9 | 7 | 0 | .563 | 398 | 273 |
| Detroit | 5 | 11 | 0 | .313 | 277 | 326 |
| Green Bay | 4 | 12 | 0 | .250 | 254 | 418 |
| Tampa Bay | 2 | 14 | 0 | .125 | 239 | 473 |
| **Western Division** | | | | | | |
| S. Francisco | 10 | 5 | 1 | .656 | 374 | 247 |
| L.A. Rams | 10 | 6 | 0 | .625 | 309 | 267 |
| Atlanta | 7 | 8 | 1 | .469 | 280 | 280 |
| New Orleans | 7 | 9 | 0 | .438 | 288 | 287 |

DEC. 24

## The Lightweight Team

The National Football League has its Refrigerator, and then it has those who could fit into a refrigerator. Here's the list of players under 170 pounds now on N.F.L. rosters:

Gerald McNeil, WR-KR, Cleveland, 146
Leonard Harris, WR, Tampa Bay, 155
Phil Epps, WR, Green Bay, 155
Paul McFadden, K, Philadelphia, 155
Willie Drewrey, WR-KR, Houston, 158
Evan Arapostathis, K-P, St. Louis, 160
Ricky Easmon, DB, Tampa Bay, 160
Tony Zendejas, K, Houston, 160

Jim Breech, K, Cincinnati, 161
Anthony Carter, WR, Minnesota, 162
Lew Barnes, WR, Chicago, 165
Joey Jones, WR, Atlanta, 165
Mickey Sutton, WR, L.A. Rams, 165
Mel Gray, RB, New Orleans, 166
Derek Holloway, WR, Washington, 166
Ernest Givins, WR, Houston, 168

SEPT. 10

## It's a game of inches, and of decimal places

The pennant races may not be very exciting this September, but how about those batting races? Heading into last night's play, the best four hitters in the National League were within 10 points of one another, as were the best three in the American. A couple of them might even wind up on the list of the closest races for the batting title in modern major league history, which looks this way:

| Year | Champion | BA | Runner-Up | BA | Margin |
|---|---|---|---|---|---|
| 1945 | George Stirnweiss, Yanks | .30854 | T. Cuccinello, White Sox | .30846 | .00008 |
| 1949 | George Kell, Tigers | .3429 | Ted Williams, Red Sox | .3428 | .0001 |
| 1931 | Chic Hafey, Cardinals | .3489 | Bill Terry, Giants | .3486 | .0003 |
| 1970 | Alex Johnson, Angels | .3290 | C. Yastrzemski, Red Sox | .3286 | .0004 |
| 1935 | Buddy Myer, Senators | .3490 | Joe Vosmik, Indians | .3484 | .0006 |
| 1982 | Willie Wilson, Royals | .3316 | Robin Yount, Brewers | .3307 | .0009 |
| 1910 | Ty Cobb, Tigers | .3851 | Nap Lajoie, Indians | .3841 | .0010 |
| 1976 | George Brett, Royals | .3333 | Hal McRae, Royals | .3321 | .0012 |
| 1911 | Honus Wagner, Pirates | .3340 | Doc Miller, Braves | .3328 | .0012 |
| 1953 | Mickey Vernon, Senators | .3372 | Al Rosen, Indians | .3356 | .0016 |
| 1928 | Goose Goslin, Senators | .3794 | Heinie Manush, Browns | .3777 | .0017 |
| 1918 | Zack Wheat, Dodgers | .3350 | Edd Roush, Reds | .3333 | .0017 |

SEPT. 16

## Don't Invite 'Em

In hitting four home runs at Pittsburgh this season, Mike Schmidt has made Three Rivers Stadium the fourth park in which he's belted more career homers than any other visiting player in National League history. But Reggie Jackson goes one better, wearing the crown exclusively at four enemy parks in the American League and sharing it at a fifth. A complete list of the most unwanted guests at current big-league stadiums:

*American League*
Tiger Stadium, Detroit, Babe Ruth, 58
Comiskey Park, Chicago, Babe Ruth, 47
Fenway Park, Boston, Babe Ruth, 38; Mickey Mantle, 38
Cleveland Stadium, Mickey Mantle, 36
Yankee Stadium, Ted Williams, 30
Memorial Stadium, Baltimore, H. Killebrew, 30
County Stadium, Milwaukee, Reggie Jackson, 29
Arlington (Tex.) Stadium, Reggie Jackson, 22
Anaheim (Calif.) Stadium, Reggie Jackson, 18
Exhibition Stadium, Toronto, Jim Rice, 16
Royals Stadium, Kansas City, Don Baylor, 16
Kingdome, Seattle, Don Baylor, 13; Reggie Jackson, 13; Jim Rice, 13
Oakland Coliseum, Reggie Jackson, 13
Metrodome, Minneapolis, Tony Armas, 10; Ron Kittle, 10; Jim Rice, 103

*National League*
Wrigley Field, Chicago, Willie Mays, 54
Atlanta-Fulton County Stadium, Johnny Bench, 32; Willie McCovey, 32
Shea Stadium, New York, Willie Stargell, 31
Riverfront Stadium, Cincinnati, Mike Schmidt, 27
Candlestick Park, San Francisco, Willie Stargell, 25
Jack Murphy Stadium, San Diego, Johnny Bench, 24
Dodger Stadium, L.A., George Foster, 23
Busch Stadium, St. Louis, Mike Schmidt, 22
Olympic Stadium, Montreal, Mike Schmidt, 22
Three Rivers, Pittsburgh, Mike Schmidt, 21
Veterans Stadium, Phila., Gary Carter, 21
Astrodome, Houston, Tony Perez, 19

SEPT. 26

# Final standings

## National League East

| Team | W | L | Pct. | GB | Str. | Div. W | Div. L | Home W | Home L | Away W | Away L |
|---|---|---|---|---|---|---|---|---|---|---|---|
| *Mets | 108 | 54 | .667 | — | W5 | 59 | 31 | 55 | 26 | 53 | 28 |
| Philadelphia | 86 | 75 | .534 | 21½ | W2 | 45 | 44 | 49 | 31 | 37 | 44 |
| St. Louis | 79 | 82 | .491 | 28½ | L4 | 45 | 44 | 42 | 39 | 37 | 43 |
| Montreal | 78 | 83 | .484 | 29½ | L2 | 46 | 44 | 36 | 44 | 42 | 39 |
| Chicago | 70 | 90 | .438 | 37 | W2 | 40 | 48 | 42 | 38 | 28 | 52 |
| Pittsburgh | 64 | 98 | .395 | 44 | L3 | 33 | 57 | 31 | 50 | 33 | 48 |

## National League West

| Team | W | L | Pct. | GB | Str. | Div. W | Div. L | Home W | Home L | Away W | Away L |
|---|---|---|---|---|---|---|---|---|---|---|---|
| *Houston | 96 | 66 | .593 | — | W5 | 56 | 34 | 52 | 29 | 44 | 37 |
| Cincinnati | 86 | 76 | .531 | 10 | L1 | 44 | 46 | 43 | 38 | 43 | 38 |
| San Francisco | 83 | 79 | .512 | 13 | W1 | 49 | 41 | 46 | 35 | 37 | 44 |
| San Diego | 74 | 88 | .457 | 22 | W1 | 43 | 47 | 43 | 38 | 31 | 50 |
| Los Angeles | 73 | 89 | .451 | 23 | L1 | 38 | 52 | 46 | 35 | 27 | 54 |
| Atlanta | 72 | 89 | .447 | 23½ | L5 | 40 | 50 | 41 | 40 | 31 | 49 |

## American League East

| Team | W | L | Pct. | GB | Str. | Div. W | Div. L | Home W | Home L | Away W | Away L |
|---|---|---|---|---|---|---|---|---|---|---|---|
| *Boston | 95 | 66 | .590 | — | L4 | 44 | 33 | 51 | 30 | 44 | 36 |
| Yankees | 90 | 72 | .556 | 5½ | W4 | 43 | 35 | 42 | 39 | 48 | 33 |
| Detroit | 87 | 75 | .537 | 8½ | W5 | 45 | 33 | 49 | 32 | 38 | 43 |
| Toronto | 86 | 76 | .531 | 9½ | L3 | 42 | 36 | 42 | 39 | 44 | 37 |
| Cleveland | 84 | 78 | .519 | 11½ | W4 | 32 | 46 | 45 | 35 | 39 | 43 |
| Milwaukee | 77 | 84 | .478 | 18 | W3 | 38 | 39 | 41 | 39 | 36 | 45 |
| Baltimore | 73 | 89 | .451 | 22½ | L4 | 28 | 50 | 37 | 42 | 36 | 47 |

## American League West

| Team | W | L | Pct. | GB | Str. | Div. W | Div. L | Home W | Home L | Away W | Away L |
|---|---|---|---|---|---|---|---|---|---|---|---|
| *California | 92 | 70 | .568 | — | L1 | 48 | 30 | 50 | 32 | 42 | 38 |
| Texas | 87 | 75 | .537 | 5 | W1 | 47 | 31 | 51 | 30 | 36 | 45 |
| Kansas City | 76 | 86 | .469 | 16 | L1 | 38 | 40 | 45 | 36 | 31 | 50 |
| Oakland | 76 | 86 | .469 | 16 | W1 | 34 | 44 | 47 | 36 | 29 | 50 |
| Chicago | 72 | 90 | .444 | 20 | L3 | 36 | 42 | 41 | 40 | 31 | 50 |
| Minnesota | 71 | 91 | .438 | 21 | W3 | 38 | 40 | 43 | 38 | 28 | 53 |
| Seattle | 67 | 95 | .414 | 25 | L9 | 32 | 46 | 41 | 41 | 26 | 54 |

*Clinched division title.

Oct. 6

## Final baseball statistics

| American League | Games | At bats | Runs | Hits | Avg. |
|---|---|---|---|---|---|
| Boggs, Boston | 149 | 580 | 107 | 207 | .357 |
| Mattingly, New York | 162 | 677 | 117 | 238 | .352 |
| Puckett, Minnesota | 161 | 680 | 119 | 223 | .328 |
| Tabler, Cleveland | 130 | 473 | 61 | 174 | .326 |
| Rice, Boston | 157 | 618 | 98 | 200 | .324 |
| Yount, Milwaukee | 140 | 522 | 82 | 163 | .312 |
| Fernandez, Toronto | 163 | 687 | 91 | 213 | .310 |
| Bradley, Seattle | 143 | 526 | 88 | 163 | .310 |
| Bell, Toronto | 159 | 641 | 101 | 198 | .309 |
| Franco, Cleveland | 149 | 599 | 80 | 183 | .306 |

**Home Runs**
Barfield, Toronto, 40; Kingman, Oakland, 35; Gaetti, Minnesota, 34; Canseco, Oakland, 33; Deer, Milwaukee, 33; Baylor, Boston, 31; Bell, Toronto, 31; Mattingly, New York, 31; Puckett, Minnesota, 31; Incaviglia, Texas, 30.

**Runs Batted In**
Carter, Cleveland, 121; Canseco, Oakland, 117; Mattingly, New York, 113; Rice, Boston, 110; Bell, Toronto, 108; Gaetti, Minnesota, 108; Barfield, Toronto, 108; Presley, Seattle, 107; Winfield, New York, 104; Buckner, Boston, 102.

**Stolen Bases**
Henderson, New York, 87; Cangelosi, Chicago, 50; Pettis, California, 50; Gibson, Detroit, 34; Wilson, Kansas City, 34; Griffin, Oakland, 33; McDowell, Texas, 33; Moseby, Toronto, 32; Butler, Cleveland, 32; Reynolds, Seattle, 30.

**Pitching** (winning percentage, 15 or more decisions)
Clemens, Boston, 24-4, .857; Rasmussen, Yankees, 18-6, .750; King, Detroit, 11-4, .733; Morris, Detroit, 21-8, .733; Eichhorn, Toronto, 14-6, .700; Schrom, Cleveland, 14-7, .667; Gubicza, Kansas City, 12-6, .667; Higuera, Milwaukee, 20-11, .645; Witt, California, 18-10, .643; Andujar, Oakland, 12-7, .632.

**Strikeouts**
Langston, Seattle, 245; Clemens, Boston, 238; Morris, Detroit, 223; Blyleven, Minnesota, 215; Witt, California, 208; Higuera, Milwaukee, 207; McCaskill, California, 202; Viola, Minnesota, 191; Correa, Texas, 189; Rijo, Oakland, 176.

**Saves**
Righetti, New York, 46; Aase, Baltimore, 34; Henke, Toronto, 27; Hernandez, Detroit, 24; Moore, California, 21; Camacho, Cleveland, 20; Harris, Texas, 20; Clear, Milwaukee, 16; Stanley, Boston, 16; Howell, Oakland, 16.

| National League | Games | At bats | Runs | Hits | Avg. |
|---|---|---|---|---|---|
| Raines, Montreal | 151 | 580 | 91 | 194 | .334 |
| Sax, Los Angeles | 157 | 633 | 91 | 210 | .332 |
| Gwynn, San Diego | 160 | 642 | 107 | 211 | .329 |
| Bass, Houston | 157 | 591 | 83 | 184 | .311 |
| Hernandez, New York | 149 | 551 | 94 | 171 | .310 |
| Hayes, Philadelphia | 158 | 610 | 107 | 186 | .305 |
| Ray, Pittsburgh | 155 | 579 | 67 | 174 | .301 |
| Knight, New York | 137 | 486 | 51 | 145 | .298 |
| Webster, Montreal | 151 | 576 | 89 | 167 | .290 |
| Schmidt, Philadelphia | 160 | 552 | 97 | 160 | .290 |

**Home Runs**
Schmidt, Philadelphia, 37; Davis, Houston, 31; Parker, Cincinnati, 31; Murphy, Atlanta, 29; Davis, Cincinnati, 27; Horner, Atlanta, 27; Strawberry, New York, 27; McReynolds, San Diego, 26; Carter, New York, 24; Morrison, Pittsburgh, 23; Stubbs, Los Angeles, 23.

**Runs Batted In**
Schmidt, Philadelphia, 119; Parker, Cincinnati, 116; Carter, New York, 105; Davis, Houston, 101; Hayes, Philadelphia, 98; McReynolds, San Diego, 96; Strawberry, New York, 93; Morrison, Pittsburgh, 88; Horner, Atlanta, 87; Maldonado, San Francisco, 85.

**Stolen Bases**
Coleman, St. Louis, 107; Davis, Cincinnati, 80; Raines, Montreal, 70; Duncan, Los Angeles, 48; Doran, Houston, 42; Samuel, Philadelphia, 42; Sax, Los Angeles, 40; Hatcher, Houston, 38; Gwynn, San Diego, 37; Bonds, Pittsburgh, 36; Webster, Montreal, 36.

**Pitching** (winning percentage, 15 or more decisions)
Ojeda, New York, 18-5, .783; Gooden, New York, 17-6, .739; Fernandez, New York, 16-6, .727; Darling, New York, 15-6, .714; Deshaies, Houston, 12-5, .706; Krukow, San Francisco, 20-9, .690; Tekulve, Philadelphia, 11-5, .688; Carman, Philadelphia, 10-5, .667; McGaffigan, Montreal, 10-5, .667; Valenzuela, Los Angeles, 21-11, .656.

**Strikeouts**
Scott, Houston, 306; Valenzuela, Los Angeles, 242; Youmans, Montreal, 202; Fernandez, New York, 200; Gooden, New York, 200; Ryan, Houston, 194; Darling, New York, 184; Welch, Los Angeles, 183; Krukow, San Francisco, 178; Palmer, Atlanta, 170.

**Saves**
Worrell, St. Louis, 36; Reardon, Montreal, 35; Smith, Houston, 33; Smith, Chicago, 31; Bedrosian, Philadelphia, 29; Franco, Cincinnati, 29; Garber, Atlanta, 29; McDowell, New York, 22; Gossage, San Diego, 21; Orosco, New York, 21.

OCT. 6

## Batting: By the numbers

Slugging average is derived by dividing total bases by times at bat. On-base average divides hits, times hit by pitch and walks by times at bat, walks, times hit by pitch and sacrifice flies. Production, developed from the work of John Thorn and Pete Palmer in *The Hidden Game of Baseball*, adds these two averages. Players eligible for these rankings are those with at least 3.1 times at bat for each of their teams' games.

| American League | | National League | |
|---|---|---|---|
| **Ranked by slugging** | | **Ranked by slugging** | |
| Mattingly, Yankees | .573 | Schmidt, Philadelphia | .547 |
| Barfield, Toronto | .559 | Strawberry, Mets | .507 |
| Puckett, Minnesota | .537 | McReynolds, San Diego | .504 |
| Bell, Toronto | .532 | Davis, Houston | .493 |
| Gaetti, Minnesota | .518 | Bass, Houston | .486 |
| Carter, Cleveland | .514 | Morrison, Pittsburgh | .482 |
| Parrish, Texas | .509 | Hayes, Philadelphia | .480 |
| Deer, Milwaukee | .494 | Dawson, Montreal | .478 |
| Gibson, Detroit | .492 | Parker, Cincinnati | .477 |
| Rice, Boston | .490 | Murphy, Atlanta | .477 |
| **Ranked by on-base average** | | **Ranked by on-base average** | |
| Boggs, Boston | .453 | Raines, Montreal | .413 |
| Bradley, Seattle | .405 | Hernandez, Mets | .413 |
| Brett, Kansas City | .401 | Sax, Los Angeles | .390 |
| Murray, Baltimore | .396 | Schmidt, Philadelphia | .390 |
| Mattingly, Yankees | .394 | Gwynn, San Diego | .381 |
| Randolph, Yankees | .393 | Hayes, Philadelphia | .379 |
| Downing, California | .389 | Smith, St. Louis | .376 |
| Yount, Milwaukee | .388 | Davis, San Francisco | .375 |
| O'Brien, Texas | .385 | Oberkfell, Atlanta | .373 |
| Rice, Boston | .384 | Doran, Houston | .368 |

| American League | | National League | |
|---|---|---|---|
| **Ranked by production** | | **Ranked by production** | |
| Mattingly, Yankees | .967 | Schmidt, Philadelphia | .937 |
| Boggs, Boston | .939 | Raines, Montreal | .889 |
| Barfield, Toronto | .927 | Strawberry, Mets | .865 |
| Puckett, Minnesota | .903 | McReynolds, San Diego | .862 |
| Brett, Kansas City | .881 | Hayes, Philadelphia | .859 |
| Bell, Toronto | .881 | Hernandez, Mets | .859 |
| Rice, Boston | .874 | Gwynn, San Diego | .848 |
| Gaetti, Minnesota | .865 | Bass, Houston | .842 |
| Gibson, Detroit | .863 | Davis, Houston | .837 |
| Murray, Baltimore | .859 | Sax, Los Angeles | .830 |

OCT. 8

## The Gate? Great!

During the first season in which each team attracted at least a million fans at home, the major leagues broke the attendance record they had set last year, jointly drawing 47.5 million. The standings of all the clubs in terms of attendance gains (+) or losses (−) from 1985 to 1986:

*American League*
1986 Gain/Loss
Cleveland, 1,471,977 (+816,796)
Texas, 1,692,021 (+579,524)
Boston, 2,147,622 (+360,989)
Kansas City, 2,320,764 (+158,047)
California, 2,655,892 (+88,465)
Yankees, 2,268,116 (+53,529)
Toronto, 2,455,477 (−13,448)
Oakland, 1,314,626 (−19,911)
Milwaukee, 1,265,041 (−95,224)
Seattle, 1,028,223 (−100,473)
Baltimore, 1,973,178 (−159,209)
Chicago, 1,424,333 (−245,555)
Detroit, 1,699,437 (−387,172)
Minnesota, 1,255,453 (−396,361)
League Total, 25,172,160 (+639,997)

*National League*
1986 Gain/Loss
San Francisco, 1,528,748 (+710,051)
Houston, 1,734,266 (+549,952)
Pittsburgh, 1,000,917 (+265,017)
Philadelphia, 1,933,335 (+102,985)
Atlanta, 1,387,181 (+37,044)
Mets, 2,762,417 (+10,980)
Cincinnati, 1,692,439 (−142,180)
St. Louis, 2,471,817 (−165,746)
Los Angeles, 3,023,208 (−241,385)
Chicago, 1,859,102 (−302,432)
Montreal, 1,128,981 (−373,513)
San Diego, 1,805,776 (−404,576)
League Total, 22,328,187 (+46,197)
GRAND TOTAL, 47,500,347 (+686,194)

OCT. 9

## Pitching: By the numbers

Control shows the ratio of strikeouts to walks. Strikeouts, walks and hits per game denote those recorded per nine innings. Pitchers are ranked in order of Earned Runs Prevented, calculated by subtracting a pitcher's Earned Run Average from the league average for the season, currently 4.20 per game in the American League and 3.73 in the National, and then multiplying that difference by the innings he has pitched, divided by 9. This statistic, developed by John Thorn and Pete Palmer in *The Hidden Game of Baseball,* gives greater credit to a pitcher with a good E.R.A. who works many innings than to one with a slightly better E.R.A. who works fewer. Thus it tends to favor starters over relief pitchers. Through regular season.

### American League

| Name team | SO/game | BB/game | Control | Hits/game | E.R.A. | Innings | Earned runs prevented |
|---|---|---|---|---|---|---|---|
| Clemens, Boston (24–4) | 8.43 | 2.37 | 3.55 | 6.34 | 2.48 | 254.00 | 47.97 |
| Eichorn, Toronto (14–6) | 9.52 | 2.58 | 3.69 | 6.02 | 1.72 | 157.00 | 42.92 |
| Witt, California (18–10) | 6.96 | 2.44 | 2.85 | 7.29 | 2.84 | 269.00 | 39.94 |
| Higuera, Milwaukee (20–11) | 7.50 | 2.68 | 2.80 | 8.19 | 2.79 | 248.33 | 38.34 |
| Morris, Detroit (21–8) | 7.52 | 2.76 | 2.72 | 7.72 | 3.27 | 267.00 | 27.01 |
| Hurst, Boston (13–8) | 8.62 | 2.58 | 3.34 | 8.72 | 2.99 | 174.33 | 22.97 |
| McCaskill, Calif. (17–10) | 7.38 | 3.36 | 2.20 | 7.56 | 3.36 | 246.33 | 22.41 |
| Righetti, Yankees (8–8) | 7.00 | 2.95 | 2.37 | 7.42 | 2.45 | 106.67 | 20.54 |
| Jackson, K.C. (11–12) | 5.57 | 3.83 | 1.46 | 8.58 | 3.20 | 185.67 | 20.23 |
| Candiotti, Cleveland (16–12) | 5.96 | 3.78 | 1.58 | 8.35 | 3.57 | 252.33 | 17.19 |

### National League

| Name team | SO/game | BB/game | Control | Hits/game | E.R.A. | Innings | Earned runs prevented |
|---|---|---|---|---|---|---|---|
| Scott, Houston (18–10) | 10.00 | 2.35 | 4.25 | 5.95 | 2.22 | 275.33 | 45.80 |
| Ojeda, Mets (18–5) | 6.13 | 2.15 | 2.85 | 7.66 | 2.57 | 217.33 | 27.83 |
| Rhoden, Pittsburgh (15–12) | 5.64 | 2.70 | 2.09 | 7.49 | 2.84 | 253.67 | 24.85 |
| Gooden, Mets (17–6) | 7.20 | 2.88 | 2.50 | 7.09 | 2.84 | 250.00 | 24.33 |
| Darling, Mets (15–6) | 6.99 | 3.08 | 2.27 | 7.71 | 2.81 | 237.00 | 23.96 |
| Cox, St. Louis (12–13) | 4.42 | 2.45 | 1.80 | 7.73 | 2.90 | 220.00 | 19.93 |
| Tudor, St. Louis (13–7) | 4.40 | 2.18 | 2.02 | 8.10 | 2.92 | 219.00 | 19.52 |
| Worrell, St. Louis (9–10) | 6.34 | 3.56 | 1.78 | 7.47 | 2.08 | 103.67 | 18.85 |
| Krukow, S.F. (20–9) | 6.54 | 2.02 | 3.24 | 7.49 | 3.05 | 245.00 | 18.27 |
| Valenzuela, L.A. (21–11) | 8.09 | 2.84 | 2.85 | 7.55 | 3.14 | 269.33 | 17.32 |

OCT. 10

# SPORTS

## All-time leaders

Players active at end of 1986 season shown in capital letters.

### Most games won by pitchers

| | W | L | Pct. |
|---|---|---|---|
| 1. Cy Young | 511 | 313 | .620 |
| 2. Walter Johnson | 416 | 279 | .599 |
| 3. Christy Mathewson | 373 | 188 | .665 |
| 3. Grover C. Alexander | 373 | 208 | .642 |
| 5. Warren Spahn | 363 | 245 | .597 |
| 6. Charles (Kid) Nichols | 361 | 208 | .634 |
| 6. James F. Galvin | 361 | 309 | .539 |
| 8. Timothy Keefe | 342 | 224 | .604 |
| 9. John G. Clarkson | 327 | 176 | .650 |
| 10. STEVE CARLTON | 323 | 229 | .585 |
| 11. Gaylord Perry | 314 | 265 | .542 |
| 12. TOM SEAVER | 311 | 205 | .603 |
| 12. PHIL NIEKRO | 311 | 261 | .544 |
| 14. DON SUTTON | 310 | 239 | .565 |
| 15. Charles (Hoss) Radbourn | 308 | 191 | .617 |
| 16. Michael F. Welch | 307 | 209 | .595 |
| 17. Eddie Plank | 305 | 181 | .628 |
| 18. Lefty Grove | 300 | 141 | .680 |
| 18. Early Wynn | 300 | 244 | .551 |
| 20. Robin Roberts | 286 | 245 | .539 |
| 21. Anthony Mullane | 285 | 213 | .572 |
| 22. Ferguson Jenkins | 284 | 226 | .557 |
| 23. Jim Kaat | 283 | 237 | .544 |
| 24. Red Ruffing | 273 | 225 | .548 |
| 25. Burleigh Grimes | 270 | 212 | .560 |

### Home Runs

1. Hank Aaron, 755
2. Babe Ruth, 714
3. Willie Mays, 660
4. Frank Robinson, 586
5. Harmon Killebrew, 573
6. REGGIE JACKSON, 548
7. Mickey Mantle, 536
8. Jimmy Foxx, 534
9. Ted Williams, 521
9. Willie McCovey, 521
11. Eddie Mathews, 512
11. Ernie Banks, 512
13. Mel Ott, 511
14. MIKE SCHMIDT, 495
15. Lou Gehrig, 493
16. Stan Musial, 475
16. Willie Stargell, 475
18. Carl Yastrzemski, 452
19. DAVE KINGMAN, 442
20. Billy Williams, 426
21. Duke Snider, 407
22. Al Kaline, 399
23. Johnny Bench, 389
24. GRAIG NETTLES, 386
25. Frank Howard, 382
26. Orlando Cepeda, 379
26. TONY PEREZ, 379
28. Norm Cash, 377
29. Rocky Colavito, 374
30. Gil Hodges, 370
31. Ralph Kiner, 369
32. Joe DiMaggio, 361
33. Johnny Mize, 359
34. Yogi Berra, 358
35. Lee May, 354
36. Dick Allen, 351
36. JIM RICE, 351
38. George Foster, 348
39. DARRELL EVANS, 347
40. Ron Santo, 342
41. Boog Powell, 339
42. Joe Adcock, 336
43. Bobby Bonds, 332
44. Hank Greenberg, 331
45. Willie Horton, 325
46. Roy Sievers, 318
47. DON BAYLOR, 315
48. Reggie Smith, 314
49. RON CEY, 312
50. Al Simmons, 307
50. Greg Luzinski, 307

### Strikeouts

#### By pitchers

1. NOLAN RYAN, 4,277
2. STEVE CARLTON, 4,040
3. TOM SEAVER, 3,640
4. Gaylord Perry, 3,534
5. Walter Johnson, 3,508
6. DON SUTTON, 3,431
7. PHIL NIEKRO, 3,278
8. Ferguson Jenkins, 3,192
9. Bob Gibson, 3,117
10. BERT BLYLEVEN, 3,090
11. Jim Bunning, 2,855
12. Mickey Lolich, 2,832
13. Cy Young, 2,819
14. Warren Spahn, 2,583
15. Bob Feller, 2,581
16. Jerry Koosman, 2,556
17. Tim Keefe, 2,538
18. Christy Mathewson, 2,505
19. Don Drysdale, 2,486
20. Jim Kaat, 2,461
21. Sam McDowell, 2,453
22. Luis Tiant, 2,416
23. Sandy Koufax, 2,396
24. Robin Roberts, 2,357
25. Early Wynn, 2,334

#### By batters

1. REGGIE JACKSON, 2,500
2. Willie Stargell, 1,936
3. TONY PEREZ, 1,867
4. DAVE KINGMAN, 1,816
5. Bobby Bonds, 1,757
6. MIKE SCHMIDT, 1,744
7. Lou Brock, 1,730
8. Mickey Mantle, 1,710
9. Harmon Killebrew, 1,699
10. Lee May, 1,570
11. Dick Allen, 1,556
12. Willie McCovey, 1,550
13. Frank Robinson, 1,532
14. Willie Mays, 1,526
15. Rick Monday, 1,513
16. Greg Luzinski, 1,495
17. Eddie Mathews, 1,487
18. Frank Howard, 1,460
19. Jim Wynn, 1,427
20. George Scott, 1,418
20. George Foster, 1,418
22. Carl Yastrzemski, 1,393
23. Hank Aaron, 1,383
24. Ron Santo, 1,343
25. GORMAN THOMAS, 1,339

**Saves**

1. Rollie Fingers, 341
2. BRUCE SUTTER, 286
3. GOOSE GOSSAGE, 278
4. Sparky Lyle, 238
5. DAN QUISENBERRY, 229
6. Hoyt Wilhelm, 227
7. GENE GARBER, 194
8. Roy Face, 193
9. Mike Marshall, 188
10. Tug McGraw, 180
11. Ron Perranoski, 179
12. KENT TEKULVE, 176
13. Lindy McDaniel, 172
14. JEFF REARDON, 162
15. Stu Miller, 154
16. Don McMahon, 153
17. Ted Abernathy, 148
18. Dave Giusti, 145
19. LEE SMITH, 144
20. Clay Carroll, 143
20. Darold Knowles, 143
22. Gary Lavelle, 135
23. Jim Brewer, 132
24. RON DAVIS, 130
25. TERRY FORSTER, 127

**Stolen Bases***

1. Lou Brock, 938
2. Ty Cobb, 892
3. Eddie Collins, 743
4. Max Carey, 738
5. Honus Wagner, 703
6. Joe Morgan, 689
7. RICKEY HENDERSON, 660
8. Bert Campaneris, 631
9. Maury Wills, 586
10. DAVEY LOPES, 555
11. Cesar Cedeno, 549
12. Luis Aparicio, 506
13. Clyde Milan, 495
14. OMAR MORENO, 487
15. Jimmy Sheckard, 474
16. WILLIE WILSON, 470
17. Bobby Bonds, 461
17. TIM RAINES, 461
19. Ron LeFlore, 455
20. Sherry Magee, 441
21. Tris Speaker, 433
22. Bob Beecher, 428
23. Frankie Frisch, 419
24. Tommy Harper, 408
25. Frank Chance, 405
25. Donie Bush, 405

*Totals since 1898, when rules were changed to present definitions.

OCT. 12

## Mets and Red Sox Win Their Pennants

The Mets won their first National League pennant in 13 years today when they rallied three times to defeat the Houston Astros, 7–6, in a 16-inning game that lasted more than four and a half hours and set records for drama and duration. It was the longest postseason game in baseball history, and one of the most gripping, and it put an elegant finishing touch to six years of rebuilding the Mets from last place to first. They won 108 games in the regular season for the best record in the big leagues, they held first place every day from April 23 and they marched the final step into the World Series today when they won a classic playoff series, four games to two.

The Astros fell on Bob Ojeda, the Mets' starting pitcher, for three runs in the first inning. Then the Astros didn't score for 12 innings. But the Mets got only two hits off the Houston starter, Bob Knepper, until the ninth, when they stood three outs from losing, but suddenly rallied for three runs and a tie.

Then the Mets broke the tie with a run in the 14th. But, two outs from losing the pennant, the Astros resurrected themselves when Billy Hatcher hit a home run off Jesse Orosco. And finally, in the 16th, the Mets stormed three runs across and looked safe at last. But the Astros fired back with two runs of their own, and still had two men on base when Orosco struck out Kevin Bass on a 3–2 pitch for the final out of the final rally.

Then the crowd of 45,718 in the Astrodome stood and applauded both teams for a rare performance. It was a performance filled with heroes, quirks and even scuff marks on baseballs. The Mets hit only .189 as a team, but still won four games. Orosco came out of the bullpen four times and won three games, including this one. And Mike Scott, the master of the split-fingered fastball, mastered the Mets twice and was voted the most valuable player of the series. If the Astros had survived, Scott would have pitched the seventh game.

Continuing to defy the skeptics who waited fruitlessly for five months for them to collapse during the regular season, the Red Sox won the American League pennant tonight with an 8–1 victory over the California Angels in the seventh and deciding game of the championship series.

The Red Sox success, capping an improbable comeback from a three-games-to-one deficit, intensified the agony and the ignominy of the Angels and their manager, Gene Mauch, who never have won a pennant, the Angels in their 26 years of existence and Mauch in his 25 years of major league managing.

Roger Clemens, making his third start of the series despite being weakened by a flu-type condition, allowed only four hits in pitching into the eighth inning. Calvin Schiraldi, the relief pitcher obtained from the Mets last winter, secured the final six outs, five on strikeouts.

"You could see in his eyes that he was going to be in control tonight," Baylor said of Clemens. In supporting Clemens, the Red Sox batters received support themselves from the Angels' defense, which in the series committed to eight errors, leading to 13 unearned runs of the 41 runs Boston scored in the series.

Dick Schofield, the sure-handed, strong-armed shortstop, and Gary Pettis, a Gold Glove center fielder last year, made the critical errors tonight that led to seven unearned runs against John Candelaria. The key hits following the errors in the second and fourth innings were a two-run single by Wade Boggs and a three-run home run by Jim Rice. The only earned Red Sox run was Dwight Evans's seventh-inning home run against Don Sutton.

Oct. 16

## Playoffs

**National League**

**Oct. 8**

| | | | | | | | | | | | | |
|---|---|---|---|---|---|---|---|---|---|---|---|---|
| New York Mets | 0 | 0 | 0 | 0 | 0 | 0 | 0 | 0 | — | 0 | 5 | 0 |
| Houston Astros | 0 | 1 | 0 | 0 | 0 | 0 | 0 | x | — | 1 | 7 | 1 |

Gooden, Orosco (8) and Carter; Scott and Ashby. W Scott (1–10). L Gooden (0–1).

**Oct. 9**

| | | | | | | | | | | | | |
|---|---|---|---|---|---|---|---|---|---|---|---|---|
| New York Mets | 0 | 0 | 0 | 2 | 3 | 0 | 0 | 0 | — | 5 | 10 | 0 |
| Houston Astros | 0 | 0 | 0 | 0 | 0 | 1 | 0 | 0 | — | 1 | 10 | 2 |

Ojeda and Carter; Ryan, Anderson (6), Lopez (8), Kerfeld (9) and Ashby. W Ojeda (1–0). L Ryan (0–1).

**Oct. 11**

| | | | | | | | | | | | | |
|---|---|---|---|---|---|---|---|---|---|---|---|---|
| Houston Astros | 2 | 2 | 0 | 0 | 0 | 0 | 1 | 0 | — | 5 | 8 | 1 |
| New York Mets | 0 | 0 | 0 | 0 | 0 | 4 | 0 | 2 | — | 6 | 10 | 1 |

Knepper, Kerfeld (8), Smith (9) and Ashby; Darling, Aguilera (7), and Carter. W Orosco (1–0). L Smith (0–1). HRs: Houston, Doran (1); New York, Strawberry (1), Dykstra (1).

**Oct. 12**

| | | | | | | | | | | | | |
|---|---|---|---|---|---|---|---|---|---|---|---|---|
| Houston Astros | 0 | 2 | 0 | 0 | 1 | 0 | 0 | 0 | — | 3 | 4 | 1 |
| New York Mets | 0 | 0 | 0 | 0 | 0 | 0 | 1 | 0 | — | 1 | 3 | 0 |

Scott and Ashby; Fernandez, McDowell (7), Sisk (9) and Carter. W Scott (2–0). L Fernandez (0–1). HRs: Houston, Ashby (1), Thon (1).

**Oct. 14**

| | | | | | | | | | | | | | |
|---|---|---|---|---|---|---|---|---|---|---|---|---|---|
| Houston Astros | 0 | 0 | 0 | 0 | 1 | 0 | 0 | 0 | 0 | 0 | 0 | — | 1 | 9 | 1 |
| New York Mets | 0 | 0 | 0 | 0 | 1 | 0 | 0 | 0 | 0 | 0 | 1 | — | 2 | 4 | 0 |

Ryan, Kerfeld (10) and Ashby; Gooden, Orosco (11) and Carter. W Orosco (2–0). L Kerfeld (0–1). HR: New York, Strawberry (2).

**Oct. 15**

| | | | | | | | | | | | | | | | | |
|---|---|---|---|---|---|---|---|---|---|---|---|---|---|---|---|---|
| New York Mets | 0 | 0 | 0 | 0 | 0 | 0 | 3 | 0 | 0 | 0 | 0 | 1 | 0 | 3 | — | 7 | 11 | 0 |
| Houston Astros | 3 | 0 | 0 | 0 | 0 | 0 | 0 | 0 | 0 | 0 | 0 | 1 | 0 | 2 | — | 6 | 11 | 1 |

Ojeda, Aguilera (6), McDowell (9), Orosco (14) and Carter; Knepper, Smith (9), Andersen (11), Lopez (14), Calhoun (16) and Ashby. W Orosco (3–0). L Lopez (0–1). HR: Houston, Hatcher (1).

## American League

**Oct. 7**

| | | | | | | | | | | | R | H | E |
|---|---|---|---|---|---|---|---|---|---|---|---|---|---|
| California Angels | 0 | 4 | 1 | 0 | 0 | 0 | 0 | 3 | 0 | — | 8 | 11 | 0 |
| Boston Red Sox | 0 | 0 | 0 | 0 | 0 | 1 | 0 | 0 | 0 | — | 1 | 5 | 1 |

Witt and Boone; Clemens, Sambito (8), Stanley (8) and Gedman. W Witt (1–0). L Clemens (0–1).

**Oct. 8**

| | | | | | | | | | | | R | H | E |
|---|---|---|---|---|---|---|---|---|---|---|---|---|---|
| California Angels | 0 | 0 | 0 | 1 | 1 | 0 | 0 | 0 | 0 | — | 2 | 11 | 3 |
| Boston Red Sox | 1 | 1 | 0 | 0 | 1 | 0 | 3 | 3 | x | — | 9 | 13 | 2 |

McCaskill, Lucas (8), Corbett (8) and Boone; Hurst and Gedman. W Hurst (1–0). L McCaskill (0–1). HRs: California, Joyner (1); Boston, Rice (1).

**Oct. 10**

| | | | | | | | | | | | R | H | E |
|---|---|---|---|---|---|---|---|---|---|---|---|---|---|
| Boston Red Sox | 0 | 1 | 0 | 0 | 0 | 0 | 2 | 0 | 0 | — | 3 | 9 | 1 |
| California Angels | 0 | 0 | 0 | 0 | 1 | 3 | 1 | 0 | 0 | — | 5 | 8 | 1 |

Boyd, Sambito (7), Schiraldi (8) and Gedman; Candelaria, Moore (7) and Boone. W Candelaria (1–0). L Boyd (0–1). HRs: California, Schofield (1), Pettis (1).

**Oct. 11**

| | | | | | | | | | | | | R | H | E |
|---|---|---|---|---|---|---|---|---|---|---|---|---|---|---|
| Boston Red Sox | 0 | 0 | 0 | 0 | 0 | 1 | 0 | 2 | 0 | 0 | — | 3 | 6 | 1 |
| California Angels | 0 | 0 | 0 | 0 | 0 | 0 | 0 | 3 | 0 | 1 | — | 4 | 11 | 2 |

Clemens, Schiraldi (9) and Gedman; Sutton, Lucas (7), Ruhle (7), Finley (8), Corbett (8) and Boone, Narron (10). W Corbett (1–0). L Schiraldi (0–1). HR, California, DeCinces (1).

**Oct. 12**

| | | | | | | | | | | | | R | H | E |
|---|---|---|---|---|---|---|---|---|---|---|---|---|---|---|
| Boston Red Sox | 0 | 2 | 0 | 0 | 0 | 0 | 0 | 4 | 0 | 1 | — | 7 | 12 | 0 |
| California Angels | 0 | 0 | 1 | 0 | 0 | 2 | 2 | 0 | 1 | 0 | — | 6 | 13 | 6 |

Hurst, Stanley (7), Sambito (9), Crawford (9), Schiraldi (11) and Gedman; Witt, Lucas (9), Moore (9), Finley (11) and Boone, Narron (10). W Crawford (1–0). L Moore (0–1). HRs: Boston, Gedman (1), Baylor (1), Henderson (1); California, Boone (1), Grich (1).

**Oct. 14**

| | | | | | | | | | | R | H | E |
|---|---|---|---|---|---|---|---|---|---|---|---|---|
| California Angels | 2 | 0 | 0 | 0 | 0 | 0 | 1 | 1 | 0 | — | 4 | 11 | 1 |
| Boston Red Sox | 2 | 0 | 5 | 0 | 1 | 0 | 2 | 0 | x | — | 10 | 16 | 1 |

McCaskill, Lucas (3), Corbett (4), Finley (7) and Boone, Narron (8); Boyd, Stanley (8) and Gedman. W Boyd (1–1). L McCaskill (0–2). HR: California, Downing (1).

**Oct. 15**

| | | | | | | | | | R | H | E |
|---|---|---|---|---|---|---|---|---|---|---|---|---|
| California Angels | 0 | 0 | 0 | 0 | 0 | 0 | 1 | 0 | — | 1 | 6 | 2 |
| Boston Red Sox | 0 | 3 | 0 | 4 | 0 | 0 | 1 | 0 | x | — | 8 | 8 | 1 |

Candelaria, Sutton (4), Moore (8) and Boone; Clemens, Schiraldi (8) and Gedman. W Clemens (1–1). L Candelaria (1–1). HRs: Boston, Rice (2), Evans (1).

Oct. 8–16

# The World Series '86: Mets Get the Magic Back, Take 7th Game and Series

By JOSEPH DURSO

The Mets brought their season of splendor to a stunning finish last night when they rallied twice to defeat the Boston Red Sox, 8–5, and win their first World Series in 17 years.

They did it with all the magic that carried them to 116 victories during the season and beyond, and that revived their fortunes after they had lost the first two games of the Series. And they shook Shea Stadium with roaring cheers, but with no postgame disorder, from the 55,032 people who watched the Mets ring down the curtain on one of the most successful seasons in baseball history.

They won their championship in the seventh game of the 83d Series and the 175th game of their baseball year, and they won it by sweeping the final two games with rousing rallies in late innings. They were two runs down in the 10th inning of the sixth game Saturday night, and scored three and won. They were three runs down to Bruce Hurst, the Red Sox's starting pitcher, last night, but stormed back with three runs in the sixth and three more in the seventh, and won it all.

Ray Knight, the Mets' 33-year-old retread at third base who seemed to have no job or future last spring, was voted the most valuable player in the Series. He hit two singles and a home run last night, and ended the Series with nine hits in 23 times at bat for a .391 batting average.

There was heavy intrigue as the 7th game began. McNamara switched pitchers, as he said he would do after the rainout provided a day of rest after the sixth game. He bypassed Dennis (Oil Can) Boyd, who was knocked around for four runs in the first inning by the Mets in the third game. And he started Hurst, his left-handed ace, who had beaten the Mets in the first and 5th games. Johnson countered by starting his right-handed hitting platoon, and even benched Len Dykstra, his leadoff "rabbit."

But, with all the platooning, the Mets got into urgent straits before the game was an inning and a half old, and they did it in a bizarre sequence.

Dwight Evans led off the second inning for the Red Sox, nearly struck out on a foul trip that eluded Gary Carter and then hit Darling's 3-and-2 pitch deep into the bleacher seats in left-center field for a home run. And the Red Sox had the lead.

Next came Rich Gedman, who hit the 1-and-1 pitch foul behind first base, where it skittered along the box-seat railing and caused a remarkable chain reaction. About a dozen fans leaned over the railing as the ball skimmed past and the railing gave way, dumping them onto the dirt track. The game was halted for almost five minutes while the ground crew repaired the railing.

Darling, who had tossed lightly during the wait, then delivered to Gedman, who nailed the first pitch to the fence in right-center. Darryl Strawberry ran back, leaped and got his glove on the ball as it went over the fence. But he couldn't hold it, and the ball plunked over the fence for a home run and a 2–0 lead.

There was more. Darling then walked Dave Henderson and got Spike Owen on a pop fly to the shortstop. Then Hurst dropped a bunt a few yards toward third base, right through the charging Knight. But Darling recovered the ball and made a strong throw to Tim Teufel at first base for the out. However, the bunt got Henderson to second, and he scored from there when Wade Boggs hit a ground single through the middle, and the Mets suddenly were three runs down.

Before Darling got the side out, Barrett outran a bunt single and shared a piece of World Series history. It was his 13th hit, typing him with Bobby Richardson of the 1964 Yankees and Lou Brock of the 1968 St. Louis Cardinals for most hits in a seven-game Series.

Darling, the 26-year-old history major from Yale, stayed until the fourth inning, when he was replaced by the left-handed Sid Fernandez. That proved to be a milestone for the Mets as their bullpen gave up no more runs until the eighth inning, and by then the game had turned toward the Mets. Fernandez led the way with two-plus innings of nearly perfect baseball.

Hurst protected his lead with another superb performance, including 11 batters in a row after a second-inning single by Knight. Then, with one down in the sixth and time slipping, the Mets took their shot.

Lee Mazzilli pinch-hit for Fernandez and singled to left field. Mookie Wilson lined the next pitch to left for a single, Mazzilli stopping at second. Teufel walked on five pitches, and the bases were loaded with Hernandez swinging. Hernandez, who played a starring role for the St. Louis Cardinals in the 1982 Series, remembered that he had sensed big things taking shape. "I told my brother in the morning, 'I'm swinging good. If I come up with people on base, I'll be a big part of this.' "

And he was. He took a strike, then lined a long single to left-center; two runs scored and the Mets were suddenly only one away.

Then came Gary Carter, who looped a pop fly into short right field. Hernandez held at first and watched Evans sprint in for the ball, then saw him dive for it. Evans couldn't hold it, but he did get up and fire the ball to second, where Hernandez was tagged out. But Teufel meanwhile was scoring, and the Mets were back in the game and back in the Series.

One inning later, Hurst was gone; one inning later, the tie was gone. In one more memorable rally, the Mets shot into the lead in the seventh inning.

The new Boston pitcher was Calvin Schiraldi, traded by the Mets to the Red Sox last winter. The first man he faced was Knight, who drove a soaring home run into the bleachers in left-center, and the Mets seized the lead.

Dykstra pinch-hit and singled to right. Then Schiraldi threw a wild pitch instead of a pitchout. When Rafael Santana bounced a single over first, Dykstra crossed and the Mets led by two.

Finally, with Joe Sambito pitching for the Red Sox, a bunt and a pair of walks gave Hernandez another shot. He lifted a sacrifice fly to center, and the Mets led by three.

But this was no night for the faint of heart. In the top of the eighth, the Red Sox came roaring back with two runs and closed it to 6–5. But Orosco became the fourth and final pitcher for the Mets and retired six straight batters. Then Darryl Strawberry unfurled a home run in the home half of the eighth, and the Mets soared to their championship.

OCT. 28

## WORLD SERIES

**Oct. 18**

Boston Red
Sox         0 0 0 0 0 0 1 0 0 — 1 5 0
New York
Mets        0 0 0 0 0 0 0 0 0 — 0 4 1

Hurst, Schiraldi (9) and Gedman; Darling, McDowell (8) and Carter. W Hurst (1–0). L Darling (0–1).

**Oct. 19**

Boston Red
Sox         0 0 3 1 2 0 2 0 1 — 9 18 0
New York
Mets        0 0 2 0 1 0 0 0 0 — 3 8 1

Clemens, Crawford (5), Stanley (7) and Gedman; Gooden, Aguilera (6), Orosco (7), Fernandez (9), Sisk (9) and Carter. W Crawford (1–0). L Gooden (0–1). HRs: Boston, Henderson (1), Evans (1).

**Oct. 21**

New York
Mets        4 0 0 0 0 0 2 1 0 — 7 13 0
Boston Red
Sox         0 0 1 0 0 0 0 0 0 — 1 5 0

Ojeda, McDowell (8) and Carter; Boyd, Sambito (8), Stanley (8) and Gedman. W Ojeda (1–0). L Boyd (0–1). HR: New York, Dykstra (1).

**Oct. 22**

| | | | |
|---|---|---|---|
| New York Mets | 0 0 0 3 0 0 2 1 0 — | 6 | 12 0 |
| Boston Red Sox | 0 0 0 0 0 0 0 2 0 — | 2 | 7 1 |

Darling, McDowell (8), Orosco (8) and Carter; Nipper, Crawford (7), Stanley (9) and Gedman. W Darling (1–1). L Nipper (0–1). HRs, New York, Carter 2 (2), Dykstra (2).

**Oct. 23**

| | | | |
|---|---|---|---|
| New York Mets | 0 0 0 0 0 0 0 1 1 — | 2 | 10 1 |
| Boston Red Sox | 0 1 1 0 2 0 0 0 x — | 4 | 12 0 |

Gooden, Fernandez (5) and Carter; Hurst and Gedman. W Hurst (2–0). L Gooden (0–2). HR: New York, Teufel (1).

**Oct. 25**

| | | | |
|---|---|---|---|
| Boston Red Sox | 1 1 0 0 0 0 1 0 0 2 — | 5 | 13 3 |
| New York Mets | 0 0 0 0 2 0 0 1 0 3 — | 6 | 8 2 |

Clemens, Schiraldi (8), Stanley (10) and Gedman; Ojeda, McDowell (8), Orosco (8), Aguilera (9) and Carter. W Aguilera (1–0). L Schiraldi (0–1). HR: Boston, Henderson (2).

**Oct. 27**

| | | | |
|---|---|---|---|
| Boston Red Sox | 0 3 0 0 0 0 0 2 0 — | 5 | 9 0 |
| New York Mets | 0 0 0 0 0 3 3 2 x — | 8 | 10 0 |

Hurst, Schiraldi (7), Sambito (7), Stanley (7), Nipper (8), Crawford and Gedman; Darling, Fernandez (4), McDowell (7), Orosco (8) and Carter. W McDowell (1–0). L Schiraldi (0–2). HRs: Boston, Evans (2), Gedman (1); New York, Knight (1), Strawberry (1).

OCT. 19–28

## MVPs

1955—Johnny Podres, Brooklyn (N.L.)
1956—Don Larsen, Yankees
1957—Lew Burdette, Milwaukee (N.L.)
1958—Bob Turley, Yankees
1959—Larry Sherry, Los Angeles, (N.L.)
1960—Bobby Richardson, Yankees
1961—Whitey Ford, Yankees
1962—Ralph Terry, Yankees
1963—Sandy Koufax, Los Angeles (N.L.)
1964—Bob Gibson, St. Louis (N.L.)
1965—Sandy Koufax, Los Angeles (N.L.)
1966—Frank Robinson, Baltimore (A.L.)
1967—Bob Gibson, St. Louis (N.L.)
1968—Mickey Lolich, Detroit (A.L.)
1969—Donn Clendenon, Mets
1970—Brooks Robinson, Baltimore (A.L.)
1971—Roberto Clemente, Pittsburgh (N.L.)
1972—Gene Tenace, Oakland (A.L.)
1973—Reggie Jackson, Oakland (A.L.)
1974—Rollie Fingers, Oakland (A.L.)
1975—Pete Rose, Cincinnati (N.L.)
1976—Johnny Bench, Cincinnati (N.L.)
1977—Reggie Jackson, Yankees
1978—Bucky Dent, Yankees
1979—Willie Stargell, Pittsburgh (N.L.)
1980—Mike Schmidt, Philadelphia (N.L.)
1981—Ron Cey, Pedro Guerrero and Steve Yeager, Los Angeles (N.L.)
1982—Darrell Porter, St. Louis (N.L.)
1983—Rick Dempsey, Baltimore (A.L.)
1984—Alan Trammell, Detroit (A.L.)
1985—Bret Saberhagen, Kansas City (A.L.)
1986—Ray Knight, Mets

OCT. 29

## Clemens, Schmidt Win Awards

Roger Clemens of the Boston Red Sox became the eighth player to win both the Cy Young and Most Valuable Player awards, and Mike Schmidt of the Philadelphia Phillies became the seventh player to win the Most Valuable Player Award three times.

Clemens, who was the third pitcher to win the American League Cy Young Award unanimously, had 19 out of the 28 first-place votes and easily outdistanced Don Mattingly of the Yankees for the Most Valuable Player Award. He won 24 games and lost 4, had an Earned Run Average of 2.48 and struck out 238 batters, including a record 20 in one game.

## Doubling Up

Statistics of the pitchers who have won both the Cy Young and Most Valuable Player awards in the same season.

|  | Don Newcombe Brooklyn, 1956 | Sandy Koufax Los Angeles, 1963 | Bob Gibson St. Louis, 1968 | Denny McLain Detroit, 1968 | Vida Blue Oakland, 1971 | Rollie Fingers Milwaukee, 1981 | Willie Hernandez Detroit, 1984 | Roger Clemens Boston, 1986 |
|---|---|---|---|---|---|---|---|---|
| Won | 27 | 25 | 22 | 31 | 24 | 6 | 9 | 24 |
| Lost | 7 | 5 | 9 | 6 | 8 | 3 | 3 | 4 |
| E.R.A. | 3.06 | 1.88 | 1.12 | 1.96 | 1.82 | 1.04 | 1.92 | 2.48 |
| Innings | 268 | 311 | 304 | 336 | 312 | 78 | 140 | 254 |
| Hits | 219 | 214 | 198 | 241 | 209 | 55 | 96 | 179 |
| Walks | 46 | 58 | 62 | 63 | 88 | 13 | 36 | 67 |
| Strikeouts | 139 | 306 | 268 | 280 | 301 | 61 | 112 | 238 |
| Complete Games | 18 | 20 | 28 | 28 | 24 | 0 | 0 | 10 |
| Saves | 0 | 0 | 0 | 0 | 0 | 28 | 32 | 0 |
| Shutouts | 5 | 11 | 13 | 6 | 8 | 0 | 0 | 1 |

Note: Don Newcombe and Sandy Koufax accomplished their doubles when only one Cy Young Award was given for both leagues. Rollie Fingers won both in a strike-shortened season.

Nov. 19

Schmidt, who led the National League with 37 home runs and 119 runs batted in while hitting .290, finished ahead of Glenn Davis of the Houston Astros, even though the Phillies were a distant second to the New York Mets in the National League's Eastern Division.

Winners of the Other Major Postseason Awards:

National League Cy Young Award: Mike Scott of the Houston Astros, who had an 18–10 record with 306 strikeouts and a 2.22 Earned Run Average. He barely beat out Fernando Valenzuela of the Los Angeles Dodgers.

National League Rookie of the Year: Todd Worrell, the St. Louis Cardinal relief pitcher who led the league with 36 saves and had a 2.03 Earned Run Average. Rob Thompson, the San Francisco second baseman, was a distant second choice.

American League Rookie of the Year: Jose Canseco, the Oakland A's' outfielder who hit 33 home runs and batted in 117 runs. He narrowly edged Wally Joyner, the California Angels' first baseman.

Nov. 13–26

## Three-Time Winners

Mike Schmidt, who also won the National League's MVP award in 1980 and 1981, joined six other players—all members of the Hall of Fame—in becoming a three-time winner. The others to win three times were Stan Musial (1943-46-48) and Roy Campanella (1951-53-55) in the National League and Jimmie Foxx (1932-33-38), Joe DiMaggio (1939-41-47), Yogi Berra (1951-54-55) and Mickey Mantle (1956-57-62) in the American League.

## The career statistics of all seven three-time winners

| Name | AB | R | H | Avg. | 2B | 3B | HR | RBI |
|---|---|---|---|---|---|---|---|---|
| Yogi Berra | 7,555 | 1,175 | 2,150 | .285 | 321 | 49 | 358 | 1,430 |
| Roy Campanella | 4,205 | 627 | 1,161 | .276 | 178 | 18 | 242 | 856 |
| Joe DiMaggio | 6,821 | 1,390 | 2,214 | .325 | 389 | 131 | 361 | 1,537 |
| Jimmie Foxx | 8,134 | 1,751 | 2,646 | .325 | 458 | 125 | 534 | 1,921 |
| Mickey Mantle | 8,102 | 1,677 | 2,415 | .298 | 344 | 72 | 536 | 1,509 |
| Stan Musial | 10,972 | 1,949 | 3,630 | .331 | 725 | 177 | 475 | 1,951 |
| Mike Schmidt | 7,292 | 1,347 | 1,954 | .268 | 352 | 57 | 495 | 1,392 |

Nov. 20

## Football Computer ranking
Division I-AA

The *New York Times*'s computer ranking of the nation's 86 Division I-AA football teams, with season records in parentheses. The top-ranked team is assigned a rating of 1.000; the ratings of other teams are percentages of that figure.

| | | | | |
|---|---|---|---|---|
| 1. Holy Cross (10–1–0) | 1.000 | | 34. Richmond (4–7–0) | .588 |
| 2. Nevada-Reno (11–0–0) | .979 | | 35. N.E. Louisiana (5–6–0) | .578 |
| 3. Pennsylvania (10–0–0) | .944 | | 36. Mississippi Valley (4–3–1) | .563 |
| 4. Appalachian State (9–1–1) | .904 | | 37. Marshall (6–4–1) | .561 |
| 5. Arkansas State (9–1–1) | .854 | | 37. Middle Tennessee (6–5–0) | .561 |
| 6. E. Illinois (10–1–0) | .848 | | 39. Boise State (5–6–0) | .559 |
| 7. Howard (8–3–0) | .830 | | 40. Montana (6–4–0) | .557 |
| 8. Ga. Southern (9–2–0) | .771 | | 41. Lafayette (6–5–0) | .549 |
| 9. E. Kentucky (8–2–1) | .767 | | 42. Illinois State (5–5–0) | .545 |
| 10. James Madison (5–5–1) | .753 | | 43. Grambling (6–4–0) | .538 |
| 11. William & Mary (9–2–0) | .728 | | 44. Eastern Washington (5–5–0) | .536 |
| 12. Delaware (8–3–0) | .715 | | 45. W. Kentucky (4–6–1) | .524 |
| 13. Furman (7–2–2) | .705 | | 46. New Hampshire (7–4–0) | .522 |
| 14. Sam Houston (9–2–0) | .699 | | 47. Western Illinois (6–5–0) | .520 |
| 14. Idaho (8–3–0) | .699 | | 48. Steven A. Austin (5–6–0) | .516 |
| 16. North Carolina A&T (9–2–0) | .692 | | 49. Tenn.-Chattanooga (4–7–0) | .514 |
| 16. Louisiana Tech (6–4–1) | .692 | | 50. Northeastern (4–6–0) | .484 |
| 18. Tennessee State (9–1–1) | .690 | | 51. Colgate (4–7–0) | .482 |
| 19. N. Arizona (7–4–0) | .663 | | 51. Bethune-Cookman (3–7–0) | .482 |
| 20. Jackson State (9–2–0) | .657 | | 53. Morehead St. (7–4–0) | .472 |
| 21. W. Carolina (6–5–0) | .655 | | 53. Florida A&M (4–6–0) | .472 |
| 22. Maine (7–4–0) | .647 | | 55. Boston U. (4–7–0) | .466 |
| 23. Southern U. (5–4–1) | .640 | | 56. S.W. Texas State (4–7–0) | .457 |
| 23. Nicholls State (9–2–0) | .640 | | 57. South Carolina St. (5–6–0) | .453 |
| 25. Murray State (7–3–1) | .630 | | 57. N.W. Louisiana (5–5–1) | .453 |
| 26. Connecticut (8–3–0) | .615 | | 59. E. Tennessee (6–5–0) | .451 |
| 26. Delaware State (7–4–0) | .615 | | 60. Lehigh (5–6–0) | .435 |
| 28. S. Illinois (7–4–0) | .611 | | 61. Alcorn State (4–5–0) | .420 |
| 29. Massachusetts (8–3–0) | .607 | | 62. Brown (5–4–1) | .416 |
| 29. N. Texas State (6–4–0) | .607 | | 63. Austin Peay (5–6–0) | .401 |
| 31. Akron (7–4–0) | .605 | | 64. Bucknell (3–7–0) | .378 |
| 31. Northern Iowa (7–3–1) | .605 | | 65. Indiana State (3–8–0) | .378 |
| 33. Cornell (8–2–0) | .597 | | 66. Dartmouth (3–6–1) | .372 |

| | |
|---|---|
| 67. S.W. Missouri State (3–7–0) | .362 |
| 68. Youngstown State (2–9–0) | .360 |
| 69. Alabama State (3–7–0) | .339 |
| 70. Weber State (3–8–0) | .335 |
| 71. Prairie View (3–8–0) | .320 |
| 72. Harvard (3–7–0) | .306 |
| 73. Montana State (3–8–0) | .289 |
| 74. McNeese State (2–9–0) | .285 |
| 75. Morgan State (1–8–0) | .283 |
| 76. Texas Southern (2–8–1) | .243 |
| 77. Citadel (3–8–0) | .231 |
| 78. Rhode Island (1–10–0) | .206 |
| 79. Yale (3–7–0) | .193 |
| 80. Idaho State (2–9–0) | .187 |
| 81. Lamar (2–9–0) | .183 |
| 82. Princeton (2–8–0) | .179 |
| 82. V.M.I. (1–10–0) | .179 |
| 84. Tennessee Tech (0–10–0) | .069 |
| 85. Davidson (0–9–0) | .029 |
| 86. Columbia (0–10–0) | −.170 |

The *New York Times*'s computer football ranking is based on analysis of each team's record, looking at who won a game, by what margin and against what quality of opposition. The quality of an opponent is calculated by examining its record against other foes. The *Times*'s computer model collapses runaway scores and takes note of a home field advantage.

Nov. 26

# Braves Pass Yanks for Top Salaries

**By MURRAY CHASS**

The Atlanta Braves, aided significantly by their trade of Claudell Washington for Ken Griffey, have supplanted the Yankees as the team with the highest average salary in baseball. This marks only the second year in the past nine years that the Yankees have not been No. 1 in the salary standing.

According to figures compiled by the Players Association for presentation to its executive board at its meeting in the Bahamas yesterday, the Braves' 1986 average salary was a record $657,657 compared with the Yankees' $617,616. The Chicago Cubs, at $601,660, and the Boston Red Sox, at $590,765, also eclipsed the record the Yankees set last year with a $546,364 average.

The Mets, who defeated the Red Sox in the World Series, ranked ninth with a $477,863 average. The Players Association computes its salary data based on players on club rosters Aug. 31, the day before rosters can expand to 40 players.

Dec. 3

## The standings

The average salaries for major league baseball teams in 1986 as compiled by the players association

| | Avg. salary | Percent change | 1985 rank |
|---|---|---|---|
| 1. Braves | $657,657 | 21.6 | 2 |
| 2. Yankees | $617,616 | 13.0 | 1 |
| 3. Cubs | $601,660 | 45.4 | 7 |
| 4. Red Sox | $590,765 | 52.8 | 13 |
| 5. Angels | $526,020 | 21.3 | 4 |
| 6. Dodgers | $496,765 | 17.1 | 6 |
| 7. Royals | $482,233 | 30.9 | 16 |
| 8. Padres | $478,719 | 19.5 | 9 |
| 9. Mets | $477,863 | 22.7 | 12 |
| 10. Tigers | $466,653 | 14.7 | 8 |
| 11. Orioles | $449,291 | 2.5 | 3 |
| 12. Astros | $433,692 | 18.4 | 17 |
| 13. Blue Jays | $423,802 | 9.8 | 15 |
| 14. Reds | $398,803 | 18.4 | 20 |
| 15. Phillies | $367,853 | −8.0 | 10 |
| 16. Twins | $364,708 | 41.3 | 23 |
| 17. Brewers | $355,714 | −17.4 | 5 |
| 18. Cardinals | $346,847 | −10.3 | 14 |
| 19. Athletics | $335,641 | −4.6 | 18 |
| 20. White Sox | $324,337 | −6.9 | 19 |
| 21. Expos | $312,875 | −0.8 | 22 |
| 22. Pirates | $299,481 | −23.7 | 11 |
| 23. Giants | $284,804 | −11.1 | 21 |
| 24. Indians | $269,868 | 22.7 | 25 |
| 25. Rangers | $242,485 | −5.9 | 24 |
| 26. Mariners | $187,850 | 10.7 | 26 |

Dec. 3

## Time at the Top

Everyone now knows that Mike Tyson became the youngest heavyweight champion in history at the age of 20 years 4 months 22 days—"and I'm going to be the oldest," he said. For that to happen, he would need to retain his crown for more than 18 years 4 months. Jersey Joe Walcott, at the age of 37 the oldest man to win the title, held it until he was 38 years 7 months old. If he should also become the oldest champ, Tyson would hold the title longer than any other heavyweight in history.

### The 10 longest world championship reigns by heavyweights

| Champion | Reign |
| --- | --- |
| Joe Louis | 11 years 8 months |
| Jack Dempsey | 7 years 2 months |
| John L. Sullivan | 7 years 1 month |
| Jack Johnson | 6 years 3 months |
| Muhammad Ali* | 5 years 11 months |
| Jim Jeffries | 5 years 11 months |
| Larry Holmes | 4 years 11 months |
| James Corbett | 4 years 6 months |
| Jess Willard | 4 years 3 months |
| Rocky Marciano | 3 years 7 months |

*Ali held the title for five days more than Jeffries

DEC. 3

## Student-Athletes, in the Real Sense

The 1986 Butkus Award to Brian Bosworth —Oklahoma linebacker and communications major with a 3.28 grade-point average— marks the 11th time in history that a player has captured a major postseason football award the same year he was elected first-team academic all-American. The 10 others:

Alan Ameche, Wisconsin, 1954 Heisman
Pete Dawkins, Army, 1958 Heisman
Merlin Olsen, Utah State, 1961 Outland
Terry Baker, Oregon State, 1962 Heisman
Bill Stanfill, Georgia, 1968 Outland
Larry Jacobson, Nebraska, 1971 Outland
Lee Roy Selmon, Oklahoma, 1975 Outland, Lombardi
Brad Budde, Southern Cal, 1979 Lombardi
Dave Rimington, Nebraska, 1981 Outland
Dave Rimington, Nebraska, 1982 Outland, Lombardi

DEC. 17

## Pro Bowl Rosters

The 1986 Pro Bowl teams selected for the Feb. 1 National Football League's all-star game at Honolulu.

### American Conference

**Offense**

Wide Receivers—Al Toon, Jets; Steve Largent, Seattle Seahawks; *-Stanley Morgan, New England Patriots; *-Mark Duper, Miami Dolphins.
Tight Ends—Todd Christensen, Los Angeles Raiders; *-Mickey Shuler, Jets.
Tackles—Anthony Munoz, Cincinnati Bengals; Cody Risien, Cleveland Browns; *-Chris Hinton, Indianapolis Colts.
Guards—Max Montoya, Cincinnati Bengals; Keith Bishop, Denver Broncos; *-Roy Foster, Miami Dolphins.
Centers—Dwight Stephenson, Miami Dolphins; *-Ray Donaldson, Indianapolis Colts.
Quarterbacks—Dan Marino, Miami Dolphins; *-John Elway, Denver Broncos.
Running Backs—Curt Warner, Seattle Seahawks; James Brooks, Cincinnati Bengals; *-Marcus Allen, Los Angeles Raiders; *-Gary Anderson, San Diego Chargers.

**Defense**

Ends—Rulon Jones, Denver Broncos; Howie Long, Los Angeles Raiders; *-Jacob Green, Seattle Seahawks.
Tackles—Bill Maas, Kansas City Chiefs; *-Bob Golic, Cleveland Browns.
Outside Linebackers—Andre Tippett, New England

Patriots; Chip Banks, Cleveland Browns; *-Mike Merriweather, Pittsburgh.
Inside Linebackers—Karl Mecklenburg, Denver Broncos; John Offerdahl, Miami Dolphins; *-Fredd Young, Seattle Seahawks.
Safeties—Deron Cherry, Kansas City Chiefs; Dennis Smith, Denver Broncos; *-Lloyd Burruss, Kansas City Chiefs.
Cornerbacks—Mike Haynes Los Angeles Raiders; Hanford Dixon, Cleveland Browns; *-Ray Clayborn, New England Patriots.

**Specialists**
Placekicker—Tony Franklin, New England Patriots.
Punter—Rohn Stark, Indianapolis Colts.
Kick-returner—Bobbie Joe Edmonds, Seattle Seahawks.
Special Teamer—Mosi Tatupu, New England Patriots.
*-Reserve.

### National Conference

**Offense**
Wide Receivers—Jerry Rice, San Francisco 49ers; Gary Clark, Washington Redskins; *-Art Monk, Washington Redskins; *-Mike Quick, Philadelphia Eagles.
Tight Ends—Mark Bavaro, Giants; *-Steve Jordan, Minnesota Vikings.
Tackles—Jimbo Covert, Chicago Bears; Jackie Slater, Los Angeles Rams; *-Brad Benson, Giants.
Guards—Dennis Harrah, Los Angeles Rams; Bill Fralic, Atlanta Falcons; *-Russ Grimm, Washington Redskins.
Centers—Jay Hilgenberg, Chicago Bears; *-Doug Smith, Los Angeles Rams.
Quarterbacks—Tommy Kramer, Minnesota Vikings; *-Jay Schroeder, Washington Redskins.
Running Backs—Eric Dickerson, Los Angeles Rams; Walter Payton, Chicago Bears; *-Joe Morris, Giants; Rueben Mayes, New Orleans.

**Defense**
Ends—Dexter Manley, Washington Redskins; Reggie White, Philadelphia Eagles; *-Leonard Marshall, Giants.
Tackles—Steve McMichael, Chicago Bears; *-Jim Burt, Giants.
Outside Linebackers—Lawrence Taylor, Giants; Wilber Marshall, Chicago Bears; *-Rickey Jackson, New Orleans Saints.
Inside Linebackers—Mike Singletary, Chicago Bears; Harry Carson, Giants; *-Carl Ekern, Los Angeles Rams.
Cornerbacks—Darrell Green, Washington Redskins; LeRoy Irvin, Los Angeles Rams; *-Jerry Gray, Los Angeles Rams.

Safeties—Dave Duerson, Chicago Bears; Ronnie Loff, San Francisco 49ers; *-Joey Browner, Minnesota Vikings.

**Specialists**
Place-kicker—Morten Anderson, New Orleans.
Punter—Sean Landetta, Giants.
Kick-returner—Vai Sikahema, St. Louis Cardinals.
Special Teamer—Ron Wolfley, St. Louis Cardinals.
*Reserve.

DEC. 18

## Teetering at the Top

Which major college football team has the best cumulative record over the years? It's Notre Dame, although second-place Michigan is gaining fast and has shaved 7 percentage points off the Irish lead this year alone. The top 10 marks among schools now in Division I-A:

|  | W–L–T | Pct. |
|---|---|---|
| Notre Dame | 651–198–40 | .754 |
| Michigan | 676–224–32 | .742 |
| Alabama | 624–218–43 | .729 |
| Texas | 645–237–31 | .723 |
| Oklahoma | 600–219–50 | .719 |
| Southern Cal. | 578–223–49 | .708 |
| Ohio State | 607–239–48 | .705 |
| Penn State | 615–266–40 | .689 |
| Nebraska | 611–276–39 | .680 |
| Tennessee | 573–257–49 | .679 |

DEC. 20

## 10 Long Seasons

Whose regular-season schedule turned out to be the toughest in all of college football? Here are the 10 schools that hoed the hardest rows, ranked according to the records of their Division I-A opponents against I-A teams other than the ranked school.

|  | W–L–T | Pct. |
|---|---|---|
| *Florida (6–5) | 64–29–3 | .682 |
| L.S.U. (9–2) | 67–36–2 | .648 |
| Notre Dame (5–6) | 68–39–1 | .631 |
| U.C.L.A. (7–3–1) | 67–39–2 | .630 |
| California (2–9) | 64–40–4 | .611 |

|  | W–L–T | Pct. |
|---|---|---|
| Oregon (5–6) | 65–41–3 | .610 |
| Oregon State (3–8) | 59–38–3 | .605 |
| Southern Cal. (7–4) | 53–35–3 | .599 |
| Washington St. (3–7–1) | 62–43–2 | .589 |
| Florida State (6–4–1) | 59–41–2 | .583 |

*The .682 winning percentage posted by Florida's opponents is the fourth highest since the N.C.A.A. began keeping track of the statistic in 1977. Higher were the .709 and the .707 by Notre Dame's opposition in 1978 and 1985, and the .688 by Auburn's foes in 1983.

DEC. 24

# Champions of 1987

### Basketball

**N.B.A.**
Team—Boston Celtics
M.V.P.—Larry Bird, Boston
Rookie of the Year—Patrick Ewing, Knicks
Scoring—Dominique Wilkins, Atl., 30.3
Rebounds—Bill Laimbeer, Detroit, 13.1
Assists—Earvin Johnson, Lakers, 12.6
Blocked Shots—Manute Bol, Wash., 4.96
Coach of Year—Mike Fratello, Atlanta

**N.C.A.A.—Men**
Division I—Louisville
Division II—Sacred Heart, Connecticut
Division III—Potsdam, New York

**N.C.A.A.—Women**
Division I—Texas
Division II—Cal Poly-Pomona
Division III—Salem St.

### Golf

**Men**
U.S. Open—Ray Floyd
U.S. Amateur—Buddy Alexander, Baton Rouge, La.
Masters—Jack Nicklaus
P.G.A. Championship—Bob Tway
British Open—Greg Norman
Vardon Trophy—Scott Hoch, Orlando, Fla.
Leading Money Winner—Greg Norman
Player of the Year—Bob Tway
Rookie of the Year—Brian Claar, Tampa, Fla.
U.S. Public Links—Bill Mayfair, Phoenix
U.S.G.A. Senior Open—Dale Douglass, Boulder, Colo.
U.S.G.A. Junior—Brian Montgomery, Bristow, Okla.
N.C.A.A. Division I—Scott Verplank, Oklahoma St.

**Women**
U.S. Open—Jane Geddes, Irving, Tex.
U.S. Amateur—Kay Cockerill, Los Gatos, Calif.
L.P.G.A.—Pat Bradley, Marco Island, Fla.
L.P.G.A. Player of the Year—Pat Bradley
Rookie Of the Year—Jody Rosenthal, Tulsa, Okla.
U.S.G.A. Senior Amateur—Constance Guthrie, Spokane, Wash.
U.S.G.A. Junior—Pat Hurst, San Leandro, Calif.
U.S.G.A. Public Links—Cindy Schreyer, Beachtree City, Ga.
N.C.A.A.—Page Dunlap, U. of Florida

### Hockey

**National Hockey League**
Stanley Cup—Montreal Canadians d. Calgary Flames
Regular Season—Patrick Division, Philadelphia Flyers; Smythe Division, Edmonton Oilers; Norris Division, Chicago Black Hawks; Adams Division, Quebec Nordiques
Most Valuable Player—Wayne Gretzky, Edmonton
Top Defenseman—Tie between Paul Coffey, Edm. and Ray Bourque, Boston
Rookie of the Year—Gary Suter, Calgary Flames
Scoring Champion—W. Gretzky, 215 pts.
Leading Goalie—Bob Froese, Phila.
Fewest Goals Allowed—Bob Froese, 2.55
Lady Byng—Mike Bossy, Islanders
M.V.P. (Playoffs)—Patrick Roy, Mont.
Coach of the Year—Glen Sather, Edm.
Lester Patrick Trophy—John MacInnes, Jack Riley

### Tennis

**International Team Champions**
Federation Cup (Women)—United States
Wightman Cup (Women)—United States

**U.S. Open Champions**
Singles—Ivan Lendl
Women's Singles—Martina Navratilova
Men's Doubles—Andres Gomez, Slobodan Zivojinovic
Women's Doubles—M. Navratilova, Pam Shriver
Mixed Doubles—Raffaella Reggi, Sergio Casal
Senior Men's Singles—Tim Gullikson
Senior Men's Doubles—Bob Lutz, Stan Smith
Senior Women's Doubles—Rosie Casals, Wendy Overton
Girls' Junior Singles—Elly Hakami
Boys' Junior Singles—Javier Sanchez

**Foreign Opens**
Wimbledon Men—Boris Becker
Wimbledon Women—M. Navratilova
French Men—Ivan Lendl
French Women—Chris Evert Lloyd

**Nabisco Masters**
Singles—Ivan Lendl
Doubles—Anders Jaryd, Stefan Edberg

**Virginia Slims Championship**
Singles—Martina Navratilova
Doubles—M. Navratilova and Pam Shriver

### Track and Field

**TAC Outdoor—Men**
100-Meter—Carl Lewis, S. Monica T.C.
200—Floyd Heard, Texas A. and M.
400—Darrell Robinson, Mazda T.C.
800—Johnny Gray, Santa Monica T.C.
1,500—Steve Scott, Asics Tiger, T.C.
3,000 Steeplechase—Henry Marsh, Athletes West
5,000—Doug Padilla, Athletes West
10,000—Gary Donakowski, Ath. W.
110-M. Hurdles—Greg Foster, World Class A.C.
400 Hurdles—Danny Harris, Ath. W.
20,000 Meter Walk—Tim Lewis, N.Y.A.C.
High Jump—Doug Nordquist, Asics Tiger, A.C.
Pole Vault—Mike Tully, N.Y.A.C.
Long Jump—Carl Lewis, S. Monica T.C.
Triple Jump—Charlie Simpkins, Nike T.C.
Shot-Put—John Brenner, Mazda T.C.
Discus—John Powell, Mazda T.C.
Hammer Throw—Bill Green, Mazda T.C.
Javelin—Tom Petranoff, Ath. W.

**TAC Outdoor—Women**
100-Meter—Pam Marshall, Mazda, T.C.
200—Pam Marshall, Mazda, T.C.
400—Diane Dixon, Atoms, T.C.
800—C. Groenendaal, Athletes West
1,500—Linda Detiefsen, Ath. West.
3,000—Mary Knisely, New Balance T.C.
5,000—Betty Springs, Ath. West.
100 Hurdles—B. Fitzgerald-Brown, Mazda, T.C.
400 Hurdles—Judi Brown-King, Ath. W.
10,000 Meter Walk—Debbi Lawrence
800 Sprint Medley Relay—Southern California Cheetahs T.C.
High Jump—L. Ritter, Pacific Coast Club
Long Jump—Carol Lewis, S. Monica T.C.
Triple Jump—Wendy Brown, Puma T.C.
Shot-Put—Ramona Pagel, unattached
Discus—Carol Cady, Stanford T.C.
Javelin—Helena Uusitalo, Finland

DEC. 28

# Sad Stats

All those year-end sports reviews neglected to make note of some remarkable achievements in major league baseball's 1986 season. For the record, then:

*Pitchers*

Lowest winning percentage (minimum of 15 decisions): .263, by Rick Sutcliffe, Chicago Cubs, 5–14.

Highest earned run average: 31.50, by Dennis Burtt, Minnesota, on 7 earned runs in 2 innings.

Worst strikeout-to-walk ratio (minimum of 100 innings pitched): 0.85, by Phil Niekro, Cleveland, on 81 strikeouts and 95 walks.

Most home runs yielded per 100 innings: 54.5, by Steve Davis, Toronto, who gave up 2 in 3⅔ innings.

Headhunter Award: To Dave Stieb, Toronto, who hit 15 batters.

*Nonpitchers**

Lowest batting average: .118, by Mark Davidson, Minnesota, on 8 for 68.

Lowest slugging percentage: .162, again by Davidson, with 11 total bases.

Most times at bat without a home run: 600, by Vince Coleman, St. Louis.

Fewest runs scored per 100 times at bat: 4.8, by Dave Hengel, Seattle, on 3 in 63 trips to the plate.

Lowest stolen-base percentage (minimum of 10 attempts): .200, by Buddy Bell, Cincinnati, 2 for 10.

Lowest fielding average (minimum of 50 games): .865, by Dale Sveum, Milwaukee.

Most strikeouts per 100 times at bat: 41.5, by Bo Jackson, Kansas City, with 34 in 82 trips to the plate.

Ron Hunt Award: To Don Baylor, Boston, hit by 35 pitches.

*Except where otherwise indicated, the requisite for each category is at least 50 times at bat.    DEC. 31

## They're A-1 in I-AA

Last week in this space was a listing of the best cumulative records over the years among all schools now playing Division I-A football. Then somebody wanted to know whether any of the Ivy League colleges figured in a similar ranking. Sure. The top records in Division I-AA:

| | W–L–T | Pct. |
|---|---|---|
| Tennessee State | 393–106–27 | .772 |
| Yale | 736–232–43 | .746 |
| Grambling | 336–113–15 | .740 |
| Florida A&M | 377–135–16 | .729 |
| Princeton | 660–266–48 | .702 |
| Harvard | 671–283–49 | .693 |

JAN. 2

## College Football: Salute to Penn State Defense

By MALCOLM MORAN

SCOTTSDALE, Ariz., Jan. 3—A few hours after the last-second climax of his second championship season, one of the proudest moments in a century of football at Penn State, Joe Paterno said he felt weary early on the morning after.

## The New York Times's final college top 20

| Rank | Team | Prev. Rank | Record | Avg. Margin of Victory | Rating | *OPPONENTS' PERFORMANCES Record | Avg. Margin of Victory |
|---|---|---|---|---|---|---|---|
| 1 | Oklahoma | 1 | 11–1–0 | 35.8 | 1.000 | 41–26–0 | 6.3 |
| 2 | Penn State | 2 | 12–0–0 | 17.5 | .972 | 41–27–2 | 6.7 |
| 3 | Miami, Fla. | 3 | 11–1–0 | 23.1 | .878 | 37–27–2 | 5.5 |
| 4 | Auburn | 5 | 10–2–0 | 23.0 | .860 | 41–28–1 | 4.0 |
| 5 | Ohio State | 8 | 10–3–0 | 12.9 | .852 | 39–28–0 | 6.0 |
| 5 | Nebraska | 9 | 10–2–0 | 23.4 | .852 | 38–32–0 | 4.7 |
| 7 | Arizona State | 13 | 10–1–1 | 17.9 | .841 | 38–30–0 | 3.3 |
| 8 | U.C.L.A. | 7 | 8–3–1 | 13.6 | .840 | 43–22–2 | 7.3 |
| 9 | Boston College | 10 | 9–3–0 | 9.0 | .822 | 40–24–0 | 4.4 |
| 10 | Alabama | 16 | 10–3–0 | 14.7 | .818 | 43–23–1 | 9.9 |
| 11 | L.S.U. | 4 | 9–3–0 | 10.1 | .813 | 48–26–3 | 8.8 |
| 12 | Michigan | 6 | 11–2–0 | 13.3 | .803 | 47–31–2 | 4.9 |
| 13 | Baylor | 18 | 9–3–0 | 10.1 | .785 | 34–25–0 | 1.9 |
| 14 | Clemson | 20 | 8–2–2 | 9.3 | .766 | 37–28–4 | 3.2 |
| 15 | Florida | 16 | 6–5–0 | 4.5 | .760 | 36–14–3 | 10.6 |
| 15 | Arizona | 19 | 9–3–0 | 12.6 | .760 | 38–26–3 | 3.0 |
| 17 | Mississippi | 22 | 8–3–1 | 6.3 | .738 | 35–22–1 | 1.6 |
| 18 | Georgia | 12 | 8–4–0 | 6.1 | .735 | 39–26–3 | 8.7 |
| 19 | Arkansas | 15 | 9–3–0 | 10.3 | .733 | 41–29–0 | 4.8 |
| 20 | Texas A&M | 11 | 9–3–0 | 13.1 | .732 | 41–31–0 | 2.3 |

The *New York Times*'s computer football ranking is based on analysis of each team's record, looking at who won a game, by what margin and against what quality of opposition. The quality of an opponent is calculated by examining its record against other foes. The *Times*'s computer model collapses runaway scores and takes note of a home-field advantage. As the season progresses, results in most recent games count for more than results in early games, so that the ranking is up to date.
The top-ranked team is assigned a rating of 1,000; the ratings of other teams are percentages of that figure.
*The opponents' won-lost record and average margin of victory shows how a particular team's opponents did in all their games before they played against that particular team.

JAN. 4, 1987

"A couple of players came into my room at 3 o'clock in the morning looking for a case of beer," the coach said. "We found one for them." The night before, the Lions used an ever-changing series of defensive coverages and ball-jarring tackling to distract, frustrate and overcome the previously top-ranked University of Miami and Vinny Testaverde in the Fiesta Bowl. The scoreboard said 14–10.

Penn State was outgained, 445 yards to 162, a margin of nearly 3 to 1. Miami held the ball 7 minutes 26 seconds longer and ran 93 offensive plays to Penn State's 59.

But more subtle figures reflected some of the methods the resourceful Lions employed to steal a game and earn the No. 1 ranking today in both news agency polls. "The things that win big games are not what you do on first and second down," Paterno said, "and they're not necessarily what you do in your own territory."

John Bruno, the Lion senior, punted nine times for an average of 43.4 yards. Even more significant was the fact that Bruno's work forced Miami to begin inside its 25-yard line six times and never farther than the Hurricane 37. The Lion kickoff coverage restricted Miami to its 25, 15 and 20.

Miami converted on 6 of 22 third-down plays, a 27.3 percent rate that was 12.6 below its level throughout the 11 Hurricane victories. When added to seven turnovers, nine penalties and at least six dropped passes, the picture becomes clearer. Testaverde, intercepted nine times all season, was picked off five times Friday night.

Penn State was No. 1 and Miami No. 2 in both the Associated Press poll of sportswriters and broadcasters and the United Press International poll of coaches. The *New York Times* computer ranking assigned Oklahoma (11–1) the No. 1 position despite the Penn State victory. The .028 difference in the two teams was based primarily on Oklahoma's average margin of victory of 35.8 points, as opposed to Penn State's 17.5.     JAN. 4, 1987

# Lady's Secret Leads Eclipse Winners

**By STEVEN CRIST**

Lady's Secret and most of her handlers were among the 10 thoroughbreds and 5 people named winners of 1986 Eclipse Awards yesterday.

Lady's Secret, the gray Secretariat filly who is a virtual cinch to be named Horse of the Year on Jan. 30, won the champion older filly title and helped win statuettes for her owner, Eugene V. Klein, her trainer, D. Wayne Lukas, and her jockey, Pat Day. Lukas and Klein also won the award last year, and Day was the champion jockey two years ago.

All the winners except the steeplechaser and the breeder, who were chosen by committees, were elected by three voting blocs whose consensus choices carried equal weight: 126 journalists affiliated with the National Turf Writers Association, 77 editorial employees of *The Daily Racing Form* and 26 racing secretaries of Thoroughbred Racing Associations member tracks.

The results in part reflected the growing importance of the seven year-end Breeders' Cup races in determining the sport's champions. Capote, Brave Raj, Smile, Lady's Secret and Manila all won Cup races at Santa Anita Nov. 1 to cement their titles, and only Lady's Secret would have won her title without having won a cup race that day.

Lukas is also the trainer, and Klein the part-owner, of Capote, the early favorite for the Kentucky Derby on May 2, who was named champion 2-year-old colt.

JAN. 7, 1987

## Eclipse Winners

**2-year-old colt:** Capote
**2-year-old filly:** Brave Raj
**3-year-old colt:** Snow Chief
**3-year-old filly:** Tiffany Lass
**Older male:** Turkoman
**Older filly or mare:** Lady's Secret
**Grass male:** Manila
**Grass female:** Estrapade
**Sprinter:** Smile
**Steeplechase:** Flatterer
**Trainer:** D. Wayne Lukas
**Breeder:** Paul Mellon
**Owner:** Eugene V. Klein
**Jockey:** Pat Day
**Apprentice jockey:** Allen Stacy

JAN. 7, 1987

# PART 7
# Culture

## Alfred I. duPont–Columbia University Awards in Broadcast Journalism

**Gold Baton**

For the program "judged to have made the greatest contribution to the public's understanding of important issues or news events, to ABC News's "Nightline" for broadcasts from South Africa.

**Silver Batons**

CBS News's "Afghanistan: Operation Blackout"
NBC News's documentary "The Real Star Wars—Defense in Space"
Public Broadcasting Service's documentary series "The Brain"
Cable News Network and the Australian Film Company, Imago, for their program "Iran: In the Name of God"
DesertWest News for a radio series on the American Sanctuary Movement
WCAU-TV, Philadelphia, for "Coverage of Move Siege."
WDVM-TV, Washington, for "Investigation of Dr. Milan Vuitch."
WCCO-TV, Minneapolis, for "The Moore Report."
Nancy Montoya and KGUN-TV, Tucson, Ariz., for outstanding reporting.
Chris-Craft Television Productions and Churchill Films for "Down for the Count—An Inside Look at Boxing."
KNX radio, Los Angeles, for "Assignment '84/'85."

**Citations were given to**

WSMV-TV, Nashville, for "Choice Cuts."
KWWL-TV, Waterloo, Iowa, for "A Town Meeting: Iowa's Future."

FEB. 6

## National Book Critics Circle Awards

**Fiction**—Anne Tyler, *The Accidental Tourist* (Knopf)
**Biography-autobiography**—Leon Edel, *Henry James: A Life* (Harper & Row)
**General nonfiction**—J. Anthony Lukas, *Common Ground: A Turbulent Decade in the Lives of Three American Families* (Knopf)
**Poetry**—Louise Glück, *The Triumph of Achilles* (Ecco Press)
**Criticism**—William H. Gass, *Habitations of the Word* (Simon & Schuster)

FEB. 18

## The George Polk Awards

(Established by Long Island University in 1949, the year after Mr. Polk, a CBS correspondent, was killed while covering the Greek civil war)

**Network television reporting**—Ted Koppel and Richard N. Kaplan of the ABC News program "Nightline" for its broadcasts from South Africa.
**Foreign reporting**—Alan Cowell of *The New York Times* for reporting from South Africa.
**Medical writing**—Lawrence K. Altman of the *Times* for his reports from Africa on AIDS.
**Career award**—George Tames of the *Times*, for his photography.
**Metropolitan reporting**—Jimmy Breslin, columnist for the *New York Daily News*, for revealing allegations that police officers had used battery-operated shock devices to torture suspects.
**International reporting**—Pete Carey, Katherine Ellison and Lewis M. Simons of *The San Jose Mercury-News* for "Hidden Billions: The Draining of the Philippines."
**National reporting**—Diana Griego and Louis Kilzer of *The Denver Post* for "The Truth about Missing Children."
**Local reporting**—Stan Jones of *The Fairbanks Daily News-Miner* for articles on corrupt leasing practices by the state of Alaska.
**Political reporting**—Frank Greve of the Knight-Ridder newspapers for a report tracing the development of President Reagan's Strategic Defense Initiative.
**Business reporting**—The Spotlight/Business team of *The Boston Globe* for articles linking the Bank of Boston to money laundering for the Mafia.
**Criticism**—Arthur C. Danto of *The Nation* for his art criticism.
**Radio reporting**—Peter Laufer of NBC Radio News for "Nightmare Abroad."
**Local television reporting**—Vic Lee, Craig Franklin and Brian McTigue of WRON-TV in San Francisco for a series, "Clean Rooms, Dirty Secrets."

MARCH 2

## Westinghouse Science Talent Search Winners

1. (tie) Wei-Jing Zhu, 16, of Brooklyn Technical High School, for a project in algebraic theory, and Wendy Kay Chung, 17, of Miami Killian Senior High School in Miami, for research into the behavior of the Caribbean fruit fly, a $20,000 college scholarship.

3. Yoriko Saito, 18, of Homewood, Ala., for biochemistry, a $15,000 scholarship.
4. George Jer-Chi Juang, 17, of Queens, N.Y., for a physics project examining the use of ferric oxyhydroxide colloids in phase conjugation devices, a $10,000 scholarship.
5. Anh Tuan Nguyen-Huynh, 17, of Chagrin Falls, Ohio.
6. Jessica Louise Boklan, 17, of Roslyn Heights, N.Y.
7. William Edward Bies, 17, of Pittsburgh, Pa.
8. Mary Elizabeth Meyerand, 17, of Glastonbury, Conn.
9. Andrew Lawrence Feig, 18, of Los Angeles, Calif.
10. Allen Wallis Inglig, 17, of Delaware, Ohio

## MARCH 4

## Sloan Science Fellowships

Ninety young scientists have been awarded $25,000 Sloan Research Fellowships under one of the oldest fellowship programs in the United States.

Following is the list of winners, their areas of study and the institutions where they will work:

Andrew B. Abel, economics, Harvard.
Richard W. Aldrich, neuroscience, Stanford.
Dana Z. Anderson, physics, University of Colorado.
Greg W. Anderson, mathematics, University of Minnesota.
Peter B. Armentrout, chemistry, University of California at Berkeley.
Michael J. Banon, neuroscience, Yale.
Mark Birkinshaw, physics, Harvard.
David E. Bloom, economics, Harvard.
Andrew B. Bocarsly, chemistry, Princeton.
Marianne Bronner-Fraser, neuroscience, University of California at Irvine.
Gary W. Brudvig, chemistry, Yale.
Charles T. Campbell, chemistry, Indiana University.
Sylvia T. Ceyer, chemistry, Massachusetts Institute of Technology.
Michael F. Christ, mathematics, Princeton.
Laurent Clozel, mathematics, University of Michigan.
Terrence J. Collins, chemistry, California Institute of Technology.
David B. Collum, chemistry, Cornell.
J. Brian Cohrey, mathematics, Oklahoma State University.
Petre S. Constantin, mathematics, University of Chicago.
Michael T. Crimmins, chemistry, University of North Carolina.
Marc Culler, mathematics, Rutgers.
Michael Dine, physics, City University of New York.
Philip H. Dybvig, economics, Yale.
Lawrence Ein, mathematics, University of Illinois, Chicago.
Nicholas M. Ercolani, mathematics, Ohio State.
Gregory S. Ezra, chemistry, Cornell.
Jeffrey A. Frankel, economics, University of California at Berkeley.
Robert Friedman, mathematics, Columbia.
David Gabai, mathematics, California Institute of Technology.
Henri A. Gillet, mathematics, University of Illinois, Chicago.
Paul Ginsparg, physics, Harvard.
Jonathan B. Goodman, mathematics, New York University.
David A. Greenberg, neuroscience, University of California at San Francisco.
Glen R. Hall, mathematics, Boston University.
Philip J. Hanlon, mathematics, University of Michigan.
John L. Harer, mathematics, University of Michigan.
Jeffrey A. Harvey, physics, Princeton.
Anthony D. J. Haymet, chemistry, University of California at Berkeley.
Carol E. Heim, economics, University of Massachusetts.
Craig J. Hogan, physics, University of Arizona.
Reuben Jih-Ru Hwu, chemistry, Johns Hopkins.
John Z. Imbrie, physics, Harvard.
Robert B. Innis, neuroscience, Yale.
Michael K. Johnson, chemistry, Louisiana State University.
Larry E. Jones, economics, Northwestern.
Aharon Kapitulnik, physics, Stanford.
Hideki Kosaki, mathematics, Tulane.
Gabriel B. Kotliar, physics, M.I.T.
Jeffrey B. Kuhn, physics, Michigan State.
Rodrigo O. Kuljis, neuroscience, Yale.
Nabil M. Lawandy, physics, Brown.
Gregory F. Lawler, mathematics, Duke.
Brian A. MacVicar, neuroscience, University of Calgary.
John H. R. Maunsell, neuroscience, University of Rochester.
Ernest J. Nordeen, neuroscience, University of Rochester.
Paul E. Olsen, physics, Columbia.
Mark J. Oreglia, physics, University of Chicago.
Michael C. Pirrung, chemistry, Stanford.
Adrianus M. M. Pruisken, physics, Columbia.
Dinakar Ramakrishnan, mathematics, Cornell.
Douglas C. Rees, chemistry, University of California at Los Angeles.
Seth Roberts, neuroscience, University of California at Berkeley.
Kenneth S. Rogoff, economics, University of Wisconsin.

Julio Rotemberg, economics, M.I.T.
Ian P. Rothwell, chemistry, Purdue.
Michael P. Schmidt, physics, Yale.
Erik S. Schweitzer, neuroscience, University of Wisconsin.
Robert A. Scott, chemistry, University of Illinois.
James A. Sethian, mathematics, University of California at Berkeley.
Martin S. Shankland, neuroscience, Harvard.
Robert S. Sheridan, chemistry, University of Wisconsin.
Mark Srednicki, physics, University of California at Santa Barbara.
Johanna Stachel, physics, State University of New York at Stony Brook.
Andrew E. Strominger, physics, Institute of Advanced Study.
Winthrop E. Sullivan, neuroscience, Princeton.
Stanislaw J. Szarek, mathematics, Case Western Reserve.
Devarajan Thirumalai, chemistry, University of Maryland.
John L. Tonry, physics, M.I.T.
Nancy S. True, chemistry, University of California at Davis.
P. Michael Tuts, physics, Columbia.
David R. Tyler, chemistry, University of Oregon.
Kenneth L. Tyler, neuroscience, Harvard.
Gianfranco Vidali, physics, Syracuse.
Ethan T. Vishniac, physics, University of Texas at Austin.
Warren S. Warren, chemistry, Princeton.
Janis C. Weeks, neuroscience, University of California at Berkeley.
Daniel P. Weitekamp, chemistry, California Institute of Technology.
Robert M. Williams, chemistry, Colorado State University.
Judith S. Young, physics, University of Massachusetts.
S. Lawrence Zipursky, neuroscience, University of California at Los Angeles.

## MARCH 9

## Science and Technology Medals

On March 12 President Reagan presented national medals for achievement in science and technology to 26 researchers.

The science winners were:

BUCHSBAUM, Solomon J., executive vice president of the Bell Telephone Laboratories at Holmdel, N.J., an expert in solid state plasmas.
COHEN, Stanley, professor of chemistry at Vanderbilt University, a cancer researcher.
CRANE, Horace R., professor at the University of Michigan, a biophysicist who made advances in DNA research and first measured the magnetic moment and spin of free electrons.
FESCHBACH, Herman, professor at the Massachusetts Institute of Technology in Cambridge, a leader in physics education.
GRAY, Harry B., professor of chemistry at California Institute of Technology at Pasadena, a pioneer in bioinorganic chemistry and inorganic photochemistry.
HENDERSON, Donald A., dean of hygiene and public health at Johns Hopkins University, chief architect of the successful campaign to eradicate smallpox.
HOFSTADTER, Robert, professor of physics at Stanford University, a 1961 Nobel laureate for work in electron scattering of protons, neutrons and other nuclei.
LAX, Peter D., director of the Courant Mathematics and Computing Laboratory, New York University, a mathematics theorist, for his contributions to the theory of partial differential equations, applied mathematics, numerical analysis and scientific computations.
LEE, Yuan Tseh, professor of chemistry at the University of California at Berkeley, a leader in molecular beam techniques.
LIEPMANN, Hans W., professor of fluid mechanics and thermodynamics at Cal Tech, whose work contributed to high-speed flight and a new generation of chemical lasers.
LIN, Tung Yen, chairman of T. Y. Lin International of San Francisco, a pioneer in structural engineering whose work includes the Rio Colorado's inverted arch bridge and the Moscone Convention Center in San Francisco.
MARVEL, Carl S., professor of chemistry at the University of Arizona, who, with his students, developed synthetic rubber, Nylon, neoprene, Mylar, Orlon and polymer for space suits.
MOUNTCASTLE, Vernon B., a Johns Hopkins neurophysiologist who developed techniques for studying the sensory systems of the brain.
OLIVER, Bernard M., program manager at the NASA Ames Research Center at Los Altos Hills, Calif., translator of physics knowledge and communications theory into practical electronics and computers and inventor of the hand-held scientific calculator.
PALADE, George E., professor emeritus at Yale University, Nobel laureate in 1974 for contributions to cell biology.
SIMON, Herbert A., professor at Carnegie Mellon University, a Nobel laureate in 1978 for contributions to understanding human problem-solving behavior and decision making within economic organizations.

STEITZ, Joan Argetsinger, professor of molecular biophysics and biochemistry at Yale University, for major contributions to the basic molecular biology of bacterial and mammalian cells.

WESTHEIMER, Frank H., Loeb professor of chemistry at Harvard University, responsible for extraordinary investigations of the mechanisms of organic and enzymic reactions.

YANG, Chen Ning, professor of physics and director of the Institute of Theoretical Physics at the State University of New York at Stony Brook, L.I.; Nobel Prize in 1975 for disproving the principle of conservation of parity.

ZYGMUND, Antoni, professor emeritus of mathematics, University of Chicago, outstanding contributions to Fourier analysis and its applications to partial differential equations and other branches of analysis.

Honored for technology achievement were:

GORDON, Bernard, of the Analogic Corporation of Boston, father of high-speed analogue-to-digital conversion.

JOHNSON, Reynold B., of Palo Alto, Calif., retired from International Business Machines, developer of magnetic disk storage for computers.

NORRIS, William C., of the Control Data Corporation of Minneapolis, for advancing microelectronics and computer technology.

PIASECKI, Frank N., of the Piasecki Aircraft Corporation of Philadelphia, developer of the tandem rotor helicopter.

STOOKEY, Stanley D., of the Corning Glass Works, Corning, N.Y., inventor of glass ceramics, which is used in Corning ware, eyeglasses and missile nose cones.

VERSNYDER, Francis, of the United Technologies Corporation of Hartford, developer of directionally solidified and crystal turbine components for jet engines.

MARCH 16

## Book Awards Given for Jewish Themes

Winners of the seventh annual Present Tense Awards, sponsored by *Present Tense* magazine and the American Jewish Committee, are:

**Biography/autobiography**—*Chaim Weitzmann: The Making of a Zionist Leader,* by Jehuda Reinharz (Oxford University Press).
**Fiction**—*That's Life,* by William Herrick (New Directions).
**History**—*The Unwanted: European Refugees in the Twentieth Century,* by Michael R. Marrus (Oxford University Press).
**Religious thought**—*The Art of Biblical Poetry,* by Robert Alter (Basic Books).
**General nonfiction**—*A Certain People: American Jews and Their Lives Today,* by Charles E. Silberman (Summit Books).

In addition, a special citation for lifetime achievement was awarded to Irving Howe, the critic, editor and author of *The World of Our Fathers.*

The awards, established by Shirley Miller Cavior of Boston and her sons, Warren, Jay and Stephen, in memory of her husband, Joel H. Cavior, are given to authors of books dealing with Jewish themes, published for the first time in English in the United States during the previous year.

MARCH 21

## The Second Annual Goldy Awards

(Presented by the Congress of Jewish Culture and 14 affiliated national and international Yiddish organizations, they are named for Abraham Goldfaden, widely regarded as the "father" of Yiddish theater more than a century ago)

Actor in a Broadway play reflecting Jewish themes: Judd Hirsch *(I'm Not Rappaport).*
Actor in a play in Yiddish: Jack Rechtzeit *(Broome Street).*
Actress in a play in English: Barbara Garrick *(Today I Am a Fountain Pen).*
Actress in a Yiddish play: Zipporah Spaisman *(Broome Street).*
Actress in a one-woman show in English: Lori Wilner *(Hannah Senesh).*
Actor in an Off-Broadway play in English: Josh Blake *(Today I Am a Fountain Pen).*
Actor in a Yiddish musical: Yankele Alperin *(A Match Made in Heaven).*
Comedienne in a Yiddish musical: Reizl Bozyk *(A Match Made in Heaven).*
Actress in an English-language musical: Rosalind Elias *(Pearls).*
Creating an innovative musical in English or Yiddish: Zalmen Mlotek and Moishe Rosenfeld (shared with the cast of the show *The Golden Land*).
Original script reflecting the Jewish experience in America: Herb Gardner *(Rappaport).*
Adaptation of a Yiddish script into a musical in English: Nahma Sandrow *(Kuni Leml).*

A script in English taken from another medium: Israel Horovitz *(Today I Am a Fountain Pen)*.
Lyrics for a musical in English adapted from Yiddish: Richard Enquist *(Kuni Leml)*.
Original score for a musical in English: Raphael Crystal *(Kuni Leml)*.
Direction of a play in Yiddish; Roger Sullivan *(Broome Street)*.
Direction of a play in English: Stanley Brechner *(Green Fields)*.
Direction of a musical in English: Ron Avni *(Kuni Leml)*.
Costumes: Neil Cooper *(Broome Street)*.
Scenic design: Eugene Gurlitz *(Green Fields)*.

APRIL 2

## The Scripps Howard Journalism Awards

Ernie Pyle Awards for Human Interest Reporting: first place, Ray Jenkins, *The Baltimore Sun;* second place, Don Duncan, *The Seattle Times*.

Walker Stone Awards for Editorial Writing: first place, Paul Greenberg, *The Pine Bluff* (Ark.) *Commercial;* second place, Richard Aregood, *The Philadelphia Daily News*.

The Edward Willis Scripps Awards for Service to the First Amendment: first place, *The Commercial Appeal,* Memphis; second place, *The Pacific Daily News,* Agana, Guam.

Edward J. Meeman Awards for Environmental Journalism. Papers under 100,000 circulation: first place, Jane Kay, *The Arizona Daily Star,* Tucson; second place, Craig Medred, *The Anchorage Daily News*. Papers over 100,000 circulation: first place, Jim Detjen and Susan FitzGerald, *The Philadelphia Inquirer;* second place, *The Boston Globe*.

Roy W. Howard Awards for Public Service Journalism: first place, *The Philadelphia Inquirer;* second place, *The Miami Herald;* honorable mention, *The Dyersburg* (Tenn.) *State Gazette*.

The Charles M. Schulz Award for Promising Cartoonist, Thomas Cheney, freelance cartoonist, Watertown, N.Y.

The Jack R. Howard Broadcast Awards for Public Service Programming. Large market television stations: first place, WCVB-TV, Boston; second place, KSTP-TV, Minneapolis. Small market television stations: first place, KGBT-TV, Harlingen, Tex.; second place, WJXT-TV, Jacksonville, Fla. Large market radio stations: KMOX, St. Louis; second place, WOR, New York. Small market radio stations, first place, WWVA, Wheeling, W.Va.; second place, WPTF, Raleigh, N.C.

APRIL 3

## The 47th Annual Awards by the Overseas Press Club

Joseph B. Treaster of *The New York Times* won first prize for the best daily newspaper or news agency reporting from abroad for his coverage of the volcano disaster in Colombia.

Joseph Lelyveld, London bureau chief of the *Times,* won for his book, *Move Your Shadow: South Africa Black and White,* published by Times Books.

Bill Moyers was honored for his "Africa: Struggle for Survival," on "The CBS Evening News." And Ted Koppel and Richard N. Kaplan won for their South Africa series on the ABC News program "Nightline."

These were the other winners:

Joseph C. Harsch, *The Christian Science Monitor,* selected commentary.
Peter Magubane, *Time* magazine, "Cry for Justice, Cry for Peace," on South Africa.
David Hume Kennerly, photographer for *Time* magazine, "Behind Closed Doors."
David Carl Turnley, photographer for *The Detroit Free Press,* "South Africa, Living under Apartheid."
Philip Till, NBC Radio Network, "T.W.A. Flight 847."
Karen Burnes, ABC Entertainment Network, "Reporter's Journal: Ethiopia."
Henry Scott Stokes, *Harper's* magazine, "Lost Samurai."
Robert J. Rosenthal, *The Philadelphia Inquirer* Sunday magazine, "South Africa: The Fires of Revolution."
Tony Auth, *The Philadelphia Inquirer,* editorial cartoons.
Michael Meyer and team, *Newsweek,* "Here Comes Korea Inc."
E. S. Browning, *The Wall Street Journal,* "Japan's Trade Issues and Tensions."
Kristin Helmore, *The Christian Science Monitor,* "The Neglected Resource: Women in the Developing World."

APRIL 17

## The National Magazine Awards

*Science 85*, for articles in the public interest, its "Technology of Peace" issue of December 1985, concerning the scientific and political issues that underlie arms control and disarmament.

Other awards included:

*Farm Journal*, for personal service
*Popular Mechanics*, for special interests
*Rolling Stone*, for reporting
*Time*, for design
*Vogue*, for photography
*The Georgia Review*, for fiction
*The Sciences*, for essays and criticism
*IEEE Spectrum*, for single-topic issue

General Excellence

*Money*, more than 1 million circulation
*Discover*, 400,000 to 1 million circulation
*3-2-1 Contact*, 100,000 to 400,000 circulation
*New England Monthly*, under 100,000 circulation

APRIL 30

## Winners of Pulitzer Prizes in Journalism, Letters and the Arts

**Public service**—*The Denver Post*, for its series on missing children, "The Truth about Missing Kids," written by three general-assignment reporters: Lou Kilzer, Diana Giego and Norman Udevitz. Despite the myth that most missing children have been abducted by strangers, they found that the majority are runaways or are involved in custody disputes.

**General news reporting**—Edna Buchanan, *The Miami Herald*, for her versatile and consistently excellent police reporting.

**Investigative reporting**—Jeffrey A. Marx and Michael M. York, *The Lexington* (Ky.) *Herald-Leader*, for their series "Playing above the Rules," which exposed improper cash payoffs to University of Kentucky basketball players and led to changes in N.C.A.A. regulations.

**Explanatory journalism**—*The New York Times*, for a series of articles on the Reagan Administration's proposal for research on a space-based missile defense system. The articles explored the scientific and technological issues and the foreign policy and political implications. The series was the work of Holcomb B. Noble, deputy science editor; Leslie H. Gelb, diplomatic writer; William J. Broad and Philip M. Boffey, science writers; Charles Mohr and Wayne Biddle, military and technology writers; and Gary Cosimini and Thomas E. Bodkin, art directors.

**Specialized reporting**—Andrew Schneider and Mary Pat Flaherty, *The Pittsburgh Press*, for a series of articles on the scientific and ethical questions raised by organ donations and transplants.

**National reporting**—Craig Flournoy and George Rodrigue, *The Dallas Morning News*, for their investigation into subsidized housing in East Texas, which uncovered patterns of racial discrimination and segregation and led to reforms; and Arthur Howe, *The Philadelphia Inquirer*, for his "enterprising and indefatigable" reporting on widespread deficiencies in the processing of tax returns by the Internal Revenue Service.

**International reporting**—Lewis M. Simons, Peter Carey and Katherine Ellison, *The San Jose Mercury News*, for a series of articles documenting large-scale transfers of wealth out of the Philippines by Ferdinand E. Marcos, then the country's president, and associates.

**Feature writing**—John Camp, *The St. Paul Pioneer Press and Dispatch*, for a series about a three-generation farm family—the Bensons of southwestern Minnesota—and their struggle to maintain their way of life.

**Criticism**—Donal Henahan, *The New York Times*, for distinguished music criticism.

**Commentary**—Jimmy Breslin, the *Daily News* (N.Y.), for columns that consistently champion the ordinary citizens of New York City.

**Editorial writing**—Jack Fuller, *The Chicago Tribune*, for his editorials on constitutional issues.

**Editorial cartooning**—Jules Feiffer, *The Village Voice*, for his weekly cartoon strip, which is characterized by sharp social commentary.

**Spot news photography**—Michel duCille and Carol Guzy, *The Miami Herald*, for their photographs of the devastation caused by the eruption last November of the Nevado del Ruiz volcano in Colombia.

**Feature photography**—Tom Gralish, *The Philadelphia Inquirer*, for two dozen photographs of homeless people in Philadelphia that appeared in the Easter issue of the *Inquirer*'s Sunday magazine.

**Fiction**—Larry McMurtry for *Lonesome Dove*, a novel about American frontier life, from Canada to Mexico, during the 1870s.

**History**—Dr. Walter A. McDougall, for *... the Heavens and the Earth: A Political History of the Space Age*, a narrative history of the early space age and the growth and power of government-sponsored technology.

**Biography**—Elizabeth Frank, for *Louise Bogan: A Portrait*, a sensitive exploration of the often chaotic life and lyrical poetry of Louise Bogan, the American poet and critic who lived from 1897 to 1970.

**Poetry**—Henry Taylor, for *The Flying Change*, which reflects his feeling for nature, especially the land of his native South.

**General nonfiction**—Joseph Lelyveld, for *Move Your Shadow: South Africa, Black and White,* an account of his experiences as a *Times* journalist returning to South Africa and examining the white fantasies that define apartheid; and J. Anthony Lukas, for *Common Ground: A Turbulent Decade in the Lives of Three American Families,* a chronicle of the effects of school desegregation in Boston on the lives of three families from 1968 to 1978.

**Music**—George Perle, for *Wind Quintet IV,* a work for flute, oboe, clarinet, French horn and bassoon.

**Drama**—No award was given.

APRIL 18

# Ring Lardner by Any Other Name: Real-Life Characters in Fiction

By WILLIAM AMOS

In *The Originals: An A–Z of Fiction's Real-Life Characters,* William Amos has matched fictional characters with their historical models. The following is excerpted from his book, published this month by Little, Brown & Company.

Ahearn, in *The Young Lions* (1948) by Irwin Shaw. Critics welcomed this as an outstanding novel of the Second World War. But Ernest Hemingway—according to his biographer, Carlos Baker—thought it a disgraceful, ignoble book, written by a coward who had never fired a shot in anger. He took the American war correspondent, Ahearn, to be a caricature of himself, and saw his younger brother, the journalist and wartime documentary filmmaker Leicester Hemingway, in Pvt. Leroy Keane, an obnoxious communications clerk striving to live up to the image of an elder brother who had been a hero of the First World War.

Brogan, Lewis, in *The Mandarins* (1954) by Simone de Beauvoir. "I've been in whorehouses all over the world and the woman there always closes the door, whether it's in Korea or India. But this woman flung the door open and called in the public and the press," lamented the American novelist Nelson Algren the day before he died [in 1981]. Interviewed by W. J. Weatherby for *The Sunday Times* of London, he was recalling his affair with Simone de Beauvoir, which led to his portrayal as Lewis Brogan. "She gave me a disguise, another name, in *The Mandarins,* but in a later book . . . she tried to make our relationship into a great international literary affair, naming me and quoting from some of my letters. . . . Hell, love letters should be private."

Harris, in *A Tramp Abroad* (1880) by Mark Twain. On being charged eight dollars for a boat trip on the Sea of Galilee, Mark Twain asked, "Do you wonder that Christ walked?" Happily, he was not then inhibited by the presence of his companion on his 1878 European tour, the Rev. Joseph Hopkins Twichell, his model for Harris. The Yale-educated son of a Connecticut farmer, Twichell was chaplain to the New York Zouaves in the Civil War and spent the rest of his life as pastor of Asylum Hill Congregational Church, Hartford, with a flock so well-heeled that Twain called the chapel "The Church of the Holy Speculators."

Hawke, Youngblood, in Herman Wouk's *Youngblood Hawke* (1962), has been taken to be the American novelist Thomas Wolfe. This identification was denied by Mr. Wouk, who said his model was the French novelist Honore de Balzac, with whom Wolfe had much in common. Mr. Wouk's choice of his character's surname, coinciding with Wolfe's *Portrait of Bascom Hawke* (1932), suggests that there may have been at least a subconscious Wolfe influence.

Lee, Lorelei, in Anita Loos's *Gentlemen Prefer Blondes* (1925). Crossing the United States by train, the author wondered why "a golden-haired birdbrain," the actress Mae

Davis, was attracting so much attention. While men fell over each other to wait upon the flaxen-haired Davis, the brunette Loos was left to struggle with a heavy suitcase. Davis had already incensed Loos by snatching away her hero, the writer H. L. Mencken; now, as the train journey progressed, it became obvious that Loos's husband, too, was much taken with the "stupid little blonde." In her autobiography, *A Girl Like I* (1966), Loos recalled how she pondered the situation. "Why did that girl so far outdistance me in allure? Why had she attracted one of the keenest minds of our era? Mencken liked me very much indeed, but in the matter of sex he preferred a witless blonde. . . . Possibly the girl's strength was rooted (like that of Samson) in her hair." Retiring to another part of the train, Loos drafted *Gentlemen Prefer Blondes*.

Leitner, Felix, in *The House of the Prophet* (1980) by Louis Auchincloss, is *The New York Herald Tribune* columnist Walter Lippmann, whose public pronouncements were at times at variance with his private behavior. After campaigning for military conscription in World War I, he sought exemption for himself, claiming he could serve his country better in some other way and pleading that his father (who would live a further 10 years) was dying. Similarly, his stance as a public moralist was belied by his affair with the wife of his friend Hamilton Fish Armstrong, editor of *Foreign Affairs*.

Llewellyn, Ivor, in *The Luck of the Bodkins* (1935) by P. G. Wodehouse. In 1930 Wodehouse was hired by the Hollywood film producer Sam Goldwyn, who is in part the model for Llewellyn. He was reputed to have given instructions for Shakespeare to be signed up to repolish *Othello*. As Goldwyn himself allegedly remarked of another occasion, this could be summed up in two words: in credible. During the filming of *These Three*, anxiety was expressed about difficulty with the censor, as the characters were lesbians. "So what's the problem?" said Goldwyn. "Make them Albanians."

Mad Hatter, the, in Lewis Carroll's *Alice's Adventures in Wonderland* (1865), is Theophilus Carter, an Oxford High Street furniture dealer and Christ Church servitor who wore his hat on the back of his head and, like Carroll's Mad Hatter, was preoccupied with time. At London's Crystal Palace in 1851 he exhibited an Alarm Bed, which tipped out its occupant at the desired hour. There is a tradition that John Tenniel, the illustrator of *Alice,* based his Mad Hatter on a Lichfield canon named Bradley. My check through a number of editions of *Crockford's Clerical Directory,* however, has failed to discover a contemporary Lichfield canon of that name.

North, Abe, in F. Scott Fitzgerald's *Tender Is the Night* (1934), is the American journalist and short-story writer Ring Lardner. Fitzgerald tried in vain to persuade an apathetic, self-despising Lardner to develop his talent as a writer.

Prynne, Amanda, in Noel Coward's *Private Lives* (1930). "Edwina and I spent all our married lives getting into other people's beds," said Lord Mountbatten, according to his biographer, Philip Ziegler. This was an exaggeration so far as he was concerned, but Lady (subsequently Countess) Mountbatten was decidedly flighty. The couple were close friends of Coward, who based Amanda Prynne on Edwina. Her married life was noted for a number of extramarital relationships—her name was linked with that of Laddie Sandford, a wealthy American polo player; with Paul Robeson, the American singer; and with Jawaharlal Nehru, the Indian statesman. With the Second World War came a social conscience that prompted her to join the St. John Ambulance Brigade, for which she did relief work in Britain during the blitz. She died, allegedly from exhaustion, touring north Borneo in her role as the brigade's superintendent in chief.

Stitch, Mrs. Algernon, in Evelyn Waugh's *Scoop* (1938) and *Officers and Gentlemen* (1955). When she caught sight of a friend disappearing underground in Sloane Street,

Mrs. Stitch followed him in her tiny car and became stuck in the gentlemen's lavatory. How would she cope with the parking restrictions of today? We know the answer because her model was Lady Diana Cooper, who upon the introduction of traffic wardens became noted for the heart-rending announcements displayed on the windscreen of her illicitly parked Mini. "Dear Warden—Taken sad child to cinemar—please forgive," she pleaded in spelling all her own. What warden could fail to be disarmed? None, until she met her match on leaving her car outside Harrods in 1984 with the note, "Old cripple's car. Gone for lunch." She returned to find a parking ticket accompanied by the message, "Hope you had a good lunch, dear." MAY 4

## The George Foster Peabody Awards for Distinguished Broadcasting for 1985

"An Early Frost," an NBC television movie about a victim of AIDS.
Johnny Carson, host of the NBC program "The Tonight Show."
"Do You Remember Love?" a CBS movie about a college professor and poet who has Alzheimer's disease.
Bob Geldof, the organizer of the Live Aid Concert to help victims of famine in Africa.
CBS News for "The Number Man—Bach at 300."
CBS News for "Whose America Is It," on conflicts created by immigration.
NBC News for "Vietnam Ten Years After."
Public television's "The MacNeil/Lehrer News Hour" for "Apartheid's People," an examination of life in South Africa.
Public television's "Frontline" for a four-part series, "Crisis in Central America."

The awards are administered by the University of Georgia School of Journalism and Mass Communications.

MAY 6

## Action for Children's Television Announced Its 14th Annual Awards for Television for Young People

The Stop, Look and Listen Award of $1,000 went to the Agency for Instructional Technology in Bloomington, Ind., for "Math Works," a public television problem-solving program, and to WMAQ-TV in Chicago for "Ready or Not," which uses humor and improvisational theater to explore teen-age issues.

Other awards in public television went to:
The Children's Television Workshop for "Sesame Street."
OWL/TV Inc., of Toronto, for "OWL/TV."
WQED, Pittsburgh, for "Wonderworks."

Other awards in commercial broadcasting went to:
ABC-TV, for "ABC Afterschool Specials."
KPIX-TV, San Francisco, for "Hot Streak."
KRON-TV, San Francisco, for "Home Turf."

Awards in cable television went to:
The Disney Channel for "Danger Bay."
Syracuse NewChannels for "The New Kid Stuff."

Awards in home video went to:
CC Studios.
Macmillan Inc.
Random House Video.
Sony Video Software.

Awards for public-service announcements went to:
KING-TV, Seattle.
Nickelodeon.

MAY 6

## 12 Journalists Named 1986 Nieman Fellows

On May 7 the Nieman Foundation at Harvard University announced the names of twelve American journalists selected to study for one year at Harvard.

The 49th annual class of Nieman Fellows will study in fields including political science, economics, constitutional law, public policy, psychology, religion, environmental studies, history and statistics. They are:
Charles Alston, 29, a reporter at the *Greensboro* (N.C.) *News & Record*.
Douglas Cumming, 34, staff writer at *The Journal* of Providence, R.I.
Michael Davis, 34, assistant managing editor–news at *The Evening Sun* of Baltimore.

Susan Dentzer, 30, general editor at *Newsweek* magazine.

Valerie Hyman, 35, senior news reporter with WSMV-TV in Nashville, Tenn.

Nancy Lee, 33, newsroom graphics editor with *The New York Times.*

Martha Matzke, 41, executive editor of *Education Week.*

Albert May, 37, Washington correspondent for *The News & Observer* of Raleigh, N.C.

Michael Meyers, 36, economics reporter for the *Minneapolis Star* and *Tribune.*

Charles Powers, 42, Nairobi, Kenya, bureau chief for *The Los Angeles Times.*

Ira Rosen, 32, producer with the CBS News program "60 Minutes."

Linda Wilson, 30, a reporter for *The Daily News* of Longview, Wash.

MAY 8

## Foreign Journalists Named to Study as Nieman Fellows

On May 27 the Nieman Foundation announced the names of eight foreign journalists who will study for a year at Harvard:

MARITES DANGUILAN-VITUG, 31 years old, a reporter for *Business Day* in Quezon City, the Philippines.

SONGPOL KAOPATUMTIP, 31, chief subeditor of *The Bangkok World,* Thailand.

JAMES EDWARD LAMB, 33, columnist with *The Vancouver Sun* in British Columbia.

FERNANDO LIMA, 31, news editor of the Mozambique news agency.

MALGORZATA NIEZABITOWSKA, 37, member of the editorial board of *The Catholic Review* in Warsaw.

SABINE ROLLBERG, 32, producer and editor of the broadcasting organization Westdeutscher Rundfunk, Cologne, West Germany.

MAHA SAMARA, 46, reporter and analyst for *An Nahar Arab and International* magazine of Beirut, Lebanon.

ANDRIES van HEERDEN, 31, assistant to the editor of *Die Vaderland* of Johannesburg.

MAY 28

# Five Tonys Are Won by "Drood"

*The Mystery of Edwin Drood,* the loose adaptation of the unfinished Dickens novel, and *I'm Not Rappaport,* Herb Gardner's play about two New York octogenarians, walked away with major honors at the 40th Annual Tony Awards ceremony last night at the Minskoff Theater.

*Edwin Drood* received five awards. It won in the best musical category, and George Rose was voted best actor in a musical. The show also won an award for Wilford Leach as director of a musical, as well as capturing honors in the original-score and musical-book categories.

These are winners of the Tony Awards:

**Best Musical**—*The Mystery of Edwin Drood.*
**Best Play**—*I'm Not Rappaport.*
**Leading Actor in a Musical**—George Rose, *The Mystery of Edwin Drood.*
**Leading Actress in a Musical**—Bernadette Peters, *Song & Dance.*
**Leading Actor in a Play**—Judd Hirsch, *I'm Not Rappaport.*
**Leading Actress in a Play**—Lily Tomlin, *The Search for Signs of Intelligent Life in the Universe.*
**Featured Actor in a Musical**—Michael Rupert, *Sweet Charity.*
**Featured Actress in a Musical**—Bebe Neuwirth, *Sweet Charity.*
**Featured Actor in a Play**—John Mahoney, *The House of Blue Leaves.*
**Featured Actress in a Play**—Swoosie Kurtz, *The House of Blue Leaves.*
**Book of a Musical**—Rupert Holmes, *The Mystery of Edwin Drood.*
**Original Score**—Rupert Holmes, *The Mystery of Edwin Drood.*
**Direction of a Play**—Jerry Zaks, *The House of Blue Leaves.*
**Direction of a Musical**—Wilford Leach, *The Mystery of Edwin Drood.*
**Scenic Design**—Tony Walton, *The House of Blue Leaves.*

Costume Design—Patricia Zipprodt, *Sweet Charity.*
Lighting Design—Pat Collins, *I'm Not Rappaport.*
Choreography—Bob Fosse, *Big Deal.*
Reproduction of a Play or Musical—*Sweet Charity.*

JUNE 2

## A Rich Legacy of Stage Hits

Alan Jay Lerner, the author of 13 Broadway musicals, died June 14. This is a list of the Broadway shows he wrote, doing both the book and lyrics except where otherwise noted:

*What's Up,* 1943; book by Mr. Lerner and Arthur Pierson, music by Frederick Loewe, 63 performances.
*The Day Before Spring,* 1945; music by Mr. Loewe, 165 performances.
*Brigadoon,* 1947; music by Mr. Loewe, 581 performances.
*Love Life,* 1948; music by Kurt Weill, 252 performances.
*Paint Your Wagon,* 1951; music by Mr. Loewe, 289 performances.
*My Fair Lady,* 1956; music by Mr. Loewe, 2,717 performances.
*Camelot,* 1960; music by Mr. Loewe, 874 performances.
*On a Clear Day You Can See Forever,* 1965; music by Burton Lane, 273 performances.
*Coco,* 1969; music by Andre Previn, 332 performances.
*Gigi,* 1973; music by Mr. Loewe, 103 performances.
*1600 Pennsylvania Avenue,* 1976; music by Leonard Bernstein, 7 performances.
*Carmelina,* 1979; music by Mr. Lane, 17 performances.
*Dance a Little Closer,* 1983; music by Charles Strouse, 1 performance.

JUNE 15

## The Humanitas Prizes

(For writers of television programs that "probe the meaning of human life" or communicate "enriching human values")

A $25,000 award to Vickie Patik, for "Do You Remember Love?" a CBS television movie about a college professor dying of Alzheimer's disease.
A $15,000 award to Robert Eisele, for "Ordinary Hero," an hour-long episode of CBS's "Cagney and Lacey," about an undocumented alien who is discovered by immigration authorities only after he breaks his back catching a mugger.
A $10,000 award to John Markus for a half-hour episode of NBC's "The Cosby Show" about a friend of Bill Cosby's daughter who thinks she is pregnant.
A $10,000 award to Josef Anderson, Fern Field and Anson Williams for "No Greater Gift," an ABC afternoon special about a dying Chicano boy offering his kidneys to a black boy.
A citation for "CBS Reports: The Vanishing Family—Crisis in Black America."
A citation to Herb Dudnick, executive producer of NBC's "Mainstreet," an after-school current events program for young people.

JUNE 20

## Reagan Picks 12 to Get National Medal of Arts

**By IRVIN MOLOTSKY**

WASHINGTON, July 6—President Reagan has selected nine American cultural figures, including three who are foreign-born, to receive the National Medal of Arts for their contributions to the nation. Three patrons of the arts have also been chosen to receive medals.

The recipients, who are to be honored with a White House luncheon on July 14, are these:
Marian Anderson, the first black artist to sing at the Metropolitan Opera.
Frank Capra, the film director and producer.
Aaron Copland, the composer.
Willem de Kooning, the artist.
Agnes de Mille, the choreographer.
Eva Le Gallienne, the actor and teacher.
Alan Lomax, the folklorist
Lewis Mumford, the philosopher and critic.
Eudora Welty, the writer.
  The patrons are:
Dominique de Menil, 78 years old, who was born in France and is a Houston art collector.
Seymour H. Knox, 88, founder of the Albright Knox Gallery in Buffalo.

The Exxon Corporation, which was cited particularly for its support of "Great Performances" on public television, for which it recently announced plans to cut financing.

This is the second year for the awards, which were proposed by President Reagan to accord to artists the same recognition that has long been given to those in science.

JULY 7

## Magician Makes the List of 25 "Genius" Winners

**By KATHLEEN TELTSCH**

The MacArthur Foundation named 25 "outstandingly talented" people yesterday to receive awards ranging from $164,000 to $300,000, one of them a 57-year-old magician who has used his skills to debunk self-styled psychics, seers and promoters of miracle cures.

The award to the magician, James Randi, of $272,000 over the next five years is a departure from the foundation's more prosaic awards, which have been given mainly to scientists, scholars and artists.

The MacArthur Fellowships, established in 1981 by the John D. and Catherine T. MacArthur Foundation, become known widely as the "search for geniuses." The no-strings, tax-free awards are intended to free the recipients from economic pressures so they can devote themselves to research or scholarship, or the creative arts.

The Chicago philanthropy, one of the wealthiest in the country, has spent $50 million on the program and made grants to 191 individuals.

JULY 15

Following is the list of winners from the MacArthur Foundation:

**PAUL R. ADAMS,** 39, professor in department of neurobiology and behavior at the State University of New York, Stony Brook, L.I.

**MILTON B. BABBITT,** 70, American composer-theorist and educator, has taught at Princeton University, both in mathematics and in the music school.

**CHRISTOPHER I. BECKWITH,** 40, chairman of the Tibetan Studies Program in the Department of Uralic and Altaic Studies at Indiana University.

**RICHARD M. A. BENSON,** 42, a specialist in photographic technologies and adjunct associate professor at Yale University.

**LESTER R. BROWN,** 52, environmentalist and author, founder of Worldwatch Institute.

**CAROLINE W. BYNUM,** 45, professor of history at the University of Washington, has written extensively about religion and women's history.

**WILLIAM A. CHRISTIAN, Jr.,** 42, a historian, sociologist and author who has concentrated on Spanish rural life.

**NANCY MARGUERITE FARRISS,** 48, professor of history at the University of Pennsylvania, has written extensively about Latin America.

**BENEDICT H. GROSS,** 36, professor of mathematics at Harvard University, best known for work on number theory.

**DARYL HINE,** 50, a poet born in British Columbia, has also written a novel and plays.

**JOHN ROBERT HORNER,** 40, curator of paleontology for the Museum of the Rockies at Montana State University.

**THOMAS C. JOE,** 51, founder of Center for the Study of Social Policy and co-author of *By the Few for the Few.*

**DAVID N. KEIGHTLEY,** 53, a professor of history at the University of California at Berkeley, a specialist on China's Bronze Age.

**ALBERT LIBCHABER,** 51, a French-born specialist in nonlinear dynamics and professor at the University of Chicago.

**DAVID PAGE,** 30, geneticist and Fellow of the Whitehead Institute of the Massachusetts Institute of Technology.

**GEORGE PERLE,** 71, composer and author and professor emeritus at the Aaron Copland School of Music at City University of New York.

**JAMES RANDI,** 57, Canadian-born professional magician is the author of a biography of Houdini and other works.

**DAVID RUDOVSKY,** 43, professor of law at the University of Pennsylvania, is an authority on the criminal justice system and a civil liberties activist and author.

**ROBERT M. SHAPLEY,** 41, associate professor of neurophysiology at Rockefeller University, a specialist in vision science.

**LEO STEINBERG,** 66, Benjamin Franklin professor of history of art at the University of Pennsylvania, is an art critic and author.

**RICHARD P. TURCO,** 43, an expert in atmospheric science and program manager with R & D Associates in Marina del Rey, Calif.

**THOMAS WHITESIDE,** 68, author and journalist who has written extensively about effects of chemical dioxin.

**ALLAN C. WILSON,** 51, professor of biochemistry at the University of California at Berkeley, has used scientific methods to develop theories on evolution.

**JAY WRIGHT,** 51, a poet whose work explores the cultures of Africa and Mexico.

**CHARLES WUORINEN,** 48, composer-in-residence with the San Francisco Symphony and an instructor at the Manhattan School of Music.

JULY 15

# 14 Are Gannett Center Fellows

Fourteen people from the news media and higher education have been named to fellowships at the Gannett Center for Media Studies at Columbia University.

Fellows typically undertake research on individuals, institutions and issues involving the mass media or technological change, according to Everette E. Dennis, executive director of the center.

These are the 1986–87 fellows and their research topics:

**Senior Fellows**
David A. Anderson, Rosenberg Centennial Professor of Law, University of Texas at Austin, "Reliance on the First Amendment in Protecting Press Freedom."
Burton Benjamin, former vice-president and senior executive producer, CBS News, "Fairness in the News Media."
Herbert J. Gans, Robert S. Lynd Professor of Sociology, Columbia University, "Television News and American Politics."
John C. Merrill, professor of journalism, Louisiana State University, "International Diplomatic Opinion and the Professionalization of Journalists."
Eleanor Singer, editor, *Public Opinion Quarterly*, and senior research scholar, Center for Social Sciences, Columbia University, "The Reporting of Risk in the Media."

**Fellows**
Ellis Cose, president, Institute for Journalism Education, University of California, Berkeley, "The Next Generation of Leaders for the Newspaper Industry."
Jerrold K. Footlick, senior editor, *Newsweek*, and editor, *Newsweek on Campus*, "Major News Organizations in Journalism Education."
Dan Schiller, associate professor of communications, Temple University, Philadelphia, "The Information Commodity."
Susan Shapiro, assistant professor of sociology, New York University, "How Media Organizations Attempt to Enhance Credibility."
Sally Bedell Smith, writer and former cultural news reporter for The New York Times, "A Biography of William S. Paley."
Susan Tifft, writer, *Time* magazine, "A Biography of the Binghams of Louisville" and "The Coming of a New Economic Order to Media Ownership."

**Research Fellows**
Lawrence T. McGill, research fellow, Center for Urban Affairs and Policy Research, Northwestern University, Evanston, Ill., "Career Paths of Journalists: The Role of Beats."
Michael Moss, staff writer, *The Atlanta Constitution and Journal*, "Media Coverage of Lingering Poverty in the South."
Christine Ogan, assistant professor of journalism, Indiana University, "New Communication Technology and the Third World."

AUG. 10

## Nobel Prizes Awarded

The Nobel Prizes were awarded between October 13 and 17. These were the winners:

**Physiology or Medicine: Dr. Rita Levi-Montalcini,** 77, a developmental biologist who holds both United States and Italian citizenship, and Dr. Stanley Cohen, 63, an American biochemist.

They were honored for major contributions to the understanding of substances that influence cell growth and the orderly development of tissues, including the nervous system. Their studies have proved important in basic research on cancer, disorders of the brain and nerves, birth defects and other health problems.

Dr. Levi-Montalcini is a senior scientist at the Institute of Cell Biology in Rome. Dr. Cohen is a professor of biochemistry at Vanderbilt University School of Medicine in Nashville. The two worked together at Washington University, St. Louis, in the 1950s.

The Nobel Assembly of the Karolinska Institute in Stockholm, in announcing the awards, said the discoveries by Drs. Levi-Montalcini and Cohen "opened new fields of widespread importance to basic science."

"As a direct consequence we may increase our understanding of many disease states such as developmental malformations, degenerative changes in senile dementia, delayed wound healing and tumor diseases," the announcement added. Tumor diseases include cancers. The most common form of dementia is Alzheimer's disease.

**Peace: Elie Wiesel,** 58, who survived Nazi death camps to become a witness against forgetfulness and violence.

Through his writings and lectures, Mr. Wiesel, a riveting public speaker, kept alive his specific experience of the camps, but sought to elevate it to a more universal level. The Nobel committee statement observed that "Wiesel's commitment, which originated in the sufferings of the Jewish people, has been widened to embrace all oppressed peoples and races."

"Elie Wiesel has emerged as one of the most important spiritual leaders and guides in an age when violence, repression and racism continue to characterize the world," said Egil Aarvik, chairman of the Norwegian Nobel Committee and a former president of the Norwegian Parliament, in awarding the prize to the resident of Manhattan.

Mr. Wiesel was born in the town of Sighet in the northern Rumanian district of Transylvania in 1928. He was deported with his family to Auschwitz when he was a boy, and then to Buchenwald. His mother and sister died at Auschwitz and his father at Buchenwald.

At the age of 16, he was liberated from Buchenwald and moved to Paris, where he adopted the French language. In 1958, he published his first book, *La Nuit (Night)*, which recounted his terrifying ordeal in the Nazi death camps.

**Physics: Dr. Ernst Ruska,** 79, Dr. Gerd Binnig, 39, and Dr. Heninrich Rohrer, 53, three pioneers in microscope design who were honored for greatly expanding humans' ability to peer deep into the smallest facets of nature.

Dr. Ruska is at the Fritz Haber Institute of the Max Planck Society in West Berlin. His electron microscope, long used as a research tool, has figured in the study of metals, viruses, protein molecules and other biological structures.

Dr. Binnig, of West Germany, and Dr. Heinrich Rohrer, of Switzerland, are members of an I.B.M. laboratory in Zurich and in 1981 invented a device—the scanning-tunneling microscope—that can map surfaces in terms of their individual atoms.

The devices stand as monuments at each end of five decades of explosive growth in microscopy.

Dr. Ruska's invention of the electron microscope opened a new era in high magnification. Because of its use in many fields of biology and medicine, the citation calls it "one of the most important inventions of this century."

Its modern descendant, the scanning-tunneling microscope, has just begun to play a role in the study of surfaces. It was developed in Zurich at the International Business Machines Research Laboratory. For the first time, on an atomic scale, it has shown the surface structures of such substances as gold, silicon, nickel and graphite.

"The scanning-tunneling microscope," the citation says, "is completely new, and we have so far only seen the beginning of its development. It is, however, clear that entirely new fields are opening up for the study of the structure of matter."

**Chemistry: Dudley R. Herschbach,** 54, Yuan T. Lee, 49, and John C. Polanyi, 57, were honored for helping to create the first detailed understanding of chemical reactions, replacing a traditional frozen picture with a way of seeing the intimate interplay of energy that transforms one kind of matter into another.

They invented a set of tools in the 1950s and 1960s that helped bring both the theory and the technology of modern physics into chemistry. Among them is a technique of using beams of molecules, fired at supersonic speeds, to study chemical reactions molecule by molecule for the first time.

Their work on "reaction dynamics" bears directly on a range of particular problems, from the burning of gases in engines to depletion of ozone in the stratosphere. It also gives a way of understanding the driving of reactions by catalysis, which is central to the industrial manufacture of chemicals and the refining of crude oil into petroleum products.

But its main import is for fundamental theory—"the lunatic fringe of science," an ebullient Dr. Herschbach said yesterday of the work of the two Americans and one Canadian. He is at Harvard University. Dr. Lee, a native of Taiwan, is at the University of California at Berkeley and Dr. Polanyi is at the University of Toronto.

**Literature: Wole Soyinka, 52,** a Nigerian playwright and poet who has been a fierce champion of political freedom in black Africa.

It was the first time the Swedish Academy had awarded the Nobel Prize to an African writer.

Mr. Soyinka, who wrote extensive poetry while in prison in Nigeria, has had his plays produced in New York and London, and he is now a visiting professor of theater at Cornell.

An academy citation said the Nigerian "in a wide cultural perspective and with poetical overtones fashions the drama of existence."

A member of the Yoruba tribe—whose rich and brooding mythologies are laced into much of his writing—Mr. Soyinka in 1960 formed the Masks drama company, which put on his play *A Dance of the Forests*. The Swedish Academy described the play as "a kind of African 'Midsummer Night's Dream' with spirits, ghosts and gods." The Yoruba god Ogun, creator and destroyer, figures prominently in this and later works.

After the outbreak of civil war in Nigeria in 1967, Mr. Soyinka appealed for a cease-fire and was arrested after trying unsuccessfully to mediate with the Ibo rebels who had broken away to form the short-lived state of Biafra. Accused of conspiring with the rebels, he was jailed for 22 months.

In prison he wrote extensively, mostly on toilet paper, producing a diary and poems that were later published under the title *A Shuttle in the Crypt*. One poem, "Live Burial," evoked his incarceration with these lines:

Sixteen paces By twenty-three.
They hold Siege against humanity
And Truth Employing time to drill through to his sanity.

**Economics: James M. Buchanan, 67,** was honored for his pioneering development of new methods for analyzing economic and political decision making.

The five-member selection committee cited Dr. Buchanan, a professor at George Mason University in Fairfax, Va., as the leading researcher in a fast-growing field of potential significance known as "public choice theory."

The selection surprised some mainstream economists because Dr. Buchanan's work straddles the boundary between economics and political science, raising issues not traditionally dealt with in the economics discipline. It strives to explain government policy decisions by the application of basic principles, just as traditional economic theory explains how consumers and businesses make choices.

Dr. Buchanan's work has particularly focused on the forces determining government spending decisions, such as the rewards or costs to politicians and voters for making changes in public expenditures. For instance, a key proposition is that politicians are like the rest of society in that they are motivated by self-interest, such as getting reelected or gaining additional power.

One conclusion derived from Dr. Buchanan's work is that, to bring significant changes in government spending or taxation, a policy initiative must be a fundamental shift in incentives. A series of piecemeal compromises among politicians will rarely yield the same result because narrower interests will prevail.

Alice Rivlin, the current president of the American Economics Association and a former director of the Congressional Budget Office, described public choice theory as an important strand of current economic thinking and the selection of Dr. Buchanan as a recognition of that fact.

OCT. 14–18

# Children's Books

Following are *The Book Review*'s choices of the 10 best illustrated children's books of 1986.

Since 1952, *The Book Review* has annually asked a panel of three judges to make a selection from among the several thousand children's books published each year. The judges this year were Augusta Baker, storyteller-in-residence at the University of South Carolina; Sybille A. Jagusch, chief of the Children's Literature Center of the Library of Congress; and Ed Koren, an illustrator whose most recent collection of drawings is entitled *Well, There's Your Problem*.

As a matter of note, William Steig has been a winner twice before and Chris Van Allsburg six times before.

*The Stranger.* Written and illustrated by Chris Van Allsburg. (Houghton Mifflin, $15.95)

*The Ugly Duckling.* By Hans Christian Andersen. Illustrated by Robert Van Nutt. (Alfred A. Knopf, $10.95)

*Flying.* Written and illustrated by Donald Crews. (Greenwillow Books, $11.75)

*The Owl Scatterer.* By Howard Norman. Illustrated by Michael McCurdy. (Atlantic Monthly Press, $13.95)

*Rembrandt Takes a Walk.* By Mark Strand. Illustrated by Red Grooms. (Clarkson N. Potter, $14.95)

*Cherries and Cherry Pits.* Written and illustrated by Vera B. Williams. (Greenwillow Books, $11.75)

*Molly's New Washing Machine.* By Laura Geringer. Illustrated by Petra Mathers. (Harper & Row, $11.95)

*Brave Irene.* Written and illustrated by William Steig. (Farrar, Straus & Giroux, $12.95)

*One Morning.* By Canna Funakoshi. Illustrated by Yohji Izawa (Picture Book Studio, $9.95)

*Pigs from A to Z.* Written and illustrated by Arthur Geisert. (Houghton Mifflin, $15.95)

Nov. 9

## Phi Beta Kappa Names Book Award Winners

Phi Beta Kappa, the national scholarly honor society, has announced the winners of its annual book awards. The awards carry prizes of $2,500 each.

These were the winners:

Maynard Mack, for *Alexander Pope: A Life.* (W. W. Norton)

Fred L. Whipple, for *The Mystery of Comets.* (Smithsonian Institution Press)

Benjamin I. Schwartz, for *The World of Thought in Ancient China.* (Belknap Press of Harvard University Press).

Dec. 6

## Editors' Choice: The Best Books of 1986

The best books of the year, chosen by the editors of *The Book Review* from those reviewed since last year's Christmas Books issue, are 7 volumes of fiction and 10 of nonfiction. The list, longer than it has been for a number of years, has six more titles than the 1985 one. Are the editors growing more generous or authors more brilliant? The tone of weekly discussions on the list that went on for more than two months, and the firm, contradictory opinions that persisted to the end, inspire caution about answering the question. (Descriptions of the books on this 19th annual list of the best books of the year are drawn from the reviews that appeared in *The Book Review.*) The list:

*Arab and Jew: Wounded Spirits in a Promised Land*, by David K. Shipler (Times Books). The chief of the Jerusalem bureau of *The New York Times* from 1979 to 1984 examines the changes in Israel since the Six-Day War of June 1967.

*Arctic Dreams: Imagination and Desire in a Northern Landscape*, by Barry Lopez (Charles Scribner's Sons). The author cannot wait to get up in the morning. What is so prodigious about him is not so much his impressive travels in the Arctic, but his happiness in them.

*Crossing the Line: A Year in the Land of Apartheid*, by William Finnegan (Harper & Row). An easy, conversational style and a talent for succinct characterization and evocation of place make William Finnegan's account of a year spent teaching in a Cape Town high school a vivid tale of South Africa's agony.

*FDR, The New York Years: 1928–1933*, by Kenneth S. Davis (Random House). *FDR, The New Deal Years: 1933–1937*, by Kenneth S. Davis (Random House). The second and third volumes in Mr. Davis's biography of Franklin Delano Roosevelt promise that when he has finished, his work will at least rival the histories of the New Deal written by Arthur M. Schlesinger, Jr., Frank Freidel and James MacGregor Burns.

*The Handmaid's Tale*, by Margaret Atwood (Houghton Mifflin Company). In the Republic of Gilead the female population is divided into classes based on functions—the Marthas (houseworkers), Econowives (workers), Handmaids (childbearers), Aunts (thought controllers) and Wives. Men (the Commanders) run the nation. Ms. Atwood's deft sardonic humor makes much of the action and dialogue in the novel funny and ominous at the same time.

*John Maynard Keynes*, vol. 1, *Hopes Betrayed 1883–1920,* by Robert Skidelsky (Elisabeth Sifton Books/Viking). This is the first biography of the economist to bring together the two sides of his early life—the formidable public person he was by the age of 30 and the circus rider of the social and homosexual whirl of Bloomsbury.

*The Life of Langston Hughes.* Vol. 1, *1902–1941. I, Too, Sing America,* By Arnold Rampersad (Oxford University Press). This biography reads like a novel, quickly and steadily sweeping the reader—with appropriate itch, anger, fear, exhilaration, triumph or pain—through the poet's life up to the beginning of World War II.

*A Machine that Would Go of Itself: The Constitution in American Culture*, by Michael Kammen (Alfred A. Knopf). This anecdotal history is committed to a survey of sentiments at the grass roots about our most fundamental political document. The bizarre ignorance of the Constitution among Americans for two centuries possibly explains the passionate fury with which political groups of every stripe have debated it.

*The Man Who Mistook His Wife for a Hat and Other Clinical Tales*, by Oliver Sacks (Summit Books). With the lucidity and power of a gifted short-story writer, Oliver Sacks, an eminent neurologist, writes with insight and compassion about two dozen patients who manifest striking peculiarities of perception, emotion, language, thought, memory or action.

*Out of India: Selected Stories*, by Ruth Prawer Jhabvala (William Morrow & Company). The 15 short stories in this collection were chosen by Ruth Prawer Jhabvala from four volumes written over the years. Her milieu is middle-class and Hindu, and her stories are mostly domestic, but she has a fine satiric eye for the modern Westernized young people who scandalize their elders and for the ashrams where young and old go on spiritual quests.

*A Perfect Spy*, by John le Carre (Alfred A. Knopf). A tense balance between the narrative drive of the plot and the artfulness of the style makes this espionage novel perhaps the best in John le Carre's oeuvre.

*The Progress of Love*, by Alice Munro (Alfred A. Knopf). Many of the 11 short stories in this collection have the moral and historical density of other people's novels.

*Roger's Version*, by John Updike (Alfred A. Knopf). Its title suggests there might be very different versions of this story from the one told by its narrator, a professor of divinity, especially when he imagines in great detail the affair his wife is having with a graduate student in science. The unresolved enigma at the heart of this challenging novel makes the arguments the professor and the scientist, who is a fundamentalist Christian, have about faith and reality deep and disturbing.

*Saints and Strangers*, by Angela Carter (Viking). The voice is literary but not precious, deep but not difficult, funny without being superficial, and indifferent to formulas. The humor in the eight stories (better to call them concoctions) in this volume is a blend of English distance and American wackiness.

*The Vanished Imam: Musa al Sadr and the Shia of Lebanon*, by Fouad Ajami (Cornell University Press). Musa al-Sadr seems to display within a single life the full range of the Middle Eastern enigma. He was born in Iran, became the inspired leader of Lebanon's Shiite community and disappeared—he is presumed dead—on a visit to Col. Muammar el-Qaddafi's Libya in 1978 when he was 50 years old. Mr. Ajami's story of his life and his people may give Americans a deeper understanding of Lebanon and the Middle East than any other book.

*Velazquez: Painter and Courtier*, by Jonathan Brown (Yale University Press). The life of the great Spanish painter Diego de Velazquez was extraordinary, and Jonathan Brown has made it enthralling. Read in context, the pictures, often interpreted by critics and artists but never so well as by Mr. Brown, mean far more than ever before.

*Whites*, by Norman Rush (Alfred A. Knopf). One of the whites in black Africa depicted in the short stories included in this collection by a former co-director of the Peace Corps in Botswana says that absence of real commitment is what makes doing good overseas so attractive to Americans now, because —no matter what happens—the visiting whites know they have done their best. The failure of American idealism and technology is the underlying subject of all the stories.

DEC. 7

# 32 from U.S. Named Rhodes Scholars

By HOWARD W. FRENCH

The names of 32 Rhodes Scholars from 24 colleges in the United States were announced yesterday.

The American students, including 11 women, 2 blacks, and a Vietnamese refugee, will join winners from 17 other countries for two years of study at Oxford University in England.

One of the winners, Hoang Nhu Tran, 21, son of a high officer in the Vietnamese Air Force who fled Vietnam with his family in 1975, became the first Vietnamese Rhodes Scholar.

Yale University led this year's list of schools represented, with four scholarships, followed by Georgetown University with three. Each of the three United States military academies was represented with one candidate.

The awards, established in 1902 in the will of Cecil Rhodes, a British colonial financier, were originally intended for young men from British colonies and from the United States and Germany, in the hope of contributing to world understanding and peace. Women have been eligible for the awards since 1976.

Scholars are now selected from India, Pakistan, Malaysia, Nigeria, Singapore, Hong Kong, the British Caribbean and Kenya, in addition to the original constituencies. Those include Canada, Australia, New Zealand, Bermuda, South Africa, Zambia, Zimbabwe and Jamaica.

In the United States, scholars were chosen from eight regions on the basis of intellectual attainment, character, leadership, and physical vigor.

At regional competitions on Saturday, the

finalists were chosen from 1,143 applicants.

*New England:* Andrew Z. Lopatin, Newton, Mass., Boston University and Brisk Rabbinical College; Robert W. Radtke, Charlestown, Mass., Columbia University; Michael S. Barr, Chevy Chase, Md., Yale University; James J. Collins, Nashua, N.H., College of the Holy Cross.

*Middle Atlantic:* Michael Gaffney, Fayetteville, N.Y., Naval Academy; Sylvia M. Mathews, Hinton, W.Va., Radcliffe College of Harvard University; Donna J. Roberts, Verona, Pa., University of Pittsburgh and Cornell University; Mark Ouweleen, Rochester, N.Y., Georgetown University.

*Southern:* Maria Weston Merritt, Franklin, Va., Wake Forest University; William H. Lipscomb, Lynchburg, Va., Duke University; Paul W. Ludwig, Signal Mountain, Tenn., University of Tennessee–Chattanooga; Barbara Petzen, Sharpsburg, Ga., Columbia University.

*Great Lakes:* Robert M. Dow, Jr., Joliet, Ill., Yale University; Jacob Weisberg, Chicago, Ill., Yale University; Daniel D. Stid, Mason, Mich., Hope College; Atul A. Gawande, Athens, Ohio, Stanford University.

*Middle West:* David H. Mehnert, Roeland Park, Kan., Princeton University; Kelly Dean Welch, Moran, Kan., Kansas State University; Laura Ruetsche, Northbrook, Ill., Carleton College; Kenneth Brashier, Aurora, S.D., University of Missouri–Columbia.

*Gulf:* Sarah H. Cleveland, Birmingham, Ala., Brown University; C. Damon Miguel Moore, Coldwater, Miss., University of Mississippi and Johns Hopkins Medical School; Susan Pepin, Tulsa, Okla., Yale University; T. Andrew Chin, Austin, Texas, University of Texas–Austin.

*Southwestern:* Kathleen L. McLaughlin, Tucson, Ariz., Boston University; John K. Tien, Cerritos, Calif., United States Military Academy and University of California–Irvine; Hoang Nhu Tran, Rohnert Park, Calif., Air Force Academy; Brett Gilbert Scharffs, Salt Lake City, Utah, Georgetown University.

*Northwestern:* Nina R. Bowen, Petersburg, Alaska, Georgetown University; Michael V. Woodhouse, Burley, Idaho, the College of Idaho; Jocelyn H. Alexander, Bozeman, Mont., Princeton University; Elizabeth M. Cousens, Tacoma, Wash., University of Puget Sound and Princeton University.   DEC. 8

## *Fatherhood* and *It* Top Sellers of '86

### By EDWIN McDOWELL

*Fatherhood*, Bill Cosby's wry observations on family life, was far and away the best-selling hardcover book in the United States in 1986, according to a survey by *The New York Times*. *It* by Stephen King, a tale of childhood horrors in a small Maine town, was the No. 1 selling book of hardcover fiction in 1986.

*Out of Africa* and *Shadows on the Grass*, a single volume of two memoirs of colonial Kenya by Isak Dinesen, was the leading paperback nonfiction title in 1986. Judith Thurman's biography, *Isak Dinesen: The Life of a Storyteller*, finished No. 6 on the same list.

*The Color Purple* by Alice Walker, an epistolary novel about the life and loves of a black woman—which had been the No. 7 best-selling fiction paperback in 1985, as well as No. 3 on the 1984 trade paperback list—rose to No. 1 in the fiction paperback category in 1986.

For the second consecutive year, *Fit for Life* by Harvey and Martin Diamond, a diet for weight loss and fitness, was the leading hardcover book in the advice and miscellaneous category, while *Women Who Love Too Much* by Robin Norwood was the No. 1 paperback title in that category.

Ratings for the hardcover lists are based on computer-processed sales figures from 2,000 bookstores in every region of the country, statistically adjusted to represent sales in all bookstores. The paperback listings also include computer-processed sales figures from representative wholesalers servicing more than 40,000 retail outlets. Although several books on the lists were published before last year, the sales figures used are only for 1986.

The autobiography of Lee Iacocca, written with William Novak, the best-selling hardcover nonfiction book in 1985 and 1984, did not place in the top 10 in 1986. But the paperback edition of the book finished No. 3 in the nonfiction category. *Lake Wobegon Days* by Garrison Keillor, which was the No. 1 hardcover fiction book in 1985, finished No. 7 in the same category in 1986 and was also No. 3 on the paperback fiction list.

Many of the best-selling authors are perennials, while others owe much of the popularity of their books to television (Mr. Cosby) or to motion pictures (*Out of Africa* spurred the sale of books by and about Isak Dinesen). The most talked-about book of 1986, James Clavell's *Whirlwind*, finished No. 5 on the hardcover fiction list, a respectable showing, since it has been in bookstores only about two months.

No author had two hardcover books on the lists, but several authors were represented more than once on the paperback list, or were best-sellers in hardcover and paperback. Mr. King's *Skeleton Crew*, for example, also held the No. 7 spot on the paperback fiction list. Tom Clancy's *Red Storm Rising* was the No. 2 hardcover fiction title in 1986, while his *Hunt for Red October*—which had been a best-seller in 1985 in both hardcover and paperback—held the No. 2 position in paperback fiction.

Jean M. Auel's *Mammoth Hunters* was the No. 4 hardcover fiction title in 1986 and the No. 8 paperback fiction title, while her *Clan of the Cave Bear* ranked No. 6 on the paperback fiction list. Danielle Steel's *Wanderlust* was the No. 6 hardcover fiction title in 1986, while her *Family Album* was No. 5 on the paperback fiction list and *Secrets* was No. 9. Gary Larson had three cartoon collections on the paperback advice and miscellaneous list: *It Came From the Far Side*, *The Far Side Gallery* and *The Far Side Gallery 2*.  JAN. 5, 1987

## Here are the Top Best-Sellers for 1986 in Six Categories:

### Hardcover Nonfiction

1. *Fatherhood*, by Bill Cosby (Dolphin/Doubleday).
2. *You're Only Old Once!*, by Dr. Seuss (Random House).
3. *His Way*, by Kitty Kelley (Bantam).
4. *James Herriot's Dog Stories*, by James Herriot (St. Martin's Press).
5. *A Day in the Life of America*, (Collins Publishers).
6. *Bus 9 to Paradise*, by Leo Buscaglia (Slack/Morrow).
7. *McMahon!*, by Jim McMahon with Bob Verdi (Warner).
8. *Necessary Losses*, by Judith Viorst (Simon & Schuster).
9. *Word for Word*, by Andrew A. Rooney (G. P. Putnam).
10. *Yeager: An Autobiography*, by Chuck Yeager and Leo Janos (Bantam).
11. *Iacocca: An Autobiography*, by Lee Iacocca and William Novak (Bantam).
12. *When All You've Ever Wanted Isn't Enough*, by Harold S. Kushner (Summit).
13. *The Triumph of Politics*, by David A. Stockman (Harper & Row).
14. *A Light in the Attic*, by Shel Silverstein (Harper & Row).
15. *One Knee Equals Two Feet*, by John Madden with Dave Anderson (Villard).

### Hardcover Fiction

1. *It*, by Stephen King (Viking).
2. *Red Storm Rising*, by Tom Clancy (G. P. Putnam).
3. *The Bourne Supremacy*, by Robert Ludlum (Random House).
4. *The Mammoth Hunters*, by Jean M. Auel (Crown Publishing).
5. *Whirlwind*, by James Clavell (William Morrow).
6. *Wanderlust*, by Danielle Steel (Delacorte Press).
7. *Lake Wobegon Days*, by Garrison Keillor (Viking).
8. *A Perfect Spy*, by John le Carre (Alfred A. Knopf).
9. *Last of the Breed*, by Louis L'Amour (Bantam).
10. *I'll Take Manhattan*, by Judith Krantz (Crown).

11. *Lie Down with Lions*, by Ken Follett (William Morrow).
12. *A Matter of Honor*, by Jeffrey Archer (Linden/Simon & Schuster).
13. *Hollywood Husbands*, by Jackie Collins (Simon & Schuster).
14. *The Prince of Tides*, by Pat Conroy (Houghton Mifflin).
15. *The Good Mother*, by Sue Miller (Harper & Row).

**Hardcover Advice and Miscellaneous**

1. *Fit for Life*, by Harvey Diamond and Marilyn Diamond (Warner).
2. *Callanetics*, by Callan Pinckney with Sallie Batson (William Morrow).
3. *The Rotation Diet*, by Martin Katahn (W. W. Norton).
4. *Webster's Ninth New Collegiate Dictionary* (Merriam-Webster).
5. *The Frugal Gourmet*, by Jeff Smith (William Morrow).

**Fiction Paperbacks**

1. *The Color Purple*, by Alice Walker (Pocket Books).
2. *The Hunt for Red October*, by Tom Clancy (Berkley).
3. *Lake Wobegon Days*, by Garrison Keillor (Penguin).
4. *If Tomorrow Comes*, by Sidney Sheldon (Warner).
5. *Family Album*, by Danielle Steel (Dell Publishing).
6. *The Clan of the Cave Bear*, by Jean M. Auel (Bantam).
7. *Skeleton Crew*, by Stephen King (Signet/New American Library).
8. *The Mammoth Hunters*, by Jean M. Auel (Bantam).
9. *Secrets*, by Danielle Steel (Dell Publishing).
10. *Lonesome Dove*, by Larry McMurtry (Pocket Books).
11. *Dark Angel*, by V. C. Andrews (Pocket Books).
12. *The Valley of Horses*, by Jean M. Auel (Bantam).
13. *The Two Mrs. Grenvilles*, by Dominick Dunne (Bantam).
14. *Hold the Dream*, by Barbara Taylor Bradford (Bantam).
15. *The Accidental Tourist*, by Anne Tyler (Berkley).

**Nonfiction Paperbacks**

1. *Out of Africa* and *Shadows on the Grass*, by Isak Dinesen (Vintage/Random House).
2. *The Road Less Traveled*, by M. Scott Peck (Touchstone/Simon & Schuster).
3. *Iacocca: An Autobiography*, by Lee Iacocca with William Novak (Bantam).
4. *The Bridge Across Forever*, by Richard Bach (Dell Publishing).
5. *Smart Women, Foolish Choices*, by Connell Cowan and Melvin Kinder (Signet/New American Library).
6. *Isak Dinesen: The Life of a Storyteller*, by Judith Thurman (St. Martin's Press).
7. *West With the Night*, by Beryl Markham (North Point Press).

**Paperback Advice and Miscellaneous**

1. *Women Who Love Too Much*, by Robin Norwood (Pocket Books).
2. *Rand McNally Road Atlas: United States, Canada, Mexico* (Rand McNally Company).
3. *Bloom County Babylon*, by Berke Breathed (Little, Brown).
4. *It Came From the Far Side*, by Gary Larson (Andrews, McMeel & Parker).
5. *The Far Side Gallery*, by Gary Larson (Andrews, McMeel & Parker).
6. *The Far Side Gallery 2*, by Gary Larson (Andrews, McMeel & Parker).
7. *Adult Children of Alcoholics*, by Janet Ceringer Woititz (Health Communications).
8. *What Color Is Your Parachute?*, by Richard Nelson Bolles (Ten Speed Press).

JAN. 5, 1987

# PART 8
# Miscellany and Living

NYT/SUZANNE DECHILLO

# Brighten the Morning After: Count the Ways

**By NANCY HARMON JENKINS**

For most people, the annual orgy of eating and drinking that began with Thanksgiving and sailed merrily through Christmas crescendoed, reaching its highest point sometime in the wee hours this morning. Though there are some dauntless souls who will stagger through yet another day of what they, at least, can still call fun, for the rest of us, the party is over. The national digestive tract is sour and the collective head aches.

A restorative, clearly, is in order.

"Pure oxygen is the best cure for a hangover," says David Outerbridge, editor of the Belfast, Me., *Republican Journal* and author of *The Hangover Handbook* (Harmony Books, 1982). "Kingsley Amis suggests vigorous sex, and the ancient Romans were partial to screech owl eggs."

British colonials considered the desert air in Cairo especially good for hangovers, while modern-day visitors in Rome claim that a visit to the vast domed space of the Pantheon performs an equally successful mind-clearing function.

From Moroccan mint tea to Fernet-Branca, the vile-tasting Italian morning-after beverage of myrrh, rhubarb and other substances, to hot chicken soup, the favorite of Jewish and Chinese grandmothers, the remedies abound. Because the chief effect of alcohol is to dehydrate the system, most doctors agree that anything that restores liquid will have a beneficial effect. Flushing salt water directly into the veins, suggested Dr. Raymond Mayewski, associate chairman of the department of medicine at the University of Rochester School of Medicine, might be the quickest restorative, though he admitted the treatment was not one to which most people would have easy access. "Normally, you'll get rid of toxins in the body over a day or two," Dr. Mayewski said. "Over time, *anything* will work."  JAN. 1

## Hangover remedies, worldwide

| Favorite Treatments | Who Uses or Where |
| --- | --- |
| Air in Cairo | British colonials |
| Bloody Marys | Americans |
| Chicken soup | Jewish and Chinese grandmothers |
| Coca-Cola syrup | Southerners |
| Fernet-Branca | Europeans, especially Italians and French |
| Hair of the dog | Long-standing Western tradition |
| Haquat broth | Chinese |
| Ice cream | People from Maine |
| Jezebel's Tea | Old South Carolina tradition |
| Juice fasts | Health spas |
| Kaopectate and morphine | London tradition, long-gone |
| Mint tea and sour lemons | Moroccans |
| Pure oxygen | Recommended by medical authorities |
| The Pantheon in Rome | American expatriates |
| Sauerkraut and bean soup | Northeastern Italians (Istria, Trieste) |
| Sauerkraut and paprika soup | Hungarians |
| Screech owl eggs | Ancient Romans |
| Spiced Mysore rasam | Indians |
| Underberg | Edward Safdie |

JAN. 1

## At Inaugural, a Taste of Old New York

**By SUZANNE M. CHARLE**

This morning, while most New Yorkers are still in bed after a night of celebrating the future, Richard Ferrugio and 50 employees will busily re-create the past.

In honor of Mayor Koch's inauguration, the 36-year-old caterer is preparing hot mulled apple cider and brandy punch, originally served at the 1710 swearing-in ceremony for Mayor Jacobus Van Cortlandt, and raisin-currant bread, served at De Witt Clinton's inaugural reception in 1803.

The 1,500 guests will sample these recipes and more at the reception scheduled for noon in the newly refurbished Italianate courthouse that was built just behind City Hall in the days when William Marcy (Boss) Tweed was head of Tammany Hall.     JAN. 1

---

### The 1986 Reception Shopping List for Mayor Koch's Third Inaugural Ceremonies

(For 1,500 guests)
- 3,000 sandwiches, including smoked turkey with dill cheese, Cajun roast beef and pita pockets with vegetables and hummus
- 800 bagels with smoked salmon and cream cheese
- 100 gallons of minestrone
- 80 loaves of bread
- 3,000 cookies
- 65 pounds of cheese
- 100 gallons of hot cider
- 50 cases of New York State wine
- 4 kegs of New Amsterdam beer

JAN. 1

---

## Newfoundland Nurtures It's Outlandish Old Nouns

**By CHRISTOPHER S. WREN**

ST. JOHN'S, Newfoundland—Only a sleveen, shimmick, tissy mawk or grum nunny-fudger could be rafted and harrished by Newfoundland English.

For while come-from-always may be nish enough to think the gate ramlatch, any yaffle of baymen from the outports, where the stun breeze faffers on the ballicatters, can still fadge in the oldest and most distinctive English spoken in North America.

The dialect of this easternmost corner of North America draws upon archaic English and Irish spoken by the hardy seafarers who began settling in Newfoundland before the Puritans landed on Plymouth Rock.

It borrows from the language of the original Indians and Eskimos of Newfoundland and Labrador and has formed words of its own to describe local flora, fauna and weather conditions.

But the most remarkable thing about Newfoundland English is that it endures, if not entirely in the capital of St. John's, then in villages and hamlets across this fogbound island, which is slightly smaller than New York State.     JAN. 3

---

### Words to Harrish a Come-From-Away

A glossary of selected Newfoundland English words.
**Sleveen:** Mean or deceitful fellow.
**Shimmick:** Dissembler or despised person.
**Mawk:** Silly or foolish fellow.
**Nunny-fudger:** Idler; shirker.
**Tissy:** Angry, irritable.
**Grum:** Morose, gloomy.

**Raft:** To upset, irritate.
**Harrish:** To torment, pester or annoy.
**Come-from-away:** An outsider.
**Nish:** Delicate, tender.
**Gate:** Habit, peculiarity.
**Ramlatch:** Something foolish or nonsensical.
**Yaffle:** A small bunch, handful of people.
**Outport:** Small coastal settlement.
**Bayman:** Outport inhabitant.
**Stun breeze:** A sea wind of at least 20 knots.
**Faffer:** To blow in chilly gusts.
**Ballicatter:** Saltwater shore ice frozen in winter.
**Fadge:** To manage, to do things for oneself.

JAN. 3

# Some Lessons from the School of Unfamiliar Fish

By NANCY HARMON JENKINS

While halibut, haddock and sole continue to be all-time favorites with American fish eaters, and shrimp—at around two pounds per person per year—is the most popular seafood of all, many unusual and unfamiliar species that can add variety and interest to fish dishes are appearing on our markets.

Some, like rougets, or red mullet, from Morocco and green-lipped mussels from New Zealand, are imports, available now because of increasing sophistication in packaging and shipping technologies. Others, like Southern catfish and mussels from Maine, are the products of aquaculture, a growing industry. And others, like squid, monkfish and sea robins, are still discarded by fishermen as trash fish. While some of these fish, especially the imported ones, may be very expensive, many more are excellent values.

It is sometimes difficult to identify unusual fish because names change from one area to another and marketers often give fish a name they think is catchier or less offensive than its proper name. Witness the green-lipped New Zealand mussels that one distributor sells as kiwi clams. Snapper is another designation given to whole varieties of saltwater fish that are unrelated to the snapper family. Tilapia is called St. Peter's fish by Israeli aquaculturists, who are promoting it as such in this country, to the confusion of restaurateurs and customers familiar with the fine Mediterranean fish called San Pietro in Italy, St.-Pierre in France and John Dory in England.

Some fishmongers misname species to make them more alluring. A recent tour of Manhattan shops revealed pollack marketed as blue snapper, hake as white snapper and mullet under the name fresh bass. "Shop for freshness and not for the name of the fish," advises Richard Lord, information director of the Fulton Fish Market.

JAN. 8

## Distinguishing the rarer varieties

| Name | Origin | How sold | Preparation |
| --- | --- | --- | --- |
| Blowfish (puffers, sea squabs) | Atlantic | Skinned and gutted whole fish, heads removed | Must be thoroughly skinned and stripped of all viscera; bread and sauté, or deep-fry |
| Bonito | North Atlantic | Whole if small; otherwise, steaks | Marinate in brine or acidulated water; grill whole fish, sauté or grill steaks |

| Name | Origin | How sold | Preparation |
|---|---|---|---|
| Buffalo fish | Canadian and New York lakes | Fillets or portions | Sauté, grill or bake |
| Catfish | Southern fish farms | Occasionally whole fish, but fillets are preferred; smoked fish available | Bread and sauté, or broil with accompanying sauce |
| Croaker; black drum; weakfish | Atlantic and Gulf of Mexico | Whole fish or fillets | Sauté or bake |
| Eels | Atlantic tidal marshes and estuaries | Whole; occasionally skinned and filleted; smoked eel available | Skin and cut into steaks or fillets; grill, deep-fry in batter or stew in sauce |
| Mako shark; dogfish | Local waters | Steaks; smaller dogfish are often in fillets | Use as swordfish; grill as steaks or kebabs, sauté or bake in sauces |
| Monkfish (anglerfish, lotte) | Local waters | Tails only, skinned | Sauté, grill, add to stews and chowders, or poach and serve cold in salad |
| Mussels | Mostly cultivated, mostly from New England | Bulk, in shells | Discard open shells; clean beards; steam in water, broth or white wine; serve hot or cold |
| Orange roughey | New Zealand | Fillets, usually frozen or thawed | Sauté, broil or bake in sauces |
| Rouget (red mullet) | Morocco | Whole fish | Grill or sauté; larger fish may be oven baked or filleted and sautéed |
| Sardines, fresh | Maine | Whole fish | Gut, split and remove backbone; grill or fry in bread crumbs or oatmeal |
| Sea robins | Local waters | Whole fish | Remove heads and skin, then fillet; bread and deep-fry or sauté |
| Skate (ray) | Local waters | Usually sold in pieces | Remove fins and skin, if necessary; marinate overnight in brine or acidulated water; poach or sauté |
| Squid (calamari) | Local waters | Whole, cleaned fish | Stuff bodies and bake; or cut into rings and deep-fry, sauté or stew in sauce; or poach and serve cold in salad |
| Tilapia (St. Peter's fish) | Cultivated fish, mostly from Israel but increasingly from Latin America and United States farms | Fillets | Broiled, sautéed or steamed |

JAN. 8

## A guide to fast-food nutrition

Estimated nutritional content of typical fast-food meals

| Company: Meal | Calories | Fat (tsp.) | Sugar (tsp.) | Sodium (mg.) |
|---|---|---|---|---|
| Wendy's: Double cheeseburger, fries, shake | 1,380 | 21 | 10 | 1,410 |
| Long John Silver's: Fish and More, soft drink | 1,096 | 17 | 8 | 2,123 |
| McDonald's: Chicken McNuggets, fries, vanilla shake | 888 | 11 | 10 | 835 |
| Burger King: Whopper, onion rings, medium Pepsi | 1,071 | 15 | 8 | 1,433 |
| Kentucky Fried Chicken: Extra Crispy dinner (dark meat), soft drink | 909 | 16 | 9 | 1,480 |

Sources: The companies

JAN. 12

## Oyster Varieties: Coast to Coast to Coast

The following are some of the oyster varieties available, if often on a limited basis, in New York restaurants and oyster bars. Prices depend on availability in the market as well as the location and style of the restaurant, but they range from around $1.15 each for local bluepoints to $1.65 for the rare Olympias.

Fishmongers usually handle only local oysters, mainly bluepoints, but a few will have a small selection from other areas.

### From Maine

**Belons:** flat shells, medium-size, very succulent with a briny, tidewater fragrance and a sharp, metallic tang; very good and constant supply, often found at better fishmongers and frequently in restaurants.

### From Cape Cod

**Chathams:** wild oysters, similar in their sweet, briny flavor to Wellfleets and Cotuits.

**Cotuits:** salty, sweet, fresh, clean taste; cultivated oysters in very limited supply.

**Wellfleets:** deep, cupped shells; for many, a superb oyster, meaty and sweetly fragrant, with a briny, seashore flavor.

### From Long Island

**Bluepoints:** medium-size, plump, sweet and, for many New Yorkers, the quintessential oyster; carried by most good fishmongers and at most oyster bars.

**Box oysters:** very large and meaty, for some consumers uncomfortably so; similar in flavor to bluepoints but less interesting; found in oyster bars.

**Wild Long Island oysters:** occasionally available, not dissimilar to bluepoints, but more pronounced in flavor; from the few remaining beds of what was once a tremendous wild resource.

### From New Jersey

**Port Norris:** New Jersey oyster beds have been devastated by the oyster parasite, MSX; Port Norris is one of the few places left from which oysters are harvested; plump with a bland but pleasantly brackish flavor.

### From Chesapeake Bay

**Chesapeakes:** Though severely decimated by MSX, the oyster harvest in the bay and its estuaries continues. Chesapeake is a generic term for oysters from the region, which are usually flat-shelled with a tangy, lightly metallic flavor and silky texture.

**Chincoteagues:** plump with a smooth shell, mild and sweet in flavor, pleasantly astringent, with metallic overtones.

**Kent Islands:** very salty, briny flavor with hint of sweetness.

### From the Gulf of Mexico

**Apalachicolas** (Florida): heavy shells; plump, pale oysters; light, subtle flavor with hints of copper; in limited supply because of storm damage to beds, but occasionally found in restaurants.

**Lake Borgnes** (Louisiana): round, curved shell; very mild, almost bland flavor; available in a few oyster bars.

### From the West Coast

**Golden Mantles** (British Columbia): large, meaty oysters with characteristic yellow-ochre stripe around the edge; variant of the Japanese Pacific oyster.

**Pacifics, or Japanese:** large with rippled shell; plump, fresh-tasting but with, for some, unpleasantly metallic aftertaste.

**Olympias:** native to the northern Pacific coast; very small, tender, sweet, briny and delicious. Rare but occasionally found in better oyster bars and restaurants.

**Westcott Bay Petites:** type of Japanese oyster, harvested small, with a fresh, scalloplike flavor in a beautiful rippled white porcelain-appearing shell.

### Other Areas

Oysters from the Canadian Maritime provinces are in short supply now, since the northern estuaries are frozen. Once they start to thaw, in late April or early May, however, look for Caraquets from New Brunswick, Bedora Lakes from Nova Scotia and Malpeques from Prince Edward Island.

A few Malpeques reach New York markets in the winter and should be sought out for their succulent texture and fresh salt tang.

Flying Foods, the wholesaler in Long Island City, Queens, imports New Zealand oysters, which are small and very flavorful, and occasionally a few other oyster varieties from foreign waters. They are found only in restaurants with fairly extensive selections.

MARCH 5

## Exercise and longevity

How calories are used by a 154-pound person

| Activities | Calories per hour |
|---|---|
| Strolling at 1 mph | 120–150 |
| Level walking at 2 mph<br>Level cycling at 5 mph | 150–240 |
| Mopping floors<br>Bowling | 240–300 |
| Tennis (doubles)<br>Raking leaves or hoeing | 300–360 |
| Disco dancing<br>Roller skating | 360–420 |
| Downhill skiing (light)<br>Splitting wood<br>Shoveling snow | 420–480 |
| Basketball<br>Jogging at 5 mph | 480–600 |
| Running at 5.5 mph<br>Cycling at 13 mph | 600–660 |
| Competitive squash<br>Cross-country skiing at 5 or more mph | More than 600 |

A continuing study of 17,000 Harvard alumni indicates that moderate exercise can significantly increase life expectancy. According to the study, which appears in the latest issue of *The New England Journal of Medicine*, men who participated weekly in activities such as walking, stair climbing and sports that used 2,000 calories or more had death rates one quarter to one third lower than those in the study who were least active. Furthermore, the death rate of older alumni who participated in the most activity was half that of those who were least active.

Source: American Heart Association

MARCH 9

## Guess Who Came to Dinner

*DINNER
Honoring
The Right Honorable
The Prime Minister of Canada
and Mrs. Mulroney*

*Angel Hair Pasta with Seafood
Romano Cheese Sauce*

*Supreme of Chicken Vol-au-Vent
Fresh Asparagus Polonaise*

*Fennel and Red Leaf Lettuce
Chèvre Cheese
Melba Toast*

*Pistachio Marquise
Petits Four*

*Sonoma-Cutrer Chardonnay 1983
Leardini Pinot Noir 1983
Schramsberg Crémant Demi Sec 1982*

*THE WHITE HOUSE
Tuesday March 18, 1986*

WASHINGTON, March 18—Following is the list of people invited to the White House dinner tonight for Prime Minister Brian Mulroney of Canada and his wife, Mila.

**Canadian Party**
Alan Gotlieb, the Canadian Ambassador, and his wife, Sandra.
Robert Anderson, of the M. A. Hanna Company, and his wife, Marjorie.
Jonathan Deitcher, of Dominion Securities Pitfield, Montreal, and his wife, Dianne.
Moses and Phyllis Deitcher, Montreal.
Paul Desmarais, of Power Corporation of Canada, and his wife, Jacqueline.
F. Ross Johnson, president, R. J. Reynolds Industries, and his wife, Laurie.
Robert Shea, of Shea Financial Group, and his wife, Gertrude.

**U.S. Guests**
Prince Karim Aga Khan and Princess Salimah Aga Khan.
Prince Sadruddin Aga Khan and Princess Catherine Aga Khan.
Dr. Giovanni Agnelli, chairman of Fiat, and Donna Marella Agnelli.
Dr. John M. Albertine, vice chairman, Farley Industries, and his wife, Mona.
Nelson and Mildred Benton, of Washington.
Winton M. Blount, Jr., chairman, Blount Inc. and former Postmaster General, and his wife, Carolyn.
Health and Human Services Secretary Otis R. Bowen and his wife, Rose.
William F. Buckley, Jr., editor in chief, *The National Review,* and his wife, Patricia.
L. Keith Bulen and Sandra M. Conovan, International Joint Commission for the United States and Canada.
Chief Justice Warren E. Burger and his wife, Elvera.
Richard R. Burt, the Ambassador to West Germany, and his wife, Gahl.
Vice President and Mrs. Bush.
Former Representative James M. Collins of Dallas and his wife, Dee.
Representative Robert W. Davis of Michigan and his wife, Marty.
Sidney Earl Dove, chairman, American Trucking Association, and his wife, Margaret.
Arthur Erickson, architect of the new Canadian Embassy.
Raymond F. Farley, president, S. C. Johnson & Sons Inc., and his wife, Mary.
Rafael Franchi, chairman, Republican National Hispanic Assembly for Virginia, and his wife, Mercedes.
Nicholas Gage, the author, and his wife, Joan.
Senator Jake Garn of Utah and his wife, Kathleen.
Frank Gifford, the sports announcer, and his wife, Astrid.
Cynthia Gregory, the ballerina, and Hilary Miller.
Michael Huffington, of Houston.
R. L. Ireland 3d, of Brown Brothers Harriman & Company, and his wife, Jacqueline.
Norma Kamali, the fashion designer, and Crist L. Zois.
Dr. Jerome Karle, 1985 Nobel Prize winner for chemistry, and his wife, Isabella.
William and Marianthi Lansdale, of Huntington Harbor, Calif.
Representative Romano L. Mazzoli of Kentucky and his wife, Helen.
Senator Mitch McConnell of Kentucky and Pam Schultz.
Larry Mizel, of Mountain Financial Services, and his wife, Carol.
Allen E. Murray, president and chairman, Mobil Corporation, and his wife, Patricia.
Kate Nelligan, actress.
Thomas M. T. Niles, the Ambassador to Canada, and his wife, Carroll.
Burl Osborne, president/editor, *Dallas Morning News,* and his wife, Betty.
Catherine Oxenberg, actress.
Mollie Parnis, fashion designer.
Walter Payton, the Chicago Bears running back, and his wife, Connie.

Ronald O. Perelman, chairman, Revlon Inc. and MacAndrews & Forbes Group Inc., and his wife, Claudia.
Christopher Plummer, actor, and his wife, Elaine.
John M. Poindexter, assistant to the President for national security affairs, and his wife, Linda.
Edmund T. Pratt, Jr., chairman, Pfizer Inc., and his wife, Jeanette.
Maureen Reagan and Dennis Revell.
Donald T. Regan, the White House chief of staff, and his wife, Ann.
Rozanne L. Ridgway, Assistant Secretary of State for European and Canadian Affairs, and Capt. Theodore Deming of the Coast Guard.
Selwa Roosevelt, the Chief of Protocol, and her husband, Archibald B. Roosevelt, Jr.
Representative Toby Roth of Wisconsin and his wife, Barbara.
Albert E. and Cynthia Schwabacher, of San Francisco.
Secretary of State George P. Shultz and his wife, Obie.
Arianna Stassinopoulos, author.
Alfred Stern, director, New York Film Festival, and his wife, Joanne, president, International Council, Museum of Modern Art.
Rosalyn Tureck, concert pianist performing for the occasion, and her guest, Diana Kitch.
Adm. James D. Watkins, chief of naval operations, and his wife, Sheila.
Thomas Wendel, history professor and chairman, Beethoven Society, and his wife, Charlotte.

MARCH 19

## Some summer sports: How they rate for fitness

The President's Council on Physical Fitness asked seven medical experts to rate the following summer activities on their effectiveness in promoting fitness. Their evaluations of each sport or exercise are based on a minimum vigorous work-out of 30 minutes to an hour, four times a week. The highest rating for effectiveness in a single category is 21, based on a scale of 0 to 3 points from each expert.

| Exercise | Cardiovascular endurance (stamina) | Muscular strength | Flexibility | Total |
|---|---|---|---|---|
| Bicycling | 19 | 16 | 9 | 44 |
| Golf* | 8 | 9 | 8 | 25 |
| Handball | 19 | 15 | 16 | 50 |
| Jogging | 21 | 17 | 9 | 47 |
| Roller skating | 18 | 15 | 13 | 46 |
| Softball | 6 | 7 | 9 | 22 |
| Squash | 19 | 15 | 16 | 50 |
| Swimming | 21 | 14 | 15 | 50 |
| Tennis | 16 | 14 | 14 | 44 |
| Walking | 13 | 11 | 7 | 31 |

*These ratings are based on the use of a golf cart or caddy. If the links are walked, the fitness value grows appreciably.
Chart courtesy of the President's Council on Physical Fitness and Sports.

MARCH 23

# Wine: State of the States

**By FRANK PRIAL**

It had to happen, I guess. A San Francisco hotel has put together a wine list that is truly American. It includes wines from 34 states. Yes, 34 states. Everyone knows about California and New York, and quite a few know now that they make wine in Oregon and Washington. But Wisconsin? And Georgia? And Hawaii and Idaho and New Jersey?

By my most recent count, wine is made commercially in 37 states. Don't expect to find them all at your corner store. Most of them are sold exclusively in the state in which they are made; in fact, a lot of them are sold only at the back door of the winery. But they're out there, and the Mark Hopkins Inter-Continental has done a service to the wine business by bringing so many of them together.

According to Marcel van Aelst, the Mark Hopkins general manager, the idea for the all-American wine list developed out of a party last year for Leon D. Adams, the grand old man of wine in America. The occasion was a party to celebrate the publication of the third edition of Mr. Adams's book, *The Wines of America*.

"We were able to assemble wines from just about every state for the party," Mr. van Aelst says, "but we soon discovered that getting a couple of bottles for a tasting and stocking the wines for a restaurant were two different things."

In fact, it took the hotel staff a year to gather the wines they wanted. "By law, we couldn't buy them ourselves," Mr. van Aelst says. "We had to go through a broker here. What made it difficult was the fact that many of these wineries are so small that they had had no experience in shipping out of state. In some cases, they were out of the wine by the time they were ready to ship it to us."

Mr. van Aelst says that he wasn't sure who was more thrilled about his wine list: guests discovering wine from their home states or the small wineries excited about having their products in a famous hotel. "They write to us and ask for copies of the wine list," he says. "Most of the guests are astonished to find that wine is made in their state. They end up insisting that their California friends try it."

What the Mark Hopkins list doesn't show is what depth some of the states have when it comes to wine. Virginia, for example, had 21 wineries at last count; Idaho, 6; Florida, 5; Mississippi, 4; and Texas, 13. Washington has 37, according to Anthony Dias Blue's book *American Wine*. Ohio has 33, Mr. Blue says, and Oregon, 31. The point being this: winemaking is no fluke; it is a serious and, in many instances, successful business.

And now for the bad news: a lot of this wine is, by any reasonable standards, rather poor stuff. Sometimes wineries are small and obscure because they are new or because they choose to be. Sometimes they are small and obscure because they deserve to be. The wines at the Mark Hopkins have been gathered together to prove a point and because it was possible to do so, not because they represent the best America has to offer.

The Mark Hopkins list says some interesting things about wine in America—aside from the fact that so many people make it. There are, for example, 19 vinifera wines on the list, 11 of them chardonnays and four of them cabernets. Twenty years ago, experts said America would never produce fine chardonnay, not even in California. Now we make it not only in California, but in Oregon, Washington, Idaho, Connecticut, Virginia, New York, Colorado, Michigan, New Mexico, New Jersey, Ohio, Rhode Island and Texas, among others.

I have nothing against the late Konstantin Frank's Rkaziteli, made from a grape he liked in his native Russia, but I wouldn't consider it representative of the best New York can do. Better a fine Baco Noir from Mark Miller's Benmarl, in the Hudson Valley, or a cabernet from the Hargrave Vineyard on Long Island.

As for California, I would not have used two wines from the Napa Valley, excellent though they both are. Such an innovative list deserves something from one of the newer regions—Eldorado County, perhaps, or Santa Barbara.

The Sparkling Scuppernong, the Magnolia Special Reserve and similar exotica I will leave to proud citizens of the states in which those wines are made. There are times when healthy chauvinism is more important than a sophisticated palate. MARCH 30

## The Mark Hopkins List

Here, for the record, is the current list at the Mark Hopkins. It applies to the wines available in the hotel's Nob Hill Restaurant:

**Alabama:** Perdido Vineyards Magnolia Special Reserve.
**Arizona:** Sonita Vineyards Chenin Blanc, 1984.
**Arkansas:** Wiederkehr Wine Cellars Cabernet Sauvignon, 1982.
**California:** Robert Mondavi Reserve Cabernet Sauvignon, 1979; Cakebread Cellars Chardonnay, 1983.
**Colorado:** Colorado Mountain Vineyards Mesa County Chardonnay, 1982.
**Connecticut:** Haight Vineyard Covertside White Table Wine.
**Florida:** Lafayette Vineyards Stover Special Reserve.
**Georgia:** Chateau Elan Muscadine.
**Hawaii:** Erdman-Tedeschi Vineyard Blanc de Noirs.
**Idaho:** Ste. Chapelle Vineyards Chardonnay, 1981.
**Illinois:** Galena Cellars Marechal Foch.
**Indiana:** St. Wendel Cellars Marechal Foch.
**Maryland:** Boordy Vineyards Vidal Blanc Semi-Dry, 1984.
**Massachusetts:** Chicama Vineyards Sea Mist Sparkling Wine Brut.
**Michigan:** Chateau Grand Traverse Chardonnay, 1981.
**Minnesota:** Alexis Bailly Vineyards Leon Millot, 1983.
**Mississippi:** Rushing Estate, Mississippi Delta Noble, 1984.
**Missouri:** Stone Hill Estate Norton Private Reserve.
**New Jersey:** Tweksbury Wine Cellars Gewurztraminer, 1983.
**New Mexico:** Binns Vineyards Private Reserve White Zinfandel.
**New York:** Woodbury Vineyards Estate Chardonnay, 1981; Vinifera Wine Cellars Rkaziteli, 1980.
**North Carolina:** Duplin Wine Cellars Sparkling Scuppernong, 1983.
**Ohio:** Markko Vineyard Chardonnay.
**Oklahoma:** Cimarron Cellars, Marechal Foch.
**Oregon:** The Eyrie Vineyards Pinot Noir.
**Pennsylvania:** Naylor Wine Cellars Chambourcin, 1982.
**Rhode Island:** Prudence Island Vineyards Chardonnay, 1982.
**South Carolina:** Truluck Vineyards Chambourcin, 1982.
**Tennessee:** Highland Manor Winery Chardonnay, 1982.
**Texas:** Llano Estacado Winery Chardonnay, 1983.
**Virginia:** Ingleside Plantation Chardonnay, 1984.
**Washington:** Chateau Ste. Michelle Cabernet Sauvignon Reserve, 1980; Preston Wine Cellars Chardonnay, 1980.
**West Virginia:** West Whitehill Winery Highland Red.
**Wisconsin:** Wollersheim Domaine Reserve Red, 1982.

MARCH 30

# Moderate Level of Exercise Brings Life-Saving Benefits

By JANE E. BRODY

Many people were pleasantly surprised by a recent finding that demanding exercise routines are not needed to reap the life-saving benefits of physical activity. Apparently you don't have to run marathons or even minimarathons to be fit. According to the new study of 17,000 Harvard alumni, a brisk three-mile "daily constitutional" should do the trick.

The study found that men who participated in moderate activity, such as walking, climbing stairs and sports that used 2,000 or more calories a week, had death rates one quarter to one third lower than their sedentary counterparts. The life-saving benefits of exercise peaked at expenditures of 3,500 calories a week, beyond which there was, in some cases, a slight detrimental effect.

But how does a person who has had trouble enough learning the caloric content of different foods begin to estimate the caloric value of different physical activities?

There are charts galore showing, for example, that to work off one piece of pecan pie, walk fast for two hours; to work off one pork chop, jog half an hour; to work off one small milk shake, bicycle 50 minutes, and so on. Such charts, however, are often misleading because the health benefits of exercise go far beyond the calories used during the activity and because many factors affect the number of calories used during various activities.

The Harvard alumni study, a continuing project under the direction of Dr. Ralph S. Paffenbarger, Jr., of Stanford University, had previously shown that moderate exercise could help prevent heart attacks. Exercise can lower blood pressure and total serum cholesterol while increasing the levels of the protective cholesterol carrier known as HDL, or high-density lipoprotein. Regular exercise helps the heart pump more blood with less effort and allows it to rest longer between beats. It aids the heart indirectly by increasing the ability of muscle cells to extract and use the oxygen delivered by the blood. Exercise also has a calming effect on the body, which can help counter stress.

But men and women do not die by heart attacks alone. The new study showed that overall mortality was significantly reduced by exercise. Another recently completed study at Harvard seems to support that notion: Researchers found that athletic women were less likely than sedentary women to develop breast cancer. The reason may be that active women have a smaller percentage of fat in their bodies; fatty tissue releases cancer-promoting estrogen into the bloodstream.

Exercise helps ward off adult-onset diabetes, strokes, osteoporosis and depression. It delays aging by slowing the decline in certain body functions, such as reaction time and responses to visual stimuli.

Exercise can counter obesity, not only by increasing caloric use but by raising the metabolism so that more calories are used during activities throughout the day, including sleep.

Many factors contribute to the number of calories used to perform a particular activity. Among them are these:

• How big you are. The more you weigh, the more calories your body must use to move around. A 175-pound person who plays recreational singles tennis for one hour uses about 70 calories more than a tennis player who weighs 120 pounds. The heavy and the light alike, however, can increase the caloric value of exercise by using a temporary weight, such as hand or ankle weights or a backpack.

• How hard and fast you perform the activity. A 60-minute stroll at two miles an hour costs a 120-pound person 165 calories, while a brisk walk at 3.5 miles an hour would use 280 calories. Jogging at 5.5 miles an hour requires 585 calories. About 100 calories are used per mile, whether the mile is covered by walking briskly or jogging.

In tennis, caloric use can vary dramatically with your skill and energy: how hard you hit the ball, how much you scramble for each shot, whether you are playing doubles or singles and how much time you spend picking up balls and chatting are all salient factors.

In swimming, caloric use depends on the stroke used and the swimmer's speed and skill.

The caloric values of all forms of exercise are also influenced by air (or water) temperature and how heavily you are dressed. Exercising in the cold when lightly dressed uses more calories because the body is also trying to keep warm.

Start by picking an activity or two you enjoy, and build gradually to the desired level. Too much too soon can result in soreness or injury. If you have been sedentary for years and are over 35, consult a physician before beginning a vigorous exercise program. This is especially important if you are at risk of heart disease—if, for example, you smoke, have high blood pressure, elevated serum cholesterol levels or a family history of heart disease.

You don't have to use up the 2,000 to 3,500 calories in a single activity. Indeed, injury and boredom are less likely if you mix activities, preferably those that exercise different muscle groups, such as walking and swimming.

Whenever possible, make exercise part of a social or athletic event, such as a hike, canoe trip or tennis match. Remember, too, that exercise can easily be fit into the busiest routines —start by walking all or part way to some destinations and by climbing stairs instead of riding elevators and escalators.   APRIL 9

## How many calories a minute?

The following table shows the calories used per minute by people of different weights performing different activities at varying rates. The values are determined by measuring the amount of oxygen used. This is an indirect measure of the amount of muscle fuel, or calories, consumed. To use the table, find your weight range and multiply the caloric value given for one minute of activity by the number of minutes you perform the activity. For weights not listed, estimate the value from the ones given.

| Activity | Weight in Pounds | | | |
|---|---|---|---|---|
| | 105–115 | 127–137 | 160–170 | 182–192 |
| Aerobic dancing | 5.83 | 6.58 | 7.83 | 8.58 |
| Badminton, singles | 4.58 | 5.16 | 6.16 | 6.75 |
| Baseball, fielder | 3.66 | 4.16 | 4.91 | 5.41 |
| Basketball | | | | |
|   Half court | 7.25 | 8.25 | 9.75 | 10.75 |
|   Full court | 9.75 | 11.16 | 13.16 | 14.50 |
| Bicycling | | | | |
|   5.5 m.p.h. | 3.16 | 3.58 | 4.25 | 4.66 |
|   10.0 m.p.h. | 5.41 | 6.16 | 7.33 | 7.91 |
|   13.0 m.p.h. | 8.58 | 9.75 | 11.50 | 12.66 |
|   Stationary, 10 m.p.h. | 5.50 | 6.25 | 7.41 | 8.16 |
|   Stationary, 20 m.p.h. | 11.66 | 13.25 | 15.58 | 17.16 |
| Calisthenics | 3.91 | 4.50 | 7.33 | 7.91 |
| Dancing | | | | |
|   Rock | 3.25 | 3.75 | 4.41 | 4.91 |
|   Square | 5.50 | 6.25 | 7.41 | 8.00 |
| Gardening, weeding and digging | 5.08 | 5.75 | 6.83 | 7.50 |
| Golf, hand cart | 3.25 | 3.75 | 4.41 | 4.91 |
| Handball, competitive | 7.83 | 8.91 | 10.50 | 11.58 |
| Hiking, 20-pound pack | | | | |
|   2 m.p.h. | 3.91 | 4.50 | 5.25 | 5.83 |
|   4 m.p.h. | 5.91 | 6.66 | 7.91 | 8.75 |
| Jogging | | | | |
|   5.5 m.p.h. | 8.58 | 9.75 | 11.50 | 12.66 |
|   6.5 m.p.h. | 8.90 | 10.20 | 12.00 | 13.20 |
|   8.0 m.p.h. | 10.40 | 11.90 | 14.10 | 15.50 |
|   9.0 m.p.h. | 12.00 | 13.80 | 16.20 | 17.80 |
| Lawn mowing, power | 3.50 | 4.00 | 4.75 | 5.16 |
| Rope skipping | | | | |
|   55 per minute | 6.66 | 7.58 | 9.00 | 9.91 |
|   95 per minute | 8.58 | 9.75 | 11.50 | 12.66 |
|   135 per minute | 15.66 | 17.83 | 21.08 | 23.25 |
| Rowing machine | | | | |
|   Easy | 3.91 | 4.50 | 5.25 | 5.83 |
|   Vigorous | 8.58 | 9.75 | 11.50 | 12.66 |
| Sawing wood, hand | 5.08 | 5.83 | 6.83 | 7.58 |
| Sexual intercourse, active partner | 3.91 | 4.50 | 5.25 | 5.83 |
| Skating | | | | |
|   Leisure | 4.58 | 5.16 | 6.16 | 8.75 |
|   Vigorous | 8.08 | 9.25 | 10.91 | 12.00 |
| Skiing | | | | |
|   Downhill | 7.75 | 8.83 | 10.41 | 11.50 |
|   Cross-country, 5 m.p.h. | 9.16 | 10.41 | 12.25 | 13.33 |
|   Cross-country, 9 m.p.h. | 13.08 | 14.83 | 17.58 | 19.33 |
| Snow shoveling | | | | |
|   Light | 7.91 | 9.08 | 10.75 | 11.83 |
|   Heavy | 13.75 | 15.66 | 18.50 | 20.41 |
| Stair climbing | | | | |
|   Normal | 5.90 | 6.70 | 7.90 | 8.80 |
|   Upstairs rapidly | 8.70 | 14.80 | 17.60 | 19.30 |
| Swimming, crawl | | | | |
|   20 yards per minute | 3.91 | 4.50 | 5.25 | 5.33 |
|   40 yards per minute | 7.83 | 8.91 | 10.50 | 11.58 |
|   55 yards per minute | 11.00 | 12.50 | 14.75 | 16.25 |
| Tennis, competitive | | | | |
|   Singles | 7.83 | 8.91 | 10.50 | 11.58 |
|   Doubles | 5.58 | 6.33 | 7.50 | 8.25 |
| Trampolining | 10.33 | 11.75 | 13.91 | 15.33 |
| Volleyball, competitive | 7.83 | 8.91 | 10.50 | 11.58 |

|  | Weight in Pounds | | | |
| --- | --- | --- | --- | --- |
| Activity | 105–115 | 127–137 | 160–170 | 182–192 |
| Walking | | | | |
| 2 m.p.h. | 2.40 | 2.80 | 3.30 | 3.60 |
| 3 m.p.h. | 3.90 | 4.50 | 5.30 | 5.80 |
| 4 m.p.h. | 4.50 | 5.20 | 6.10 | 6.80 |

Adapted from *Diet Free* by Dr. Charles T. Kuntzleman (Rodale Press, 1981).

APRIL 9

# Great Trees

By ERIK ECKHOLM

The Louis Vieux, reigning king of American elms has been dethroned.

The emphatic defeat of the 99-foot tree in Kansas by a 125-foot elm in Virginia is the most surprising news from this year's reckoning of the country's largest trees.

Word of the Kansas tree's loss of status came in the American Forestry Association's 1986 register of the largest living specimen of each of the 650-odd species of trees in the nation. For nearly half a century the association has kept score on the giants, a search for arboreal greatness intended to build appreciation for trees of all sizes.

The Louis Vieux, named for a 19th-century pioneer who once owned it, is so admired in its prairie homeland that it was officially designated a one-tree state forest.

Inspired by the toppling of this legendary champion, tree hunters, hobbyists who search for record-breaking trees in the interests of conservation and personal glory, carry on their quest. All across the country, big-tree hunters scan the treetops for potential champions wherever they walk, run, drive, canoe or fly.

New York has 13 national champions, but they are not always the most romantic of species. One is the nation's largest poison sumac, a 16-foot menace to unwary tree climbers, on Robins Island in Peconic Bay, Suffolk County.

In the nation's big-tree leagues, New York's standing wilts by comparison with the leaders: Florida has 99 champions, Michigan 75 and California 68.

But Florida has an unfair advantage, observed Paul W. Thompson, the Michigan coordinator. "They have a hundred species down there that occur nowhere else in the country," he said. "All they have to do is find a specimen, and it has no competition."

The biggest tree in the country is the General Sherman, California's famous giant sequoia. It is 275 feet tall, has a girth of 83 feet and a crown spread of 107 feet.

The biggest is not the highest, an honor borne by a coast redwood, also in California, that at 362 feet is 57 feet higher than the Statue of Liberty.

It is 87 feet higher than the General Sherman but has a thinner trunk and a less impressive upper spread, for fewer points in the scoring system. Total points are determined by adding the tree's height in feet, its girth in inches and one fourth of its average crown spread in feet.

Champions come in all shapes and sizes: the littlest is a 13-foot American snowbell in Texas with a girth of just 8 inches and a spread of 15 feet.

APRIL 20

## The biggest trees In America

Champion trees from selected species. Circumference is measured in inches 4½ feet above ground. Total points are figured by adding height in feet, circumference, and one-fourth of crown spread in feet.

| Species | Height (feet) | Circumference | Spread (feet) | Total points | Location |
|---|---|---|---|---|---|
| Apple (common) | 35 | 132 | 44 | 178 | Santa Fe, N.M. |
| Ash (white) | 95 | 304 | 82 | 420 | Palisades, N.Y. |
| Avocado | 42 | 87 | 54 | 142 | Hallandale, Fla. |
| Beech (American) | 130 | 222 | 75 | 371 | Ashtabula County, Ohio |
| Birch (gray) | 59 | 63 | 43 | 133 | East Windsor, Conn. |
| Cherry (black) | 93 | 222 | 122 | 346 | Allegan County, Mich. |
| Douglas Fir (coast) | 221 | 545 | 61 | 781 | Olympic Nat. Park, Wash. |
| Elm (American) | 125 | 284 | 124 | 440 | Southampton Co., Va. |
| Eucalyptus (longbeak) | 171 | 178 | 68 | 386 | Kern County, Calif. |
| Hickory (sand) | 94 | 133 | 86 | 248 | Vineland, N.J. |
| Locust (black) | 96 | 280 | 92 | 399 | Dansville, N.Y. |
| Magnolia (southern) | 86 | 243 | 96 | 363 | Bladen Co., N.C. |
| Maple (bigleaf) | 101 | 419 | 90 | 542 | Jewell, Ore. |
| Mesquite (velvet) | 55 | 180 | 76 | 254 | Coronado Nat. Forest, Ariz. |
| Oak (white) | 107 | 414 | 145 | 557 | Wye Mills, Md. |
| Peach | 57 | 77 | 42 | 144 | Sacramento, Calif. |
| Pine (ponderosa) | 223 | 287 | 68 | 527 | Plumas, Calif. |
| Poison Sumac | 16 | 34 | 17 | 54 | Robins Island, N.Y. |
| Redwood (coast) | 362 | 629 | 74 | 1,010 | Humboldt Redwoods State Park, Calif. |
| Rhododendron (rosebay) | 40 | 25 | 22 | 70 | Ocones Co., S.C. |
| Sassafras | 76 | 253 | 69 | 346 | Owensboro, Ky. |
| Sequoia (giant) | 275 | 998 | 107 | 1,300 | Sequoia Nat. Park, Calif. |
| Spruce (blue) | 148 | 167 | 34 | 324 | Rio Blanca Co. Colo. |
| Sycamore | 129 | 582 | 105 | 737 | Jeromesville, Ohio |
| Walnut (black) | 122 | 271 | 134 | 426 | Humboldt Co., Calif. |
| Willow (weeping) | 97 | 286 | 106 | 410 | Asheville, N.C. |
| Yellow Poplar | 124 | 363 | 122 | 516 | Bedford, Va. |

Source: American Forestry Association

## Metropolitan Diary

Reading about the recent disbarring of a rogue lawyer, the thought occurred to Gary S. Novick, M.D.: If he were to be found incompetent as a physician, could he then be dismembered by his peers? This, of course, led Dr. Novick to compile a list of terms describing the violent act of dismissal peculiar to particular trades or professions.

Judge—Disrobed
Hairdresser—Distressed
Banker—Disinterested
Team Owner—Disenfranchised
Shepherd—Distended
Magician—Disillusioned
Gambler—Discarded
Secretary—Defiled
Furniture Refinisher—Distained
Mountain Climber—Disinclined
Knight—Demoted
Accountant—Disfigured
U.N. Representative—Disassembled
Jockey—Distracted
Detective—Dissolved
Waiter—Disordered
Calligrapher—Described
Cleaner—Depressed
Electrician—Delighted
Innkeeper—Dislodged
Cowboy—Deranged

APRIL 30

## Metropolitan Diary

Follow-up on Gary S. Novick's original list of terms that describe the act of dismissal peculiar to particular trades, professions or people. These, from David I. Obel, Vernon D. MacLaren, Morrie Goldfischer, Marcia Lloyd, Susan W. Buckley, Hara Reiser, J. Louise Soule, Jon Kalos, Ellen Cohn, Albert Komishane, Esther and Maria Castano, Herman Schmertz, Ron Meyers, Eva Neisser, Peter M. Spinner and Tom Bradshaw.

Musician—Disconcerted
Pig farmer—Disgruntled
Florist—Deflowered
Cardiologist—Disheartened
Volcanologist—Disrupted
Pastry chef—Deserted
Camp counselor—Debunked
Weather forecaster—Disgusted
Actor—Departed
Pants presser—Decreased
Skirt maker—Depleted
Cantor—Disenchanted
Quilt maker—Dispatched
Feminist—Dismssed
Manicurist—Defiled
Butcher—Delivered
Detective—Dissolved
Fisherman—Debated
Seismologist—Defaulted
Podiatrist—Defeated
Jim Palmer—Debriefed
Hamlet—Disdained

JUNE 4

## Power Anyone? Tennis Is "In"

### By BARBARA GAMAREKIAN

**W**ASHINGTON, May 10—Power equals success in the nation's capital, and as the czar of Washington tennis, Allie Ritzenberg wields his own brand of power. For tennis is the hot game here these days, and he is the man who signals thumbs up or thumbs down on membership in St. Albans Tennis Club, one of the city's most exclusive.

The No. 1 court is, of course, the one at 1600 Pennsylvania Avenue. Nothing beats playing tennis in the shadow of the White House. But St. Albans, a club run by Mr. Ritzenberg that is owned by and affiliated with a private school for boys on the National Cathedral grounds, comes a close second. Some wait as long as 10 years to get membership. "I got in when I was in the White House," said Jack Valenti, head of the Motion Picture Association of America, who first came to Washington as a White House aide in the Johnson Administration. "The easiest way to get into any club in this town is when you are in government, in Congress or the Cabinet, or as a White House aide."

What has happened in recent years, he said, "is that you now have a 7 A.M. tennis group that is heavyweight government—it's a convivial game and it's fast for busy, important people. Very few high-ranking government people can take time out to play golf; if you want to stay alive socially with them, you've got to play tennis."  MAY 11

## Allie Ritzenberg's Rating of Washington Tennis Players

**Best Disciplined:** William H. Webster, Director, F.B.I.
**Best at Analyzing Opponent's Game:** Walter Mondale
**Best Footwork:** George P. Shultz
**Best Ball Hawk:** Zbigniew Brzezinski
**Best Drop Shot:** Carl Rowan
**Most Versatile:** Representative Les Aspin
**Most Consistent:** the journalist Elizabeth Drew
**Best Touch:** the artist Sam Gilliam
**Most Probing:** the journalist Seymour Hersh
**Best Percentage Player:** Senator Paul Laxalt
**Toughest Fighter:** Senator Howard M. Metzenbaum
**Most Casual:** Senator John Warner
**Greatest Variety of Shots:** Senator John Heinz
**Most Promising:** Representative Timothy E. Wirth
**Best Dressed:** Katharine Graham
**Best Conditioned:** Joseph Califano
**Most Relaxed:** Nina Auchincloss Straight

MAY 11

# Lexicon

By DAVID E. ROSENBAUM

The prevailing wisdom in Washington is that sweeping changes in the Federal income tax system will be enacted before the end of the summer. In the meantime, however, there will be plenty of talk about tax rates and tax breaks as the legislation wends its way through the Senate and a House-Senate conference.

To understand the debate, it helps to understand some of the unusual jargon now current among tax writers and lobbyists.

Oilgas'n'timber—Always mentioned like this in one breath, these are the special interests most favored by the Senate Finance Committee. The panel's tax bill would repeal tax breaks enjoyed by most people and most other industries, but it would leave those of the oil, gas and timber industries basically intact.

Packwood—An intransitive verb meaning the act of changing one's position 180 degrees, as in, "I think the senator will Packwood on the Saudi arms sale." The verb entered common usage on Capitol Hill last month after Senator Bob Packwood of Oregon, the Republican who is chairman of the Finance Committee, scrapped his first tax plan, which entailed even more tax preferences than the existing law, and offered a new one that would remove most preferences.

Transition rule—The euphemism for a special tax break put in a bill to win a particular lawmaker's support. For example, to make sure that Representative Claude Pepper, the Florida Democrat who is chairman of the House Rules Committee, would be supportive, the House Ways and Means Committee adopted transition rules to help Mr. Pepper's constituents by providing special exemptions from the general tax rules for a new football stadium for the Miami Dolphins, a convention center on Miami Beach and a redevelopment project in Miami.

Zero out—The act of not paying any taxes. For example, the Packwood bill would continue to allow tax-exempt municipal bonds, and wealthy people could zero out if all their income came from such bonds. However, the bill's stiff minimum tax on corporations would prevent a profitable company like General Dynamics, which has used so many writeoffs that it has not paid taxes in years, from zeroing out any longer.

Gucci gantlet—The corridors outside the the House Ways and Means Committee and Senate Finance Committee meeting rooms where hundreds of lobbyists congregate while tax bills are being drafted in closed session.

The term refers to the fancy shoes (mostly tassled loafers) sported by nearly all the male lobbyists. MAY 19

# The Summer Insect Invasion; How to Control the Hordes

**By CALVIN SIMS**

Insects have been around longer, much longer, than humans have, and no household is going to win the war against them. But with the right tools and a little knowledge, individual battles can be won.

The arrival of rising temperatures and high humidity has increased the metabolism and activity of such pests as cockroaches, silverfish, moths, carpet beetles, flies and termites. For centuries, people have fought them with rocks, clubs, fire, shoes, dusts, sprays and traps. Pesticide experts say that when these efforts don't work, the householder has usually either failed to eliminate the source of the infestation or used the wrong pesticide.

"The first thing to do to get rid of unwanted bugs is to figure out what caused them—starting with sanitation," said Ed Raffensperger, a professor of entomology at Cornell University.

Pests invade the home in search of food, water and shelter, and loose garbage is a major attraction. The common house fly is attracted by garbage, manure, grass clippings and other decaying matter. When the food supply is cut off, the insects either die or seek provisions elsewhere. Many infestations can be eliminated by thorough cleaning.

In both apartments and homes, unsealed cracks and holes in walls and around pipes give pests easy access. Seal these entry points with steel wool or other flexible fireproof material, Dr. Raffensperger suggests. He said homeowners should clean regularly under kitchen and bathroom sinks, in food cabinets and in hard-to-reach cracks and crevices. In addition, he said, wipe niches around faucets and sink fixtures and stop all water leaks and drips. Most insects need a good water source to survive.

Dr. Raffensperger also recommended feeding pets during the day and removing dishes before night because many nocturnal pests, especially cockroaches, are attracted by a pet food dish left on the floor.

## What the bugs do and how to stop them

| Pest | Habits | Control |
|---|---|---|
| **Ants (carpenter)** Black, one-half to three-quarters inch long. Very common to Eastern and Midwestern United States. | These ants normally nest outdoors in trees, but some nest in structural wood that is moist and decaying. They do not eat wood but excavate it for nesting space, causing considerable damage. The ants feed on dead insects, pollen and household foods such as cookie crumbs, fruits, meat scraps and other sweets. | Try to find the nest even though this is difficult. Look for sawdust dropping from a beam or listen for rustling noises. If the nest is found, spray or dust with bendiocarb, malathion, propoxur, diazinon or chlorpyrifos. If nest cannot be found or ants persist, call an exterminator. |

| Pest | Habits | Control |
|---|---|---|
| **Ants (house)** Black, brown or red, usually wingless. They live in colonies with a complex division of labor. | Attracted from outdoors by greasy or sweet food. | First step is to find the nest by watching where they are coming from or where they are going after feeding. Apply insecticide to window frames, baseboards, cracks, around electrical outlets, plumbing and heating pipes, sinks, bathtubs, kitchen cupboards and any out-of-sight area where ants may enter. Chlorpyrifos, diazinon, malathion and propoxur are recommended. |
| **Bedbugs** Squat, oval and chestnut brown. | Bedbugs are active only at night, usually before dawn. During the day they hide in cracks and crevices in walls, floors, beds and furniture. Many live close to sleeping areas and attack humans. Their bite causes itching and burning sensations and a colorless lump. They enter the home on second hand articles or through wires, plumbing and gutters. | Treat cracks and crevices in floors, walls, baseboards, seams and bottoms of mattresses, furniture and other hiding places with a premium grade of malathion or pyrethrum. |
| **Beetles (carpet)** Black or variegated. | Carpet beetles are sometimes seen on window sills in the spring. Their larvae, which are covered with golden brown hair, feed on furs and woolens, in particular sweaters, fur coats and carpets. They prefer undisturbed areas and may feed on stored grain products, pollen and the corpses of other insects. They also eat synthetic fibers that have perspiration and food stains. | First line of defense is cleanliness. Carpets and clothing should be cleaned regularly, especially carpets, to prevent wool lint, a major food source, from accumulating. Use malathion, methoxychlor or diazinon. |
| **Beetles (powder post)** Small, brown and usually less than a quarter inch long. They attack seasoned wood. | These beetles breed in flooring, paneling, furniture and other wood. They can cause severe structural damage. Basements, barns and storage sheds are common places to find them. Their presence is indicated by small holes and fine sawdust. | Powder post beetles usually do not infest painted or varnished wood. Deodorized kerosene can be used to paint or spray the infested surface. In severe cases, an exterminator should be used. |

| Pest | Habits | Control |
|---|---|---|
| **Cockroaches**<br>Broad and flattened with six long legs | Cockroaches hide in cracks, crevices, and other dark places during the day and come out at night to feed. They prefer warm, moist places such as the kitchen and bathroom where there is a source of food, mainly garbage. Wet house plants, underneath appliances and wet clothes are prime nesting places. | Sanitation is the key to eliminating cockroaches. Clean up spilled foods, including crumbs, immediately; do not leave dirty dishes, and keep food boxes tightly closed. Effective insecticides are chlorpyrifos, diazinon, malathion and propoxur. Cockroach traps are also available. A mixture of boric acid and sugar or Combat bait trays can also be used. |
| **Fleas**<br>Small, dark brown, shorter than a quarter inch. | Fleas are usually more of a problem for pets than for humans. They attach themselves to pets to suck blood and lay eggs. The eggs fall off the animal into its bedding, the floor or furniture, where they develop into adults. Domestic fleas do not transmit disease but they do bite humans. Pets may develop allergies and diseases. | Use flea powder, spray, dip or shampoo on pet to eliminate fleas. For home, thoroughly vacuum rugs and floor and dispose of the vacuum bag. Then apply bendiocarb, chlorpyrifos, malathion or methoxychlor to kill the larvae. If fleas persist, call an exterminator. |
| **Flies (house)**<br>Four-winged insect with dark longitudinal stripes on middle body. | House flies are strongly suspected of transmitting disease. They breed and feed in large numbers in dumps, sewers, garbage, manure, grass and weed clippings and other decaying matter. | Do not allow materials where they breed and feed to accumulate. Keep trash can clean and tightly covered. Use window and door screens to keep them from entering home. For large numbers of flies in home, use aerosol spray labeled for flying insects. Pyrethrum or allethrin in a pressurized can or "No Pest" strips are recommended. |
| **Mosquitoes**<br>Biting insects that suck blood from humans. | Mosquitoes breed any place there is still water: old tires, drain spouts, a child's wading pool, street basins, etc. | Drain all water containers to prevent breeding. Use pyrethrum or allethrin or "No Pest" strips. |
| **Moths (clothes)**<br>Yellowish-tan or buff with one-half-inch wingspan. Larvae are usually whitish with dark heads. | Larvae feed on fabric containing wool or other animal fiber. Usually found in dark, undisturbed places, often where clothing is stored or beneath furniture. Some larvae spin a cocoon from the fibers they feed on, camouflaging themselves. Damage to material goes unnoticed until holes appear. | Protect uninfested goods with repellents such as naphthalene flakes or paradichlorobenzene crystals. Use malathion, methoxychlor or diazinon in infested areas. Vacuum wool lint from between floor boards. |

| Pest | Habits | Control |
|---|---|---|
| **Pests (cereal, pantry)** Indian meal moths, saw-toothed grain beetles, flour moths and weevils. | These insects attack cereals, flour, herbs, spices, dried fruits, dried dog food and fish food and other pantry items. | To stop these pests from spreading, destroy infested food and clean shelves and cupboards thoroughly. Remove food and dishes and treat corners with methoxychlor; malathion, propoxur or diazinon. Wait until surfaces dry before replacing contents. Keep fresh supplies in air-tight clear jars where larvae are easily noticeable. Keep pet food in tightly closed containers. |
| **Silverfish** Wingless with silver scales, long feelers and bristly tails. | Silverfish thrive in damp, dark places. They damage books and other paper products when they eat materials high in protein such as the starch in glues and pastes of books and wallpapers. They cause wallpaper to peel. Silverfish are active at night and hide during the day. | Methoxychlor, propoxur, diazinon or malathion should be applied to cracks and where pipes go through walls. |
| **Termites** Pale social insects with soft bodies and wings. | Termites destroy wood. They eat through wood leaving no exterior indication that they are present until the structure gives way. Wood in contact with soil is particularly susceptible, but termites sometimes build mud tunnels over obstacles to reach wood. | No insecticides available to consumers eliminate termites. See an exterminator immediately. |
| **Wasps and Hornets** Large winged insects with black and yellow stripes. | Usually seen near houses where they make a nest in a cavity of a wall or under the eaves or in a loft. They can be seen drinking nectar from flowers and the juices of ripe fruit. As a defense, they deliver a painful sting. | Exterminate nest at night when wasps are less aggressive. Use propoxur, carbaryl or malathion formulated in pressurized cans. |

This chart was prepared in collaboration with Carolyn Klass and Ed Raffensperger, Department of Entomology, Cornell University; Phil Koehler, United States Department of Agriculture Insects Affecting Man and Animals Research Center, Gainesville, Fla., and Stanley Green, University of Pennsylvania Cooperative Extension Service. All pesticides listed were recommended by the entomologists. No endorsement of products is intended nor is criticism of unnamed products implied. For additional information and advice on pest control, call or write your local cooperative extension service.

**MAY 29**

## Not-So-Vital Statistics on Senator Packwood

WASHINGTON, May 29—Senator Bob Packwood, a 53-year-old Republican, has represented Oregon in the Senate since 1967 and, as chairman of the Finance Committee, recently oversaw the evolution of a tax revision bill that many, including the Senator himself, at first gave little chance of succeeding. After months of work, however, the committee unanimously approved the bill just after midnight May 8, and it appears likely to pass when the full Senate, in televised debate, takes it up next Wednesday. Some insights into Mr. Packwood, as provided by the Senator:

**Height:** 5 feet 11 inches.
**Weight:** 180 pounds.
**Shirt collar:** 15½
**Waist:** 36.
**Sleeve:** 34.
**Shoe size:** 9½.
**Eyesight:** Wears contact lenses; has had operations on both eyes for cataracts.
**Allergies:** None.
**Favorite food:** Tacos.
**First-choice dinner:** Pork chops.
**Nighttime snacks:** None.
**Sweet tooth?** No.
**Current reading:** John Colville's *The Fringes of Power (10 Downing Street Diaries 1939–55).*
**Favorite book:** Any novel by Thomas Hardy.
**Favorite television show:** News shows.
**Favorite game:** Charades.
**Favorite song:** "Good Vibrations."
**Favorite musical instrument:** Piano.
**Favorite performer:** Frank Sinatra.
**Favorite time of day:** Early morning.
**Favorite vacation spot:** Oregon coast.
**Pet peeves:** People who are late.
**Biggest surprise on arrival in Washington:** The humidity.
**Hobbies:** Squash, listening to classical music.
**Clothing styles:** Casual.
**Kind of car:** '73 Buick station wagon.
**Favorite sport:** playing squash, small-boat sailing.
**Personal heroes:** Thomas Jefferson, Winston Churchill.
**Favorite president:** Jefferson.
**Religion:** Unitarian-Universalist.
**Favorite saying:** "Judgment comes from experience and great judgment comes from bad experience."
**Political superstition:** None.
**Lucky number:** None.
**Fondest memory:** Wedding day.
**Most memorable moment in career:** The night the Senate Finance Committee unanimously approved the tax revision bill.
**Most difficult moment in career:** Having to say no to President Nixon personally when he lobbied for Judge Clement Haynsworth's nomination to the Supreme Court.

## May 30

## Not-So-Vital Statistics on Admiral Crowe

WASHINGTON, June 11—Adm. William J. Crowe has occupied the post of Chairman of the Joint Chiefs of Staff since October. An Oklahoma native and a Navy officer with more than 43 years of service, he previously served as Commander of American forces in the Pacific and has held commands in the Middle East and southern Europe as well. As the first officer to be promoted to Chairman of the Joint Chiefs from a unified command rather than from the top ranks of his own service, Admiral Crowe has become an important participant in the debate on restructuring the responsibilities of the Joint Chiefs. Here are some insights into the admiral, as supplied by him:

**Height:** 6 feet.
**Weight:** 198 pounds.
**Shirt collar:** 16½.
**Sleeve:** 34.
**Overcoat size:** 44 long.
**Shoe size:** 9½ D.
**Hat size:** 7¼.
**Eyesight:** 20/20.
**Favorite food:** Pasta. "To paraphrase Will Rogers, I've never met a pasta I didn't like."
**First-choice dinner:** Same.
**Nighttime snack:** Ice cream.
**Sweet tooth?** Yes, for chocolate truffles.
**Favorite drink:** Bourbon.
**Current reading:** *Mr. Clemens and Mark Twain,* by Justin Kaplan.
**Favorite magazine:** *Mad.*
**Favorite books:** Historical novels.
**Favorite television show:** "Cheers."
**Favorite actor:** Jimmy Stewart.
**Favorite actress:** Ava Gardner.
**Favorite game:** Chess.
**Favorite song:** "Battle Hymn of the Republic."
**Favorite instrument:** Clarinet.
**Favorite performer:** Dean Martin.
**Favorite city:** San Francisco.
**Favorite vacation spot:** Oklahoma's lake country.
**Favorite time of day:** Late evening.

**Pet peeve:** Lawyers.
**Biggest surprise on arrival in Washington:** How little things had changed.
**Hobbies:** Reading history.
**Kind of car:** Dodge station wagon.
**Favorite sport:** Tennis.
**Clothing styles:** Sweaters.
**Pajamas:** None.
**Personal heroes:** Robert E. Lee.
**Favorite president:** Abraham Lincoln.
**Religion:** Methodist.
**Guiding philosophy:** Common sense.
**Favorite saying:** "Always conduct yourself so you will be welcome to return to your hometown." From a graduation speech delivered by James V. Forrestal, then Secretary of the Navy, to William Crowe's class at Annapolis.
**Lucky number:** 6.
**Fondest memory:** Meeting wife.
**Most memorable moment in career:** Being promoted to rear admiral.
**Most difficult moment in career:** "Too many to remember."

JUNE 12

# Wine Talk

By FRANK J. PRIAL

Adding a good year to a vintage chart is always a pleasure, and 1985 was for the most part a very good year. California, France, Italy and Germany all made good wines—not as much as in 1984, in some instances, but certainly as good and often much better.

The chart itself is different this year. It lists Champagne and California wines. Champagne is normally a blend of several vintages; it carries a vintage date only in exceptional years. Even so, the wine is produced every year, and the yearly quality affects its price. As the chart shows, more and more vintage years are being declared in Champagne.

The California figures are very general, given the considerable variety of wine-producing regions within the state. But California vintage reports usually are understood to refer principally to the well-known North Coast wine region: Napa, Sonoma and Mendocino and the area south of San Francisco in Santa Clara County. When someone says, "1968 was a legendary year in California," it's assumed the reference is not to the Central Valley.

In addition, extra vintages of Beaujolais have been added. Though Beaujolais should be drunk young, that doesn't mean that, for example, all 1983s are finished or that there are not still a few drinkable 82s and 81s in someone's cellar. Just don't buy any older than 1984.

A group called the American Wine Society came up with the idea of putting three or four golden oldies at the end of its chart, and we picked up on the idea, if not always the organization's choices. One of the best vintage charts is compiled by Jean-Claude Vrinat, owner of the restaurant Taillevent in Paris. Rather than attenuate his choices, he pushes his chart all the way back to 1928. This is fine if, like Mr. Vrinat, one has a cellar full of 28s, 29s, 45s and 61s.

Mr. Vrinat's chart is not produced in a vacuum. He consults other restaurateurs and many of the famous wine producers whose bottles he sells. The vintage chart here is similar, in that it reflects personal tastes but also represents the input of many knowledgeable people.

Once again, the ratings are based on a system of 20, à la Francaise, so to speak. Ten is more common in this country, except for the system used by Robert M. Parker, Jr., editor of *The Wine Advocate,* whose ratings are on a scale of 100. The chart's letter code describes the readiness of the wine for drinking.

Bear several things in mind when using any vintage chart. Regardless of how many little symbols and numbers it may show, it is little more than a casual guide. Just as it cannot possibly deal with the enormous diversity of California, it cannot encompass the nuances of any one vintage in France.

### Vintage chart/1975–1985

| Wine | '75 | '76 | '77 | '78 | '79 | '80 | '81 | '82 | '83 | '84 | '85 | Past Glories |
|---|---|---|---|---|---|---|---|---|---|---|---|---|
| Beaujolais | — | — | — | — | — | — | 15D | 15D | 18C | 14C | 18C | — |
| Bordeaux red | 17B | 16C | 14D | 18B | 17B | 14C | 17B | 19A | 17A | 13B | 18A | '55, '61, '70 |
| Burgundy red | 11C | 16C | 14D | 18B | 15C | 14C | 15C | 16B | 18A | 13B | 18A | '69, '71 |
| Burgundy white | 13C | 16C | 14D | 18C | 15C | 12D | 13D | 17C | 17B | 12C | 18A | '69, '73 |
| Rhône | 14C | 18C | 15D | 18C | 16C | 17C | 16C | 17B | 18A | 12B | 19A | '61, '70 |
| Sauternes | 19B | 17C | 15D | 17B | 15B | 17C | 18B | 17A | 18A | 14B | 15A | '61, '67, '73 |
| Champagne | 16 | 18 | NV | NV | 17 | NV | 16 | 16 | 15 | NV | 15 | — |
| Rhine | 18C | 19C | 12D | 13D | 16C | 12D | 16C | 12D | 16C | 10D | 17B | '71 |
| Mosel-Saar-Ruwer | 18C | 19C | 12D | 13D | 16C | 12D | 15D | 13D | 17C | 10D | 18B | '71 |
| Amarone (Veneto) | 18C | 14C | 16C | 14D | 16C | 14C | 12D | 18B | 17B | 10D | 18A | '71, '74 |
| Barolo (Piedmont) | 10D | 11D | 11D | 19C | 16C | 15C | 11D | 19B | 17B | 10D | 19A | '70, '71, '74 |
| Chianti (Tuscany) | 18C | 12D | 18D | 19C | 16C | 15C | 14D | 18B | 18B | 10D | 18A | '70, '71 |
| California: Cabernet | 16C | 14C | 15D | 17C | 13D | 17C | 15C | 15C | 17B | 18A | 19A | '68, '70, '74 |
| Chardonnay | 16C | 15D | 14D | 16C | 15D | 18C | 16C | 17C | 17B | 18A | 19A | — |

*NV:* Nonvintage
*Numbers:* 0 (worst) to 20 (best)
*Letters:* A: wine needs more bottle age; B: can be drunk now but probably would be better with more age; C: ready now; D: may still be good, but approach with caution

JUNE 18

# 13 (Count 'em) Toasts

**W**ASHINGTON, July 1—On the Fourth of July in 1778, *The Pennsylvania Packet* reported, the "honorable" Congress celebrated the anniversary of Independence "at the City Tavern in this metropolis."

According to the Library of Congress's "Letters of Delegates to Congress," the President of Congress, Henry Laurens of South Carolina, offered a few toasts. In fact, he offered 13:

1. The United States of America.
2. The Protector of the Rights of Mankind.
3. The Friendly European Powers.
4. The happy era of the independence of America.
5. The Commander in Chief of the American Forces.
6. The American Arms by land and sea.
7. The Glorious 19th of April 1775.
8. The Glorious 26th of December 1776.
9. The Glorious 16th of October 1777.
10. The 28th of June, twice Glorious, 1776 and 1778.
11. May the Arts and Sciences flourish in America.
12. May the People continue Free forever.
13. May the Union of the United States be perpetual.

(Toast No. 7 referred to the Battle of Lexington and Concord at the start of the war; No. 8 to the Battle of Trenton; No. 9 to the defeat at Saratoga, N.Y., of General Burgoyne, who formally surrendered Oct. 17, 1777; and No. 10 to the beating off of the British naval attack on Charleston, S.C., in 1776, and the Battle of Monmouth Courthouse, N.J., in 1778.)

The Library of Congress editors did not state whether *The Pennsylvania Packet* reported what was in Laurens's toasting cup (ale was popular then, as was rum, but it also might have been wine).

Nor was it reported whether the 13th toast was uttered as clearly as the first.  JULY 2

## One Traveler's Packing List of Provisions

By NANCY HARMON JENKINS

Traveling in China is not like traveling anywhere else in the world. Prpared for a third world experience, you may well be surprised at the level of amenities. (One that always pleases foreigners is the Chinese custom of providing a large thermos of boiling hot water in every hotel room, even the most humble.) On the other hand, if you expect luxury services outside large Western-style hotels in major cities, you are in for a rude awakening. (Next to that thermos of hot water, you may find a tea mug containing the remains of the last guest's cup of tea.) Accommodations are often Spartan and toilet facilities, in particular, can be—well, crude at best.

Just back from a four-week tour of China myself, I am full of well-meaning advice for my fellow travelers. For peace of mind, here are a few rules and unfamiliar customs to remember, as well as a short list of items to tuck in your suitcase or backpack. They will add to the weight of your luggage, but they may make your trip far more comfortable than if you had left them behind.

First, the rules:

1. Reserve hotel space before you begin your trip and keep your reservation number handy. Hotel rooms are often hard to come by, especially in the major cities, and Chinese hotel keepers are notorious for last-minute cancellations. Also, Western names are cumbersome for the Chinese, but a number is a number and is less likely to be misunderstood.

2. Remember that state-run restaurants—and most restaurants in China are still owned and operated by the government—have rigid schedules. In most cities, lunch is not served after 1:00 P.M. and dinner not after 7:30, sometimes earlier. There is no breaching this rule: Tears and fainting spells are of no avail. The cook has gone home, the stove is shut down and there is no more food. If you want to dine in a special restaurant, arrive early—11:30 is the best bet for lunch, no later than 6:30 for dinner. Adjust your eating schedule to conform to Chinese custom. Otherwise, you will eat all your meals in Western-style hotels, one of the dreariest ways to experience food in China.

3. If you value privacy, or just like to rest in the altogether in your room, lock your hotel room door. Chinese in the People's Republic do not have the same concept of privacy as visitors from the West. If your room door is not locked, anyone may come in at any moment for any reason. It may well be a student of English, in which case the first question will be: "How old are you?" Do not be ashamed to lie. To the Chinese, you always look younger than you are.

Now for the list:

Swiss army knife. I do not think anyone should go anywhere in the world without a Swiss army knife. It need not be the five-pound variety complete with fish scaler and ivory toothpick that my young son considers essential, but a knife with a couple of blades, a corkscrew, bottle opener and hole punch is a useful item in any traveler's bag (though not in carry-on luggage, as it might be confiscated by airport security personnel). In China especially, if you buy fresh fruit from a market stall —and you may wish to because it is seldom served at meals—you will want to peel it before eating.

Toilet paper and/or tissues. Toilet paper, when available, is as rough and uncomfortable as the pages of a Sears Roebuck catalogue. If you go to the north of China you will most likely come down with a cold—almost everyone does because of the dry, dusty air—so you will need to blow your nose frequently. You will also need paper to use for table napkins, seldom provided, and for wiping off bowls, glasses and chopsticks—a perfectly acceptable thing to do, so my Chinese friends advise me.

Food. Chocolate bars, if that's what you like, although some travelers take peanut butter. I do not because it sticks to the roof of my mouth and makes it difficult to talk. There is an abundance of good food in China but often it is not available when you most crave it.

Plastic bags. Small plastic sandwich bags or larger refrigerator bags can be used in a variety of ways, some that you might not imagine beforehand. If you neglected to bring chocolate or peanut butter, you will find the bags handy for wrapping up leftover food from the table for midnight snacks. They are also useful for carrying the underwear you rinsed out at night that wasn't dry when it was time to leave the hotel in the morning. Then, too, the markets are full of interesting things to buy, but decidedly short on shopping bags.

Maps. Doubtless for reasons of state security, there are no good maps available in China. A map of the whole country will help you figure out where you are and at the same time make new friends. When you open it in public, you will be surrounded by Chinese trying to figure out where they are, too.

Collapsible mug or plastic cup. As noted above, though boiling water is always available, clean cups may be in short supply. Best to carry your own: If it isn't clean, at least it carries only your own germs.

Towel. If you have room, a small bath towel may well be one of the most comforting items you can carry. Hotels often provide miniature towels that, while charming, hardly do the job. A towel also makes a useful pillowcase when necessary, as on an overnight train.

Soap. Often unavailable, soap, when provided, may be harsher than what you are used to. Take your own, in a soap dish. Also be sure to take plenty of shampoo.

Alcoholic beverages. Beer is the most common alcoholic drink in China, and it is only slightly alcoholic. The alternative is the infamous maotai, a sort of white lightning that may become repugnant the third or fourth time around. If you like a drink before dinner, take your own. It need not be elaborate: If you can't live without margaritas, you probably should not be in China anyway.

Instant coffee. You will find coffee distressingly unavailable in many parts of China.

Tea. Odd as it may seem, tea—in bags, for convenience—is a useful item. Chinese tea is almost invariably jasmine, a lovely tea that tastes cloying when taken in excess. Bags of black Ceylon or India tea or herbal infusions provide a welcome alternative.

Phrase book. It is frustrating and limiting anywhere in the world to be unable to speak the language, but at least in Germany or Argentina one can read the street signs. In China, unless you have studied long and hard, you can neither speak nor read. However, there are a few phrase books available that translate from English into Pinyin, the Chinese system of Romanization. Even if you never need to use it, a phrase book is a comfort in your pocket.

Medications. If you use any special medications, you know to take plenty along with you wherever you go. You might also pack a small medicine box of nonprescription pharmaceuticals that can be useful in minor emergencies; aspirin, antacid, iodine, antihistamines and Band-Aids come immediately to mind. It is sensible to take along an extra pair of eyeglasses or, if you wear contact lenses, lens cleaning solution. If you feel you can't get along without a hair dryer, take a battery-operated one.

JULY 20

## Dinner for Pakistan's Prime Minister

WASHINGTON, July 16—Prime Minister Mohammad Khan Junejo of Pakistan is in the United States for a weeklong visit, including four days of talks and ceremony in Washington. Tonight he was the guest of honor at a state dinner at the White House.

Following are the menu and guest list, as provided by the White House:

The President & Mrs. Reagan
The Prime Minister of The Islamic Republic of Pakistan
Miss F. Junejo
Miss S. Junejo
Mr. Mohammad Asad Ali Khan Junejo
The Minister for Foreign Affairs & Mrs. Yaqub-Khan
Mian Mohammad Yasin Khan Wattoo (Minister for Finance & Economic Affairs)
Hon. Mian Mohammad Nawaz Sharif (Chief Minister of Punjab)
Hon. Arbab Mohammad Jahangir Khan (Chief Minister of Northwest Frontier Province)
The Ambassador of the Islamic Republic of Pakistan & Mrs. Azim
Air Chief Marshal Jamal Ahmad Khan (Chief of Air Staff, PAF)
Mr. A. G. N. Kazi (Deputy Chairman, Planning Commission)
Mr. Abdul Sattar (Secretary, Foreign Affairs)
Hon. & Mrs. Michael H. Armacost (Bonny) (Under Secretary of State for Political Affairs)
Mr. & Mrs. John F. Akers (Susan) (President & CEO, I.B.M. Corporation)
The Secretary of the Treasury & Mrs. Baker (Susan)
Mr. Hector Barreto & Ms. Ana Favrow-Barreto (daughter) (President, U.S. Hispanic Chamber of Commerce)
Mr. & Mrs. Bruce Boxleitner (Kitty) (Actor, "Scarecrow & Mrs. King")
Hon. (Judge) & Mrs. James L. Buckley (Ann) (Judge, U.S. Court of Appeals for the District of Columbia)
Mr. & Mrs. James E. Burke (Diane) (Chairman, Johnson & Johnson)
The Vice President & Mrs. Bush (Barbara)
Hon. (Sen.) John H. Chafee (R/Rhode Island)
Hon. (Rep.) Rod Chandler (R/Washington)
Hon. (Dr.) Lynne V. Cheney & Hon. (Rep.) Richard B. Cheney (Chairman, National Endowment for the Humanities—R/Wyoming)
Hon. (Sen.) & Mrs. Thad Cochran (Rose) (R/Mississippi)
Hon. & Mrs. Barber B. Conable, Jr. (Charlotte) (President, World Bank)
Mr. Robert Denning (Denning & Fourcade Inc., N.Y.C.)
Mr. & Mrs. John W. Dixon (Doris) (Chairman & CEO, E-Systems Inc.)
Dr. & Mrs. Lloyd H. Elliott (Evelyn—"Betty") (President, George Washington University)
Mr. & Mrs. David Flynn (Mrs.: Jane Seymour, actress)
Mr. & Mrs. Eugene Fodor (Susan) (Violinist, performing)
Mr. & Mrs. Horton Foote (Lillian) (Screenwriter)
Mr. Vincent Fourcade (Denning & Fourcade Inc., N.Y.C.)
Mr. & Mrs. Julian Gingold (Irene), Irvington, N.Y.
Mr. & Mrs. Lawrence Goodman (Muriel), Pacific Palisades, Calif.
Hon. (Sen.) & Mrs. Howell Heflin (Elizabeth Ann) (D/Alabama)
Hon. (Amb.) Deane R. Hinton (American Ambassador to Pakistan)
Hon. (Mayor) & Mrs. William H. Hudnut (Susie) (Mayor of Indianapolis)
Mr. & Mrs. Harold Johnson (Elma), Sands Point, N.Y.

Mr. & Mrs. Karl Karcher (Margaret), Anaheim, Calif.
Mr. & Mrs. George Keller (Adelaide) (Chairman, Chevron Corporation)
Miss Darci Kistler (Ballerina, N.Y.C. Ballet)
Mr. Alan Ladd, Jr., & Miss Tracy Ladd (Metro-Goldwyn-Mayer).
Mr. & Mrs. James Lehrer (Kate) ("The MacNeil/Lehrer News Hour")
Prof. Glenn Lowry & Prof. Linda Datcher-Lowry (Mr.: Economist, Harvard—Mrs.: Tufts)
Hon. & Mrs. William H. Luers (Wendy) (President, Metropolitan Museum of Art, and former Ambassador)
Hon. & Mrs. Cecil B. Lyon (Elizabeth), Hancock, N.H. (former Ambassador)
Hon. & Mrs. John O. Marsh, Jr. (Glenn Ann) (Secretary of the Army)
Miss Mary T. Meagher (Olympic gold medalist—swimming)
Mr. & Mrs. Pat Murphy (Betty) (Publisher, *Arizona Republic & Phoenix Gazette*)
Hon. & Mrs. Richard W. Murphy (Anne) (Assistant Secretary of State for Near Eastern & South Asian Affairs)
Dr. & Mrs. David Paton (Diane Brokaw) (Mr.: Opthalmologist with volunteer medical program. Mrs.: Executive Director, The President's Committee on the Arts & the Humanities)
Mr. & Mrs. George Peppard (Joyce) (Actor)
The Secretary of Housing & Urban Development & Mrs. Pierce (Barbara)
Hon. (Adm.) John M. Poindexter & the Rev. Linda A. Poindexter (Assistant to the President for National Security Affairs)
Ms. Maureen E. Reagan
Hon. & Mrs. Donald T. Regan (Ann) (Chief of Staff to the President)
Mr. & Mrs. Frank Richardson (Nancy) (Mr.: Executive vice-president, Wesray Capital Corporation—Mrs.: Editor, *House & Garden* magazine)
The Chief of Protocol Selwa Roosevelt & Mr. Archibald B. Roosevelt, Jr.
Mrs. Gloria Sachs (Fashion designer)
Mr. & Mrs. Norman Sandler (Raeanne) (White House Correspondent, UPI)
Hon. (Rep.) & Mrs. F. James Sensenbrenner (Cheryl) (R/Wisconsin)
Mr. Joseph Shapiro & Miss Janet Lottero (White House Correspondent, *U.S. News & World Report*)
The Secretary of State & Mrs. Shultz ("Obie")
Hon. (Rep.) & Mrs. Ike Skelton (Susie) (D/Missouri)
Hon. (Judge) & Mrs. Kenneth W. Starr (Alice) (Judge, U.S. Court of Appeals for the District of Columbia)
Hon. Caspar W. Weinberger (Secretary of Defense)
Gen. & Mrs. John A. Wickham, Jr. (Ann) (Chief of Staff, U.S. Army)

JULY 17

---

DINNER
Honoring
His Excellency
The Prime Minister of the Islamic Republic of Pakistan

Salmon Mousse of Smoked Trout
Tarragon Sauce
Herbed Toast Rounds

Supreme of Chicken with Basil
Morel Sauce
Saffron Rice
Tiny Beans & Summer Squash

Port du Salut Cheese
Watercress & Shiitake Mushrooms
Radish Dressing

Plum & Pineapple Sorbet
Petits Fours Sec

SAINTSBURY Chardonnay 1984
CHARLES F. SHAW Napa Valley Gamay 1985
CULBERTSON Cuvée de Frontignan Demi-Sec

THE WHITE HOUSE
Wednesday, July 16, 1986

JULY 17

## Not-So-Vital Statistics on Rep. Mike Synar

**W**ASHINGTON, Aug. 3—Representative Mike Synar, a four-term Democrat from Oklahoma, stepped to the center of the budget wrangling on Capitol Hill with his legal challenge to the budget-balancing law. His suit contesting its constitutionality won in the Supreme Court last month, and the Congress and Administration are now struggling to find another way to impose some discipline on the budget.

A 35-year-old native of Oklahoma and a graduate of the University of Oklahoma, Mr. Synar, who serves on the Government Operations and Judiciary committees, has established a reputation as a maverick member of the moderate to conservative Oklahoma delegation. Some insights into the congressman, as supplied by him and his staff:

Height—5 feet 11¾ inches
Weight—165 pounds
Shirt collar—16
Waist—34
Sleeve—34
Overcoat size—40
Shoe size—9
Eyesight—20/20
Allergies—none
Favorite food—turkey and dressing
First-choice dinner—barbecued chicken
Nighttime snacks—chocolate cake, cashews
Sweet tooth?—yes
Favorite wine—St. Clement Chardonnay
Favorite drink—Diet Coke
Current Reading—*Lake Wobegon Days*
Favorite magazine—*Newsweek*
Favorite television show—"St. Elsewhere," evening news
Favorite actor—Paul Newman
Favorite game—charades
Favorite song—"Moon River"
Favorite musical instrument—guitar
Favorite performer—Robin Williams
Favorite time of day—night
Favorite vacation spot—Grand Lake, Okla.
Favorite city—Washington, D.C.
Pet peeves—being late
Biggest surprise on arrival in Washington—humidity
Hobbies—hunting, fishing
Kind of car—1970 Mustang
Favorite sport—basketball
Clothing styles—casual
Personal heroes—father
Favorite President—Thomas Jefferson
Religion—Episcopalian
Guiding philosophy—Be enthusiastic; don't take yourself too seriously
Political superstition—none
Lucky number—4
Fondest memory—Being in 4-H
Most memorable moment in career—getting elected
Most difficult moment in career—deciding whether to sue on budget law

AUG. 4

## The Flavors of Ice-Cream Parlors: Nostalgic to New; The Scoop on Store-Bought Brands

**A**ccording to the International Association of Ice Cream Manufacturers, a Washington-based trade group, in a country of chocolate lovers, vanilla is the most popular ice-cream flavor, accounting for 31.02 percent of all ice-cream sales. That's down from 51 percent a decade ago. Then comes chocolate.

In a blind taste test, five experts sampled vanilla and chocolate of 13 commercial brands of ice cream: Baskin-Robbins (vanilla and French vanilla, as well as chocolate), Ben & Jerry's, Breyers, Carvel, Dolly Madison, Frusen Glädjé, Häagen-Dazs, Howard Johnson's, Louis Sherry, Schrafft's, Sealtest, Sedutto and Steve's (no plain chocolate available). The criteria for judging these products included flavor, texture and overall quality.

The following chart is the result of their sampling efforts. "N.A." indicates that information was not available from the manufacturer. The serving size is four ounces, the standard used by many manufacturers. Butterfat is the source of an ice cream's richness and half its calories, mostly in the form of saturated fat. Air is whipped into all ice creams. Overrun is a measure of how much that air swells the volume of the original mix. Ice cream with 100 percent overrun is 50 percent air. (Federal authorities limit overrun by specifying that ice cream may not weigh less than 4.5 pounds per gallon.)

As a group, the vanillas tasted by panelists fared better than the chocolates, with rich, creamy Sedutto and Häagen-Dazs vanillas coming in first and second, or second and first, on everyone's list. No store-bought brand of chocolate ice cream was judged excellent.

AUG. 20

| Brand | Cost per serving | Calories per serving | Percent butterfat | Percent overrun | Mg. calcium | Comments (taste, texture, etc.) |
|---|---|---|---|---|---|---|
| **VANILLA** | | | | | | |
| **Excellent** | | | | | | |
| Häagen-Dazs | $0.50 | 267 | 16% | 20% | N.A. | Caramel sweet vanilla/creamy, smooth |
| Sedutto | .43 | N.A. | 16% | 50% | N.A. | Rich caramel vanilla/creamy, smooth |
| **Good** | | | | | | |
| Frusen Glädjé | .50 | 250 | 15.4% | 20% | 200 | Good/smooth |
| Steve's | .50 | 268 | 16% | 20% | N.A. | A little too sweet/creamy |
| **Fair** | | | | | | |
| Baskin-Robbins (vanilla) | .69 | 235 | 12% | N.A. | 136 | Too sweet/fluffy |
| Ben & Jerry's | .50 | 267 | 15% | 20% | 142.8 | Bland/fluffy |
| Carvel | .65 | 196 | 10% | 40% | 184 | Bland/smooth |
| Dolly Madison | .38 | 150 | N.A. | N.A. | N.A. | Sweet, slight aftertaste/smooth |
| Howard Johnson's | .38 | 210 | 16.5% | 55% | N.A. | Bland/cottony |
| Louis Sherry | .40 | 150 | N.A. | N.A. | N.A. | Artificial/airy, smooth |
| Sealtest | .37 | 140 | 10.2% | 100% | 100 | Artificial/cottony |
| **Others** | | | | | | |
| Baskin-Robbins (French vanilla) | .69 | 290 | 12% | N.A. | 127.1 | Burned caramel/dense, chalky |
| Breyers | .48 | 150 | 12% | 90% | 100 | Overcooked/chalky |
| Schrafft's | .49 | 220 | 17% | 45% | N.A. | Bland/grainy |
| **CHOCOLATE** | | | | | | |
| **Good** | | | | | | |
| Ben & Jerry's | .50 | 290 | 15% | 20% | 101.5 | Strong cocoa-powder/silky |
| Häagen-Dazs | .50 | 283 | 16% | 20% | N.A. | Good, tangy/smooth |
| Howard Johnson's | .38 | 221 | 16% | 55% | N.A. | Slightly cooked/dense but smooth |
| Schrafft's | .49 | 240 | 16% | 43% | N.A. | Complex cocoa/smooth |
| Sedutto | .43 | N.A. | 13% | 50% | N.A. | Cocoa/creamy |

| Brand | Cost per serving | Calories per serving | Percent butterfat | Percent overrun | Mg. calcium | Comments (taste, texture, etc.) |
|---|---|---|---|---|---|---|
| **Fair** | | | | | | |
| Baskin-Robbins | .69 | 264 | 12% | N.A. | 115.2 | Sightly burned/chalky |
| Breyers | .48 | 160 | 9.7% | 90% | 80 | Vaguely chocolate/fluffy |
| Dolly Madison | .38 | 150 | N.A. | N.A. | N.A. | Too sweet, bland/gummy |
| Frusen Glädjé | .50 | 260 | 14.8% | 20% | 150 | Slightly bitter/grainy |
| Louis Sherry | .40 | 150 | N.A. | N.A. | N.A. | Too sweet, bland/mousselike |
| **Others** | | | | | | |
| Carvel | .65 | 196 | 10% | 40% | 164 | Sour, artificial/dense |
| Sealtest | .37 | 140 | 9.9% | 100% | 80 | Caramel, artificial/gritty |

AUG. 20

## Meat Is Getting Trimmer for a Comeback Fight

**By MARIAN BURROS**

Beef has gone on a diet, its battle with fat a well-publicized fact.

Following the slimming efforts that made pork and chicken more appealing, beef is trying to compete in the meat case as a trimmer, lower-fat version of its former self.

After a decade of fighting consumer demands for leaner, as well as safer, beef—a period when the per capita consumption of beef dropped from 94.4 pounds to 79.1 pounds a year—cattlemen have acknowledged the complaints and done something about them. The industry has gone on the offensive on three fronts, working back from the retail meat case to the feedlot and, finally, to the breeder.

• To provide consumers with leaner beef, packing houses and retail stores are trimming more external fat. Instead of retail cuts with one-half to three-quarters of an inch of fat, many stores, including ShopRite in New York and Kings in New Jersey, are offering beef that is fully trimmed or has only a quarter-inch of fat.

• Cattle are spending less time in feedlots so they will develop less fat. Instead of the standard 160 days, they are being fed for 110 to 115 days.

• Genetically leaner cattle such as Chianina from Italy are being crossbred with traditional beef cattle to produce leaner animals.

In keeping with the emphasis on leanness, next year the Department of Agriculture will allow beef with 5 percent fat to be called "extra lean," beef with 10 percent fat or less "lean" or "low fat." As an added lure to consumers worried about hormones and antibiotics in beef, some cattlemen have reduced or eliminated their use. These claims, however, go unregulated by the Government, although the Agriculture Department says it plans within six months to publish a proposal that would help monitor their accuracy.

Yet it is still too early to tell whether the beef industry has lured enough consumers back from the fish counter.

To find out if the new beef is actually leaner and what the trade-offs are in taste and price, *The New York Times* had 11 brands of beef tested for fat content and conducted a taste test, comparing the leaner beef with ordinary choice and prime beef from the supermarket. There were more than a few surprises, including the debunking of the belief that fatter beef tastes better than leaner.

I cooked and tasted 12 cuts of beef—an additional prime cut was added for tasting—for flavor and texture by oven broiling and charcoal grilling outdoors until just rare to medium-rare. Predictably, the two brands with the least fat were the driest; in the other samples, flavor was not affected by fat content.

The tenderness and juiciness of steaks of the same brand sometimes varied. For example, one sample of Brae Beef was extremely tender, but a bit mushy and not very beefy in flavor; another was very beefy and juicy, but less tender. On the other hand, one choice steak from Kings was very tender and fairly beefy; another was not flavorful at all. One piece of prime steak was characteristically juicy but had only a moderately beefy flavor. But overall and regardless of price, there was little qualitative difference in taste.

If leanness is an important characteristic by which the consumer judges beef, buying the most costly brands may be unnecessary. The ordinary good grade can be as lean as the exotic brands, flavorful but more economical.

OCT. 8

## How lean is lean beef?

| Brand name | % Fat content | Calories* Total | % Fat | Price per pound Regular | Trimmed | Taste |
|---|---|---|---|---|---|---|
| Key Lite | 3.18 | 117 | 29 | — | N.A.† | Chewy, fairly meaty; from gristly and dry to tender |
| Certified Natural Light Beef | 3.25 | 113 | 30 | 5.99 | 7.45 | A bit chewy, somewhat dry, not meaty |
| Brae Beef | 4.18 | 125 | 38 | — | 23.95 | From tender to mushy; juicy; meaty |
| Piedmonte | 4.22 | 129 | 38 | 15.00 | 32.10 | Tender, slightly dry, fairly meaty |
| Giant Lean | 4.49 | 136 | 41 | 4.59 | 6.36 | Very tender, slightly dry; meaty |
| Maverick's Naturalite | 4.97 | 135 | 45 | 7.99 | 9.62 | Juicy, good meaty taste, tender |
| Choice (Kings) | 5.12 | 135 | 47 | 5.69 | 6.81 | Very tender; one piece meaty, the other not |
| Lean Limousin | 5.81 | 139 | 53 | 11.33§ | 16.84 | Tender, meaty, fairly juicy |
| Coleman Natural Beef | 5.96 | 142 | 54 | 7.99 | 12.43 | From tender to slightly tough; meaty flavor |
| A & P Grain-Fed Thin Trim | 6.43 | 147 | 59 | 4.69 | 7.07 | Dry, grassy, moderately tender |
| Certified Angus Beef | 6.9 | 148 | 63 | 7.49 | 10.01 | From tender to slightly chewy, a little dry, not very meaty |

*Calories per 3.5-ounce serving.
†Not available.
§Meat sold by the package: eight 12-ounce Omaha strip steaks are $67.95 by mail; the larger the order, the lower the cost.

OCT. 8

# Personal Health

**By JANE BRODY**

The cholesterol-conscious American is eating less red meat, fewer eggs, more poultry and slightly more fish than two decades ago. Chicken and turkey franks, turkey ham and turkey pastrami have taken their place beside the fattier beef and pork versions, and ground turkey has begun to invade the market for ground beef.

But in choosing among protein-rich foods, people often make dietary changes that are no improvement. In some cases, as in substituting cheese for red meat, the changes are more likely to harm than help. Also confusing is the fact that some foods people have been told to eat—for example, veal—actually have more cholesterol than does beef. And after years of being told to avoid cholesterol-rich shrimp and fatty fish, suddenly these are said to be OK, even desirable.

With the link between dietary fat and cholesterol and the risk of coronary heart disease ever more firmly established, the American Heart Association has further reduced recommended consumption levels. The new guidelines suggest a maximum of 30 percent of calories from fat, with at most 10 percent from saturated fats, and a daily cholesterol intake of 100 milligrams for each 1,000 calories consumed (to a maximum of 300 milligrams a day).

The following facts can help in making healthier choices among sources of protein.

Cholesterol is a waxy alcohol found only in animals. In foods it is usually, although not always, associated with fat. Thus, whole milk (3.7 percent butterfat) contains seven times as much cholesterol as fat-free skim milk. In the body, cholesterol is carried in the blood by three types of proteins. Two of them—low-density and very-low-density lipoproteins (LDLs and VLDLs)—encourage the formation of cholesterol-laden plaques in human arteries, whereas high-density lipoprotein (HDL) apparently helps rid the body of cholesterol.

Food fats are made up of three types of fatty acids that influence cholesterol levels in the blood: saturated, monounsaturated and polyunsaturated. Highly saturated fats, such as beef fat, lard and butterfat, are hard at room temperature; they tend to raise blood levels of artery-damaging cholesterol. However, monounsaturated fats, such as olive oil, and polyunsaturates, such as corn and soybean oils, tend to reduce cholesterol levels in the blood.

The kinds and amounts of fats in the diet may affect blood cholesterol levels more than the actual amount of cholesterol consumed, which is why low-fat but higher-cholesterol veal is preferred to naturally fattier beef. On the other hand, it is not advisable to consume large amounts of polyunsaturated fats because, while they lower the damaging LDL and VLDL cholesterol in the blood, they also reduce the protective HDL cholesterol. Recent studies of monounsaturated fats, however, suggest that these may reduce harmful cholesterol levels without affecting HDL cholesterol.

Still, no one should go on a diet high in any type of fat. High-fat diets are associated with increased cancer risk and obesity. All fats, saturated or not, are highly caloric, providing the body with nine calories per gram of fat, or two and a quarter times as many calories as equal amounts of starch, sugar or protein.

Nov. 5

# Fats and cholesterol in popular protein foods

(All values are for cooked or ready-to-eat food)

| Food | Serving Size (ounces, except where indicated) | Calories | Protein (grams) | Percent Calories From Fat | Percent Calories From Saturated Fat | Cholesterol (milligrams) |
|---|---|---|---|---|---|---|
| **Fresh Red Meats** (trimmed of fat, cooked medium) | | | | | | |
| Beef, ground, extra lean (17% fat raw) | 3.5 | 250 | 25 | 58 | 23 | 82 |
| Beef, ground, regular (27% fat raw) | 3.5 | 287 | 23 | 66 | 26 | 87 |
| Beef, round | 3.5 | 184 | 28 | 34 | 12 | 82 |
| Brisket | 3.5 | 263 | 28 | 54 | 21 | 91 |
| Flank steak | 3.5 | 244 | 28 | 51 | 22 | 71 |
| Lamb leg roast | 3.5 | 191 | 28 | 38 | 16 | 89 |
| Lamb loin chop, broiled | 3.5 | 215 | 30 | 42 | 17 | 94 |
| Liver, fried | 3.5 | 217 | 27 | 36 | 12 | 482 |
| Pork loin roast | 3.5 | 240 | 27 | 52 | 16 | 90 |
| Sirloin | 3.5 | 208 | 30 | 37 | 15 | 89 |
| Spareribs | 3.5 | 397 | 29 | 67 | 27 | 121 |
| Veal cutlet, fried | 3.5 | 183 | 33 | 42 | 20 | 127 |
| Veal rib roast | 3.5 | 175 | 26 | 37 | 15 | 131 |
| **Poultry** | | | | | | |
| Chicken, with skin, roast | 3.5 | 239 | 27 | 51 | 14 | 88 |
| Chicken, no skin, roast | 3.5 | 190 | 29 | 37 | 10 | 89 |
| Turkey, light meat, no skin | 3.5 | 157 | 30 | 18 | 6 | 69 |
| **Fish** | | | | | | |
| Clams | 3.5 | 98 | 16 | 6 | 0 | 39 |
| Cod | 3.5 | 98 | 22 | 8 | 1 | 74 |
| Flounder | 3.5 | 99 | 21 | 12 | 2 | 54 |
| Mackerel | 3.5 | 199 | 27 | 77 | 20 | 100 |
| Ocean perch | 3.5 | 110 | 23 | 13 | 3 | 53 |
| Salmon | 3.5 | 182 | 27 | 24 | 5 | 93 |
| Scallops | 3.5 | 112 | 23 | 8 | 1 | 56 |
| Shrimp | 3.5 | 116 | 24 | 15 | 2 | 156 |
| Tuna | 3.5 | 181 | 32 | 41 | 10 | 48 |
| **Processed "Meats"** | | | | | | |
| Bologna, beef and pork | 2 | 178 | 7 | 81 | 31 | 32 |
| Bologna, turkey | 2 | 114 | 8 | 68 | — | 56 |
| Canadian bacon | 2 | 89 | 12 | 40 | 13 | 28 |
| Chicken roll | 2 | 90 | 11 | 42 | 12 | 28 |
| Franks, beef | 2 franks | 284 | 11 | 81 | 34 | 54 |
| Franks, turkey | 2 franks | 204 | 13 | 70 | — | 96 |
| Ham, extra lean (5% fat) | 2 | 74 | 11 | 34 | 11 | 26 |
| Ham, turkey | 2 | 73 | 11 | 36 | 12 | — |
| Italian sausage | 3.5 | 323 | 20 | 72 | 25 | 78 |

| Food | Serving Size (ounces, except where indicated) | Calories | Protein (grams) | Percent Calories From Fat | Percent Calories From Saturated Fat | Cholesterol (milligrams) |
|---|---|---|---|---|---|---|
| **Dairy Products and Eggs** | | | | | | |
| Cheddar | 1 | 114 | 7 | 74 | 47 | 30 |
| Cottage cheese (1% fat) | 4 | 82 | 14 | 13 | 8 | 5 |
| Cream cheese | 1 | 99 | 2 | 90 | 57 | 31 |
| Egg whites | 3 lg | 49 | 10 | 0 | 0 | 0 |
| Eggs, whole | 2 lg | 158 | 12 | 63 | 19 | 548 |
| Feta | 1 | 75 | 4 | 72 | 51 | 25 |
| Milk, skim | 8 | 90 | 9 | 11 | 4 | 5 |
| Milk, whole | 8 | 157 | 8 | 51 | 32 | 35 |
| Mozzarella, part skim | 1 | 72 | 7 | 56 | 36 | 16 |
| Neufchâtel | 1 | 74 | 3 | 80 | 51 | 22 |
| Ricotta, part skim | 4 | 171 | 14 | 52 | 32 | 38 |
| Swiss | 1 | 107 | 8 | 66 | 42 | 26 |
| Yogurt, plain low-fat | 8 | 144 | 12 | 22 | 14 | 14 |
| **Nuts and Beans** | | | | | | |
| Almond butter | 2 tbs | 202 | 5 | 84 | 8 | 0 |
| Kidney beans | 1 cup | 218 | 14 | 4 | — | 0 |
| Lentils | 1 cup | 212 | 16 | 0 | 0 | 0 |
| Peanut butter | 2 tbs | 190 | 9 | 77 | 13 | 0 |
| Peanuts | 1 | 161 | 7 | 78 | 11 | 0 |
| Tofu | 4 | 86 | 9 | 52 | 10 | 0 |
| Walnuts | 1 | 182 | 4 | 86 | 8 | 0 |

—No data available

Source: U.S. Agriculture Department

Nov. 5

# Observer: The Depth of Fashion

### By RUSSELL BAKER

The 125 most publicized things that could get you, listed in alphabetical order:

Acid rain
Airplane hijacker
Alzheimer's disease
Asbestos
Avalanche
Bald tire
Barracuda
Beirut
Black widow spider
Bottle without safety cap
Botulism
Bribe-taking elevator inspector
Broken ladder rung
Caffeine
Cancer-causing additive
Carbon monoxide
Careless deer hunter
Casual sex
Chemical-factory leak
Chemical preservative
Chewing tobacco
Child in satanic possession
Cholesterol
Cigarettes
Confused anesthetist
Crococile-infested swamp
Damp climate
Dental overbite
Dioxin
Diverticulitis
Drifting cigarette smoke
Drunk driver
Earthquake
Eating antique paint
Emotional repression
Emphysema
Enraged bull
Escaped jungle cat
Excess body weight
Exhausted air traffic controller
Fallen live wire
Faulty brakes
Faulty smoke detector
Fiber shortage
Fire ant invasion
Fire in crowded theater
Forgetting annual checkup
Gasoline fumes
Giant rat of Borneo
Giant squid
Gingivitis
Hatred of exercise
H bomb explosion
High blood pressure
Homicidal lunatic
Hostile poltergeist
Hurricane
Icy highway patch
Ignoring infected cut
Ileitis
Inadequately cooked pork
Inferior genes
Insouciant surgeon
Killer bee attack
Killer whale
Lack of calcium
Lead in water
Legionnaire's disease
Lifeboat insufficiency at sea
Lightning
Low blood pressure
Lower back pain
Manic-depressive illness
Mercury-tainted fish
Microwave emissions
Midlife crisis
Model-airplane-glue fumes
Narcotics desperadoes
Osteomyelitis
Ozone breakdown
PCBs
Pesticide in groundwater
Phlebitis

Phone call in thunderstorm
Plaque
Poisonous mushroom
Police pursuit of speeder
Poor posture
Psittacosis
Psychopathic burglar
Quicksand
Rabid-raccoon bite
Radiation leak from TV set
Radon in house
Reactor meltdown
Roller skate on stair
Rotting oak overhanging house
Runaway electric carving knife
Rusty roller coaster rail
Salt
Scorpion
Sharks
Skyscraper dropping windows
Slipped disk
Slippery bathtub
Steroids
Stress
Stroke
Sugar
Suntan
Terrorist bombing
Tetanus
Tidal wave
Toppling construction crane
Toxic waste
Unbuckled seat belt
Uncontrollable skid
Ungrounded wire
Unhelmeted motorcycle ride
Unsupervised fireworks show
Unvented garage
Venomous snake
Volcanic explosion
Whisky
Worn-out windshield wipers

Nov. 8

# Western White House

WASHINGTON, Nov. 25—President and Mrs. Reagan will once again spend the Thanksgiving holiday weekend at their California ranch.

And once again there will be a traditional family dinner on Thanksgiving, including two family favorites: "monkey" bread (which is made in ring molds) and a turkey stuffed with corn bread dressing.

Joining the Reagans will be the President's brother, Neil, and his wife, Bess; the Reagans' son, Ron, and his wife, Doria, and Mr. Reagan's daughter, Maureen, and her husband, Dennis.

## The Menu

Turkey with Corn Bread Dressing
Cranberries
String Beans with Almonds
Monkey Bread
Mashed Potatoes
Salad
Pumpkin Pie with Whipped Cream

**Mrs. Reagan's Recipe for Corn Bread Dressing**
1 box corn bread stuffing mix
1 pan homemade corn bread
1 package chicken livers
Chopped parsley
1 small stalk celery
3 large onions
Turkey giblets, cooked
Poultry seasoning and white pepper (to taste)

1. Chop chicken livers and sauté in butter. Add finely chopped onions, parsley and celery. Add seasoning to taste.

2. Crumble homemade corn bread and add box of corn bread stuffing mix. Then add chicken liver mixture and stuff turkey.

BASTING TIP: After cooking giblets, divide broth in half. Use half for basting after adding one chicken bouillon cube plus one cube butter. Baste frequently. Retain remaining broth for gravy of your choice.

Nov. 26

# Major Personality Study Finds That Traits Are Mostly Inherited

By DANIEL GOLEMAN

The genetic makeup of a child is a stronger influence on personality than child rearing, according to the first study to examine identical twins reared in different families. The findings shatter a widespread belief among experts and laymen alike in the primacy of family influence and are sure to engender fierce debate.

The findings are the first major results to emerge from a long-term project at the University of Minnesota in which, since 1979, more than 350 pairs of twins have gone through six days of extensive testing that has included analysis of blood, brain waves, intelligence and allergies.

The results on personality are being reviewed for publication by the *Journal of Personality and Social Psychology*. Although there has been wide press coverage of pairs of twins reared apart who met for the first time in the course of the study, the personality results are the first significant scientific data to be announced.

For most of the traits measured, more than half the variation was found to be due to heredity, leaving less than half determined by the influence of parents, home environment and other experiences in life.

The Minnesota findings stand in sharp contradiction to standard wisdom on nature versus nurture in forming adult personality. Virtually all major theories since Freud have given far more importance to environment, or nurture, than to genes, or nature.

The traits were measured using a personality questionnaire developed by Auke Tellegen, a psychologist at the University of Minnesota who was one of the principal researchers. The questionnaire assesses many major aspects of personality, including aggressiveness, striving for achievement and the need for personal intimacy.

For example, agreement with the statement "When I work with others, I like to take charge" is an indication of the trait called social potency, or leadership, while agreement with the sentence "I often keep working on a problem, even if I am very tired" indicates the need for achievement.

Among traits found most strongly determined by heredity were leadership and, surprisingly, traditionalism or obedience to authority. "One would not expect the tendency to believe in traditional values and the strict enforcement of rules to be more an inherited than learned trait," said David Lykken, a psychologist in the Minnesota project. "But we found that, in some mysterious way, it is one of traits with the strongest genetic influence."

Dec. 2

## The Roots of Personality

The degree to which 11 key traits of personality are estimated to be inherited, as gauged by tests with twins. Traits were measured by the Multidimensional Personality Questionnaire, developed by Auke Tellegen at the University of Minnesota.

**Social Potency  61%**
A person high in this trait is masterful, a forceful leader who likes to be the center of attention.

**Traditionalism  60%**
Follows rules and authority, endorses high moral standards and strict discipline.

**Stress Reaction  55%**
Feels vulnerable and sensitive and is given to worries and easily upset.

**Absorption  55%**
Has a vivid imagination readily captured by rich experience; relinquishes sense of reality.

**Alienation 55%**
Feels mistreated and used, that "the world is out to get me."

**Well-Being 54%**
Has a cheerful disposition, feels confident and optimistic.

**Harm Avoidance 51%**
Shuns the excitement of risk and danger, prefers the safe route even if it is tedious.

**Aggression 48%**
Is physically aggressive and vindictive, has taste for violence and is "out to get the world."

**Achievement 46%**
Works hard, strives for mastery and puts work and accomplishment ahead of other things.

**Control 43%**
Is cautious and plodding, rational and sensible, likes carefully planned events.

**Social Closeness 33%**
Prefers emotional intimacy and close ties, turns to others for comfort and help.

DEC. 2

## The way we live

In a study that examines trends in American households and families, the Census Bureau reported last week that American men and women are marrying later than ever before and that more than 1 American adult in 10 lives alone—three times as many as in 1960. Some statistics from the study follow:

**Median age at first marriage**

|       | 1960 | 1965 | 1970 | 1975 | 1980 | 1985 | 1986 |
|-------|------|------|------|------|------|------|------|
| Men   | 22.8 | 22.8 | 23.2 | 23.5 | 24.7 | 25.5 | 25.7 |
| Women | 20.3 | 20.6 | 20.8 | 21.1 | 22.0 | 23.3 | 23.1 |

**Percent of men and women never married**

| Men          | 1950 | 1960 | 1970 | 1980 | 1985 | 1986 |
|--------------|------|------|------|------|------|------|
| 20 to 24 years | 59.0 | 53.1 | 54.7 | 68.8 | 75.6 | 75.5 |
| 25 to 29 years | 23.8 | 20.8 | 19.1 | 33.1 | 38.7 | 41.4 |
| 30 to 34 years | 13.2 | 11.9 | 9.4  | 15.9 | 20.8 | 22.2 |

| Women        | 1950 | 1960 | 1970 | 1980 | 1985 | 1986 |
|--------------|------|------|------|------|------|------|
| 20 to 24 years | 32.3 | 28.4 | 35.8 | 50.2 | 58.5 | 57.9 |
| 25 to 29 years | 13.3 | 10.5 | 10.5 | 20.9 | 26.4 | 28.1 |
| 30 to 34 years | 9.3  | 6.9  | 6.2  | 9.5  | 13.5 | 14.2 |

Source: Bureau of the Census

DEC. 14

**Unmarried couples living together**
(as a percent of all households)

| 1960 | 1970 | 1980 | 1985 | 1986 |
|------|------|------|------|------|
| 0.8  | 0.8  | 2.0  | 2.3  | 2.5  |

**One-person households**
(as a percent of all households)

| 1960 | 1970 | 1980 | 1985 | 1986 |
|------|------|------|------|------|
| 13   | 17   | 23   | 24   | 24   |

## In Wages, Sexes May Be Forever Unequal

By PAUL LEWIS

PARIS—Throughout the industrial world, women are catching up with men in education and earning power. But if some current trends continue, they may never achieve equality.

According to the Organization for Economic Cooperation and Development, women claim a much higher share of places in higher education than they did a decade ago. In the United States, Canada, Norway, Sweden and Denmark, the proportion of women at universities and other institutions of higher education is roughly in line with their proportion in the population, and in a few instances is higher. But many countries, including Japan, Luxembourg, Switzerland and Britain, are lagging in this regard.

The O.E.C.D. found that the gap between what men and women earn is narrowing but persists despite legislation in most of its 24 member nations requiring equal pay for equal work.

The findings are in two recent reports, one on education and the other on women's roles in the economy, that grew out of decade-long studies. Each country supplied its own data. The statistics show women's earnings are closest to men's in Australia, the Scandinavian countries and the Netherlands; O.E.C.D. officials said the figures turned in by Italy and Portugal are not credible. The data from the United States, while not readily comparable to that provided by other countries, suggest that American women are singularly disadvantaged in their earnings.

The percentage of working-age men who are employed has been falling in most Western countries as a result of the prolonged decline of manufacturing. At the same time, the percentage of women in the labor force has risen. Despite women's gains in education, however, most of the new positions they fill are service jobs that require few skills and pay comparatively poorly.

Part of the explanation, according to the O.E.C.D., is that women are still underrepresented in the most prestigious schools, such as France's *grands ecoles*, and specialize in subjects least likely to lead to well-paid jobs. Women tend to concentrate in literature, languages, education and sociology, for example, while young men dominate science, engineering, business studies and law.

But the O.E.C.D. also found that in any given job category men are paid more than women. The report said women tended to be kept in less lucrative positions and to receive less overtime, for example.

"Serious inequalities between girls and boys and between men and women persist," the report said. "A serious gap remains between the official objectives and actual practice."

DEC. 21

## Gains in education and employment by women in selected countries

**Percentage of female students in universities and other institutions of higher education**

|  | 1970 | 1975 | 1980 | 1981 | 1982 | 1983 |
|---|---|---|---|---|---|---|
| Australia | 32.7 | | | | | 46.2 |
| Austria | 29.2 | | | | | 41.1 |
| Belgium | 28.6 | | | | | 39.7 |
| Britain | | 35.8 | 36.4 | | | |
| Canada | 37.4 | | | | | 51.0 |
| Denmark | 36.7 | | | | 48.9 | |
| Finland | 48.4 | | | | | 47.7 |
| France | | 57.1 | | 49.1 | | |
| Japan | 28.2 | | | | | 34.5 |
| Luxembourg | 37.5 | | | | | 35.0 |
| Netherlands | 27.7 | | | | 41.9 | |
| New Zealand | 39.2 | | | | | 41.7 |
| Norway | 28.1 | | | | 48.8 | |
| Spain | 26.7 | | | | | 46.8 |
| Sweden | 42.4 | | | 46.2 | | |
| Switzerland | 22.5 | | | | | 32.8 |
| Turkey | 18.9 | | | | | 33.7 |
| United States | 41.3 | | 51.4 | | | |
| West Germany | 26.9 | | | | 42.0 | |
| Yugoslavia | 39.4 | | | | | 44.9 |

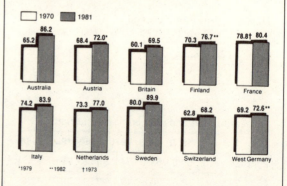

**Average hourly earnings in non-agricultural activities of full-time female workers as a percentage of those of men**

**UNITED STATES**
Earnings of full-time female employees as a percentage of full-time male earnings, by sector

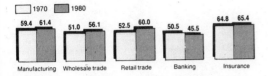

**Percentage of men and women of working age employed full-time or part-time**

|  | Men | | Women | |
|---|---|---|---|---|
|  | 1975 | 1983 | 1975 | 1983 |
| Britain | 92.2 | 87.9 | 55.3 | 57.7 |
| France | 84.4 | 79.4 | 49.9 | 52.1 |
| Japan | 89.7 | 89.1 | 51.7 | 57.2 |
| Netherlands | 83.2 | 80.3 | 31.0 | 38.7 |
| Sweden | 89.2 | 85.9 | 67.6 | 76.6 |
| United States | 84.7 | 84.7 | 53.2 | 61.9 |
| West Germany | 87.0 | 80.0 | 49.6 | 49.6 |

Source: Organization for Economic Cooperation and Development

DEC. 21

# Index

abortion, 208–10
Access, 163–64
Adams, Eddie L., 194
Adams, Leon D., 404
*Admiral Nakhimov,* 52
advertising agencies, 242–44
Aeromexico Flight 498, 159–61
Africa:
    economic crisis in, 34–36
    life in, 35
    malnutrition and poverty in, 36
    survival difficult in, 35–36
    UN aid to, 33
Africa Fund, 112
Agca, Mehmet Ali, 22–23
Aghazadeh, Gholam Reza, 63
agriculture, *see* farmers
Agriculture Department, U.S., 425
airlines:
    accidents and, 25, 84, 159–61
    future rankings of, 238–39
    operating costs of, 236–37
Alabama, 155
Alaska, 186, 188
Alfano, Peter, 331–32
Algren, Nelson, 380
*Alice's Adventures in Wonderland* (Carroll), 381
Allied-Signal Corporation, 245
All-Star Game, 342, 345–46
Alma-Ata riots, 81
American Association of University Professors, 191
American Bar Association, 130
American Forestry Association, 408
American Heart Association, 427
American Hospital Association, 98
American League, 325, 346–47, 350
    in All-Star Game, 342, 345
    playoffs of, 356–58
American Motors Corporation (AMC), 38, 236, 248
American Petroleum Institute, 249
American Protestant Health Association, 98
Americans for Democratic Action, 209
American Stock Exchange (Amex), 273, 281, 285, 296
    gainers and losers on, 275, 283, 297–98, 308
    most active issues on, 309
American Viewpoint, 232
*American Wine* (Blue), 404
American Wine Society, 417
Ameritrust Corporation, 269
Amis, Kingsley, 396
Amos, William, 380–82
Anaya, Toney, 194
Anderson, Clayton & Company, 254–55
Anderson, Dave, 333–36
Andersson, Arne, 338
Andújar, Joaquín, 321
Antarctica, 84
antidrug legislation, 223–24
Apple, R.W., Jr., 202
Applebome, Peter, 158–59, 167
Aquino, Benigno S., Jr., 73
Aquino, Corazon C., 43
    ascendancy to presidency by, 11–12
    cease-fire negotiated by, 73
    in Philippine elections, 4
    U.S. recognition of, 7–11
Argentina, 3
Armacost, Samuel H., 300
Armada Corporation, 240
arms control:
    glossary for, 64–65
    public opinion on, 226–27
    tentative agreements on, 64
    U.S. and Soviet proposals on, 44–46, 64
Armstrong, Neil A., 92
arts awards, 379–80, 384–85
Ashburn, Richie, 341
Asselstine, James K., 126
Associated Press, 370
Association of Southeast Asian Nations, 43
asteroids, 110
astronauts:
    asteroids named for, 110
    on *Challenger,* 88, 91, 110
Atlanta Braves, 342, 364
Atoms Track Club, 339
auto age, 86–87
automobile industry:
    adjustments forced on, 262–63
    base-model price list of, 239
    four-wheel-drive models of, 248–49

automobile industry *(cont'd)*
    importance of size in, 260–61
    of Japan, 248, 261, 263
    profitability of, 237–38
automobile racing, 341
automotive research, 236
aviation safety, 161
awards:
    in arts, 379–80, 384–85
    in baseball, 346–47, 361–63
    genius, 385–86
    for heroism, 119, 176, 196–97
    for journalism, 374, 378–80, 382–83, 386
    for magazines, 379
    for science, 374–77
    for television, 374, 382, 384
    for theater, 377–78, 383–84
    for writing, 374, 377, 379–80, 384, 388–91
    *see also specific awards*

bachelor's degrees, 147, 240
Bagci, Omer, 23
Baker, Augusta, 388
Baker, Russell, 430–31
Ballesteros, Steve, 333
Balzac, Honoré de, 380
Banc One, 269
BankAmerica Corporation, 240, 268
    Armacost and, 300–1
Bankers Trust Company, 288
Bank of England, 295
bankruptcies, 252–53
banks:
    commercial, 277, 304–5
    earnings of, 266–67
    first-quarter results of, 278
    growth of, 269–70
    investment, 266, 279, 287, 294–96
    loans to Argentina by, 3
    in Middle West, 269–70
    non-loan profits of, 288
    profit pressure at, 301
    profits of, 277
    savings and loan associations as, 304–6
    second-quarter results of, 288–89
    size and success of, 268–69
    third quarter results of, 302–3
Bannister, Roger, 338
banquets:
    of Hirohito, 31
    for prime minister of Pakistan, 421–22
    at Western White House, 431
    at White House, 402–3, 421–22
Barmash, Isadore, 254
Barrett, Marty, 359–60
baseball:
    All-Star Game of, 342, 345–46
    All-Star voting in, 343–45
    all-time leaders in, 355–56
    attendance gains and losses of, 353–54
    award winners of, 346–47, 361–63
    base stealers in, 346
    batters hit by pitches in, 347
    batting races in, 350
    batting statistics for, 352–53
    best players in, 342–44
    coaches and managers in, 322–23
    computer predictions for, 325
    consecutive-game streaks in, 341
    drug abuse in, 320–21
    final standings for, 351
    final statistics for, 352–54
    going from minors to majors in, 330
    home run records in, 350
    pennant winners in, 356–58
    pitching statistics for, 354
    players' poll in, 342–43
    salaries in, 315, 321, 324, 364
    scouting for, 332
    successful franchises in, 347–48
    top strikeout games in, 329
    World Series of, 359–61
    worst statistics in, 368
baseball parks, 350
basketball, college, 367
    championship games of, 323–24
    coaches of, 318–19
basketball, professional:
    centers in, 331
    champions of, 367
    draft picks in, 340–41
    drug abuse in, 319–20
    steals in, 322
Ted Bates Worldwide, 242–43
Baylor, Don, 347
Bay Street, 289

BBDO International, 243
Beamon, Bob, 339
Beauvoir, Simone de, 380
Beef, 425–26
Bennett, William J., 94, 95
Berg, Eric N., 3, 266–67, 268, 277, 288, 301
Berke, Richard L., 162, 168–69, 197–98
Berkow, Ira, 322–23, 329
Berman, Stephen, 301
Bernstein, Joseph E., 17
Bernstein, Richard, 16
Berra, Dale, 320–21
Berra, Yogi, 322–23, 362
Berry, Ray, 316
best book selections, 388–91
best sellers, 392–94
Bethesda Naval Medical Center, 151
Biaggi, Mario, 40
Biderman, Mark, 267
Big Bang Day, 295
*Big Chill, The,* 286
Black & Decker Corporation, 291
*Black Enterprise,* 242
blacks:
    businesses owned by, 241–42
    in 1986 elections, 185–86
    in South Africa, 29
    wages earned by, 97
Black Sea, sinking of Soviet liner in, 52
Blanck, Max, 106–7
Bleakley, Fred R., 294–95
Blix, Hans, 31
Blue, Anthony Dias, 404
Bogdanowicz-Bindert, Christine A., 3
Boggs, Wade, 329, 359
Bond, Christopher, 177
bonds:
    bank profits spurred by, 277
    corporate, 310
    heavy demand for, 310
    junk, 280, 303–4, 310
bookstores, 254
Bortel, Allan G., 304
Boston Corporation, 268
Boston Red Sox, 329, 345–46, 364
    pennant won by, 356–58
    in World Series, 359–61
Bosworth, Brian, 365
boxing, 365

Boyd, Dennis (Oil Can), 359
Boyd, Gerald M., 92, 232–33
Bradley, Phil, 329
Breau, John B., 185
Brinkley, Joel, 13–14, 98, 156, 188
British Open, 335–36
Broad, William J., 88–91
broadcasters, 314
Brock, Lou, 360
Brody, Jane E., 405–7, 427
Brown, Harold, 257
Brown, Michael W., 195
Broyhill, James T., 179, 185
Bruno, John, 370
Bryan, Charles F., 237
Bubka, Sergei, 338
Budget, U.S. (1987):
   evolution of, 136–37
   House's approval of, 123–26
   programs retained in, 134–35
budget-balancing amendment, 109–10
budget-balancing law:
   cuts required by, 87
   Supreme Court decision on, 143–44
Burger, Warren E., 133, 144, 166, 222–23
Burns, John F., 38
Burros, Marian, 425–26
Bush, George, 162, 179
business, businesses:
   black-owned, 241–42
   directors of, 239, 240
   industry and, 235–64
   investments in South Africa of, 48–50, 65–66
   public opinion on, 218–19
   retail, 254
   small, 258–60
   social issues as interest of, 116–17
   Tax Reform Act and, 258–60
   transition tax rules beneficial to, 246–48
   write-offs for, 260
business holdings of Mormon Church, 85
Butkus Award winners, 365
Butterfield, Fox, 163–64

Cabell, Enos, 321
California, 188
California Angels, 356–58

calories, 401, 406–8
campaign debts, 197–98
campaign funds:
   PACs' contributions to, 108–9, 162–63, 168–69
   of Republican vs. Democratic senators, 152–54
Campanella, Roy, 362
Canada, securities industry of, 289–90
Candelaria, John, 357
Canseco, Jose, 362
capital appreciation funds, 311–12
Capote, 370
car-buying habits, 236
Carlucci, Frank C., 75–76
Carnegie, Andrew, 119
Carnegie Hero Fund Commission, 119, 176, 196–97
Carroll, Lewis, 381
Carruthers, Garrey, 194
Carter, Gary, 359–60
Carter, Jimmy, 107, 130, 198
Carter, Theophilus, 381
Cary, Larry, 107
Castro, Fidel, 165
Catholic Conference, U.S., 165
CBS Inc., 256–58
   board of, 257
   upheaval at, 257–58
Census Bureau, U.S., 145, 199
Central America, 214, 229
*Challenger* space shuttle:
   crew of, 88, 91, 110
   explosion of, 88–91, 204–5
   final minute of, 93–94
   presidential commission on, 92
   public opinion since, 204–6
Charle, Suzanne M., 397
Chase Manhattan, 269
Chass, Murray, 346, 364
Chemical New York Corporation, 288
chemicals, agricultural, 128–29
Cheney, Dick, 17–18
Chernobyl nuclear reactor:
   accident at, 29–31, 126, 127–28
   safety features of, 127–28
chess, 62–63
Chevron Corporation, 249
Chicago Bears, 316
Chicago Cubs, 364
Chicago White Sox, 347
children:
   books for, 388–89

   personalities of, 432
   space travel approved by, 204–6
China, People's Republic of:
   foreign investments in, 38–39
   traveling to, 419–20
   U.S. joint ventures with, 39
Chirac, Jacques, 16
cholesterol, 427–29
Chrysler Corporation, 237–38, 248, 261
Cisneros, Henry G., 195
Citibank, 269
Citicorp, 268, 288, 300
Citter, Rick, 224
City, The (London), 294
*City & State*, 195
civil service:
   Federal, 142, 158–59
   international, 57
Claiborne, Harry E., 145
Clausen, A. W., 300
Clean Water Act (1977), 134
Clemens, Roger, 342
   in All-Star Game, 345
   as Most Valuable Player, 361–62
   in playoffs, 357
   20-strikeout game of, 329–30
Clinton, De Witt, 397
Clymer, Adam, 204–5, 208–9, 215–16, 218, 222–24, 226, 231–32
coaches:
   of baseball teams, 322–23
   of basketball teams, 318–19
   of track and field teams, 338–39
cocaine:
   in professional sports, 319–21
   student use of, 143
Coffee, John C., Jr., 286
Cole, Alyson, 112
Coleman, Daniel, 432
colleges:
   bachelor's degrees conferred by, 147
   doctorates conferred by, 187–88
   endowments of, 167
   fees paid to guest lecturers by, 190–91
   investments in South Africa and, 112–13
   *see also* education; students
Commerce Department, U.S., 173

commercial banks, 277
  savings and loans vs., 304–5
  see also banks
Commission on Executive, Legislative, and Judicial Salaries, 195
Common Cause, 152
communications industry, 244–45, 256–58
comparable worth, 194–95
Compton, Joel L., 194
computer technology, 293, 325
Conference of Mayors, U.S., 195
Congress, U.S., 144, 147, 171–72, 174
  on assistance to U.N., 46
  budget resolution of, 134–35
  on immigration legislation, 172–73
  on national speed limit, 175
  PACs and, 108–9
  see also House of Representatives, U.S.; Senate, U.S.
congressmen, 195
Connally, John B., 197
Connecticut, 132, 188
Connolly, John D., 273
Conrail, 134
Constitution, U.S., 144, 209
Consumer Price Index, 173
Continental Basketball Association, 319
Continental Illinois Corporation, 269–70
Contras, see Iran-Contra affair; Nicaraguan rebel aid
Conway, Robert M., 294
Cooper, Gordon, 144
Cooper, Lady Diana, 382
Corallo, Anthony (Tony Ducks), 192
corn, U.S. production of, 33
corporate bonds, 310
corporate social policies, 116–17
corporations, 259–60
  see also business, businesses
corruption inquiries, 110–11
Cosby, Bill, 190–91, 392–93
Council on Economic Priorities, 116
Court of Appeals, U.S., 130–32
Coward, Noel, 381
Cram, Steve, 337–38
Cranston, Alan, 37, 177, 185

credit cards, interest rates on, 240–41
Credit-Suisse First Boston Corporation, 294, 310
crime, 194
  insider trading as, 279–80, 286–87
Crist, Steven, 370
Crocker National Corporation, 301
Crossette, Barbara, 73
Crowe, William J., 416–17
Crown Books, 254
Crudele, John, 293, 306
Cuba, political prisoners released by, 165–66
cultural news, 373–94
Cummings, Judith, 159
Cunningham, Billy, 318
Cy Young Award winners, 346–47, 361–62

*Daily Race Form,* 370
B. Dalton, 254
Daniels, Lee A., 249
Daniloff, Nicholas S., 57–58
Darling, Ron, 359–60
Davis, Glenn, 362
Davis, Mae, 380–81
Dayton-Hudson Corporation, 254
Dean Witter Reynolds, 273
death penalty:
  Anaya on, 194
  Supreme Court on, 120
Dedeurwaerder, Jose, 236
Defense Department, U.S., 93, 123
de la Madrid, Miguel, 228
Delaware, 156
Delcap Fund 1, 311–12
DeLeon, José, 347
Democrat, Republican Independent Voter Education (DRIVE), 168–69
Democratic Party:
  campaign funds raised for, 152–54
  gain in House by, 177, 179, 185–86
  Senate controlled by, 176–77, 178–79, 185–86
Democratic Senatorial Campaign Committee, 152
demography, 80–81
denationalization, 14–15

Dent, Richard, 316
Denton, Jeremiah, 185
Desmarais, Henry R., 98
Detroit Tigers, 347
DeVoe, Raymond F., Jr., 272–73
Diamond, Stuart, 126–28
DiBona, Charles J., 249
Dickens, Charles, 383
Diller, Barry, 264
DiMaggio, Joe, 362
Dingman, Michael D., 245
Dionne, E. J., Jr., 176–77, 178–79, 207–8, 211
Diouf, Abdou, 35
director insurance, 240
Distilling and Cattle Feeding Company, 272
Ditka, Mike, 316
Divall, Linda, 232
divestment:
  by businesses, 48–50, 65–66
  by colleges, 112–13
divorce rates, 111
doctorates, 187–88
doctors, disciplining of, 188–90
Dole, Bob, 171, 176
Domenici, Pete V., 134
Dominion Securities Pitfield Ltd., 289
Doubleday, Nelson, Jr., 348
Doubleday & Company, 348
Dow Jones industrial average, 281
  historic closes of, 271
  largest one-day declines in, 293
  severe drops in, 266
  stock market in step with, 272–73
  stocks included in, 271–72
  surges in, 270
Doyle Dane Bernbach Group, 243
Drew, John, 319
Drexel Burnham Lambert, 280, 310
droughts, 154–56
drugs:
  glamorizing use of, 224
  Mexican trafficking in, 229
  over-the-counter, 238
  public concern over, 223–25
  student use of, 143
  see also cocaine
drug testing, 224, 225
Dumas, Charlie, 338
Dunaway, Jim, 338

Alfred I. duPont-Columbia University Awards in Broadcast Journalism, 374
Durso, Joseph, 347–48, 359–60
Dykstra, Len, 359–60

Eagleton, Thomas F., 179
East, James P., 179
Eastern Airlines, 236–37
Eberfeld, Norm, 347
Eckholm, Erik, 408
Eclipse Award winners, 370–71
economic problems:
 in Africa, 34–36
 of Mexico, 228–29
 in Southeast Asia, 43
education:
 Alaska's spending for, 186
 of women, 433–35
 *see also* colleges; students
Education Department, U.S., 94, 147, 187–88
 on teaching, 95, 96
Ehlen, James G., Jr., 277
800-meter run, 339
Einhorn, Steven G., 273
Eisenhower, Dwight D., 202
Eisner, Michael, 264
election of 1986:
 blacks and, 185–86
 for governor, 177, 179, 184–85
 for House, 177–78, 179, 180–82, 227
 regional power changes and, 177–78
 for Senate, 176–77, 178–79, 183, 185–86
 voters and nonvoters compared for, 178
election of 1988, 233
Ellis Island Medal of Honor recipients, 169–70
Employee Benefit Research Institute, 174
employment, 53, 132
endowments:
 for high school graduates, 164–65
 of universities, 167
Energy Department, U.S., 93
English dialects, 397–98
Enrile, Juan Ponce, 9–10
Environmental Protection Agency (EPA), 128–29
Ermita, Eduardo, 73

Espy, Mike, 186
Eurobonds, 291–92, 294
Euroequities, 291–92
Europe, 261–62
 capital markets of, 291–92
 governments trusted in, 207–8
 on military reply to terrorism, 211-12
Evans, Dwight, 359–60
executive branch officials, 195
exercise, 403, 405
 calories used in, 401, 406–8
 longevity and, 401
 moderate levels of, 405–7

Fabrikant, Geraldine, 255–57, 264
farmers:
 chemicals used by, 128–29
 market share of, 32–33
 public sympathy for, 210–11
Farnsworth, Clyde H., 32–33
fast food, 400
fat:
 in beef, 425–26
 cholesterol and, 427–29
*Fatherhood* (Cosby), 392–93
Feder, Barnaby J., 116–17
Federal Aviation Administration, 159
Federal Bankruptcy Code, Chapter 11 of, 252
Federal Bureau of Investigation, 57
Federal Election Commission, 162, 168–69, 197
Federal employees, 142
Federal Reserve Board, 306
Federation of State Medical Boards, 188
fellowships, 375–76, 382–83, 385–86
Fernandez, Sid, 360
Ferrugio, Richard, 397
fictional characters, 380–82
finance, markets and, 265–312
fires, 106–7
First Boston Corporation, 280, 310
First Chicago Corporation, 269
First Indiana Bankcorp, 269
First Interstate Bancorp, 300
fish, 398–99
Fisher, John F., 269
Fisher, Lawrence E., 255

Fiske, Edward B., 95
Fitzgerald, F. Scott, 381
Florida, 188, 199
Foley, Thomas S., 17
football, college:
 award winners of, 365
 best cumulative records in, 366, 369
 computer ranking for, 363–64
 final standings for, 369–70
 predictions for, 347
 toughest schedules in, 366-67
football, professional:
 best rushing performances in, 314
 draft picks in, 327
 favorite team in, 234
 final standings for, 349
 hall of fame members of, 318
 leading receivers in, 314
 lightweight team of, 349
 predictions for, 348–49
 Pro Bowl teams selected for, 365–66
 Super Bowl results in, 316–17
Ford, Gerald R., 231
Ford Motor Company, 237–38, 248, 261
foreign aid:
 recipients of, 32
 from UN, 33
 from U.S., 31–32
Forest Service, U.S., 168
44 Wall Street Equity, 311–12
401(k) retirement plans, 258
four-wheel-drive vehicles, 248–49
Foxx, Jimmie, 362
France, 207–8, 211, 262
 Chirac as premier of, 16
 denationalization for, 14–15
 NATO and, 68
Frank, Konstantin, 404–5
Frank, Peter H., 254–55
Freehan, Bill, 347
French, Howard W., 391–92
Freud, Sigmund, 432
Frost, Bob, 49
Fuerbringer, Jonathan, 123, 142
Fulton Fish Market, 398
Fund for America's Future, 162
Furman Selz Mager Dietz & Birney Inc., 255

Gagliardo, Greg, 334

Gallup, George, 231
Gallup International, 207
Gallup Organization, 230
Gallup Polls, 219, 223
Gamarekian, Barbara, 410–11
Gannett Center Fellowship
    winners, 386
Gannett Company, 244–45
Garcia, Richard R., 194
Garcia Estevez, Carmello, 165
Gardner, Herb, 383
gasoline consumption, 96–97
    *see also* oil, oil industry
Gedman, Rich, 346, 359
Gehrig, Lou, 342
Gemma, Peter, 209
General Electric (GE), 50
General Motors Corporation
    (GM), 248, 262–63
    divestment by, 65
    size of, 260–61
General Sherman, 408
generation gap, 224–25
genius awards, 385–86
*Gentlemen Prefer Blondes*
    (Loos), 380–81
Georgia, 155
Georgia Tech University, 318
Gerasimov, Gennadi I., 66
Germany, Federal Republic of
    (West), 207–8, 211, 262
Gibson, William E., 268
Gilbert, William W., 194
Gilpin, Kenneth N., 245
*Girl Like I, A* (Loos), 381
Giscard D'Estaing, Valéry, 15
Giuliani, Rudolph W., 192
Glenn, John, 144, 198
Goldaper, Sam, 319
Goldman, Sachs & Company,
    273, 277, 287
Goldman, Sachs International,
    294
Goldwyn, Sam, 381
Goldy Award winners, 377–78
golf, 333–37, 367
Golf Association, U.S. (USGA),
    335
golf courses:
    designing of, 331–32
    for U.S. Opens, 333–36
Gomez Blanco, Juan, 165
Gooden, Dwight, 330–31, 342,
    345
Goodwin, Michael, 320–21

Gorbachev, Mikhail S., 202
    at Reykjavík summit, 64, 66,
        67–68, 226
    Soviet demography and, 81
    Soviet leadership shake-up by,
        5–6
Gordon, Michael R., 44
Gordon Capital Corporation, 289
Gottesman, Alan J., 242
government corruption, 110–11,
    212–13
governorships:
    1986 races for, 184–85
    Republican gains in, 177, 179
Graddick, Charles, 177
graduation rates, 94–95
Graefe, Frederick, 98
Grantham, Charles, 319
Gray, William H., 3d, 58
Great Britain, 207–8, 211, 262
    U.S. investment banks in,
        294–96
    on U.S. raid on Libya, 215–16
Greener, William, 179
Greenhouse, Linda, 39–40, 113,
    166
Greenhouse, Steven, 269–70
Griffey, Ken, 364
gross domestic production, 43
Gruet, Jean-Claude, 238
Gruntal Inc., 293
guest lecturers, fees charged by,
    190–91
Gun Control Act (1968), 113
guns, 86
    House on sale of, 113–16
Guskin, Alan E., 112
Gutfreund, John H., 303
Guzman, Michael A., 194
Gwertzman, Bernard, 31–32, 57,
    64

Haberman, Clyde, 2–3, 217
Haft, Robert, 254
Hagg, Gunder, 338
Hale, Steve, 318
Hall, Bradley, 196
Halloran, Richard, 145
Hamilton, Brutus, 338–39
Hammonds, Keith H., 48–50
*Hangover Handbook, The*
    (Outerbridge), 396
hangover remedies, 396
Harris, Isaac, 106–7
Hart, Gary, 177

Hart, Peter D., 232
Harvard University, 167
    Nieman Foundation at, 190
health, 427–29
    President Reagan's, 151–52
    *see also* exercise
Health and Human Services
    Department, U.S. (HHS),
    98, 146, 188
health care:
    spending for, 146–47
    *see also* hospitals
Health Care Financing
    Administration, 98
heart surgery, mortality rates
    after, 156–58
heavyweight champions, 365
Heebner, G. Kenneth, 285, 312
Hefner, W. G., 18
Hemingway, Ernest, 380
Henderson, Dave, 359
Henderson, Rickey, 342
Henley Group Inc., 245–46
Hennessy, John M., 294
Hernandez, Keith, 320–21, 360
Hershey, Robert D., Jr., 173
Hicks, Jonathan P., 241–42
*Hidden Game of Baseball, The*
    (Palmer and Thorn), 325
high-density lipoproteins
    (HDLs), 406, 427
Higuera, Ted, 345–46
hijackings:
    casualty lists for, 56
    in Karachi, 55–56
hiring biases, 53–54
Hirohito, Emperor of Japan, 31
hockey, 367
Hofman, Rob, 50
Hohn, Uwe, 338
Holderman, James B., 190
Holloway, Tommy, 91
Holusha, John, 65, 236, 237–38,
    248, 260–61, 262–63
Homan, Paul M., 269–70
Home Shopping Network Inc.,
    285, 312
Mark Hopkins Inter-Continental
    Hotel, 404–5
horse racing, 328, 370–71
hospitals, 146–47
    death rates of, 98–106
    VA, 156–58
hostages:
    arms shipments to Iran and,

72–73, 75–76
  as missing in Lebanon, 26–27, 71
  release from Lebanon of, 70–71
  U.S. arms trades for, 71–73, 74–75, 77–79, 231
  in West Virginia Penitentiary, 84
Hough, Charlie, 345–46
House of Representatives, U.S., 154
  on aid to Nicaraguan rebels, 17–21, 39–43, 214
  on antidrug legislation, 223–24
  Appropriations for Foreign Operations Subcommittee of, 31
  blacks elected to, 185–86
  Democratic gains in, 177, 179, 185–86
  Federal officials impeached by, 145
  Intergovernmental Relations and Human Relations Subcommittee of, 156
  in 1986 election, 177–78, 179, 180–82, 227
  1987 budget plan approved by, 123–26
  portrait of electorate and, 180–82
  public opinion on, 227–28
  roll call votes of, 18–21, 40–43, 59–61, 114–16, 123–26, 148–51
  Rules Committee of, 411
  on sale of guns, 113–16
  sanctions on South Africa approved by, 58–61
  shifting balances in, 177–78
  on trade legislation, 32–33, 148–51
  Ways and Means Committee of, 171, 411
  see also Congress, U.S.; Senate, U.S.
Houston Astros, 322
  in playoffs, 356–57
Howard, Elston, 322
Howard, James J., 175
Howser, Dick, 345
Hubbell, Carl, 345
Humanitas Prize winners, 384
Humphrey, Hubert H., 198

Hunt, Guy, 177
Hunt, H. L., 252
Hunt, Lamar, 252
Hunt, Nelson Bunker, 252–53
Hunt, Ron, 347
Hunt, W. Herbert, 252–53
Hurst, Bruce, 359–60
Hurt, William, 286

Icahn, Carl, 303
ice cream, 423–25
Iceland summit meeting, see Reykjavík summit meeting
ideological alignments, 202–4
immigration, public opinion on, 219–22
Immigration Reform and Control Act, 172
*I'm Not Rappaport* (Gardner), 383
impeachments, 145
imported textiles, legislation to place limits on, 148–51
India, 32
Individual Retirement Accounts (IRAs), 258, 259
industry, industries:
  advertising, 242–44
  airlines, 236–37, 238–39
  automobile, 236, 237–38, 239, 248–49, 260–61, 262–63
  business and, 235–64
  communications, 244–45, 256–58
  insurance, 240
  motion pictures, 264
  oil, 4, 63, 69, 70, 79, 249–50, 252–53
  pet food, 254–55
  relationship of military spending to, 261–62
inherited traits, 432
insects, 412–15
insider trading, 279–80, 286–87
insurance industry, 240
interest rates:
  on credit card purchases, 240–41
  stock markets and, 273, 293, 306
Interfaith Center on Corporate Responsibility, 65, 116–17
International Association of Ice Cream Manufacturers, 423
International Association of

Machinists and Aerospace Workers, 237
International Atomic Energy Agency, 31
International Brotherhood of Teamsters, 168–69
international civil service, 57
international events, 1–81
international funds, 311
International Thomson Organization, 256
investment banking firms, 266, 287
  capital positions of, 279
  of U.S. in Britain, 294–96
  see also underwriters
investments:
  in China, 38–39
  IRAs as, 259
  in Northern Ireland, 53
  in South Africa, see divestment
Investor Responsibility Research Center, 49
Iran:
  oil ministers of, 63
  U.S. embassy in, 231
  U.S. military aid sent to, 71–75, 77–79
Iran-Contra affair, 75–76, 230, 232–34
Iran-Iraq war, 79
Ireland, Northern, 211
  hiring bias opposed in, 53–54
Islamic Holy War, 70
Israel, 211
Istanbul, terrorism in, 54–55
*It* (King), 392–93
Italy, 207–8, 211

Jackson, Reggie, 350
Jacobsen, David P., 70–71
Jagusch, Sybille A., 388
James, George, 135–36
Janofsky, Michael, 348–49
Japan, 262
  automobile industry of, 248, 261, 263
  financial institutions of, 287–88, 290
  payments to Marcos by, 14
  public opinion in, 217–18
  U.S. trade relations with, 2
  as world power, 217–18
javelin, 338
Javier Blanco, Francisco, 168

Jay, John, 133
Jenkins, Nancy Harmon, 396, 398, 419–20
Jews, terrorist acts against, 54–55
job growth, 132
John Paul II, 22–24
Johnson, Davey, 359
Johnson, Dirk, 24–25
Johnson, Lyndon B., 410
Johnson Space Center, 91
Johnston, Lloyd D., 143
joint ventures, Sino-American, 39
Jones, Robert Trent, 331–32
Jones, Thomas E., 268
journalism awards, 374, 378–80, 382–83, 386
*Journal of Personality and Social Psychology*, 432
Joyner, Wally, 342, 362
Junejo, Mohammad Khan, 421–22
junk bonds, 280, 303–4, 310
Juppé, Alain, 15
Justice Department, U.S., 76, 86, 107, 130

Kaldor, Mary, 262
Kamm, Henry, 54–55
Kansas City Royals, 325, 346
Karachi, hijacking in, 55–56
Karpov, Anatoly, 62
Kasparov, Gary, 62–63
Kaufman, Henry, 303
Kazakhstan, 80–81
Keller, Bill, 80–81, 93
Keller, George M., 249
Keller, Maryann N., 238
Kennedy, Edward M., 62
Kennedy, Robert F., 113
Kennedy Space Center, 89, 90
Kentucky Derby, 328, 370
Kermes, Kenneth, 291
Khomeini, Ayatollah Ruhollah, 72
Kifner, John, 70–71
Kilborn, Peter T., 70
King, Martin Luther, Jr., 112, 113, 185
King, Stephen, 392–93
Kirk, Paul G., Jr., 179
Kite, Tom, 333
Klein, Eugene V., 370
Kline, Kevin, 286
Klott, Gary, 258–60

Knepper, Bob, 356
Knight, Jonathan, 191
Knight, Ray, 359–60
Koch, Edward I., 135
  inaugural reception for, 397
  N.Y.C. government corruption and, 212–13
  salary of, 194–95
Kohut, Andrew, 230
Kolbin, Gennadi V., 80
Korea, Republic of (South), 231, 263
Koren, Ed, 388
Kramer, William C., 161
Kratochvilova, Jarmila, 339
Kusserow, Richard P., 188

Labor Department, U.S., 107, 142
Lady's Secretary, 370
Lambert, Bruce, 194–95
Land-Rover-Leyland International Holdings, 248
Lange, David, 43
Langenberg, Rena, 197
Langer, Bernhard, 333
language, 397–98, 410
Laning, Robert A., 156
Lardner, Ring, 381
Latin America, debts of, 3, 8
Lauber, John, 161
Laurens, Henry, 418–19
Laxalt, Paul, 10, 177
Leach, Wilford, 383
Lebanon:
  hostages missing in, 26–27, 71
  U.S. hostage freed in, 70–71
Lebo, Jeff, 318
Lee Kuan Yew, 43
Legg Mason Wood Walker Inc., 272–73
Lehrer, James, 190
Leonard, Jeff, 321
Lerner, Alan Jay, 384
"Letters of Delegates to Congress" (Library of Congress), 418–19
Levine, Dennis B., 286
Lewin, Tamar, 106–7, 240, 286
Lewis, Ann F., 209
Lewis, Carl, 339
Lewis, Paul, 14–15, 261–62, 433–34
Liberty Weekend, 142
  cleanup after, 144–45

Library of Congress, U.S., 418–19
Libya, 211
  key military forces of, 22
  major trading partners of, 2–3, 29
  U.S. air raid on, 27, 215–16
  U.S. relations with, 27–28
Lietzke, Bruce, 333
Lindenauer, Geoffrey G., 213
Lindsey, Robert, 160–61
Lipper, Michael, 311
Lipper Analytical Services, 285, 311
litigations, 239, 240
Litsky, Frank, 337–39
Little, Brown Company, 256
*Lloyds Bank Review*, 262
Lo, Robert, 38
Loews Corporation, 256–57
Lohr, Steve, 53–54, 79, 291–92
Lolley, Beverly, 159
longevity, 401
long-jump, 328–29
Loos, Anita, 380–81
Lord, Richard, 398
Los Angeles Dodgers, 325, 345, 347–48
Louis Vieux, 408
low-density lipoproteins (LDLs), 427
Lubasch, Arnold H., 192
*Luck of the Bodkins, The* (Wodehouse), 381
Lugar, Richard G., 4, 37, 61–62
Lukas, D. Wayne, 370
Lydenberg, Steven, 116
Lykken, David, 432

MacArthur, Douglas, 144
MacArthur Fellowship winners, 385–86
McAuliffe, Christa, 88–90, 205
MacBride, Sean, 53
MacBride Principles, 53–54
McCurdy, Dave, 18
McDermott, James J., 3
McDowell, Edwin, 392–93
McLeod Young Weir Ltd., 289
McNamara, John, 359
MacNeil, Robert, 190
Maeroff, Gene I., 112
Mafia commission, 192–93
magazine awards, 379
mail carriers, 158–59

Malbin, Michael, 162
malnutrition, African, 36
management, nuclear reactor, 126
*Mandarins, The* (Beauvoir), 380
mandatory retirement, 174–75
Manion, Daniel A., 130
Mansfield, Mike, 2
Mantle, Mickey, 362
Manufacturers Hanover
    Corporation, 288
marathons, 326
Marcos, Ferdinand E.:
    bank deposits made by, 14
    Manhattan property owned by,
      17
    personal fortune of, 13–14
    in Philippine elections, 4
    Philippines fled by, 7–11
    retinue of, 13
Marcos, Imelda, 7, 9, 17
marijuana, 224
maritime disasters:
    recent, 52–53
    of Soviet Union, 52
Market and Opinion Research
    International, 211, 216
market research, 236
markets:
    farmers' share of, 32–33
    finance and, 265–312
    for oil, 70
    for pain relievers, 238
    for textbooks, 256
Markey, Edward J., 126, 128
Markham, James M., 67–68
marriage rates, 111, 433
Martin, Douglas, 289–90
Martin, Robin, 50
Martinez, Michael, 345–46
Maryland, 155
Mastercard, 240–41
Masters Tournaments, 335–36
Mattingly, Don, 242, 361
Mauch, Gene, 356–57
Maxwell, John C., Jr., 255
Maxwell, Robert, 294
Mayewski, Raymond, 396
mayors, salaries of, 194–95
Mayor's Liberty Medal
    recipients, 135–36
Mazza, N. Douglas, 248
Mazzilli, Lee, 360
Mboumoua, William Eteki, 33
Medal of Freedom winners,
    122–23

Medal of Liberty winners, 97
Media General Financial
    Services, 273, 281, 296
Medicaid, 146–47
medical errors, preventable,
    156–58
Medicare, 98, 146–47
Meese, Edwin, 3d, special
    prosecutor requested by,
    75–76
Meislin, Richard J., 212–13,
    230–31
Mencken, H. L., 381
menus:
    for Hirohito's banquet, 31
    for Koch's inaugural reception,
      397
    for Reagan's Thanksgiving
      dinner, 431
    for White House dinners, 402,
      422
mergers and acquisitions, 303–4
    in advertising industry, 242–44
    biggest, 311
    in communications industry,
      244–45
    in pet food industry, 254–55
    in publishing industry, 255–56
Messer, Velma, 119
metropolitan statistical areas,
    145–46
Metzenbaum, Howard M., 174
Mexico:
    economic problems of, 228–29
    U.S. relations with, 229–30
Miami, University of, 370
"Miami Vice," 224
Middle Atlantic states, heat and
    drought in, 154–56
Middle East, terrorist links to,
    25–26
Middle West, 269–70
milers, 337–38
military aid:
    hostage releases and, 72–73,
      77–79
    for Iran, 71–75, 77–79
    for Nicaraguan rebels, 18–21,
      39–43, 48, 74, 75–76
    for Saudi Arabia, 37–38
military forces:
    conventional, 67–68
    of Libya, 22
military spending, 93, 123
    industrial performance and,

      261–62
Milwaukee Brewers, 345
Mitchell, George J., 152
Mitterrand, François, 14–15, 16
mob figures:
    convictions of, 192–93
    trials of, 118
Molotsky, Irvin, 384–85
Montreal Expos, 347
Moore, Arch A., Jr., 84
Moore, Jesse W., 89, 90
Moore, W. Henson, 185
Moran, Malcolm, 369–70
J.P. Morgan & Company, 305
Morgan Guaranty Trust
    Company, 288
Morgan Stanley & Company, 280
Mormon Church, 85
mortality rates:
    after heart surgery, 156–58
    of hospitals, 98–106, 156–58
Most Valuable Player Award
    winners, 361–63
Motion Picture Association of
    America, 410
motion pictures industry, 264
Mountbatten, Lord and Lady, 381
MRCA Information Services, 255
murders, 158–59
Murphy, Art, 264
Murphy, Dale, 341, 342
Murphy, Eddie, 264
Musial, Stan, 362
mutual funds:
    first quarter performance of,
      277
    second-quarter performance
      of, 285–86
    fourth-quarter performance of,
      311–12
Mydans, Seth, 7–11
*Mystery of Edwin Drood, The*
    (Dickens), 383
*My Years with General Motors*
    (Sloan), 260

Nader, Ralph, 198
Nakasone, Yasuhiro, 217
Naples, Fla., 146
Nasdaq issues, 273, 281, 296
    gainers and losers among, 274,
      284, 299–300
    most active, 309–10
National Academy of Sciences
    members, 121–22

National Aeronautics and Space Administration (NASA), 88–89, 91, 92, 204
  on final minute of *Challenger*, 93–94
National Association of College and University Business Officers, 167
National Basketball Association (NBA), 319
National Basketball Players Association, 319
National Book Critics Circle Award winners, 374
National Council of Churches, 116–17
National Divestment Protest Day, 112
National Education Association, 94
national events, 83–199
National Forest Management Act, 168
National Forests, 168
National Institute on Drug Abuse, 143
National League, 325, 346–48, 350
  in All-Star Game, 342, 345
  playoffs of, 356–57
National Magazine Award winners, 379
National Medal of Arts winners, 384–85
national pride, 207–8
National Pro-Life Political Action Committee, 209
National Rifle Association, 113
National Safety Council, 107
National Security Council (NSC), 75–76
national speed limit, 175
National Transportation Safety Board, 161
National Turf Writers Association, 370
"Nation at Risk, A" (Bennett), 94
NATO (North Atlantic Treaty Organization), 67–68
Nazer, Hisham, 70
NBC-TV, 224
NCNB Corporation, 268
Needham Harper Worldwide, 243
Nelson, David C., 194
Nelson, Ricky, 84

Nesbitt, Stephen A., 90
Neuharth, Allen H., 244
Nevada, 188
Neve Shalom Synagogue, 54–55
New England Mutual Life Insurance Company, 163
New England Patriots, 316
New England Zenith Capital Growth, 285, 312
Newfoundland, 397–98
New Jersey, 132, 188
New Jersey Nets, 319
New Mexico, 194
newspapers, 244
New York City, property owned by Marcos in, 17
New York City corruption inquiries:
  figures in, 110–11
  public attitude toward, 212–13
New York Mercantile Exchange, 70
New York Mets, 320–21, 325, 364
  financial score card of, 348
  home attendance of, 347–48
  pennant won by, 356–57
  in World Series, 359–61
New York State, 188
  Factory Investigating Commission of, 107
  job growth in, 132
  Labor History Association of, 107
New York Stock Exchange (NYSE):
  busiest trading days on, 294
  gainers and losers on, 276, 282–83, 296–97, 307
  index of common stocks of, 273
  most active issues on, 309
  top volume sessions on, 270
*New York Times*/CBS News Polls, 185–86, 202–34
New York Yankees, 320–21, 322, 325, 342, 346, 347–48, 360, 364
New Zealand, 43
Nicaragua, 229
Nicaraguan rebel aid:
  administration commitment to, 74, 214
  House on, 17–21, 39–43, 214
  public opinion on, 214–15
  Senate on, 48

  U.S. funds diverted to, 75–76
Nicholson, Robert W., Jr., 90–91
Nicklaus, Jack, 333–38
Niekro, Phil, 323
Nieman Fellows, 382–83
99th Congress, *see* Congress, U.S.
Nipper, Al, 329
Nixon, Richard, M., 230, 231
Nobel Prize winners, 53, 387–88
Noble, Kenneth B., 174, 195
Nofziger, Lyn, 190
Nomura Securities Company, 290, 301
nonvoters, 178
Nordheimer, Jon, 165
North Atlantic Treaty Organization (NATO), 67–68
North Carolina, 155
North Carolina, University of, 318
North Sea, oil production in, 4
Nova, Scott, 112
Novick, Gary S., 410
nuclear accidents:
  at Chernobyl, 29–31, 126, 127–28
  mismanagement as cause of, 126, 128
nuclear reactors, 126–28
  best and worst, 126–27
  management of, 126
  proposed, 127
  safety features of, 127–28
Nuclear Regulatory Commission, 126, 128
nuclear tests, 21
Nunn, Sam, 93

Obey, David R., 31
O'Brien, Parry, 338
Occupational Safety and Health Administration (OSHA), 107, 142
OECD (Organization for Economic Cooperation and Development), 262, 433–34
*Officers and Gentlemen* (Waugh), 381–82
oil, oil industry, 273
  bankruptcies in, 252–53
  capital spending plans in, 249–50
  North Sea production of, 4
  OPEC's cut in output of, 79

OPEC's quota agreements on, 69, 249
  rankings of OPEC producers of, 63
  surge in prices of, 70
Ojeda, Bob, 356
Oklahoma, University of, 370
O'Leary, Albert W., 144–45
Olympics, 339
100-meter dash, 337
O'Neill, Thomas P., Jr., 179
Open, U.S., 333–37
Oppenheimer & Company, 267
Organization for Economic Cooperation and Development (OECD), 262, 433–34
Organization of African Unity, 35
Organization of Petroleum Exporting Countries (OPEC):
  current ranking producers in, 63
  Iranian oil minister in key role in, 63
  oil output cut by, 79
  quota agreements of, 69, 249
  Saudis seek price meeting for, 70
*Originals: An A–Z of Fiction's Real-Life Characters, The* (Amos), 380–82
Orosco, Jesse, 356, 360
OSHA (Occupational Safety and Health Administration), 107, 142
Ospina, Alberto, 24–25
Outerbridge, David, 396
Overseas Press Club Award winners, 378
over-the-counter (OTC) stocks, *see* Nasdaq issues
Owen, Jack, 98
Owen, Richard, 192
Owens, Spike, 329
oysters, 400–401

packing, 419–20
Packwood, Bob, 246, 411, 416
PACs, *see* political action committees
Paffenbarger, Ralph S., Jr., 406
pain relievers, 238
Pakistan, hijacking account given by, 55–56

Palestine Liberation Organization, 211
Paley, William S., 257
Palme, Olof, 211
Palmer, John L., 174
Palmer, Pete, 325
Pan American World Airways Flight 73 hijacking, 55–56
Panetta, Leon E., 171
Parade of Sail, 137
Paramount Pictures Corporation, 264
Parker, Dave, 321
Parker, Robert M., Jr., 417
Paterno, Joe, 369–70
Patrick, Michael, 167
George Foster Peabody Award for Distinguished Broadcasting, 382
Pear, Robert, 146–47, 172, 219–20
Pearl Harbor attack, 231
Pennel, John, 338
Penn State, 369–70
*Pennsylvania Packet,* 418–19
Penrod Drilling Company, 252–53
Pepper, Claude, 174, 411
Perelman, Ronald, 303
Perez de Cuellar, Javier, 57
Perlez, Jane, 17
Perot, H. Ross, 262
Persico, Carmine (Junior), 192
personality, 432–33
personnel systems, 57
pet food, 254–55
Pet Food Institute, 255
Pettis, Gary, 357
PGA (Professional Golfers Association), 336
Phelps, Ken, 329
Phi Beta Kappa book award winners, 389
Philadelphia, Pa., 145
Philadelphia 76ers, 318
Philippines, 43
  Aquino's ascendancy to presidency of, 11–12
  casino earnings in, 14
  cease-fire in, 73
  Communist rebels in, 73–74
  Marcos's flight from, 7–11
  Senate on elections in, 4–5
  U.S. observers for elections in, 4

Phillips, Edward E., 163
physical fitness, 401, 403
Pickens, T. Boone, 303
Placid Oil Company, 252–53
plane crashes:
  in Antarctica, 84
  international, 84, 160
  midair, 159–61
Planned Parenthood, 208–9
pole vault, 338–39
political action committees (PACs):
  of Bush, 162
  campaign funds raised by, 108–9, 162–63, 168–69
  of Teamsters, 168–69
political prisoners:
  Cuban release of, 165–66
  Sakharov's list of, 79–80
George Polk Award winners, 374
Pollack, Andrew, 300
population:
  of metropolitan statistical areas, 145–46
  of Soviet Union, 80–81
  of states, 199
*Portrait of Bascom Hawke* (Wolfe), 380
poverty, African, 36
J. D. Power & Associates, 236
Power Report on Automotive Marketing, 236
Praxis Biologics Inc., 246
prayers for peace, 68–69
Present Tense Award winners, 377
presidential campaign debts, 197–98
Presidential Commission on the Space Shuttle *Challenger,* 92
*Pretty in Pink,* 264
Prial, Frank, 404–5, 417–18
prison riots, 84–85
*Private Lives* (Coward), 381
privatization, French-owned companies in line for, 15
Professional Golfers Association (PGA), 336
protectionist legislation, 32–33, 148–51
Public Citizens Health Research Group, 98
public opinion, 201–34
  on abortion issue, 208–10
  on aid to Nicaraguan rebels, 214–15

public opinion (cont'd)
  on arms control, 226–27
  on big business, 218–19
  on drug use, 223–25
  in Europe, 207–8, 211, 215–16
  on farm issues, 210–11
  on football teams, 234
  on government corruption, 212–13
  on House candidates, 227–28
  ideological alignments and, 202–4
  on immigration, 219–22
  on Japan's world role, 217–18
  on Mexican economy, 228–29
  on 1986 elections, 185–86, 227
  on Reagan, 202, 215–16, 226–27, 230–34
  on space travel, 204–6
  on Supreme Court, 222–23
  on terrorism, 206–7, 211–12
  on trust in government, 207–8
  on U.S.-Mexican relations, 229–30
  on U.S. raid on Libya, 215–16
public stock offerings, 245–46
Puerto Rico, 168
Pulitzer Prize winners, 379–80
Purnick, Joyce, 144–45

Quaker Oats, 254–55
Quint, Michael, 310

radio stations, 244
Raffensperger, Ed, 412
Ralston Purina Company, 254–55
Ramos, Fidel V., 9–11
Reagan, Nancy, 151
Reagan, Ronald, 107, 109, 161, 172, 190, 211, 214
  on arms control, 226–27
  arms for Saudis backed by, 37
  on arms to Iran, 71–72
  awards presented by, 122–23, 128, 384–85
  *Challenger* explosion and, 88, 92
  congressional budget resolution and, 134
  Defense Department budget proposed by, 93
  Democratic control of Senate and, 176–77, 178–79
  federal court appointments by, 130–32, 222–23

  health problems of, 151–52
  honesty and integrity of, 232
  House votes on aid to Nicaraguan rebels and, 17–18, 39–40
  as liar, 232–33
  Medals of Freedom presented by, 122–23
  1987 budget plan and, 123
  popularity of, 202, 215–16, 226–27, 230–34
  public school education and, 95
  at Reykjavík meeting, 64, 66, 67–68, 226–27
  Senate votes on aid to Nicaraguan rebels and, 48
  South African sanctions and, 58–62
  Soviet freeing of Daniloff and, 57–58
  Soviet relations and, 227
  special prosecutor appointment urged by, 76
  on Star Wars, 226, 261–62
  Supreme Court's 1985–1986 term and, 143–44
  on tax legislation, 250
  Thanksgiving dinner of, 431
  trade bill veto of, 148
  urological examination of, 151
  White House Fellows announced by, 128
Realtors PAC, 162
Red Army Faction, 211
Reed, Sally, 187–88
Rehnquist, William H., 223
  Senate confirmation of, 166–67
Reinhold, Robert, 194
*Republican Journal*, 396
Republican National Committee, 179
Republican Party:
  black voters and, 185–86
  campaign funds raised for, 152–54
  and Democrats' control of Senate, 176–77, 178–79, 185
  governorships won by, 177, 179
Republicbank Dallas, 253, 268
retirement, mandatory, 174–75
retirement plans, 258, 259
Reykjavík summit meeting, 64, 66, 67–68
  as failure, 226
  public opinion and, 226–27

Reynolds, Craig, 322–23
Rhodes Scholars, 391–92
Richardson, Bobby, 360
Richardson, Michael Ray, 319–20
Righetti, Dave, 346
Rimer, Sara, 24
Ritzenberg, Allie, 410–11
Robbins, William, 210–11
Roberts, Steven V., 4, 17–18, 37, 48, 58, 61–62, 148, 152, 171
Rockefeller, Winthrop, 194
*Roe* v. *Wade,* 208
Rogers, William P., 92
Roman Catholics, 53
Rookie of the Year Award winners, 362
Roosevelt, Franklin D., 202, 231
Rose, George, 383
Rose, Pete, 341
Rosenbaum, David E., 246, 250, 411–12
Rostenkowski, Dan, 171
L. F. Rothschild, Unterberg, Towbin Inc., 243
Ryder, Henry W., 337–38

Saatchi & Saatchi Company, 242–44
Sabah, Ali Khalifa al-, 79
Saberhagen, Bret, 346
Sadat, Jihan el-, 190
safety, workplace, 106–8, 142
sailing ships, 137–41
St. Albans Tennis Club, 410
St. Louis Cardinals, 360
Sakharov, Andrei D., 79–80
salaries, wages:
  with bachelor's or master's degree, 240
  of baseball players, 315, 321, 324, 364
  of blacks vs. whites, 97
  Eastern's battle over, 236–37
  of guest lecturers, 190–91
  for judges, congressmen and executive branch officials, 195–96
  of mayors, 194–95
  of teachers, 186–87
  of women, 433–35
Salerno, Anthony (Fat Tony), 192
Salomon Brothers Inc., 238, 290, 310
  junk bond financing by, 303–4
  as No. 1 underwriter, 280, 304

Salonga, Jovito R., 17
Salpukas, Agis, 236–37
Sambito, Joe, 360
Sanchez Pruna, Jose, 165
Sanford, Terry, 185
San Francisco, Calif., 145
Sanitation Department, N.Y.C., 144–45
Santana, Rafael, 360
Saplin, Stan, 338
Saturn, 239
Saudi Arabia:
  OPEC price meeting sought by, 70
  Senate approval of arms for, 37–38
savings and loan associations, 304–6
Scalia, Antonin, 166, 223
Schmemann, Serge, 5–6, 62, 66–67
Schmidt, Mike, 350
  as Most Valuable Player, 361–62
Schmidt, William E., 190
Schmitt, Eric, 273, 281, 296
Schnittker, John A., 33
Schofield, Dick, 357
scholars, 391–92
schools:
  Bennett on, 94
  best ways of teaching in, 95, 96
  graduation rates of, 94–95
  in U.S., 94–96
Schumer, Charles E., 240
Science and Technology Medal winners, 376–77
science awards, 374–77
*Scientific American*, 337–38
Sciolino, Elaine, 33, 46–47, 57
*Scoop* (Waugh), 381–82
S corporations, 259–60
Scott, Foresman & Company, 255–56
Scott, Joe, 237
Scott, Mike, 356, 362
Scripps Howard Journalism Award winners, 378
Seagle, Gene J., 293
Securities and Exchange Commission (SEC), 279–80, 286
Securities Data Company, 280
Senate, U.S., 113
  aid to Nicaraguan rebels approved by, 48
  Armed Services Committee of, 93
  arms to Saudis approved by, 37–38
  budget-balancing amendment defeated by, 109–10
  Budget Committee of, 134
  Democrats gain control of, 176–77, 178–79, 185–86
  Finance Committee of, 411
  Foreign Relations Committee of, 61–62
  Judiciary Committee of, 130, 166
  in 1986 election, 176–77, 178–79, 183, 185–86
  1987 budget plan and, 123
  on Philippine elections, 4–5
  Rehnquist confirmed by, 166–67
  roll call votes of, 37–38, 48, 62, 109–10, 166–67, 173
  on South African sanctions by, 61–62
  on Tax Reform, 246–48, 250
  *see also* Congress, U.S.; House of Representatives, U.S.
SFN Companies, 256
Shabecoff, Philip, 168
Sharp, Margaret, 262
Shaun, Gabriel, 54
Shaw, Irwin, 380
Shcherbina, Boris Y., 30
Shearson Lehman Brothers Inc., 304
Shelby, Richard C., 185
Shenon, Philip, 130, 145
Sherrill, H. Virgil, 335
Sherrill, Patrick H., 158–59
Shinnecock Hills golf course, 333–35
Shipler, David K., 206, 214
Shiraldi, Calvin, 357, 360
shootings, 158–59
shot put, 338
Shultz, George P., 31–32, 226
  on aid to Africa, 33, 34
  Southeast Asia toured by, 43
Shultz, Virginia, 24
Simon, Paul, 130
Simons, Howard, 190
Simpson, Alan K., 172
Sims, Calvin, 412
Singapore, 43
Sino-American joint ventures, 39
Sloan, Alfred P., Jr., 260–61
Sloan Science Fellowship winners, 375–76
small business, 258–60
Smith, Dean, 318–19
Smith, Frank L., 95
Smith, Kenny, 318
Smith, Lonnie, 321
Smith, Rob, 159
Smith, Roger B., 65
Smith, T. Burton, 151
Smith, Timothy, 65, 116–17
social issues, corporations' interest in, 116–17
Social Security benefits, 173–74
Solomentsev, Mikhail, 80
South, heat and drought in, 154–56
South Africa, Republic of, 53, 285–86
  changes in, 29
  GM's withdrawal from, 65
  House's approval of sanctions on, 58–61
  largest U.S. employers in, 66
  Senate's approval of sanctions on, 61–62
  U.S. business divestments in, 48–50, 65–66
  U.S. college divestments in, 112–13
  U.S. trade with, 39, 47
South Carolina, 156
South Carolina, University of, 190–91
Southeast Asia, economic downturn of, 43
Southern Regional Council, Voter Education Project at, 185
South-Western Publishing Company, 256
Soviet Union, 214
  arms control proposals of, 44–46, 64
  Chernobyl nuclear accident, in, 29–31, 126, 127–28
  Communist Party and government hierarchies of, 6–7
  Daniloff freed by, 57–58
  diplomats of, U.S. expulsion of, 67
  ethnic diversity of, 80–81

Soviet Union *(cont'd)*
  Gorbachev's shake-up of leadership of, 5–6
  key indicators released by, 70
  maritime disasters of, 52
  Reagan's handling of, 227
  Sakharov's list of political prisoners in, 79–80
  Southeast Asia and, 43
  in Star Wars debate, 44, 46, 64, 226
  U.S. diplomats expelled by, 66–67
  U.S. in variety of negotiations with, 50–52
  U.S. relations with, 64
  world-chess championship held in, 62–63
soybeans, U.S. production of, 33
space shuttles, 88–92
  explosion of, 88–91, 93–94
  planned schedule for, 91–92
space travel, children enthusiastic about, 204–6
Spain, 207–8
special prosecutors:
  listing of, 76–77
  Meese's request for, 75–76
spies, 57–58
sports, sports news, 313–71
  automobile racing in, 341
  baseball in, 315, 320–25, 329–31, 332, 341–48, 350–63, 364, 368
  basketball in, 318–20, 322, 331, 367
  boxing in, 365
  broadcasters in, 314
  coaches and managers in, 318–19, 322–23
  exercise and, 401, 405–8
  football in, 234, 314, 316–18, 327, 347, 348–49, 363–67
  golf in, 331–37, 367
  hockey in, 367
  horse racing in, 328, 370–71
  summer, 403
  tennis and, 367–68, 410–11
  track and field in, 326, 337–39, 368
Stadler, Craig, 333
W. R. Stamler, 50
Standard & Poor's 500-stock index, 273, 285, 311
Stanley Works, 48–49

Star Wars:
  Reagan on, 226, 261–62
  Soviets vs. U.S. on, 44, 46, 64, 226
State Department, U.S., 31–32, 66
state medical boards, doctors disciplined by, 188–90
Statue of Liberty–Ellis Island Foundation, 135
Steinbrenner, George, 322
Stern, David, 319
Sterngold, James, 287, 303
Stevens, William K., 84
Stevenson, Richard W., 242–43, 252–53
stock market:
  Dow Jones industrial average in step with, 272–73
  four-year climb of, 291
  interest rates and, 273, 293, 306
  use of computer and, 293
stock mutual funds, 311
stocks:
  in Dow Jones industrial average, 271–72
  four-year climb of, 290
  illegal trading of, 279–80, 286–87
  public offerings of, 245–46
  second quarter evaluation of, 281
  third-quarter evaluation of, 296–300
Stockton, William, 228, 229
Stop, Look and Listen Award winners, 382
Strategic Defense Initiative, *see* Star Wars
Strategic Investments Fund, 285
Strawberry, Darryl, 359–60
Strong, Richard, 285
Strong Opportunity Fund, 285
Stuart, Reginald, 175
Student Loan Marketing Association, 291
students:
  cocaine used by, 143
  funds and jobs for, 163–64
  *see also* colleges; education
Sullivan, Leon, 116
Sullivan Principles, 53, 116
Sumitomo Bank Ltd., 287–88
summer sports, 403
Suntrust Banks, 268

Super Bowls, 316–17
Supreme Court, U.S.:
  on abortion, 208
  Associate Justices of, 166
  Chief Justices of, 133, 166–67
  on death penalty, 120
  justices of, 144
  1985–86 term of, 143–44
  public opinion on, 222–23
Suzuki Samurai, 248
Sweden, 211
Synar, Mike, 423

Tagliabue, John, 22–23, 63
Taubman, Philip, 52
taxi service, 193
tax rates, 259, 260
Tax Reform:
  bipartisan passage of, 250
  evolution of, 251–52
  highlights of, 250–51
  IRAs and, 258
  jargon of, 411–12
  small business and, 258–60
  transition rules for, 246–48
Taylor, Austin, 289
Taylor, Stuart, 120
Taylor, Stuart, Jr., 143–44
teachers, teaching, 95, 96
  average income of, 186–87
technology, computer, 293, 325
television awards, 374, 382, 384
Tellegen, Auke, 432
Teltsch, Kathleen, 385–86
*Tender Is The Night* (Fitzgerald), 381
Tenniel, John, 381
tennis, 367–68
  in Washington, D.C., 410–11
Tenold, Terry, 168
terrorism:
  business travel and, 24–25
  European attitudes toward, 211–12
  in Istanbul, 54–55
  Middle East links to, 25–26
  military reply to, 211–12
  public attitudes toward, 206–7, 211–12
  twelve months of, 25–26
  victims of, 24, 55
  *see also* hijackings; hostages
Testaverde, Vinny, 370
Texas Rangers, 346
Texas, University of, 167

textbook publishers, 255–56
Thanksgiving dinner, 431
Thatcher, Margaret, 216
theatrical awards, 377–78, 383–84
Thompson, Fred, 339
Thompson, Paul W., 408
Thorn, John, 325
Thoroughbred Racing Associations, 370
Three Mile Island nuclear accident, 128
Tilney, Corder, 50
Time Inc., 255–56
*Times* (London), 216, 380
Tisch, Laurence A., 256–57
toasts, 418–19
Tolchin, Martin, 108
Tokyo Broadcasting System, 217
Toner, Robin, 94
Tony Award winners, 383–84
Torrance, Jack, 338
track and field, 326, 337–39, 368
trade:
    deficit, in U.S., 12–13
    of Libya, 2–3, 29
    between U.S. and Japan, 2
    between U.S. and South Africa, 39, 47
trade legislation:
    to curtail imported textiles, 148–51
    farm provisions of, 32–33
*Tramp Abroad, A* (Twain), 380
travel, 419–20
trees, 408–9
Trevino, Lee, 335–36
Triangle Shirtwaist Company fire, 106–7
Truman, Harry S., 231
TWA Flight 840, explosion on, 25
Twain, Mark, 380
Tweed, William Marcy (Boss), 397
Twichell, Joseph Hopkins, 380
Twin Torch Inn, 197
Tyson, Mike, 365
Tyson, Patrick, 107

Ueberroth, Peter, 320–21
underwriters:
    leading, 280–81, 310–11
    Salomon Brothers as, 280, 304
    *see also* investment banking firms

unemployment rates, 53
United Nations:
    aid to Africa debated by, 33
    outstanding contributions to, 28
    personnel system of, 57
    survival in Africa described at, 35
    U.S. Mission to, 46
    U.S. outvoted in, 46–47
United Press International, 370
United Services Gold Shares, 285
United States:
    air raid on Libya by, 27, 215–16
    Aquino recognized as president by, 7–11
    arms control proposals of, 44–46, 64
    arms sent to Iran by, 71–75, 77–79
    Chinese joint ventures with, 39
    Cuban political prisoners in, 165–66
    diplomats of, Soviet expulsion of, 66–67
    Euroequity issues sold in, 291–92
    farming in, 32–33, 128–29, 210–11
    foreign aid from, 31–32
    government trust in, 207–8
    on hospital mortality rates, 98–106
    hostages in Lebanon and, 26, 70–71
    ideological alignments in, 202–4
    investment banks of, in Britain, 294–96
    investments in Northern Ireland by, 53
    Japanese trade relations with, 2
    Libyan relations with, 27–28
    loans to Argentina by, 3
    Mexican relations with, 229–30
    nuclear reactor safety in, 126–28
    Philippine elections and observers from, 4
    South African divestment and, 48–50, 65–66, 112–13
    South African trade with, 39, 47
    Soviet diplomats expelled by, 67

    Soviet relations with, 64
    Soviets in variety of negotiations with, 50–52
    in Star Wars debate, 44, 46, 64, 226
    state of schools in, 94–96
    trade deficit of, 12–13
    U.N. votes against, 46–47
    wines of, 404–5
universities, *see* colleges
USA/Mobil national outdoor championships, 339
*USA Today,* 244
Utah Jazz, 319

Valenti, Jack, 410–11
Valenzuela, Fernando, 345, 362
van Aelst, Marcel, 404
Van Cortlandt, Jacobus, 397
*Variety,* 264
Vartan, Vartanig G., 272–73, 285–86, 311–12
Ver, Fabian C., 7, 9–10, 13
Vercelli, Larry J., 158
Veterans Administration (VA) hospitals, 156–58
VF Corporation, 50
Vilas-Fischer Associates, 238
vintage charts, 417–18
V-J Day, 144
voters:
    nonvoters vs., 178
    portrait of, 180–82
Vrinat, Jean-Claude, 417

Waite, Terry, 70–71
Walcott, Jersey Joe, 365
Waldenbooks, 254
Walker, William, 262
Warsaw Pact, 67–68
Washington, Claudell, 364
*Washington Post,* 190
Washington Senators, 347
water, U.S. standards for, 134
Watergate affair, 230
Wattenberg, Martin, 232
Waugh, Evelyn, 381–82
Weatherby, W. J., 380
Weill, Sanford I., 240
Weinberger, Caspar W., 93
Weinraub, Bernard, 71–72, 75–76, 151
Weisman, Steven R., 55
Weiss, Ted, 156
Wells Fargo & Company, 301

Wertheimer, Fred, 151
Westinghouse, 14
Westinghouse Science Talent
    Search winners, 374–75
West Virginia Penitentiary, 84
"What Works: Research about
    Teaching and Learning"
    (U.S. Department of Education),
    95, 96
wheat, U.S. production of, 33
White, Gordon, 347
White House Fellows, 128
Williams, Lena, 185–86
Wilson, Jerry, 185
Wilson, Mookie, 360
*Wine Advocate,* 417
wine:
    of U.S., 404–5
    vintage chart of, 417–18
*Wines of America, The* (Adams),
    404
Wirth, Timothy E., 177
Wirthlin, Richard B., 226
Wodehouse, P.G., 381
Wolfe, Sidney, 98
Wolfe, Thomas, 380
Wolff, Craig, 342
women, 187
    earning power and education
        of, 433–35
    in track events, 337, 339
workplace safety, 106–8, 142
World Bank, 300
world chess championship, 62–63
Worrell, Todd, 362
Wouk, Herman, 380
Wren, Christopher S., 397
write-offs, 260
writing awards, 374, 377,
    379–80, 384, 388–91
Wyman, Thomas H., 256

Yapp, George J., 255
Yeltsin, Boris N., 30–31
Yeoman, Wayne A., 236–37
Yeutter, Clayton K., 148
Young, Coleman A., 195
Young, D. Robert, 119
*Youngblood Hawke* (Wouk), 380
*Young Lions, The* (Shaw), 380
Yugoslavia, 263
*Yunque, el,* 168

Zakharov, Gennadi F., 58
Zschau, Ed, 177, 185